# Nicknames and Sobriquets of U.S. Cities and States

by
## Joseph Nathan Kane
and
## Gerard L. Alexander

Second Edition

# The Scarecrow Press, Inc.
# Metuchen, N.J.        1970

# Preface

Joseph Nathan Kane in his book "1,000 Facts Worth Knowing" published in 1938, out of print for more than a score of years, devoted a small section to nicknames. Thirteen years later, Gerard L. Alexander compiled "Nicknames of American Cities, Towns and Villages (Past and Present)," published by the Special Libraries Association, which is also out of print.

A mutual friendship and interest of the authors resulted in this larger and more complete list to which explanatory text has been added. The idea was broached to Scarecrow Press and it appeared as a book in 1965. Five years of additional research have disclosed about 6,000 additional listings. Still unfound are further nicknames which it is hoped will be collected in a future edition.

# Contents

## Introduction

Practically all the states, cities and towns in the United States, regardless of location, size or age, have nicknames. Some of them are well known, others are seldom used and rarely printed. Very few nicknames of states, cities and towns are official or adopted by legislative action. Often it is usual for a locality to have more than one definite nickname.

Nicknames have been conferred in numerous ways by chambers of commerce, literary sources, advertising executives, publicity representatives and by rival cities.

Over the years, some cities have acquired so many nicknames that each has lost its importance. These may be completely diversified and bear no relation to each other. New York City, for example, is called America's Leading Tourist Resort, The Babylonian Bedlam, The Capital of the World, The City of Skyscrapers, The Coliseum City, The Empire City, The Entertainment Capital of the World, The Front Office of American Business, The Metropolis, The Money Town, The Nation's First City, The Seat of Empire, The World's Fair City, The World's Metropolis, just to mention a few.

In the same vein, nicknames of one locality may be so similar in meaning to others that they may be easily interchanged with little loss. Boston, for example, is known as Beantown, the City of Baked Beans, the City of Bean Eaters or the Home of Baked Beans.

The most common form of nicknames is the descriptive one: The Battlefield City, The Border City, The Classic City, The Cockade City, The College City, The Crescent City, The Druid City, The Dynamic City, The Empire City, The Executive City, The Exposition City, The Family City, The Frosty City, The Golden City, The Historic City, The Lookout City, The Prison City, The Stone City.

### Industry
Another form of nickname associates the city with its most prominent industry: The Aluminum City, The Atomic

7

Energy City, The Auto City, The Automobile City, The Beer City, The Bituminous City, The Bran Town, The Brass City, The Brewing City, The Butter City, The Camera City, The Canoe City, The Car Shop City, The Cash Register City, The Celery City, The Celluloid City, The Cement City, The Ceramic City, The Cereal Food Center, the Chemurgic City, The Clay City, The Chair City, The Chemical City, The Chocolate City, The Cigar City, The Circus City, The Clipper City, The Clock City, The Coal City, The Coke City, The Collar City, The Copper City, The Cordage City, The Cream City, The Crystal City, The Dairy City, The Electrical City, The Flour City, The Flower City, The Furniture City, The Granite City, The Gypsum City, The Hardware City, The Hat City, The Insurance City, The Iron City, The Kodak City, The Lock City, The Lumber City, The Marble City, The Missile City, The Motor City, The Nail City, The Oil City, The Paper City, The Pearl City, The Plow City, The Pottery City, The Pretzel City, The Railroad City, The Rubber City, The Salmon City, The Salt City, The Sawdust City, The Ship-building City, The Shoe City, The Shovel City, The Silk City, The Silver City, The Smelter City, The Spindle City, The Sponge City, The Steel City, The Sweat-shop Capital, The Tannery City, The Textile City, The Thread City, The Tube City, The Wool City.

## Geography

Geographical attributes often account for the nicknames of cities. Examples are: The Bay City, The Bayou City, The Bluff City, The Canal City, The Canyon City, The Cavern City, The City by the Lake, The City by the Sea, The City on the Gulf, The Falls City, The Hill City, The Lake City, The Mile-High City, The Mound City, The Mountain City, The Natural Gas City, The Port City, The Scholarship City, The Science City, The Windy City.

## Local

Nicknames are often specifically limited to locality: Arizona's First Capital, Arkansas' Only Seaport, Benton County's Fastest Growing City, Colorado's Second City, Delaware's Summer Capital, Idaho's Farm Market, Iowa's Own City, Maine's Fastest Growing Industrial and Recreational Area, Michigan's Most Famous Summer Resort, Montana's Largest and Friendliest City, New York's First Capital, Rhode Island's Most Historic Town, South Arkansas' Busy Port City, South Carolina's Capital City, South Dakota's City of Opportunity, Tallest Town in Oregon, Tennessee's Beauty Spot, Tip of Cape Cod, Trade Center of Southwest Georgia.

## Botany

Flowers, trees and shrubs lend their influence to nicknames: The Camellia City, The Christmas Tree City, The Dogwood City, The Elm City, The Evergreen City, The Floral City, The Flower City, The Forest City, The Holly City, The Iris City, The Lawn City, The Lilac City, The Magnolia City, The Maple City, The Oak City, The Oleander City, The Orchard City, The Palm City, The Palmetto City, The Peony Center, The Rose City, The Sycamore City, The Tulip City.

## Sports

Sports and games often serve as the nucleus for nicknames: Golf Capital, Hockey Capital of the Nation, Home of Baseball, Home of the Packers, Packer's Town, Polo Capital of, Ski Capital of.

## Nationality - Religion

Nationality and religion have inspired nicknames for some cities: Czech Bethlehem, Deutsch Athens, Dutch City, Dutchtown, German Athens, Mormon City, Polish City, Quaker City, Quaker Town.

## Meaningless

Many cities have adopted nicknames so bland and colorless that they have lost their importance and original individuality and are no longer distinctive or meaningful, such as: The Capital City, The City Beautiful, The City of Churches, The City of Homes, The City of Opportunity, The City of Roses, The City of Trees, The City With a Future, The Convention City, The Friendly City, The Gate City, The Gateway City, The Gem City, The Hub City, The Magic City, The Progressive City, The Queen City.

## Hyperbole

Many nicknames are inspired by wishful thinking and hyperbole, such as: The Best Known City, The Cleanest Beach in the World, The Cleanest Big City in the World, The Closest State to Heaven, The Dancingest Town in the U.S., The Fastest Growing City, The Finest Beach in the World, The Friendliest Town, The Most Beautiful City, The Most Historic City, The Nation's Most Beautiful City, The Proudest Small Town in America, The Safest Spot in the World, The South's Fastest Growing City, The South's Greatest City, The South's Most Beautiful and Interesting City, The Tourist's Paradise, The Town Where Summer is Air Conditioned, The Town With the Most to Offer Industry, The West's Most Western Town, The Winter Playground of America.

## Slander

Just as proud local citizenry are eager to accent these encomiums, there are jealous or hostile groups who swing the pendulum in the opposite direction to foster such slander as: Bad Birmingham, Hangtown, Mobtown, The Modern Gomorrah, The Murder Capital of, Sin City, Sinema City, The Sodom of, The Wickedest City of.

## Geography (Foreign)

Many cities resort to associations with European countries and cities for their nicknames, such as: The Alexandria of, The Athens of, The Birmingham of, The Carlsbad of, The Eden of, The Edinburgh of, The Essen of, The Gibraltar of, The Heidelberg of, The Lyons of, The Manchester of, The Naples of, The Paris of, The South Sea Island of, The Switzerland of, The Thermopylae of, The Venice of.

## Geography (United States)

Some cities claim a fancied or non-existant relationship with a better known community, such as: The Atlantic City of, The Boston of, The Brooklyn of, The Chicago of, The Coney Island of, The Denver of, The Detroit of, The Greenwich Village of, The Hartford of, The Hudson of, The Kansas City of, The Las Vegas of, The Lexington of, The Little Louisville of, The Lowell of, The Minneapolis of, The Newport of, The Niagara of, The Pittsburgh of, The Plymouth of, The Saratoga of, The Spokane of, The West Point of.

## Picturesque - Fanciful

Other cities prefer a picturesque or fanciful name, such as: Buckle on the Kansas Wheat Belt, City Built on Oil, Soil and Toil, City Where Mexico Meets Uncle Sam, City Where Oil Flows, Gas Blows and Glass Glows, City Where Progress and Pleasures are Partners, City Where Summer Winters, City Where There are no Strangers--Just Friends, City Where Work and Play are Only Minutes Away, Land of Cheese, Trees and Ocean Breeze, Magic Mascot of the Plains, The Peerless Princess of the Plains.

## Food

Foods often serve as the basis of cities' nicknames. Here is a partial list roughly subdivided into classifications: The Honey Capital, The Pretzel City, The Rice City, The Scrapple City.

FRUITS: The Apple City, The Berry City, The Blueberry Capital, The Cherry City, The Citrus Center, The Home of the Tangerine, The Lemon Center, The Orange Capital, The Peach Bowl, The Peach Capital, The Pear City, The Raisin Capital, The Strawberry Capital, The Watermelon Capital.

MEAT: The Bratwurst Capital, The Broiler Capital, The Holstein Capital, The Pheasant Capital, The Pork City, The Turkey Capital.

NUTS: The Filbert Center, The Land of Hazel Nuts, The Maple Center, The Peanut City, The Pecan Capital, The Walnut City.

SEA FOOD: The Clam Town, The Crawfish Town, The Home of the Famous Silver King Tarpon, The Lake Trout Capital, The Sailfish Capital, The Salmon City, The Salt Water Trout Capital, The Sea Turtle Capital.

VEGETABLES: America's Carrot Capital, Bean Town, The Celery City, The Green Bean Center, The Lettuce Center, The Potato Capital, The Pumpkin Capital, The Spinach Capital, The Tomato Capital.

## Book Titles

Nicknames are often taken from the title, the subtitle, the text or characters in books and stories: Green Felt Jungle, Money Town, Sodom by the Sea.

## Made-Up Names

Coined names, made-up words and meaningless combinations of letters are sometimes used: Arkopolis, Bostonia, Cornopolis, Dupontia, Gotham, Hogopolis, Jacksonopolis, Mushroomopolis, Pigopolis, Porkopolis, Soo, Squawkiewood, Touropolis, Tusselburgh.

## Humorous

Humorous or facetious names often lampoon a town: Annie's Town, Betsytown, Bumgannon, Lunchburg, Tater Town, Taterville, Unsainted Anthony.

Towns often acquire nicknames based upon the birth of some outstanding individual: Birthplace of Calvin Coolidge, Birthplace of Daniel Webster, Birthplace of Harry S Truman, Birthplace of McKinley.

Other birthplaces are commemorated such as the Birthplace of American Liberty, Birthplace of Aviation, Birthplace of California, Birthplace of Dixie, Birthplace of Liberty, Birthplace of Maine, Birthplace of Oklahoma, Birthplace of Radio, Birthplace of Speed, Birthplace of The Nation, Birthplace of The Republican Party, Birthplace of United States Naval Aviation.

Some cities have acquired their nicknames from some event associated with their history: The Home of the Apple Blossom Festival, The Home of the Boll Weevil Monument, The Home of the Comstock Lode, The Home of the Florida Derby, The Home of the Mining Barons, The Home of the Miss Universe Pageant, The Home of the Pacific Fleet, The Home of the Snake River Stampede, The Home of the World Famous Glass Bottom Boats.

Historical and literary allusions aften account for some nicknames: The Cradle of Liberty, The Cradle of Secession, The Mission City, The Modern Phoenix, Paul Bunyan's Capital, The Rebel Capital.

Peculiarly, nicknames of some cities may be contrary and at cross purposes with each other such as The Sleepy Town and The World's Greatest Workshop; The Babylonian Bedlam and The Wonder City; The Crime Capital and The Metropolis of the West; The Gas House of the Nation and The Nation's Headquarters.

### Joint - Collective
Many cities have jointly adopted the same nickname with neighboring cities which is often used individually or collectively: Dual Cities, Fall Cities, Quad Cities, Tri-Cities, Twin Cities.

### Abbreviations and Nicknames
Abbreviations and word contractions often serve as nicknames: Alex City, Ark City, Billtown, Bison City, Chi, El-ay, Frisco, Jax, Jeff City, Jimtown, L. A., Philly, Sacto, San Berdoo.

In every state, one city bears the nickname "The Capital City" or "The Capitol City." Capital and capitol are often interchanged, either correctly or incorrectly, so that it is impossible to state which is correct or which was originally intended.

Another point of argument or dispute is the use of the article "a" and "the" in the nicknames. Both are often used, in some instances neither are used, and in other cases are interchanged: A City of Homes, The City of Homes, A City of Opportunity, The City of Opportunity, A City of Trees, The City of Trees.

In some instances, both the "a" and the "the" are omitted.

12

In similar vein, an identical situation arises with regard to the use of "of" and "to." The Gateway of the South, The Gateway to the South, The Gateway of the West, The Gateway to the West.

Another variation is the use of the singular and the plural; City of Diversified Industry, City of Diversified Industries.

When a locality has a particular designation, it is possible that it may also have an unlimited number of variations. To illustrate the point, a city might be called The Celery Capital, The Celery Capital of Michigan, The Celery Capital of the United States, The Celery Capital of the World, The Celery City, The Celery City of Michigan, The Celery City of the United States, The Celery City of the World, Michigan's Celery City, The United States' Celery City, The World's Celery City. The ramifications may be extended indefinitely.

As the nuances are unlimited, a complete list of all the combinations of one city would be a mighty undertaking and when multiplied by the large number of places listed in this book, would make an encyclopedia minute by comparison. Furthermore, this overspecialization would decrease rather than increase the utility value of this book. Consequently, the temptation to strive for bulk has been disregarded, and no effort has been made to list all the existing possible names and combinations. However, exceptions have been made in instances where the deviations have become almost as commonplace and acceptable as the original name.

Often the publication of a brochure, map or publicity circular, the handicraft of word-outpouring by a promotion direction, tries to bring about a new image or concept. This is one of the prolific sources of nicknames and, being in print, remains for posterity.

Occasionally, nicknames are coined by some orator or political campaigner and find their way into the language.

Nicknames of cities often undergo a metamorphosis and revisions are made. Sometimes the change is proportionate to the inflated ego and exaggeration of the publicity director. Again, many nicknames have completely outlived their usefulness, or the purpose for which they were originally intended. The Town may become The City, The Hub of the Territory may change to The Hub of the State.

Where a city has more than one nickname, the nicknames have been listed alphabetically without attempting to grade them in importance or value.

The source or origin of many nicknames is unknown. In many instances, the authorities differ as to the reason of selection and consequently several versions exist. Where there are several different explanations, they have been listed without attempting to rate their importance.

When the nickname is descriptive or self-explanatory such as The Capital City, The City of Beauty, The Friendly City, The Progressive City, no attempt has been made to explain the obvious. Also, when no logical explanation can be given, it is likewise omitted.

The listing or inclusion of a nickname does not necessarily imply that it is official, in constant use or is approved by this book.

Certain nicknames are appropriate, others are not appropriate; others are sheer hyperbole, still others are misnomers while some have been judiciously named.

Some are grammatically incorrect, plurals being used for singulars and vice versa. Apostrophe marks are often applied in the wrong places. Hyphens are occasionally used unnecessarily and often omitted when required.

All known nicknames have been recorded impartially as this book is a record, not apologia or propaganda.

In addition to the informative material, this book portrays the field to the publicity departments and public relations executives of the various cities and enables them to revalue their efforts. It may stimulate them to strive for originality or adopt the platitudes of repetition if they desire. If this compilation serves to encourage the former, it will have well served its purpose.

The authors realize that this book is not the end-all on the subject. There are many places in the United States for which no nicknames are known. This may be because the place has none or that it is so limited that it has not escaped local confines, or that it is oral and has not been captured by print. If any of these sites have been omitted, or others inherit new nicknames, we would like to hear of them for inclusion in future editions. Advice from chambers of

14

commerce and local officials will be especially appreciated.

It would be remiss not to thank the librarians, historians, public officials, city and state agencies and individuals whose assistance has been of inestimable value in the compilation of this book. As the authors primarily used the facilities of the New York Public Library, the Library of Congress and the Free Library of Philadelphia, special thanks are due their staffs who obligingly facilitated this work.

Geographical Index
Cities

ALABAMA

ALBERTVILLE | The Friendly City
ALEXANDER CITY | Alex City
The City with a Great Civic
Pride and a Sound Business
Climate
The Industrial and Recreational
Center of East Alabama
ANDALUSIA | The Gem City of Southern Alabama
ANNISTON | Annie's Town (named for Mrs.
Annie Scott Tyler)
The Brooklyn of the South
The City of Churches
The Magic City
The Model City (town laid out
before plots were sold to the
public)
The Model City of Alabama
The Pearl of the South
The Soil Pipe Center of the
World (manufactures cast
iron soil pipe and plumbers
specials)
ATMORE | The City Where Industry Profits
The City With Room to Stretch
and Grow in
AUBURN | The Loveliest Village of the
Plains
The Village of the Plains
BESSEMER | The Iron City (steel furnaces)
BIRMINGHAM | Bad Birmingham
The City Beautiful
The City of Executives
The City Where the Mighty Smith
Stands (the Vulcan statue)
The City With a Heart in the
Heart of Dixie

17

BIRMINGHAM (Cont'd)

The Emerging Industrial Center
The Football Capital of the South
(Legion Field holds 75,000
people)
The Home of Vulcan (statue)
The Industrial Center of the
Great South (major iron and
steel production center in the
south)
The Industrial Center of the
Southeast
The Industrial City Beautiful
The Industrial City of Dixie
The Industrial City of the South
The Inland Metropolis
The Magic City
The Magic City of the South
The Mineral City of the South
The Murder Capital of the World
(1932)
The Pittsburgh of the South
The Youngest of the World's
Great Cities (settled in 1813,
Jones Valley)

CITRONELLE

The Oil Capital of Alabama
(more than 200 producing oil
wells in the vicinity)

DECATUR

The City of Achievement
The City of Hospitality
The City Where River, Air, Rail
and Highway Meet
The City With Opportunity For
All
The Four-Leaf Clover City (short
circle tours from this hub en-
compass the numerous moun-
tain and lake attractions)
The Hub of the North Alabama
Resort Areas
The Northern Gateway to Ala-
bama
The Saturday Town
The South's Most Strategic and
Distribution Center
The South's Most Strategic Indus-
trial and Distributional Center
The Wonder City

| | |
|---|---|
| DEMOPOLIS | The City of People |
| | The City of the People (founded in 1817 by Napoleonic exiles) |
| | The Peoples' City |
| | The Wine and Olive Colony |
| DOTHAN | The City of Pines and Flowers |
| | The Home of the National Peanut Festival |
| | The Perfect Spot to Work, to Play, to Enjoy Life |
| ENTERPRISE | The Home of the Boll Weevil Monument (dedicated 1919) |
| | The Peanut Capital of the World (peanut oil mills, peanut butter factory, peanut shelling plants) |
| EUFAULA | The Bluff City (bluff rises 150 feet on the west bank of the Chattahoochee River) |
| | The Bluff City of the Chattahoochee |
| FAIRHOPE | The Eastern Shore of Mobile Bay (on a bluff above Mobile Bay) |
| | The Home of the Jubilee (marine life in summer months comes to the beach line and the cry of "jubilee" is made when a catch is made) |
| FLORENCE | The City of Beautiful Churches, Homes and Buildings |
| | The City of Outstanding Educational Advantages |
| | The Home of Florence State College (the oldest teacher's institution in the south) |
| | The Tri-Cities (with Sheffield and Tuscumbia on the Tennessee River) |
| FOLEY | The Heart of the American Riviera (on the Gulf of Mexico) |
| | The Town where Industry's Contribution to the Community Is Appreciated |
| GADSDEN | The Queen City of Alabama |
| | The Queen City of the Coosa (Coosa River) |
| GREENVILLE | The Camellia City |

GUNTERSVILLE                The Boat Racing Capital of the
                                South (Dixie Cup Races)
HUNTSVILLE                  The City of Contrasts
                            The City of Governors (Thomas
                                Bibb, Gabriel Moore, Clement
                                Comer Clay, Reuben Chapman,
                                John Winston, David P. Lewis)
                            The City of Gracious Living
                            The First Capital of the State
                                (1819)
                            The Geographical Center of the
                                South
                            The Guided Missile Research and
                                Space Flight Center (U. S.
                                Army Missile Command)
                            The Hub of the Powerful Tennes-
                                see Valley
                            The Industrial City of North Ala-
                                bama
                            The Rocket Capital of the Nation
                                (where Redstone rocket was
                                designed and placed in orbit)
                            The Rocket City (The Jupiter
                                "C" rocket was perfected
                                here)
                            Rocket City, U. S. A.
                            The Space Capital of the Nation
                            The Space Capital of the World
                                (George C. Marshall Space
                                Flight Center)
                            The Watercress Capital of the
                                World
JASPER                      The Home of Hospitality
MOBILE                      Alabama's City in Motion
                            Alabama's Only Port City (on the
                                west side of the Mobile River)
                            The Charm Spot of the Deep
                                South
                            The City of Five Flags
                            The City of Six Flags
                            The Gulf City (on the Gulf of
                                Mexico)
                            The Picnic City
                            The Port City (the only seaport
                                in Alabama)
                            The Sportland of the Gulf
MONROEVILLE                 The Hub of Southwest Alabama

| | |
|---|---|
| MONROEVILLE (Cont'd) | (county seat of Monroe County) |
| MONTEVALLO | The Heart of Alabama (in the exact geographical center) |
| MONTGOMERY | One of America's Most Interesting Cities |
| | The Birthplace of Dixie |
| | The Capital City (134, 393 population in 1960) |
| | The City of Beauty |
| | The City of Opportunity |
| | The Cow Town of the South |
| | The Cradle of the Confederacy (the first capital of the Confederacy) |
| | The Thriving Capital City |
| MUSCLE SHOALS | The Aluminum City (home of second largest producer of aluminum in U. S. ) |
| | The Niagara of the South (the Tennessee River drops 134 feet in almost 40 miles) |
| | The Space Age City |
| OPELIKA | The Industrial and Trading Center of East Alabama |
| | The Trading Center of East Alabama |
| OZARK | The City of Churches |
| | The Helicopter Capital of the World |
| | The Home of Fort Rucker, the Army Aviation Center |
| PHENIX CITY | The City of Progress and Opportunity |
| | The Hub of the Chattahoochee Valley |
| | The Wickedest City in America (title of book by Edwin Strickland) |
| ROBERTSDALE | The Hub City |
| SELMA | The Queen City of the Black Belt (black belt soil of cotton and soybean plantations) |
| | The Electrical Center of America |
| SHEFFIELD | The Iron City on the Tennessee River |
| | The Tri-Cities (with Florence and Tuscumbia) |

| | |
|---|---|
| SYLACAUGA | The Marble City (marble quarries |
| TALLADEGA | The Bride of the Mountains (in the foothills of the Appalachian Mountains) |
| TRUSSVILLE | The City With Small Town Hospitality (1960 population 2, 510) |
| TUSCALOOSA | The Athens of Alabama (University of Alabama) |
| | The City of Oaks |
| | The Druid City (oak trees and mistletoes) |
| TUSCUMBIA | The Home of Helen Keller ("Ivy Green" now a state shrine) |
| | The Tri-Cities (with Florence and Sheffield) |

## ALASKA

| | |
|---|---|
| ANCHORAGE | The Air Crossroads of the World (SAS field on Europe-Orient flight) |
| | The Chicago of the North |
| | The Crossroads of the World |
| | The Financial Center of Alaska |
| | The Front Door Entrance to an Alaska Vacation |
| | The Hub City |
| | The International Polar Air Cross Roads of the World |
| | The Largest City in the Largest State (1960 population 44, 237) |
| | The Most Air-Minded City in the World |
| | The Nerve Center of Alaska |
| CORDOVA | Alaska's Friendly City |
| | The Friendly City |
| | The Razor Clam Capital of the World |
| DOUGLAS | The Ideal Home Community |
| FAIRBANKS | The Friendly Frontier City |
| | The Gateway to the Arctic |
| | The Golden Heart Metropolis of the Interior |
| | The Golden Heart of Alaska |
| | The Golden Heart of the North |
| | The Kansas City of Alaska |

| | |
|---|---|
| HAINES | The Strawberry Capital of Alaska |
| HOMER | The City Where People Like to Live (1960) population 1, 247) |
| | The City Where The Trail Ends and The Sea Begins |
| | The Shangri-la of Alaska |
| JUNEAU | Alaska's Capital City (1960) population 6, 797) |
| | Alaska's Scenic Capital |
| | America's Most Scenic Capital |
| | The Capital City |
| | The Capital City of Alaska |
| | The Capital of an Empire |
| | The Convention City |
| | The Gateway to Glacier Bay National Monument |
| | The Scenic and Recreation Center of Alaska |
| | The Scenic City of Nightless Summer Days |
| KENAI | The Oil Capital of Alaska |
| | The Village With A Past, The City With A Future |
| KETCHIKAN | Alaska's First City |
| | The Canned Salmon Capital of the World |
| | The First City |
| | The Gateway to Adventure |
| | The Gateway to Adventure on North America's Spectacular Marine Highway |
| | The Gateway to Salt and Freshwater Fishing, Hunting, Scenic Beauty and Fun |
| | The Gateway Port of Alaska |
| | The Salmon Capital of Alaska |
| | The Salmon Capital of the World |
| | The Totem City (contains more totem poles than any other city in the world) |
| | The World's Salmon Capital |
| KODIAK | The Home of the World's Largest Bear |
| | The King Crab Capital of the World |
| KOTZEBUE | The Eskimo Village |
| NORTH POLE | The Home of Santa Claus |

| | |
|---|---|
| NOME | The Famed Gold Rush Town |
| PETERSBURG | Alaska's Little Norway |
| | The Center of Southeast Alaska's Vacationland |
| | The Hospitality Center of Alaska |
| | The Little Norway of Alaska |
| | The Shrimp Capital of Alaska |
| POINT BARROW | The Top of the World |
| SELDOVIA | The City of Seclusion |
| SEWARD | The Gateway to Kenai Peninsula (between Cook Inlet and Prince William Sound) |
| | The Gateway City (on Resurrection Bay) |
| SITKA | Alaska's Most Scenic Historic Playground |
| | Alaska's Number One Tourist City |
| | The City By The Sea In Beautiful Southeastern Alaska |
| | The City Where Scenic Grandeur, History, Legend and Bustling Modern Economy Are Blended Into Everyday Life |
| | The First Capital City |
| | The Paris of the Pacific |
| | The Portal to Romance (title of book by Barrett Willoughby) |
| | The Russian-American Capital |
| | The Showplace of Southeast Alaska |
| SKAGWAY | The Gateway to the Yukon |
| SOLDATNA | The Hub of the Kenai Peninsula |
| TOK | The Crossroads of Alaska |
| | The Million Dollar Camp |
| VALDEZ | The Copper City |
| | The Gateway to the Interior |
| | The Photographer's Paradise |
| | The Switzerland of Alaska |
| WRANGELL | The Center of Scenic Southeast Alaska |
| | The Gateway to the Stikine |
| | The Hub of Thlingit Totem Land |
| | The Lumber Capital of Alaska |
| | The Lumber Export Capital of Alaska |

ARIZONA

| | |
|---|---|
| AGUILA | The Lettuce Center of the Nation |
| AJO | The Gateway to Sonoyta, Mexico and the Gulf of Lower California |
| BISBEE | Arizona's Copper Capital |
| | The Gateway to Fort Huachuca (U. S. electronic proving ground) |
| BOWIE | The City in the Garden of the Sun |
| | The Gateway to Chiricahua National Monument (Cochise County, S. E. Arizona) |
| CHANDLER | The City where Summer Winters |
| | The Five Star City in the Valley of the Sun |
| | The Green Spot in Arizona's Famous Valley of the Sun |
| DOUGLAS | The City where Progress and Pleasure Are Partners |
| | The Friendly City in the Heart of the Old West |
| FLAGSTAFF | Friendly Fabulous Flagstaff |
| | The Business, Finance, Industry, Shopping and Transportation Hub |
| | The Center of Everything in Northern Arizona |
| | The Center of North Arizona's Scenic Vacationland (on the Coconino Plateau) |
| | The City in the Center of the Most Amazing and Beautiful Country in the World |
| | The City in the Heart of Coconino National Forest |
| | The City in the Pines (ponderosa pine forests) |
| | The City of Seven Wonders |
| | The County Seat of Coconino County |
| | The Home of Ten Thousand Friendly People (1960 pop. 18,214) |
| | The Hub of Arizona's Lumber Industry |

| | |
|---|---|
| FLAGSTAFF (Cont'd) | Touropolis of America (three major tour routes enter the city) |
| FORT HUACHUCA | The Electronic Center of the Southwest |
| GLENDALE | The City in the Valley of the Sun |
| | The Land of Perpetual Harvest |
| | The New Car Capital of Arizona (factory representatives of all major automobile concerns located here) |
| GLOBE | The Capital City of the County with a Copper Bottom (county seat of Gila County noted for its copper mines) |
| | The Gateway to Arizona's Scenic and Recreational Area |
| JEROME | The Largest Ghost Town in America (1960 population 243) |
| KAYENTA | The Gateway to Monument Valley (red sandstone buttes 1,000 feet high in N. E. Arizona and S. E. Utah) |
| KINGMAN | The Gateway to Hoover Dam (726 feet high on Colorado River between Clara County, Nev. and Mohave County, Ariz.) |
| | The Gateway to "Wanderland" in Mohave County, Arizona |
| MESA | Arizona's Third Largest City (1960 population 33, 772) |
| | The City in the Heart of Arizona Vacationland |
| | The City where It's June in January Along the Romantic Apache Trail |
| | The Gem City in Arizona's Valley of the Sun |
| | The Heart of the Romantic Southwest in the Valley of the Sun |
| | The Little City of Charm (1960 population 33, 772) |
| MIAMI | The Concentrator City |
| PHOENIX | America's Favorite Sun and Fun Vacationland |

| | |
|---|---|
| PHOENIX (Cont'd) | The Capital City (1960 population 439, 170) |
| | The Capital City of Arizona (1889) |
| | The City in Arizona's Valley of the Sun |
| | The City where Summer Winters |
| | The Heart of the Sun Country |
| | The Metropolis of the Desert |
| | The Palm City |
| | The Profit Center of the Southwest |
| | The Southwest's Sightseeing Center |
| | The Valley in the Sun (Salt River Valley) |
| | The Youngest Big City in the United States (settled 1870; 1960 population 439, 170) |
| PORTAL | The Yosemite of Arizona (Cave Creek Canyon in Chiricahua Mountains) |
| PRESCOTT | Arizona's First Capital (first territorial legislature 1864, also 1877-1889) |
| | The Center of the Nation's Greatest Concentration of Varied Natural Attractions |
| | The Center of Yavapai (seat of Yavapai County) |
| | The City Rich in Western Tradition |
| | The Cowboy Capital |
| | The First Capital of Arizona (1864-65) |
| | The Mile High City (altitude 5, 346 feet) |
| | The Mile High City of Health |
| | The Sentinel City in the Pines (in the Sierra Madre mountains) |
| QUARTZSITE | The Hottest Town (average July temp. 108. 7°) |
| | The Nation's Hottest Town |
| SALOME | The City where She Danced (town named for Mrs. Grace Salome Pratt) |

| | |
|---|---|
| SAN CARLOS | Hell's Forty Acres (on the San Carlos Indian Reservation) |
| SCOTTSDALE | The Fun'n Excitement Center |
| | The West's Most Western Community |
| | The West's Most Western Town (new buildings simulate frontier structures) |
| SUN CITY | The Town That Changed America's Viewpoint on Retirement Living |
| | The Twin City (with Youngstown, Ariz.) |
| TEMPE | The Home of the Fabulous Sun Devil Athletic Team and Arizona State University |
| | The Swell Place to Live |
| | The Valley's College Town (Arizona State University) |
| TOMBSTONE | The City of Health, History, Hospitality |
| | The City of Sunshine and Silver (famous mining center) |
| | The Town Too Tough To Die (water flooded the mines in 1886, but the people did not leave) |
| TUCSON | America's First City of Sunshine |
| | Arizona's Second Largest City |
| | The Ancient and Honorable Pueblo |
| | The City of Sunshine |
| | The City where Winter Wears a Tan |
| | The Heart of the Old Southwest |
| | The Heart of the Scenic Southwest |
| | The Home of the University of Arizona |
| | The New Pueblo |
| | The Old Pueblo (oldest city in Arizona, first settlement 1776) |
| | The Retirement Center of the Nation |
| | The Southwest Sun Country (about 3,800 hours of sunshine a year) |
| | The Sunshine Capital of the Southwest |
| | The Sunshine City |

| TUCSON (Cont'd) | The Western Gateway to Mexico (65 miles to Nogales, Mexico) The Wonderful Weather Land |
|---|---|
| WICKENBURG | A Bit of the Old West Transplanted in the Twentieth Century America's Dude Ranch Capital The Dude Ranch Capital of the World |
| WILLCOX | A Good Place to Know, Go, Visit, Stay The Cattle Capital and Agricultural Center of the Great Southwest The Cattle Capital of the Nation The Cattle Capital of the World The City in the Heart of the Southwest Wonderland |
| WINSLOW | The Center of Northern Arizona's Scenic Beauty The City in the Heart of the Nation's Sunniest State The Gateway to Hopiland and Navajoland (Hopi Indians and Navajo Indians) The Gateway to Zane Grey's Tonto Basin and Navajoland The Largest City in Northern Arizona |
| YOUNGSTOWN | The Twin City (with Sun City, Ariz.) |
| YUMA | The City where You Can Work, Live, Play, the Western Way The Sunshine Capital of the United States |

## ARKANSAS

| ALMA | The Crossroads for North-South, East-West Traffic |
|---|---|
| ARKANSAS CITY | Ark City |
| BENTON | The Gateway to the Bauxite Fields (discovered 1887 in the Ouachita Mountains) |
| BENTONVILLE | The Gateway to the Northwest |
| BERRYVILLE | The Center City of the Ozarks |

BERRYVILLE (Cont'd)    The Turkey Capital of Arkansas
                       (turkey farms)
                       The Turkey Capital of the Ozarks
BLYTHEVILLE            The City of Churches
                       The City where Cotton Is King
                       The Home of the National Cotton
                       Picking Contest
BULL SHOALS            The Capital of the Big Lake (Bull
                       Shoals Lake)
CAMDEN                 South Arkansas' Busy Port City
                       (on Ouachita River)
                       The Queen City of the Ouchita
CONWAY                 The City of Opportunity
CROSSETT               The Forestry Capital of the Nation
DECATUR                The Community of Friendly People
DOVER                  The Gateway to the Ozarks (be-
                       tween Little Rock and Fort
                       Smith)
EL DORADO              The Commercial, Cultural and
                       Industrial Center of South
                       Arkansas
                       The Oil Capital of Arkansas (oil
                       discovered 1921)
EUREKA SPRINGS         America's Little Switzerland
                       (mountain resort)
                       The "Believe It Or Not" Town
                       The Capital Resort of the Ozarks
                       (oldest resort in the Ozark
                       Region)
                       The Little Switzerland of Amer-
                       ica
                       The Town of "Up and Down"
FAYETTEVILLE           America's Little Switzerland
                       (highest point in Arkansas
                       Ozarks)
                       Northwest Arkansas' Largest City
                       The Athens of Arkansas
                       The City That Progress Built
                       The Gateway to Scenic Boston
                       Mountains
                       The Gateway to the Boston Moun-
                       tains
FLIPPIN                The Gateway to Blue Shoals Lake
                       and Dam
FORREST CITY           The Hoist Capital of America
                       (Yale and Towne Inc. plant)

| | |
|---|---|
| FORT SMITH | America's Industrial City |
| | Arkansas' Industrial Center |
| | The Center City |
| | The City of Balance |
| | The City of Your Future |
| | The Growing City of Industry and Recreation |
| | The Gateway to the Beautiful Ozark Playground |
| | The Leading Industrial City in Arkansas |
| | The Southwestern Factory City |
| GENTRY | The Typical Ozark Home Town |
| GRAVETTE | The World's Largest Black Walnut Factory |
| GREEN FOREST | The Tomato Capital of the Ozarks |
| HARRISON | The Hub of the Ozarks (in the Arkansas Ozarks) |
| | The Metropolis of a Fast Growing Commercial and Agricultural Area |
| | The Ozark Wonderland |
| HAZEN | The Rice Center of the U. S. A. |
| HEBER SPRINGS | The Gateway to Giant Greer's Ferry Lake |
| HELENA | Arkansas' Only Seaport (on the Mississippi River) |
| | The City of Industrial Opportunity |
| | The Twin Cities (with West Helena) |
| HOPE | Southwest Arkansas' Most Conveniently Located City |
| | The Watermelon Capital of the U. S. |
| HOT SPRINGS | America's Greatest Health and Resort Center |
| | America's Greatest Health and Rest Center |
| | America's Own Spa (the only health resort in the U. S. where the natural hot waters which flow from the earth are owned, controlled and endorsed by the U. S. government) |
| | Arkansas' Largest Health and Pleasure Resort |
| | The Carlsbad of America |

| | |
|---|---|
| HOT SPRINGS (Cont'd) | The City where the World Bathes and Plays |
| | The Nation's Health Resort (famous hot springs and spas) |
| | The Valley of Vapors |
| | The Vapor City (steam from the hot springs) |
| HUNTSVILLE | The Friendly City |
| JONESBORO | The City Ready for Tomorrow (home of Arkansas State College) |
| LAKE VILLAGE | Home of the Big Black Bass |
| LITTLE ROCK | Arkopolis |
| | The Capital City (1960 population 107,813), (only city in the nation with three capitals) |
| | The City of Roses |
| | The City of Three Capitals (three capital buildings remain, each of a different era) |
| | The Geographic Cultural and Economic Center |
| MOUNTAIN HOME | The Center of the Most Popular Resort Section in the Ozarks |
| | The Fishing Capital of the Ozarks (White River, Norfork Lake, Bull Shoals Lake) |
| | The Gateway to Lake Norfolk |
| NASHVILLE | The Peach Capital of Arkansas |
| PARIS | The Gateway to Mt. Magazine |
| PINE BLUFF | The City of Gigantic Industries, Unparalleled Schools |
| | The City of Magnificent Churches, Beautiful Homes |
| | The City of Peace and Plenty |
| | The Gateway to Southeast Arkansas |
| | The Trade Center for Southeast Arkansas |
| ROGERS | The Heartland of the Beaver Lake Area |
| RUSSELLVILLE | The Home of Arkansas Polytechnic College |
| SPRINGDALE | The Agricultural and Industrial Center of Northwest Arkansas |
| | The Main Street of Northwest Arkansas |

SPRINGDALE (Cont'd)        The Rodeo of the Ozarks Town
STUTTGART                  The Duck Hunting Capital of the
                             World
TEXARKANA                  The Twin Cities (twin cities on
                             the Arkansas-Texas border:
                             Texarkana, Ark., and Texar-
                             kana, Texas)
VAN BUREN                  The Kopper Kettle
WASHINGTON                 The Birthplace of Texas
                           The Cradle of Arkansas History
WEST HELENA                The Twin Cities (with Helena)
WEST MEMPHIS               The Fastest Growing City in East-
                             ern Arkansas
                           The Gateway to the Southwest
WILCOX                     The Cattle Center
WINSLOW                    The Pioneer Resort Town

## CALIFORNIA

ALAMEDA                    The Isle of Pleasant Living (east-
                             ern shore of San Francisco
                             Bay)
ALBANY                     The City of Homes
ALTADENA                   The Community of the Deodars
                             (trees)
ALTURAS                    The Home of the Mule-tail Deer
ANAHEIM                    The City of Beautiful Parks
                           The City of Good Living
                           The Family City
                           The Fun N' Convention City
                           The Home of Disney Land
                           The Ideal Year 'Round Commun-
                             ity
                           The Recreation Center
ANGWIN                     The City Set on a Hill
ATOLIA                     The Sin City
ATWATER                    The Center for Good Living,
                             Agriculture, Recreation and
                             Industry
                           The City That Is Near Every-
                             thing
AVALON                     The Port of Friendliness
AZUZA                      The Gateway to the San Gabriels
BALDWIN PARK               The Gateway to the Orange Em-
                             pire
BANNING                    The Gateway to the Desert and
                             Idyllwild Mountain Resort

| | |
|---|---|
| BEAUMONT | The Center of San Gorgonio Mountains |
| BENICIA | The Athens of California |
| | The City of Industrial Opportunity |
| BERKELEY | The Athens of the West (the University of California) |
| | The Balanced City |
| BEVERLY HILLS | The Garden Spot of the World |
| BISHOP | The Sportsmans Town |
| | The World Gliding Center |
| BLUE LAKE | The Gateway to the Great Mad River Valley |
| | The Place where the Sunshine and Sea Meet |
| BUENO PARK | The Center of the Southland |
| BURLINGAME | One of California's Choicest Communities |
| CAMBRIA | The Village where the Pines Meet the Sea |
| CASTRO VALLEY | The City Big Enough for Opportunity - Small Enough for Friendliness |
| | The Family Community |
| | The Heart of Good Living |
| CASTROVILLE | The Artichoke Capital of the World |
| CHICO | The Almond Capital of the World (almond processing plants) |
| | The Almond Center of the World (produces 20 percent of the world's supply) |
| CHOWCHILLA | A Nice Place to Live |
| | The City With a Big Future |
| CHULA VISTA | California's Fastest Growing City |
| | The City for Gracious Living |
| | The City where Industry is Wanted and Growing |
| | The City where Year-round Living Is a Pleasure |
| | The City which Tops the World for Sunshine and Sociability |
| | The Good Place to Live |
| | The Lemon Capitol of the World |
| | The Vacation Land |
| CLAREMONT | A Bit of New England with a Sombrero on It |
| | Claremont, the Beautiful |

CLAREMONT (Cont'd)    The City of Living and Learning
                      The College Town Amid the
                          Orange Groves (Pomona Col-
                          lege, Scripps College for Wo-
                          men, Claremont Men's Col-
                          lege, Claremont Graduate
                          School, Harvey Mudd College)
COALINGA              The Heart of the Westside of
                          Fresno County
COLTON                The Hub City
                      The Industrial City
COMMERCE              The Model City
                      The Modern City
COMPTON               The Hub City
CONCORD               The City of Dynamic Opportunity
CORNING               The Center of the Olive Industry
CORONA                The Circle City (three mile cir-
                          cular boulevard surrounding
                          the business district)
                      The Lemon Capital
CULVER CITY           The Business Center for Greater
                          Los Angeles
DEATH VALLEY          America's Bottom
                      America's Low Spot
DELANO                The Land of Promise
DEL MONTE             The Twenty-Thousand Acre Play-
                          ground
DINUBA                The Center of the Most Produc-
                          tive Agricultural Area in the
                          Nation
                      Raisinland, U. S. A.
DIXON                 The City of Diversified Opportun-
                          ity
DOWNEY                The City with a Future Unlimited
EL CERRITO            The City Keyed to Your Way of
                          Living
                      The City of Gracious Living
                      The City that Knows where It Is
                          Going
                      The City with a View
                      The Dynamic City
                      The Prime Residential Community
                          in the Bay Area
ELSINORE              The Scenic Health Resort of Cali-
                          fornia
FONTANA               The Neighborly Friendly Commun-
                          ity

FORTUNA                 The City where Nature Smiles
                           the Year 'Round
                        The Friendly City
FRESNO                  The Agricultural and Recreational
                           Center of California
                        The Bustling Center of Industry,
                           Agriculture, Wholesale Trade
                           and Shipping
                        The Gateway to Yosemite Sequoia
                           and King Canyon Parks
                        The Raisin Center of the World
                        The Scenic Hub of the Golden
                           State
                        The Sweet Wine Capital of the
                           World
FULLERTON               The City of Excellence in Living
                        The City of Hospitality
GARDEN GROVE            The Planned Growing City
GARDENA                 The Little Las Vegas
                        The Poker City
                        The Poker-Playing Capital of the
                           West
GLENDALE                The Jewel City
                        The Queen of the Valley (San Fer-
                           nando Valley)
GUSTINE                 The Home of the World's Largest
                           Walnut Tree
HALF MOON BAY           Spanish Town
HAWTHORNE               The Aircraft Center of the West
                        The City of Progress and Security
HOLLYWOOD               Filmdom
                        Filmland
                        The Big-Headed Burg
                        The Celluloid City
                        The Cinema Capital (moving pic-
                           ture studios opened 1911)
                        The Cinema Village
                        The Cinemaland
                        The Cinematown
                        The Circle City
                        The City of Galloping Tin-Types
                        The Fairyland
                        The Film Capital
                        The Film Capital of the World
                        The Film City
                        The Flicker Capital

| | |
|---|---|
| HOLLYWOOD (Cont'd) | The Flicker City |
| | The Flicker Lane |
| | The Glamour City |
| | The Land of Promise |
| | The Movie Village |
| | The Movieland |
| | The Screenland |
| | The Sinemaland |
| | The Squawkiewood |
| | The Stardom |
| | The Starland |
| | The Studioland |
| HOLTVILLE | America's Carrot Capital (in Imperial Valley) |
| INDIO | The Center of All Vacation Fun |
| | The Date Capital of the United States (produces about 90 percent of all dates grown in the United States) |
| | The Date Capital of the World |
| | The Desert Wonderland (Coachella Valley) |
| | Southern California's Desert Playground |
| INGLEWOOD | The Harbor of the Air (numerous aircraft plants) |
| ISLETON | The Asparagus Capital of the World |
| KINGSBURG | The Largest Watermelon Shipping Center in California |
| LAGUNA BEACH | The City of Serene Living |
| LAKE TAHOE | (see also Nevada) |
| | America's All-Year Playground |
| | The Cesspool for Gambling Joints |
| | The City with a Hole in the Middle |
| | The Coming Vegas |
| | The Recreational Slum |
| | The Sierra "Coney Island" (a pleasure resort in Brooklyn, N. Y. ) |
| LANCASTER | The Heart of the Antelope Valley |
| LINDSAY | The City in the Garden of the Sun |
| LODI | America's Sherryland |
| | The Home of the Flame Tokay Grape |
| LONG BEACH | The City by the Sea |

LONG BEACH (Cont'd)          The City of Investments where
                               Commerce and Industry Thrive
                             The Gem of Beaches
                             The Home of the Miss Universe
                               Pageant
                             The International City
                             The Land of Industrial Opportun-
                               ities
                             The Most Versatile Port on the
                               West Coast
                             The Natural Gateway to Southern
                               California's Endless Charm
                             The Pride of the Pacific
                             The Proud Port of the Pacific
                             The Queen of the Beaches
                             The Star of the Southland
                             The World Center of Oceanology
                               (Battelle Memorial Institute,
                               Ocean Science and Engineering,
                               Inc., etc.)
                             The Year 'Round Convention and
                               Resort Metropolis of the Pa-
                               cific
                             The Year 'Round Playground of
                               the Pacific
LOS ALTOS                    The City of Trees
                             The Garden Spot of the World
                               Famous Santa Clara Valley
LOS ANGELES                  Cleveland with Palm Trees
                             El-Ay
                             Elay
                             L. A.
                             Las Diablos
                             Nineteen Suburbs in Search of a
                               Metropolis
                             The Angel City
                             The Capital of Crackpots
                             The Catchall of Suckers
                             The Circus Without a Tent
                             The Citrus Metropolis
                             The City Built in a Day
                             The City Built on Sand
                             The City Metropolis
                             The City of Angels
                             The City of Dreadful Joy
                             The City of Excitement

LOS ANGELES (Cont'd)      The City of Flowers
                          The City of Liquid Sunshine
                          The City of Make Believe
                          The City of Sunshine
                          The Collection of Freeways in
                            Search of a City
                          The Community of Trees
                          The Detroit of Airplanes
                          The Exciting City
                          The Exciting World City
                          The Fabulous City
                          The House Built on Sand
                          The Land of the Afternoon
                          The Lost Angels
                          The Mecca of Crackpots
                          The Metropolis of Isms
                          The Metropolis of the Pacific
                            Coast
                          The Metropolis of the West
                          The Motion Picture Center of the
                            World
                          The Movie City
                          The Murder City (where Senator
                            Robert Francis Kennedy was
                            assassinated)
                          The Nation's Smog Capital
                          The Old Pueblo
                          The Original Site of Californica-
                            tion
                          The Paradise Sullied
                          The Place where Fun Never Stops
                          The Queen of the Cow Countries
                          The Seaport of Iowa (facetious)
                          The Second Murder City (assassi-
                            nation of Senator R. F. Kennedy)
                          The Smog City
                          The Spawning Ground of Realtors
                          Two Newarks
                          The Ultimate City (title of book by
                            Christopher Rand)
                          The Upper Sandusky West
                          The Westernmost Suburb of Des
                            Moines
                          The World of Variety
                          The Year-Round Convention City
LOS BANOS                 The Center for Agriculture, In-
                            dustry and Recreation

McLOUD                    The Blackberry Capital of the
                             World
MADERA                    The Gem City of the Wealthy San
                             Joaquin Valley
MANTECA                   The Butter City (dairy production
                             center, Spanish word for but-
                             ter)
                          The Crossroads of California
MARIPOSA                  The Western Gateway City
MARYSVILLE                The Peach Bowl of the United
                             States
MERCED                    The Gateway to Yosemite
MILL VALLEY               The Gateway to Muir Woods
MODESTO                   The City That Is Only Two Hours
                             to the Sierras on the Sea (on
                             the Tuolumne River)
                          The Peach Capital of the World
MONROVIA                  The City in Motion
                          The Gem City of the Foothills
MONTEBELLO                The City Between the Mountains
                             and the Sea
                          The City of Flowers
                          The City of Gardens
                          The City of Homes
                          The City of Industry
                          The Fastest Growing City in Los
                             Angeles County (1960 popula-
                             tion 32, 097)
MONTEREY                  America's Famous Summer and
                             Winter Resort
                          The Capital of Old California
                             (capital of old California from
                             1776 to the end of 1849 and de
                             facto from 1770-1776)
                          The City of History and Romance
                          The City where America Began
                             in the West (site discovered in
                             1542 by Juan Rodriguez Cabril-
                             lo)
                          The First American Capital West
                             of the Rockies (capital of Alta
                             California under the Spanish,
                             Mexican and United States
                             Flags)
                          The Year Round Golf Capital of
                             the World

| | |
|---|---|
| MORGAN HILL | The Dam End of Santa Clara County |
| | The Land of Opportunity |
| NAPA | The Southeastern Entrance to the Redwood Empire (97 percent of the world's great redwoods) |
| | The Table Wine Center of the World (applied also to Napa County) |
| NATIONAL CITY | The City where Summers are Mild and Winters are Warm |
| NEVADA CITY | The Gateway to the Great Tahoe National Forest |
| | The Gateway to the Sportsman's Paradise |
| NORTH HOLLYWOOD | The Gateway to the San Fernando Valley (a part of the City of Los Angeles) |
| OAKDALE | The City in Central California Convenient to Everything |
| | The Ladino Clover Center of America (grazing for beef cattle, originally imported from Italy) |
| OAKLAND | The City of Progress and Prosperity |
| | The Detroit of the West (manufacturing center) |
| | The Wester City of Ships (site of U. S. Army Port of Embarkation, Naval Supply Depot, etc.) |
| OCEANSIDE | The Gateway to Camp Pendleton |
| | The Gateway to San Luis Rey Mission |
| ONTARIO | The City That Charms |
| OROVILLE | The District Incomparable |
| PACIFIC GROVE | The Leading Family Resort Summer and Winter |
| | The Model Family Resort, Summer and Winter |
| PALM DESERT | The Winter Golf Mecca |
| PALM SPRINGS | America's Desert Resort |
| | America's Foremost Desert Resort |
| | The Capital of Sunshine |
| | The City That Is Just for Fun |
| | The Golf Capital of the World (over 20 challenging courses) |

| | |
|---|---|
| PALM SPRINGS (Cont'd) | The Lost Resort |
| | The Oasis in the Desert (in the Upper Colorado desert) |
| | The Swimming Pool City (over 4,000 pools) |
| | The Winter Golf Capital of the World |
| | The World's Winter Golf Capital |
| PALO ALTO | The Garden Spot of Peninsular (at foothills of Coast Range Mountains) |
| | The Home of Stanford University |
| | The Ideal Home and Recreational Center |
| | The Ultra Modern City |
| PARAMOUNT | The City of Roses |
| PASADENA | The City of Roses |
| | The Crown City |
| | The Crown City of the Valley |
| | The Crown of the Valley |
| | The Hub of the Fabulous Gulf Coast |
| | The Town That Roses Built (famous annual parade on January first, and football tournament) |
| PETALUMA | The Egg Basket of the World (egg production center) |
| | The Future Manufacturing Center of the West where Rail and Water Transportation Meet (used in 1906) |
| | The Lowell of the West |
| | The White Leghorn City of the West |
| | The World's Egg Basket |
| PIEDMONT | The Queen of the Hills |
| PISMO BEACH | The City where the Sun Spends the Winter |
| PITTSBURG | The Industrial Capital of California |
| | The Industrial City of the West (steel plant, numerous factories) |
| PLACERVILLE | Hangtown (numerous hangings in pioneer days) |
| POMONA | The Inland City Beautiful |

| | |
|---|---|
| PORTERVILLE | The Friendly City |
| PORTOFINO | Southern California's Most Modern Resort |
| REDLANDS | The Busy Business Center |
| | The Gem City |
| | The Gem of the Valley |
| | The Radiant Garden Spot of California |
| | The Show Place of Southern California |
| RICHMOND | The Fastest Growing Industrial Community (1960 population 71, 854) |
| | The Largest City of Contra Costa County, California |
| RIDGECREST | The Desert Community |
| RIPON | The Almond Capitol of California |
| | The Home of the Ripon Almond Blossom Festival |
| RIVERSIDE | The City of Exceptional Beauty |
| | The City of Friendliness and Beauty |
| | The City of Individuality and Charm |
| | The Home of the Orange |
| | The Mission City |
| SACRAMENTO | New Helvetia (founded August 12, 1839 by Captain John Augustus Sutter; first settlement of white men in interior California) |
| | Sacto (contraction of word, first and last syllable of Sacramento) |
| | The Almond Capital of the World |
| | The Capital City (1960 population 191, 667) |
| | The City of the Plains |
| | The City of Trees |
| | The City where California Began (founded August 12, 1839 by Captain John Augustine Sutter; first settlement of white men in interior California) |
| | The Golden City |
| | The Heart of California |
| | The Land of Romance and Recreation |
| | The Queen of the Golden Empire |

| | |
|---|---|
| ST. HELENA | The City in the Heart of Colorful Napa Valley |
| | The Table Wine Center of the World |
| SAN ANSELMO | The Hub |
| SAN BERNARDINO | The City of Mineral Springs |
| | The Gate City |
| | The Leading Inland City of the South (on the edge of the Mojave Desert at the base of the San Bernardino Mountains, about sixty miles inland) |
| | The Playground of Southern California |
| | San Berdoo |
| SAN BRUNO | The City with a Future |
| | The Friendliest Spot on the King's Highway |
| SAN CLEMENTE | The City That Climate Built |
| | The Spanish Village |
| SAN DIEGO | America's Only International Playground |
| | California at Its Best |
| | The Air Capital of the West |
| | The Birthplace of California (discovered 1542 by Cabrillo) |
| | The City Built Around a Park |
| | The City by the Sea |
| | The City where California and Mexico Meet the Blue Pacific |
| | The City where California Began (visited in 1539 by Father Marcos and his followers from the desert side) |
| | The Gateway to California |
| | The Italy of America |
| | The Jewel City of California |
| | The Kingdom of the Sun |
| | The Place where California Began |
| | The Plymouth of the Pacific Coast (first permanent white settlement on the Pacific Coast) |
| | The Plymouth of the West |
| SAN FRANCISCO | America's Most Exciting City |
| | America's Most Friendly Fascinating City |

SAN FRANCISCO (Cont'd)        America's Paris
                              Frisco
                              The Bagdad by the Bay
                              The Bay City
                              The City Beautiful
                              The City by the Golden Gate
                              The City by the Sea
                              The City Cosmopolitan
                              The City for Romantics
                              The City of a Hundred Hills
                              The City of Bridges
                              The City of Firsts
                              The City of Many Adventures
                              The City of Miracles
                              The City of One Hundred Hills
                              The City of the Golden Gate
                              The City on the Golden Hills
                                  (title of book by Herb Caen
                                  and Dong Kingman)
                              The City where the Far East
                                  Meets the Far West
                              The Cosmopolitan City
                              The Cosmopolitan City of the
                                  West
                              The Cosmopolitan San Francisco
                              The Cultural Center of the West
                              The Exposition City
                              The Financial Center of the West
                              The Financial Center of the World
                              The Gateway to the Orient
                              The Gateway to the Far East
                              The Golden City
                              The Golden Gate City
                              The Market of Three Barbarian
                                  Tribes
                              The Mushroom City
                              The Nation's Western Capital
                              The Old Gold Hill
                              The Paris of America
                              The Phoenix of the Pacific
                              The Poor Man's Paradise
                              The Port O'Missing Men
                              The Port of Gold
                              The Queen City
                              The Queen City of the Pacific
                              The Queen City of the Pacific
                                  Coast

| | |
|---|---|
| SAN FRANCISCO (Cont'd) | The Queen City of the West |
| | The Queen of the Pacific |
| | The Sand Hills of the Eastern Barbarians |
| | The Suicide Capital of the United States |
| | The Timeless Wonderland |
| | The United Nations' Conference Center (United Nations Conference on International Organization of 46 nations opened April 25, 1945) |
| | The Western Gate |
| SAN JOSE | The Garden City |
| SAN LEANDRO | The Cherry City of California |
| | The Home of Sunshine and Flowers |
| SAN LUIS OBISPO | The City of the Mountain Peaks |
| | Southern California's Big "Oh" |
| SAN MARCOS | The City in the Valley of Discovery |
| SAN MATEO | The Center of Transportation to All Points |
| | The City with the Nation's Most Perfect Year 'Round Climate |
| | The Growing Center of Administrative Offices |
| | The Retail Shopping Center of the Peninsula |
| SAN PABLO | The City of Pride and Progress |
| | The Little City with the Big Inferiority Complex |
| SAN RAFAEL | The City of Health (St. Raphael, Patron Saint of Good Health) |
| | The City where Past and Future Make a Prosperous Present |
| | The Heart of Marvelous Marin County |
| | The Missing City of Marin |
| SANTA ANA | The City of Resources |
| SANTA BARBARA | California's Enchanting City |
| | California's World Famous All-Year Resort |
| | The City by the Sea |
| | The City where Hospitality is a Tradition |

| | |
|---|---|
| SANTA BARBARA (Cont'd) | The Newport of the Pacific |
| | The Queen of the Missions (Mission Santa Barbara founded 1786) |
| SANTA CRUZ | Scenic California's Scenic Playground |
| | The World's Most Famous Playground |
| SANTA MARIA | The Missile Capital of the West |
| | The Valley of the Gardens (numerous seed farms) |
| SANTA MONICA | The City for Oceans of Fun |
| | The City where the Mountains Meet the Sea |
| | The City where Wilshire Boulevard Meets the Pacific |
| SANTA PAULA | The Lemon Center |
| SANTA ROSA | The City Designed for Living |
| SAUSALITO | The Greenwich Village of the West (literary groups) |
| SELMA | The Raisin Capital of the World |
| SHAFTER | The Potato Capital |
| SOLVANG | Little Denmark (established in 1912 as a settlement for Danes; has Danish church, college and schools) |
| STOCKTON | A Variety of Recreational Opportunities |
| | California's Inland Harber (on Stockton channel and San Joaquin River) |
| | The Center of California |
| | The City That Has Something for You |
| | The Gateway to the San Joaquin Valley |
| | The Heart of America's Number One Agricultural Area |
| | The Home of Diamond Walnuts |
| | The Industrial and Distributing Center of the Pacific Coast Empire |
| | The Industrial Hub of the West |
| | The Manufacturing City of the Pacific |
| SUNNYVALE | The City with a Built-In Future |
| TERMINAL ISLAND | A Little Sea by the Sea of Happy |

TERMINAL ISLAND (Cont'd)    Rest and Reverie
THOUSAND OAKS               The Bel Air of Conejo
TRACY                       The City where Agriculture and
                               Industries Meet
TWENTY-NINE PALMS           The Northernmost Oasis in Amer-
                               ica
UKIAH                       The Home of Bartlett Pears
UPLAND                      The City of Good Health, Living
                               and Business
                            The Western Shangri-La
VALLEJO                     The Navy Town (home of Mare
                               Island Naval Shipyard and Cali-
                               fornia Maritime Academy)
VENTURA                     The Poinsettia City
WALNUT CREEK                The Paradise in a Nut Shell
WATSONVILLE                 The Apple City
                            The Strawberry Capital of the
                               World
WEST COVINA                 The Headquarters City of East
                               San Gabriel Valley
WESTMINSTER                 The Heart of Orange County
WHITTIER                    A Municipal Poem of Beauty,
                               Sunshine, Health, Prosperity
                               and Happiness
                            The Finest Home and Cultural
                               Community in Southern Cali-
                               fornia
                            The Best Town of its Age in
                               This Glorious Climate
                            The Home Town of Richard Nixon
                            The Magic Little City (founded in
                               1887 by Quakers)
                            The Quaker City (founded in 1887
                               by Quakers)
WILLITS                     The Good Little Town
WILMINGTON                  The Heart of the Harbor
YORBA LINDA                 The Birthplace of President Rich-
                               ard Nixon
YUBA CITY                   The Peach Bowl of the U. S.

## COLORADO

ALAMOSA                     The City at the Crossroads of
                               Trans-Americas Highway and
                               the Navajo Trail
ASPEN                       Ski Capital U. S. A.
BOULDER                     The City where Mountains and

BOULDER (Cont'd)

Plains Mcet (at the foot of
the Flatirons which rises
1,000 feet above the city)
The Gateway to Colorado's Scenic
Region
The Gateway to Roosevelt National
Forest and Rocky Mountain Na-
tional Park
The Home of the University of
Colorado
The Wonderland of America

BRIGHTON

Brighton's Future Is Bright

BRUSH

America's Sugar Bowl (Great
Western Beet Sugar Factory,
beet slicing capacity about
1,600 tons daily)

CENTRAL CITY

The Richest Square Mile on
Earth

COLORADO SPRINGS

The City of Sunshine
The Little Lunnon (London) (many
Britishers live here)
The Newport of the West

DENVER

The Capital City (1960 population
493,887)
The Capital of the Rocky Moun-
tain Empire
The City of the Plains
The Convention City
The Dynamic Metropolis of the
Rocky Mountain Empire
The Friendly City in the Sky
The Gateway to the Rockies
The Industrial, Commercial and
Cultural Capital
The Little Capital
The Mile High City (alt. 5,280 ft.)
The Mining Town with a Heart
The Queen City of the Plains
The Queen City of the West
The Western Capital
The White Collar City

DURANGO

The Switzerland of America (altitude 6,505 feet)

EMPIRE

The Eastern Approach to Ber-
thoud Pass

ESTES PARK

Resort Town, U.S.A. (near Rocky
Mountain National Park)

| | |
|---|---|
| FORT COLLINS | Eden of the Closest State to Heaven |
| | The City of Beautiful Parks |
| | The City of Magnificent Mountains |
| | The City of Panoramic Boulevards |
| | The City of Plentiful Plains |
| | The Fascinating Foothills City (about 40 miles from Fort Collins Mountain Park) |
| | The Gateway to the Poudre (River) |
| | The Home of the Colorado Aggies (Colorado Agricultural and Mechanical College) |
| | The Lamb and Cattle Capital of the West ( large lamb-feeding center) |
| | The Lilac City |
| | The Safest Spot in the World |
| FORT MORGAN | The City of Lights |
| GEORGETOWN | The Historic Doorway to Colorado's Finest See and Ski Country |
| | The Silver Queen of the Rockies (at the foot of the Continental Divide) |
| | The Ski Capital of Colorado |
| GLENWOOD SPRINGS | The Kissingen of America |
| GRAND JUNCTION | The City with Foresight |
| | The Headquarters City |
| | The Hub City of Western Colorado and Eastern Utah |
| | The Hub of the Scenic West (Grand Mesa National Forest) |
| | The Uranium Capital of the World |
| | The Vacation Center of a Fabulous Land of Contrasts |
| LEADVILLE | The Cloud City (altitude 10, 188 feet, claimed to be the highest incorporated city in the U. S. ) |
| | The Magic City |
| LIMON | The Gateway to the Rockies |
| LOVELAND | America's Sweetheart City (popular mailing address for valentines) |
| | The Sweetheart Town |
| MONTE VISTA | The Potato Capital of the West |
| OURAY | The Gem City of the Rockies |

| | |
|---|---|
| OURAY (Cont'd) | The Gem of the Rockies |
| | The Switzerland of America |
| PUEBLO | Colorado's Second City |
| | The City of Homes and Industry |
| | The Fountain City |
| | The Manufacturing City of the Rocky Mountain Region |
| | The Steel City of the West (plant of Colorado Fuel and Iron Corp. ) |
| SALIDA | Nature's Wonderland |
| | The City Atop the Nation's Roof Garden (altitude 7, 038 feet) |
| | The City in the Valley of the Arkansas |
| | The City of Dreams |
| | The City on the Highway to Heaven (altitude 7, 038 feet) |
| | The Closest State to Heaven |
| | The Crossroads to Wonderland |
| | The Gem City |
| | The Gem of the Ocean |
| | The Heart of the Rockies |
| | The Hospitality City of the Rockies |
| | The Lovely Gateway to the Passes |
| | The Portal to the Quint States |
| | The Roof Garden of America (altitude 7, 038 feet) |
| | The Sportsman's Paradise |
| | The Town with a Heart |
| STEAMBOAT SPRINGS | The Gateway to the Routt National Forest |
| | Ski Town, U. S. A. |
| | The Winter and Summer Playground |
| TRINIDAD | The City Where the Santa Fe Trail of the Prairies Meets the Mountains of the Historical West |
| VAIL | The Baby of the Colorado Ski Resorts |
| WALSH | The Broom Corn Center |

## CONNECTICUT

| | |
|---|---|
| ANSONIA | The Industrial Heart of the Naugatuck Valley |

BRIDGEPORT                          The Essen of America
                                    The Industrial Capital of Amer-
                                       ica
                                    The Industrial Capital of Con-
                                       necticut
                                    The Park City
                                    The Proud City
                                    The Recreation Center for Gener-
                                       ations
BRISTOL                             The City of Opportunity
                                    The Clock Center of the World
                                       (numerous clock factories, site
                                       of American Clock and Watch
                                       Museum)
CLINTON                             The Truly Colonial Town
DANBURY                             The City in the Country
                                    The Gateway to Candlewood Lake
                                    The Gateway to New England
                                    The Hat City (numerous hat fac-
                                       tories; first one opened in
                                       1780)
                                    The Hat City of the World
                                    The Space Age City
EAST HAMPTON                        The Bell Town (site of bell fac-
                                       tories since 1808)
                                    The Bell Town of America
EAST WINDSOR HILL                   The Town to Grow With
FARMINGTON                          The Mother of Towns (settled
                                       1640)
GREENWICH                           The Friendliest Town (foster chil-
                                       dren invited for supper)
                                    The Gateway to New England
GROTON                              The World's Submarine Capital
                                       (the Nautilus first atomic-
                                       powered submarine built here
                                       and launched January 21, 1954)
GUILFORD                            The City where the Heritage of
                                       the Past Lends Warmth to the
                                       Present
                                    The Shore Village (on Long Is-
                                       land Sound)
                                    The Shrine of Old Homes
HARTFORD                            The Capital City (1960 population
                                       162, 176)
                                    The Charter Oak City (the consti-
                                       tution of Connecticut hidden in

| | |
|---|---|
| HARTFORD (Cont'd) | hollow of an oak tree) |
| | The City Beautiful |
| | The Convention City of the East |
| | The East Coast Megalopolis |
| | The Insurance Capital of the World |
| | The Insurance City (home office of about 40 insurance companies with combined assets over 12 billion) |
| | The Major Insurance City |
| | The Nation's Insurance Capital |
| LITCHFIELD | The Ultimate City |
| MANCHESTER | The City of Village Charm (in the valley of the Connecticut River) |
| MERIDEN | The Complete Shopping Center |
| | The Heart of Connecticut |
| | The Silver City (home of International Silver Co. and other silverware manufacturers) |
| MIDDLETOWN | The Forest City |
| MYSTIC | The Cradle of Square Riggers (famous shipbuilding center about 1850's) |
| | The Home of Yachtsmen |
| | The Port of Last Call |
| | The Seaport Village (developed by Marine Historical Association) |
| | Williamsburg of the Sea |
| NAUGATUCK | The Hub of Connecticut's Naugatuck River Valley |
| NEW BRITAIN | The Hardware City (production of builders' hardware) |
| | The Hardware City of the World |
| | The Wonderful Place to Live, Work, Play |
| NEW CANAAN | The Next Station to Heaven |
| NEW HAVEN | One of the First American Cities of the Industrial Age |
| | The City of Elms |
| | The City of the Future |
| | The Elm City |
| | The Yankee Athens (site of Yale University) |
| NEW LONDON | The City Just a Step From the Past, in Step with the Present |

NEW LONDON (Cont'd)            and Stepping Toward the Future
                              The Hills Against the Sky Town
                              The Ideal City in All Seasons
                              The Whaling City (industry cen-
                                  tered here from 1784 to 1850)
                              The Utopia of the North Atlantic
NORWALK                        The Athens of New England
                              The Charming Spot in Which to
                                  Live and Work
                              The City of Homes
                              The City of Science
                              The Clam Town
                              The Community of Substance
                              The Derby City (first derby hat
                                  in the U. S. made here)
                              The Gateway of New England
                              The Gateway to All New England
                              The Hat Town
                              The New England Garden Spot
                              The Place to Live
                              The Progressive City with a
                                  Bright Future
                              The Shoe and Slipper City
                              The Thrifty New England Com-
                                  munity Steeped in Colonial
                                  Tradition and Democracy
                              The Twin City (with South Nor-
                                  walk)
                              The Well Balanced City with Op-
                                  portunities for All
                              The World's Oyster Capital
NORWICH                        The Rose of New England (fa-
                                  mous Memorial Rose Garden
                                  honoring World War II dead)
ROCKVILLE                      The Loom City
SOUTH NORWALK                  The Twin City (with Norwalk,
                                  Conn. )
SOUTH WINDSOR                  The Town with Grow Power
STAMFORD                       The City in Step with Tomorrow
                              The City of Research
                              The Cultural Hub
                              The Fastest Growing City in the
                                  County (Fairfield County)
                              The Fastest Growing Municipality
                                  in the State
                              The Home of the Metered Maid
                                  System

STAMFORD (Cont'd)          The Lock City (Yale and Towne
                              factory was located here)
                           The Research City
STRATFORD                  The Town with a Future (1960
                              population 45,012)
THOMASTON                  The Clock City (Seth Thomas
                              clocks made 1813)
THOMPSON                   The Indianapolis of the East
                              (Thompson Speedway)
TORRINGTON                 The Most Accessible City
WATERBURY                  The Brass Center of the World
                           The Brass City (large brass in-
                              dustry)
                           The Center of Industrial Develop-
                              ment in Western Connecticut
                           The City where Things Are Hap-
                              pening
                           The Crossroads of Connecticut
                           The Gateway to the Litchfield
                              Hills
                           The Key City of Naugatuck Valley
WESTPORT                   The Town of Homes
WILLIMANTIC                The Eastern Connecticut Center
                           The Thread City (mill of Ameri-
                              can Thread Company)
WINDSOR                    The Heart of the New England
                              Tobacco Farm Land
WINSTED                    The Gateway to the Berkshires
                           The Laurel City (mountain laurel)

DELAWARE

DOVER                      The Capital City (1960 population
                              7,230, state capital in 1777)
                           The Capital of the First State
                           The First City of the First State
                              (became capital May 12,
                              1777)
                           The Home of Latex Rubber
MILFORD                    The Heart of Delaware
NEW CASTLE                 The Gateway to the Miss Universe
                              Highway
REHOBOTH BEACH             Delaware's Summer Capital (pop-
                              ular summer resort on the At-
                              lantic Ocean)
                           The Nation's Summer Capital
                              (because of the large number

REHOBOTH BEACH (Cont'd)   of vacationists from Washing-
ton, D. C.)
Washington-By-The Sea (near
Washington, D. C.)

WILMINGTON        Dupont Town (home of the E. I.
du Pont de Nemours & Co.)
Dupontonia (see above)
Quaker Town (formerly used be-
cause of Quaker residents)
The Chemical Capital of the
World
The First City of the First State
(first settlement established
by the Swedes in the territory
which later was the first to
ratify the Constitution)
The Financial Center of the Del-
Mar-Va Peninsula
The Heart of the Harbor
The Port of Personal Service
(on Delaware River)

## DISTRICT OF COLUMBIA

WASHINGTON        Capital City, U. S. A.
The Capital City
The Capital of a Great Nation
The Capital of America
The Capital of Miserable Huts
The Capital of the Vast Republic
The Center of History in the
Making
The City Beautiful
The City in a Forest
The City of a Thousand Thrills
The City of Conversation
The City of Houses Without
Streets
The City of Lost Footsteps
The City of Magnificent Distances
(so-called by Jose Correo de
Serra, once Minister from
Portugal)
The City of Receptions
The City of Streets Without
Houses
The City of Trees Without Houses

WASHINGTON (Cont'd)          The City of Washington
                             The Commercial Empire of the
                                 United States
                             The Court City of a Nation
                             The Crossroads of the World
                             The Embryonic Capital
                             The Executive City
                             The Federal Capital
                             The Federal City
                             The Federal Seat
                             The Federal Site
                             The Federal Town
                             The Foundling Capital
                             The Gas House of the Nation
                             The Grand Emporium of the West
                             The Grand Metropolis
                             The Great Dismal
                             The Great Serbonian Bog
                             The Great White City
                             The Heart of America
                             The Magnificent Capitol
                             The Metropolis of the Country
                             The Metropolitan City
                             The Mighty Capital
                             The Most Beautiful City in Amer-
                                 ica
                             The Mud-Hole City
                             The National Capital
                             The Nation's Capital
                             The Nation's Headquarters
                             The Nation's State
                             The New Capital
                             The New City of Washington
                             The New Settlement
                             The News Capital of the World
                             The Political Front
                             The Problem Capitol of the World
                             The Second Rome
                             The Virgin Capital
                             The Wilderness City
                             The World's Most Beautiful City
                             The Young Capital
                             Washington, B. C. --Before Corn

                        FLORIDA

ANNA MARIA                   The Choicest Spot in All Florida

ANNA MARIA (Cont'd)          The Island You'll Love
APALACHICOLA                 The City of the Friendly People
                             The Gateway to the Apalachicola
                                System
                             The Natural Port City
                             The Old City with a New Future
                             The Sportman's Paradise
APOPKA                       The City of Families, Faith and
                                Friendship
                             The Fern City of Florida
ARCADIA                      The City of Character in a Land
                                of Beauty
                             The Land of Contrast
ASTATULA                     The Center of Central Florida
                                (on Lake Harris)
AUBURNDALE                   The City in the Heart of the Cit-
                                rus Belt and Holiday Highlands
AVON PARK                    The City with the Mile Long Mall
                             The Friendliest Little City
                             The Jacaranda City with the Mile
                                Long Mall
BARTOW                       The City of Oaks
                             The City of Oaks and Azaleas
BELLEVIEW                    Florida's Last Frontier
                             The City where You Can Have
                                Fun and Live Better
                             The Gateway to the Tropics
                             The Ideal Location for Vacation
                                and Home
                             The Land of Opportunity
                             The Progressive Community
                             The Progressive Community with
                                a Bright Future
                             The Region of Great Natural Won-
                                ders
BLOUNTSTOWN                  The Agricultural and Timber Em-
                                pire (richest timber producing
                                area of Florida)
                             The Hub of the Great Apalachicola
                                Valley
                             The Kingdom of Opportunity
                             The Paradise of Fishing, Hunting
                                and Swimming
BOCA RATON                   The Golden City of the Gold
                                Coast
                             The Water Polo Capital of Florida
BONIFAY                      The Ideal Spot for Retirement

| | |
|---|---|
| BONIFAY (Cont'd) | The Right Climate for Business and Family Living |
| BONITA SPRINGS | The Fisherman's Paradise |
| | The Vacationer's Dreamland |
| BOYNTON BEACH | A Fine Place to Live |
| | The Gateway to "Sailfish Alley" |
| BRADENTON | The Friendly City |
| | South Florida's Oldest Pioneer Village |
| BRANDON | A Good Place to Live--Better |
| | The Sightseeing Hub of the West Coast of Central Florida |
| BRANFORD | The City of Beauty |
| | The City of Beauty on the Suwannee River |
| BROOKSVILLE | The City of Seven Hills |
| | The Home of the Tangerine |
| | The Sunrise of Opportunity |
| CAPE CANAVERAL | The Space Hub |
| CAPE CORAL | Florida's Waterfront Wonderland |
| | The City of the Future |
| | The City with a Future |
| | The Waterfront Wonderland |
| CAPE KENNEDY | The Spaceport, U. S. A. (rockets, satellites) |
| CARRABELLE | A Great Place to Visit, A Wonderful Place to Live |
| | The City in the Heart of Florida's Gulf Fishing |
| | The City where Civic Pride is City-Wide |
| | The Fisherman's Paradise |
| CASEY KEY | Florida's West Coast's Finest Vacation Spot |
| CHATTAHOOCHEE | Hub City of Good Living |
| | Hub City of Recreation |
| | The Hub City of Transportation |
| CHIEFLAND | The Watermelon Capital |
| | The Watermelon Center Festival |
| CLEARWATER | Florida's Newest Convention City |
| | The City with a Sparkle |
| | The Home of the World Champion Clearwater Bombers |
| | The Springtime City |
| | The Winter Home of the National League Philadelphia Phillies (baseball club) |

| | |
|---|---|
| CLERMONT | The Gem of the Hills (amid 17 lakes and hills) |
| | The Hub of Florida |
| CLEWISTON | America's Sweetest Town (sugar cane fields) |
| | Capital of Florida's Sugar Industry (largest sugar mill in the U. S.) |
| | The City in the Heart of the Everglades |
| | The Progressive Community |
| | The Queen City of Florida's Sugar Bowl |
| COCOA | The Citrus Center (shipping point for Indian River Citrus fruits) |
| | The Salt Water Trout Capital of the World |
| COCOA BEACH | Missile Land, U. S. A. |
| | The Center of Activity for America's Space Program |
| | The City at the Portal to the Universe |
| | The Cosmopolitan Community with the Warmth of a Small Town |
| | The Resort Area of Cape Kennedy |
| | The Surfing Capital of the South (wave formations) |
| | The World's Best Beach |
| CORAL GABLES | Florida's Showcase Community |
| | The City Beautiful (part of Greater Miami) |
| | The City Planned for Perfect Living |
| CRESCENT CITY | The Gateway to the Bass Capital of the World |
| CRESTVIEW | The Center for Giant Blueberry Bushes |
| | The Hub City in the Heart of Florida's West Country |
| | The Hub City of Northwest Florida |
| | The Real Paradise for Family Living |
| CROSS CITY | The City Way Down Upon the Suwannee River |
| DADE CITY | The Home of the Pioneer Florida Museum |
| DANIA | The Antiques Center of the South |
| | The City where Life Is Worth Living |

| | |
|---|---|
| DANIA (Cont'd) | The Cruise Capital of the World |
| | The Tomato Capital of the World |
| | The Tomato Center of the World |
| | The Tourist Mecca and Antiques Center of the South |
| DAVENPORT | Florida's Biggest Little Town |
| | The Town in the Gateway to the Beautiful Red Section of Florida |
| | The Town on the Ridge in the Heart of Orangeland |
| DAYTONA BEACH | Florida's Newest Metropolitan Industrial Area |
| | Florida's Vacation Capital |
| | Florida's Year Round Playground |
| | The All-Year Vacationland |
| | The Fun Capital of the South |
| | The Ideal Year-Round Resort |
| | The Prettiest Resort in the World |
| | The Resort Area |
| | The Summer Fun Capital of the South (founded 1870) |
| | The World's Largest Family Resort |
| | The World's Most Famous Beach (23 miles long, 500 feet wide at low tide) |
| DE BARY | The Fastest Growing Friendly Retirement Community |
| DEERFIELD BEACH | The City in the Heart of the Gold Coast |
| | The Heart of the Gold Coast |
| | The Miracle City of the Gold Coast |
| | The Northern Gateway to Broward County |
| DE LAND | The Athens of Florida (home of Stetson University) |
| | The City Located in the Very Heart of Florida |
| | The Home of Stetson University |
| | The Home of Stetson University and Florida Military School |
| | The Land of Flowers |
| | The Land of Sunshine |
| DELRAY BEACH | Florida's Dissimilar Resort |

DELRAY BEACH (Cont'd)    The City in Florida with a Dif-
                            ference
DESTIN                   The City in the Heart of North-
                            west Florida's Miracle Strip
                         The City in the Heart of the Mir-
                            acle Strip
                         The World's Luckiest Fishing
                            Village (fishing area for red
                            snapper, etc.)
DUNEDIN                  Florida's Boating Capital on the
                            Gulf
                         The City of Beautiful Homes
DUNNELLON                Home of Rainbow Springs (larg-
                            est in Florida)
                         Home of the World's Largest Bass
                         The Community where Business
                            and Pleasure Live in Complete
                            Harmony
                         The Community where You Work
                            and Play the Same Day
                         The Kingdom of the Sun (on the
                            Withlacoochee River)
EAU GALLIE               The Gateway to the Missile Test
                            Center
                         The Gateway to the Space Pro-
                            gram
                         The Harbor City (land-locked
                            harbor on the Indian River)
                         The Progressive City
EDGEWATER                The City of Progress
                         The City on Florida's Famous
                            East Coast and the Indian River
                         The Gateway to Nova (Nova Indus-
                            trial Area)
                         The Place in the Sun to Visit, to
                            Play, to Work, to Live
                         The World's Safest Bathing Beach
ENGLEWOOD                The City where Life Is Lived
                            Every Day of the Year
                         Your Tropical "Home Town"
EUSTIS                   The Center of Our Nation's Play-
                            ground (on east shore of Lake
                            Eustis)
                         The City for a Vacation or a Life-
                            time of Real Living
                         The City in the Heart of Central
                            Florida's Water Wonderland

| | |
|---|---|
| EUSTIS | The Orange Capital of the World |
| | The Winter and Summer Vacation Center of Florida |
| | The World Capital of the Orange-Growing Industry |
| EVERGLADES | The Fisherman's Paradise |
| | The Western Water Gate (the way to 2,100 square miles of Everglades National Park) |
| | The Western Water Gateway (to Everglades National Park) |
| | The Wonderland of the Ten Thousand Islands |
| FERNANDINA BEACH | The Buccaneer City (favorite port for pirates) |
| | The Ocean City (on Amelia Island) |
| FORT LAUDERDALE | Florida's Tropical Paradise |
| | The All-Year Vacation City |
| | The Beach that Made Fort Lauderdale Famous |
| | The Boating Capital of the World |
| | The Gateway to the Everglades |
| | The Home Town in the American Tropics |
| | The Place to Go in Florida |
| | The Sunshine City |
| | The Tropical Wonderland |
| | The Venice of America (more than 165 miles of lagoons, canals and rivers flow within its boundaries) |
| FORT MEADE | The City in Florida's Fun-Filled Holiday Highlands |
| | The City in the Heart of Florida's Citrus, Phosphate, Recreation, History, Cattle |
| FORT MYERS | The City of Homes |
| | The City of Palms (Thomas Alva Edison advocated the planting of palms throughout the city) |
| | The City where the American Tropics Begin |
| | The Gladioli Capital of the World |
| | The Jewel City of the Florida West |
| | The New Resort Area of Florida |
| FORT MYERS BEACH | The Tropical Island Wonderland |

FORT MYERS BEACH                in the Gulf of Mexico (on Es-
(Cont'd)                            tero Island)
FORT PIERCE                     Florida's Finest Agricultural In-
                                    dustrial and Resort Community
                                The Capitol of Florida's Trea-
                                    sure Coast (about two millions
                                    in Spanish and U. S. gold was
                                    recovered in 1964)
                                The City in the Heart of the
                                    World Famous Indian River Cit-
                                    rus Country
                                The Vacationland for the Whole
                                    Family
FORT WALTON                     The Heart of Florida's Miracle
                                    Strip
FROSTPROOF                      The Friendly City of the High-
                                    lands
GAINESVILLE                     Florida's Center for Science,
                                    Education, Medicine
                                North Central Florida's Shopping
                                    Center
                                North Central Florida's Shopping
                                    Headquarters
                                The Home of the University of
                                    Florida
                                The University City (University of
                                    Florida)
GROVELAND                       A Good Place to Live, Work and
                                    Play
                                The City in the Center of Sunland
HAINES CITY                     The City in the Heart of Florida
                                The Community where You Can
                                    Live, Work, Relax
                                The Gateway to the Holiday High-
                                    lands
                                The Heart of Florida
                                The Inland Paradise of Florida
                                The Picturesque Heart of Central
                                    Florida
HALLANDALE                      The City where Your Dreams of
                                    Florida Living Come True
                                The Home of the Florida Derby
HASTINGS                        Florida's Potato Capital (multi-
                                    million dollar industry)
HIALEAH                         Florida's Fastest Growing City
                                The City for Family Living at Its
                                    Best

| | |
|---|---|
| HIALEAH (Cont'd) | The Fastest Growing Industrial Area in the Southeast |
| | The South Florida Hub |
| | The Taxpayer's Haven |
| HIGH SPRINGS | The Ideal Living City in the Heart of Florida |
| HOBE SOUND | The Gateway to the Famous Gold Coast |
| HOLLY HILL | The City in the Heart of the Daytona Beach Resort Area |
| | The City with a Heart |
| HOLLYWOOD | Florida's Golfingest City |
| | The Dream City Come True |
| | The Heart of the Gold Coast |
| | There's Something for Everyone in Hollywood |
| HOMESTEAD | The City of Bicycles |
| IMMOKALEE | The Watermelon Capital |
| | The Watermelon Capital of Florida |
| INDIANTOWN | The Community Planned for Pleasant Living |
| ISLAMORADA | The City in the Florida Keys |
| | The Crown Jewel of the Florida Keys |
| | The Sportfishing Capital of the World |
| JACKSONVILLE | Florida's Gateway City |
| | Florida's Hub of Fun |
| | Jax |
| | The Biggest City in Area in the Free World (827 square miles) |
| | The Bold New City of the South |
| | The City of Pleasant Memories |
| | The City on the Go |
| | The Colorful Key Center for Defense Activities |
| | The Communication Center of Florida |
| | The Deep Water Port |
| | The Distribution Center of the Southeast |
| | The Finance Center of Florida |
| | The Friendly City of Endless Charm |
| | The Gate City of Florida (world port and commercial center) |

| | |
|---|---|
| JACKSONVILLE (Cont'd) | The Gateway City |
| | The Gateway to All Florida |
| | The Hartford of the South (numerous insurance companies) |
| | The Hub of Fun |
| | The Hub of History |
| | The Hub of Progress |
| | The Ideal Convention City |
| | The Ideal Place to Work, Live, Play |
| | The Ideal Year Round Vacation Spot |
| | The Industrial and Distribution Center |
| | The Insurance Center of the South |
| | The Key National Defense Center |
| | The Naval Center of the South |
| | The Popular Vacationland |
| | The Tourist and Convention Center |
| | The World's Finest Beach |
| JENSEN BEACH | The Friendly Community in Martin County |
| | The Sea Turtle Capital of the World |
| JUPITER | The First City in Famous Palm Beach County |
| | The Gateway to Tropical Florida's First Resort |
| KEY BISCAYNE | The Island Paradise |
| | The Island Paradise Minutes from Miami |
| KEY COLONY BEACH | The Complete Vacation Resort City |
| | The Gem of Florida's Keys |
| KEY WEST | America's Singapore |
| | America's Southernmost City (county seat of Monroe County) |
| | The Center of America's Clear Havana Industry |
| | The Cigar Capital of the World (popular in the 1870's) |
| | The Island City of Old World Charm |
| | The Nation's Other Capital (Nixon's home and office) |
| | The Nation's Southernmost City |

| | |
|---|---|
| KEY WEST (Cont'd) | (near extreme end of Florida Keys) |
| | The Southernmost City in the Continental United States |
| KISSIMMEE | The Cow Capital of Florida |
| LA BELLE | The City Among the Oaks |
| | The City at the Crossroads of Southwest Florida |
| | The City where the Fun of Living Comes "Naturally" |
| | The Tranquil Living in a Natural Paradise |
| LAKE ALFRED | One of Florida's Finest Smaller Communities |
| | The City at the Crossroads of Holiday Highlands |
| | The City in the Heart of the Citrus Area |
| LAKE CITY | Florida's New Gateway |
| | The Forestry Capital of Florida |
| | The Highway Hub (two interstate routes, five primary highways) |
| | The Hub of North Central Florida's Scenic Wonderland |
| LAKE HAMPTON | Florida's Complete Family Outdoor Recreation Center |
| LAKE MARY | The Hidden Jewel of Central Florida |
| | The Village Idea for Retirement, for Raising a Family and for Placid Everyday Living |
| | The Village Not for Tourists, Not for Excitement But for Modest Tranquil Healthful Living |
| LAKE PLACID | The Caladium Capital of the World (a tropical American plant of the arum family) |
| | The Roof Garden of Florida |
| LAKE WALES | Florida's Attraction Showcase |
| | The City of the Carillon (the Bok Tower, 71 bells weighing from 12 pounds to 11 tons) |
| LAKE WEIR | The City for Family Fun in the Florida Sun |
| | The Year Around Living at Its Best |

LAKE WEIR (Cont'd)          The Very Center of the Sunshine
                            State
LAKE WORTH                  The City of Lake Worth where
                            the Fun Begins
                            The City where the Tropics Be-
                            gin
                            The Gold Coast in Florida
                            The Heart of the Palm Beaches
                            (south of Palm Beach)
                            The Recreation Mecca of the
                            Fabulous Southeastern Coast
                            of Florida
                            The Shuffleboard Capital (32 shuf-
                            fleboard courts in the heart of
                            the business district)
LAKELAND                    Florida's Eighth City
                            Polk County's Largest City
                            The City Nearer to Everywhere
                            in Florida
                            The City of Lakes (19 lakes)
                            The City where Industry Finds a
                            Favorable Climate
                            The City Wonder-full for Business
                            The Heart of the Citrus Industry
                            The Hub of Florida's Scenic Won-
                            derland (19 lakes within city
                            limits)
                            The Imperial Polk (in Polk Coun-
                            ty)
                            The Vacation for a Lifetime
                            The Welcome to the City of Lakes
                            The World's Citrus Center (about
                            90 percent of the crop is grown
                            here)
LANTANA                     The Gem on the Ocean
LARGO                       Florida's Most Friendly Commun-
                            ity
                            The Fair City (site of the Pinel-
                            las County Fair and Horse
                            Show)
                            The Hub of Pinellas County
LEESBURG                    The Action Center of Florida's
                            "Holiday Highlands"
                            The Community where the Big
                            Bass Bite
                            The Community with a Heart in

LEESBURG (Cont'd)                    the Heart of Fabulous Florida
                                     The Watermelon Capital of Flor-
                                         ida
LEHIGH ACRES                         Florida's Country Club Town
LONGBOAT KEY                         Florida's West Coast Beach Re-
                                         sort
                                     The Casual Family Beach Resort
                                         in the Center of Florida's
                                         West Coast
                                     The City on the Lazy Blue Wa-
                                         ters of the Gulf of Mexico
                                     The World's Finest Natural White
                                         Sand Beaches
MACCLENNY                            North Florida's Gretna Green
                                         (numerous marriages performed
                                         by judges)
MAITLAND                             The Central Florida's City of Big
                                         Opportunity
                                     The Small Town with the Bustling
                                         Activity of a Growing City
MARATHON                             The Fisherman's Paradise
                                     The Heart of the Florida Keys
                                         (second largest community in
                                         Florida Keys)
                                     The Resort Town where the Fish-
                                         erman Is King
MARGATE                              The City That Started with a Plan
MELBOURNE                            Crossroads to the Universe
                                     The Mid-Way City (midway be-
                                         tween Jacksonville and Miami,
                                         Fla.)
MERRITT ISLAND                       The Launch Pad to Progress
MIAMI                                Florida's Magic City
                                     Greater Miami Means More
                                     The Air Capital of the World
                                     The City of Opportunities
                                     The Gateway of the Americas
                                     The Greatest Vacation Spot of All
                                     The Hub of All South Florida's
                                         Sun-Fun Vacationland
                                     The Jewel City of the Sunshine
                                         State
                                     The Magic City
                                     The Metropolis of Southeastern
                                         Florida
                                     The Paradise of the South
                                     The Playground of the Americas

MIAMI (Cont'd)

The South Sea Isles of America
The Sunshine Capital of the World
The Tropic Metropolis
The Twin Cities (with Miami Beach)
The Wonder City of the World
The World's Largest Import-Export Air Cargo Terminal

MIAMI BEACH

A Fun Festival Place
America's Year Round Playground
The Capital of Florida's Enchanting Gold Coast
The City of Magic Islands and Waterways
The City where the Palms Meet the Sea
The City where the Welcome's Warm as the Sunshine
The Convention Center of the United States
The Fabulous City in the Sun
The Gold Coast City
The Magic City
The Photogenic Sun Capital of the East
The Playground of the Americas
The Riviera of America
The Shangri-La of the Western Hemisphere
The Sister City in the Sun
The Sun and Fun Capital of the World
The Twin Cities (with Miami, Fla.)
The Vacationland of a Thousand Pleasures
The World's Greatest Resort
The Year Round Playground of the Americas
Vacationland, U. S. A.

MONTICELLO

The Garden Spot of Northwest Florida (county seat of Jefferson County)

NAPLES

One of the Fastest Growing Resort Centers
The City on the Gulf (Gulf of Mexico)
The Gateway to the 10, 000 Islands

| | |
|---|---|
| NAPLES (Cont'd) | The Refuge From Resorts |
| NEW PORT RICHEY | The Gateway to Tropical Florida |
| NEW SMYRNA | The World's Largest Safest Bathing Beach (on the banks of the North Indian River) |
| NEWBERRY | The Little City of Big Opportunity |
| NICEVILLE | The Home of Eglin Air Force Base (with Valparaiso, Fla.) |
| | Twin Cities on the Bay (with Valparaiso, Fla.) |
| OCALA | The Heart of Florida's Fun-Land (county seat of Marion County) |
| | The Heart of Florida's Thoroughbred Country |
| | The Thoroughbred Capital of Florida (outstanding horse farms) |
| OCEAN CITY | The Home of Pure Water |
| OKEECHOBEE | The Chicago of the South |
| | The Year-Round Sportsman's Paradise (on Lake Okeechobee) |
| ORLANDO | Florida's City Beautiful |
| | Florida's Transportation Hub |
| | The Action Center of Florida |
| | The Action City |
| | The Birthplace of Speed |
| | The City Beautiful |
| | The City Beautiful in the Heart of Florida |
| | The City with Unexcelled Opportunities for Good Living |
| | The Growingest City in the South |
| | The Modern City on the Move |
| | The Very Heart of Florida (largest inland city in Florida) |
| ORMOND BEACH | The Birthplace of Speed (automobile races began about 1902) |
| | The Parrot's Paradise |
| ORMAND BY THE SEA | Retire, Relax, Relive |
| PAHOKEE | The City with an Area of Agricultural Achievement |
| | The Garden of the Glades |
| | The Nation's Sugar Bowl |
| | The Sugar Bowl of America |
| PALATKA | The City where Industry and Recreation Meet |
| | The Bass Capital of the World |
| | The City where Work and Play |

72

PALATKA (Cont'd)              Are Only Minutes Away
                             The Gem City
PALM BAY                     The City in the Heart of the Dy-
                                namic Cape Kennedy Area
                             The City Programmed for Pro-
                                gress
PALM BEACH                   The Center of a Sportsman's
                                Paradise
                             The Golden Coast of Florida
                             The Home of the Winter White
                                House
                             The Mecca for Champions in
                                Many Fields
                             The World's Premier Winter Re-
                                sort (a 14 mile island connected
                                by several bridges to West
                                Palm Beach)
PALM SPRINGS                 The Delightful Residential Com-
                                munity in the Heart of the
                                Palm Beaches
                             The Garden Spot of the Palm
                                Beaches
                             The Ideal Family Community
PALMETTO                     The Gateway to Tropical Florida
PANAMA CITY                  The City in Beautiful Bay County
                                (on St. Andrew Bay)
                             The City of Destiny
                             The City on the Cool Gulf Coast
                                (an indentation of the Gulf of
                                Mexico)
                             The City with the World's Whitest
                                Beaches
                             The Industrial and Resort Center
PENSACOLA                    Florida's City of Five Flags
                             The Annapolis of the Air
                             The Birthplace of U.S. Naval Avi-
                                ation (naval air training school
                                opened 1914)
                             The City of Camelias
                             The City of Five Flags
                             The City of Pleasant Living
                             The Cradle of Naval Aviation
                             The Florida Plus City
                             The Garden Spot of the South
                             The Gateway to Florida
                             The Gateway to the Gulf Coast
                             The Gulf Coast City

PENSACOLA (Cont'd)

The Industrial Center of West Florida

The Metropolis of West Florida

The Nearest Florida Resort to Most of the Nation

The Panama Port

The Pleasant All-Year Vacation Center

The Scenic City of Five Flags at the Top of the Gulf of Mexico

The Typical Resort City

PERRY

The Gateway to All Florida (county seat of Taylor county)

PINE ISLAND

The Home of Fishingest Bridge

PINELLAS PARK

The Hub of Pinellas County

PLANT CITY

Just a Real Nice Town

The City in the Heart of the Great New Central Florida Vacationland

The City Most Convenient to All Florida

The City of Hospitality and Charm

The City where the Sun Beams Brighter with "Ole" Florida's Hospitality

The Eastern Gateway to Hillsborough County

The Neighborly Satisfying Community for Living

The Winter Strawberry Capital of the World

POMPANO BEACH

A Study in Contrasts

The City for Year Round Fishing Variety

The City in the Shadow of the Famed Hillsboro Light

The City of Contrasts

The City Right in the Center of Things

The City That's a Study in Contrasts

The City where Your Vacation Dreams Are Fulfilled

The Convenient Vacationland

The Family Oasis of Safe Ocean Beaches

The Gem of the Gold Coast

POMPANO BEACH (Cont'd)   The Heart of the Gold Coast
                         The New Playground of America (be-
                             tween Palm Beach and Miami)
                         The Perfect Playground for the
                             Young in Heart
                         The Sparkling Sand, Golden Sun-
                             shine on the Atlantic Shore
                         Truly Izaak Walton's Headquarters
PORT EVERGLADES          The Cruise Capital of the South
                         Florida's Deep Water Harbor
                         The Largest Port on the Lower
                             East Coast
                         The Souths No. 1 Cruise-Ship Port
PORT ST. JOE             Florida's Fabulous Frontier Coast
                         The City with a Future
                         The Constitution City (where the
                             Florida constitution was drawn
                             up in 1839)
PUNTA GORDA              The Home of the Famous Silver
                             King Tarpon
                         The Sportsman's Paradise
                             (on Charlotte Harbor)
QUINCY                   The City at the Top in Florida
                         The City in the Heart of Florida's
                             Future
                         The City in the Heart of Florida's
                             "tall country"
                         The City of Tobacco
                         The City where Families Enjoy
                             Florida Living in a Beautiful
                             and Historic Setting
                         The City where Historic Pride
                             and Civic Progress Unite in
                             the Industrial and Cultural
                             Heart of Northwest Florida
                         The City where the Old and the
                             New Combine
                         The Highest City in Florida
                         The Industrial Heart of Florida's
                             Future
                         The Shade Tobacco Capital (multi-
                             million dollar crop of cigar
                             wrapper tobacco)
                         The Shade-Grown Tobacco Capital
RIVIERA BEACH            Everything Your Vacation Heart
                             Desires Can Be Found in Riv-
                             iera Beach

| | |
|---|---|
| RIVIERA BEACH (Cont'd) | The Center of the Palm Beaches (on Singer Island) |
| | The Sun Smiles Happily on Industry in Riviera Beach where There Is Everything to Make You Happy |
| RUSKIN | The Area of Opportunity |
| | The City Centered in the Heart of the Suncoast |
| | The Place to Live, Relax and Play. . . on Miles of Water |
| | The Salad Bowl of America |
| | The Salad Bowl of the Nation |
| ST. AUGUSTINE | America's Oldest City (where Juan Ponce de Leon landed on April 3, 1513) |
| | The Ancient City |
| | The Fountain of Youth City |
| | The Nation's Oldest City (continuous existence since 1565) |
| | The Oldest City in the United States (permanent white settlement 1565) |
| | The Summer and Winter Year 'Round Resort (on Matanzas Bay) |
| ST. CLOUD | The Fisherman's Paradise |
| ST. PETERSBURG | One of America's Greatest Playgrounds |
| | The City for Living |
| | The City of Good Living |
| | The City of Homes |
| | The City of the Unburied Dead |
| | The City with a Million Ambassadors |
| | The Happy People Place |
| | The Sunshine City |
| | Tops in Sun'n Fun |
| ST. PETERSBURG BEACH | The City on the Gulf of Mexico |
| SANFORD | The Celery City |
| | The City of Gracious Living |
| | The World's Celery Center (20% of celery production in the U.S.) |
| SARASOTA | Florida's Entertainment Capital |
| | Florida's Great Gulf Beach Resort Area |

| | |
|---|---|
| SARASOTA (Cont'd) | The City of Attractions |
| | The Sunshine City |
| SEBRING | A Good Place to Visit |
| | A Wonderful Place to Live |
| | The Golfing Capital of Florida |
| | The Hub of the Florida Peninsula |
| SILVER SPRINGS | Nature's Underwater Fairyland |
| | One of the Great Natural Wonders of the World |
| | The Camping Ground of the Seminole Indians |
| | The Community of Eight Thrilling Attractions |
| | The Home of World Famous Glass Bottom Boats |
| | The Underwater Motion Picture Capital of the World |
| SNEADS | The Eastern Gateway to Jackson County |
| STARKE | Florida's Winter Strawberry Market |
| | The Berry Capitol of the World |
| | The Friendly City |
| | The Heart of Florida's Crown |
| | The Heart of Florida's Strawberry Market |
| | The Strawberry City |
| STUART | The Sailfish Capital of the World |
| SURFSIDE | The Resort where Fun Never Sets |
| | The Sunny Community of Leisurely Living and Happy Holidays |
| TALLAHASSEE | The Capital City (1960 population 48,174) |
| | The Capital City of Fabulous Florida |
| | The Southland at its Best |
| TAMPA | Florida's Convention Center |
| | Florida's Gulf Coast Metropolis |
| | Florida's Metropolitan Distributing Center |
| | Florida's Second Largest City |
| | Florida's Treasure City |
| | Florida's Year 'Round City |
| | The Center of Florida's Exciting West Coast |
| | The Cigar Capitol of America |
| | The Cigar City |

| | |
|---|---|
| TAMPA (Cont'd) | The City of Diversity |
| | The City where a Wealth of Pleasure Awaits You Spring or Summer, Fall or Winter |
| | The Gateway to the Caribbean |
| | The Gateway to World Ports |
| | The Hub of Florida's West Coast |
| | The Hub of the Great Orange, Grapefruit and Winter Strawberry Producing Section in the United States |
| | The Industrial Hub of Florida |
| | The Sightseeing Center of Florida |
| | The Spanish Town |
| | The Trade Capital of Florida's West Coast |
| | The Treasure City |
| TARPON SPRINGS | The Sponge City (sponge divers) |
| | The Venice of the South (bordered on three sides by water, the Gulf of Mexico, the Anclote River and Lake Tarpon) |
| TAVARES | The City Beautiful |
| | The City That Has Everything for Enjoyable Living |
| | The County Seat of Lovely Lake County |
| | The Crossroads of Florida |
| TITUSVILLE | The City of Progress |
| | The Gateway to the Galaxies (rocket sites) |
| | The Missile City |
| | The Tour Entrance to the Kennedy Space Center |
| TREASURE ISLAND | The Vacationland Without Equal |
| UMATILLA | The Gateway to Ocala National Forest |
| | The Sportsman's Town (near Florida's best hunting area) |
| VALPARAISO | Twin Cities on the Bay (with Niceville, Fla.) |
| VERO BEACH | The City of Homes |
| | The Gem of the Florida East Coast |
| WEST PALM BEACH | First on the Fun Coast of Florida |
| | Florida's All-Year Resort |

WEST PALM BEACH (Cont'd) The Center of America's Fastest
                                Growing Area
                          The City where Pleasure Begins
                          The Fast Growing City
                          The Metropolitan Center of Trop-
                                ical Florida's First Resort
                                Area
                          Tropical Florida's First Resort
WINTER HAVEN              Central Florida's Lake Region
                          The Citrus Capital of the World
                          The Citrus Center of the World
                          The City of Homes
                          The City of Hundred Lakes
                          The Heart of Florida's Citrus
                                Industry
                          The Holiday Highlands
                          The Home of Beautiful Cypress
                                Gardens
                          The Prettiest Little Town This
                                Side of Heaven
WINTER PARK              The City of Homes
                          The Town That Has Become a
                                University (Rollins College)
ZELLWOOD                 The Vegetable Bowl (major crops
                                are corn, celery, radish, let-
                                tuce and beans)
ZEPHYRHILLS             The City of Pure Water

GEORGIA

AIKEN                    One of the Most Favorable Re-
                                sorts of the South
ALBANY                   The Artesian City (numerous
                                artesian wells)
                          The City of Opportunity
                          The Trade Center of Southwest
                                Georgia (seat of Dougherty
                                County)
ALMA                     The Queen City
AMERICUS                 Georgia's Mobile Home Center
                          The Home of Andersonville
ASHBURN                  The Bountiful Country
ATHENS                   The Athens You Will Want to See
                          The Classic City of the South
                                (home of the University of
                                Georgia, opened 1801, and
                                named for the Greek City)

| | |
|---|---|
| ATHENS (Cont'd) | ✓The Home of the University of Georgia |
| ATLANTA | The Business Hub of the Southeast |
| | The Capital City (1960 population 487, 455) |
| | The Citadel of the Confederacy |
| | The City of Beautiful Homes and Thriving Industry |
| | The City of Homes |
| | The City Without Precedent, Without Comparison |
| | The Confederate Supply Depot |
| | The Dogwood City |
| | The Federal City |
| | The Gate City |
| | The Gate City to the South |
| | The Gateway of the South |
| | The Hub of the Southeast |
| | The Ideal City (book by R. Brown) |
| | The Ideal Convention City |
| | The Insurance City |
| | The Manufacturing and Industrial Metropolis of the Southeast |
| | The Metropolis of a New South |
| | The New Kind of City |
| | The New National City |
| | The New York of the South |
| | The Railroad City |
| | The Southern Crossroads City |
| | The Well-balanced Metropolis |
| | The Winter Golf Capital of America |
| AUGUSTA | A Wonderful Place to Live |
| | A Wonderful Place to Live, to Work, to Play |
| | Georgia's Second Oldest City |
| | Golf Capital of the U. S. |
| | The Battlefield of the Revolution (American Revolution) |
| | The Center of a Rich and Highly Diversified Agricultural Empire |
| | The City of Beautiful Churches |
| | The City of Beautiful Homes |
| | The Distribution Center of the Southeast |

| AUGUSTA (Cont'd) | The Friendly City |
| | The Garden City of the South |
| | The Gateway of the Southeast |
| | The Golf Capital of America (site of the Masters Invitation Tournament) |
| | The Heart of Eastern Georgia and Western South Carolina |
| | The Leading Resort City |
| | The Lowell of the South (textile manufacturing) |
| | The Progressive City |
| | The Winter Golf Capital of the World |
| BAINBRIDGE | Georgia's First Inland Port |
| BARNESVILLE | The Home of Gordon College |
| BAXLEY | The Turpentine Capital of the World |
| BLACKSHEAR | The Heart of Tobacco Land |
| BLAKELY | The Peanut Capital of the World |
| BREMEN | The Clothing Center of the South |
| BRUNSWICK | Georgia's Golden Isles |
| | Georgia's Ocean Port |
| | The City of Beauty |
| | The City of Opportunities |
| | The Gateway to Your Georgia Vacationland |
| | The Georgia Vacationland |
| | The Ideal Vacationland |
| | The Progressive City |
| | The Progressive City Planning Today for the Events of Tomorrow |
| BUFORD | The Leather City |
| CAIRO | The Collard and Pickle Capital |
| CALHOUN | The Cherokee Indian Capital |
| CAMILLA | The Hub City |
| CANTON | The Broiler City |
| CARROLLTON | The Friendly City |
| CEDARTOWN | The Only Cedartown in the U. S. A. |
| CLAXTON | The Fruit Cake Capital |
| | The Home of the World Famous Claxton Fruit Cake |
| CLAYTON | Georgia's Mountain Resort |
| CLEVELAND | The Mountain Gateway |
| COLLEGE PARK | Atlanta's Airport City |

| | |
|---|---|
| COLUMBUS | The South's Oldest Industrial City (planned 1827) |
| COMMERCE | The Home of Georgia Belle Peach |
| CORNELIA | The Home of the Big Red Apple |
| CUMMING | The Gateway to Lake Lanier |
| DALTON | The Tufted Textile Center of the World |
| DAWSON | The Spanish Peanut Center of the World |
| | The World's Largest Spanish Peanut Market |
| DOUGLAS | The Friendly City |
| DOUGLASVILLE | The Dynamic City |
| DUBLIN | The City That's 'Dublin' Daily |
| EAST POINT | A Community Well Planned, Well Developed, Well Equipped for Commerce, Industry and Family Life |
| | A Good Place to Live, to Work and to Rear Your Family |
| | The City of Homes and Industry |
| | The City where People Are Happy and Industry Flourishes |
| | The City You Can Be Proud to Live and Work in |
| | The Diversified Industry City |
| | The South's Fastest Growing City |
| EASTMAN | The Candy Capital of Georgia |
| ELBERTON | The Granite Center of the World |
| | The Granite City |
| FITZGERALD | The Colony City (settled in 1895 by a colony of Union veterans) |
| | The Heart of the South Georgia Empire |
| FOLKSTON | The Land of the Trembling Earth |
| FORT BENNING | The West Point of the South |
| FORT VALLEY | The Best Pecan Producing Area in the South |
| | The Peach Center |
| GAINESVILLE | The Poultry Capital of the World |
| GRIFFIN | The Pimiento Center of the World |
| HAWKINSVILLE | The City of 13 Highways |
| HAZLEHURST | The Friendly City |
| HINESVILLE | The Home of Fort Stewart |
| JEKYLL ISLAND | America's Year-round Holiday Island |

| | |
|---|---|
| JEKYLL ISLAND (Cont'd) | Georgia's Fabulous Year Round Beach Resort |
| | Georgia's Island of Friendliness and Hospitality |
| | Georgia's Playground for Family Fun |
| | Georgia's Year-round Family Beach Resort |
| | Georgia's Year Round Family Resort |
| | One of Georgia's Golden Isles |
| | The Golden Isle in a By-gone Golden Age |
| | The Island where the Sand Whispers to the Sea |
| | The Year-round Convention and Meeting Center |
| JESUP | The City Building For Today and Planning For Tomorrow |
| | The City of Progress |
| LA GRANGE | Crossroads of the South |
| | The Largest Cotton Manufacturing Center in the State |
| LOUISVILLE | The Old Slave Market |
| LYONS | The Tobacco Center |
| MACON | The City on the Move |
| | The Friendly City in the Heart of Georgia |
| | The Heart of Georgia (about six miles from the geographical center) |
| | The Heart of the Southeast |
| | The South's Most Beautiful and Interesting City |
| MANCHESTER | The Little White House |
| METTER | The Home of Better Living |
| MIDWAY | Georgia's Cradle of the Revolution |
| | The Cradle of the Revolution |
| MONROE | The Birthplace of the 'Buddy Poppy' |
| MOULTRIE | A Better Place to Work and Play |
| | The Progressive Community |
| | South Georgia's Market Place |
| NASHVILLE | The Bright Leaf Tobacco Center |
| NEWNAN | The City of Homes |
| PEARSON | The Heart of the Turpentine Industry |

| | |
|---|---|
| PERRY | The Motel City |
| QUITMAN | The Camellia City |
| ROCKMART | The City on the Move |
| ROME | The City of Fine Educational Institutions (Shorter College) |
| | The City of Seven Hills |
| | The City of the Seven Hills (like Rome, Italy, built on seven hills) |
| | The Hub of Northwest Georgia |
| | The Versatile City |
| ST. SIMONS ISLAND | The Georgia Vacationland |
| | The Golden Isles of Georgia |
| | The Land of the Old South |
| SANDERSVILLE | The Kaolin Center of the World |
| SAVANNAH | America's Most Beautiful City |
| | Georgia's Colonial Capital |
| | Georgia's Colonial Capital City |
| | Georgia's First City (founded 1733) |
| | The City of Historical Charm |
| | The City of Southern Charm |
| | The Cradle of Georgia (founded Feb. 12, 1773 by James Edward Oglethorpe, English nobleman, as a colony and buffer state against the Spaniards in Florida) |
| | The First City of the South (settled Feb. 12, 1773 by General James Edward Oglethorpe) |
| | The Forest City |
| | The Forest City of the South |
| | The Garden City |
| | The Hostess City of the South |
| | The Mother City of Georgia |
| | The Sugar Bowl of the Southeast |
| SEA ISLAND | A Great Place to Vacation, a Wonderful Place to Live |
| | The Georgia Vacationland |
| | The Golden Isles of Georgia |
| | The Land of the Old South |
| SMYRNA | The Jonquil City |
| STATESBORO | The Tourist City |
| SUMMERVILLE | The City of Young Men |
| SWAINSBORO | The Pine Tree Country |
| SYLVANIA | The Home of the Famous "Jacksonboro Legend" |

| | |
|---|---|
| SYLVANIA (Cont'd) | The Welcome Station City |
| SYLVESTER | The Heart of Hunting Land |
| THOMASTON | Tire Cord Capital of the U. S. |
| THOMASVILLE | The City of Roses |
| | The Famous Winter Resort for Northern Invalids and Pleasure Seekers (used in 1895) |
| | The Key Junction to the Southeast |
| | The Original Winter Resort of the South |
| | The Rose City (rose gardens and annual rose show) |
| THOMSON | The Camellia City of the South |
| TIFTON | The Tomato Plant Capital |
| TOCCOA | The Furniture, Thread and Steel City |
| VALDOSTA | The Airways of America (near Moody Air Force Base) |
| | The Naval Stores Capitol of the World (largest inland naval stores market) |
| | The Vale of Beauty |
| VIDALIA | The Modern Town for Modern Living |
| WARM SPRINGS | The Little White House City (home of Franklin Delano Roosevelt) |
| WARNER ROBINS | The Home of Air Materiel Command |
| WASHINGTON | The City of Ante-Bellum Homes |
| WAYCROSS | Georgia's "Welcome World" City |
| | The Center City of Southern Georgia |
| | The Diversified City |
| | The Gateway to Okefenokee Swamp |
| | The Land of the Trembling Earth |
| WAYNESBORO | The Bird Dog Capital of the World |
| WEST POINT | The Home of Textiles |
| WINDER | The Work Clothing Center of the World |

## HAWAII

| | |
|---|---|
| HILO | The City of Orchids |
| | The Crescent City |
| | The Gateway to the Volcanoes |
| | The Orchid Capital of Hawaii |

HONOLULU                        The Capital City (1960 population
                                  294, 179)
                                The Center of Pineapple Industry
                                The Crossroads of the Pacific
                                The Exciting City of Welcome
WAIKIKI                         The Birthplace of Surfing

## IDAHO

AMERICAN FALLS                  The Power City (second largest
                                  artificial reservoir in the
                                  United States)
BOISE                           The Capital City (1960 population
                                  34, 481)
                                The City of Beautiful Homes
                                The City of Trees
                                The Nation's Largest Basque
                                  Colony
                                The Pacific Northwest's Most
                                  Progressive Community
                                The Tree City
                                The Western Mecca for Enjoyment
                                  Unlimited
                                The Woods
BURLEY                          The Best Lighted Town in the
                                  West (light, power and water
                                  obtained from the Minidoka
                                  Project)
                                The Jewel of the Gem State
CALDWELL                        Idaho's Farm Market
COEUR D'ALENE                   The Beautiful City by a Beautiful
                                  Lake
                                The City by the Lake (Lake
                                  Coeur d' Alene)
                                The Convention and Recreation
                                  Center of the Northwest
                                The Famous Playground of the
                                  Wondrous Northwest
                                The Heart of the Emerald Em-
                                  pire in the North Idaho Scenic
                                  Land
                                The Only Town in the U. S. with
                                  an Apostrophe in Its Name
CRAIGMONT                       The Second Largest Grain Ship-
                                  ping Center of the Northwest
GOODING                         The Commercial Center of Irri-
                                  gated Idaho

JEROME                          The Geographical Center of
                                    Magic Valley
KELLOGG                         The Home of Idaho's Greatest
                                    Mines
LEWISTON                        Idaho's Oldest Incorporated City
                                Idaho's Only Seaport (at the con-
                                    fluence of the Snake and Clear-
                                    water Rivers)
                                The Banana Belt City
                                The First Territorial Capital (of
                                    Idaho)
                                The Seaport for the Land-locked
                                    State of Idaho
MOSCOW                          The City of Homes, Churches and
                                    Fine Schools (University of
                                    Idaho)
NAMPA                           The City of Expanding Industry
                                The Home of the Snake River
                                    Stampede (a rodeo staged dur-
                                    ing July)
POCATELLO                       The Gate City to the Great North-
                                    west
SUN VALLEY                      America's Foremost Year 'Round
                                    Sports Center
                                The All-Year Sports Center
                                The Gateway to America's Last
                                    Wilderness
TWIN FALLS                      Idaho's Finest Residential Com-
                                    munity
                                One of America's Fastest Grow-
                                    ing Cities (1960 population
                                    20,126)
                                The Hub of the Magic Valley
                                    (headquarters for the Sawtooth
                                    National Forest)
WENDELL                         The Center of Gooding County

## ILLINOIS

ALTON                           The City That Came Back (Anti-
                                    abolitionist riot 1837, abolition-
                                    ist Elijah P. Lovejoy killed and
                                    printing presses destroyed)
                                Tusselburgh (evidently referring
                                    to above)
BLOOMINGTON                     It's Pleasant to Live in
                                The Hub of Illinois

| | |
|---|---|
| BLOOMINGTON (Cont'd) | The Prairie City |
| | The Twin City (with Normal, Ill.) |
| BYRON | The Hudson of the West (on Rock River) |
| CAIRO | The Goose Capital of the World |
| CANTON | A Good Place to Live, Work, Play |
| CARBONDALE | The Crossroads of the Continent (division headquarters for the Illinois Central Railroad) |
| CENTRALIA | The Gateway to Egypt (name applied to southern quarter of Illinois, Egyptian motifs on several buildings) |
| | The Oil Center of Illinois |
| | The Population Center, U. S. A. |
| CHAMPAIGN | The Twin Cities (with Urbana, Ill.) |
| CHICAGO | America's No. 1 Contrary City |
| | America's Riviera |
| | Chi |
| | Hogopolis |
| | Old Chi |
| | Pigopolis |
| | Porkopolis |
| | The Big Town |
| | The Breezy Town |
| | The Center of Innovation and Culture |
| | The City Beautiful |
| | The City by the Lake |
| | The City of Extremes |
| | The City of Big Shoulders |
| | The City of the Lakes |
| | The City of the Lakes and Praries |
| | The City of Winds |
| | The City with Two Faces |
| | The Convention City |
| | The Cornopolis |
| | The Country's Greatest Rail Center |
| | The Crime Capital |
| | The Gangland |
| | The Garden City |
| | The Gem of the Prairies |
| | The Golf Capital of the Midwest |
| | The Home of the Loop |

| | |
|---|---|
| CHICAGO (Cont'd) | The Host City of the Nation |
| | The Hub of American Merchandising |
| | The Lake City |
| | The Leading Convention City in the Country |
| | The Metropolis of the West |
| | The Midland Metropolis |
| | The Midwest Golf Capital |
| | The Midwest Metropolis |
| | The Mighty Metropolis |
| | The Miracle City of the Midwest |
| | The Nation's No. 1 Convention City |
| | The Phoenix City |
| | The Pork City |
| | The Prairie |
| | The Queen of the Lakes |
| | The Western Metropolis |
| | The White City |
| | The Windy City |
| | The World's Fair City |
| | The World's Largest Railroad Center |
| | The World's Railroad Capital |
| | The World's Railroad Mecca |
| DE KALB | The Barbed Wire Capital of the World (barb wire invented and manufactured there in 1873) |
| DECATUR | Playtown, U. S. A. |
| | The Soybean Capital of the World (numerous processing mills) |
| | The Soybean Center |
| DUNDEE | Santa's Village |
| EAST MOLINE | America's Farm Implement Capital (plant of International Harvester Co. ) |
| | The Quad Cities (with Moline, Ill. , Rock Island, Ill. , and Davenport, Iowa) |
| EFFINGHAM | The Heart of the U. S. A. |
| ELGIN | The Community with its Sites Set on Tomorrow |
| EUREKA | The Pumpkin Capital of the World |
| EVANSTON | The Finest New England Village in the Middle West |
| | The Historical City of Homes |

| | |
|---|---|
| EVANSTON (Cont'd) | The Ideal Home Community |
| GALENA | The City Time Forgot |
| | The Crescent City of the North-west |
| GALESBURG | The College City (Knox College) |
| | The World's Greatest Mule Market |
| GRIGGSVILLE | The Purple Martin Capital of the World (numerous insect-devouring purple martens) |
| | The World's Largest Cardinal Gardens |
| HARVARD | America's Milk Center (Starline Model Dairy Farm) |
| | The Milk Center of the World |
| JOLIET | The Pittsburgh of the West (several hundred manufacturing plants) |
| KEWANEE | The Hog Capital of the World |
| LOMBARD | The Lilac Town |
| MACOMB | The World's Largest Art Pottery City (site of the Haeger Potteries, Inc.) |
| MATTOON | The Center of Agricultural, Commercial, Industrial Oil Transportation |
| | The Center of Agriculture, Commerce, Industry, Oil and Transportation |
| | The City Noted for Diversification |
| MOLINE | The Farm Machinery Capitol of America |
| | The Plow City (John Deere began plow manufacture in 1847) |
| | The Quad Cities (with East Moline, Ill., Rock Island, Ill., and Davenport, Iowa) |
| | The Tri-Cities (with Rock Island, Ill., and Davenport, Iowa) |
| MONMOUTH | The Prime Beef Center of the World |
| MOOSEHEART | The City of Childhood (children's home of Loyal Order of Moose) |
| NAUVOO | The City Beautiful (on the east bank of the Mississippi River) |
| NORMAL | The Twin City (with Bloomington, Ill.) |

| OAK PARK | The Saints Rest (settled in 1833) |
| PANA | City of Roses |
| | One of the World's Largest Rose Growing Centers |
| PEKIN | The Celestial City |
| PEORIA | Illinois' Second City (1960 population 103, 162) |
| | The Bright Spot of America |
| | The Center of Midwest Friendliness |
| | The City Pledged to Progress |
| | The Progressive City |
| | The Whiskey Town (site of the world's largest distillery, Hiram Walker & Sons) |
| PULLMAN | The City of Brick (part of Chicago) |
| QUINCY | The Gem City |
| | The Gem City in the Heart of the Great Mississippi Valley |
| | The Gem City of the Middle West |
| | The Gem City of the West |
| | The Model City |
| | The Most Beautiful of All Western Cities |
| ROCK ISLAND | The Quad Cities (with East Moline, Ill., Moline, Ill., and Davenport, Iowa) |
| | The Tri-Cities (with Moline, Ill., and Davenport, Iowa) |
| ROCKFORD | Illinois' Second Industrial City |
| | Illinois' Second Largest City |
| | The City at the Top in Illinois |
| | The City of Beautiful Homes |
| | The Crossroads of the Middle West |
| | The Forest City |
| | The Nation's Second Largest Machine-tool Center |
| | The Rich Agricultural and Industrial Heartland of Mid-America |
| SPRINGFIELD | A Great American Shrine (Lincoln Tomb State Memorial) |
| | A Progressive American City |
| | An Important Convention and Conference City |

| | |
|---|---|
| SPRINGFIELD (Cont'd) | Illinois' Capital City (selected 1837) |
| | The Capital City (1960 population 83, 271) |
| | The City of Flowers |
| | The Flower City |
| | The Home of Abraham Lincoln |
| URBANA | The Twin Cities (with Champaign, Ill. ) |
| VANDALIA | Wilderness Capital of Lincoln's Land (capital of Illinois from 1820 to 1839) |
| WEST FRANKFORT | The Geographic Center of Industrial Southern Illinois |
| | The Heart of a Dispersed City of Towns |
| WESTCHESTER | The Gateway to the Tollroads |

## INDIANA

| | |
|---|---|
| ALBION | The Heart of the Indiana Lake Country |
| ANDERSON | Mid-America's Industrial Center |
| ANGOLA | The Center of Activity (the boundaries of three states, Indiana, Ohio and Michigan, meet at the northeast tip of Starke County of which Angola is the county seat) |
| | Mid-America's Finest Vacationland |
| ATTICA | The Gem City of the Wabash (on the Wabash and Erie Canal) |
| BEDFORD | The Home of the Nation's Building Stone |
| | The Stone City (the heart of the Indiana limestone district) |
| BLOOMINGTON | The Gateway to Scenic Southern Indiana |
| BOONVILLE | The Lincoln City |
| BRAZIL | The Clay City (about a dozen factories making clay products from local clay) |
| CARROLLTOWN | Tailholt (featured in James Whitcomb Riley's poem "The Little Town O'Tailholt") |

| | |
|---|---|
| COLUMBUS | The City of Better Living |
| CONNERSVILLE | Little Detroit (five makes of automobiles once manufactured there) |
| CRAWFORDSVILLE | The Athens of America (referring to the literary figures who once lived in the town, General Lew Wallace, Maurice Thompson, Meredith Nicholson, etc.) |
| | The Athens of Indiana |
| | The Home of Ben Hur (General Lew Wallace's study) |
| | The Hoosier Athens (Wabash College) |
| DANVILLE | The Gable Town (gabled roofs) |
| ELKHART | The Band City (produces over 60 percent of band instruments) |
| | The Lake Capital of the Hoosier State |
| | The Musical Instrument Capital of the World (band instruments manufactured) |
| | The World's Largest Mobile Home Manufacturing Center |
| EVANSVILLE | The Air Crossroads of America |
| | The City in the Valley of Opportunity |
| | The City of Opportunity |
| | The Refrigeration Capital of the World |
| FORT WAYNE | The Birthplace of Night Baseball (game played under "rays of electric light" on June 2, 1882) |
| | The Center of the World's Magnet Wire Production |
| | The Gateway to the Northern Indiana Lake Region |
| | The Hub of the Great North-Central Industrial and Agricultural America |
| | The Summit City |
| FOUNTAIN CITY | Grand Central Station of the Underground Railroad (home of Quaker Levi Coffin, major terminus of Underground Railroad during the Civil War) |

| | |
|---|---|
| FRANKFORT | The City Substantial |
| FRENCH LICK | America's Greatest Health and Pleasure Resort (mineral waters, Pluto water bottled here, luxury hotels) |
| | America's Sports Mecca |
| | The Carlsbad of America |
| | The Home of the Famous Pluto Mineral Springs |
| GARY | America's Magic City (it didn't exist at the turn of the century)  . |
| | The Center of Industry |
| | The Gateway to Indiana Dunes |
| | The Gateway to Vast Farm and Industrial Markets |
| | The Magic City |
| | The Playground of the Dunes |
| | The Steel City (U. S. Steel Corp. mill) |
| | The Steel-Making City |
| GENEVA | The Limberlost Country (the Limberlost swamp region made famous in the books of Gene Stratton Porter) |
| GOSHEN | The Maple City |
| GREENSBURG | The City with a Future |
| | The Tower Tree City (the tower of the courthouse contains a growing tree) |
| | The Tree City |
| GREENWOOD | The Town of Happy Homes |
| INDIANAPOLIS | America's Greatest Inland City |
| | The Capital City (1960 population 476, 258) |
| | The City That Has the Resources to Fit Your Business Needs |
| | The Crossroads of America |
| | The Hoosier Capital |
| | The Hoosier City |
| | The Hub of the Nation-wide Transportation System (7 interstate highways, 6 major railroads, 6 airlines, 125 truck lines) |
| | The Opportunity City |
| | The Railroad City |
| JASPER | The Chair and Desk City |

| | |
|---|---|
| JASPER (Cont'd) | The Nation's Wood Capital (manufacture of wood office furniture) |
| JEFFERSONVILLE | Indiana's Gateway City (terminal of the American Commercial Barge Line) |
| | The Falls Cities (with New Albany, Ind., and Louisville, Ky.) |
| KOKOMO | The City of Firsts |
| | The City of the First Automobile |
| LAFAYETTE | The Star City (on the Wabash River) |
| | The Twin Cities (with West Lafayette, Ind.) |
| LA PORTE | Indiana's Finest Home Town |
| | The City of Lakes (seven lakes partially in the city) |
| | The Maple City |
| LEBANON | The Friendliest City in the State |
| LEESBURG | The Gateway of the Lake Region (Tippecanoe Lake) |
| LOGANSPORT | The City of Bridges (situated at the confluence of the Wabash and Eel Rivers) |
| MADISON | The City 'Neath the Hills (on the Ohio River) |
| MARION | The Queen City of the Gas Belt (gas and oil discovered in 1880's) |
| MARTINSVILLE | The Artesian City (artesian wells supply mineral water) |
| MICHIGAN CITY | Indiana's Summer Playground |
| | The Capital of Duneland (located in the famous sand dune country at the southern end of Lake Michigan) |
| | The Largest Resort Center in Indiana |
| MIDDLETOWN | The Typical American City |
| MISHAWAKA | The City in the Valley of Promise |
| MITCHELL | The Home of Astronaut Virgil (Gus) Grissom |
| | The Largest Small City in Indiana (1960 population 3,552) |
| MONTPELIER | The Oil City |
| MORGANTOWN | The Gateway to Brown County |
| MUNCIE | Middletown U.S.A. (two books |

MUNCIE (Cont'd)

about Muncie by sociologists
Robert S. and Helen M. Lynd
entitled "Middletown" and
"Middletown in Transition")
The Magic City
The Typical American City (on
the White River, 1960 popula-
tion 68, 603)

NEW ALBANY

A Good Place to Live, Work and
Play
The Falls Cities (with Jefferson-
ville, Ind., and Louisville, Ky.)
The Home of the Robert E. Lee
(the famous steamboat was
built there)
The Plywood Capital of the World
The Real Hoosier City

NEW CASTLE

The City with a Planned Future
The City of Roses

NEW HARMONY

The Athens of America (on Wabash River)

PAOLI

The Crossroads of Southern Indiana

PERU

The Circus City (winter headquarters of numerous circuses)
The Circus City of the World

PLAINFIELD

The Friendly Folk's Village
The Village of Friendly Folk

RICHMOND

The Quaker City of the West
(founded 1806 by the Society
of Friends)
The Rose Center of the United
States

ROANOKE

The Athens of Indiana (Roanoke
Classical Seminary, considered
ultimate in culture in 1860's)

ROCKVILLE

The Covered Bridge Capital of
the World (38 bridges in Parke
County)

SALEM

The Athens of the West

SEYMOUR

The Crossroads of America
The Crossroads of Southern Indiana
The Gateway of Southern Indiana
(between the White River and
the Vernon Fork of the Musca-
tatuck)

SOUTH BEND              The Major World Tool and Die
                         Training Center
TERRE HAUTE            Boomtown, U. S. A. (derisive title
                         for numerous gas explosions in
                         1963)
                       The Pittsburgh of the Big West
                       The Switzerland of America
                       The Sycamore City
VINCENNES              The Citadel of the Old Northwest
                         (fort erected here in 1732)
WABASH                 The First Electrically Lighted
                         City in the World
                       The Rock City (Wabash River over
                         white stones and rocks)
WARSAW                 The Gateway to the Indiana Lake
                         Area (Winona, Center and Pike)
WASHINGTON             The Garden Spot of Southern Indi-
                         ana
WEST LAFAYETTE         The Twin Cities (with Lafayette,
                         Ind. )

## IOWA

ALGONA                 The Friendly City
                       The Gateway to West Bend Grotto
BURLINGTON             The Orchard City
                       The Porkopolis of Iowa
CEDAR FALLS            The Garden City
                       The Home of Quaker Oats
                       The Lawn City
CEDAR RAPIDS           The Metropolis of Industry
                       The Parlor City
                       The Rapid City (swift rapids)
CHARLES CITY           The Birthplace of the Farm Trac-
                         tor
DAVENPORT              Dynamic Davenport
                       The City of Beauty
                       The Port of Hospitality on the
                         Great Father of Waters
                       The Progressive City with the
                         Rich Heritage and Charm of
                         the Old River Days
                       The Quad Cities (with East Mo-
                         line, Moline, and Rock Island,
                         Ill. )
                       The Queen City
                       The Tri-Cities (with Moline and

Davenport, Iowa                                         97

| | |
|---|---|
| DAVENPORT (Cont'd) | Rock Island, Ill. ) |
| DECORAH | The Switzerland of Iowa |
| DE WITT | The Prime Beef Center of the World |
| DENVER | The Pheasant Country |
| DES MOINES | Iowa's Own City |
| | The Action Capitol of the Midwest |
| | The Capital City (1960 population 208,982; capital in 1857) |
| | The Center of the Midwest and the Country (250 miles from Minneapolis and St. Paul; 140 miles from Omaha; 340 miles from Chicago; 300 miles from St. Louis and 200 miles from Kansas City) |
| | The City of Certainties |
| | The Largest Insurance Center in the West (about fifty insurance companies) |
| DUBUQUE | Iowa's Industrial, Scenic and Cultured City |
| | The City for Family Fun and Action |
| | The City of Progress |
| | The Heidelberg of America (Germanic influence in architecture and schools) |
| | The Key City |
| | The Key City of Iowa |
| | The Little Heidelberg of America |
| | The Queen City of the Northwest |
| FORT DODGE | The Gypsum City (one of the largest gypsum producing centers) |
| IOWA CITY | The Athens of America |
| | The Athens of Iowa |
| JEFFERSON | The Community of Hospitable People |
| | The Home of the Mahanay Memorial Carillon Tower |
| KEOKUK | A Good Place to Live, Work and Do Business |
| | The City That Holds the Key to Mid-America |
| | The City That Is Attracting New Industry |

| | |
|---|---|
| KEOKUK (Cont'd) | The Gate City (foot of the Mississippi River) |
| | The Home of George M. Verity |
| | The Power City (Keokum Dam drains about 120,000 square mile area) |
| | The Progressive City |
| LE CLAIRE | The Birthplace of Buffalo Bill Cody |
| MARSHALLTOWN | The City of Progress with Pride and Purpose |
| | The Convention City of Iowa |
| MASON CITY | The Friendly and Progressive City |
| | The Home of the "Music Man" (Meredith Willson) |
| MONONA | The Heart of the Corn Country |
| MUSCATINE | The Pearl City (pearl button production |
| | The Port City of the Corn Belt |
| NEW HAMPTON | The Petunia Capital |
| OTTUMWA | Today's City with Tomorrow's Vision |
| PLEASANTVILLE | The Rose City |
| ST. DONATUS | The Picturesque Old World Village |
| SHENANDOAH | The World's Largest Seed and Nursery Center |
| SIOUX CITY | The City of Distinction |
| | The City where the Industrial East Meets the Agricultural West |
| | The Foremost Industrial Center of Iowa |
| | The Home Market for the Great Northwest |
| | The Industrial City of Iowa |
| | The Livestock, Grain and Industrial Capital of the Great Northwest |
| | The World's Central Livestock Market |

KANSAS

| | |
|---|---|
| ABILENE | The Biggest Little City (1960 population 6,746) |
| | The Center of the Great Kansas |

ABILENE (Cont'd)                 Agricultural Empire
                                 The City of the Plains (on Smoky
                                     Hill River)
                                 The Gem of the Plains
                                 The Good Size Town for Knowing
                                     Your Neighbor
                                 The Greyhound City (about sixty
                                     percent of America's grey-
                                     hound dogs born and bred here)
                                 The Growing City of Opportunity
                                 The Heart of History and Ro-
                                     mance in Kansas
                                 The Health Center and Principal
                                     Trade Center of North Central
                                     Kansas
ARKANSAS CITY                    The Ark City (on Mississippi
                                     River)
BURLINGAME                       The City where the Trail Meets
                                     Rail (Santa Fe Trail)
CALDWELL                         The Queen City of the Border
CAWKER CITY                      The Biggest Little Town in Kan-
                                     sas
CEDAR VALE                       The Quail Haven
COFFEYVILLE                      The Cow Town (settled in 1870,
                                     formerly used)
COLBY                            The Golden Buckle on the Wheat
                                     Belt (the heart of wheat belt)
CONCORDIA                        The City of Concord
                                 The City That Is Big Enough to
                                     Serve You and Small Enough
                                     to Know You
                                 The City with Unity in the Com-
                                     munity
DODGE CITY                       The Biggest Little City in the
                                     U. S. A. (1960 population 13, 520)
                                 The Buckle on the Kansas Wheat
                                     Belt
                                 The Cowboy Capital
                                 The Cowboy Capital of the World
                                 The Home of World Famous Front
                                     Street and Boot Hill
                                 The Queen City of the Cow Towns
                                 The Queen of the Cow Towns
                                 The Shipping Center of the South-
                                     west
                                 The Wickedest Little City in
                                     America

| | |
|---|---|
| EMPORIA | The Educational Center of the West (site of Kansas State Teachers College and College of Emporia) |
| | The Loveliest Site in the World for a Town |
| FORT LEAVENWORTH | The City where the History of the West Begins (fort erected in 1827 as protection from Indians) |
| GARDEN CITY | The Family Town |
| | The Garden Spot of the West |
| GOODLAND | The Heart of the Wheat Land |
| GREAT BEND | The Oil Capital in the Heart of the Wheat Belt (oil wells) |
| HUGOTON | The Gas Capital of the World |
| | The Natural Gas Capital of the U. S. |
| HUTCHINSON | The Salt City (extensive salt beds underlying the city) |
| INDEPENDENCE | The Buckle on the Oil Belt (oil and gas) |
| | The City where the Accent Is on Family |
| | The Queen City of Southeast Kansas |
| KINSLEY | Half Way and a Place to Stay (between Dodge City and Great Bend) |
| LEAVENWORTH | The City where Progress Profits Growth |
| | The Cottonwood City |
| | The First City of Kansas |
| | The Sight-Seeing City of the Middle West |
| LIBERAL | The Pancake Center |
| | The Pancake Center of the World |
| MANHATTAN | The City where People Play and Prosper |
| | The Complete Community |
| | The Kansas Water Sports Capital |
| NORTON | The Pheasant Capital of Kansas |
| OGDEN | The Last Place on the Map |
| OLATHE | The Cowboy Boot Capital (boot factories) |
| OVERBROOK | Don't Overlook Overbrook |

SALINA                        The City where North and South
                                  Meet East and West
                              The Convention City
                              The Metropolis of Central and
                                  Northwest Kansas
                              The Proven Progressive City
SHAWNEE                       The Gateway of Kansas
SMITH CENTER                  The "Home on the Range" Birth-
                                  place
TOPEKA                        The Capital City (1960 population
                                  119, 484)
                              The Center of the Nation
VICTORIA                      The Cathedral of the Plains (St.
                                  Fidelis Church)
WELLINGTON                    The Wheat Capital of the World
WICHITA                       Kansas' Premier City
                              One of the World's Great Airplane
                                  Manufacturing Centers (Beech,
                                  Boeing, Cessna, etc.)
                              The Air Capital (four major air-
                                  lines unite)
                              The Air Capital of America
                              The Air Capital of the Nation
                              The Air Capital of the World
                              The City of Conventions
                              The City of Industry
                              The Cow Capital
                              The Magic Mascot of the Plains
                              The Peerless Princess of the
                                  Plains
WILLIAMSTOWN                  Billtown

                          KENTUCKY

ASHLAND                       The Busy Friendly City
                              The City where Coal Meets Iron
                                  (steel mill)
BOWLING GREEN                 Southern Kentucky's Largest Shop-
                                  ping Center
                              The City where Folks Are Not
                                  Too Busy to Be Friendly
                              The Confederate State Capital of
                                  Kentucky (during the Confeder-
                                  ate occupation)
CAVE CITY                     The Gateway to the Mammoth Cave
CORBIN                        The Hub of the Valley of Parks
                                  (near Cumberland Falls, Lake

CORBIN (Cont'd)                    Cumberland and Levi Jackson
                                   Wilderness Road State Park)
COVINGTON                          The Dixie Gateway (at confluence
                                   of Ohio and Licking rivers op-
                                   posite Cincinnati, Ohio)
FLORENCE                           The City where Hospitality of the
                                   South Begins
FRANKFORT                          The Bluegrass Capital (selected
                                   in 1792)
                                   The Capital City (1960 pop. 18,365)
                                   The Diversified Community
                                   The Heart of America
                                   The Heart of Kentucky
                                   The Historic Frankfort (founded
                                   in 1786)
HARRODSBURG                        The Birthplace of Western Amer-
                                   ica
HENDERSON                          The Gateway to the Greatest Va-
                                   cation Land in Mid-America
                                   The Land of Outdoor Fun
LEXINGTON                          One of the Nation's Largest
                                   Spring Lamb Producing Centers
                                   One of the South's Foremost Edu-
                                   cational Centers
                                   The Athens of the West (Univer-
                                   sity of Kentucky)
                                   The Belle City of the Bluegrass
                                   Regions
                                   The Bluegrass Capital
                                   The Capital of the Bluegrass Re-
                                   gion
                                   The Capital of the Horse World
                                   The Chief City of the Bluegrass
                                   Region
                                   The Dimple of the Bluegrass
                                   The Heart of Kentucky's Blue
                                   Grass Region (about 1,200
                                   square miles)
                                   The Retail, Wholesale, Industrial,
                                   Medical Institutional Center of
                                   Kentucky
                                   The Thoroughbred, Standard-
                                   bred and Saddle Horse Center
                                   of America
                                   The Trade Center of the Rich
                                   Blue Grass, Tobacco and Live-
                                   stock Region

| | |
|---|---|
| LEXINGTON (Cont'd) | The World's Largest Loose-Leaf Tobacco Market |
| LOUISVILLE | The Bustling River Port |
| | The City by the Falls (Ohio River) |
| | The City of Beautiful Churches |
| | The City of Homes |
| | The City of the Falls |
| | The Convention City |
| | The Falls Cities (with Jeffersonville and New Albany, Ind.) |
| | The Falls City (on the Ohio River) |
| | The Gateway City (on the Ohio River) |
| | The Gateway to the South |
| | The Growing Industrial, Financial and Educational Center |
| | The Home of the Kentucky Derby |
| | The Metropolis of the New South |
| | The Nation's Thoroughfare |
| MURRAY | The Birthplace of Radio (Nathan B. Stubblefield radio pioneer) |
| | The Friendliest Little "Big Town" in Kentucky (1960 population 9,303) |
| PADUCAH | America's Newest Industrial Center |
| | The Capital of Western Kentucky |
| | The Medical Center |
| WINCHESTER | The Center of the Blue Grass Area |

## LOUISIANA

| | |
|---|---|
| ALEXANDRIA | The Crossroads of Louisiana (on the Red River) |
| | The Geographical Crossroads of Louisiana |
| | The Hub City (center of the industrial area of the state) |
| | The Twin Cities on the Red River in the Heart of Louisiana (with Pineville) |
| BATON ROUGE | America's Most Beautiful Capitol |
| | Louisiana's Fastest Growing City |
| | The Capital City (1960 population 152,419) |

| | |
|---|---|
| BATON ROUGE (Cont'd) | The Chemical Center of the South |
| | The Farthest Inland Deep Water Port |
| | The Home of Louisiana State University |
| BOGALUSA | The Magic City of the Green Empire (founded 1906) |
| BOSSIER CITY | The City Situated in Strategic Northwest Louisiana |
| | The Growingest City in Louisiana |
| BREAUX BRIDGE | The Crawfish Capital of the World |
| BURAS | The Center of the Louisiana Orange Industry |
| CROWLEY | The Rice Capital of Louisiana |
| | The Rice Capital of the World |
| | The Rice Center of America |
| | The Rice City of America |
| FORT JESSUP | The Cradle of the Mexican War (troops from the fort were sent to Texas during the Revolution from Mexico) |
| FRANKLIN | The Cleanest City in Louisiana |
| GONZALEZ | Jambalaya Capital of the World |
| | The City of Southern Friendliness and Charm |
| HAMMOND | The Strawberry Capital of America |
| HOUMA | The Oyster Center of the State |
| | The Venice of America |
| INDEPENDENCE | Little Italy |
| JENNINGS | Louisiana's Cleanest City |
| | The Cradle of Louisiana Oil ( the first oil well in the state flowed Sept. 21, 1901) |
| | The Garden Spot of Louisiana |
| LAFAYETTE | The Azalea Trail City |
| | The City in the Heart of South Central Louisiana (on the Vermilion River) |
| | The French Louisiana |
| | The Hub of Southwestern Louisiana |
| LAKE CHARLES | The Rice Capital of Louisiana |
| | The Sea Gate to the Southwest (on the Calcasieu River, 37 miles from the Gulf of Mexico) |
| MARKSVILLE | The Fishing Shangri-La of the South |

| | |
|---|---|
| MINDEN | The Home of Champions (athletic teams and the Louis-Annes precision drill team) |
| MONROE | The Twin Cities (with West Monroe) |
| | The Twin Cities of the Ouachita (with West Monroe) |
| NATCHITOCHES | The Up-to-Date Oldest Town in Louisiana (French trading post established in 1714) |
| NEW IBERIA | The Queen City of the Teche (a stream flowing into the Atchafalaya Bayou) |
| NEW ORLEANS | America's Most Hedonistic City |
| | America's Most Interesting City |
| | The Air Hub of the Americas |
| | The Alexandria of America |
| | The City Care Forgot |
| | The City of Charm |
| | The City of Contrasts |
| | The Crawfish Town |
| | The Crescent City (it curves around the Mississippi) |
| | The Gateway to the World |
| | The Great South Gate (entrance to the Gulf of Mexico) |
| | The Gulf City (on the Gulf of Mexico) |
| | The Heart of America's New Commercial Frontier |
| | The Heart of Dixie |
| | The Hub of the Americas |
| | The International City |
| | The Key of the Great Valley |
| | The Mardi Gras Metropolis |
| | The Metropolis of the South |
| | The Old French Town |
| | The Paris of America |
| | The Queen of the South |
| | The South's Greatest City (founded in 1718; 1960 population 627, 525) |
| | The Winter Capital of America |
| PINEVILLE | The Crossroads of Louisiana |
| | The Twin Cities on the Red River in the Heart of Louisiana (with Alexandria) |

| | |
|---|---|
| RAYNE | The Frog Market of the Nation |
| RUSTON | The Land of Good Living |
| ST. FRANCISVILLE | The Town Two Miles Long and Two Yards Wide (1960 population 1, 661) |
| SHREVEPORT | The Capital City of the Land of Ark-La-Tex |
| | The City of Churches |
| | The City on the Grow |
| | The New City in the Old South (incorporated 1839) |
| | The Pipeline Capitol of America (during the oil and gas boom of the 1920's and 1930's) |
| | The Pivot City of the Central South |
| | The Pivot City of the South |
| | The Queen City of the Ark-La-Tex (located geographically near the borders of Texas and Arkansas) |
| SLIDELL | The City Geared to Space-Age Families |
| | The City of Good Living |
| | The City with a Bright Future |
| WEST MONROE | The Twin Cities (with Monroe, La. ) |
| | The Twin Cities of the Ouachita (with Monroe, La. ) |

## MAINE

| | |
|---|---|
| AUBURN | The City of Homes |
| | The Industrial Heart of Maine |
| | The Shire City of Androscoggin County |
| | The Shoe City (about 15 shoe factories) |
| | The Twin Cities (with Lewiston) |
| AUGUSTA | The Capital City (1960 population 21, 680) |
| | The City of Manifold Advantages |
| | The City of Year-around Recreation |
| BANGOR | The Center of Maine |
| | The Gateway to the North Woods |
| | The Greatest Lumber Market in |

BANGOR (Cont'd)

the World (not claimed now)
The Lumber City
The Metropolis of the Northeast
The Queen City (1960 population 38, 912)
The Queen City of the East
The Twin Cities (with Brewer; Bangor on the east bank, Brewer on the west bank of the Penobscot River)

BAR HARBOR

Maine's Most Famous Coast Resort (on Mount Desert Island, on Frenchman Bay)
The Lobster Center of the World

BATH

The Shipping City (on the Kennebec River, claims to have launched more ships than any other place in the world)

BELFAST

The Biggest Little City in Maine
The Broiler Capital of Maine
The Broiler Capital of New England
The Capital of the Broiler Industry
The Shire City of Waldo County

BETHEL

The Gateway to Maine from the White Mountains
The Ideal Place in Which to Live, Work and Play (in the Rangeley Lake area, on the Androscoggin River)

BIDDEFORD

The City where Life Is Different
The Gateway to Maine (on the Saco River)
The Major Market of York County (with Saco, Me. )
The Nation's Best Recreational Area - Four Season Fun
The Twin Cities (with Saco, Me., opposite sides of the Saco River)

BINGHAM

The City where Historic Yesterday Greets Dynamic Tomorrow

BOOTHBAY HARBOR

The Boating Capital of New England
The Yachting Capital of New England

| | |
|---|---|
| BREWER | The Twin Cities (with Bangor, Me., opposite sides of the Penobscot River) |
| BRIDGTON | The Vacation Fun Spot of Western Maine (12 lakes in the town) |
| | The Wonderland of Lakes |
| CALAIS | The International City (International Bridge to St. Stephens, New Brunswick, Canada) |
| CAMDEN | The City where the Mountains Meet the Sea (on Penobscot Bay) |
| | The Gem of Penobscot Bay |
| CARIBOU | The Hub of Aroostook County |
| | The Northeastern-most City in the U.S. |
| CHINA | The Family Vacation Resort |
| DAMARISCOTTA | The Twin Towns (with Newcastle, Me.) |
| | The Twin Villages (with Newcastle; Damariscotta on the east bank of the Damariscotta River opposite Newcastle) |
| DENMARK | A Place to Live, Work or Play |
| EASTPORT | The Sardine Capital of the U.S. |
| ELLSWORTH | The City at the Crossroads Down East |
| FARMINGTON | The Gateway to Rangeley and Sugarloaf |
| | The Gateway to the Rangeley Lakes |
| | The Shire Town and Hub of the County (Franklin County) |
| FORT KENT | The Gateway to Canada's St. Lawrence Seaway (at the junction of the Fish and St. John River) |
| | The Gateway to the Allagash Country |
| | The Gateway to the Fish River Chain of Lakes |
| FREEPORT | The Birthplace of Maine (where the commissioners of the District of Maine and the Commonwealth of Massachusetts signed an agreement for the separation) |

FRYEBURG                      The Friendly Prosperous Town
                              The Place for Vacations Year
                                  'Round and for Year 'Round
                                  Living
HARRISON                      A Family Community for Your
                                  Maine Vacation
                              The Friendly Village
HOULTON                       The Garden of Maine (Aroostook
                                  County agricultural center)
                              The Shopping Center of Northern
                                  Maine
                              The Town Just Rite for Your
                                  Plant Site
JACKMAN                       The Gateway to Real Vacation
                                  Pleasure
                              The Switzerland of Maine
KENNEBUNK                     The "Maine" Idea in Recreation
KINGFIELD                     The Little City in the Woods
KITTERY                       The Gateway to Maine
LAKEWOOD                      The Broadway Colony in the
                                  Heart of Maine (Lakewood
                                  Playhouse and Summer colony)
LEWISTON                      The Home City
                              The Ideal Working City
                              The Industrial Center
                              The Industrial Heart of Maine
                              The Progressive, Prosperous and
                                  Peaceful Community
                              The Spindle City (largest textile
                                  manufacturing center in Maine;
                                  the home of Bates Mfg. Co.)
                              The Twin Cities (with Auburn,
                                  Me.)
                              The Working City
MONHEGAN                      The Fortunate Island (in Knox
                                  County, island in the Atlantic
                                  Ocean)
MOSCOW                        The City where Historic Yester-
                                  day Greets Dynamic Tomorrow
MOUNT KATAHDIN                America's Alarm City
NAPLES                        The Heart of the Region
NEWCASTLE                     The Twin Towns (with Damaris-
                                  cotta, Me.)
                              The Twin Villages (on the west
                                  bank of the Damariscotta
                                  River opposite Damariscotta
                                  on the east bank)

| | |
|---|---|
| NORWAY | Maine's Fastest Growing Industrial and Recreational Area |
| | The Fastest Growing Community in Maine |
| | The Snowshoe Town of America |
| OGUNQUIT | Ogunquit Is the Sea |
| | The Beautiful Place by the Sea (scenic three-mile beach whose Indian name means "beautiful place by the sea") |
| OLD ORCHARD BEACH | Sun and Fun! Sand 'N Sea! |
| | The All-Round Playground (seashore resort) |
| | The City of Sun and Fun, Sand 'N Sea |
| | The Cleanest Beach in the World |
| | The Finest Beach in the World (700 feet wide at low tide) |
| | The Playground of the Nation |
| | The Playground of Vacationland |
| OLD TOWN | The Canoe City (industrial city on the Penobscot River where world-famed canoes are manufactured) |
| PARIS | Maine's Fastest Growing Industrial and Recreational Area |
| | The City on the Hill |
| | The Fastest Growing Community in Maine (1960 population 3,601) |
| PATTEN | The Northern Gateway to the Natural Paradise Baxter Park |
| | The Unspoiled Beauty Spot of Northern Maine |
| PEAKS ISLAND | The Island of Easy Living (part of Portland, Maine) |
| PITTSFIELD | The Center of Progress in Maine (on the Sebasticook River) |
| PORTLAND | A Wonderful Place to Live, to Work and Play |
| | America's Sunrise Gateway |
| | The Beautiful City by the Sea |
| | The Beautiful Town That Is Seated by the Sea |
| | The Forest City |
| | The Gateway to Vacationland |

| | |
|---|---|
| PORTLAND (Cont'd) | The Hill City |
| | The Vacation City on Casco Bay |
| RAYMOND | The Tall Tower Town |
| ROCKLAND | The Metropolis of the Penobscot Bay Region |
| RUMFORD | Maine's Outstanding Winter Sports Center |
| SACO | The City where Life Is Different |
| | The Gateway to Maine (on the Saco River) |
| | The Major Market of York County (with Biddeford, Me. ) |
| | The Twin Cities (with Biddeford) |
| SANFORD | The Up and Coming City (in York County, 1960 population 10, 936) |
| SEARSPORT | The Fastest Growing Deep Water Seaport in Maine (Penobscot Bay) |
| | The Home of Old Sea Captains |
| | The Home of World Famous Sea Captains |
| SEBAGO LAKE | The Town of Sandy Beaches |
| SKOWHEGAN | The Friendliest Town in New England (on the Kennebec River, 1960 population 6, 667) |
| SOUTH BERWICK | The Parish of Unity |
| STOCKTON SPRINGS | The Home of the World's Largest Black Walnut Processing Plant |
| | The Home of the World Famous Stockton Cheese |
| VINALHAVEN | Maine's Most Enchanting Island |
| WATERVILLE | The Elm City |
| WELLS | One of New England's Most Famous Coast Resorts |
| WISCASSET | The Modern Town Rich in History (historic homes built in the 1790's and early 1800's) |
| YARMOUTH | The Coastal Town of Charm and Beauty (on Casco Bay) |

## MARYLAND

| | |
|---|---|
| ANNAPOLIS | Crabtown (crab fishing) |
| | The Ancient City (Capital of Maryland in 1694) |
| | The Athens of America |
| | The Capital City (1960 pop. 23, 385) |

| | |
|---|---|
| ANNAPOLIS (Cont'd) | The City where Land and Water Meet |
| | The Crabtown-on-the-Bay (crab fishing) |
| | The First Peace Time Capitol of the United States |
| | The Gateway to the South |
| | The Heart of Maryland |
| | The Modern City with a Colonial Setting |
| | The Venice of America (many creeks and streams) |
| BALTIMORE | Maryland's Largest City (1960 population 939,024) |
| | The Aviation Center of the East |
| | The Birthplace of the Star Spangled Banner |
| | The Convention City |
| | The Mobtown (lawless element which prevailed particularly during the Civil War) |
| | The Monumental City (first city to erect a monument to George Washington, cornerstone laid July 4, 1815) |
| | The National Anthem City (where the Star Spangled Banner was written) |
| | The Nation's Most Hospitable City |
| BETHESDA | The Western Gateway to the Nation's Capital |
| CHEVY CHASE | The Suburb of Washington |
| CRISFIELD | The Seafood Capital of the World (on Tangier Sound, part of Chesapeake Bay) |
| CUMBERLAND | The Heart of the Potomac Highlands (eastern end of Georges Creek) |
| | The Queen City |
| | The Transportation City |
| EASTON | The Colonial Capital of the Eastern Shore (unofficial) |
| | The Newport of the Eastern Shore |
| ELKTON | Gretna Green |
| | Gretna Green of Maryland |

| | |
|---|---|
| ELKTON (Cont'd) | Head of Elk |
| FREDERICK | The City in Marylands Historic Heartland |
| | The Heart of Industry |
| | The Hub of History |
| OCEAN CITY | A City There's a Lot to Like About |
| | Maryland's Playground |
| | The Fort Lauderdale of the Eastern Shore |
| | The White Marlin Capital of the World |
| POCOMOKE CITY | Home of the National Bass Round-Up |
| SALISBURY | The Tennis Capital of the World (U. S. Indoor Tennis Tournaments are held here) |

## MASSACHUSETTS

| | |
|---|---|
| AMESBURY | The Carriage Center of the World |
| AMHERST | The Distinguished and Friendly Community |
| ASHFIELD | The Little Switzerland |
| BELLINGHAM | The Growing Community Centered in a Growing Market |
| BEVERLY | The Birthplace of the American Navy (the schooner "Hannah" was armed, outfitted and commissioned by George Washington in 1775 as the first ship of the American Navy) |
| | The City in the Country by the Sea |
| | The Garden City |
| | The Heart of the Famous North Shore (on the Atlantic Ocean) |
| BOSTON | Beantown |
| | Bostonia |
| | The American Athens |
| | The Athens |
| | The Athens of America |
| | The Athens of the New World |
| | The Athens of the United States |
| | The Athens of the West |
| | The Bay Horse |

BOSTON (Cont'd)

The Bitches' Heaven
The Birthplace of Freedom
The Capital City (1960 population 697, 197)
The Capital of New England
The City of Baked Beans
The City of Bean Eaters
The City of Firsts
The City of Kind Hearts
The City of Notions
The City of Paul Revere
The Classic City
The Cradle of the American Revolution
The Home of Baked Beans
The Home of the Homeless Ballet
The Hub
The Hub of New England
The Hub of the Commonwealth
The Hub of the Solar System (so called by Oliver Wendell Holmes)
The Hub of the Universe (statement attributed to Oliver Wendell Holmes)
The Hub Town
The Literary Emporium
The Major Cultural Center of the World
The Metropolis of New England
The Modern Athens
The Mother City of America
The Panhandler's Heaven
The Puritan City
The Puritan Zion
The Tri-Mountain City (the three hills on which it was originally built)
Tremont

BRAINTREE

The Future Industrial Capital of the South Shore

BROCKTON

The City of Shoes (shoe products)
The Industrial City

BROOKLINE

The Richest Town in the World
The Town of Millionaires (a residential suburb of Boston)

CAMBRIDGE

The Athens of America

| | |
|---|---|
| CAMBRIDGE (Cont'd) | The Center of History, Education and Industry |
| | The Geographical Center of the Metropolitan Boston Area |
| | The Hub of a New World (title of book by Christopher Rand) |
| | The Outstanding American City |
| | The University City (Harvard University, Radcliffe College, Massachusetts Institute of Technology, etc.) |
| CHATHAM | The First Stop of the East Wind (on Cape Cod) |
| | The Town where Summer Is Air-Conditioned (Atlantic Ocean on one side, Nantucket Sound on the other) |
| CHELSEA | The City of Transformations |
| CHICOPEE | The Fastest Growing City in New England |
| | The Future Minded City (1960 population 61,553) |
| | The Hub of Fast Transportation |
| CONCORD | The Cradle of Liberty (battle fought April 19, 1775) |
| | The Golden Age Haven |
| DEDHAM | The Birthplace of Democracy |
| | The Sober-Minded (settled in 1636) |
| DENNIS | The Heart of Cape Cod |
| EASTHAM | Vacationland, U.S.A. |
| EVERETT | The Industrial Half-Sister |
| FALL RIVER | The Border City |
| | The City of Falling Water |
| | The Scholarship City (numerous scholarships offered) |
| | The Spindle City (cotton and textile mills) |
| FITCHBURG | The Mercantile Center |
| FOXBORO | The City on the Crossroads of the Expressways |
| FRAMINGHAM | The Diversified Manufacturing Community |
| GLOUCESTER | America's First and Most Historic Fishing Port |
| GREAT BARRINGTON | The Winter Playground |
| GREENFIELD | The Dream-town |
| | The Well-balanced Community |

| | |
|---|---|
| HAVERHILL | America's Oldest Industrial City |
| | The Place by the Winding River |
| | The Queen Shoe City of the World |
| | The Shoe Town |
| HOLYOKE | A City in the Country |
| | The City at the Heart of Industrial New England |
| | The City of Diversified Industries |
| | The City of Uninterrupted Electric Power |
| | The Fine Writing Paper Center of the World |
| | The Industrial City |
| | The Largest Industrial City in Western Massachusetts |
| | The Paper City (better-grade writing paper produced) |
| HUDSON | The Crossroads of Industrial Development |
| IPSWICH | The Birthplace of American Independence |
| LAWRENCE | The City where Modern America Began |
| | The City where Visitors Meet Hospitality |
| | The Immigrant City |
| | The Worsted Mill Capital of the World |
| LEOMINSTER | The Baby City (became a city in 1915) |
| | The Comb City (in 1845 had 24 factories making combs) |
| LEXINGTON | The Birthplace of American Liberty |
| | The Cradle of Liberty (Minute Men resisted British troops, April 19, 1775) |
| LOWELL | The City of Magic |
| | The City of Spindles |
| | The Manchester of America (Manchester, England, cotton manufacturing city) |
| | The Modern American Athens (Lowell Technical Institute) |
| | The Spindle City (cotton and woolen mills) |

LUDLOW                          The Industrial Center
LYNN                            Shoe Capital of the World
                                The Center of Distribution
                                The City of Shoes
                                The City of Soles
                                The Machine City
                                The Shoe City (manufacturing be-
                                   gan 1635)
MALDEN                          The Ideal City
                                The Proud City with a Bright
                                   Future
MARBLEHEAD                      The Birthplace of the American
                                   Navy
                                The City where Tradition Lingers
                                The Greatest Town for Fishing
                                   in New England (seacoast on
                                   Massachusetts Bay and Atlan-
                                   tic Ocean)
                                The Yachting Capital of the
                                   World
                                The Yachting Center of the
                                   World
MARTHAS VINEYARD                One Hundred Square Miles of
                                   Picturesque Pleasure
                                The Friendly Island (in Atlantic
                                   Ocean)
MELROSE                         The City of Homes and Gracious
                                   Living
MIDDLETOWN                      Santa's Lookout
NANTUCKET                       The Far Away Island (30 miles
                                   off the Massachusetts coast
                                   in the Atlantic Ocean)
                                The Far Away Land (30 miles
                                   off the mainland in the Atlan-
                                   tic Ocean)
NEW BEDFORD                     The Economy Gateway
                                The Gateway to Cape Cod
                                The Leading Scallop Port of the
                                   World
                                The Trading Center
                                The Whaling Capital of the World
                                The Whaling City (at one time
                                   the greatest whaling port in
                                   the world)
NEWBURYPORT                     The Birthplace of the United
                                   States Coast Guard
                                The City of Captains' Houses

| | |
|---|---|
| NEWBURYPORT (Cont'd) | The City of Industry |
| | The City with a Blending of Past and Present on the Banks of the Merrimac |
| | The Yankee City |
| NEWTON | The Commuter's Haven (a suburb of Boston, Mass. ) |
| | The Garden City |
| | The Tin Horn Village |
| NORTHAMPTON | The Heart of the Pioneer Valley |
| | The Meadow City |
| NORTON | The Typical New England City |
| ORANGE | The Home of Minute Tapioca |
| | The Sport Parachuting Center of the United States of America |
| PEABODY | The Leather City (tanneries) |
| PITTSFIELD | The Center of Culture |
| | The City of Culture |
| | The Heart of the Berkshires (on the Housatonic River) |
| | The Heart of the Famous Berkshire Hills |
| | The Industrial City |
| | The Middle Town of New England |
| | The Mill Town |
| | The Show Country of New England |
| | The Vacation Land in the Center of the Berkshires |
| | The Youthful Community |
| PLAINVILLE | The World's Largest Specialty Jewelry Manufacturing Center |
| PLYMOUTH | America's Home Town |
| | Pilgrim Land |
| | The First Town of America (December 1620, Pilgrims made first permanent settlement north of Virginia) |
| | The Land of the Pilgrims, Sun and Sand |
| | The Nation's Birthplace |
| PROVINCETOWN | The Port of the Pilgrims |
| | The Tip of Cape Cod (projects into Cape Cod Bay and Atlantic Ocean, first landing place of Pilgrims, Nov. 11, 1620) |
| QUINCY | The Birthplace of Liberty |

QUINCY (Cont'd)          The Birthplace of the Second and
                         Sixth Presidents (John Adams
                         and his son, John Quincy
                         Adams)
                         The City of Presidents
                         The Fastest Growing City in
                         Massachusetts
                         The Granite City
                         The Shipbuilding City

ROCKPORT                 The City at the Tip of Cape Ann
                         The Most Popular Summer Re-
                         sort in New England

SALEM                    New England's Treasure House
                         The Center of the Beautiful North
                         Shore of Massachusetts
                         The City of Homes
                         The City of Peace
                         The City of Witches (famous
                         witchcraft trials in colonial
                         days about 1692)
                         The City where History Blends
                         with Progress
                         The Most Historic City in the
                         East
                         The Paradise of New England
                         The Witch City
                         The Witchcraft City

SALISBURY BEACH          Five Miles of Smiles, Sea, Sand
                         and Fun
                         New England's Playground on the
                         Atlantic
                         The Jones Beach of New England

SANDWICH                 The Home of Sandwich Glass
                         (manufactured from 1825 to
                         1887)

SAUGUS                   The Birthplace of America's Iron
                         and Steel Industry

SCITUATE                 The Vacation or Year Round
                         Home City (on the Atlantic
                         Ocean)

SHELBURNE FALLS          The Town of Tumbling Waters
                         (center of the hydroelectric
                         plants of the New England
                         Power Company)

SOMERVILLE               The City of Hills
                         The City of Homes
                         The Heart of New England

| | |
|---|---|
| SOUTHBRIDGE | The Eye of the Commonwealth (ophthalmic products) |
| | The Heart of New England |
| SPRINGFIELD | A Host Without Parallel |
| | One of the Most Accessible Cities in the Eastern States |
| | The Best Convention Point in the East |
| | The City of Homes |
| | The City Rich in Tradition and Opportunity |
| | The Crossroads of New England |
| | The Dean of the 27 Springfields in the U. S. A. |
| | The Distribution Center of the Northeast |
| | The Home of More Than 4, 000 Commerical Travelers |
| | The Metropolis of Western Massachusetts |
| | The Rifle City (National Armory established April 2, 1794) |
| TANGLEWOOD | America's First Summer Festival |
| TAUNTON | The Christmas City |
| | The Cradle of American Liberty (a Liberty Pole was erected October 1774) |
| | The Largest City for Its Size (1960 population 41, 132) |
| | The Stove City |
| WALTHAM | The City of Five-Score Industries |
| | The Heartland of Industry and Electronics |
| | The Precision City |
| WAREHAM | The City where Strangers Become Friends |
| | The City where the Land Meets the Water |
| | The Place to Live, Relax and Play--Night and Day |
| WELLESLEY | The Town of Schools-- and a College (Wellesley College for women, Babson Institute for men) |
| WESTBORO | The Crossroads of New England |
| WESTFIELD | The Whip City (manufacturers of whips) |

| | |
|---|---|
| WEYMOUTH | An Aggregate of Villages |
| WILLIAMSTOWN | The Village Beautiful |
| WINCHENDON | The Toy Town (manufacturing center) |
| WOBURN | The Home of a Yankee Count |
| | The Tanning City |
| WOODS HOLE | America's Naples (on the southwestern tip of Cape Cod) |
| WORCHESTER | The City in the Heart of Massachusetts Vacationland |
| | The City of Diversified Industries |
| | The City of Prosperity |
| | The Faithful City (from its motto "Floreat Semper Civitas Fidelis") |
| | The Heart of the Bay State |
| | The Heart of the Commonwealth |
| | The Heart of the Massachusetts Vacationland |
| | The Population Center |
| | The Rail Center of New England |

## MICHIGAN

| | |
|---|---|
| ADRIAN | The Maple City of Michigan (shade trees) |
| ANN ARBOR | The Research Center of the Midwest (University of Michigan) |
| BATTLE CREEK | The Best Known City in the World (1960 population 44,169) |
| | The Best Known City of Its Size in the World (1960 population 44,169) |
| | The Breakfast Food City |
| | The Cereal Food Center of the World |
| | The Health City |
| | The Health Food City |
| BAY CITY | The City where the Summer Trails Begin (on Lake Huron) |
| BEAVERTON | The City Growing with Plastics |
| BELDING | The Land of Chief Wabasis |
| BELLAIRE | America's "Bit O' Ireland" in County O' Antrim |
| BENTON HARBOR | Michigan's Most Famous Summer Resort |

| | |
|---|---|
| BENTON  HARBOR (Cont'd) | The Heart of the Fruit Belt |
| | The Twin-Cities (with St. Joseph) |
| BLANEY PARK | The Playground of Paul Bunyon |
| | (Bunyon Museum) |
| BOYNE CITY | The All-Season Vacationland |
| BRIGHTON | The Center of Sixty-One Lakes |
| BRONSON | The City the Depression Passed |
| | Up |
| CADILLAC | The Friendliest Area in Northern |
| | Lower Michigan |
| CLARE | The Gateway to the North |
| DEARBORN | Michigan's Dynamic City |
| | Michigan's Fastest Growing City |
| | Michigan's Fastest Growing Com- |
| | munity |
| | The City of Advantages |
| DETROIT | Detroit the Beautiful |
| | Dynamic Detroit |
| | Fordtown (Ford Motor Company) |
| | The Auto City |
| | The Automobile Capital of the |
| | World |
| | The Automobile City |
| | The Automobile City of the World |
| | The Automotive Capital of the |
| | World |
| | The Beautiful City of the Straits |
| | The City of Destiny |
| | The City of Straits |
| | The City of the Straits (on the |
| | strait connecting Lake Saint |
| | Clair and Lake Erie) |
| | The City of Twentieth Century |
| | America |
| | The Dynamic City |
| | The Greatest Automobile Capital |
| | The Most Beautiful City |
| | The Motor Capital of the World |
| | The Motor City |
| | The Overgrown Small Town |
| EATON RAPIDS | The Wool City |
| ELK RAPIDS | The City for a Vacation of a Life- |
| | time |
| | The Entrance to the Chain-O- |
| | Lakes |
| FLINT | The Automobile Center (Buick, |
| | Chevrolet companies,  etc. ) |

| | |
|---|---|
| FLINT (Cont'd) | The Country Music Capital of the North |
| | The Home of Buick |
| | The Vehicle City (largest General Motors plant) |
| FRANKFORT | The Gateway to the Proposed Sleeping Bear National Park |
| | The Gliding and Soaring Center of the United States |
| GAYLORD | The Ski Capitol of Michigan |
| GLADSTONE | The All Year Round Vacation Center |
| GRAND RAPIDS | The City in the Heart of 250 Sparkling Lakes and Streams |
| | The Furniture Capital of America |
| | The Furniture Center of the World (high-grade furniture) |
| | The Furniture City |
| | The Gateway to the Water Wonderland |
| GRAYLING | The Source of the Au Sable (Au Sable River) |
| HAMTRAMCK | The Polish City (Polish community, a part of Detroit) |
| HARRISON | The City where the North Begins |
| HOLLAND | The Clean, Colorful Tulip City on Scenic Lake Macatawa |
| | The Dutch City (settled in 1847 by the Dutch) |
| | The Tulip Center of America |
| | The Tulip City |
| HONOR | The Gateway to Sleeping Bear Dunes |
| HOUGHTON | America's First Mining Capital (site of Michigan College of Mining) |
| IRONWOOD | The Center of the Gogebic Iron Range (open pits and underground mines) |
| JACKSON | Jacksonopolis |
| | The Home of Illuminated Cascades (about 500 acres outside the city limits, illuminated cascades, winding canals and lagoons) |
| | The Prison City |
| | The Rose City |

| | |
|---|---|
| KALAMAZOO | The Celery City |
| LAKE CITY | The Center of a Marvelous Natural Playground |
| LANSING | The Capital City (1960 population 107, 807) |
| LIVONIA | The City where Ambition Meets Opportunity |
| MACKINAC ISLAND | The Bermuda of the North (island 3 miles long, 2 miles wide) |
| | The Fudge Capital of the World |
| | The Showplace of the Lakes |
| | The Summer Wonderland (state park, resort) |
| MACKINAW CITY | The Gateway to Mackinac Island and the Upper Peninsula of Michigan |
| MANISTEE | The Salt City (salt deposits) |
| MARQUETTE | The Center of All There Is to See in the Upper Peninsula |
| | The Four Season's Playground |
| | The Queen City of Lake Superior |
| | The Queen City of the Northland |
| MEARS | The Gateway to the Sand Dune Mountains |
| MESICK | The Mushroom Capital |
| MORLEY | The Gateway to the Water Wonderland |
| MOUNT CLEMENS | America's Bath City (famous mineral springs) |
| | The Health City (mineral waters) |
| MOUNT PLEASANT | The Oil Capital |
| MUNISING | The Gateway to Pictured Rocks (37 miles of cliffs and odd formations about 5 miles northeast) |
| | The Naples of America |
| MUSKEGON | The Gambling Queen |
| | The Lumber City of the World |
| | The Lumber Queen |
| | The Lumber Queen of the World |
| | The Red Light Queen |
| | The Saloon Queen |
| | The Sawdust City |
| NEW BUFFALO | The Gateway to Michigan |
| NEWAYGO | America's Little Switzerland |
| NILES | The Four Flags City (the only locality in Michigan under four |

NILES (Cont'd)                    flags, France, England, Spain
                                  and the United States)
OWOSSO                            The Friendly City
PETOSKEY                          Northern Michigan's Shopping
                                  Center
ROCKFORD                          The Biggest Little City in Mich-
                                  igan (1960 population 2, 074)
ROGERS CITY                       The Limestone City (limestone
                                  quarries)
ROYAL OAK                         The City of Homes (suburb of
                                  Detroit)
                                  The Gateway to Eastern Michigan
SAGINAW                           The City of Opportunities
                                  The Industrial Center
ST. JOHNS                         The Hub of Michigan
ST. JOSEPH                        The Twin Cities (with Benton Har-
                                  bor, Mich. )
ST. LOUIS                         The Geographical Center of
                                  Michigan
SAULT STE. MARIE                  Soo (Soo Locks, St. Mary's Falls
                                  Ship Canal)
                                  The Gateway of Lake Superior
SUTTONS BAY                       The Alpine Village
TAWAS CITY                        Perchville, U. S. A.
TRAVERSE CITY                     The Cherry Capital of the World
                                  The Cherry City
WAYLAND                           The Cow Town
WAYNE                             The Center of Civic and Indus-
                                  trial Opportunity
WHITE CLOUD                       The City where the North Begins
                                  and the Pure Waters Flow
WHITE ROCK                        Michigan's Most Renowned Phan-
                                  tom City
WHITEHALL                         The City for Every Vacation
                                  Pleasure
WYANDOTTE                         The City of Good Homes
                                  The Heart of Down River's Chem-
                                  ical Empire (numerous chem-
                                  ical plants)

## MINNESOTA

AITKIN                            The Turkey Capital
AURORA                            The City Down on the Mesabi
                                  (on eastern edge of the Mesabi
                                  iron range)
BARNUM                            An Arrowhead Egg Basket (poul-

BARNUM (Cont'd)            try raising industry)
BEAVER BAY                A North Shore Haven (at the
                             mouth of the Beaver River)
BEMIDJI                   One of America's Fifty Best Va-
                             cation Spots
                          The Headwaters of the Mississippi
                          The Home of Paul Bunyan
BENA                      The City where the Partridge
                             Finds a Refuge
BLACKDUCK                 The Hunter's Rendezvous (on
                             Blackduck Lake)
BLOOMINGTON               The City with a Future
BRAINERD                  Paul Bunyon's Capital (27-foot
                             animated Bunyon statue)
                          The Capital of the Paul Bunyon
                             Playground
                          The Hub City
BUHL                      The Springs of Health and Pits
                             of Wealth (open pit mines)
CARLTON                   The Birthplace of the Northern
                             Pacific (where the first spike
                             was driven)
CASS LAKE                 The Capital of the Chippewa Na-
                             tion (Indian tribe)
                          The Permanent Home of the Pine
CLOQUET                   The Modern Phoenix (built on the
                             ashes of an earlier town)
COLERAINE                 The Model Village (1960 popula-
                             tion 1, 346)
COOK                      The Home of the Christmas Tree
                             Industry
CROSBY                    The Cuyuna Capital (eastern end
                             of the Cuyuna iron range)
DULUTH                    The Air-Conditioned City
                          The Air-Conditioned Duluth
                          The Center of the Universe (1960
                             population 106, 884)
                          The City of Destiny
                          The City on a Mountain
                          The City where the Prairie
                             Meets the Sea (Lake Superior)
                          The Coolest Summer City
                          The Gateway to the World
                          The Hay Fever Relief Haven of
                             America
                          The Metropolis of the Unsalted
                             Seas

| | |
|---|---|
| DULUTH (Cont'd) | The Old Maid City, Looking Under Her Bed Every Night for an Ocean |
| | The Ore and Grain Port |
| | The Popular Convention City |
| | The Recreational, Industrial City |
| | The Summer City |
| | The Twin Ports (with Superior, Wisc.) |
| | The Westernmost Port on America's Fourth Seacoast |
| | The Year 'Round Playground |
| | The Zenith City |
| | The Zenith City of the Unsalted Sea (its position on the Great Lakes) |
| ELY | The Capital of the Vermilion Range (Vermilion iron range) |
| | The City where the Wilderness Begins |
| | The Gate to the Sportsman's Eden |
| | The Gateway to the Sportsman's Eden |
| EVELETH | The Hill Top City (alt. 1,574 ft.) |
| | The Hockey Capital of the Nation |
| FARIBAULT | The Athens of the Northwest |
| | The Peony Center of the World (won peony prize at the Century of Progress Exposition 1933) |
| FERGUS FALLS | The City Beautiful in the Land O' Lakes |
| | The Queen City of the Otter Tail Empire |
| GILBERT | The Village of Destiny |
| GRAND MARAIS | The Place where Lake Meets Forest (on Lake Superior) |
| GRAND PORTAGE | The Gateway to Isle Royale National Park |
| | The Oldest Settlement in Minnesota (central depot of the Northwest Company in 1792) |
| HIBBING | America's Iron Capital |
| | America's Mining Capital |
| | The Iron Ore Capital of the World (1960 pop. 17,731) |

| | |
|---|---|
| HIBBING (Cont'd) | The Richest Village on Earth |
| | The Town That Moved Overnight |
| HOVLAND | The Lake Trout Capital |
| INTERNATIONAL FALLS | The Trail's End (across the Rainy River from Fort Frances, Ontario, Canada) |
| MINNEAPOLIS | America's Safest Big City |
| | The Center of the Flour Milling Industry |
| | The City in Touch with Tomorrow |
| | The City of Industry |
| | The City of Lakes |
| | The City of Lakes and Mills (title of book) |
| | The City to Watch |
| | The Dual Cities (with St. Paul) |
| | The Fast-Growing Nerve Center for America's Great Northland Empire |
| | The Flour City (extensive milling) |
| | The Flour Milling Capital of the World |
| | The Gateway City |
| | The Milltown |
| | The Sawdust City |
| | The Twin Cities (with St. Paul) |
| | The Twin City (with St. Paul) |
| | The Twins (with St. Paul) |
| MOOSE LAKE | The Southern Gateway (between Superior and St. Paul) |
| MOUNTAIN LAKE | The Birthplace of the Mesabi |
| NORTHFIELD | America's Holstein Capital |
| | The City of Cows, Colleges and Contentment (St. Olaf and Carleton College) |
| | The Holstein Capital of America |
| OWATONNA | The Butter Capital of the World |
| | The Typical American City |
| PROCTOR | The Hub |
| REDWOOD FALLS | The Scenic City of Southern Minnesota |
| ROCHESTER | The Busiest Potential Metropolitan Market |
| ST. CLOUD | The City where the Mississippi Becomes Mighty |
| | The Granite City (first quarry opened 1868) |

ST. PAUL

Pig's Eye
The Boston of the West
The Capital City (1960 population
    313, 411)
The City in the Land of Lakes
The Dual Cities (with Minneapolis)
The Gateway to the Famed North-
    woods
The Gateway to the Northwest
The Gem City
The Ideal American City
The North Star City
The Saintly City
The Twin Cities (with Minneap-
    olis)
The Twin City (with Minneapolis)
The Twins (with Minneapolis)
The Winter Sport Capital of the
    Nation

VIRGINIA

The Queen City of the Iron Range
The Queen City of the Range

WADENA

The Vacation Land

WALKER

The Vacationer's Paradise (in
    the Chippewa National Forest)

WINONA

Minnesota's Outdoor Playground
The Gate City (on Mississippi
    River)

WORTHINGTON

The Business Heart of South-
    western Minnesota
The Turkey Capital of Minnesota
The Turkey Capital of the World

## MISSISSIPPI

BAY ST. LOUIS

The Praline Capital of the World

BILOXI

America's Riviera (27 mile sand
    beach)
Heart of the Fabulous Gulf Coast
    Country
Mississippi's Great Resort and
    Historic Center
Nation's Seafood Center
The Oldest French City in the
    United States
The Year 'Round Resort and Con-
    vention Center

| | |
|---|---|
| BROOKHAVEN | The Homeseeker's Paradise |
| | The Hospitality Capital of the New South |
| | The Industrial Paradise |
| | The Perfect Place for Growing Up |
| CANTON | The Historic Town of the Old South--Now a Progressive City |
| CLARKSDALE | The Golden Buckle on the Cotton Belt |
| CLEVELAND | So Near to So Much |
| | The City of Opportunity |
| | The Home of Delta State College |
| | The Hub of the Delta |
| COLUMBUS | The City where Industrial and Agricultural Activities Are Blended with Dairying and Livestock Production |
| | The Friendly City |
| | The Town with the Most to Offer Industry |
| CORINTH | The City That Smiles Back |
| | The City where Dixie Welcomes You |
| GREENVILLE | Mississippi's Largest River Port |
| | One of Mississippi's Fastest Growing Cities |
| | The City where Main Street Meets the River and Joins Main Street Mid-America |
| | The Metropolis of the Mississippi Delta |
| | The Port City of the Delta |
| GREENWOOD | One of the World's Largest Long-staple Cotton Markets |
| | The City in the Heart of Mississippi's Rich Delta |
| | The City with a Future |
| | The City with an Aristocratic Past |
| | The City with an Exciting Future |
| | The Medical Center of the Mississippi Delta (location of Greenwood-Leflore Hospital) |
| | The Sportsman's Paradise |
| GRENADA | The Heart of North Mississippi |

GRENADA (Cont'd)

GULFPORT

   and Beautiful Grenada Lake

   America's Riviera (on Gulf of Mexico)

   The All Year Playground of the Old South

   The Central City of the Metropolitan Mississippi Gulf Coast

   The City in the Center of Mid-America's Riviera Year 'Round Resort

   The City in the Center where the Action Is

   The City where Your Ship Comes In

   The City with a Future

   The Home of Mississippi's Annual Deep Sea Fishing Rodeo (the largest deep sea fishing event in the world)

   The Hospitality City

HOLLY SPRINGS

   The Athens of the South

   The City of Roses

   The Educational, Cultural and Business Center

JACKSON

   A City of Rich Cultural and Residential Charm

   Chimneyville

   One of the Fastest Growing Cities in the Nation

   One of the South's Fastest Growing Cities

   The Agricultural Capital

   The Balanced Community of Opportunity and Happy Homes

   The Capital City (1960 population 144, 422)

   The Capital of America's State of Opportunity

   The Center of Commerce and Agriculture

   The Center of Year 'Round Recreation

   The City at the Crossroads of the Old and New South

   The City of Fine Homes, Churches, and Schools

   The City that Means Business and

| | |
|---|---|
| JACKSON (Cont'd) | and the Good Life Too |
| | The City where a New South Is in the Making |
| | The City where the Old South and the New South Meet |
| | The Crape Myrtle City |
| | The Crossroads of the Old and the New South |
| | The Crossroads of the South |
| | The Educational Capital |
| | The Friendly City |
| | The Industrial Capital |
| | The Oil Capital |
| | The Oil Center for Mississippi |
| | The Vivid Capital of the Old South |
| LAUREL | Magnolia's Largest Industrial City |
| | Mississippi's Industrial City (canning, sweet potato, starch manufacturing, masonite) |
| | The Chemurgic City (pine lumber converted into masonite) |
| | The Magnolia's State Industrial City |
| | The Oil Capital of Mississippi |
| LONG BEACH | The Friendly City |
| MC COMB | The Camellia City of America |
| | The Charm Circle of the South |
| | The City of Camellias |
| MERIDIAN | The Heart of the New South |
| NATCHEZ | The Bluff City (alluvial bluffs overlooking the Mississippi River) |
| | The City where the Charm, Culture and Traditions of the Old South Blend in a Modern City |
| | The City where the Old South Still Lives |
| | The Historic City of America (explored in 1682 by La Salle) |
| OXFORD | The Home of "Ole Miss" (The University of Mississippi) |
| PASCAGOULA | Mississippi's Industrial Seaport |
| | The Industrial and Recreational Paradise |
| PASS CHRISTIAN | Nature's Gift to the Gulf Coast |

| | |
|---|---|
| PASS CHRISTIAN (Cont'd) | The City where You Can Live and Enjoy Life |
| PICAYUNE | The Gateway to the Future in Space |
| | The Tung Oil Center of America |
| | The Tung Tree Capital of the World |
| STARKVILLE | The Dairy Center of the South |
| TUPELO | Mississippi's Best Example of the New South |
| | Mississippi's Finest Example of the New South |
| | The Capital of the Great Chickasaw Nation |
| | The City where Industry, Agriculture and Cultural Life All Balance |
| | The City Without City Limits |
| | The City Without Limits |
| | The Community Working Together for the Future |
| | The First TVA City (first contract with the Tennessee Valley Authority to purchase electricity signed November 11, 1933) |
| | The Former Capital of the Chickasaw Nation |
| VICKSBURG | The Gibraltar of America (on the Mississippi River, reputed to have been an impregnable fortification in the War of Secession, fell July 4, 1863 after seige of one year) |
| | The Gibraltar of Louisiana |
| | The Gibraltar of the Confederacy |
| | The Gibraltar of the South |
| | The Hill City (206 feet altitude) |
| | The Key City |
| WEST POINT | The Point of Opportunity |
| YAZOO CITY | Mississippi's Thriving Industrial Center |
| | The City where the Delta Begins |
| | The Gateway to the Delta (low flat on the Yazoo River) |
| | The Oil Capital of Mississippi |

MISSOURI

| | |
|---|---|
| ASH GROVE | The Area Shopping Crossroads |
| | The Friendly Community, the Home of Friendly People |
| AURORA | The Tri-County Trading Center |
| BOLIVAR | The Largest Shopping Center in the Pomme de Terre Area |
| BUTLER | The West Gate to the Land-O-Lakes |
| CAPE GIRADEAU | The City of Roses |
| CARTHAGE | The City at the Crossroads of Mid-America |
| | The Crossroads of Mid-America |
| | The Home of World Famous Carthage Marble |
| | The Ideal Place to Stay or Play |
| | The Pure Bred Jersey Capital of America |
| CASSVILLE | The City of Seven Valleys |
| | The Hub of the Scenic Ozarks (near Roaring River State Park) |
| | The Once Confederate Capital of America (1861) |
| CLINTON | The Queen City of the Golden Valley |
| | The Sportsman's Paradise |
| COLUMBIA | The Athens of the Midwest (home of the University of Missouri) |
| CRANE | The Home of 'Old Hickory' Ham and Bacon |
| DE SOTO | The Fountain City (numerous artesian wells) |
| EL DORADO SPRINGS | The City where Gracious Living and Fine Churches Offer a Life of Contentment for Businessman, Worker, Retired and the Sportsman |
| | The Land of Lakes Shopping Center |
| | The Wonder City in the Middle of the Land of Lakes |
| ELDON | The Gateway to Lake of the Ozarks (12 miles from Bagnell Dam) |
| FAYETTE | The Mother of Counties (organiz- |

FAYETTE (Cont'd) ed January 13, 1816 from
which 46 counties were formed,
36 in Missouri and 10 in Iowa)

FORSYTH The Twin Lakes Capital of the
Ozarks (Lake Taneycomo and
Bull Shoals Lake)

GREENFIELD The Headwaters of Stockton Lake

HANNIBAL The Bluff City (Cardiff Hill and
Lovers' Leap)

The Boyhood Home of Mark Twain

The Capital of Youth (Tom and
Huck monument, Mark Twain's
characters)

The St. Petersburg of Tom Saw-
yer

INDEPENDENCE The City where the West Begins
(starting place in 1849 of
Santa Fe and Oregon Trails)

The Gateway to the West

The Queen City of the Trails

JEFFERSON CITY Jeff City (named for Thomas Jefferson)

The Capital City (1960 pop. 28,228)

The Convention City

JOPLIN The Center of Mid-American
Industrial Progress

The Crossroads of America

The Crossroads of Mid America

The Fastest Growing Chemical
Center in the Great Midwest

The Gateway to the Ozarks

The Town That "Jack" Built

KANSAS CITY The City of the Future

The Gateway to the West and the
Southwest

The Greatest Primary Winter
Wheat Market

The Heart of America

The Heart of the United States
of America

The Home of the Athletics (baseball team)

The Metropolis of the Missouri
Valley

The Mushroomopolis

The Nation's Largest Winter
Wheat Market

| | |
|---|---|
| KANSAS CITY (Cont'd) | The Overgrown Cow Town |
| | The Steak Center of the Nation (Kansas City Livestock Exchange and Stockyards) |
| KNOB NOSTER | The Gateway to the Whiteman Air Force Base |
| LAMAR | The Birthplace of Harry S Truman |
| LEBANON | Near to Everything Everywhere |
| LINCOLN | Benton County's Fastest Growing City |
| MARCELINE | The Magic City |
| MARSHALL | The Center of a Lively Industrial and Agricultural Trade Area |
| | The City Beautiful |
| | The City with a Great Potential for Growth |
| | The Mother of the West |
| MEXICO | The Capital of Little Dixie |
| | The Fire Clay and Horse Capital of the World |
| | The Fireclay Capital (manufactures clay products) |
| | The Fireclay Capital of the World |
| | The Saddle Horse Capital of the World |
| | The World's Saddle Horse Capital |
| MOBERLY | The City in the Heart of the Heartland |
| | The Magic City |
| MONETT | The Big "M" of the Ozarks |
| | The Gateway to Outdoor Fishing and Hunting Activities |
| NEOSHO | The City of Springs |
| | The Flower Box City |
| | The Flowerbox City |
| NEVADA | The Bushwacker's Capital (headquarters of several Confederate detachments in the War of Secession) |
| NOEL | The Christmas City |
| OSCEOLA | A Key Spot in the Future of Kaysinger Reservoir |
| | The Home of the World's Finest Catfish |

| | |
|---|---|
| PIERCE CITY | A Diversified Agricultural and Industrial Community |
| POPLAR BLUFF | The Eastern Gateway to the Ozarks |
| RICHMOND HEIGHTS | The City of Homes |
| ROCKAWAY BEACH | The Perfect Vacation Spot |
| ROGERSVILLE | The Coon Capitol of the World |
| ROLLA | The Scientific Center |
| ST. CHARLES | The First Capital of Missouri (1821-1826) |
| | The Last Outpost of Civilization |
| STE GENEVIEVE | The Oldest City West of the Mississippi |
| ST. JOSEPH | The City Worth While |
| | The Home of Jesse James |
| ST. LOUIS | America's Great Central Market and Tourist City |
| | America's Shoe Capital |
| | Paincourt |
| | The Child of the River |
| | The City of a Thousand Sights |
| | The City of Culture and Entertainment |
| | The City of Learning |
| | The City of the French |
| | The Convention City |
| | The Family City |
| | The Future Great City of the World |
| | The Gateway Arch City |
| | The Gateway of the West |
| | The Gateway to Space |
| | The Gateway to the American West |
| | The Gateway to the Centers of the Aerospace Industry |
| | The Gateway to the West |
| | The Great River City (on the Mississippi River) |
| | The Heart of the Midwest |
| | The Historical and Cultural Center |
| | The Holiday City |
| | The Home of the World's Largest Brewery (Anheuser-Busch Brewery) |

138

| ST. LOUIS (Cont'd) | The Hub of American Inland Navigation |
|---|---|
| | The Hub of the New High-Speed Interstate Highway System |
| | The Largest Metropolis in the Mississippi Valley |
| | The Memphis of the American Nile |
| | The Mound City |
| | The Parent of the West |
| | The Parking Lot City |
| | The Pride of the Mississippi Valley |
| | The Queen City of the Mississippi |
| | The Showboat City |
| | The Solid City |
| | The Vacation City |
| | The Vatican City |
| SARCOXIE | The Peony Capitol of the World |
| SEDALIA | A Good Place to Live, Work and Enjoy Life |
| | The City where North and South Meet East and West |
| | The Convention City |
| | The Gateway to the Lake of the Ozarks |
| | The Gateway to the Land O' Lakes |
| | The Home of the State Fair |
| | The Queen City of the Prairies |
| SENECA | The Northeastern Gateway to the Grand Lake Resort Area |
| SOUTH WEST CITY | The Busy Agricultural Community |
| SPRINGFIELD | The Dairy, Agricultural and Industrial Center |
| | The Gateway to Four Ozark Vacation Areas |
| | The Gateway to the Southern Ozarks |
| | The Queen City of the Ozarks |
| STOCKTON | A Wonderful Place to Rear Your Family Beneath Wide-Open Missouri Skies |
| | The Best Town in the State by a Damsite |

| | |
|---|---|
| STOCKTON (Cont'd) | The City at the Water's Edge |
| | The City where "Fish Are Jumpin' and the Livin' Is Easy" |
| | The City where Game in Its Wild State Abounds |
| | The City where You Can Live in the City Limits and Be on the Lake |
| | The City where You Have the Splendor of Four Seasons |
| | The Haven to Retire in, Away From the Rush |
| TRENTON | The City with a Future |
| UNIONVILLE | The Feeder Calf Capital of the World |
| WARSAW | The City of Opportunity, Recreation, Retirement |
| | The Gunstock Capitol of the World |
| | The Most Opportune Locality of the Middle West |
| | The Spoonbill Capital of the World |
| WASHINGTON | Missouri's Most Industrially Diversified Small City |
| | The Corncob Pipe Capital of the World |
| | The Place to Live |
| | The Williamsburg of the Mid West |
| WEST PLAINS | The Feeder Pig Capitol of the World |
| WILLOW SPRINGS | The Gateway to the South |
| WINDSOR | The North Gateway to the Kaysinger Dam and Reservoir Area |

## MONTANA

| | |
|---|---|
| ANACONDA | The City on the Top of the Rockies |
| | The Home of the Largest Copper Producing Smelter and Smokestack in the World (585 feet, Anaconda Mining Co.) |
| | The St. Moritz of the Rockies |

ANACONDA (Cont'd)

BILLINGS

BROADUS

BUTTE

(winter sport resort)

The Smelter City (one of the largest non-ferrous producing plants)

A Great Intermountain Transportation Center

America's Ideal Vacation Land

Montana's Only Billion Dollar Market

The Capital of the Midland Empire

The City in the Heart of the Nation's Famous Dude Ranch Country

The City in the Mountain Country

The Civics Center of the Midland Empire

The Commercial Center of the Midland Empire

The Fun Capital of the Vacation State

The Gateway to America's Wonderland

The Gateway to the West (on the west bank of the Yellowstone River)

The Land of Shining Mountains

The Magic City

The Midland Empire City

The Midland Empire Magic City

The Queen City of the Midland Empire

The Silver Dollar City

The Star of the Big Sky Country

The Sun City of the Big Sky Country

The Biggest Little Town in the West (1960 population 628)

One of America's Most Unique Cities

One of the Most Colorful Cities in America

The Black Heart of Montana

The Center of Montana's Wonderland

The Copper City (numerous

BUTTE (Cont'd)

CUT BANK

EUREKA

FORSYTH
GLENDIVE

GREAT FALLS

HELENA

JORDAN

KALISPELL

LAUREL

large copper mines)

The Heart of Montana's Magic-land

The Only Electric Lighted Cemetery in the United States

The Richest Hill on Earth (one of the world's greatest mining cities)

Montana's Friendly Community

The Oil Capital of Montana (about 1, 200 oil wells and 100 gas wells)

The Christmas Tree Capital of the Nation

The Christmas Tree Capital of the World

The City of Trees

The City with a Future to Share

The Gateway to the Historic Northwest (seat of Dawson County)

Montana's Largest and Friendliest City (55, 357 population in 1960)

The Electric City (hydroelectric power plant on the Missouri River)

The Niagara of the West (hydro electric plants on the Great Falls of the Missouri)

The Capital City (20, 227 population in 1960)

The Queen of the Mountains

The Lonesomest Town in the World (1960 population 557)

The Center of a Land of Enchantment (the Swan Range on the east, the Whitefish Range to the north)

The Hub of the Beautiful Flathead Valley

The Northwest Montana's Business and Shopping Center

The Frontier of Industrial Opportunity

The Hub of Montana's Vast Vacationland

The Scenic Gateway

| | |
|---|---|
| LAUREL (Cont'd) | The Sportsman's Paradise |
| LIBBY | Nature's Play Ground |
| LIVINGSTON | The Home of the Original Trout Derby (National Trout Derby) |
| MILES CITY | The Cow Capital of the West (about 25 percent of Montana's cattle and sheep) |
| MISSOULA | The Garden City |
| | The Medical Center of Western Montana |
| | The Place to Enjoy Yourself |
| PHILIPSBURG | The Year-Round Sportsman's Paradise |
| SIDNEY | The Heart of the Yellowstone Valley |

## NEBRASKA

| | |
|---|---|
| ALLIANCE | The Cattle Capital of Nebraska |
| BASSETT | The Home of Famous Sand Hill Beef |
| BLAIR | The City where Commerce, Farming, Industry and Education Thrive Together |
| | The Eastern Gateway to Nebraska-land |
| BOYS TOWN | The City of Little Men (home for destitute boys) |
| BROWNVILLE | Historic Brownville, where Nebraska Begins (three miles north of the Kansas border) |
| BURWELL | The Friendliest Little City in Nebraska |
| CHADRON | Nebraskaland's Big Game Capital |
| | The Southern Gateway to the Black Hills |
| CRAWFORD | The Big Game Capital of Nebraska |
| | The City in the Heart of the Pine Ridge |
| FREMONT | A Good Place to Live, Work and Play |
| | The City where Agriculture and Industry Meet |
| | The Trade Center of Mid-East Nebraska |
| GERING | The Best Lighted City in the |

| | |
|---|---|
| GERING (Cont'd) | World |
| | The City in the Heart of Irrigation |
| GOTHENBURG | The City in the Heart of the Irrigated Platte Valley |
| | The Pony Express City |
| GRAND ISLAND | A Good Place to Work and Live |
| | Nebraska's Third City |
| | The Progressive City |
| HASTINGS | The City of Liquid Gold (abundant water supply) |
| | The Crossroads of the Nation |
| | The Fastest Growing City in the State |
| KEARNEY | The Hub of the Nation (center of Platte Valley) |
| LINCOLN | The Capital City (1960 population 128,521) |
| | The City Worthy of a Noble Name |
| | The Cornhusker Capital City |
| | The Hartford of the West (insurance companies) |
| | The Holy City |
| | The Lilac City |
| | The Loveliest Modern City in Mid-America |
| MC COOK | The Center of a Fisherman's Paradise |
| | The Oil Capital of Southwest Nebraska |
| | The Retail Center of Southwest Nebraska and Northeast Kansas |
| MINDEN | The Christmas City |
| | The Home of Harold Warp's Pioneer Village |
| NEBRASKA CITY | The Town That Gave the World a Great Idea (Arbor Day) |
| NORFOLK | Nebraska's Game Paradise |
| | North Nebraska's Largest City |
| | The Host City (Northeast Nebraska) |
| | The Southern Gateway to the Lewis and Clark Lake |
| NORTH PLATTE | The Home of Buffalo Bill |
| OGALLALA | Nebraska's Sport Center |
| | The Cowboy Capital of Nebraska (the end of the Old Texas |

OGALLALA (Cont'd)              Trail terminal)
                               The Electronics Capital of the
                                  Midwest
                               The Gateway to the Nebraska
                                  Panhandle
                               The Home of Lake McConaugy
                                  and Kingsley Dam
                               The Official Cowboy Capital of
                                  Nebraska
OMAHA                          Boy's Town
                               The City of Recreation and Cul-
                                  ture
                               The Crossroads of the Nation
                               The Gate City of the West
                               The Gateway to Nebraska's
                                  Vacationland
                               The Gateway to the West
                               The New York of Nebraska
                               The Steak Capital of the World
                               The World's Largest Livestock
                                  and Meat Packing Center
PLAINVIEW                      Nebraska's Friendly City
SCOTTS BLUFF                   The Service Center for Indus-
                                  trial Agriculture
SIDNEY                         The City where the Hospitality
                                  of the Old West Remains
                               The Home of Historical Fort
                                  Sidney
                               The Recreation Hub of the His-
                                  torical Colorful West
VALENTINE                      The City with a Heart
                               The Heart City of the Sandhills
                               The Home of the Original Long
                                  Horns
                               Valentine Has Everything
                               Your One-Stop Sports Paradise
WAHOO                          The Heart of the Nation
WILBER                         The Czech Capital of Nebraska
YORK                           The City at the Crossroads of
                                  Nebraskaland's Best Hunting
                                  Country
                               The City where There Are No
                                  Strangers--Just New Friends


                               NEVADA

AUSTIN                         The Silver Boom Town

| | |
|---|---|
| BEATTY | The Chicago of Nevada |
| | The Gateway to Death Valley |
| BOULDER CITY | The Garden City of Clark County |
| | The Garden City of Southern Nevada |
| | The Gateway to the Lake Mead Recreational Area |
| CARSON CITY | The Capital City (territorial capital in 1861, state capital 1864) |
| | The Gateway to Lake Tahoe and Yosemite Valley |
| | The Smallest Capital in America (5, 163 population in 1960) |
| ELKO | The Cattle Country |
| | The Metropolis of Eastern Nevada (1960 population 6, 298) |
| | The Ranching Center |
| ELY | The Gateway to Scenic Adventure |
| FALLON | The Heart of Western Nevada's Agricultural Region |
| | The Oasis of Nevada |
| GARDNERVILLE | The Twin Cities (with Minden, Nev. ) |
| GENOA | The Oldest Town in Nevada (settled in 1845 by Mormon emigrants) |
| LAKE TAHOE | (see also Lake Tahoe, Calif. ) |
| LAS VEGAS | Nevada's Largest City |
| | One of America's Fastest Growing Cities |
| | Playtown, U. S. A. |
| | The All-Season Convention-Vacation Location |
| | The All-Year Resort and Recreation Center |
| | The Booming Convention City |
| | The Broadway of the Desert (lighted main street) |
| | The City of Chance |
| | The City of Destiny |
| | The City of Little Wedding Churches |
| | The City of Luck |
| | The City That Has Everything for Everyone--Anytime |
| | The City That Is Still a Frontier Town (used 1939) |

LAS VEGAS (Cont'd)          The City where the Action Is
                            The City where the Fun Begins
                                and Never Ends
                            The City Without Clocks (book by
                                Ed Reid)
                            The Convention Capital of the
                                West
                            The Desert Babylon
                            The Early West in Modern Splen-
                                dor
                            The Entertainment Capital of the
                                World
                            The Favored Vacation Package
                                of Western America
                            The Fun Capital of the World
                            The Gambler's Mecca
                            The Gambler's Paradise on
                                Earth
                            The Gateway to Lake Mead and
                                Hoover Dam
                            The Gateway to Pleasure
                            The Glamor and Action Capital
                                of the World
                            The Great Convention-Vacation
                                Location
                            The Green Felt Jungle (book by
                                Ed Reid and Ovid Demaris)
                            The Hub City of the Scenic South-
                                west
                            The Hub of a Vast Scenic and
                                Sports Wonderland
                            The Leading Entertainment Mec-
                                ca
                            The Luxury Resort Town
                            The Metropolis of Southern Ne-
                                vada
                            The Monte Carlo of the West
                            The Nation's Great New Conven-
                                tion City
                            The Never-Closed Casino City
                            The Place where Every Day's
                                a Holiday
                            The Play Around the Clock
                                Time
                            The Playground of the Desert
                            The Playground of the "Now"

**LAS VEGAS** (Cont'd)

    Set
The Playground of the World
The Scenic Sportland
The Sin City
The Spectacular Convention Center
The Splendor of the West
The Sun, Fun and Action Town
The Town Blessed By An Ideal Year-Round Climate
The Twenty-Four Hour Gambling City
The World Famous Resort and Convention Center
The World Renowned Strip
The World's Largest Gambling Center
The Year-Round Center for Major Spectator Events

**LOVELOCK**
The Agricultural Town

**MINDEN**
The Twin Cities (with Gardnerville, Nev.)

**RENO**
The Biggest Little City in the World (51,470 population in 1960)
The Center of Summer and Winter Sports
The Twin Cities by the Truckee (with Sparks, Nev.)

**SPARKS**
The City with Promise
The Twin Cities by the Truckee (with Reno, Nev.)

**TONOPAH**
The Queen of the Silver Camps (1900's)
The Silver Town

**VIRGINIA CITY**
The City of Illusion (novel by Vardis Fisher)
The City That Saved the Union (silver from the Comstock mines shipped to President Lincoln bolstered the buying power of the Union army)
The Home of the Comstock Lode (one of the richest fissure vein deposits of gold and silver ever found)
The Queen of the Comstock Lode

| VIRGINIA CITY (Cont'd) | The World's Liveliest Ghost Town |
| WELLS | The Gateway to the Ruby Mountains |
| WINNEMUCCA | The Center for Ranching |

## NEW HAMPSHIRE

| BERLIN | The Chemical City |
| | The City for the Full Life |
| | The City in the White Mountains |
| | The City That Trees Built |
| | The First Ski Club City |
| BETHLEHEM | The Heart of the White Mountains |
| BOW | The Birthplace of Mary Baker Eddy |
| CONCORD | The Capital City (28,991 population in 1960) |
| DOVER | The Easterly Gateway to the Lakes and White Mountains Regions |
| | The Garrison City (the guardian fort and defender of the state) |
| FRANKLIN | Gateway to the White Mountains |
| | The Birthplace of Daniel Webster |
| GLEN | The City in the Center of the White Mountains |
| HAMPTON BEACH | The Favorite Family Seaside Resort (on the Atlantic Ocean) |
| HENNIKER | The Only Henniker on Earth |
| JEFFERSON | Santa's Village |
| LACONIA | The City in the Heart of the Lakes Region |
| | The City of the Lakes |
| | The City on the Lakes (on Lake Winnipesaukee, overlooks four lakes) |
| LANCASTER | The Friendly Town in the Friendly State |
| | Santa's Village |
| MANCHESTER | The City in the Very Heart of New England |
| | The City of Opportunity |
| | The Manchester of America |
| | The Queen City |

| | |
|---|---|
| MANCHESTER (Cont'd) | The Queen City of New Hampshire |
| | The Queen City of the Merrimack Valley (on the Merrimack River) |
| MEREDITH | The Latchkey to the White Mountains |
| | The Town That Is Going Places |
| MERRIMACK | The Fastest Growing Town in Hillsboro County |
| MOUNT WASHINGTON | The Goliath of All North-eastern North America |
| NASHUA | The Gate City (on the Nashua River) |
| | The Gate City of New Hampshire |
| NEWPORT | The Sunshine Town |
| NORTH CONWAY | The Most Complete Year 'Round Resort Town in the White Mountains |
| | The Year 'Round Vacation Town in the White Mountains |
| NORTH WALPOLE | Steamtown, U. S. A. |
| PORTSMOUTH | An Old Town By the Sea |
| | The New World Port (only natural deepwater harbor between the ports of Portland, Me., and Boston, Mass.) |
| | The Port City (New Hampshire's only seaport) |
| ROCHESTER | The City of Friendly People |
| | The City of Governors |
| | The Gateway to Vacationland |
| RUMNEY | The Crutch Capital of the World (crutch manufacturing) |
| TILTON | The Boy's Town of New England (Spaulding Youth Center) |
| WINNIPESAUKEE | The Smile of the Great Spirit (name used by the Indians for Lake Winnipesaukee) |
| WOLFEBORO | The Oldest Summer Resort in America (founded 1759) |
| WONALANCET | The Sled Dog Center of the U. S. (location of Chinook Kennels) |

## NEW JERSEY

| | |
|---|---|
| ASBURY PARK | Health City, U. S. A. |

| | |
|---|---|
| ASBURY PARK (Cont'd) | One of America's Foremost All Year Resorts |
| | The All Year Home Town |
| | The Beauty Spot of the North Jersey Coast (on the Atlantic Ocean) |
| | The City-By-The-Sea |
| | The Nation's Great All-Year Resort |
| | The Nation's Great All-Year Resort City-by-the-Sea |
| | The Nation's Great Resort City-by-the-Sea |
| | The Resort of Enjoyment |
| ATLANTIC CITY | America's Bagdad by the Sea (on the Atlantic Ocean) |
| | America's Ocean Playground |
| | The Biggest Little City in America |
| | The City of Fun and Frolic |
| | The City of Health and Recreation |
| | The City where the Action Is |
| | The Coastline of Health and Happiness |
| | The Four-Season Resort for Health, Rest and Pleasure |
| | The Host with the Most |
| | The Number One Host of the Jersey Coast |
| | The Playground of the World |
| | The Queen of Resorts |
| | The Skyline of Romance |
| | The Vacation Capital of the Nation |
| | The Vacation City Supreme |
| | The World's Playground |
| | The Year 'Round Vacation Playland |
| AVALON | The City Cooler By a Mile |
| | The Gem of the Jersey Coast |
| BAYONNE | The Oil City (refineries and tanks, pipeline to Longview, Texas) |
| BELMAR | The Fisherman's Paradise |
| | The Modern Little City |
| BRADLEY BEACH | The Friendly Resort City |
| CAMDEN | The Capital of Radio (home of the |

| | |
|---|---|
| CAMDEN (Cont'd) | RCA-Victor Manufacturing Co.) |
| | The Home of National Industries |
| CAPE MAY | America's Most Distinctive Seashore Vacationland |
| | The Nation's Oldest Seashore Resort (settled about 1664) |
| DOVER | The Business Heart of the Lakeland Area |
| | The Pittsburgh of New Jersey (industrial area) |
| EAST BRUNSWICK | The Center of the World's Biggest Market |
| | The Gateway to a Fabulous Market |
| ELIZABETH | Betsytown (humorous varient) |
| | The Rail and Harbor City |
| GARFIELD | The City of Industrial Peace |
| GLASSBORO | The Summit Town (where President L. B. Johnson conferred with Soviet Premier Kosygin) |
| HAMMONTON | The Garden Spot of the Garden State |
| HARVEY CEDARS | America's Greatest Family Resort |
| | The High Point of Long Beach Island |
| HOBOKEN | The Gibraltar of Democracy |
| | The Little Eden |
| | The Mile Square City |
| JERSEY CITY | The American City of Opportunity |
| | The City That Has Everything for Industry |
| KEARNY | The Heart of America's Industrial War Front |
| LONG BRANCH | America's First Seashore Resort (summer home of President Garfield) |
| MADISON | The Rose City (rose-growing center) |
| METUCHEN | The Brainy Borough |
| MILLVILLE | The Holly City of America |
| MOUNT LAUREL | The Balanced Community |
| NEW BRUNSWICK | The Industrial and Cultural Center of New Jersey |
| NEWARK | One of America's Outstanding Cities |

| | |
|---|---|
| NEWARK (Cont'd) | The Birmingham of America |
| | The City of Industry |
| | The Milwaukee of the East (production of beer and ale) |
| OCEAN CITY | America's Greatest Family Resort (on island between Great Egg Harbor and Atlantic City) |
| OCEAN GROVE | Neptune Township's Ocean Front |
| | The First Choice in Family Resorts |
| PATERSON | The American Lyons (a mill town producing nylon, rayon, silk, wool and textile dyes) |
| | The Cotton Town of the U. S. A. |
| | The Cradle of American Industry (planned as an industrial town by Alexander Hamilton and Society for Establishing Useful Manufactures 1791) |
| | The Federal City (Alexander Hamilton and others planned this city expecting it to serve as the capital of the U.S.) |
| | The Lyons of America |
| | The Silk City (silk manufacturing) |
| PERTH AMBOY | The City by the Sea (on Raritan Bay) |
| | The Clay Center |
| | The Shopping Center of the Raritan Bay Area |
| PLAINFIELD | The Queen City in the Garden State |
| | The Queen City of New Jersey |
| PRINCETON | The Most Beautiful College Town in America (Princeton University) |
| RARITAN | The Friendly Town of Friendly People |
| SEA ISLE CITY | The Sea and Sand Vacationland |
| STONE HARBOR | The Clean and Quiet Resort |
| | The Finest in Tennis on the Jersey Coast |
| | The Venice of America (seashore community, sheltered waterways) |

| | |
|---|---|
| TRENTON | The Capital City (1960 population 114, 167) |
| VENTNOR CITY | The All-Year Residential Resort |
| WEST CALDWELL | An Ideal Community in Which to Live, Work and Play |
| WEST PORTAL | Little Switzerland |
| WILDWOOD | Five Miles of Health and Happiness |
| | The Family Vacation Spot |
| | The Tent City (popular summer resort, tents replaced by solid buildings) |
| | The World's Finest and Safest Bathing Beach (on Atlantic Ocean) |

## NEW MEXICO

| | |
|---|---|
| ACOMA | The Sky City (steep cliffs) |
| ALAMOGORDO | The Rocket City (near site of first man-made atomic explosion of July 16, 1945 at White Sands Proving Ground) |
| ALBUQUERQUE | One of the World's Leading Convention Centers |
| | The Duke City (the Duke of Albuquerque created by Henry IV of Castile, brother of Queen Elizabeth) |
| | The Metropolis of New Mexico |
| CARLSBAD | The Cavern City (about 25 miles from Carlsbad Caverns National Park) |
| CLAYTON | The Friendly Town |
| CLOVIS | The Cattle Capital of the Southwest |
| DULCE | The Home of the Jicarilla Apache Tribe |
| FARMINGTON | The Energy Capital of the West (producer of gas and oil, terminus of two natural gas pipelines) |
| GALLUP | The Indian Capital (site of the Intertribal Indian Ceremonial) |
| | The Indian Capital of the World |
| GRANTS | The Uranium Capital of the |

GRANTS (Cont'd)                World (processing mills for
                                uranium)
JEMEZ PUEBLO                   Track and Field Town, U. S. A.
LOS ALAMOS                     The Atomic City
                               The Capital of the Atomic Age
                                  (Los Alamos Scientific Labor-
                                  atory)
LOVINGTON                      The City where Oil and Water
                                  Mix (the Oil Patch area and
                                  fertile soil)
MOUNTAINAIR                    The Gateway to Ancient Cities
RATON                          The Gate City
SANTA FE                       The Capital City (1960 population
                                  34, 676)
                               The Capital City Different
                               The Center of Prehistoric, His-
                                  toric and Scenic Interest
                               The City Different
                               The Oldest and Quaintest City in
                                  the United States (believed to
                                  have been settled by Indians
                                  in 1210 and by Europeans in
                                  1610)
                               The Royal City
SILVER CITY                    The Gateway to the Gila Wilder-
                                  ness (headquarters for Gila
                                  National Forest)
TAOS                           The Art Center of the Southwest
                               The Northern New Mexico's Most
                                  Unique Vacationland
TUCUMCARI                      A Wonderful Place of Recreation-
                                  al Enjoyment

                        NEW YORK

ALBANY                         The Capital City (1960 population
                                  129, 726)
                               The Capital of the Empire State
                               The City of Homes
                               The Cradle of the American
                                  Union (Benjamin Franklin pro-
                                  posed a federal union of 13
                                  colonies at the congress of
                                  1754)
                               The Edinburgh of America
                               The Governmental, Educational
                                  Recreational Center

| | |
|---|---|
| ALBANY (Cont'd) | The Historic and Colorful Capital of the Empire State |
| | The Hub of the Empire State's Capital District |
| | The Oldest Chartered City in the United States (an exaggerated claim) |
| | The Oldest City in the United States Operating Under Its Original Charter |
| AMSTERDAM | The Carpet City |
| | The Carpet City of the World (the foremost manufacturing city for carpets and rugs) |
| | The City of Diversified Industries |
| | The City of Rugs |
| | The Foot of the Adirondacks (on the Mohawk River and the New York Barge Canal) |
| AUBURN | The Cordage City (cord manufacturing) |
| AURIESVILLE | The Land of the Crosses |
| AUSAUBLE CHASM | The Grand Canyon of the East (scenic attraction) |
| | The Yosemite of the East |
| BEMUS POINT | The Muskie Capital of New York |
| | The Village Right in the Middle of Things on Beautiful Chautaqua Lake |
| BINGHAMTON | The Bran Town |
| | The Parlor Town |
| BRANT LAKE | The Center of the Summer-time World in the Great North Woods |
| BREWSTER | The Hub of the Harlem Valley |
| BROOKLYN | The Bedroom of New York (one of the boroughs of New York City, primarily a residential sector) |
| | The Church City |
| | The City of Churches |
| | The City of Homes |
| | The Dormitory of New York |
| | The Greatest City's Greatest Borough |
| BUFFALO | An Overgrown Village |

BUFFALO (Cont'd)

One of America's Most Important Inland Fort Centers

The Beautiful City of Homes, Diversified Business and Progressive Outlook

The Bison City (the scientific name for buffalo)

The Center of America's Greatest Market

The Center of Industrial and Atomic Development

The City of Flour (flour and feed milling)

The City of Good Neighbors

The City of Homes

The City of Progressive Outlook

The City of Trees

The Electric City of the Future

The First and Last Major U. S. Port of Call on the Seaway Route

The Flour City

The Flour Milling Capital of the World

The Gateway City to Canada

The Gateway to Picturesque Canada

The Gateway to the Heartland of America

The Metropolis in a Forest of Trees (more than 40,000 city-owned trees)

The Most Accessible City on the North American Continent

The National, Industrial, Scientific, Educational and Cultural Center

The Pathway to Progress

The Queen City of the Great Lakes

The Queen City of the Lakes

The Queen of the Lakes

The Rail Center

The Second Largest Railroad Center in the United States (12 freight terminals, 5 passenger terminals)

| | |
|---|---|
| BUFFALO (Cont'd) | The Transport Center of the Nation |
| | The Wonder City of America |
| CANANDAIGUA | The Chosen Spot in the Beautiful Finger Lakes |
| CAPE VINCENT | Gateway to the Thousand Islands |
| | The Black Bass Capital of the World |
| | The Home of the Gamey Black Bass |
| CARTHAGE | The Gateway to the Adirondacks and the 1,000 Island Region |
| CITY ISLAND | The Hub of New York's Boating Center |
| COLTON | The Center of the St. Lawrence Valley Vacationland |
| COLD SPRING HARBOR | Bungtown |
| CONEY ISLAND | Sodom by the Sea (title of book by Oliver Pilat and Jo Ranson) |
| COOPERSTOWN | The Birthplace of Baseball |
| | The Heart of the Leatherstocking Land |
| | The Home of Baseball (where Abner Doubleday introduced the game) |
| | The Home of James Fenimore Cooper |
| | The Village of Great Museums (the Baseball Museum, the Farmers Museum, etc.) |
| | The Village of Museums |
| | The Village where Nature Smiles |
| CORNING | The Crystal City (Steuben Glass Center and Steuben factory) |
| | The Major Glass Center (the 200-inch lens for Mt. Palomar's Telescope was made here) |
| CORTLAND | The County Seat of Cortland County |
| | The Typewriter Capital of the World |
| DUNKIRK | New York's Lake Erie Vacationland in Beautiful Chautauqua County |
| ELLENVILLE | Ellenville is Everythingville |
| ELMIRA | The Center of Commerce |
| | The Glider Capital of America |

ELMIRA (Cont'd)            The Glider Capital of the World
FORT ANNE                  The Gateway to the North
FREDONIA                   The Most Beautiful Village in New
                             York State (a description by
                             Chauncey M. Depew)
FULTON                     The Power City
GARDEN CITY                The Cathedral Town (Protestant
                             Episcopal Cathedral of the
                             Incarnation, in the Sea of the
                             Episcopal Diocese)
GENEVA                     The Heart of the Finger Lakes
                             Vacationland
GLENS FALLS                Hometown, U. S. A.
                           The Gateway to the Adirondacks
GOSHEN                     The Cradle of the Trotter (two
                             famous trotting tracks)
GREENPORT                  The Community That Has Every-
                             thing
HAMPTON                    Long Island's World Famous
                             Ocean Playground
HAMPTON BAYS               Long Island's Ocean Playground
HANCOCK                    The Switzerland of the Catskills
HARRIMAN                   The Gateway to the Southern
                             Catskills
HEMPSTEAD                  The Hub of Nassau
                           The Hub of Nassau County
HYDE PARK                  The Home of Franklin Delano
                             Roosevelt (national shrine)
INDIAN LAKE                The Heart of the Adirondacks
ISLIP                      The Industrial Dynamo
                           The Residential Haven
                           The Town with a Split Personality
ITHACA                     The Educational Center
JOHNSON CITY               The Shoe City (site of Endicott-
                             Johnson Corp., shoe factory)
KINGSTON                   The Colonial City (first capital of
                             New York State, 1777)
                           The First Capital of New York
                           The Gateway to the Catskills
                             (Catskill Mountains)
                           New York's First Capital
                           New York State's First Capital
LAKE GEORGE                America's Family Playground
                           Storytown, U. S. A.
                           The Queen of America's Lakes
                           The Queen of American Lakes
                           The Queen of the American Lakes

| | |
|---|---|
| LAKE GEORGE (Cont'd) | The Resort Area of the Adirondacks |
| LAKE LUZERNE | The Gateway to the Adirondacks (Adirondack Mountains) |
| LAKE PLACID | America's Switzerland (in the Adirondack Mountains on Mirror Lake) |
| | Nation's Finest Winter Sports Center |
| | New York State's Complete All-Season Resort |
| | One of America's Oldest Playgrounds |
| | The Olympic Village |
| | The Summer Vacationland and Winter Wonderland |
| LOCKPORT | The Buying Center for Thousands |
| | The Hub of the Great Niagara Fruit Belt |
| | The Well-Balanced Community |
| LONG BEACH | America's Healthiest City |
| | The City by the Sea (the Atlantic Ocean) |
| | The Ideal Vacation Resort |
| | The Ideal Vacation Resort and Year 'Round Residential Community |
| LONG LAKE | The Magnificent Mountain Wonderland |
| MALONE | The Big Little City |
| | The City Famous for Friendliness |
| | The Community of Opportunity |
| | The Star of the North |
| MASSENA | The Aluminum City (Aluminum Company of America's smelting plant) |
| | The Gateway of the North |
| | The Gateway to Vacationland |
| | The Heart of the Famous St. Lawrence Seaway |
| | The Seaway Vactionland |
| MATTITUCK | The Friendly Village |
| MEXICO | The Mother of Towns |
| MIDDLETOWN | The Gateway to Upstate |
| MONROE | The Place where There Is Everything for Everyone |
| MONTAUK | America's Riviera |

| | |
|---|---|
| MONTAUK (Cont'd) | The Miami Beach of the North |
| MONTICELLO | The Catskills and County Cross-roads of the Center for Action |
| | The Home of the Mighty M (Monticello Raceway) |
| NEWARK | The Rose Capital of America (rose cultivation, annual rose festival) |
| NEW ROCHELLE | The City Alive |
| | The City of Huguenots (settled by the Huguenots in 1689) |
| | The Park City |
| | The Queen City of the Sound (Long Island Sound) |
| NEW YORK CITY | America's Leading Tourist Resort |
| | Father Knickerbocker (referring to the type of trousers worn by the early Dutch settlers) |
| | Gotham (name given to New York City by Washington Irving in the Salamagundi Papers, 1807) |
| | The Babylonian Bedlam (allusion to the confusion of tongues at Babel, described in Genesis XI) |
| | The Bagdad of the Subway |
| | The Bagdad on the Hudson |
| | The Banking Center of the World |
| | The Big Apple |
| | The Big Burg |
| | The Big City |
| | The Big Town |
| | The Biggest Gateway to Immigrants |
| | The Burg |
| | The Business Capital of the Nation |
| | The Business Capital of the World |
| | The Capital of Finance |
| | The Capital of the World |
| | The Center of the World (Trygve Lie, first United Nations secretary on Sept. 7, 1962) |
| | The City |
| | The City of Golden Dreams |
| | The City of Islands (the borough of Manhattan and numerous |

NEW YORK CITY (Cont'd)

other small islands within the
city limits)

The City at the Crossroads of
High Diplomacy

The City of Friendly People

The City of Orchestras (music
center and "Tin Pan Alley")

The City of Skycrapers (the tallest
building in the world; the Empire State building, the Chrys-
ler Building, 60 Wall Tower,
etc. )

The City of Superlatives

The City of the World

The City of Towers

The City That Belongs to the
World

The City That Never Sleeps

The City with Everything

The Cleanest Big City in the
World

The Coliseum City

The Commercial Emporium

The Crossroads of the World

The Cuisine Capital of the World

The Cultural Center of the Nation

The Empire City

The Entertainment Capital of the
World

The Fashion Capital of the World

The Financial Capital of the World

The First City of the World (the
most populated city in the
United States, approximately 8
million)

The Friendly City

The Frog and Toe

The Front Office of American
Business

The Fun City

The Fun City on the Hudson

The Greatest All-Year Round Vacation City

The Greatest Industrial Center in
the World

The Headquarters of World Bank-
ing

NEW YORK CITY (Cont'd)   The Hong Kong of the Hudson
The Host of the World
The Hub City of the World
The Hub of Transport
The Land of Surprising Contrasts
The Mecca of Telephone Men
The Melting Pot (drama by Israel
   Zangwill, 1908)
The Metropolis
The Metropolis of a Continent
The Metropolis of America
The Metropolitan City
The Mighty Manhattan
The Modern Gomorrah (one of the
   cities of the plains destroyed
   by fire and brimstone because
   of wickedness, mentioned in
   the Old Testament)
The Money Town
The Most Colorful Exciting City
   in the World
The Movie-Making City
The Nation's First City
The Nation's Greatest City
The Nation's Largest Communica-
   tions Center
The Nation's Largest Port
The Port of Many Ports
The Science City
The Seat of Empire (named in
   1784 by George Washington)
The Super City
The University of Telephony
The Vacation City
The Wonder City
The World Capital of Fashion
The World's Capital City
The World's Fair City
The World's Financial Capital
The World's Metropolis
The World's Most Exciting All
   Year Round Vacation Center

NIAGARA FALLS   America's Scenic Wonderland
Nature's Mighty Masterpiece
The Cataract City (descriptive)
The City of Business
The City of Fine Schools

| | |
|---|---|
| NIAGARA FALLS (Cont'd) | The City of Homes |
| | The City of Industry |
| | The City of Scenic Marvels |
| | The Honeymoon City (a favorite vacation spot for honeymoon couples) |
| | The King of Power |
| | The Nearby Wonder of the World |
| | The Power City (hydroelectric stations) |
| | The Power City of Scenic Wonders |
| | The Powerhouse of the Niagara Frontier |
| | The Quality City |
| | The Queen of Beauty |
| | The Scenic Gateway to America |
| NORTH POLE | Santa's Workshop (toy factory) |
| | Village of Breathtaking Beauty and Enchantment |
| | Village of Enchantment |
| OGDENSBURG | A Community on the Move for a Century and a Half with More to Offer for the Future |
| | An Entire City of Friendly People |
| | Enjoyment in History Relived |
| | The City Historical and Enjoyable |
| | The Friendliest City on any International Border |
| | The Gateway to International Fun for the Entire Family |
| OLD FORGE | The Year 'Round Vacationland |
| ONEIDA | A Bit of America at Its Best |
| ONEONTA | The City of Hills (west of the Catskill Mountain region) |
| | The Manufacturing City |
| OYSTER BAY | The Home of Theodore Roosevelt |
| PORCHESTER | The Sin City |
| POTSDAM | The Business and Cultural Center of the St. Lawrence Valley |
| | The Education, Culture, Business Distribution Center of the St. Lawrence Valley |
| RIPLEY | The Gretna Green (on Lake Erie) |
| RIVERHEAD | The Gateway to the Hamptons |
| | The Hub of Eastern Long Island |
| | The Ideal Town in which to Live, Work, Shop and Play |

| | |
|---|---|
| RIVERHEAD (Cont'd) | The Town where Your Summer Fun Begins |
| ROCHESTER | Lake Ontario's Westernmost American Seaport |
| | The Aquaduct City |
| | The Camera Center |
| | The Camera City |
| | The City Built by Hands |
| | The City of Giant Industry |
| | The City of Great Industry |
| | The City of Homes |
| | The City of Many Industries |
| | The City of Quality Products |
| | The City of Varied Industries |
| | The Emerging Metropolis |
| | The Flour City |
| | The Flower City |
| | The Friendliest City |
| | The Gateway to Vacationland |
| | The Home of One of the Nation's Largest Skilled Technical Work Forces |
| | The Kodak City |
| | The Photographic and Optical Center of the World |
| | The Photography Capital |
| | The Power City |
| | The Quality City |
| | The Snapshot City |
| | The World's Largest Lilac Center |
| ROME | The Copper City (about 10 percent of the copper factories of the U. S. ) |
| RYE | America's Premier Playground |
| | The Border Town |
| SARANAC LAKE | The Little City in the Adirondacks |
| SARATOGA SPRINGS | America's Most Wonderful Spa |
| | Fun Country, U. S. A. |
| | The Capitol of Thoroughbred Racing |
| | The Convention City |
| | The Home of America's Greatest Spa |
| | The Home of Health, History and Horse |
| | The Invevitable Spa City |
| | The Queen of the Spas |

| | |
|---|---|
| SARATOGA SPRINGS (Cont'd) | The Spa City |
| SCHENECTADY | Dorp |
| | Old Dorp |
| | The City of Flourishing Industries |
| | The City of Magic |
| | The City that Lights and Hauls the World |
| | The Electric City (site of the General Electric Co.) |
| | The Electrical City (site of the General Electric Co.) |
| | The Gateway to the West (on the Mohawk River) |
| | The Magic City |
| SCHROON LAKE | The Cultural Center of the Adirondacks |
| | The Family Vacationland |
| | The Heart of the Adirondack Vacationland |
| | The Playground of the Adirondacks (summer resort) |
| SHARON SPRINGS | America's Mountain Spring (White sulphur spring four barrels a minute) |
| SHELTER ISLAND | The Vacationer's Paradise |
| SOMERS | The Birthplace of the American Circus |
| | The Circus Capital |
| | The Cradle of the American Circus |
| SPECULATOR | The City in the Lake District of the Adirondacks |
| | The Land of Beautiful Lakes |
| | The Vacationland of Unlimited Enjoyment |
| SYRACUSE | The Central City |
| | The City of Conventions |
| | The City of Isms |
| | The City of Salt |
| | The City of the Plains |
| | The Crossroads of New York State |
| | The Electronics Capital of the World |
| | The Fair City |
| | The Heart of New York State |

| | |
|---|---|
| SYRACUSE (Cont'd) | The Hub of the Empire State |
| | The Ideal Residential City |
| | The Salt City (salt springs and salt brine) |
| | The Telegraphic Hub |
| | The Venice of America |
| THERESA | The Gateway to Twelve Beautiful Lakes |
| TICONDEROGA | America's Most Historic Town |
| | The Land where History Was Made |
| TROY | The Collar City (factories manufacturing Arrow shirts and collars) |
| | The Tide-Water City (at head of the Hudson River) |
| TRUMANSBURG | The City in the Heart of the Finger Lakes |
| TUPPER LAKE | The Crossroads of the Adirondacks |
| UTICA | The Beautiful City of Homes in the Historic Mohawk Valley |
| | The City of the Crossroads of the Empire State |
| | The City of Successful Diversified Industry |
| | The Crossroads of New York |
| | The Gateway to the Adirondacks |
| | The Heart of America's Richest Market |
| | The Hub of the Empire State |
| | The Watering-Pot of America |
| WALTON | The Foothills of the Catskills |
| | The Heart and Hub of Delaware County |
| WARRENSBURG | The Queen Village of the Adirondacks |
| WATERTOWN | The City of Pleasant Living and Industry |
| | The City where Industry Thrives |
| | The Gateway to the St. Lawrence Power and Seaway |
| | The Gateway to the Thousand Islands |
| | The Hydro-Electric City |
| | The Metropolis of Northern New York |

| | |
|---|---|
| WATERTOWN (Cont'd) | The Woolworth Town (Frank H. Woolworth established the first 5 and 10 cent store here) |
| WATKINS GLEN | The Heart of the Lake Country |
| | The Vacation Center |
| | Your Vacation Center |
| WELLS | A Truly Year 'Round Vacation Land |
| WESTPORT | The City where the Adirondacks Meet Lake Champlain |
| WHITE PLAINS | The Heart of Westchester (Westchester County) |
| WHITEHALL | The Birthplace of the U.S. Navy |
| WILLIAMSVILLE | The Gateway to Niagara Falls |
| YONKERS | The City Next to the Greatest City in the World |
| | The City of Graceful Living |
| | The Queen City of the Hudson |
| | The Terrace City |

## NORTH CAROLINA

| | |
|---|---|
| ASHEVILLE | One of the Leading Health and Tourist Resorts of the East |
| | The Capital City of the Land of the Sky |
| | The City in the Land of the Sky (altitude 2, 250 feet) |
| | The City in the Sky |
| | The City where Spring Spends the Winter |
| | The Land of the Sky (altitude 1, 980 feet to 3, 020 feet) |
| | The Popular Convention City |
| | The Preeminent Vacation Center |
| BLOWING ROCK | The Heart of North Carolina's Holiday Highland |
| | The Southern Holiday Highland |
| BOONE | The Home of the "Horn of the West" (historical drama story of Daniel Boone) |
| | The Horn of the West |
| | The Hub of the "Holiday Highlands" |
| BREVARD | The Home of the Brevard Music Center |
| | The Music Center of the South |

BREVARD (Cont'd)                  (Brevard Music Center)
                                 The Popular Summer Resort
BURLINGTON                       The Home of State's First Indus-
                                   trial Training Center
CAROLINA BEACH                   The States Largest Oceanside
                                   Resort Town
CHAPEL HILL                      The Capital of the Southern Mind
                                   (University of North Carolina)
CHARLOTTE                        The Action City
                                 The City of Churches
                                 The City where the Southeast
                                   Gets Its Money
                                 The Heart of the Piedmont
                                 The Home City
                                 The Hornets' Nest
                                 The Queen City
                                 The Spearhead of the New South
CHEROKEE                         The Gateway to the Great Smoky
                                   Mountains National Park
CLAYTON                          The Tobacco and Farming Center
CONCORD                          The Gateway to the Friendly City
DRAPER                           The Tri-City (with Leaksville and
                                   Spray, N. C.)
EDENTON                          The Cradle of the Colony (one of
                                   the oldest communities)
FAYETTEVILLE                     The City of Historical Heritage
FRANKLIN                         The Gem Capital of the World
                                   (numerous ruby mines)
GASTONIA                         The Pacemaker of the Piedmont
                                 What We Make Makes Us
GOLDSBORO                        The Community of Progress
                                 The Friendly City of Progress
                                 The Heart of Eastern North Caro-
                                   lina
GREENSBORO                       The Center of the Greatest Man-
                                   ufacturing Area in the South
                                 The City of Charm
                                 The Pivot of the Piedmont
HATTERAS                         The Blue Marlin Capital of the
                                   World
HATTERAS ISLAND                  The Graveyard of the Atlantic
HENDERSON                        The Bird Sanctuary
                                 The City where Hospitality Never
                                   Ceases
                                 The City with a Future
                                 The Gateway to the South (North
                                   Carolina's Most Northern City)

| | |
|---|---|
| HENDERSON (Cont'd) | One of the Leading Tobacco Markets for Bright Leaf Tobacco |
| HENDERSONVILLE | The City of Four Glorious Seasons |
| | The Dancingest Town in the United States (numerous street and other public dances) |
| | The Flower, Fruit, Vegetable Center |
| | The Resort City of Blue Ridge |
| | The Summer and Health Resort |
| | Your Cool Mountain Vacationland |
| HICKORY | The Best Balanced City |
| HIGH POINT | The Furniture City (about 90 furniture factories) |
| | The Furniture City of the World |
| | The Furniture Production Center of the U. S. |
| | The Industrial City |
| HIGHLANDS | The Highest Incorporated Town in Eastern America |
| JACKSONVILLE | The City on the Go |
| KANNAPOLIS | The Towel City (site of Cannon Mills) |
| LEAKSVILLE | The Tri-City (with Spray and Draper, N. C. ) |
| LEXINGTON | The City Four-Dimensional |
| | The Winter Golf Capital of America |
| LITTLE SWITZERLAND | The Beauty Spot of the Blue Ridge |
| MURPHY | The Great Smokies' Mountain Lake Neighbor |
| | The Land of Lakes and Trout Streams |
| | The Land of the Sky |
| | The Mountain Lake Vacationland |
| | The Southern Gateway to the Great Smokies |
| NEW BERN | The All-Year Resort Center |
| | The Historic Center of North Carolina |
| | The Hub of Coastal Carolina |
| | The Land of Enchanting Waters |
| OCRACOKE | North Carolina's Pleasure Island |
| PINEHURST | Golftown, U. S. A. |
| | The Winter Golf Capital of America |

| | |
|---|---|
| RALEIGH | The Capital City (1960 pop. 93,931) |
| | The City of Oaks |
| | The Oak City |
| | The Trading Center |
| ROANOKE RAPIDS | The Northeastern North Carolina Industrial Center |
| ROCKY MOUNT | The Gate to the Old South (on the Tar River) |
| SANFORD | The Brick Capital of the United States |
| | The City where Business and Friendship Thrive |
| | The Gateway to the Famous Sandhills |
| | The Heart of North Carolina |
| SEALEVEL | The Home of the Green Sea Horse |
| SOUTHERN PINES | The Mid-South Resort |
| SPRAY | The Tri-City (with Leaksville and Draper, N. C.) |
| SPRUCE PINE | The Mineral City (feldspar and kaolin) |
| STATESVILLE | The City of Progress |
| | The Crossroads of Tomorrow |
| THOMASVILLE | The Chair Capital of the World |
| | The Chair City (furniture manufacturing since 1870) |
| TRYON | The City in the Famous Thermal Belt of North Carolina |
| | The Friendliest Town in America (in the Blue Ridge Mountains) |
| WAYNESVILLE | The Gateway to the Great Smoky Mountains State Park |
| | The Vacation and Health Resort |
| WELDON | The Rock Fish Capital of the World (on the Roanoke River) |
| | Rockfish Capital |
| WHITE LAKE | The Nation's Safest Beach |
| WILSON | The Greatest Show in Tobaccoland (bright-leaf tobacco market) |
| WINSTON-SALEM | The Camel City (a brand cigarette manufactured by the R. J. Reynolds Tobacco Company) |
| | The City Founded Upon Cooperation |
| | The City of Culture, History, Industry |

WINSTON-SALEM (Cont'd)   The City of History, Culture,
                                     Education, Industry
                                     The Twin Cities (Winston and
                                     Salem consolidated in 1913)
                                     The Twin City (Winston and Sa-
                                     lem consolidated in 1913)

## NORTH DAKOTA

BISMARCK                 The Capital City (1960 population
                                     27, 670)
                                     The Capital of Opportunity
                                     The City Beside the Broad Mis-
                                     souri
                                     The Fastest Growing City in the
                                     Northwest
                                     The Medical Center of North
                                     Dakota

DEVILS LAKE              The Satanic City (a synonym for
                                     devil)

DICKINSON               A Good Place to Visit, a Good
                                     Place to Live
                                     North Dakota's Queen City
                                     The City That Is Big Enough to
                                     Serve You, Yet Small Enough
                                     to Know You
                                     The Gateway of America's Scenic
                                     Wonderland
                                     The Gateway to the West
                                     The Queen City
                                     The Queen City of the Prairies
                                     The Threshold of Theodore
                                     Roosevelt National Memorial
                                     Park

ENDERLIN                The City That Is Friendly, Pro-
                                     gressive, Alive
                                     The Tri-County City That Is
                                     Friendly, Progressive, Alive

FARGO                   A Fine Residential Center
                                     An Important Livestock Center
                                     The Bread Basket of the World
                                     The Distribution Center for the
                                     Great Northwest
                                     The Food Basket of the World
                                   The Gateway City
                                   The Gateway City to the Bread
                                   Basket of the World

FARGO (Cont'd)          The Land of Business Opportunity
                        The Mainline City (by air, rail
                            and highway)
                        The Metropolis of North Dakota
                        The Natural Location for Agri-
                            cultural Industry
GARRISON                Mid-America's Fast Growing
                            Exciting New Playground
                        The Fishing and Hunting Head-
                            quarters for Gigantic Lake
                            Garrison
GRAFTON                 Every Year a Growth Year for
                            Grafton
                        Growing Grafton Leads North Da-
                            kota
                        The Agricultural Breadbasket
                            Center of North America
                        The Center of the Red River Val-
                            ley Bread Basket
                        The Nation's No. 3 Potato Center,
                            Soon the First
                        The True Center of the Rich Red
                            River Valley
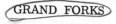GRAND FORKS    The City with a Heart
                        The Heart of North Dakota
                        The Home of the University of
                            North Dakota
                        The Only Grand Forks in the Na-
                            tion
JAMESTOWN               Jimtown
                        The City with a Future
                        The Home of the World's Largest
                            Buffalo
MARMARTH                The City of Trees
MEDORA                  The Cow Town
MINOT                   North Dakota's Favorite Conven-
                            tion City
                        The Continental Crossroads
                        The Gateway to Garrison Dam
                        The Hub of Recreational North
                            Dakota
                        The Magic City (referring to its
                            fast growth)
NEW TOWN                The Old West's Newest City
STANTON                 The Home of Sakakawea
                        The Most Historic Spot in North
                            Dakota

| | |
|---|---|
| STANTON (Cont'd) | The Power City |
| VALLEY CITY | The City Beautiful |
| WILLISTON | A Good Place to Work, Live and Play |
| | The Capitol of a Great Empire |
| | The City where the Best Begins |

## OHIO

| | |
|---|---|
| AKRON | The Center of the World's Rubber Manufacturing |
| | The City of Opportunity |
| | The Heart of America's Workshop |
| | The Rubber Capital of the United States (numerous factories producing tires and other rubber products) |
| | The Rubber Capital of the World |
| | The Rubber City |
| | The Summit City (950 feet altitude, highest point of old Ohio and Erie Canal) |
| | The Tire Capital of the World |
| | The Tire City of the United States |
| BAINBRIDGE | The Cradle of Dental Education (school for dentists opened in 1826 by Dr. John Harris) |
| BARBERTON | The Largest Industrial City of Its Size in Ohio |
| | The Magic City |
| BERLIN | The Heart of Amish Territory |
| | Swiss Cheese |
| CADIZ | The Proudest Small Town in America (1960 population 3, 259) |
| CANTON | The Gateway to the Midwest |
| CEDAR POINT | The Atlantic City of the Great Lakes |
| | The Atlantic City of the Middle West (resort area on Sandusky Bay) |
| CHILLICOTHE | Ohio's First Capital |
| CINCINNATI | America's Paris |
| | Pigopolis |
| | Porkopolis |

CINCINNATI (Cont'd)          The Athens of the Middle West
                             The Beautiful City
                             The Birmingham of America
                             The City of Personality
                             The Conservative Cincinnati
                             The Contented City
                             The Crossroads of the Nation
                             The Floral City
                             The Gateway to the South
                             The Paris of America
                             The Queen City
                             The Queen City of the Ohio
                             The Queen City of the Ohio River
                             The Queen City of the West
                             The Queen of the Ohio (Ohio
                                River)
                             The Queen of the West
                             The Ragtown (manufacture of
                                cloaks and suits often refer-
                                red to in the trade as "rags")

CLEVELAND                    Lake Erie's Vacation City
                             The Advertising Center
                             The Best Location in the Nation
                             The Capital City of a Great
                                Trade Empire
                             The City That Cooperates
                             The First City in American
                                Spirit
                             The Forest City
                             The Lighting Capital of the
                                World (General Electric Com-
                                pany's lamp division)
                             The Modern Athens
                             The Overgrown Country Town
                             The Queen of Lake Erie
                             The University of Light (General
                                Electric Company's lamp di-
                                vision)
                             The Vacation City

COLUMBUS                     Ohio's Beautiful Capital
                             The Capital City (1960 pop. 471,316)
                             The Heart of a Great State
                             The Middle of Marketing America
                             The Rose Capital of the World

CONNEAUT                     The Plymouth of the Western Re-
                                serve (first settlers in Ohio,
                                July 4, 1796)

| | |
|---|---|
| CRESTLINE | The Railroad Center Since 1850 |
| DAYTON | The Aviation City |
| | The Birthplace of Aviation (Wright-Patterson Air Force Base) |
| | The Cash Register City (National Cash Register Co. factory) |
| | The City Beautiful |
| | The City of Beauty |
| | The City of Industry |
| | The City of Progress |
| | The Cradle of Aviation (Wright-Patterson Air Force Base) |
| | The Cradle of Creativity |
| | The Crossroads of Your National Market |
| | The Gem City |
| | The Gem City of Ohio |
| | The Home of the Wright Brothers |
| | The Pioneering Center of Aviation |
| | The World Famous Manufacturing Center |
| DELPHOS | The Heart of Industrial America |
| DENNISON | The Clay Pipe Center of the World |
| DOVER | The Home of Warther Museum (world famous carvings) |
| EAST LIVERPOOL | The Ceramic City (leading pottery center) |
| | The Pottery Center |
| ELYRIA | The City of Beauty and Unlimited Opportunities |
| | The City of Diversified Products |
| | The Growth Market in Lorain County |
| FAIRBORN | Ohio's Most Progressive City |
| GALLIPOLIS | The City of the Gauls (settled by the French in 1790) |
| HAMILTON | The Postmark of Distinctive Trademarks (Gen. Arthur St. Clair built Fort Hamilton in 1791) |
| HAYDENVILLE | The Ideal Town |
| LAKESIDE | The Chautauqua of the Great Lakes (summer conference |

LAKESIDE (Cont'd)                grounds on the southern shore
                                 of Lake Erie)
LAKEWOOD                         The City of Homes
LIMA                             A City of Fine Homes and Streets
                                 The Hub of a $500,000 Trading
                                   Area
                                 The Pipeline Center of the Nation
LORAIN                           One of the Fastest Growing Areas
                                   in the Nation
MARIETTA                         A Town for Those in Love with
                                   Life
                                 Ohio's First City
                                 Ohio's Oldest and Most Beautiful
                                   City (settled by 48 people in
                                   1788)
                                 The Birthplace of the Northwest
                                   Territory
                                 The City of Diversified Industries
                                 The City of Many Cultural Ad-
                                   vantages
                                 The Most Historic City in the
                                   Northwest Territory (first
                                   civil government in the North-
                                   west Territory when Arthur
                                   St. Clair took the oath of gov-
                                   ernor in 1788)
MARION                           The Shovel City of the World
NILES                            The Birthplace of Mc Kinley
                                   (President William Mc Kinley
                                   born Jan. 29, 1843)
                                 The Haven for Industry, Com-
                                   merce and Good Living
PORTSMOUTH                       The City where Southern Hospital-
                                   ity Begins (on the Ohio River)
                                 The Steel City (iron and steel
                                   factory built 1872)
SABINA                           The Eden of Ohio
SALEM                            Ohio's City of Friends
                                 The Quaker City (founded in 1801
                                   by Quakers)
SANDUSKY                         The Gateway to Lake Erie
                                 The Gateway to the Ohio Lake
                                   Erie Islands (on Sandusky Bay
                                   of Lake Erie)
SIDNEY                           The Industrial City
SPRINGFIELD                      The Champion City
                                 The City of Progress

| | |
|---|---|
| SPRINGFIELD (Cont'd) | The Flower City |
| | The Hub of Historic Ohio |
| | The Hub of Historical Ohio |
| | The Progressively Growing Well-Seasoned City |
| STEUBENVILLE | The Best Town Site on the Ohio (on the Ohio River, 1960 population 32, 495) |
| SUGARCREEK | The Swiss Cheese Center of Ohio (numerous factories) |
| TOLEDO | One of America's Great Cities |
| | One of the Busiest Freshwater Ports in the World (on the Maumee River flowing into Lake Erie) |
| | The Busiest Freshwater Port in the World |
| | The Central Gateway of the Great Lakes |
| | The City where Coal and Iron Meet |
| | The City where the Seaway Meets the Turnpike |
| | The Corn City |
| | The Glass Capital of the World (numerous glass factories) |
| | The Glass Center (factories of Owens-Illinois Glass Co., Ford Glass Co., Libby-Owens, etc.) |
| | The Mud Hen City |
| | The Pivot City of the Great Lakes (on Lake Erie) |
| | The World's Largest Coal-Shipping Port |
| UHRICHSVILLE | The Clay Pipe Center of the World |
| UPPER SANDUSKY | The Friendly Community of Beauty and Industry |
| | The Home of the Wyandot Indians |
| | The Indian Village (home of Wyandot Indians) |
| VAN WERT | The Nation's Peony Center |
| WARREN | The Home of Little Steel (steel mills) |
| YOUNGSTOWN | The Capital City |
| | The Capital City of a Great Industrial Empire |

| | |
|---|---|
| YOUNGSTOWN (Cont'd) | The Gateway to the Old Western Reserve |
| | The Land of Flowing Springs |
| | The Recreational, Educational and Cultural Center of Northeastern Ohio |
| ZANESVILLE | America's Typical City |
| | The Capital City (Ohio's capital from 1810-1812) |
| | The Pottery City (pottery, tile, glass manufacturing) |
| | The "Y" Bridge City (bridge built in the form of the letter "Y") |

## OKLAHOMA

| | |
|---|---|
| ARDMORE | The Capital of South Central Oklahoma |
| BARTLESVILLE | America's Ideal Family Center |
| | The City with a Future |
| CHANDLER | The Largest Pecan Shipping Center in America |
| | The Pecan Capital of the World |
| CLAREMORE | The Best Known Little City in America (1960 population 6, 639) |
| DRUMRIGHT | The Friendliest Town in Oklahoma |
| | The Gateway to the Lakes |
| | The Pipeline Capital of the World |
| ENID | The Queen City of the Cherokee Strip |
| GROVE | The Friendly Community |
| | The Spot for a Home and Life of Joy |
| GUTHRIE | The Birthplace of Oklahoma (first state capital 1907) |
| | The Fraternal Capital of the Southwest (largest Scottish Rite Temple) |
| HUGO | The Circus Town, U.S.A. |
| KENTON | The Cowboy Capital (used before Oklahoma became a state) |
| KETCHUM | The Home of the First Fully Automatic Non-Attended Dial |

| | |
|---|---|
| KETCHUM (Cont'd) | Telephone Switchboard in the United States |
| LAWTON | The Post City (U. S. Army and Fort Lawton) |
| | The Rollicking, Hilarious Tent and Shack City |
| MUSKOGEE | The City of Beauty |
| | The City of History |
| | The Established City |
| NOWATA | The Home of Championship Cowboys |
| | The World's Largest Shallow Oil Field |
| OKLAHOMA CITY | The Capital City (1960 population 324, 253) |
| | The Capital of Soonerland |
| | The Central City of the Great Southwest |
| | The City of 1, 000 Lakes (actually 1, 514 lakes ranging from a few acres to 100, 000 acre-foot Elm Creek Reservoir) |
| | The Hub of the Great Southwest |
| | The Industrial Frontier of America |
| | The Land of Perpetual Prosperity |
| | The Sedate Capital of the Bible Belt |
| | The Town where Oil Derricks Loom in Almost Any Yard |
| | The Town where the Office Ledger Has Replaced the Horse Pistol |
| OKMULGEE | The City where Oil Flows, Gas Flows and Glass Glows |
| PONCA CITY | The City Built on Oil, Soil and Toil |
| PRYOR | The Gateway from South and West to Ozark Playgrounds |
| SALINA | The Oldest White Settlement in the State (founded by Pierre Chouteaux, explorer, in 1796) |
| SEILING | The Little Louisville of the Southwest |
| SNYDER | The Home of World's Finest Granite |
| TAHLEQUAH | The Former Capital of the Cherokee Indian Nation |

TULSA
> The City Beautiful
> The Fair Little City
> The Home of Diamond Products
> The Home of the International Petroleum Exposition
> The Magic City
> The Most Eastern Western Metropolis
> The Most Northern Southern City
> The Oil Capital
> The Oil Capital of the World
> The Young Man's Capital of the World

VINITA
> The Ozark's Western Gateway (on the Texas Road, formerly the Osage Trace)
> The Second Oldest Settlement in Oklahoma

## OREGON

ALBANY
> The Hole in the Ground (altitude 216 feet; the current washed away a section near the mouth of the Calapooya River)
> The Hub City
> The Hub of the Willamette Valley

ASHLAND
> The American Carlsbad (mineral springs)
> The City of Spas (lithia water mineral springs)
> The Gateway
> The Granite City (marble works 1865)
> The Home Town of Southern Oregon

ASTORIA
> The First Port on the Columbia
> The Salmon City (on the Columbia River)

AURORA
> The Dutchtown (founded in 1857 by Dr. William Keil and German settlers)

BAKER
> The Denver of Oregon
> The Friendly City on the Oregon Trail
> The Gold Coast of Oregon (gold

BAKER (Cont'd)
    discovered on Griffin Creek 1861)
    The Switzerland of America

COOS BAY
    The Lumber Port of the World
    The World's Largest Lumber Shipping Port

COQUILLE
    The Gem City of Cedar Empire (on the Coquille River)

CORNELIUS
    The Corntown

CORVALLIS
    The Heart of the Valley (Willamette Valley)
    The Ideal Community

DIAMOND LAKE
    Gem of the Cascades
    The Home of the Rainbow Trout

ENTERPRISE
    The Gateway to Wallowa National Forest

EUGENE
    Skinner's Mudhole (Eugene F. Skinner established his land claim in 1846 near the Eugene and Willamette Rivers)
    The Spokane of Oregon
    Western Oregon's Leading Industrial and Marketing Center

FOREST GROVE
    Oregon's Own Homebase for Fun, Culture and Scenic Splendor
    The City Between the City and the Sea

GARIBALDI
    Little Holland (numerous dikes)

HILLSBORO
    The Filbert Center of the United States

LA GRANDE
    The Hub of Northeast Oregon (foot of Blue Mountains)

LAKEVIEW
    The Tallest Town in Oregon (elevation 4, 800 feet)

LANCASTER
    The Fightin'est Town on the River

MC MINNVILLE
    The Walnut City

MEDFORD
    The Bustling Western City (population about 25, 000)
    The Fun Capitol of Southern Oregon
    The Land of Incredible Beauty and Great Livability
    The Pear City (annual pear pack of the district about 4, 000 carloads)
    The Vacationland Unlimited

NEWBERG
    The Quaker City (founded by Quakers)

| | |
|---|---|
| NEWPORT | The Dungeness Crab Capital of the World |
| NORTH BEND | The City of Progress (city government 1903) |
| ONTARIO | The Brightest Spot in Eastern Oregon |
| | The Capital of Eastern Oregon |
| OREGON CITY | The City of Firsts |
| PENDLETON | The Round-Up City (Pendleton's first round-up, 1912) |
| PORTLAND | America's Newest Convention City |
| | Little Stumptown (contempuously so-called in the early days by non-residents because there were so many stumps in the streets, sometimes painted white so they could be seen in the dark) |
| | The Beautiful City of Roses |
| | The Capital of the Land of Out-Doors |
| | The City in the Evergreen Playground |
| | The City of Homes |
| | The City of Roses |
| | The Convention City |
| | The Country's Largest Lumber Shipping Center |
| | The Lumber Manufacturing Center of the Pacific Northwest |
| | The Lumber Industry's Capital |
| | The Metropolis of the State of Oregon |
| | The Rose City |
| | The Spinster City |
| | The Sub-Treasury of the Pacific Northwest |
| | The Summer Capital |
| PRINEVILLE | The Agate Capital of the U. S. (agates, jasper, chalcedony, quartz crystals, etc. ) |
| | The Country where the Climate Invites You Out-of-Doors |
| | The Cowboy Capital of Oregon |
| REDMOND | The Hub of Central Oregon |
| | Tailhold |

| | |
|---|---|
| ROSEBURG | The Lumber Capital of the Nation |
| | The Timber Capital of the Nation |
| SALEM | An All American City of the Great Northwest |
| | Oregon's Beautiful Capital City |
| | The Capital City (1960 population 49, 142) |
| | The Capital City of Good Living, Commerce and Industry |
| | The Charmed Land of Unequalled Beauty |
| | The Cherry City |
| | The City of Diversified Industry |
| | The City of Orderly Growth |
| | The City of Unexcelled Opportunities for Business and Industry |
| | The City where Advantages Abound for Business |
| | The Fisherman's Paradise |
| | The Gateway to the Great Northwest Market |
| | The Happy City Life |
| | The Heart of the Pacific Wonderland |
| SEASIDE | The Playground of the Northwest |
| STAYTON | The Green Bean Center |
| TILLAMOOK | The Land of Cheese, Trees and Ocean Breeze (on the Pacific Ocean) |
| WOODBURN | The Berry City |

## PENNSYLVANIA

| | |
|---|---|
| ALIQUIPPA | The Dynamic Area of Growth |
| | The Focal Point of Industrial America |
| | The Phenominal Example of American Growth |
| ALLENTOWN | The Cement City |
| | The Hub of the Greater Lehigh Valley |
| | The Queen City |
| | The Queen City of the Lehigh Valley (on the Lehigh River) |
| | The Scrapple City |

ALTOONA

    The City of Home Owners
    The Mountain City (altitude about
      1, 170 feet, east base of Alle-
      gheny Mountains)
    The Pleasant Place to Live and
      Work
    The Railroad City (shops and
      yards of Pennsylvania Rail-
      road)

AMBLER
    One of Pennsylvania's Fastest
      Growing Communities
    The Hub of Homes and Industries

BEDFORD
    The Mineral Springs City (resort
      area popular since 1795)
    The Resort and Convention Play-
      ground of the Alleghenies
    The World's Best Little Town

BEDFORD SPRINGS    The Carlsbad of America

BELLEFONTE
    The City of Governors
    The City of the Belles

BERLIN
    The Scenic City (in Brothers Val-
      ley)

BERWICK
    The Car Shop City (American Car
      and Foundry plant)

BETHLEHEM
    Allentown's Sister City
    America's Christmas City
    The Christmas City
    The Historic Bethlehem
    The Hub of the Great Lehigh
      Valley
    The Star City with a Great Future
    The Steel City (Bethlehem Steel
      Co., plant and coke works)

BLOOMSBURG    An Ideal Place to Work and Live

BLOSSBURG    The Tannery City

BRADFORD
    The Growing Industrial Center of
      Northwestern Pennsylvania
    The High Grade Oil Metropolis
      of the World
    The Metropolitan Center of Mc-
      Kean County
    The Natural Gas City

BUSHKILL
    The Niagara of Pennsylvania (300-
      foot series of falls)

CARLISLE
    The City of Molly Pitcher (grave
      of Molly Pitcher, heroine of
      Battle of Monmouth)

| | |
|---|---|
| CARLISLE (Cont'd) | The Crossroads of American History |
| | The Crossroads of History |
| | The Crystal Center of the World (manufacturing of quartz crystals for radio sets, etc.) |
| CHESTER | The Ship-Building City (on the Delaware River) |
| COATESVILLE | A Good Place in which to Work and Live |
| CONNELLSVILLE | The Bituminous City |
| | The Iron Ore City |
| COUDERSPORT | The Ice Mine City (a vertical shaft 40 feet deep, 8 feet wide and 10 feet long containing ice formations during the spring, continuing through the summer and disappearing in the winter) |
| DOWNINGTOWN | The Gateway to the Pennsylvania Dutch Country |
| DOYLESTOWN | Home of the Mercer Museum |
| EASTON | The Transportation City |
| EBENSBURG | The Lookout City (altitude 2,022 feet) |
| ELKLAND | The Dairy City |
| ELLWOOD CITY | A Good Place to Live, Work and Play |
| | Ellwood City Encourages Enterprise |
| | The City of Diversified Industry |
| EMPORIUM | The Land of the Endless Mountains |
| EPHRATA | The Community where Living Is at Its Best |
| | The Home of Miss America 1954 |
| ERIE | The City of Diversified Industry and Commerce |
| | The Gem City of the Lakes |
| | The Harbor City (only lake port in Pennsylvania, located on Lake Erie) |
| GETTYSBURG | The Battlefield City (bloodiest battle of the War of Secession, July 1-3, 1863, loss 23,001 men) |
| | The Nation's Greatest Historic Shrine |

| | |
|---|---|
| GREENSBURG | The City Progressive |
| | The Community Progressive |
| | The Tunnel City (bituminous coal mines) |
| HANOVER | The Shoe City |
| HARRISBURG | Pennsylvania's Capital City |
| | The Capital City (1960 population 79, 697) |
| | The Center of the Northeast |
| | The City That Puts Business on the Go |
| | The Courteous Capital City |
| | The Heart of Distribution |
| | The Heart of the Commonwealth |
| | The Host City to Conventions |
| | The Hub of the Interstate and U. S. Highways |
| | The State City |
| | The Transportation King of the Mid-East |
| HAZLETON | Pennsylvania's Highest City |
| | The "Can Do" City |
| | The Crossroads of Tomorrow |
| HERSHEY | Chocolate Town, U. S. A. (Hershey Chocolates) |
| | Progress Through Vision |
| | The Chocolate City |
| | The Chocolate Crossroads of the World |
| | The Chocolate Town |
| | The Golf Capital of Pennsylvania |
| HOLLIDAYSBURG | The Canal City (in the 1830's a canal and railroad terminus) |
| | The Portage City (to Johnstown, Pa.) |
| HUMMELSTOWN | The Brownstone City |
| HUNTINGDON | Pennsylvania's New Vacationland |
| | The Scenic Land of the Standing Stone (upright stone column [tribal totem pole] which is the symbol of the Indian lore) |
| INDIANA | The Christmas Tree Capital of the World |
| JEANNETTE | The Friendly City with a Future |
| | The Glass City |
| JERSEY SHORE | The Fair Play City (settled in 1785) |

| | |
|---|---|
| JOHNSONBURG | The Paper City (Castanea Paper Company) |
| JOHNSTOWN | The Cradle of the Steel Industry |
| | The Flood City (disastrous flood May 31, 1889) |
| | The Flood Free City |
| | The Friendly City |
| KANE | Air Conditioned By Nature (2, 200 feet above the sea) |
| | The Summit City (2, 013 feet altitude) |
| | The Weedless City (the city ordinance requires elimination of weeds) |
| | The Winter Sports City |
| | The Year-Round Health and Recreational Resort |
| LANCASTER | America's Garden Spot |
| | America's Oldest Inland City |
| | Pennsylvania's Above-Average Market of Industry and Agriculture |
| | The Arsenal (rifles and cannons were forged during the Revolutionary War) |
| | The Bread-Basket (during the Revolutionary War the farmlands supplied the Army) |
| | The Buying Center of a Quarter Million People |
| | The City in the Heart of Pennsylvania Dutch Country |
| | The Heart of Pennsylvania Dutch Country |
| | The Metropolis of "Dutchland" |
| | The Oldest Inland City in the United States |
| | The Pretzel City |
| | The Red Rose City |
| LATROBE | The Birthplace of Professional Football |
| LEBANON | The Iron Mountain City (Cornall ore mines in operation since 1742, largest iron mines in eastern U. S.) |
| LEWISBURG | The College City (Bucknell University established 1846) |

LOCK HAVEN                  The Eastern Gateway to Bucktail
                           State Park
                           The Private Flying Capital of the
                           World (headquarters of the
                           Piper Airplane Company)
                           The Sawdust City (lumbering)

MC KEESPORT                The City in the Heart of Indus-
                           trial America
                           The Tube City (plant of National
                           Tube Co. )

MANHEIM                    The Rose City (on December 4,
                           1772 "Baron" von Stiegel, a
                           trustee of the Manheim Luth-
                           eran Congregation deeded a
                           plot of ground to them with
                           the stipulation that "in the
                           month of June forever here-
                           after the rent of one red rose
                           if the same shall be lawfully
                           demanded" shall be paid)

MAUCH CHUNK                The Switchback City (since 1827
                           site of first switchback rail-
                           way)

MEADVILLE                  The Hub of Industrial America
MECHANICSBURG              Big City Benefits with Small
                           Town Advantages

MERCER                     The Hub of the Highways
MONROEVILLE                The Gateway to Pittsburgh
                           The Nation's Residential Research
                           Center
                           The Residential Research Center
                           of the Nation

MOUNT JOY                  The Garden Spot of Pennsylvania
                           The Hub of the Richest Farming
                           District of the U. S.
                           The Ideal Industrial Town
                           The Town where Natural Beauty
                           and Industry Meet to Create

NAZARETH                   The City where Industry Pros-
                           pers, You Will Too

NEW CASTLE                 The City with Its Sights on Its
                           Future
                           The Gateway to the Miss Universe
                           Highway (U. S. 301)

NEW KENSINGTON             The Aluminum City (Aluminum
                           Company of America plant)

| | |
|---|---|
| NEW KENSINGTON<br>(Cont'd) | The Center of Allegheny Valley's Business and Industrial Activity |
| | The City of Growing Industries |
| NORRIS TOWN | The Aqueduct City |
| OIL CITY | The Derrick City (site of derricks used since 1860 discovery of oil) |
| PHILADELPHIA | A Glorious Past...A Brilliant Present...Looking Forward to an Exciting Future |
| | America's Convention City |
| | America's Great Convention City |
| | Philly |
| | The Birthplace of American Independence |
| | The Birthplace of American Liberty (Declaration of Independence signed July 4, 1776) |
| | The Birthplace of the Nation |
| | The City of Brotherly Love |
| | The City of Churches |
| | The City of Firsts |
| | The City of Homes |
| | The City of Penn (William Penn settled in 1682) |
| | The Cradle of Liberty |
| | The Cradle of the Revolution |
| | The Gateway to the United States |
| | The Modern City of Great Historical Interest |
| | The Native City of Benjamin Franklin |
| | The Pacesetter of Progress |
| | The Quaker City (settled by William Penn and Quaker colony) |
| | The Quakertown |
| | The Rebel Capital |
| | The Sleepy Town |
| | The World's Greatest Workshop |
| | The World's Largest Fresh-Water Port |
| PITTSBURGH | A City Excitingly Alive and Progressive |
| | The Big Smoke |
| | The Big Smoky |

PITTSBURGH (Cont'd)        The Birmingham of America
                           The Center of Eastern Steel
                               Making
                           The City of Bridges (Liberty
                               Bridge, Smithfield St. Bridge,
                               Ft. Pitt Bridge, etc.)
                           The City of Steel (U. S. Steel
                               Corp.)
                           The City of the Longest Sunday
                           The City of the Unexpected
                           The Coal City
                           The Forge of the Universe
                           The Gateway Between East and
                               West
                           The Gateway Center
                           The Gateway to the West
                           The Greatest Steel City in the
                               World
                           The Industrial City of the West
                           The Iron City
                           The Most Bridged City in the
                               World
                           The Renaissance City of America
                           The Smoky City
                           The Steel Capital of the World
                           The Steel City
                           The World's Workshop

POTTSVILLE                 The Coal City (southern gateway
                               to the anthracite region)

READING                    Penn's Town (founded in 1748 by
                               Thomas and Richard Penn,
                               sons of William Penn)
                           The Brewing City
                           The Capital of Pennsylvania Ger-
                               man Land
                           The Center of the World's Best
                               Market
                           The City of Progress
                           The Industrial Metropolis
                           The Pretzel City (J. T. Adams
                               Pretzel Bakery, established
                               1873)
                           The Textile City

ROCHESTER                  The Gateway to the West where
                               the Ohio and the Beaver Riv-
                               ers Meet

SCRANTON                   America's Year 'Round Playground

| | |
|---|---|
| SCRANTON (Cont'd) | The Anthracite Capital of the World (coal mines) |
| | The Anthracite Center of the World |
| | The Anthracite City |
| | The City of Black Diamonds (coal) |
| | The Electric City (first electric streetcar line on which fares were collected, 1886) |
| | The Friendly City |
| | The Wonderful Convention City |
| | The World's Largest Anthracite Coal Mining City |
| SMETHPORT | The Bucktail City (Bucktail Regiment organized in 1861 by Gen. Thomas L. Kane) |
| SOMERSET | Eastern Gateway to Laurel Highlands |
| | Growing Progressive Community |
| | The Frosty City |
| | The Roof Garden of Pennsylvania (Mt. Davis, altitude 3,240 feet) |
| | The Summer and Winter Paradise |
| STATE COLLEGE 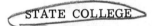 | The Educational-Cultural Community |
| | The Penn State City (site of Pennsylvania State College) |
| STROUDSBURG | The Gateway to the Poconos (about fourteen miles from the heart of the Pocono Mountains) |
| TITUSVILLE | The Gateway to the Galaxies |
| | The Town That Outlives and Outgrew the Oil Boom (first successful oil well drilled 1859, Drake well) |
| UNION CITY | The Chair Center of the World |
| UNIONTOWN | The City of Coal Kings |
| | The Coke City |
| WARREN | The City of Industrial Opportunity |
| WASHINGTON | The Crossroads of the Nation |
| WAYNESBURG | The Catacomb City |
| WELLSBORO | The Canyon City (Pine Creek Gorge, the Grand Canyon of Pennsylvania) |
| | The Pennsylvania Athens |
| WEST CHESTER | An Alluring Attractive Suburban |

| | |
|---|---|
| WEST CHESTER (Cont'd) | Municipality |
| | The Athens of Pennsylvania |
| | The Heart of Historic America |
| | The Shopping Center of Chester County |
| WILKES-BARRE | The Black Diamond City (coal) |
| | The Diamond City |
| | The Heart of the Valley That Warms a Nation (Wyoming Valley) |
| WILKINSBURG | The City of Churches |
| WILLIAMSPORT | The Birthplace and Home of Little League Baseball |
| | The Lumber City |
| | The Queen City |
| | The Sawdust City of America (sawmills in the 1900's) |
| | The Scenic Capital of Central Pennsylvania (on the west branch of the Susquehanna River) |
| YORK | The Castle City |
| | The City of Diversified Industry and Civic Achievement |
| | The Community of Craftsmen |
| | The Distribution Point, U. S. A. |
| | The First Capital of the United States |
| | The Plough-Share City |
| | The White Rose City (refers to symbol of York in struggle against Lancaster in the struggle (1455-1471) for possession of the English throne) |

## RHODE ISLAND

| | |
|---|---|
| BRISTOL | The City where Things Are Shipshape and Bristol Fast |
| CENTRAL FALLS | The Twin Cities (with Pawtucket, R. I.) |
| CUMBERLAND | The Mineral Pocket of New England (iron, copper and other minerals have been found within its borders) |
| EAST GREENWICH | The Heart of Rhode Island |
| JAMESTOWN | A Safe Place for Children |

| | |
|---|---|
| JAMESTOWN (Cont'd) | The City where the Breezes Blow (on Conanicut Island) |
| JOHNSTON | The Friendly City |
| | The Friendly Town |
| LINCOLN | Historic and Scenic Lincoln |
| MIDDLETOWN | The Woods (on Aquidneck Island between Newport and Portsmouth) |
| NEW SHOREHAM | America's Bermuda (on Block Island) |
| | The Bermuda of the North |
| | The Fisherman's Paradise of the North Atlantic |
| NEWPORT | America's City of History |
| | America's First Resort (in the 1720's a famous vacation resort of Carolina and West Indies planters and merchants) |
| | America's First Vacationland |
| | America's Oldest Summer Resort |
| | America's Society Capital |
| | Rhode Island's Most Historic Town |
| | The Capital of Vacation Land |
| | The City By the Sea |
| | The City of Contrasts |
| | The Historic Showplace of America |
| | The Naval Center |
| | The Queen of the Resorts |
| | The Queen of Summer Resorts |
| | The Queen of World Resorts |
| | The Summer Capital of Society |
| | The Summer Resort |
| | The Yachting Capital of the World |
| NORTH KINGSTOWN | The Home of the Atlantic Sea Bees |
| PAWTUCKET | The Birthplace of America's Cotton Industry |
| | The Birthplace of the American Cotton Industry (Samuel Slater established his mill in 1790) |
| | The Cradle of the American Textile Industry |
| | The Heart of the Blackstone Valley |

| | |
|---|---|
| PAWTUCKET (Cont'd) | The Twin Cities (with Central Falls, R. I. ) |
| PORTSMOUTH | The Home for Your Business |
| | The Home for Your Family |
| | The Home of the Portsmouth Compact |
| | The Vacation Center |
| PROVIDENCE | America in Miniature |
| | The Bee-hive of Industry |
| | The Big Money Center You Never Heard Much About |
| | The Capital City (1960 population 207, 498) |
| | The Center of U. S. Jewelry Production |
| | The Cradle of American Independence |
| | The Cultural and Economic Center of Southeastern New England |
| | The First City of America's First Vacationland |
| | The Gateway of Southern New England |
| | The Modern City with a Proud Heritage |
| | The Perry Davis' Pain Killer City |
| | The Roger Williams City (founded in 1636 by Roger Williams) |
| | The Southern Gateway of New England |
| WICKFORD | The Art Center of Rhode Island |
| | The Venice of America (on Narragansett Bay) |

## SOUTH CAROLINA

| | |
|---|---|
| ABBEVILLE | The Cradle and the Grave of the Confederacy (secession movement originated Nov. 22, 1860, last cabinet meeting of President Jefferson Davis May 2, 1865) |
| AIKEN | One of the Most Fashionable Winter Resorts of the South |

| | |
|---|---|
| AIKEN (Cont'd) | One of the Most Favorable Winter Resorts of the South |
| | The City in the Land of the Pines |
| | The Polo Capital of the South |
| | The Sports Center of the South (steeplechase and horse show annual events) |
| ALLENDALE | The Tourist Mecca of the South (numerous tourist accomodations) |
| ANDERSON | A Place to Live, a Place to Work |
| BATESBURG | The Only Twin-Cities in South Carolina (with Leesville, S. C.) |
| BEAUFORT | The Capital of the Sea Islands |
| | The City in the Heart of the Coastal Sea Islands |
| | The Gateway to the Carolina Sea Islands |
| | The Home of Parris Island (U. S. Marine Corps East Coast Recruit Depot) |
| | The Nation's Most Historic Area |
| | The Newport of the South |
| CHARLESTON | America's Most Historic City |
| | The Air Capital of the Carolinas |
| | The Capital of the Carolinas |
| | The Capital of the Coastal Empire of South Carolina |
| | The Capital of the Plantations |
| | The City by the Sea |
| | The City of Churches |
| | The City of History and Romance |
| | The City of Secession (first ordinance of secession, 1860) |
| | The Cradle of Secession |
| | The Earthquake City |
| | The Historic Seaport City |
| | The Holy City |
| | The Palmetto City |
| | The Plumb Line Port to Panama |
| | The Queen City of the Sea |
| | The Queen City of the South |
| CHERAW | The Prettiest Town in Dixie |
| COLUMBIA | South Carolina's Capital City |
| | The Capital City (1960 population 97,433) |

COLUMBIA (Cont'd)        The Gateway to the South
                         The Golden Rule City
CONWAY                   The City By the Waccamaw
                         The Gateway to the Grand Strand
DILLON                   The Gateway to the Palmetto
                           State
ELLENTON                 The H-Bomb's Home Town
FLORENCE                 The Home of South Carolina's
                           Little Arlington (veterans of
                           five wars buried in the na-
                           tional cemetery established in
                           1868)
                         The Magic City
GAFFNEY                  The Hub of the Southeast
GREENVILLE               The Textile Center of the World
                           (textile finishing and garment
                           production)
GREENWOOD                The Widest Street in the World
HARTSVILLE               The City of Lovely Gardens
LATTA                    The Gateway to the Palmetto
                           State
LEESVILLE                The Only Twin-Cities in South
                           Carolina (with Batesburg, S. C.)
MANNING                  The Prettiest Small Town Be-
                           tween New York and Miami
                         The Prettiest (Small) Town Be-
                           tween New York and Maine
MULLINS                  The Tobacco Capital of South
                           Carolina
NEWBERRY                 The City of Friendly Folks
SPARTANBURG              The Crossroads of the New South
                         The Hub City of the Southeast
                         The South's Largest Producer of
                           Cotton Cloth
SUMMERTON                The Home of the World's Only
                           Landlocked Striped Rock Bass
SUMMERVILLE              The Flower Town in the Pines
SUMTER                   The Gamecock City (named for
                           General Thomas Sumter "the
                           gamecock of the Revolution")

### SOUTH DAKOTA

ABERDEEN                 A Good Place to Live
                         The Convention Hub of the Da-
                           kotas
                         The Hub City (in the James River

ABERDEEN (Cont'd)

BELLE FOURCHE

BROOKINGS

CANTON

CUSTER CITY

DEADWOOD

EDGEMONT

HOT SPRINGS

HOWARD

HURON

Valley)
The Hub City of the Dakotas (four
railroads in the area resemble
the spokes of a wheel)
The Home of the Famed Black
Hills Round-Up
The Northern Gateway to the
Black Hills
The Home City
The Home of South Dakota State
College
The Gateway to the Newton Hills
State Park
The Town where the Action Is
The Town with a Gunsmoke Fla-
vor
The Historic City of the Black
Hills (gold discoveries about
1876)
The Twin Cities of the Northern
Black Hills of South Dakota
The Uranium Center of South
Dakota (uranium and vanadium
extraction mills)
The City in a Valley where Re-
cuperation, Rehabilitation,
Rest and Relaxation with Rec-
reation and Scenic Beauty
Abound
The City of Healing Waters (min-
eral springs)
The Southern Gateway to the
Black Hills
The Pheasant Paradise of Amer-
ica
The Center of the World's Larg-
est Irrigation Power Naviga-
tion Flood Control Project
The Central City of South Dakota
The City with Future Unlimited
The Convention Headquarters for
the Dakotas
The Fair City (site of the South
Dakota State Fair)
The Natural City (geographically
nearest both the center of
population of the entire state

HURON (Cont'd)                    and population center of that
                                  portion of the state lying east
                                  of the Missouri River)
                                  The Pheasant Capital of the
                                  World
KADOKA                            The Gateway to the Badlands
                                  The Gateway to the Badlands
                                  and Pine Ridge Indian Reser-
                                  vation
KEYSTONE                          The Home of the World-Famous
                                  Mount Rushmore National
                                  Memorial
LAKE ANDES                        The Fish City (site of state fish
                                  hatchery)
LEAD                              Over a Mile High, a Mile Long,
                                  a Mile Wide and a Mile Deep
                                  The Mile High City
                                  The Twin Cities of the Northern
                                  Black Hills of South Dakota
MADISON                           The City That Says "Welcome
                                  Neighbor"
                                  The Land of Longtails
                                  The Water City (Lake Madison
                                  and Lake Herman)
MARTIN                            The Metropolis of the Pine Ridge
                                  Reservation Country
MILBANK                           The Granite City (Milbank granite
                                  quarries)
MITCHELL                          A Pleasant Place to Visit
                                  A Wonderful Place to Live
                                  South Dakota's City of Opportun-
                                  ity
                                  South Dakota's Opportunity City
                                  The Educational Centre
                                  The Home of the World's Only
                                  Corn Palace
                                  The Marketing and Shopping Cen-
                                  ter
                                  The Medical Center
                                  The Recreational Center
MOBRIDGE                          The Northern Pike Capital of
                                  the World
PIERRE                            A Real Western City
                                  The Capital City (1960 population
                                  10, 088)
                                  The Center of Commerce
                                  The Center of Great Wealth

| | |
|---|---|
| PIERRE (Cont'd) | The Center of the Sunshine State |
| | The City in the Center of Hunting Lands |
| | The City in the Heart of Western Ranch Land |
| | The Coming City of the Great North West |
| | The Future Great City |
| | The Gateway to the Black Hills |
| | The Home of Friendly People |
| | The Home of the Giant Oahe Dam |
| | The Metropolis of the Northwest |
| | The Railroad Center |
| | The Railroad Town |
| | The Site of the Oahe Dam |
| RAPID CITY | The Denver of South Dakota |
| | The Eastern Gateway to the Black Hills |
| | The Eastern Gateway to the Mountainous Black Hills where East Meets West and the Friendly Hospitality |
| | The Fastest Growing City in the Upper Midwest |
| | The Gate City |
| | The Gateway City of the Hills |
| | The Gateway to the Black Hills |
| REDFIELD | The Birthplace of South Dakota's Pheasant Hunting |
| SIOUX FALLS | The Crossroads of the Nation |
| | The Gateway to the Dakotas |
| | The Gateway to the West |
| | The Growing City |
| | The Pheasant Capital of the World |
| | The Progressive City |
| | The Progressive Gateway City to the Dakotas |
| | The Queen City |
| SPEARFISH | Home of the World-Famous Black Hills Passion Play |
| | The Queen City |
| | The Queen City of the Hills (the Black Hills) |
| SPENCER | The Granite City |
| STURGIS | The Key City of the Black Hills |
| VERMILLION | The Home of the University of |

| VERMILLION (Cont'd) | South Dakota |
| | The University City (University of South Dakota) |
| WALL | The Gateway to the Badlands National Park |
| | The Northern Gateway to the Badlands National Monument |
| WATERTOWN | South Dakota's Newest Convention City |
| | The Lake City (on Lake Kampeska) |
| WEBSTER | The Gateway to Coteau Lake Region |
| | The Gateway to the Lake Region |
| | The Petunia Capital of the World |
| WINNER | The Gateway to the Black Hills |
| YANKTON | The City where Your Dream Vacation Can Become a Reality |
| | The Gateway to South Dakota's Vacation Wonderland |
| | The Mother City |
| | The Mother City of the Dakotas (oldest city in Dakota territory, territorial capital 1861) |
| | The Port of Entry to the Missouri Great Lakes |
| | The Recreation Paradise on Beautiful Lewis and Clark Lake |

## TENNESSEE

| ALCOA | The Twin Cities (with Maryville, Tenn. ) |
| ATHENS | The City where Business and Industry Thrive and People Enjoy a Wide Variety of Year Around Recreation |
| | The Progressive City |
| BRISTOL | The City in the Heart of Eastern America (see also Virginia) |
| | The Outdoorman's Paradise |
| | The Shopping Center of the Appalachians (see also Virginia) |
| | The Tri-Cities (with Johnson City and Kingsport, Tenn. ) |
| | Twin Cities (with Bristol, Va. ) |
| CHATTANOOGA | One of America's Most Interest- |

| | |
|---|---|
| CHATTANOOGA (Cont'd) | ing Cities |
| | The Dynamo of Dixie |
| | The Gate City |
| | The Mountain City |
| | The Scenic Center of the South |
| CLARKSVILLE | One of the Fastest Developing Areas in the Nation |
| CLEVELAND | A Good Place to Aim For |
| COPPERHILL | The Painters' Paradise |
| DYERSBURG | The City Thriving From the Fertile Banks of Ole Man River |
| ERWIN | The Gateway to the Smoky Mountains |
| GATLINBURG | The Convention Center of the Great Smokies |
| | The Convention City of the Great Smokies |
| | The Fastest Growing Mountain Resort |
| | The Gateway Resort Town of Your Smokies |
| | The Gateway to the Great Smokies (the Great Smoky Mountains National Park) |
| | The Gateway to the Smokies |
| | The Handicraft Capital of the United States |
| | The Host Resort to the Nation |
| GLEASON | Taterville |
| | The Tater Town |
| GREENVILLE | One of the Country's Leading Burley Markets |
| JACKSON | The Home of Casey Jones |
| JOHNSON CITY | The Gateway to the Smokies |
| | The Tri-Cities (with Bristol and Kingsport, Tenn. ) |
| KINGSPORT | The City of Diversified Industry (planned 1916) |
| | The Tri-Cities (with Bristol and Johnson City, Tenn. ) |
| KNOXVILLE | The City of the Great Smokies |
| | The Gateway to the Great Smoky Mountains National Park |
| | The Gateway to the Smokies |
| | The Marble City |
| | The Metropolis of East Tennessee |

| | |
|---|---|
| KNOXVILLE (Cont'd) | The Queen City of the Mountains |
| MARYVILLE | The Twin Cities (with Alcoa, Tenn.) |
| MEMPHIS | Babylon on the Bluff |
| | Big Shelby |
| | Crumptown |
| | Homicide Headquarters |
| | Queen of the American Nile |
| | Sodom of the South |
| | The Bluff City |
| | The City at the Crossroads of the South |
| | The City Beautiful |
| | The City of Hospitality |
| | The City of Opportunity |
| | The City of Tradition |
| | The Commercial Metropolis of West Tennessee |
| | The Convention City in the Heart of the South |
| | The Cotton Center |
| | The Crossroads of the Mid-South |
| | The First City |
| | The Gateway to the South |
| | The Innkeeper's City |
| | The Murder Capital of America |
| | The Nation's Cleanest City |
| | The Place of Good Abode |
| | The Progressive City |
| | The Tri-State Capital (Arkansas-Tennessee-Mississippi) |
| | The World's Largest Hardwood Lumber Market |
| | The World's Largest Spot Cotton Market |
| MORRISTOWN | The City Always Expanding |
| | The City Rich in History |
| | The Cleanest City in the United States |
| | The Home of the Tennessee Valley Industrial District |
| | The Lakeway to the Smokies |
| | The Vacation Wonderland |
| NASHVILLE | Music City, U.S.A. (origination point of Grand Old Opry and other shows) |
| | Tennessee's Beauty Spot |

| | |
|---|---|
| NASHVILLE (Cont'd) | The Athens of the South (Nashville contains a replica of the Parthenon) |
| | The Capital City (1960 population 170, 874) |
| | The Capital City of Industrial Progress |
| | The Capital City of Tennessee |
| | The City Beautiful |
| | The City of Diversified Interests |
| | The City of Opportunity |
| | The City of Rocks |
| | The Country Music Capital of the World |
| | The Dimple of the Universe |
| | The Gateway of the South |
| | The Iris City |
| | The Plus City |
| | The Rock City |
| | The Wall Street of the South |
| NEWPORT | The Gateway to the Smokies |
| OAK RIDGE | The Atomic Capital of the World |
| | The Atomic City |
| | The Atomic Energy City (manufacture of atomic bomb) |
| | The City on the Move |
| SAVANNAH | The Home of the National Catfish Derby |
| | The Place where Sportsmen Meet |
| | The World's Finest Catfish Waters |
| SHELBYVILLE | The Walking Horse Capital of the World |
| TULLAHOMA | The Thermopylae of Middle Tennessee (winter headquarters of Gen. Braxton Bragg fell to Union General Rosecrans on July 3, 1863) |

## TEXAS

| | |
|---|---|
| ABILENE | Texas' Only Atlas Missile Sites |
| | The Athens of the West (Hardin-Simmons University, McMurray and Abilene Christian colleges) |
| | The Key City of West Texas |

| | |
|---|---|
| ALICE | The Sweetheart of South Texas |
| ALPINE | The Roof Garden of Texas (altitude 4,484 feet) |
| | The Roof Garden Resort of Texas |
| ALVIN | The Center of the Action in the Tremendous Houston-Gulf Coast |
| | The Crossroads to the Gulf |
| AMARILLO | The Metropolis of an Agricultural Empire |
| | The Metropolis of the Panhandle |
| | The Plains Empire City |
| | The Queen City of the Panhandle |
| ARLINGTON | The City in the Heart of America's Future |
| AUSTIN | The Big Heart of Texas |
| | The Boom Town Without Oil |
| | The Capital City (1960 pop. 186,545) |
| | The City of the Violet Crown (located on violet-crowned hills) |
| | The Friendly City |
| | The Fun-tier Capital of Texas |
| | The Ideal Home City |
| BAY CITY | The Deep South of Texas (on Bay Prairie) |
| BEAUMONT | The Birthplace of the Modern Oil Industry |
| | The City where Great East Texas Meets the Sea |
| | The City where Main Street Meets the World |
| | The Industrial Giant of Far Southwest Texas |
| | The Port City |
| | The Queen of the Neches (on the Sabine-Neches waterway) |
| BENJAMIN | The Big Cattle Country |
| BORGER | The Boomtown |
| | The Industrial Center of the Panhandle |
| BRADY | The Heart of Texas |
| BRENHAM | The Heart of Your Texas Market |
| BROWNSVILLE | The Capital of the Rio Grande Valley |
| | The City where Mexico Meets Uncle Sam (across the river is Matamoras, Mexico) |

| | |
|---|---|
| BROWNSVILLE (Cont'd) | The Metropolis of the Magic Valley |
| CANTON | The Capital of the "Free State" of Van Zandt County |
| | The Home of the Famous "First Monday" Trades Day |
| CARRIZO SPRINGS | The Hub of the Winter Garden (in Dimmit County) |
| CHILDRESS | The City of the Plains (county seat of Childress County) |
| CLEBURNE | The Gateway to Lake "Whitney" |
| CLEVELAND | The Entrance to Sam Houston National Forest |
| | The Gateway to the Lakes |
| CORPUS CHRISTI | Texas's Sparkling City By the Sea |
| | The City where Texas Meets the Sea (on Corpus Christi Bay) |
| | The Fastest Growing City in Texas (1960 population 167,690) |
| | The Gateway to Padre Island |
| | The Jewel on the Gulf of Mexico |
| | The Sparkling City By the Sea |
| | The Sun City |
| CROCKETT | Paradise in the Pines |
| CRYSTAL CITY | The Spinach Capital of the World |
| | The World's Spinach Capital (a statue of Popeye stands in Popeye Park) |
| DALLAS | Athens of the Southwest |
| | Big "D" |
| | The All-American Town |
| | The Bright Spot |
| | The City Deep in the Heart of Texas |
| | The City of Homes |
| | The City of Opportunity |
| | The City of the Hour |
| | The City with a Future |
| | The Electronics Aerospace Center |
| | The Fastest Growing City |
| | The Financial Center of the Southwest |
| | The High Point for Travel Fun |
| | The Metropolis of North Texas |
| | The Metropolis of the Southwest |
| | The Murder Capital of the World |

| | |
|---|---|
| DALLAS (Cont'd) | (so-called after the assassination of President John Fitzgerald Kennedy) |
| | The Southwest's Leading Financial Manufacturing and Distribution Center |
| | The Sports Center of the Southwest |
| DEL RIO | The Queen City of the Rio Grande |
| DENISON | Texas' First Stop |
| | The Gate City (in northeastern Grayson County) |
| | The Home of Denison Dam |
| | The Home of Eisenhower's Birthplace |
| | The Home of Eisenhower's Birth-Place and Denison Dam-Lake Texoma |
| DENTON | The City Half a World from the "Hubbub" |
| | The City Half an Hour from the Hub |
| | The City on the Move |
| | The Fun Place |
| DUNCAN | The Oil Well Cementing Capital of the World |
| EDGEWOOD | The Center of the Rich Gas and Sulphur Fields |
| EL PASO | The City in the Southwest Sun Country |
| | The Crossroads City |
| | The Crossroads of America |
| | The Crossroads of the Americas |
| | The Exciting International City |
| | The Gateway to Mexico |
| | The Host City of the Sunland Empire |
| | The Hub of the International Southwest |
| | The International City |
| | The Largest City in the Most Favored Climate Area in America |
| FORT WORTH | The Arsenal of Democracy |
| | The Chicago of the Southwest |
| | The City of Beautiful Heights |
| | The City of Delight |

| | |
|---|---|
| FORT WORTH (Cont'd) | The City of Lakes |
| | The City of Western Charm and Hospitality |
| | The City where the West Begins |
| | The City Worth Looking Into |
| | The Cow Town (largest livestock marketing and processing center south of Kansas City) |
| | The Fort Town |
| | The Friendly City |
| | The Friendly City of the Southwest |
| | The Fun Spot of the Southwest |
| | The Gateway to the West |
| | The Gateway to West Texas |
| | The Hub of Banking and Insurance Interests |
| | The Lake City |
| | The Medical Center (17 hospitals and 85 private clinics) |
| | The Panther City |
| | The Queen City of the Plains |
| | The Queen City of the Prairies |
| | The Second Largest Aircraft Production Center in the Country |
| | The Stage Coach Town |
| | The World's Greatest Storehouse of Raw Material |
| GALVESTON | America's Port of Quickest Dispatch |
| | The Oldest Port in the West Gulf |
| | The Oleander City |
| | The Oleander City by the Sea |
| | The Oleander City of Texas |
| | The Port and Playground of the Southwest (on Gulf of Mexico) |
| | The Port of the Southwest |
| | The Queen City |
| | The Seaport of the West |
| | The Space Port USA |
| | The Treasure Island of the Southwest |
| GARLAND | The Wonderful Place to Live and Work |
| GLADEWATER | The City in the Heart of the East |

| | |
|---|---|
| GLADEWATER (Cont'd) | Texas Oil Fields |
| GONZALES | A Great Place to Live |
| | The City where the Fight for Texas Liberty Began |
| | The Lexington of Texas |
| | The Mecca for History Lovers |
| | The Opportunity for History |
| | The Playground for Vacationers |
| GRAND PRAIRIE | The Center of the Aircraft Industry |
| HARLINGEN | The Growing City of the Lower Rio Grande Valley of Texas |
| | The Key City in the Lower Rio Grande Valley |
| | The Retirement Center |
| HENDERSON | The Crape Myrtle City |
| HEREFORD | The City Without a Toothache (low dental decay rate) |
| HILLTOP LAKES | America's Most Complete Resort |
| HOUSTON | America's Growingest City |
| | Land of the Big Rich |
| | Nature's Gift to Texas |
| | Southwest's Foremost Educational Center |
| | Space City, U. S. A. |
| | Space Headquarters, U. S. A. |
| | The Bayou City |
| | The Booming Oil Rich City |
| | The City of Gracious Living |
| | The City of Magnolias |
| | The City That Built Its Seaport |
| | The Command Post for the Nation's Manned Space Exploration |
| | The Cultural Center of the Southwest |
| | The Fashion Capital of the Nation |
| | The Fastest Growing of the Nation's Major Cities |
| | The First City in Texas |
| | The First Cotton Port |
| | The Headquarters of the International Oil Tool Trade |
| | The Home of America's Greatest Petrochemical Industry Complex |
| | The Home of Astronauts |

| | |
|---|---|
| HOUSTON (Cont'd) | The Land of the Big Inch (oil pipe line) |
| | The Land of the Big Rich |
| | The Largest City in the South |
| | The Largest City in the Southwest |
| | The Leading Commercial Financial and Distribution Center |
| | The Leading Industrial City of the Southwest |
| | The Leading Spot Cotton Market |
| | The Magnolia City |
| | The Metropolis of the West |
| | The Miracle City |
| | The Murder Capital of the World |
| | The Nation's Most Exciting New Convention Center |
| | The Natural Gas Pipeline Capital of the Nation |
| | The Oil Center of the World |
| | The Petroleum World Center |
| | The Space Center |
| | The World's Heart Transplant Capital |
| | The World's Petroleum Capital |
| HUGHES SPRINGS | The Home of the East Texas Peach Festival |
| HURST | The Strategic Geographical Location for Industry |
| HUNTSVILLE | The Mount Vernon of Texas (last home and burial place of Sam Houston) |
| JACKSONVILLE | The Tourist Mecca of East Texas |
| JASPER | The Gateway to East Texas' Enchanting Vacationland |
| JEFFERSON | The Gateway to Texas |
| | The Living Page From Texas History |
| | The Williamsburg of Texas |
| JOHNSON CITY | The Home Town of Lyndon B. Johnson |
| | The Peach Center of Texas |
| JUNCTION | The Yosemite of Texas |
| KERRVILLE | The City in the Heart 'o the Hills |
| KILEEN | The Gateway to Ft. Hood |
| LAREDO | The Gate City (on the Rio Grande River which separates it from Nuevo Laredo, Texas) |

| | |
|---|---|
| LAREDO (Cont'd) | The Gateway City |
| | The Gateway to Mexico |
| LIBERTY | The Hub of the Industrial Gulf Coast |
| LONE STAR | The City of Youth, Industry, Recreation |
| | The City to Grow With |
| LUBBOCK | Texas' Largest Isolated Market |
| | The Cottonseed Oil Capital of the World |
| | The Home of Texas Tech (Texas Technological College) |
| | The Hub City of the South Plains |
| | The Hub of Agriculture |
| | The Hub of Beauty |
| | The Hub of Civic Pride |
| | The Hub of Education |
| | The Hub of Industry and Oil |
| | The Hub of Livestock Processing |
| | The Hub of the Plains (county seat of Lubbock County) |
| | The Industrial, Agricultural and Educational Center of the South Plains of Texas |
| MC ALLEN | The City of Palms |
| MC KINNEY | The Home of Prosperous Agriculture Business and Industry |
| MABANK | The Friendliest Town on the Lake |
| MARLIN | The Bluebonnet Capital |
| | The Southwest's Greatest Health Resort |
| MARSHALL | The Golden Gateway to the Great Gulf Southwest |
| | The Home of Lady Bird Johnson |
| | The Industrial Rocket Center |
| | The Oil, Gas, Steel, Chemical, Clay, Lumber Center |
| | The Recreation and Industrial Center of East Texas |
| MIDLAND | The City of Fine Homes |
| | The Financial Center |
| | The Headquarters City of the Permian Basin |
| | The Oil Center |
| | The Recreation Center |
| | The Transportation Center |
| MINEOLA | The Gateway to the Pines |

| MINEOLA (Cont'd) | The Watermelon Center |
| MISSION | The Home of the Texas Grapefruit (Ruby Red) |
| NACOGDOCHES | The City where History and Progress Join Hands |
| | The Historic Center of East Texas |
| ODESSA | A City where Growth Has Become a Habit |
| | America's Newest Industrial Frontier |
| | The City of Dreams |
| | The New Industrial Frontier of the Southwest |
| | The Oil City of the Southwest (Penn field opened 1929, Crowden field 1930) |
| ORANGE | The City where Water Means Pleasure, Progress and Prosperity |
| | The Gateway to Texas and the Astrodome |
| | The Water Wonderland |
| PALACIOS | The Encampment City |
| PALESTINE | The Home of Texas Dogwood Trails |
| | The Homesteader's Paradise (in the center of Anderson County) |
| PAMPA | The City at the Top O' Texas |
| | The City where Wheat Grows and Oil Flows |
| | The Friendly City |
| PANNA MARIA | The Polish City in Texas (established 1854 by Catholic Poles) |
| PARIS | The Industrial Center of the Red River Valley |
| PASADENA | The Hub of the Fabulous Golden Gulf Coast |
| | The Industrial Center of the South |
| PECOS | The World's First Rodeo |
| PERRYTON | The Oil and Gas Center of the Great Anadarko Basin |
| | The Wheat Heart of the Nation |
| PHARR | The City of Palms |
| | The Industrial Frontier of the Magic Lower Rio Grande Valley of Texas |

| | |
|---|---|
| PITTSBURG | The Home of East Texas' Peach Festival |
| PLANO | The Manufacturing Research and Development Center of the Southwest |
| PORT ARTHUR | The City of Homes |
| POTEET | The Strawberry Capital of Texas |
| RANGER | The City of Flowing Gold (oil wells) |
| RICHARDSON | The Electronic City of the Southwest |
| ROBY | The Best in the West |
| | The Good Home Town |
| SAN ANGELO | The City of Angels |
| SAN ANTONIO | The Alamo City (March 6, 1837 Alamo siege climaxed) |
| | The Citadel of History |
| | The City in the Sun |
| | The City of Contrast and Romance |
| | The City of Contrasts |
| | The City of Flaming Adventure |
| | The City of Missions |
| | The City where Life Is Different |
| | The Cradle of Texas Liberty |
| | The Free State of Bexar |
| | The Gateway to Mexico |
| | The Gateway to Old Mexico |
| | The Hemis Fair City |
| | The Mission City |
| | The Mother City of an Empire |
| | The Old Garrison |
| | The Venice of the Prairie (canals winding through the streets) |
| | The Winter Playground of America |
| | St. Anthony's Town (mission authorized 1716) |
| | Unsainted Anthony |
| | When You See San Antonio, You See Texas |
| SAN AUGUSTINE | The Cradle of Texas |
| SHAMROCK | The Greenest Spot in the Golden Spread of Texas |
| STONEWALL | The Home of LBJ (President Lyndon Baines Johnson) |
| | The Peach Capital of Texas |
| SURFSIDE | The Gateway to Gulf of Mexico |

| | |
|---|---|
| SWEETWATER | The Last of the Western Frontier |
| | The West Texas Industrial City |
| TEMPLE | The Population Center of Texas |
| TRINITY | The City with Natural Beauty the Year 'Round |
| | The Headquarters of Lake Livingston |
| TEXARKANA | The Twin Cities (with Texarkana, Ark.; twin cities on the Arkansas-Texas border) |
| TYLER | The Floral Metropolis of East Texas |
| | The Rose Capital |
| | The Rose Capital of America |
| | The Rose Capital of the World |
| | The Wonderful Place to Live |
| UVALDE | The City Beautiful |
| | The Honey Capital of the United States |
| | The Honey Capital of the World |
| | The Town of Many Opportunities |
| VERNON | The City Beautiful |
| VICTORIA | The City with a Future For All Industry |
| WACO | The Athens of Texas (home of Baylor University) |
| | The City on the Grow |
| | The Heart of the Texas Funtier |
| | The Hub of Texas |
| | The Palace of King Cotton |
| | The Queen of the Brazos (on the Brazos River) |
| | The Target of Opportunity |
| WEATHERFORD | The Watermelon Capital of the World |
| WEST COLUMBIA | The Birthplace of a Republic (the first congress of the Republic of Texas assembled on October 3, 1836 at Columbia) |
| | The First Capital of the Republic of Texas |
| YOAKUM | A City of Homes, Schools and Churches |
| | The City By Accident |
| | The Hub City of South Texas (in western Lavaca County) |

YOAKUM  (Cont'd)          The Tomato Capital of South Cen-
                          tral Texas

                          UTAH

BRIGHAM CITY             The City of Peaches (peach pro-
                          duction)
                          The Gateway to the Bear River
                          Migratory Bird Refuge
CORINNE                  The Burg on the Bear (Bear
                          River)
                          The Gentile City
KANAB                    The Little Hollywood (a favorite
                          movie location)
MOAB                     The Uranium Capital of the
                          World (discovery by Charles
                          Steen in 1952)
OGDEN                    The City of Diversified Industry
                          The City where Business and
                          Happy Living Flourish
                          The Transportation Hub of the
                          West
                          The West's Fastest-Growing
                          Transportation and Industrial
                          Center
PRICE                    The Gateway to the Canyonlands
                          and Highlands of Southeastern
                          Utah
                          The Heart of a Hunter's Paradise
PROVO                    The Center of Scenic Utah
                          The City of Beauty, Progress
                          and Culture
                          The Gateway to Vacation-Land
                          The Host to the West's Scenic
                          Wonder-Ways
                          The Pioneer Mormon City
SALT LAKE CITY           Deseret
                          The Capital City (1960 population
                          189, 454)
                          The Center of Scenic America
                          The City by the Great Salt Lake
                          The City of Opportunities
                          The City of the Saints (home of
                          the Church of Jesus Christ
                          of Latter-Day Saints)
                          The Crossroads of the West
                          The Great Salt Lake City

SALT LAKE CITY (Cont'd)    The Mormon City
                           The Mormon's Mecca
                           The New Jerusalem
                           The Utah Zion
                           Zion
SALTAIR                    The Coney Island of the West

## VERMONT

BARRE                      The Friendly Place to Live and
                             Work
                           The Granite Center of the World
                             (granite quarries)
BENNINGTON                 The Southwestern Gateway to the
                             Historic Four Season Vacation-
                             land
                           The Williamsburg of the North
                           Vermont's Most Historic Town
                             (British expedition defeated
                             August 16, 1777 by General
                             John Stark)
BRATTLEBORO                The City where Vermont Begins
                             (on the Connecticut River)
                           The Organ Town (organ produc-
                             tion)
                           The Southeastern Gateway to Ver-
                             mont
BURLINGTON                 The City of Homes and Parks
                           The Land of Amazing Variety
                             and Contrasts
                           The Queen City
                           The Queen City of Vermont
                           The Year 'Round Vacationland
HARDWICK                   The Granite Center
KILLINGTON                 The Four Mountains of Fun
LUDLOW                     Ludlow Is a Snow Town, Ludlow
                             Is a Fun Town, Ludlow Has
                             Everything
MANCHESTER                 The Four Season Resort and
                             Cultural Center
                           This Pleasant Land Among the
                             Mountains
MONTPELIER                 The Capital City (1960 population
                             8,782)
                           The Green Mountain City
NEWPORT                    The City in the Northeast King-
                             dom

| | |
|---|---|
| NEWPORT (Cont'd) | The Four-Season Community |
| | The Holiday Harbor of Vermont |
| PLYMOUTH | The Birthplace of Calvin Coolidge (July 4, 1872) |
| PROCTOR | The Marble Capital of the United States (home of Vermont Marble Company) |
| RUTLAND | The Center of the Marble Industry |
| | The Community on the Move |
| | The Heart of the Green Mountains |
| | The Marble City (large marble quarries) |
| | The Year Around Playground |
| ST. ALBANS | The Railroad City (yards and shops of the Central Vermont Railway) |
| ST. JOHNSBURY | The Maple Center of the World |
| | The Maple Sugar Center of the World |
| | The Ski Crossroads of the World |
| SPRINGFIELD | The Black River Valley Area of Vermont |
| | The Black River Valley of Vermont |
| | The Cradle of Industry |
| | The Four-Season Area |
| | The Gateway to Picturesque Precision Valley |
| | The Industrial Center of Vermont |
| | The Springboard Into the Four Season Area |
| STOWE | The All Year Round Vacationland |
| | The Cool and Sunny Paradise |
| | The Gateway to Smuggler's Notch (between Mt. Mansfield and the Sterling Mountains) |
| | The Ski Capital of the East (a single and two double chair lifts, three T-bar lifts, etc. ) |
| | The Skier's Heaven |
| | The Snow Paradise |
| WAITSFIELD | The Peaceful Valley in the Heart of the Green Mountains |
| WATERBURY | The City Located in the Heart and Center of Vermont |
| | The Gateway to the Mount Mans- |

| | |
|---|---|
| WATERBURY (Cont'd) | field Area |
| | The Recreation Crossroads of Vermont |
| | Vermont's Recreation Crossroads |
| WELLS RIVER | The Crossroads of Northern New England |
| WINDSOR | The Birthplace of the Republic of Vermont |

## VIRGINIA

| | |
|---|---|
| ALBERTA | The Land of the Pines |
| ALEXANDRIA | The Heart of the Nation's Heritage |
| | The Historic Home Town of General George Washington |
| | The Home Town of George Washington |
| APPALACHIA | The Center of the Coal Fields |
| ARLINGTON | The Bedroom of Washington (residential area of many persons working in the nation's capital) |
| | The City of the Slain (Arlington National Cemetery) |
| | The Resting Place of the Unknown American Hero (in Arlington National Cemetery) |
| ASHLAND | The Slash Town (1848 health resort Slash Cottage) |
| BEDFORD | The Mineral Springs City (limestone, sulphur, iron and sweet water springs) (see also Pa.) |
| BERRYVILLE | Battletown (name applied to local tavern where fights were frequent) |
| BLACKSBURG | A Good Place to Live and Work |
| | The City in Pace with the Space Age |
| | The City where Industry and Education Meet (home of Virginia Polytechnic Institute) |
| | The Community that Builds Health Minds and Bodies |
| | The Space Age Community |
| BLACKSTONE | The Heart of the Old Dominion |
| | The Lunchstone |

BLUEFIELD                    Nature's Air-Conditioned City
                             (adjoining Bluefield, W. Va.)
                             Twin Cities (with Bluefield, W. Va.)
BOYKINS                      Tarrara City
BRISTOL                      The City in the Heart of Eastern
                             America (see also Tennessee)
                             The Shopping Center of the Ap-
                             palachians (see also Tennessee)
                             Twin Cities (with Bristol, Tenn.)
CHARLOTTESVILLE              Jefferson's Country (in Albemarle
                             County)
                             The Heart of Historic Virginia
                             The Home of the Albemarle Pip-
                             pin (extensive peach and apple
                             orchards)
CHASE CITY                   Christiansville
CHINCOTEAGUE                 The Sportsman's Paradise (on the
                             eastern shore of Chincoteague
                             Bay)
CHRISTIANSBURG               The Gateway to the Southwest (on
                             the Blue Ridge Plateau)
CLARKSVILLE                  The Friendliest Town on Earth
                             The Old Mart (tobacco market)
                             Virginia's Vacation Paradise on
                             Beautiful Buggs Island Lake
CLIFTON FORGE                The City That's Scenic, Busy
                             and Friendly
CLINCHPORT                   The Frog Level
COLONIAL BEACH               Las Vegas on the Potomac (river
                             resort on Potomac River)
COLONIAL HEIGHTS             The City Located in the Heart of
                             Virginia's Industry
                             The City on the Highway of Pro-
                             gress
                             The Most Promising Industrial
                             Community of the Future
CULPEPER                     A Beautiful Community in Beauti-
                             ful Virginia
                             A High and Pleasant Situation
                             The Hub of Northern Virginia
DAMASCUS                     The Gateway to Three Local
                             Slogan States: Virginia, Ten-
                             nessee, North Carolina
DANVILLE                     The Bright Leaf Tobacco Market
                             of the World
                             The Capital City of South Side
                             Virginia

DANVILLE (Cont'd)              The Capital City of Southern Vir-
                                  ginia
                               The City of Churches (over 100
                                  sanctuaries of various denomi-
                                  nations)
                               The City on the Dan (Dan River)
                               The Home of the Dan River Mills
                                  (largest single-unit textile
                                  mill in the world)
                               The Home of the World's Largest
                                  Single-Unit Textile Mill
                               The Last Capital of the Confed-
                                  eracy (April 3-10, 1865 occu-
                                  pied by Jefferson Davis and
                                  his cabinet after the evacuation
                                  of Richmond)
                               The World's Best Tobacco Mar-
                                  ket
                               Virginia's Largest Market for
                                  Bright Leaf Tobacco
DRAKES BRANCH                  Ducks' Puddle
DUNGANNON                      Bumgannon
EDINBURG                       The Granary of the Confederacy
FALLS CHURCH                   A Good Place to Work...In and
                                  From
FREDERICKSBURG                 America's Most Historic City
                                  (numerous battles between
                                  1861-1865)
                               George Washington's Boyhood
                                  Home
                               The Boyhood Home of George
                                  Washington
                               The Cockpit of the Civil War
                               The Friendly City
                               The Gateway to Historyland
                               The Land of Washington
FRONT ROYAL                    The City where the Shenandoah
                                  National Park Begins
                               The City where the Skyline Drive
                                  Begins
                               Northern Entrance to the Skyline
                                  Drive, Shenandoah National
                                  Park
GRETNA                         The Junction
HAMILTON                       Harmony
HAMPTON                        Crab Town (oyster and fishing in-
                                  dustry)

HAMPTON (Cont'd)              The Oldest Continuous English
                             Speaking Settlement in America
                             (settled in 1610)
HAMPTON ROADS                The World's Greatest Harbor (the
                             James, Nansemund and Eliza-
                             beth Rivers flow into Ches-
                             apeake Bay)
HARRISONBURG                 The City with the Planned Future
                             The Turkey Capital of the East
                             The Turkey Capital of the Nation
                             The World's Turkey Capital
                             Virginia's Biggest Little City
                             (1960 population 11, 916)
HILLSVILLE                   The Hill Town
HOLLAND                      Holland's Corner
HOPEWELL                     The Chemical Capital of Virginia
                             The Wonder City (on the James
                             River)
                             Virginia's Inland Port
INDEPENDENCE                 Pinhook
JAMESTOWN                    The Birthplace of the Nation
                             (English colony, permanent
                             settlement in 1607)
LEXINGTON                    The Athens of Virginia (home of
                             Washington and Lee University)
                             The Shrine of the South (home of
                             Virginia Military Institute,
                             burial place of Stonewall Jack-
                             son, etc. )
LYNCHBURG                    Lunchburg (humorous)
                             The Center of Old Virginia
                             The City of Charming Houses
                             The City of Friendliness, Culture
                             and Traditions
                             The City of Hills (overlooking the
                             James River)
                             The City of Industry and Oppor-
                             tunity
                             The City where Good Living Is
                             the Custom
                             The Community of Culture and
                             Traditions
                             The Friendly City
                             The Hill City
                             The Industrial, Geographical His-
                             toric and Transportation Center
                             of Virginia

| | |
|---|---|
| LYNCHBURG (Cont'd) | The Modern City |
| | The Progressive Metropolis |
| MANASSAS | The Town Rich in History |
| MARTINSVILLE | The Furniture City (numerous furniture factories) |
| | The Sweatshirt Capital of the World |
| MOUNT VERNON | The Home of Our First President |
| NEW MARKET | The Western Gateway to the Skyline Drive |
| NEWPORT NEWS | The City of Ships and Shipbuilding |
| | The World's Greatest Harbor (James River) |
| NORFOLK | The Capital of the Most Historic Resort Area in America |
| | The City By the Sea |
| | The City that Does Things |
| | The Industrial Vacation and Seafood Shopping Center |
| | Vacationland, U. S. A. |
| PENNINGTON GAP | The Gap (in Cumberland Mountains) |
| PETERSBURG | America's Most Historic City |
| | The City Industrially Sound and Historically Great |
| | The City of Industrial Opportunity |
| | The City with a Past |
| | The Cockade City (Captain Richard Mc Roe and his company of volunteers wore a cockade) |
| | The Cockade of the Union (nickname given by President James Madison---50,000 Confederate troops defended the city for ten months against 113,000 Federal besiegers) |
| | The Crossroads of History |
| PORTSMOUTH | The Hub of Historic Shrines |
| | The Hub of the Scenic Historic Tidewater Region at the Base of Chesapeake Bay |
| | The Industrial Center |
| | The Modern City |
| | The Navy's First City of the Sea (Norfolk Naval Shipyard) |

PULASKI                    The Gem City
RICHMOND                   America's Fastest Growing In-
                             dustrial City
                           An Interesting Past, a Prosper-
                             ous Present, an Unlimited
                             Future
                           Byrd Town (foundation laid in
                             1733 by William Byrd II)
                           One of the World's Largest Man-
                             ufacturers of Cigarettes __
                           The Capital City (1960 population
                             219, 958)
                           The Capital of the Confederacy
                           The Capital of the Old South
                           The City of Monuments
                           The City of Romance and Rebel-
                             lion
                           The City of Seven Hills
                           The Cockade City
                           The Confederate Capital
                           The Gateway to the South
                           The Modern Rome
                           The Monument City
                           The Nine Hills
                           The Queen City of the South
                           The Queen on the James (James
                             River)
                           The Tobacco Capital of the World
ROANOKE                    The Magic City
                           The Magic City of the South
                           The Magic City of Virginia
                           The Shopping Center of Western
                             Virginia
                           The Star City of the South (mam-
                             moth man-made star shining
                             atop Mill Mountain)
RODA                       The Happy Hollow
SINGERS GLEN               The Glen
SMITHFIELD                 The Home of the Smithfield Ham
SOUTH HILL                 The Third Largest Tobacco Mar-
                             ket in Virginia
STAUNTON                   The Birthplace of Woodrow Wilson
                           The Queen City of the Shenandoah
                             Valley
SUFFOLK                    The Fastest Growing Area in
                             Virginia
                           The Home of Planters Peanuts

| | |
|---|---|
| SUFFOLK (Cont'd) | The Peanut City (processing plant of Planters Peanuts) |
| | The World's Largest Peanut Center |
| TOMS BROOK | The Brook |
| VICTORIA | The City in the Heart of Southside Virginia |
| | The Town of Hospitality and Progress |
| VIRGINIA BEACH | America's Historyland Playground |
| | The City where the Pines Meet the Sea |
| | The Fun Shines Brightest in the Summer Time |
| | The Garden Spot for Golf |
| | The Land of Play and Plenty |
| | The Vacationist's Paradise |
| | Virginia's Atlantic City |
| WACHAPREAGUE | The Oldest Sport Fishing Center in Virginia |
| WAYNESBORO | A Wonderful Place to Visit and a Better Place to Live |
| | The City where the Blue Ridge Parkway Joins the Skyline Drive |
| | The Hub of Scenic and Historic Western Virginia |
| WILLIAMSBURG | The Capital of Colonial Virginia |
| | The City that Turned Back Time |
| | The Colonial Capital of Virginia |
| | The Community where the Future May Learn from the Past |
| | The Historic City |
| | The Restored Colonial City (a project supported by John D. Rockefeller, Jr.) |
| | Virginia Colony's Elegant Old Capital |
| WINCHESTER | The Apple Capital |
| | The Apple Capital in the Beautiful Shenandoah Valley |
| | The City in the Beautiful Shenandoah Valley |
| | The City in the Heart of the Shenandoah Valley of Virginia |
| | The City Rich in History with a Wealth of Charm |

WINCHESTER (Cont'd)                 The City where the South Begins
                                    at the Gateway to the Beauti-
                                    ful Shenandoah Valley
                                  The Home of the Apple Blossom
                                    Festival
                                  The Home of the World Famous
                                    Annual Shenandoah Apple Blos-
                                    som Festival
                                  The Northern Gateway to the
                                    Beautiful Shenandoah Valley
                                  The Northern Gateway to the
                                    Shenandoah Valley
WYTHEVILLE                        The Hub of Southwest Virginia
YORKTOWN                          The Waterloo of the Revolution
                                    (October 19, 1781 General
                                    Cornwallis surrendered)

## WASHINGTON

ABERDEEN                          The Plank Island
                                  The Twin Cities (with Hoquiam,
                                    Grays Harbor)
ANACORTES                         The Magic City (on Fidalgo Is-
                                    land)
                                  The Ship Harbor
                                  The Squaw Harbor
AUBURN                            The Slaughter House (named for
                                    Lt. W. A. Slaughter, renamed
                                    Auburn in 1893)
BANGOR                            The Three Spits
BELLINGHAM                        The Tulip City (tulip cultivation)
BREMERTON                         The Home of the Pacific Fleet
                                    (Puget Sound Navy Yard)
                                  The String Town
BUCKLEY                           The City of Good Water (on the
                                    White River)
BURLEY                            The Circle City
CAMAS                             The City of Paper (Crown-Zeller-
                                    bach mills)
CARBONADO                         The Model Mining Community
                                    (ceased operations about 1920)
CARNATION                         The Home of the Contented Cows
                                    (Carnation Milk Products Com-
                                    pany Farms)
                                  The Milk City
CASHMERE                          The Home of Aplets, the Confec-
                                    tion of the Fairies (apple juice

| | |
|---|---|
| CASHMERE (Cont'd) | flavored enriched by walnuts and spices) |
| CENTRALIA | The Hub City (junction of the Chehalis and Skookumchuck Rivers) |
| | The Hub City of Southwestern Washington |
| CHEHALIS | The Friendly City |
| CHELAN | The Deep Water (Lake Chelan, bottom 400 feet below sea level) |
| CHENEY | The Depot Springs |
| CLARKSTON | Jawbone Flats (original name, changed in 1900 to Clarkston) |
| COLBY | The Coal Bay |
| CONCONULLY | The Money Hole (a mountain recess settled in 1886 by prospectors) |
| COULEE CITY | The Engineers' Town (junction point of the railroad and stage lines) |
| COUPEVILLE | The Port of Sea Captains (first of whom was Captain Thomas Coupe who settled in 1852) |
| COYLE | The Fisherman's Harbor |
| DAYTON | The City of Shady Walks and Pleasant Lawns |
| EDMONDS | The Princess City of Puget Sound (between Seattle and Everett) |
| ELLENSBURG | The Robbers' Roost (original name in 1867) |
| | The Rodeo City (rodeo held on Labor Day weekend) |
| ENUMCLAW | The Home of the Evil Spirits |
| EVERETT | The City of Smokestacks |
| | The Lumbering Center |
| FALL CITY | The Falls (on the Snoqualmie River) |
| | The Landing (original name) |
| FERNDALE | The Gem of the Nooksack Valley (on the Nooksack River) |
| FRUITLAND | The Robbers' Roost (early rendezvous for cattle thieves and desperadoes) |
| GRANITE FALLS | The Portage (the Stillaquamish River and the Pilchuck River) |
| HILLYARD | The Horse Plains |

| | |
|---|---|
| HOQUIAM | The Twin Cities (with Aberdeen, the Grays Harbor Cities)<br>The Board Foot (saw mills) |
| INDEX | The Tourist's Paradise (near Snoqualmie National Forest) |
| KAHLOTUS | The Hole-in-the-Ground (Indian word, town on Washtucna Lake) |
| KALAMA | The City where Rail Meets Water (Northern Pacific Railroad at confluence of Columbia and Kalama Rivers)<br>The Town where Rail Meets Water (the Northern Pacific and the Columbia River) |
| KENNEWICK | The Grassy Place (irrigated farmlands)<br>The Tri-Cities (with Richland and Pasco) |
| KITTITAS | The Land of Bread |
| LA CONNER | The Venice of Puget Sound (sloughs and marshes) |
| LATAH | The Hangman Creek |
| LONGVIEW | The City Practical That Vision Built (first planned city in the northwest, dedicated 1923) |
| MANETTE | The String Town |
| MARYSVILLE | The Home of the Strawberry Festival |
| MASON CITY | The All-Electric Community (prefabricated) |
| MAZAMA | Goat Creek |
| MESA | The Table-Land |
| MONROE | Park Place<br>The Model Municipality |
| MONTESANO | Mount Zion |
| MUKILTEO | Good Camping Ground |
| OCOSTA | Ocosta by the Sea (on Grays Harbor) |
| OLYMPIA | The Bear's Place (domicile of the brown bear)<br>The Capital City (1960 population 18,273)<br>The Capital of the Evergreen State |
| ORONDO | The Town Which Held the Key |
| PAHA | The Big Water |
| PALISADES | The Beulah Land |

| | |
|---|---|
| PALOUSE | The Grass Lands |
| PASCO | The Tri-Cities (with Richland and Kennewick) |
| PATAHA | Favorsburg (town site plotted in 1882 by "Vine" Favor) |
| | Waterstown (former name) |
| POMONA | The Roman Goddess of Fruit Trees (whose name was Pomona) |
| PORT ANGELES | Our Lady of the Angels |
| | The City where the Mountains Meet the Sea (between the Olympic range and Strait of Juan de Fuca) |
| PORT GAMBLE | Boston |
| | The Brightness of the Noonday Sun |
| PORT MADISON | The Oleman House |
| PORT TOWNSEND | The Key City (a key city on Port Townsend Bay in the sailing boat era) |
| | The Key City of Puget Sound (on the Olympic Peninsular) |
| | The Port of Entry (on the Olympic Peninsula where the Straight of Juan de Fuca joins Puget Sound) |
| PULLMAN | The Home of State College of Washington |
| | The Three Forks |
| PUYALLUP | The Generous People |
| QUILCENE | The Salt Water People |
| RENTON | The Jet Transport Capital of the World (Boeing plant) |
| RICHLAND | The Town the Atom Built (Hanford Engineer Works) |
| | The Tri-Cities (with Kennewick and Pasco) |
| RUBY | The Babylon of Washington Territory (a lawless wide open town when formed) |
| SEATTLE | The Boating Capital of the World |
| | The Cannery City |
| | The City of Eternal Views (vistas of lakes, mountains and sound waters) |
| | The City of Homes |

| | |
|---|---|
| SEATTLE (Cont'd) | The City of Seven Hills |
| | The Commercial Center in the Pacific Northwest |
| | The Cosmopolitan Seaport |
| | The Evergreen Playground |
| | The Gateway to Alaska |
| | The Gateway to the Orient |
| | The Great Sports Resort Community |
| | The International Melting Pot |
| | The Little Portage (between Puget Sound and Lake Washington) |
| | The Metropolis of the Pacific Northwest |
| | The Most Scenic City on the Continent |
| | The Nation's Most Beautiful City |
| | The Northwest Gateway |
| | The Queen City |
| | The Queen City of the Pacific |
| | The Queen City of the Sound |
| | The Visually Exciting City |
| | The World Port |
| | The World's Greatest Halibut Port |
| SEQUIM | The Smooth Water |
| | The Still Water |
| SHELTON | Christmas Town, U. S. A. (famous for its Christmas tree crop) |
| | The Strong Water |
| SKAMOKAWA | Little Venice (on Skamokawa Creek) |
| | The Smoke on the Water |
| SNOHOMISH | The Hub (at the confluence of the Pilchuck and Snohomish Rivers) |
| SPOKANE | The Center of the Vast Inland Empire |
| | The Friendly City |
| | The Heart of the Inland Empire |
| | The Home of the Mining Barons |
| | The Metropolis of the Inland Empire |
| | The Minneapolis of the West |
| | The Trading Center of the Inland Empire |

| | |
|---|---|
| SPRINGDALE | The Squire City |
| SUNNYSIDE | The Holy City (Christian Co-operative Movement settlement in 1898) |
| TACOMA | The Center of Industry |
| | The City of Destiny |
| | The City of Fine Hotels |
| | The Commencement City |
| | The Evergreen Playground |
| | The Forest Products Capital of America |
| | The Gateway to Mount Ranier |
| | The Lumber Capital |
| | The Lumber Capital of America |
| | The Lumber Capital of the World |
| | The Nearest Metropolitan Center to All Five Gateways of Ranier National Park |
| TOUCHET | The White Stallion (original name designated by Lewis and Clark) |
| TUKWILA | The Land of Hazel Nuts |
| TUMWATER | The Falls (on the Deschutes River) |
| | The New Market |
| | The Waterfalls |
| UNION | Another Clyde City |
| | The Venice of the Pacific |
| UTSALADDY | The Land of Berries |
| VANCOUVER | Columbia City (on the Columbia River) |
| VASHON | The Metropolis of Vashon Island (midway between Seattle and Tacoma) |
| WALLA WALLA | The Cradle of Pacific Northwest History |
| | The Place of Many Waters |
| WATERVILLE | The Jumper's Flats (claim jumping) |
| | The Sour Dough Flats |
| WENATCHEE | The Apple Capital |
| | The Apple Capital of the World |
| | The Gateway to the Valley of Perfect Apples |
| | The Home of Apple Blossom Festival |
| WILBUR | The Goosetown (in 1888 Samuel Wilbur Condit shot a tame gander believing it was a wild goose) |

| | |
|---|---|
| WILLAPA | The Venice of the Northwest (on the Willapa River) |
| WISHRAM | The Food Emporium |
| YAKIMA | The Eastern Gateway to Mt. Ranier National Park |
| | The Fruit Bowl of the Nation |

## WEST VIRGINIA

| | |
|---|---|
| BECKLEY | The Smokeless Coal Capital of the World (center of coal mining and natural gas region) |
| BLUEFIELD | Nature's Air-Conditioned City |
| | The Air Conditioned City (adjoining Bluefield, Va.) |
| | The City where the Mountains Meet the Sky |
| | The Gateway to the Great Coal Fields of Southern West Virginia |
| | The Metropolis of the Southern West Virginia Coal Fields |
| | Twin Cities (with Bluefield, Va.) |
| CHARLESTON | The Capital City (1960 population 85, 796) |
| | The Chemical City (produces calcium chlorine, iodine, etc.) |
| ELKINS | The Vacation Capital of the Appalachian Highlands (on the Tygarts Valley River) |
| HUNTINGTON | The Gateway City (southwestern section of W. Va.) |
| MARTINSBURG | The Chief Industrial City of the Eastern Panhandle |
| MIDDLEWAY | The Wizard's Clip |
| MORGANTOWN | The Home of West Virginia University (founded 1867) |
| MOUNDSVILLE | The City of Industrial Potentialities |
| PARKERSBURG | The City of Wonderful Living with Industrial Prosperity |
| SHEPHERDSTOWN | The Oldest Town in West Virginia (established 1732) |
| SOUTH CHARLESTON | The Chemical Center of the World |
| WELCH | Little New York (closely built congested area) |

| | |
|---|---|
| WHEELING | The Chief City of West Virginia (1960 population 53, 500) (3rd in pop. ) |
| | The City of Beautiful Parks (Oglebay Park, largest in W. Va. ) |
| | The City of Historic Lore (first visitor, Captain de Bienville, 1749) |
| | The City of Magnificent Stores |
| | The City of Thriving Industries |
| | The Nail City |
| | The Trading Center |

## WISCONSIN

| | |
|---|---|
| ANTIGO | The City where Potatoes Are King (potato-growing region) |
| APPLETON | The Crescent City |
| BELOIT | A Metropolitan Community of Opportunity |
| | One of Wisconsin's Fastest Growing Cities |
| CLINTONVILLE | The Home of Four Wheel Drive Trucks |
| COLBY | The Midget City |
| CRIVITZ | The Gateway to the Lakes and Streams of the Thunder Mountain Region (on the Peshtigo River) |
| DELAVAN | The Circus Capital of America in the Nineteenth Century |
| | The Cradle of the American Circus |
| DE PERE | America's Number One Small City (on the Fox River) |
| | The City of Historic Charm |
| | The Home of the Norbertines (St. Norbert College) |
| EAU CLAIRE | The City Blessed in Many Ways |
| | The City of the Green Light |
| | The Friendly Door to Wisconsin's Indianhead Country |
| | The Key City of Central Northwest Wisconsin |
| FOND DU LAC | The Fountain City |
| GREEN BAY | The Home of the Packers (sta- |

GREEN BAY (Cont'd)                    dium and playing field of the
                                      professional football team
                                      known as the Green Bay Pack-
                                      ers)
                                      The Packers Town
                                      The Port of Distinction
                                      Titletown, U. S. A. (because of
                                      Packers, championship foot-
                                      ball team)

HAYWARD                               The Musky Capitol (excellant
                                      musky fishing)

IRON RIVER                            The Blueberry Capital of the Na-
                                      tion

KAUKAUNA                              The Electric City (municipally
                                      owned and operated hydroelec-
                                      tric power and water facilities)
                                      The Friendly City

LA CROSSE                             The Gateway City (on the Missis-
                                      sippi River at the confluence
                                      of the Black and La Crosse
                                      Rivers)

LAKE GENEVA                           The Newport of Chicago Society
                                      (a summer residential colony
                                      which received its impetus in
                                      1871 as a result of the Chi-
                                      cago fire)

MADISON                               The Capital City (1960 population
                                      126, 706)
                                      The City Built on an Isthmus (be-
                                      tween Lakes Monona and Men-
                                      dota)
                                      The City of Beautiful Homes and
                                      Thriving Industry
                                      The City of Parks
                                      The Cultural Center
                                      The Four Lake City
                                      The Four Lakes City (Lakes Men-
                                      dota, Monona, Waubesa and
                                      Kegonsa)
                                      The Home of the University of
                                      Wisconsin
                                      The Ideal Convention and Vaca-
                                      tion City
                                      The Key Shopping and Manufactur-
                                      ing Center
                                      The Lake City
                                      The Most Beautiful Little City in

MADISON (Cont'd)

America (1960 population 126, 706)

The Recreational Center

MANITOWOC

The Clipper City (a shipbuilding center where clipper ships were built from 1860 to 1880)

MARINETTE

The Queen City (named for Queen Marinette of the Menominee indian tribe)

MARSHFIELD

The Crossroads of Wisconsin

The Modern City

MENASHA

The Twin Cities (with Neenah, Wis. )

MERRILL

The City of Parks

The Natural Trading Center

MILWAUKEE

America's Machine Shop

Great for Business, Great for Living and Growing Greater

Milwaukee the Beautiful

The American Munich

The Beer Capital of America (numerous breweries)

The Beer City

The Blonde Beauty of the Lakes

The Brewing Capital of the World (Blatz Brewery, Pabst Brewery, etc. )

The Bright Spot

The City Beautiful

The City of Fountains

The City of Homes

The City where Beer Is Famous

The Cream City (from the color of bricks manufactured there)

The Cream White City of the Unsalted Seas

The Deutsch-Athens (German immigrants)

The Fair White City

The Foam City

The Friendly City

The German Athens (German immigrants)

The Home of the Braves

The Industrial City

The Middlewest Center for Diversified Manufacture

| | |
|---|---|
| MILWAUKEE (Cont'd) | The Railway Metropolis of the West |
| | There's More in Milwaukee |
| | Wisconsin's Beautiful Capitol City |
| MINERAL POINT | The Shake-Rag City (Shake Rag Street where women waved rags and dishcloths to summon miners on an opposite hill to return for dinner) |
| MONROE | America's Swiss Cheese Capital (about 300 factories) |
| | The Swiss Cheese Capital of the United States (numerous factories) |
| NEENAH | The Paper City (numerous paper mills) |
| | The Paper City of the World (numerous paper producing mills) |
| | The Twin Cities (with Menasha, Wis. ) |
| NEW GLARUS | Little Switzerland (numerous Swiss colonist descendants) |
| NEW RICHMOND | The City Beautiful |
| ORFORDVILLE | The Grass Roots of America |
| OSHKOSH | The City of Industry, Recreation, Business |
| | The City of Opportunity |
| | The Heart of the Fox Valley Area |
| | The Sawdust City |
| PARK FALLS | The City in the Center of the Beautiful North Woods |
| | The City in the Heart of the Chequamegon National Forest |
| | The Fun Town (popular recreation area) |
| | The Vacation Wonderland |
| | The Vacationland of Northern Wisconsin |
| PLYMOUTH | The Cheese Capitol of the World |
| PORT WING | The Hub of Lake Superior's Beautiful South Shore Drive |
| PRAIRIE DU CHIEN | America's Wild Life Preserver |
| | The Gateway to the Winneshiek (Winneshiek Bluff) |
| | The Historical City (seen in 1673 by Joliet and Marquette) |

PRENTICE        The Friendly Village (1960 popula-
                tion 427)

RACINE          Kringleville (after the Dane's
                favorite pastry)
                The Belle City
                The Belle City of the Lakes (on
                Lake Michigan)
                The City of Advantages
                The Czech Bethlehem (Bohemian
                settlement)
                The Danish Capital of the United
                States (one-third of its popula-
                tion of Danish descent)
                Wisconsin's Second City (actually
                now third city in population in
                1960, population 89, 144)

RHINELANDER     The Capital of the Heart O' the
                Lakes (trading center for hunt-
                ers, campers, fishermen)
                The Home of the Hodag (beast of
                frightening appearance)

RIPON           The Birthplace of the Republican
                Party (organized Feb. 28, 1854)
                The City of the Twin Spires (the
                spires on College Hill of the
                Grace Lutheran and Congrega-
                tional Churches)

SHEBOYGAN       The Bratwurst Capital of the
                World (German settlement)
                The Chair City (industry declined
                about 1918)
                The City of Cheese, Chairs, Chil-
                dren and Churches (seldom
                used after 1940)
                The Evergreen City
                Wurst City of the World (smoked
                sausage and bratwurst produc-
                tion)

STEVENS POINT   The City of Wonderful Water (on
                Plover and Wisconsin Rivers)

STURGEON BAY    The Canal City (canal connecting
                Green Bay with Lake Michigan)

SUPERIOR        America's Most Westerly Inland
                Port (at head of Lake Super-
                ior)
                America's Second Port (on Lake
                Superior)

SUPERIOR (Cont'd)                The City of One Hundred Lakes
                                          and Streams
                                 The City of Smiles
                                 The City of the Northland
                                 The City where Spring Spends the
                                          Summer
                                 The Consumer Cooperative Cen-
                                          ter of the United States
                                 The Eye of the Northwest
                                 The Four Season City
                                 The Hub of North America
                                 The Playground of Presidents
                                 The Summer Capital of America
                                          (on Lake Superior)
                                 The Transportation Center of
                                          North America (grain center
                                          and shipping terminus for
                                          copper and iron)
                                 The Twin Ports (with Duluth,
                                          Minn. )

THREE LAKES                      The Midwest's Winter Sports
                                          Mecca
VIROQUA                          The Tobacco Center
WAUKESHA                         The City with a Future
                                 The Hub of the Fastest Growing
                                          County in the State
                                 The Spring City (medicinal springs)
WAUSAU                           The Forest City
WEST ALLIS                       The City of Homes and Diversified
                                          Industries
                                 The Saratoga of the West (medi-
                                          cinal springs)
WISCONSIN DELLS                  America's Scenic Wonderland
                                          (on the Wisconsin River, lined
                                          by rock formations)
WISCONSIN RAPIDS                 The Geographic Heart of the
                                          State (on the Wisconsin River)

## WYOMING

AFTON                            The Switzerland of America (6, 134
                                          feet altitude)
BASIN                            Bean Town (marketing center for
                                          the bean crop)
                                 The Garden City (a tree and
                                          shrub planting campaign was
                                          instituted in 1910)

CASPER — The Convention City  
The Geographic Center of the Oil Industry in the Rocky Mountains  
The Growing City  
The Hub  
The Hub City (seat of Natrona County)  
The Magic City of the Plains  
The Oil Capital of the Rockies (oil fields, 3 major oil refineries, 400 oil affiliated concerns)  
The Oil City  
The Progress City of the Rockies  
Wyoming's Most Progressive City (about 40,000 population)  

CHEYENNE — Hell on Wheels (formerly used)  
The Capital City (1960 population 43,505)  
The Home of Frontier Days  
The Magic City of the Plains  
The Magic City of the West  

DOUGLAS — The Tent Town (name conferred in 1886 when the town was founded)  

DUBOIS — The Rock Capital of the Nation  
EVANSTON — The Most Typical Western City in Wyoming  

GLENDO — Wyoming's Big Little Town  
GLENROCK — The Oil City (oil refinery)  
JACKSON — The Last of the Old West and the Best of the New  
The New Height in American Skiing (in Teton National Forest, 4,135 feet vertical rise)  

KEMMERER — The Gateway to Western Wyoming's Wonderland  
LANDER — The Apple City  
The City where the Rails and the Trails Begin (western terminus of the Chicago and Northwestern Railway)  
The Push Root City  
LARAMIE — The Athens of Wyoming (home of the University of Wyoming)  
The Gem City

| | |
|---|---|
| LOVELL | The City of Roses |
| | The Rose Town |
| POWELL | The City where Oil and Water Mix |
| | The Friendly Little City in the Prosperous Shoshone Valley |
| | The Home of Northwest Community College |
| | The Oasis in Mountain Country |
| ROCK SPRINGS | The City of Industry in the Land of Sage and Sun |
| | The Gateway to Yellowstone and Teton National Parks |
| SARATOGA | America's Newest Family Playground |
| | The Small Town with a Big Welcome |
| | The Town where the Trout Leap in Main Street |
| SHERIDAN | The Center of the Dude Ranch Industry |
| | The City in "The Big Horns" |
| | The City in the Heart of "The Big Horns" |
| | The City in the Shadow of the Big Horn |
| | The City where the West Remains |
| | The Headquarters of the Big Horn National Forest |
| | The Optimist City |
| THERMOPOLIS | The City of Heat (thermal springs) |
| | The Health Center of the West (hot springs) |
| | The Home of the World's Largest Mineral Hot Springs |
| | The Recreation Center of the West |
| | The World's Largest Mineral Hot Springs (13,000 gallons flow per minute) |
| | Wyoming's Year 'Round Health and Scenic Center |

## A

| | |
|---|---|
| ACTION CAPITOL OF THE MIDWEST | Des Moines, Iowa |
| ACTION CENTER OF FLORIDA | Orlando, Fla. |
| ACTION CENTER OF FLORIDA'S "HOLIDAY HIGHLANDS" | Leesburg, Fla. |
| ACTION CITY | Charlotte, N. C. |
| ACTION CITY | Orlando, Fla. |
| ADVERTISING CENTER | Cleveland, Ohio |
| AGATE CAPITAL OF THE U. S. | Prineville, Ore. |
| AGGREGATE OF VILLAGES | Weymouth, Mass. |
| AGRICULTURAL AND INDUSTRIAL CENTER OF NORTHWEST ARKANSAS | Springdale, Ark. |
| AGRICULTURAL AND RECREATIONAL CENTER OF CALIFORNIA | Fresno, Calif. |
| AGRICULTURAL AND TIMBER EMPIRE | Blountstown, Fla. |
| AGRICULTURAL BREADBASKET CENTER OF NORTH AMERICA | Grafton, N. D. |
| AGRICULTURAL CAPITAL | Jackson, Miss. |
| AGRICULTURAL TOWN | Lovelock, Nev. |
| AIR CAPITAL | Wichita, Kan. |
| AIR CAPITAL OF AMERICA | Wichita, Kan. |
| AIR CAPITAL OF THE CAROLINAS | Charleston, S. C. |
| AIR CAPITAL OF THE NATION | Wichita, Kan. |
| AIR CAPITAL OF THE WEST | San Diego, Calif. |
| AIR CAPITAL OF THE WORLD | Miami, Fla. |
| AIR CAPITAL OF THE WORLD | Wichita, Kan. |
| AIR CONDITIONED BY NATURE | Kane, Pa. |
| AIR-CONDITIONED CITY | Bluefield, W. Va. |
| AIR-CONDITIONED CITY | Duluth, Minn. |
| AIR-CONDITIONED DULUTH | Duluth, Minn. |
| AIRCRAFT CENTER OF THE WEST | Hawthorne, Calif. |
| AIR CROSSROADS OF AMERICA | Evansville, Ind. |
| AIR CROSSROADS OF THE WORLD | Anchorage, Alaska |
| AIRWAYS OF AMERICA | Valdosta, Ga. |
| AIR HUB OF THE AMERICAS | New Orleans, La. |
| ALABAMA'S CITY IN MOTION | Mobile, Ala. |
| ALABAMA'S ONLY PORT CITY | Mobile, Ala. |

ALAMO CITY | San Antonio, Tex.
ALASKA'S CAPITAL CITY | Juneau, Alaska
ALASKA'S FIRST CITY | Ketchikan, Alaska
ALASKA'S FRIENDLY CITY | Cordova, Alaska
ALASKA'S LITTLE NORWAY | Petersburg, Alaska
ALASKA'S MOST SCENIC HISTORIC
PLAYGROUND | Sitka, Alaska
ALASKA'S NUMBER ONE TOURIST
CITY | Sitka, Alaska
ALASKA'S SCENIC CAPITAL | Juneau, Alaska
ALEX CITY | Alexander City, Ala.
ALEXANDRIA OF AMERICA | New Orleans, La.

ALL-AMERICAN CITY

While the term "All-American City" is often referred to as a nickname, it is an award sponsored by the National Municipal League and Look Magazine. Its use is authorized for one year only. The cities so honored and the years in which the awards were made are listed at the conclusion of this general index beginning with page 417.

ALL AMERICAN CITY OF THE GREAT
NORTHWEST | Salem, Ore.
ALL-AMERICAN TOWN | Dallas, Tex.
ALL-ELECTRIC COMMUNITY | Mason City, Wash.
ALL-ROUND PLAYGROUND | Old Orchard Beach,
| Me.
ALL-SEASON CONVENTION VACATION
LOCATION | Las Vegas, Nev.
ALL-SEASON VACATIONLAND | Boyne City, Mich.
ALL YEAR HOME TOWN | Asbury Park, N. J.
ALL YEAR PLAYGROUND OF THE
OLD SOUTH | Gulfport, Miss.
ALL YEAR RESIDENTIAL RESORT | Ventnor City, N. J.
ALL-YEAR RESORT AND RECREATION
CENTER | Las Vegas, Nev.
ALL-YEAR RESORT CENTER | New Bern, N. C.
ALL YEAR ROUND VACATION
CENTER | Gladstone, Mich.
ALL YEAR ROUND VACATIONLAND | Stowe, Vt.
ALL-YEAR SPORTS CENTER | Sun Valley, Idaho
ALL YEAR VACATION CITY | Fort Lauderdale,
| Fla.
ALL-YEAR VACATIONLAND | Daytona Beach, Fla.
ALLENTOWN'S SISTER CITY | Bethlehem, Pa.
ALLURING ATTRACTIVE SUBURBAN
MUNICIPALITY | West Chester, Pa.
ALMOND CAPITAL OF THE WORLD | Chico, Calif.
ALMOND CAPITAL OF THE WORLD | Sacramento, Calif.

240

| | |
|---|---|
| ALMOND CAPITOL OF CALIFORNIA | Ripon, Calif. |
| ALMOND CENTER OF THE WORLD | Chico, Calif. |
| ALPINE VILLAGE | Suttons Bay, Mich. |
| ALUMINUM CITY | Massena, N. Y. |
| ALUMINUM CITY | Muscle Shoals, Ala. |
| ALUMINUM CITY | New Kensington, Pa. |
| AMERICA IN MINIATURE | Providence, R. I. |
| AMERICA'S ALARM CITY | Mount Katahdin, Me. |
| AMERICA'S ALL-YEAR PLAYGROUND | Lake Tahoe, Calif. |
| AMERICA'S BAGDAD BY THE SEA | Atlantic City, N. J. |
| AMERICA'S BATH CITY | Mount Clemons, Mich. |
| AMERICA'S BERMUDA | New Shoreham, R. I. |
| AMERICA'S "BIT O' IRELAND" IN COUNTY O'ANTRIM | Bellaire, Mich. |
| AMERICA'S BOTTOM | Death Valley, Calif. |
| AMERICA'S CARROT CAPITAL | Holtville, Calif. |
| AMERICA'S CHRISTMAS CITY | Bethlehem, Pa. |
| AMERICA'S CITY OF HISTORY | Newport, R. I. |
| AMERICA'S CONVENTION CITY | Philadelphia, Pa. |
| AMERICA'S DESERT RESORT | Palm Springs, Calif. |
| AMERICA'S DUDE RANCH CAPITAL | Wickenburg, Ariz. |
| AMERICA'S FAMILY PLAYGROUND | Lake George, N. Y. |
| AMERICA'S FAMOUS SUMMER AND WINTER RESORT | Monterey, Calif. |
| AMERICA'S FARM IMPLEMENT CAPITAL | East Moline, Ill. |
| AMERICA'S FASTEST GROWING INDUSTRIAL CITY | Richmond, Va. |
| AMERICA'S FAVORITE SUN AND FUN VACATIONLAND | Phoenix, Ariz. |
| AMERICA'S FIRST AND MOST HISTORIC FISHING PORT | Gloucester, Mass. |
| AMERICA'S FIRST CITY OF SUNSHINE | Tucson, Ariz. |
| AMERICA'S FIRST MINING CAPITAL | Houghton, Mich. |
| AMERICA'S FIRST RESORT | Newport, R. I. |
| AMERICA'S FIRST SEASHORE RESORT | Long Branch, N. J. |
| AMERICA'S FIRST SUMMER FESTIVAL | Tanglewood, Mass. |
| AMERICA'S FIRST VACATIONLAND | Newport, R. I. |
| AMERICA'S FOREMOST DESERT RESORT | Palm Beach, Calif. |
| AMERICA'S FOREMOST YEAR 'ROUND SPORTS CENTER | Sun Valley, Idaho |
| AMERICA'S GARDEN SPOT | Lancaster, Pa. |
| AMERICA'S GREAT CENTRAL MARKET AND TOURIST CITY | St. Louis, Mo. |
| AMERICA'S GREAT CONVENTION CITY | Philadelphia, Pa. |

| | |
|---|---|
| AMERICA'S GREATEST FAMILY RE-SORT | Harvey Cedars, N.J. |
| AMERICA'S GREATEST FAMILY RE-SORT | Ocean City, N.J. |
| AMERICA'S GREATEST HEALTH AND PLEASURE RESORT | French Lick, Ind. |
| AMERICA'S GREATEST HEALTH AND RESORT CENTER | Hot Springs, Ark. |
| AMERICA'S GREATEST HEALTH AND REST CENTER | Hot Springs, Ark. |
| AMERICA'S GREATEST INLAND CITY | Indianapolis, Ind. |
| AMERICA'S HEALTHIEST CITY | Long Beach, N.Y. |
| AMERICA'S HISTORYLAND PLAY-GROUND | Virginia Beach, Va. |
| AMERICA'S HOLSTEIN CAPITAL | Northfield, Minn. |
| AMERICA'S HOME TOWN | Plymouth, Mass. |
| AMERICA'S IDEAL FAMILY CENTER | Bartlesville, Okla. |
| AMERICA'S IDEAL VACATION LAND | Billings, Mont. |
| AMERICA'S INDUSTRIAL CITY | Fort Smith, Ark. |
| AMERICA'S IRON CAPITAL | Hibbing, Minn. |
| AMERICA'S LEADING TOURIST RE-SORT | New York, N.Y. |
| AMERICA'S LITTLE SWITZERLAND | Eureka Springs, Ark. |
| AMERICA'S LITTLE SWITZERLAND | Fayetteville, Ark. |
| AMERICA'S LITTLE SWITZERLAND | Newaygo, Mich. |
| AMERICA'S LOW SPOT | Death Valley, Calif. |
| AMERICA'S MACHINE SHOP | Milwaukee, Wis. |
| AMERICA'S MAGIC CITY | Gary, Ind. |
| AMERICA'S MILK CENTER | Harvard, Ill. |
| AMERICA'S MINING CAPITAL | Hibbing, Minn. |
| AMERICA'S MOST BEAUTIFUL CAP-ITOL | Baton Rouge, La. |
| AMERICA'S MOST BEAUTIFUL CITY | Savannah, Ga. |
| AMERICA'S MOST COMPLETE RE-SORT | Hilltop Lakes, Tex. |
| AMERICA'S MOST DISTINCTIVE SEA-SHORE VACATIONLAND | Cape May, N.J. |
| AMERICA'S MOST EXCITING CITY | San Francisco, Calif. |
| AMERICA'S MOST FRIENDLY FAS-CINATING CITY | San Francisco, Calif. |
| AMERICA'S MOST HEDONISTIC CITY | New Orleans, La. |
| AMERICA'S MOST HISTORIC CITY | Charleston, S.C. |
| AMERICA'S MOST HISTORIC CITY | Fredericksburg, Va. |
| AMERICA'S MOST HISTORIC CITY | Petersburg, Va. |
| AMERICA'S MOST HISTORIC TOWN | Ticonderoga, N.Y. |
| AMERICA'S MOST INTERESTING CITY | New Orleans, La. |
| AMERICA'S MOST SCENIC CAPITAL | Juneau, Alaska |

| | | |
|---|---|---|
| AMERICA'S MOST WESTERLY INLAND PORT | | Superior, Wis. |
| AMERICA'S MOST WONDERFUL SPA | | Saratoga Springs, N. Y. |
| AMERICA'S MOUNTAIN SPRING | | Sharon Springs, N. Y. |
| AMERICA'S NAPLES | | Woods Hole, Mass. |
| AMERICA'S NEWEST CONVENTION CITY | | Portland, Ore. |
| AMERICA'S NEWEST FAMILY PLAY-GROUND | | Saratoga, Wyo. |
| AMERICA'S NEWEST INDUSTRIAL CENTER | | Paducah, Ky. |
| AMERICA'S NEWEST INDUSTRIAL FRONTIER | | Odessa, Tex. |
| AMERICA'S NO. 1 CONTRARY CITY | | Chicago, Ill. |
| AMERICA'S NO. 1 SMALL CITY | | De Pere, Wis. |
| AMERICA'S OCEAN PLAYGROUND | | Atlantic City, N. J. |
| AMERICA'S OLDEST CITY | | St. Augustine, Fla. |
| AMERICA'S OLDEST INDUSTRIAL CITY | | Haverhill, Mass. |
| AMERICA'S OLDEST INLAND CITY | | Lancaster, Pa. |
| AMERICA'S OLDEST SUMMER RE-SORT | | Newport, R. I. |
| AMERICA'S ONLY INTERNATIONAL PLAYGROUND | | San Diego, Calif. |
| AMERICA'S OWN SPA | | Hot Springs, Ark. |
| AMERICA'S PARIS | | Cincinnati, Ohio |
| AMERICA'S PARIS | | San Francisco, Calif. |
| AMERICA'S PORT OF QUICKEST DIS-PATCH | | Galveston, Tex. |
| AMERICA'S PREMIER PLAYGROUND | | Rye, N. Y. |
| AMERICA'S RIVIERA | | Biloxi, Minn. |
| AMERICA'S RIVIERA | | Chicago, Ill. |
| AMERICA'S RIVIERA | | Gulfport, Miss. |
| AMERICA'S RIVIERA | | Montauk, N. Y. |
| AMERICA'S SAFEST BIG CITY | | Minneapolis, Minn. |
| AMERICA'S SCENIC WONDERLAND | | Niagara Falls, N. Y. |
| AMERICA'S SCENIC WONDERLAND | | Wisconsin Dells, Wis. |
| AMERICA'S SECOND PORT | | Superior, Wis. |
| AMERICA'S SHERRYLAND | | Lodi, Calif. |
| AMERICA'S SHOE CAPITAL | | St. Louis, Mo. |
| AMERICA'S SINGAPORE | | Key West, Fla. |
| AMERICA'S SOCIETY CAPITAL | | Newport, R. I. |
| AMERICA'S SOUTHERNMOST CITY | | Key West, Fla. |
| AMERICA'S SPORTS MECCA | | French Lick, Ind. |
| AMERICA'S SUGAR BOWL | | Brush, Colo. |

| | |
|---|---|
| AMERICA'S SUNRISE GATEWAY | Portland, Me. |
| AMERICA'S SWEETEST TOWN | Clewiston, Fla. |
| AMERICA'S SWEETHEART CITY | Loveland, Colo. |
| AMERICA'S SWISS CHEESE CAPITAL | Monroe, Wis. |
| AMERICA'S SWITZERLAND | Lake Placid, N.Y. |
| AMERICA'S TYPICAL CITY | Zanesville, Ohio |
| AMERICA'S WILD LIFE PRESERVER | Prairie du Chien, Wis. |
| AMERICA'S YEAR 'ROUND HOLIDAY ISLAND | Jekyll Island, Ga. |
| AMERICA'S YEAR 'ROUND PLAY-GROUND | Miami Beach, Fla. |
| AMERICA'S YEAR 'ROUND PLAY-GROUND | Scranton, Pa. |
| AMERICAN ATHENS | Boston, Mass. |
| AMERICAN CARLSBAD | Ashland, Ore. |
| AMERICAN CITY OF OPPORTUNITY | Jersey City, N.J. |
| AMERICAN LYONS | Paterson, N.J. |
| AMERICAN MUNICH | Milwaukee, Wis. |
| ANCIENT AND HONORABLE PUEBLO | Tucson, Ariz. |
| ANCIENT CITY | Annapolis, Md. |
| ANCIENT CITY | St. Augustine, Fla. |
| ANGEL CITY | Los Angeles, Calif. |
| ANNAPOLIS OF THE AIR | Pensacola, Fla. |
| ANNIE'S TOWN | Anniston, Ala. |
| ANOTHER CLYDE CITY | Union, Wash. |
| ANTHRACITE CAPITAL OF THE WORLD | Scranton, Pa. |
| ANTHRACITE CENTER OF THE WORLD | Scranton, Pa. |
| ANTHRACITE CITY | Scranton, Pa. |
| ANTIQUES CENTER OF THE SOUTH | Dania, Fla. |
| APPLE CAPITAL | Wenatchee, Wash. |
| APPLE CAPITAL | Winchester, Va. |
| APPLE CAPITAL IN THE BEAUTIFUL SHENANDOAH VALLEY | Winchester, Va. |
| APPLE CAPITAL OF THE WORLD | Wenatchee, Wash. |
| APPLE CITY | Lander, Wyo. |
| APPLE CITY | Watsonville, Calif. |
| AQUEDUCT CITY | Norristown, Pa. |
| AQUEDUCT CITY | Rochester, N.Y. |
| AREA OF OPPORTUNITY | Ruskin, Fla. |
| AREA SHOPPING CROSSROADS | Ash Grove, Mo. |
| ARIZONA'S COPPER CAPITAL | Bisbee, Ariz. |
| ARIZONA'S FIRST CAPITAL | Prescott, Ariz. |
| ARIZONA'S SECOND LARGEST CITY | Tucson, Ariz. |
| ARIZONA'S THIRD LARGEST CITY | Mesa, Ariz. |
| ARK CITY | Arkansas City, Ark. |

| | |
|---|---|
| ARKANSAS' INDUSTRIAL CENTER | Fort Smith, Ark. |
| ARKANSAS' LARGEST HEALTH AND PLEASURE RESORT | Hot Springs, Ark. |
| ARKANSAS' ONLY SEAPORT | Helena, Ark. |
| ARKOPOLIS | Little Rock, Ark. |
| ARROWHEAD EGG BASKET | Barnum, Minn. |
| ARSENAL | Lancaster, Pa. |
| ARSENAL OF DEMOCRACY | Fort Worth, Tex. |
| ART CENTER OF RHODE ISLAND | Wickford, R. I. |
| ART CENTER OF THE SOUTHWEST | Taos, N. M. |
| ARTESIAN CITY | Albany, Ga. |
| ARTESIAN CITY | Martinsville, Ind. |
| ARTICHOKE CAPITAL OF THE WORLD | Castroville, Calif. |
| ASPARAGUS CAPITAL OF THE WORLD | Isleton, Calif. |
| ATHENS | Boston, Mass. |
| ATHENS OF ALABAMA | Tuscaloosa, Ala. |
| ATHENS OF AMERICA | Annapolis, Md. |
| ATHENS OF AMERICA | Boston, Mass. |
| ATHENS OF AMERICA | Cambridge, Mass. |
| ATHENS OF AMERICA | Crawfordsville, Ind. |
| ATHENS OF AMERICA | Iowa City, Iowa |
| ATHENS OF AMERICA | New Harmony, Ind. |
| ATHENS OF ARKANSAS | Fayetteville, Ark. |
| ATHENS OF CALIFORNIA | Benicia, Calif. |
| ATHENS OF FLORIDA | De Land, Fla. |
| ATHENS OF INDIANA | Crawfordsville, Ind. |
| ATHENS OF INDIANA | Roanoke, Ind. |
| ATHENS OF IOWA | Iowa City, Iowa |
| ATHENS OF NEW ENGLAND | Norwalk, Conn. |
| ATHENS OF PENNSYLVANIA | West Chester, Pa. |
| ATHENS OF TEXAS | Waco, Texas |
| ATHENS OF THE MIDDLE WEST | Cincinnati, Ohio |
| ATHENS OF THE MIDWEST | Columbia, Mo. |
| ATHENS OF THE NEW WORLD | Boston, Mass. |
| ATHENS OF THE NORTHWEST | Faribault, Minn. |
| ATHENS OF THE SOUTH | Holly Springs, Miss. |
| ATHENS OF THE SOUTH | Nashville, Tenn. |
| ATHENS OF THE SOUTHWEST | Dallas, Tex. |
| ATHENS OF THE UNITED STATES | Boston, Mass. |
| ATHENS OF THE WEST | Abilene, Tex. |
| ATHENS OF THE WEST | Berkeley, Calif. |
| ATHENS OF THE WEST | Boston, Mass. |
| ATHENS OF THE WEST | Lexington, Ky. |
| ATHENS OF THE WEST | Salem, Ind. |
| ATHENS OF VIRGINIA | Lexington, Va. |

245

| | |
|---|---|
| ATHENS OF WYOMING | Laramie, Wyo. |
| ATHENS YOU WILL WANT TO SEE | Athens, Ga. |
| ATLANTA'S AIRPORT CITY | College Park, Ga. |
| ATLANTIC CITY OF THE GREAT LAKES | Cedar Point, Ohio |
| ATLANTIC CITY OF THE MIDDLE WEST | Cedar Point, Ohio |
| ATOMIC CAPITAL OF THE WORLD | Oak Ridge, Tenn. |
| ATOMIC CITY | Los Alamos, N. M. |
| ATOMIC CITY | Oak Ridge, Tenn. |
| ATOMIC ENERGY CITY | Oak Ridge, Tenn. |
| AUTO CITY | Detroit, Mich. |
| AUTOMOBILE CAPITAL OF THE WORLD | Detroit, Mich. |
| AUTOMOBILE CENTER | Flint, Mich. |
| AUTOMOBILE CITY | Detroit, Mich. |
| AUTOMOBILE CITY OF THE WORLD | Detroit, Mich. |
| AUTOMOTIVE CAPITAL OF THE WORLD | Detroit, Mich. |
| AVIATION CENTER OF THE EAST | Baltimore, Md. |
| AVIATION CITY | Dayton, Ohio |
| AZALIA TRAIL CITY | Lafayette, La. |

B

| | |
|---|---|
| BABY CITY | Leominster, Mass. |
| BABY OF THE COLORADO SKI RE-SORTS | Vail, Colo. |
| BABYLON OF WASHINGTON TERRI-TORY | Ruby, Wash. |
| BABYLON ON THE BLUFF | Memphis, Tenn. |
| BABYLONIAN BEDLAM | New York, N. Y. |
| BAD BIRMINGHAM | Birmingham, Ala. |
| BAGDAD BY THE BAY | San Francisco, Calif. |
| BAGDAD OF THE SUBWAY | New York, N. Y. |
| BAGDAD ON THE HUDSON | New York, N. Y. |
| BALANCED CITY | Berkeley, Calif. |
| BALANCED COMMUNITY | Mount Laurel, N. J. |
| BALANCED COMMUNITY OF OPPOR-TUNITY AND HAPPY HOMES | Jackson, Miss. |
| BANANA BELT CITY | Lewiston, Idaho |
| BAND CITY | Elkhart, Ind. |
| BANKING CENTER OF THE WORLD | New York, N. Y. |
| BARBED WIRE CAPITAL OF THE WORLD | De Kalb, Ill. |
| BASS CAPITAL OF THE WORLD | Palatka, Fla. |
| BATTLEFIELD CITY | Gettysburg, Pa. |

| | |
|---|---|
| BATTLEFIELD OF THE REVOLUTION | Augusta, Ga. |
| BATTLETOWN | Berryville, Va. |
| BAY CITY | San Francisco, Calif. |
| BAY HORSE | Boston, Mass. |
| BAYOU CITY | Houston, Tex. |
| BEACH THAT MADE FORT LAUDERDALE FAMOUS | Fort Lauderdale, Fla. |
| BEAN TOWN | Basin, Wyo. |
| BEANTOWN | Boston, Mass |
| BEAR'S PLACE | Olympia, Wash. |
| BEAUTIFUL CITY | Cincinnati, Ohio |
| BEAUTIFUL CITY BY A BEAUTIFUL LAKE | Coeur d'Alene, Idaho |
| BEAUTIFUL CITY BY THE SEA | Portland, Me. |
| BEAUTIFUL CITY OF HOMES, DIVERSIFIED BUSINESS AND PROGRESSIVE OUTLOOK | Buffalo, N. Y. |
| BEAUTIFUL CITY OF HOMES IN THE HISTORIC MOHAWK VALLEY | Utica, N. Y. |
| BEAUTIFUL CITY OF ROSES | Portland, Ore. |
| BEAUTIFUL CITY OF THE STRAITS | Detroit, Mich. |
| BEAUTIFUL PLACE BY THE SEA | Ogunquit, Me. |
| BEAUTIFUL COMMUNITY IN BEAUTIFUL VIRGINIA | Culpeper, Va. |
| BEAUTIFUL TOWN THAT IS SEATED BY THE SEA | Portland, Me. |
| BEAUTY SPOT OF THE BLUE RIDGE | Little Switzerland, N. C. |
| BEAUTY SPOT OF THE NORTH JERSEY COAST | Asbury Park, N. J. |
| BEDROOM OF NEW YORK | Brooklyn, N. Y. |
| BEDROOM OF WASHINGTON | Arlington, Va. |
| BEE-HIVE OF INDUSTRY | Providence, R. I. |
| BEER CAPITAL OF AMERICA | Milwaukee, Wis. |
| BEER CITY | Milwaukee, Wis. |
| BEL AIR OF CONEJO | Thousand Oaks, Calif. |
| "BELIEVE IT OR NOT" TOWN | Eureka Springs, Ark. |
| BELL TOWN | East Hampton, Conn. |
| BELL TOWN OF AMERICA | East Hampton, Conn. |
| BELLE CITY | Racine, Wis. |
| BELLE CITY OF THE BLUEGRASS REGIONS | Lexington, Ky. |
| BELLE CITY OF THE LAKES | Racine, Wis. |

| | |
|---|---|
| BENTON COUNTY'S FASTEST GROWING CITY | Lincoln, Mo. |
| BERMUDA OF THE NORTH | Mackinac Island, Mich. |
| BERMUDA OF THE NORTH | New Shoreham, R. I. |
| BERRY CAPITOL OF THE WORLD | Starke, Fla. |
| BERRY CITY | Woodburn, Ore. |
| BEST BALANCED CITY | Hickory, N. C. |
| BEST CONVENTION POINT IN THE EAST | Springfield, Mass. |
| BEST IN THE WEST | Roby, Tex. |
| BEST KNOWN CITY IN THE WORLD | Battle Creek, Mich. |
| BEST KNOW CITY OF ITS SIZE IN THE WORLD | Battle Creek, Mich. |
| BEST KNOWN LITTLE CITY IN AMERICA | Claremore, Okla. |
| BEST LIGHTED CITY IN THE WORLD | Gering, Neb. |
| BEST LIGHTED TOWN IN THE WEST | Burley, Idaho |
| BEST LOCATION IN THE NATION | Cleveland, Ohio |
| BEST PECAN PRODUCING AREA IN THE SOUTH | Fort Valley, Ga. |
| BEST TOWN IN THE STATE BY A DAMSITE | Stockton, Mo. |
| BEST TOWN OF ITS AGE IN THIS GLORIOUS CLIMATE | Whittier, Calif. |
| BEST TOWN SITE ON THE OHIO | Steubenville, Ohio |
| BETSYTOWN | Elizabeth, N. J. |
| BETTER PLACE TO WORK AND PLAY | Moultrie, Ga. |
| BEULAH LAND | Palisades, Wash. |
| BIG APPLE | New York, N. Y. |
| BIG BURG | New York, N. Y. |
| BIG CATTLE COUNTRY | Benjamin, Tex. |
| BIG CITY | New York, N. Y. |
| BIG CITY BENEFITS WITH SMALL TOWN ADVANTAGES | Mechanicsburg, Pa. |
| BIG "D" | Dallas, Tex. |
| BIG GAME CAPITAL OF NEBRASKA | Crawford, Neb. |
| BIG HEART OF TEXAS | Austin, Tex. |
| BIG LITTLE CITY | Malone, N. Y. |
| BIG "M" OF THE OZARKS | Monett, Mo. |
| BIG MONEY CENTER YOU NEVER HEARD MUCH ABOUT | Providence, R. I. |
| BIG SHELBY | Memphis, Tenn. |
| BIG SMOKE | Pittsburgh, Pa. |
| BIG SMOKY | Pittsburgh, Pa. |
| BIG TOWN | Chicago, Ill. |
| BIG TOWN | New York, N. Y. |

248

| | |
|---|---|
| BIG WATER | Paha, Wash. |
| BIGGEST CITY IN AREA IN THE FREE WORLD | Jacksonville, Fla. |
| @BIGGEST GATEWAY TO IMMIGRANTS | New York, N. Y. |
| BIGGEST LITTLE CITY | Abilene, Kan. |
| BIGGEST LITTLE CITY IN AMERICA | Atlantic City, N. J. |
| BIGGEST LITTLE CITY IN MAINE | Belfast, Me. |
| BIGGEST LITTLE CITY IN MICHIGAN | Rockford, Mich. |
| BIGGEST LITTLE CITY IN THE U. S. A. | Dodge City, Kan. |
| BIGGEST LITTLE CITY IN THE WORLD | Reno, Nev. |
| BIGGEST LITTLE TOWN IN KANSAS | Cawker City, Kan. |
| BIGGEST LITTLE TOWN IN THE WEST | Broadus, Mont. |
| @BIG-HEADED BURG | Hollywood, Calif. |
| @BILLTOWN | Williamstown, Kan. |
| BIRD DOG CAPITAL OF THE WORLD | Waynesborg, Ga. |
| BIRD SANCTUARY | Henderson, N. C. |
| BIRMINGHAM OF AMERICA | Cincinnati, Ohio |
| @ BIRMINGHAM OF AMERICA | Newark, N. J. |
| BIRMINGHAM OF AMERICA | Pittsburgh, Pa. |
| @ BIRTHPLACE AND HOME OF LITTLE LEAGUE BASEBALL | Williamsport, Pa. |
| BIRTHPLACE OF A REPUBLIC | West Columbia, Tex. |
| @BIRTHPLACE OF AMERICA'S COTTON INDUSTRY | Pawtucket, R. I. |
| BIRTHPLACE OF AMERICA'S IRON AND STEEL INDUSTRY | Saugus, Mass. |
| BIRTHPLACE OF AMERICAN INDE-PENDENCE | Ipswich, Mass. |
| BIRTHPLACE OF AMERICAN INDE-PENDENCE | Philadelphia, Pa. |
| BIRTHPLACE OF AMERICAN LIBERTY | Lexington, Mass. |
| @BIRTHPLACE OF AMERICAN LIBERTY | Philadelphia, Pa. |
| @BIRTHPLACE OF AVIATION | Dayton, Ohio |
| ·BIRTHPLACE OF BASEBALL | Cooperstown, N. Y. |
| BIRTHPLACE OF BUFFALO BILL CODY | Le Claire, Iowa |
| @BIRTHPLACE OF CALIFORNIA | San Diego, Calif. |
| BIRTHPLACE OF CALVIN COOLIDGE | Plymouth, Vt. |
| BIRTHPLACE OF DANIEL WEBSTER | Franklin, N. H. |
| BIRTHPLACE OF DEMOCRACY | Dedham, Mass. |
| @ BIRTHPLACE OF DIXIE | Montgomery, Ala. |
| @ BIRTHPLACE OF FREEDOM | Boston, Mass. |
| BIRTHPLACE OF HARRY S. TRUMAN | Lamar, Mo. |
| @BIRTHPLACE OF LIBERTY | Quincy, Mass. |
| BIRTHPLACE OF MC KINLEY | Niles, Ohio |
| BIRTHPLACE OF MAINE | Freeport, Me. |

| | |
|---|---|
| BIRTHPLACE OF MARY BAKER EDDY | Bow, N. H. |
| BIRTHPLACE OF NIGHT BASEBALL | Fort Wayne, Ind. |
| BIRTHPLACE OF OKLAHOMA | Guthrie, Okla. |
| BIRTHPLACE OF PRESIDENT RICHARD M. NIXON | Yorba Linda, Calif. |
| BIRTHPLACE OF PROFESSIONAL FOOTBALL | Latrobe, Pa. |
| BIRTHPLACE OF RADIO | Murray, Ky. |
| BIRTHPLACE OF SOUTH DAKOTA'S PHEASANT HUNTING | Redfield, S. D. |
| BIRTHPLACE OF SPEED | Ormond Beach, Fla. |
| BIRTHPLACE OF SURFING | Waikiki, Hawaii |
| BIRTHPLACE OF TEXAS | Washington, Ark. |
| BIRTHPLACE OF THE AMERICAN CIRCUS | Somers, N. Y. |
| BIRTHPLACE OF THE AMERICAN COTTON INDUSTRY | Pawtucket, R. I. |
| BIRTHPLACE OF THE AMERICAN NAVY | Beverly, Mass. |
| BIRTHPLACE OF THE 'BUDDY POPPY' | Monroe, Ga. |
| BIRTHPLACE OF THE FARM TRACTOR | Charles City, Iowa |
| BIRTHPLACE OF THE MESABI | Mountain, Lake, Minn. |
| BIRTHPLACE OF THE MODERN OIL INDUSTRY | Beaumont, Tex. |
| BIRTHPLACE OF THE NATION | Jamestown, Va. |
| BIRTHPLACE OF THE NATION | Philadelphia, Pa. |
| BIRTHPLACE OF THE NORTHERN PACIFIC | Carlton, Minn. |
| BIRTHPLACE OF THE NORTHWEST TERRITORY | Marietta, Ohio |
| BIRTHPLACE OF THE REPUBLIC OF VERMONT | Windsor, Vt. |
| BIRTHPLACE OF THE REPUBLICAN PARTY | Ripon, Wis. |
| BIRTHPLACE OF THE SECOND AND SIXTH PRESIDENTS | Quincy, Mass. |
| BIRTHPLACE OF THE STAR SPANGLED BANNER | Baltimore, Md. |
| BIRTHPLACE OF THE UNITED STATES COAST GUARD | Newburyport, Mass. |
| BIRTHPLACE OF THE U.S. NAVY | Whitehall, N. Y. |
| BIRTHPLACE OF U.S. NAVAL AVIATION | Pensacola, Fla. |
| BIRTHPLACE OF WESTERN AMERICA | Harrodsburg, Ky. |

| | |
|---|---|
| BIRTHPLACE OF WOODROW WILSON | Staunton, Va. |
| BISON CITY | Buffalo, N. Y. |
| BIT OF AMERICA AT ITS BEST | Oneida, N. Y. |
| BIT OF NEW ENGLAND WITH A SOMBRERO ON IT | Claremont, Calif. |
| BIT OF THE OLD WEST TRANS-PLANTED IN THE TWENTIETH CENTURY | Wickenburg, Ariz. |
| BITCHES HEAVEN | Boston, Mass. |
| BITUMINOUS CITY | Connellsville, Pa. |
| BLACK BASS CAPITAL OF THE WORLD | Cape Vincent, N. Y. |
| BLACK DIAMOND CITY | Wilkes-Barre, Pa. |
| BLACK HEART OF MONTANA | Butte, Mont. |
| BLACK RIVER VALLEY AREA OF VERMONT | Springfield, Vt. |
| BLACK RIVER VALLEY OF VERMONT | Springfield, Vt. |
| BLACKBERRY CAPITAL OF THE WORLD | McLoud, Calif. |
| BLONDE BEAUTY OF THE LAKES | Milwaukee, Wis. |
| BLUE MARLIN CAPITAL OF THE WORLD | Hatteras, N. C. |
| BLUEBERRY CAPITAL OF THE NA-TION | Iron River, Wis. |
| BLUEBONNET CAPITAL | Marlin, Tex. |
| BLUEGRASS CAPITAL | Frankfort, Ky. |
| BLUEGRASS CAPITAL | Lexington, Ky. |
| BLUFF CITY | Eufaula, Ala. |
| BLUFF CITY | Hannibal, Mo. |
| BLUFF CITY | Memphis, Tenn. |
| BLUFF CITY | Natchez, Miss. |
| BLUFF CITY OF THE CHATTAHOO-CHEE | Eufaula, Ala. |
| BOARD FOOT | Hoquiam, Wash. |
| BOATING CAPITAL OF NEW ENGLAND | Boothbay Harbor, Me. |
| BOATING CAPITAL OF THE WORLD | Fort Lauderdale, Fla. |
| BOATING CAPITAL OF THE WORLD | Seattle, Wash. |
| BOAT RACING CAPITAL OF THE SOUTH | Guntersville, Ala. |
| BOLD NEW CITY OF THE SOUTH | Jacksonville, Fla. |
| BOOM TOWN WITHOUT OIL | Austin, Tex. |
| BOOMING CONVENTION CITY | Las Vegas, Nev. |
| BOOMING OIL RICH CITY | Houston, Tex. |
| BORDER CITY | Fall River, Mass. |
| BOOMTOWN | Borger, Tex. |
| BOOMTOWN, U. S. A. | Terre Haute, Ind. |

| | |
|---|---|
| BORDER TOWN | Rye, N. Y. |
| BOSTON | Port Gamble, Wash. |
| BOSTON OF THE WEST | St. Paul, Minn. |
| BOSTONIA | Boston, Mass. |
| BOUNTIFUL COUNTRY | Ashburn, Ga. |
| BOYHOOD HOME OF GEORGE WASH-INGTON | Fredericksburg, Va. |
| BOYHOOD HOME OF MARK TWAIN | Hannibal, Mo. |
| BOY'S TOWN | Omaha, Neb. |
| BOY'S TOWN OF NEW ENGLAND | Tilton, N. H. |
| BRAINY BOROUGH | Metuchen, N. J. |
| BRAN TOWN | Binghampton, N. Y. |
| BRASS CENTER OF THE WORLD | Waterbury, Conn. |
| BRASS CITY | Waterbury, Conn. |
| BRATWURST CAPITAL OF THE WORLD | Sheboygan, Wis. |
| BREAD-BASKET | Lancaster, Pa. |
| BREAD BASKET OF THE WORLD | Fargo, N. D. |
| BREAKFAST FOOD CITY | Battle Creek, Mich. |
| BREEZY TOWN | Chicago, Ill. |
| BREWING CAPITAL OF THE WORLD | Milwaukee, Wis. |
| BREWING CITY | Reading, Pa. |
| BRICK CAPITAL OF U. S. A. | Sanford, N. C. |
| BRIDE OF THE MOUNTAINS | Talladega, Ala. |
| BRIGHT LEAF TOBACCO CENTER | Nashville, Ga. |
| BRIGHT LEAF TOBACCO MARKET OF THE WORLD | Danville, Va. |
| BRIGHT SPOT | Dallas, Tex. |
| BRIGHT SPOT | Milwaukee, Wis. |
| BRIGHT SPOT OF AMERICA | Peoria, Ill. |
| BRIGHTEST SPOT IN EASTERN OREGON | Ontario, Ore. |
| BRIGHTNESS OF THE NOONDAY SUN | Port Gamble, Wash. |
| BRIGHTON'S FUTURE IS BRIGHT | Brighton, Colo. |
| BROADWAY COLONY IN THE HEART OF MAINE | Lakewood, Me. |
| BROADWAY OF THE DESERT | Las Vegas, Nev. |
| BROILER CAPITAL OF MAINE | Belfast, Me. |
| BROILER CAPITAL OF NEW ENGLAND | Belfast, Me. |
| BROILER CITY | Canton, Ga. |
| BROOK | Toms Brook, Va. |
| BROOKLYN OF THE SOUTH | Anniston, Ala. |
| BROOM CORN CENTER | Walsh, Colo. |
| BROWNSTONE CITY | Hummelstown, Pa. |
| BUCCANEER CITY | Fernandina Beach, Fla. |
| BUCKLE ON THE KANSAS WHEAT BELT | Dodge City, Kan. |

| | |
|---|---|
| BUCKLE ON THE OIL BELT | Independence, Kan. |
| BUCKTAIL CITY | Smethport, Pa. |
| BUMGANNON | Dungannon, Va. |
| BUNGTOWN | Cold Spring Harbor, N. Y. |
| BURG | New York, N. Y. |
| BURG ON THE BEAR | Corinne, Utah |
| BUSHWACKERS' CAPITAL | Nevada, Mo. |
| BUSIEST FRESHWATER PORT IN THE WORLD | Toledo, Ohio |
| BUSINESS AND CULTURAL CENTER OF THE ST. LAWRENCE VALLEY | Potsdam, N. Y. |
| BUSINESS CAPITAL OF THE NATION | New York, N. Y. |
| BUSINESS CAPITAL OF THE WORLD | New York, N. Y. |
| BUSINESS CENTER FOR GREATER LOS ANGELES | Culver City, Calif. |
| BUSINESS, FINANCE, INDUSTRY, SHOPPING AND TRANSPORTATION HUB | Flagstaff, Ariz. |
| BUSINESS HEART OF SOUTHWESTERN MINNESOTA | Worthington, Minn. |
| BUSINESS HEART OF THE LAKELAND AREA | Dover, N. J. |
| BUSINESS HUB OF THE SOUTHEAST | Atlanta, Ga. |
| BUSINESS POTENTIAL METROPOLITAN MARKET | Rochester, Minn. |
| BUSTLING RIVER PORT | Louisville, Ky. |
| BUSTLING CENTER OF INDUSTRY, AGRICULTURE, WHOLESALE TRADE AND SHIPPING | Fresno, Calif. |
| BUSTLING WESTERN CITY | Medford, Ore. |
| BUSY AGRICULTURAL COMMUNITY | Southwest City, Mo. |
| BUSY BUSINESS CENTER | Redlands, Calif. |
| BUSY FRIENDLY CITY | Ashland, Ky. |
| BUTTER CAPITAL OF THE WORLD | Owatonna, Minn. |
| BUTTER CITY | Manteca, Calif. |
| BUYING CENTER FOR THOUSANDS | Lockport, N. Y. |
| BUYING CENTER OF A QUARTER MILLION PEOPLE | Lancaster, Pa. |
| BYRD TOWN | Richmond, Va. |

C

| | |
|---|---|
| CALADIUM CAPITAL OF THE WORLD | Lake Placid, Fla. |
| CALIFORNIA AT ITS BEST | San Diego, Calif. |
| CALIFORNIA'S ENCHANTING CITY | Santa Barbara, Calif. |

CALIFORNIA'S FASTEST GROWING

| | |
|---|---|
| CITY | Chula Vista, Calif. |
| CALIFORNIA'S INLAND HARBOR | Stockton, Calif. |
| CALIFORNIA'S WORLD-FAMOUS ALL-YEAR RESORT | Santa Barbara, Calif. |
| CAMEL CITY | Winston-Salem, N.C. |
| CAMELLIA CITY | Greenville, Ala. |
| CAMELLIA CITY | Quitman, Ga. |
| CAMELLIA CITY OF AMERICA | McComb, Miss. |
| CAMELLIA CITY OF THE SOUTH | Thomson, Ga. |
| CAMERA CENTER | Rochester, N.Y. |
| CAMERA CITY | Rochester, N.Y. |
| CAMPING GROUND OF THE SEMINOLE INDIANS | Silver Springs, Fla. |
| 'CAN DO' CITY | Hazleton, Pa. |
| CANAL CITY | Hollidaysburg, Pa. |
| CANAL CITY | Sturgeon Bay, Wis. |
| CANDY CAPITAL OF GEORGIA | Eastman, Ga. |
| CANNED SALMON CAPITAL OF THE WORLD | Ketchikan, Alaska |
| CANNERY CITY | Seattle, Wash. |
| CANNON CITY | Kannapolis, N.C. |
| CANOE CITY | Old Town, Me. |
| CANYON CITY | Wellsboro, Pa. |
| CAPITAL CITY | Albany, N.Y. |
| CAPITAL CITY | Annapolis, Md. |
| CAPITAL CITY | Atlanta, Ga. |
| CAPITAL CITY | Augusta, Me. |
| CAPITAL CITY | Austin, Tex. |
| CAPITAL CITY | Baton Rouge, La. |
| CAPITAL CITY | Bismarck, N.D. |
| CAPITAL CITY | Boise, Idaho |
| CAPITAL CITY | Boston, Mass. |
| CAPITAL CITY | Carson City, Nev. |
| CAPITAL CITY | Charleston, W.Va. |
| CAPITAL CITY | Cheyenne, Wyo. |
| CAPITAL CITY | Columbia, S.C. |
| CAPITAL CITY | Columbus, Ohio |
| CAPITAL CITY | Concord, N.H. |
| CAPITAL CITY | Denver, Colo. |
| CAPITAL CITY | Des Moines, Iowa |
| CAPITAL CITY | Dover, Del. |
| CAPITAL CITY | Frankfort, Ky. |
| CAPITAL CITY | Harrisburg, Pa. |
| CAPITAL CITY | Hartford, Conn. |
| CAPITAL CITY | Helena, Mont. |
| CAPITAL CITY | Honolulu, Hawaii |
| CAPITAL CITY | Indianapolis, Ind. |

| | |
|---|---|
| CAPITAL CITY | Jackson, Miss. |
| CAPITAL CITY | Jefferson City, Mo. |
| CAPITAL CITY | Juneau, Alaska |
| CAPITAL CITY | Lansing, Mich. |
| CAPITAL CITY | Lincoln, Neb. |
| CAPITAL CITY | Little Rock, Ark. |
| CAPITAL CITY | Madison, Wis. |
| CAPITAL CITY | Montgomery, Ala. |
| CAPITAL CITY | Montpelier, Vt. |
| CAPITAL CITY | Nashville, Tenn. |
| CAPITAL CITY | Oklahoma City, Okla. |
| CAPITAL CITY | Olympia, Wash. |
| CAPITAL CITY | Phoenix, Ariz. |
| CAPITAL CITY | Pierre, S. D. |
| CAPITAL CITY | Providence, R. I. |
| CAPITAL CITY | Raleigh, N. C. |
| CAPITAL CITY | Richmond, Va. |
| CAPITAL CITY | Sacramento, Calif. |
| CAPITAL CITY | St. Paul, Minn. |
| CAPITAL CITY | Salem, Ore. |
| CAPITAL CITY | Salt Lake City, Utah |
| CAPITAL CITY | Santa Fe, N. M. |
| CAPITAL CITY | Springfield, Ill. |
| CAPITAL CITY | Tallahassee, Fla. |
| CAPITAL CITY | Topeka, Kan. |
| CAPITAL CITY | Trenton, N. J. |
| CAPITAL CITY | Washington, D. C. |
| CAPITAL CITY | Youngstown, Ohio |
| CAPITAL CITY | Zanesville, Ohio |
| CAPITAL CITY DIFFERENT | Santa Fe, N. M. |
| CAPITAL CITY OF A GREAT IN-DUSTRIAL EMPIRE | Youngstown, Ohio |
| CAPITAL CITY OF A GREAT NATION | Washington, D. C. |
| CAPITAL CITY OF A GREAT TRADE EMPIRE | Cleveland, Ohio |
| CAPITAL CITY OF ALASKA | Juneau, Alaska |
| CAPITAL CITY OF ARIZONA | Phoenix, Ariz. |
| CAPITAL CITY OF FABULOUS FLORIDA | Tallahassee, Fla. |
| CAPITAL CITY OF GOOD LIVING, COMMERCE AND INDUSTRY | Salem, Ore. |
| CAPITAL CITY OF INDUSTRIAL PRO-GRESS | Nashville, Tenn. |
| CAPITAL CITY OF SOUTHERN VIR-GINIA | Danville, Va. |
| CAPITAL CITY OF SOUTHSIDE VIR-GINIA | Danville, Va. |
| CAPITAL CITY OF TENNESSEE | Nashville, Tenn. |

| | |
|---|---|
| CAPITAL CITY OF THE COUNTRY WITH A COPPER BOTTOM | Globe, Ariz. |
| CAPITAL CITY OF THE LAND OF ARK-LA-TEX | Shreveport, La. |
| CAPITAL CITY OF THE LAND OF THE SKY | Asheville, N. C. |
| CAPITAL CITY, U. S. A. | Washington, D. C. |
| CAPITAL OF AMERICA | Washington, D. C. |
| CAPITAL OF AMERICA'S STATE OF OPPORTUNITY | Jackson, Miss. |
| CAPITAL OF AN EMPIRE | Juneau, Alaska |
| CAPITAL OF COLONIAL VIRGINIA | Williamsburg, Va. |
| CAPITAL OF CRACKPOTS | Los Angeles, Calif. |
| CAPITAL OF DUNELAND | Michigan City, Ind. |
| CAPITAL OF EASTERN OREGON | Ontario, Ore. |
| CAPITAL OF FINANCE | New York, N. Y. |
| CAPITAL OF FLORIDA'S ENCHANTING GOLD COAST | Miami Beach, Fla. |
| CAPITAL OF FLORIDA'S SUGAR IN- DUSTRY | Clewiston, Fla. |
| CAPITAL OF LITTLE DIXIE | Mexico, Mo. |
| CAPITAL OF MISERABLE HUTS | Washington, D. C. |
| CAPITAL OF NEW ENGLAND | Boston, Mass. |
| CAPITAL OF OLD CALIFORNIA | Monterey, Calif. |
| CAPITAL OF OPPORTUNITY | Bismarck, N. D. |
| CAPITAL OF PENNSYLVANIA GER- MAN-LAND | Reading, Pa. |
| CAPITAL OF RADIO | Camden, N. J. |
| CAPITAL OF SOONERLAND | Oklahoma City, Okla. |
| CAPITAL OF SOUTH CENTRAL OKLAHOMA | Ardmore, Okla. |
| CAPITAL OF SUNSHINE | Palm Springs, Calif. |
| CAPITAL OF THE ATOMIC AGE | Los Alamos, N. M. |
| CAPITAL OF THE BIG LAKE | Bull Shoals, Ark. |
| CAPITAL OF THE BLUE-GRASS REGION | Lexington, Ky. |
| CAPITAL OF THE BROILER INDUSTRY | Belfast, Me. |
| CAPITAL OF THE CAROLINAS | Charleston, S. C. |
| CAPITAL OF THE CHIPPEWA NATION | Cass Lake, Minn. |
| CAPITAL OF THE COASTAL EMPIRE OF SOUTH CAROLINA | Charleston, S. C. |
| CAPITAL OF THE CONFEDERACY | Richmond, Va. |
| CAPITAL OF THE EMPIRE STATE | Albany, N. Y. |
| CAPITAL OF THE EVERGREEN CLUB | Olympia, Wash. |
| CAPITAL OF THE FIRST STATE | Dover, Del. |
| CAPITAL OF THE "FREE STATE" OF VAN ZANDT COUNTY | Canton, Tex. |

256

| | |
|---|---|
| CAPITAL OF THE GREAT CHICKASAW NATION | Tupelo, Miss. |
| CAPITAL OF THE HEART O' THE LAKES | Rhinelander, Wis. |
| CAPITAL OF THE HORSE WORLD | Lexington, Ky. |
| CAPITAL OF THE LAND OF OUT-DOORS | Portland, Ore. |
| CAPITAL OF THE MIDLAND EMPIRE | Billings, Mont. |
| CAPITAL OF THE MOST HISTORIC RESORT AREA IN AMERICA | Norfolk, Va. |
| CAPITAL OF THE OLD SOUTH | Richmond, Va. |
| CAPITAL OF THE PAUL BUNYAN PLAYGROUND | Brainerd, Mich. |
| CAPITAL OF THE PLANTATIONS | Charleston, S. C. |
| CAPITAL OF THE RIO GRANDE VAL-LEY | Brownsville, Tex. |
| CAPITAL OF THE ROCKY MOUNTAIN EMPIRE | Denver, Colo. |
| CAPITAL OF THE SEA ISLANDS | Beaufort, S. C. |
| CAPITAL OF THE SOUTHERN MIND | Chapel Hill, N. C. |
| CAPITAL OF THE VAST REPUBLIC | Washington, D. C. |
| CAPITAL OF THE VERMILION RANGE | Ely, Minn. |
| CAPITAL OF THE WORLD | New York, N. Y. |
| CAPITAL OF VACATIONLAND | Newport, R. I. |
| CAPITAL OF WESTERN KENTUCKY | Paducah, Ky. |
| CAPITAL OF YOUTH | Hannibal, Mo. |
| CAPITAL RESORT OF THE OZARKS | Eureka Springs, Ark. |
| CAPITOL CITY | Little Rock, Ark. |
| CAPITOL OF A GREAT EMPIRE | Williston, N. D. |
| CAPITOL OF FLORIDA'S TREASURE COAST | Fort Pierce, Fla. |
| CAPITOL OF THOROUGHBRED RACING | Saratoga Springs, N. Y. |
| CAR SHOP CITY | Berwick, Pa. |
| CARLSBAD OF AMERICA | Bedford Springs, Pa. |
| CARLSBAD OF AMERICA | French Lick, Ind. |
| CARLSBAD OF AMERICA | Hot Springs, Ark. |
| CARPET CITY | Amsterdam, N. Y. |
| CARPET CITY OF THE WORLD | Amsterdam, N. Y. |
| CARRIAGE CENTER OF THE WORLD | Amesbury, Mass. |
| CASH REGISTER CITY | Dayton, Ohio |
| CASTLE CITY | York, Pa. |
| CASUAL FAMILY BEACH RESORT IN THE CENTER OF FLORIDA'S WEST COAST | Longboat Key, Fla. |
| CATACOMB CITY | Waynesburg, Pa. |
| CATARACT CITY | Niagara Falls, N. Y. |

| | |
|---|---|
| CATCHALL OF SUCKERS | Los Angeles, Calif. |
| CATHEDRAL OF THE PLAINS | Victoria, Kan. |
| CATHEDRAL TOWN | Garden City, N. Y. |
| CATSKILLS AND COUNTY CROSSROADS OF THE CENTER FOR ACTION | Monticello, N. Y. |
| CATTLE CAPITAL AND AGRICULTURAL CENTER OF THE GREAT SOUTHWEST | Willcox, Ariz. |
| CATTLE CAPITAL OF NEBRASKA | Alliance, Neb. |
| CATTLE CAPITAL OF THE NATION | Willcox, Ariz. |
| CATTLE CAPITAL OF THE SOUTHWEST | Clovis, N. M. |
| CATTLE CAPITAL OF THE WORLD | Willcox, Ariz. |
| CATTLE CENTER | Willcox, Ariz. |
| CATTLE COUNTRY | Elko, Nev. |
| CAVERN CITY | Carlsbad, N. M. |
| CELERY CITY | Kalamazoo, Mich. |
| CELERY CITY | Sanford, Fla. |
| CELESTIAL CITY | Pekin, Ill. |
| CELLULOID CITY | Hollywood, Calif. |
| CEMENT CITY | Allentown, Pa. |
| CENTER CITY | Fort Smith, Ark. |
| CENTER CITY OF SOUTHERN GEORGIA | Waycross, Ga. |
| CENTER CITY OF THE OZARKS | Berryville, Ark. |
| CENTER FOR AGRICULTURE, INDUSTRY AND RECREATION | Los Banos, Calif. |
| CENTER FOR GIANT BLUEBERRY BUSHES | Crestview, Fla. |
| CENTER FOR GOOD LIVING, AGRICULTURE, RECREATION AND INDUSTRY | Atwater, Calif. |
| CENTER FOR RANCHING | Winnemucca, Nev. |
| CENTER OF A FISHERMAN'S PARADISE | McCook, Neb. |
| CENTER OF A LAND OF ENCHANTMENT | Kalispell, Mont. |
| CENTER OF A LIVELY INDUSTRIAL AND AGRICULTURAL TRADE AREA | Marshall, Mo. |
| CENTER OF A MARVELOUS NATURAL PLAYGROUND | Lake City, Mich. |
| CENTER OF A RICH AND HIGHLY DIVERSIFIED AGRICULTURAL EMPIRE | Augusta, Ga. |
| CENTER OF A SPORTSMAN'S PARADISE | Palm Beach, Fla. |
| CENTER OF ACTIVITY | Angola, Ind. |
| CENTER OF ACTIVITY FOR AMERICA'S SPACE PROGRAM | Cocoa Beach, Fla. |

258

| | |
|---|---|
| CENTER OF AGRICULTURAL, COMMERCIAL, INDUSTRIAL OIL TRANSPORTATION | Mattoon, Ill. |
| CENTER OF AGRICULTURE, COMMERCE, INDUSTRY OIL AND TRANSPORTATION | Mattoon, Ill. |
| CENTER OF ALL THERE IS TO SEE IN THE UPPER PENINSULA | Marquette, Mich. |
| CENTER OF ALL VACATION FUN | Indio, Calif. |
| CENTER OF ALLEGHENY VALLEY'S BUSINESS AND INDUSTRIAL ACTIVITY | New Kensington, Pa. |
| CENTER OF AMERICA'S FASTEST GROWING AREA | West Palm Beach, Fla. |
| CENTER OF AMERICA'S GREATEST MARKET | Buffalo, N. Y. |
| CENTER OF CALIFORNIA | Stockton, Calif. |
| CENTER OF CENTRAL FLORIDA | Astatula, Fla. |
| CENTER OF CIVIC AND INDUSTRIAL OPPORTUNITY | Wayne, Mich. |
| CENTER OF COMMERCE | Elmira, N. Y. |
| CENTER OF COMMERCE | Pierre, S. D. |
| CENTER OF COMMERCE AND CULTURE | Jackson, Miss. |
| CENTER OF CULTURE | Pittsfield, Mass. |
| CENTER OF DISTRIBUTION | Lynn, Mass. |
| CENTER OF EASTERN STEEL MAKING | Pittsburgh, Pa. |
| CENTER OF EVERYTHING IN NORTHERN ARIZONA | Flagstaff, Ariz. |
| CENTER OF FLORIDA'S EXCITING WEST COAST | Tampa, Fla. |
| CENTER OF GOODING COUNTY | Wendell, Idaho |
| CENTER OF GREAT WEALTH | Pierre, S. D. |
| CENTER OF HISTORY, EDUCATION AND INDUSTRY | Cambridge, Mass. |
| CENTER OF HISTORY IN THE MAKING | Washington, D. C. |
| CENTER OF INDUSTRIAL AND ATOMIC DEVELOPMENT | Buffalo, N. Y. |
| CENTER OF INDUSTRIAL DEVELOPMENT IN WESTERN CONNECTICUT | Waterbury, Conn. |
| CENTER OF INDUSTRY | Gary, Ind. |
| CENTER OF INDUSTRY | Tacoma, Wash. |
| CENTER OF INNOVATION AND CULTURE | Chicago, Ill. |
| CENTER OF MAINE | Bangor, Me. |

| | |
|---|---|
| CENTER OF MID-AMERICAN INDUS-<br>TRIAL PROGRESS | Joplin, Mo. |
| CENTER OF MIDWEST FRIENDLINESS | Peoria, Ill. |
| CENTER OF MONTANA'S WONDER-<br>LAND | Butte, Mont. |
| CENTER OF NORTH ARIZONA'S SCENIC<br>VACATIONLAND | Flagstaff, Ariz. |
| CENTER OF NORTHERN ARIZONA'S<br>SCENIC BEAUTY | Winslow, Ariz. |
| CENTER OF OLD VIRGINIA | Lynchburg, Va. |
| CENTER OF OUR NATION'S PLAY-<br>GROUND | Eustis, Fla. |
| CENTER OF PREHISTORIC, HISTORIC<br>AND SCENIC INTEREST | Santa Fe, N. M. |
| CENTER OF PROGRESS IN MAINE | Pittsfield, Me. |
| CENTER OF SAN GORGONIO MOUN-<br>TAINS | Beaumont, Calif. |
| CENTER OF SCENIC AMERICA | Salt Lake City,<br>Utah |
| CENTER OF SCENIC SOUTHEAST<br>ALASKA | Wrangell, Alaska |
| CENTER OF SCENIC UTAH | Provo, Utah |
| CENTER OF SIXTY-ONE LAKES | Brighton, Mich. |
| CENTER OF SOUTHEAST ALASKA'S<br>VACATIONLAND | Petersburg, Alaska |
| CENTER OF SUMMER AND WINTER<br>SPORTS | Reno, Nev. |
| CENTER OF THE ACTION IN THE<br>TREMENDOUS HOUSTON-GULF<br>COAST | Alvin, Tex. |
| CENTER OF THE AIRCRAFT INDUSTRY | Grand Prairie, Tex. |
| CENTER OF THE BEAUTIFUL NORTH<br>SHORE OF MASSACHUSETTS | Salem, Mass. |
| CENTER OF THE BLUE GRASS AREA | Winchester, Ky. |
| CENTER OF THE COAL FIELDS | Appalachia, Va. |
| CENTER OF THE DUDE RANCH IN-<br>DUSTRY | Sheridan, Wyo. |
| CENTER OF THE FLOUR MILLING<br>INDUSTRY | Minneapolis, Minn. |
| CENTER OF THE GOGEBIC IRON<br>RANGE | Ironwood, Mich. |
| CENTER OF THE GREAT KANSAS<br>AGRICULTURAL EMPIRE | Abilene, Kan. |
| CENTER OF THE GREATEST MANU-<br>FACTURING AREA IN THE SOUTH | Greensboro, N. C. |
| CENTER OF THE LOUISIANA ORANGE<br>INDUSTRY | Buras, La. |
| CENTER OF THE MARBLE INDUSTRY | Rutland, Vt. |

| | |
|---|---|
| CENTER OF THE MIDWEST AND THE COUNTRY | Des Moines, Iowa |
| CENTER OF THE MOST POPULAR RESORT SECTION IN THE OZARKS | Mountain Home, Ark. |
| CENTER OF THE MOST PRODUCTIVE AGRICULTURAL AREA IN THE NATION | Dinuba, Calif. |
| CENTER OF THE NATION | Topeka, Kan. |
| CENTER OF THE NATION'S GREATEST CONCENTRATION OF VARIED NATURAL ATTRACTIONS | Prescott, Ariz. |
| CENTER OF THE NORTHEAST | Harrisburg, Pa. |
| CENTER OF THE OLIVE INDUSTRY | Corning, Calif. |
| CENTER OF THE PALM BEACHES | Riviera Beach, Fla. |
| CENTER OF THE PINEAPPLE INDUSTRY | Honolulu, Hawaii |
| CENTER OF THE RED RIVER VALLEY BREAD BASKET | Grafton, N. D. |
| CENTER OF THE RICH GAS AND SULPHUR FIELDS | Edgewood, Tex. |
| CENTER OF THE ST. LAWRENCE VALLEY VACATIONLAND | Colton, N. Y. |
| CENTER OF THE SOUTHLAND | Bueno Park, Calif. |
| CENTER OF THE SUMMER-TIME WORLD IN THE GREAT NORTH WOODS | Brant Lake, N. Y. |
| CENTER OF THE SUNSHINE STATE | Pierre, S. D. |
| CENTER OF THE UNIVERSE | Duluth, Minn. |
| CENTER OF THE VAST INLAND EMPIRE | Spokane, Wash. |
| CENTER OF THE WORLD | New York, N. Y. |
| CENTER OF THE WORLD'S BEST MARKET | Reading, Pa. |
| CENTER OF THE WORLD'S BIGGEST MARKET | East Brunswick, N. J. |
| CENTER OF THE WORLD'S LARGEST IRRIGATION, POWER NAVIGATION FLOOD CONTROL PROJECT | Huron, S. D. |
| CENTER OF THE WORLD'S MAGNET WIRE PRODUCTION | Ft. Wayne, Ind. |
| CENTER OF THE WORLD'S RUBBER MANUFACTURING | Akron, Ohio |
| CENTER OF TRANSPORTATION TO ALL POINTS | San Mateo, Calif. |
| CENTER OF U. S. JEWELRY PRODUCTION | Providence, R. I. |
| CENTER OF YAVAPAI | Prescott, Ariz. |
| CENTER OF YEAR 'ROUND RECRE- | |

| | |
|---|---|
| ...ATION | Jackson, Miss. |
| CENTRAL CITY | Syracuse, N. Y. |
| CENTRAL CITY OF SOUTH DAKOTA | Huron, S. D. |
| CENTRAL CITY OF THE GREAT SOUTHWEST | Oklahoma City, Okla. |
| CENTRAL CITY OF THE METROPOLITAN MISSISSIPPI GULF COAST | Gulfport, Miss. |
| CENTRAL FLORIDA'S CITY OF BIG OPPORTUNITY | Maitland, Fla. |
| CENTRAL FLORIDA'S LAKE REGION | Winter Haven, Fla. |
| CENTRAL GATEWAY OF THE GREAT LAKES | Toledo, Ohio |
| CERAMIC CITY | East Liverpool, Ohio |
| CEREAL FOOD CENTER OF THE WORLD | Battle Creek, Mich. |
| CESSPOOL FOR GAMBLING JOINTS | Lake Tahoe, Calif. |
| CHAIR AND DESK CITY | Jasper, Ind. |
| CHAIR CAPITAL OF THE WORLD | Thomasville, N. C. |
| CHAIR CENTER OF THE WORLD | Union City, Pa. |
| CHAIR CITY | Sheboygan, Wis. |
| CHAIR CITY | Thomasville, N. C. |
| CHAMPION CITY | Springfield, Ohio |
| CHARM CIRCLE OF THE SOUTH | McComb, Miss. |
| CHARM SPOT OF THE DEEP SOUTH | Mobile, Ala. |
| CHARMED LAND OF UNEQUALLED BEAUTY | Salem, Ore. |
| CHARMING SPOT IN WHICH TO LIVE AND WORK | Norwalk, Conn. |
| CHARTER OAK CITY | Hartford, Conn. |
| CHAUTAUQUA OF THE GREAT LAKES | Lakeside, Ohio |
| CHEESE CAPITOL OF THE WORLD | Plymouth, Wis. |
| CHEMICAL CAPITAL OF THE WORLD | Wilmington, Del. |
| CHEMICAL CAPITAL OF VIRGINIA | Hopewell, Va. |
| CHEMICAL CENTER OF THE SOUTH | Baton Rouge, La. |
| CHEMICAL CENTER OF THE WORLD | South Charleston, W. Va. |
| CHEMICAL CITY | Berlin, N. H. |
| CHEMICAL CITY | Charleston, W. Va. |
| CHEMURGIC CITY | Laurel, Miss. |
| CHEROKEE INDIAN CAPITAL | Calhoun, Ga. |
| CHERRY CAPITAL OF THE WORLD | Traverse City, Mich. |
| CHERRY CITY | Salem, Ore. |
| CHERRY CITY | Traverse City, Mich. |
| CHERRY CITY OF CALIFORNIA | San Leandro, Calif. |
| CHI | Chicago, Ill. |
| CHICAGO OF NEVADA | Beatty, Nev. |
| CHICAGO OF THE NORTH | Anchorage, Alaska |

| | |
|---|---|
| CHICAGO OF THE SOUTH | Okeechobee, Fla. |
| CHICAGO OF THE SOUTHWEST | Fort Worth, Tex. |
| CHIEF CITY OF THE BLUEGRASS REGION | Lexington, Ky. |
| CHIEF CITY OF WEST VIRGINIA | Wheeling, W. Va. |
| CHIEF INDUSTRIAL CITY OF THE EASTERN PANHANDLE | Martinsburg, W. Va. |
| CHILD OF THE RIVER | St. Louis, Mo. |
| CHIMNEYVILLE | Jackson, Miss. |
| CHOCOLATE CITY | Hershey, Pa. |
| CHOCOLATE CROSSROADS OF THE WORLD | Hershey, Pa. |
| CHOCOLATE TOWN | Hershey, Pa. |
| CHOCOLATE TOWN, U. S. A. | Hershey, Pa. |
| CHOICEST SPOT IN ALL FLORIDA | Anna Maria, Fla. |
| CHOSEN SPOT IN THE BEAUTIFUL FINGER LAKES | Canandaigua, N. Y. |
| CHRISTIANSVILLE | Chase City, Va. |
| CHRISTMAS CITY | Bethlehem, Pa. |
| CHRISTMAS CITY | Minden, Neb. |
| CHRISTMAS CITY | Noel, Mo. |
| CHRISTMAS CITY | Taunton, Mass. |
| CHRISTMAS TOWN, U. S. A. | Shelton, Wash. |
| CHRISTMAS TREE CAPITAL OF THE NATION | Eureka, Mont. |
| CHRISTMAS TREE CAPITAL OF THE WORLD | Eureka, Mont. |
| CHRISTMAS TREE CAPITAL OF THE WORLD | Indiana, Pa. |
| CHURCH CITY | Brooklyn, N. Y. |
| CIGAR CAPITAL OF AMERICA | Tampa, Fla. |
| CIGAR CAPITAL OF THE WORLD | Key West, Fla. |
| CIGAR CITY | Tampa, Fla. |
| CINEMA CAPITAL | Hollywood, Calif. |
| CINEMALAND | Hollywood, Calif. |
| CINEMATOWN | Hollywood, Calif. |
| CINEMA VILLAGE | Hollywood, Calif. |
| CIRCLE CITY | Corona, Calif. |
| CIRCLE CITY | Hollywood, Calif. |
| CIRCUS CAPITAL | Somers, N. Y. |
| CIRCUS CAPITAL OF AMERICA IN THE NINETEENTH CENTURY | Delavan, Wis. |
| CIRCUS CITY | Burley, Wash. |
| CIRCUS CITY | Peru, Ind. |
| CIRCUS CITY OF THE WORLD | Peru, Ind. |
| CIRCUS TOWN, U. S. A. | Hugo, Okla. |
| CIRCUS WITHOUT A TENT | Los Angeles, Calif. |
| CITADEL OF HISTORY | San Antonio, Tex. |

| | |
|---|---|
| CITADEL OF THE CONFEDERACY | Atlanta, Ga. |
| CITADEL OF THE OLD NORTHWEST | Vincennes, Ind. |
| CITRUS CAPITAL OF THE WORLD | Winter Haven, Fla. |
| CITRUS CENTER | Cocoa, Fla. |
| CITRUS METROPOLIS | Los Angeles, Calif. |
| CITRUS CENTER OF THE WORLD | Winter Haven, Fla. |
| CITY | New York, N.Y. |
| CITY ALIVE | New Rochelle, N.Y. |
| CITY ALWAYS EXPANDING | Morristown, Tenn. |
| CITY AMONG THE OAKS | La Belle, Fla. |
| CITY AT THE CROSSROADS DOWN EAST | Ellsworth, Me. |
| CITY AT THE CROSSROADS OF HIGH DIPLOMACY | New York, N.Y. |
| CITY AT THE CROSSROADS OF HOLIDAY HIGHLANDS | Lake Alfred, Fla. |
| CITY AT THE CROSSROADS OF MID-AMERICA | Carthage, Mo. |
| CITY AT THE CROSSROADS OF NEBRASKALAND'S BEST HUNTING COUNTRY | York, Neb. |
| CITY AT THE CROSSROADS OF THE EMPIRE STATE | Utica, N.Y. |
| CITY AT THE CROSSROADS OF SOUTHWEST FLORIDA | La Belle, Fla. |
| CITY AT THE CROSSROADS OF THE OLD AND NEW SOUTH | Jackson, Miss. |
| CITY AT THE CROSSROADS OF THE SOUTH | Memphis, Tenn. |
| CITY AT THE CROSSROADS OF TRANS-AMERICA'S HIGHWAY AND THE NAVAJO TRAIL | Alamosa, Colo. |
| CITY AT THE HEART OF INDUSTRIAL NEW ENGLAND | Holyoke, Mass. |
| CITY AT THE PORTAL TO THE UNIVERSE | Cocoa Beach, Fla. |
| CITY AT THE TIP OF CAPE ANN | Rockport, Mass. |
| CITY AT THE TOP IN FLORIDA | Quincy, Fla. |
| CITY AT THE TOP IN ILLINOIS | Rockford, Ill. |
| CITY AT THE TOP O' TEXAS | Pampa, Tex. |
| CITY AT THE WATER'S EDGE | Stockton, Mo. |
| CITY ATOP THE NATION'S ROOF GARDEN | Salida, Colo. |
| CITY BEAUTIFUL | Birmingham, Ala. |
| CITY BEAUTIFUL | Chicago, Ill. |
| CITY BEAUTIFUL | Coral Gables, Fla. |
| CITY BEAUTIFUL | Dayton, Ohio |
| CITY BEAUTIFUL | Hartford, Conn. |

| | |
|---|---|
| CITY BEAUTIFUL | Marshall, Mo. |
| CITY BEAUTIFUL | Memphis, Tenn. |
| CITY BEAUTIFUL | Milwaukee, Wis. |
| CITY BEAUTIFUL | Nashville, Tenn. |
| CITY BEAUTIFUL | Nauvoo, Ill. |
| CITY BEAUTIFUL | New Richmond, Wis. |
| CITY BEAUTIFUL | Orlando, Fla. |
| CITY BEAUTIFUL | San Francisco, Calif. |
| CITY BEAUTIFUL | Tavares, Fla. |
| CITY BEAUTIFUL | Tulsa, Okla. |
| CITY BEAUTIFUL | Uvalde, Tex. |
| CITY BEAUTIFUL | Valley City, N. D. |
| CITY BEAUTIFUL | Vernon, Tex. |
| CITY BEAUTIFUL | Washington, D. C. |
| CITY BEAUTIFUL IN THE HEART OF FLORIDA | Orlando, Fla. |
| CITY BEAUTIFUL IN THE LAND O'LAKES | Fergus Falls, Minn. |
| CITY BESIDE THE BROAD MISSOURI | Bismarck, N. D. |
| CITY BETWEEN THE CITY AND THE SEA | Forest Grove, Ore. |
| CITY BETWEEN THE MOUNTAINS AND THE SEA | Montebello, Calif. |
| CITY BIG ENOUGH FOR OPPORTUNITY - SMALL ENOUGH FOR FRIENDLINESS | Castro Valley, Calif. |
| CITY BLESSED IN MANY WAYS | Eau Claire, Wis. |
| CITY BUILDING FOR TODAY AND PLANNING FOR TOMORROW | Jesup, Ga. |
| CITY BUILT AROUND A PARK | San Diego, Calif. |
| CITY BUILT IN A DAY | Los Angeles, Calif. |
| CITY BUILT ON OIL, SOIL AND TOIL | Ponca City, Okla. |
| CITY BUILT ON SAND | Los Angeles, Calif. |
| CITY BUILT BY HANDS | Rochester, N. Y. |
| CITY BUILT ON AN ISTHMUS | Madison, Wis. |
| CITY BY ACCIDENT | Yoakum, Tex. |
| CITY BY THE FALLS | Louisville, Ky. |
| CITY BY THE GOLDEN GATE | San Francisco, Calif. |
| CITY BY THE GREAT SALT LAKE | Salt Lake City, Utah |
| CITY BY THE LAKE | Chicago, Ill. |
| CITY BY THE LAKE | Coeur d'Alene, Idaho |
| CITY-BY-THE-SEA | Asbury Park, N. J. |
| CITY BY THE SEA | Charleston, S. C. |
| CITY BY THE SEA | Long Beach, Calif. |
| CITY BY THE SEA | Long Beach, N. Y. |
| CITY BY THE SEA | Newport, R. I. |
| CITY BY THE SEA | Norfolk, Va. |

265

| | |
|---|---|
| CITY BY THE SEA | Perth Amboy, N. J. |
| CITY BY THE SEA | San Diego, Calif. |
| CITY BY THE SEA | San Francisco, Calif. |
| CITY BY THE SEA | Santa Barbara, Calif. |
| CITY BY THE SEA IN BEAUTIFUL SOUTHEASTERN ALASKA | Sitka, Alaska |
| CITY BY THE WACCAMAW | Conway, S. C. |
| CITY CARE FORGOT | New Orleans, La. |
| CITY CENTERED IN THE HEART OF THE SUNCOAST | Ruskin, Fla. |
| CITY COOLER BY A MILE | Avalon, N. J. |
| CITY COSMOPOLITAN | San Francisco, Calif. |
| CITY DEEP IN THE HEART OF TEXAS | Dallas, Tex. |
| CITY DESIGNED FOR LIVING | Santa Rosa, Calif. |
| CITY DIFFERENT | Santa Fe, N. M. |
| CITY DOWN ON THE MESABI | Aurora, Minn. |
| CITY EXCITINGLY ALIVE AND PROGRESSIVE | Pittsburgh, Pa. |
| CITY FAMOUS FOR FRIENDLINESS | Malone, N. Y. |
| CITY FOR A VACATION OF A LIFETIME | Elk Rapids, Mich. |
| CITY FOR A VACATION OR A LIFETIME OF REAL LIVING | Eustis, Fla. |
| CITY FOR EVERY VACATION PLEASURE | Whitehall, Mich. |
| CITY FOR FAMILY FUN AND ACTION | Dubuque, Iowa |
| CITY FOR FAMILY FUN IN THE FLORIDA SUN | Lake Weir, Fla. |
| CITY FOR FAMILY LIVING AT ITS BEST | Hialeah, Fla. |
| CITY FOR GRACIOUS LIVING | Chula Vista, Calif. |
| CITY FOR LIVING | St. Petersburg, Fla. |
| CITY FOR OCEANS OF FUN | Santa Monica, Calif. |
| CITY FOR ROMANTICS | San Francisco, Calif. |
| CITY FOR YEAR ROUND FISHING VARIETY | Pompano, Beach, Fla. |
| CITY FOR THE FULL LIFE | Berlin, N. H. |
| CITY FOUNDED UPON COOPERATION | Winston-Salem, N. C. |
| CITY FOUR DIMENSIONAL | Lexington, N. C. |
| CITY GEARED TO SPACE-AGE FAMILIES | Slidell, La. |
| CITY GROWING WITH PLASTICS | Beaverton, Mich. |
| CITY HALF A WORLD FROM THE "HUBBUB" | Denton, Tex. |
| CITY HALF AN HOUR FROM THE HUB | Denton, Tex. |

| | |
|---|---|
| CITY HISTORICAL AND ENJOYABLE | Ogdensburg, N. Y. |
| CITY IN A FOREST | Washington, D. C. |
| CITY IN A VALLEY WHERE RECUPER-ATION, REHABILITATION, REST AND RELAXATION WITH RECREATION AND SCENIC BEAUTY ABOUND | Hot Springs, S. D. |
| CITY IN ARIZONA'S VALLEY OF THE SUN | Phoenix, Ariz. |
| CITY IN BEAUTIFUL BAY COUNTY | Panama City, Fla. |
| CITY IN CENTRAL CALIFORNIA CON-VENIENT TO EVERYTHING | Oakdale, Calif. |
| CITY IN FLORIDA WITH A DIFFER-ENCE | Delray Beach, Fla. |
| CITY IN FLORIDA'S FUN-FILLED HOLIDAY HIGHLANDS | Fort Meade, Fla. |
| CITY IN MARYLAND'S HISTORIC HEARTLAND | Frederick, Md. |
| CITY IN MOTION | Monrovia, Calif. |
| CITY IN PACE WITH THE SPACE AGE | Blacksburg, Va. |
| CITY IN STEP WITH TOMORROW | Stamford, Conn. |
| CITY IN THE BEAUTIFUL SHENAN-DOAH VALLEY | Winchester, Va. |
| CITY IN "THE BIG HORNS" | Sheridan, Wyo. |
| CITY IN THE CENTER OF HUNTING LANDS | Pierre, S. D. |
| CITY IN THE CENTER OF MID-AMERICA'S RIVIERA YEAR 'ROUND RESORT | Gulfport, Miss. |
| CITY IN THE CENTER OF SUNLAND | Groveland, Fla. |
| CITY IN THE CENTER OF THE BEAU-TIFUL NORTH WOODS | Park Falls, Wis. |
| CITY IN THE CENTER OF THE MOST AMAZING AND BEAUTIFUL COUN-TRY IN THE WORLD | Flagstaff, Ariz. |
| CITY IN THE CENTER OF THE WHITE MOUNTAINS | Glen, N. H. |
| CITY IN THE CENTER WHERE THE ACTION IS | Gulfport, Miss. |
| CITY IN THE COUNTRY | Danbury, Conn. |
| CITY IN THE COUNTRY | Holyoke, Mass. |
| CITY IN THE COUNTRY BY THE SEA | Beverly, Mass. |
| CITY IN THE EVERGREEN PLAY-GROUND | Portland, Ore. |
| CITY IN THE FAMOUS THERMAL BELT OF NORTH CAROLINA | Tryon, N. C. |
| CITY IN THE FLORIDA KEYS | Islamorada, Fla. |
| CITY IN THE GARDEN OF THE SUN | Bowie, Ariz. |
| CITY IN THE GARDEN OF THE SUN | Lindsay, Calif. |

| | |
|---|---|
| CITY IN THE HEART OF AMERICA'S FUTURE | Arlington, Tex. |
| CITY IN THE HEART OF ARIZONA VACATIONLAND | Mesa, Ariz. |
| CITY IN THE HEART OF CENTRAL FLORIDA'S WATER WONDERLAND | Eustis, Fla. |
| CITY IN THE HEART OF COCONINO NATIONAL FOREST | Flagstaff, Ariz. |
| CITY IN THE HEART OF COLORFUL NAPA VALLEY | St. Helena, Calif. |
| CITY IN THE HEART OF EASTERN AMERICA | Bristol, Tenn. -Va. |
| CITY IN THE HEART OF FLORIDA | Haines City, Fla. |
| CITY IN THE HEART OF FLORIDA'S CITRUS, PHOSPHATE, RECREATION, HISTORY, CATTLE | Fort Meade, Fla. |
| CITY IN THE HEART OF FLORIDA'S GULF FISHING | Carrabelle, Fla. |
| CITY IN THE HEART OF FLORIDA'S FUTURE | Quincy, Fla. |
| CITY IN THE HEART OF FLORIDA'S "TALL COUNTRY" | Quincy, Fla. |
| CITY IN THE HEART OF INDUSTRIAL AMERICA | Mc Keesport, Pa. |
| CITY IN THE HEART OF IRRIGATION | Gering, Neb. |
| CITY IN THE HEART OF MASSACHU-SETTS VACATIONLAND | Worcester, Mass. |
| CITY IN THE HEART OF MISSISSIP-PI'S RICH DELTA | Greenwood, Miss. |
| CITY IN THE HEART OF NORTHWEST FLORIDA'S MIRACLE STRIP | Destin, Fla. |
| CITY IN THE HEART OF PENNSYL-VANIA DUTCH COUNTRY | Lancaster, Pa. |
| CITY IN THE HEART OF SOUTH CEN-TRAL LOUISIANA | Lafayette, La. |
| CITY IN THE HEART OF SOUTHSIDE VIRGINIA | Victoria, Va. |
| CITY IN THE HEART OF "THE BIG HORNS" | Sheridan, Wyo. |
| CITY IN THE HEART OF THE CITRUS AREA | Lake Alfred, Fla. |
| CITY IN THE HEART OF THE CHE-QUAMEGON NATIONAL FOREST | Park Falls, Wis. |
| CITY IN THE HEART OF THE CITRUS BELT AND HOLIDAY HIGHLANDS | Auburndale, Fla. |
| CITY IN THE HEART OF THE COASTAL SEA ISLANDS | Beaufort, S. C. |
| CITY IN THE HEART OF THE DAYTONA | |

|  |  |
|---|---|
| BEACH RESORT AREA | Holly Hill, Fla. |
| CITY IN THE HEART OF THE DYNAMIC CAPE KENNEDY AREA | Palm Bay, Fla. |
| CITY IN THE HEART OF THE EAST TEXAS OIL FIELDS | Gladewater, Tex. |
| CITY IN THE HEART OF THE EVERGLADES | Clewiston, Fla. |
| CITY IN THE HEART OF THE FINGER LAKES | Trumansburg, N. Y. |
| CITY IN THE HEART OF THE GOLD COAST | Deerfield, Fla. |
| CITY IN THE HEART OF THE GREAT NEW CENTRAL FLORIDA VACATIONLAND | Plant City, Fla. |
| CITY IN THE HEART OF THE HEARTLAND | Moberly, Mo. |
| CITY IN THE HEART OF THE IRRIGATED PLATTE VALLEY | Gothenburg, Neb. |
| CITY IN THE HEART O'THE HILLS | Kerrville, Tex. |
| CITY IN THE HEART OF THE LAKES REGION | Laconia, N. H. |
| CITY IN THE HEART OF THE MIRACLE STRIP | Destin, Fla. |
| CITY IN THE HEART OF THE NATION'S FAMOUS DUDE RANCH COUNTRY | Billings, Mont. |
| CITY IN THE HEART OF THE NATION'S SUNNIEST STATE | Winslow, Ariz. |
| CITY IN THE HEART OF THE PINE RIDGE | Crawford, Neb. |
| CITY IN THE HEART OF THE SHENANDOAH VALLEY OF VIRGINIA | Winchester, Va. |
| CITY IN THE HEART OF THE SOUTHWEST WONDERLAND | Willcox, Ariz. |
| CITY IN THE HEART OF THE WORLD FAMOUS INDIAN RIVER CITRUS COUNTRY | Fort Pierce, Fla. |
| CITY IN THE HEART OF TWO HUNDRED AND FIFTY SPARKLING LAKES AND STREAMS | Grand Rapids, Mich. |
| CITY IN THE LAKE DISTRICT OF THE ADIRONDACKS | Speculator, N. Y. |
| CITY IN THE HEART OF WESTERN RANCH LAND | Pierre, S. D. |
| CITY IN THE LAND OF CHIEF WABASIS | Belding, Mich. |
| CITY IN THE LAND OF LAKES | St. Paul, Minn. |
| CITY IN THE LAND OF THE PINES | Aiken, S. C. |

269

| | |
|---|---|
| CITY IN THE LAND OF THE SKY | Asheville, N. C. |
| CITY IN THE MOUNTAIN COUNTRY | Billings, Mont. |
| CITY IN THE NORTHEAST KINGDOM | Newport, Vt. |
| CITY IN THE PINES | Flagstaff, Ariz. |
| CITY IN THE SHADOW OF THE BIG HORN | Sheridan, Wyo. |
| CITY IN THE SHADOW OF THE FAMED HILLSBORO LIGHT | Pompano Beach, Fla. |
| CITY IN THE SKY | Asheville, N. C. |
| CITY IN THE SOUTHWEST SUN COUNTRY | El Paso, Tex. |
| CITY IN THE SUN | San Antonio, Tex. |
| CITY IN THE VALLEY OF DISCOVERY | San Marcos, Calif. |
| CITY IN THE VALLEY OF THE ARKANSAS | Salida, Colo. |
| CITY IN THE VALLEY OF OPPORTUNITY | Evansville, Ind. |
| CITY IN THE VALLEY OF PROMISE | Mishawaka, Ind. |
| CITY IN THE VALLEY OF THE SUN | Glendale, Ariz. |
| CITY IN THE VERY HEART OF NEW ENGLAND | Manchester, N. H. |
| CITY IN THE WHITE MOUNTAINS | Berlin, N. H. |
| CITY IN TOUCH WITH TOMORROW | Minneapolis, Minn. |
| CITY INDUSTRIALLY SOUND AND HISTORICALLY GREAT | Petersburg, Va. |
| CITY JUST A STEP FROM THE PAST, IN STEP WITH THE PRESENT AND STEPPING TOWARD THE FUTURE | New London, Conn. |
| CITY KEYED TO YOUR WAY OF LIVING | El Cerrito, Calif. |
| CITY LOCATED IN THE HEART AND CENTER OF VERMONT | Waterbury, Vt. |
| CITY LOCATED IN THE HEART OF VIRGINIA'S INDUSTRY | Colonial Heights, Va. |
| CITY LOCATED IN THE VERY HEART OF FLORIDA | Deland, Fla. |
| CITY METROPOLIS | Los Angeles, Calif. |
| CITY MOST CONVENIENT TO ALL FLORIDA | Plant City, Fla. |
| CITY NEARER TO EVERYWHERE IN FLORIDA | Lakeland, Fla. |
| CITY 'NEATH THE HILLS | Madison, Ind. |
| CITY NEXT TO THE GREATEST CITY IN THE WORLD | Yonkers, N. Y. |
| CITY NOTED FOR DIVERSIFICATION | Mattoon, Ill. |
| CITY OF A HUNDRED HILLS | San Francisco, Calif. |
| CITY OF A THOUSAND SIGHTS | St. Louis, Mo. |

| | |
|---|---|
| CITY OF A THOUSAND THRILLS | Washington, D. C. |
| CITY OF ACHIEVEMENT | Decatur, Ala. |
| CITY OF ADVANTAGES | Dearborn, Mich. |
| CITY OF ADVANTAGES | Racine, Wis. |
| CITY OF ANGELS | Los Angeles, Calif. |
| CITY OF ANGELS | San Angelo, Tex. |
| CITY OF ANTE-BELLUM HOMES | Washington, Ga. |
| CITY OF ATTRACTIONS | Sarasota, Fla. |
| CITY OF BAKED BEANS | Boston, Mass. |
| CITY OF BALANCE | Fort Smith, Ark. |
| CITY OF BEAN EATERS | Boston, Mass. |
| CITY OF BEAUTIFUL CHURCHES | Augusta, Ga. |
| CITY OF BEAUTIFUL CHURCHES | Louisville, Ky. |
| CITY OF BEAUTIFUL CHURCHES, HOMES AND BUILDINGS | Florence, Ala. |
| CITY OF BEAUTIFUL HEIGHTS | Fort Worth, Tex. |
| CITY OF BEAUTIFUL HOMES | Augusta, Ga. |
| CITY OF BEAUTIFUL HOMES | Boise, Idaho |
| CITY OF BEAUTIFUL HOMES | Dunedin, Fla. |
| CITY OF BEAUTIFUL HOMES | Rockford, Ill. |
| CITY OF BEAUTIFUL HOMES AND THRIVING INDUSTRY | Atlanta, Ga. |
| CITY OF BEAUTIFUL HOMES AND THRIVING INDUSTRY | Madison, Wis. |
| CITY OF BEAUTIFUL LAKES | Anaheim, Calif. |
| CITY OF BEAUTIFUL PARKS | Fort Collins, Colo. |
| CITY OF BEAUTIFUL PARKS | Wheeling, W. Va. |
| CITY OF BEAUTY | Branford, Fla. |
| CITY OF BEAUTY | Brunswick, Ga. |
| CITY OF BEAUTY | Davenport, Iowa |
| CITY OF BEAUTY | Dayton, Ohio |
| CITY OF BEAUTY | Montgomery, Ala. |
| CITY OF BEAUTY | Muskogee, Okla. |
| CITY OF BEAUTY AND UNLIMITED OPPORTUNITIES | Elyria, Ohio |
| CITY OF BEAUTY ON THE SUWANNEE RIVER | Branford, Fla. |
| CITY OF BEAUTY, PROGRESS AND CULTURE | Provo, Utah |
| CITY OF BETTER LIVING | Columbus, Ind. |
| CITY OF BICYCLES | Homestead, Fla. |
| CITY OF BLACK DIAMONDS | Scranton, Pa. |
| CITY OF BRICK | Pullman, Ill. |
| CITY OF BRIDGES | Logansport, Ind. |
| CITY OF BRIDGES | Pittsburgh, Pa. |
| CITY OF BRIDGES | San Francisco, Calif. |
| CITY OF BROTHERLY LOVE | Philadelphia, Pa. |

| | |
|---|---|
| CITY OF BUSINESS | Niagara Falls, N. Y. |
| CITY OF CAMELLIAS | McComb, Miss. |
| CITY OF CAMELLIAS | Pensacola, Fla. |
| CITY OF CAPTAINS' HOUSES | Newburyport, Mass. |
| CITY OF CERTAINTIES | Des Moines, Iowa |
| CITY OF CHANCE | Las Vegas, Nev. |
| CITY OF CHARACTER IN A LAND OF BEAUTY | Arcadia, Fla. |
| CITY OF CHARM | Greensboro, N. C. |
| CITY OF CHARM | New Orleans, La. |
| CITY OF CHARMING HOUSES | Lynchburg, Va. |
| CITY OF CHEESE, CHAIRS, CHILDREN AND CHURCHES | Sheboygan, Wis. |
| CITY OF CHILDHOOD | Mooseheart, Ill. |
| CITY OF CHURCHES | Anniston, Ala. |
| CITY OF CHURCHES | Blytheville, Ark. |
| CITY OF CHURCHES | Brooklyn, N. Y. |
| CITY OF CHURCHES | Charleston, S. C. |
| CITY OF CHURCHES | Charlotte, N. C. |
| CITY OF CHURCHES | Danville, Va. |
| CITY OF CHURCHES | Ozark, Ala. |
| CITY OF CHURCHES | Philadelphia, Pa. |
| CITY OF CHURCHES | Shreveport, La. |
| CITY OF CHURCHES | Wilkinsburg, Pa. |
| CITY OF COAL KINGS | Uniontown, Pa. |
| CITY OF CONCORD | Concordia, Kan. |
| CITY OF CONTRAST AND ROMANCE | San Antonio, Tex. |
| CITY OF CONTRASTS | Huntsville, Ala. |
| CITY OF CONTRASTS | New Orleans, La. |
| CITY OF CONTRASTS | Newport, R. I. |
| CITY OF CONTRASTS | Pompano Beach, Fla. |
| CITY OF CONTRASTS | San Antonio, Tex. |
| CITY OF CONVENTIONS | Syracuse, N. Y. |
| CITY OF CONVENTIONS | Wichita, Kan. |
| CITY OF CONVERSATION | Washington, D. C. |
| CITY OF COWS, COLLEGES AND CONTENTMENT | Northfield, Minn. |
| CITY OF CULTURE | Pittsfield, Mass. |
| CITY OF CULTURE AND ENTERTAINMENT | St. Louis, Mo. |
| CITY OF CULTURE, HISTORY, INDUSTRY | Winston-Salem, N. C. |
| CITY OF DELIGHT | Fort Worth, Tex. |
| CITY OF DESTINY | Detroit, Mich. |
| CITY OF DESTINY | Duluth, Minn. |
| CITY OF DESTINY | Las Vegas, Nev. |
| CITY OF DESTINY | Panama City, Fla. |
| CITY OF DESTINY | Tacoma, Wash. |

| | |
|---|---|
| CITY OF DISTINCTION | Sioux City, Iowa |
| CITY OF DIVERSIFIED INDUSTRIES | Amsterdam, N. Y. |
| CITY OF DIVERSIFIED INDUSTRIES | Holyoke, Mass. |
| CITY OF DIVERSIFIED INDUSTRIES | Marietta, Ohio |
| CITY OF DIVERSIFIED INDUSTRIES | Worcester, Mass. |
| CITY OF DIVERSIFIED INDUSTRIES AND CIVIC ACHIEVEMENT | York, Pa. |
| CITY OF DIVERSIFIED INDUSTRY | Ellwood City, Pa. |
| CITY OF DIVERSIFIED INDUSTRY | Kingsport, Tenn. |
| CITY OF DIVERSIFIED INDUSTRY | Ogden, Utah |
| CITY OF DIVERSIFIED INDUSTRY | Salem, Ore. |
| CITY OF DIVERSIFIED INDUSTRY AND COMMERCE | Erie, Pa. |
| CITY OF DIVERSIFIED INTERESTS | Nashville, Tenn. |
| CITY OF DIVERSIFIED OPPORTUNITY | Dixon, Calif. |
| CITY OF DIVERSIFIED PRODUCTS | Elyria, Ohio |
| CITY OF DIVERSITY | Tampa, Fla. |
| CITY OF DREADFUL JOY | Los Angeles, Calif. |
| CITY OF DREAMS | Odessa, Tex. |
| CITY OF DREAMS | Salida, Colo. |
| CITY OF DYNAMIC OPPORTUNITY | Concord, Calif. |
| CITY OF ELMS | New Haven, Conn. |
| CITY OF ETERNAL VIEWS | Seattle, Wash. |
| CITY OF EXCELLENCE IN LIVING | Fullerton, Calif. |
| CITY OF EXCEPTIONAL BEAUTY | Riverside, Calif. |
| CITY OF EXCITEMENT | Los Angeles, Calif. |
| CITY OF EXECUTIVES | Birmingham, Ala. |
| CITY OF EXPANDING INDUSTRY | Nampa, Idaho |
| CITY OF EXTREMES | Chicago, Ill. |
| CITY OF FALLING WATER | Fall River, Mass. |
| CITY OF FAMILIES, FAITH AND FRIENDSHIP | Apopka, Fla. |
| CITY OF FINE EDUCATIONAL INSTITUTIONS | Rome, Ga. |
| CITY OF FINE HOMES | Midland, Tex. |
| CITY OF FINE HOMES AND STREETS | Lima, Ohio |
| CITY OF FINE HOMES, CHURCHES AND SCHOOLS | Jackson, Miss. |
| CITY OF FINE HOTELS | Tacoma, Wash. |
| CITY OF FINE SCHOOLS | Niagara Falls, N. Y. |
| CITY OF FIRSTS | Boston, Mass. |
| CITY OF FIRSTS | Kokomo, Ind. |
| CITY OF FIRSTS | Oregon City, Ore. |
| CITY OF FIRSTS | Philadelphia, Pa. |
| CITY OF FIRSTS | San Francisco, Calif. |
| CITY OF FIVE FLAGS | Mobile, Ala. |

273

| | |
|---|---|
| CITY OF FIVE FLAGS | Pensacola, Fla. |
| CITY OF FIVE-SCORE INDUSTRIES | Waltham, Mass. |
| CITY OF FLAMING ADVENTURE | San Antonio, Tex. |
| CITY OF FLOUR | Buffalo, N. Y. |
| CITY OF FLOURISHING INDUSTRIES | Schenectady, N. Y. |
| CITY OF FLOWERS | Los Angeles, Calif. |
| CITY OF FLOWERS | Montebello, Calif. |
| CITY OF FLOWERS | Springfield, Ill. |
| CITY OF FLOWING GOLD | Ranger, Tex. |
| CITY OF FLOWERS AND SUNSHINE | Los Angeles, Calif. |
| CITY OF FOUNTAINS | Milwaukee, Wis. |
| CITY OF FOUR GLORIOUS SEASONS | Hendersonville, N. C. |
| CITY OF FRIENDLINESS AND BEAUTY | Riverside, Calif. |
| CITY OF FRIENDLINESS, CULTURE AND TRADITIONS | Lynchburg, Va. |
| CITY OF FRIENDLY FOLKS | Newberry, S. C. |
| CITY OF FRIENDLY PEOPLE | New York, N. Y. |
| CITY OF FRIENDLY PEOPLE | Rochester, N. H. |
| CITY OF FUN AND FROLIC | Atlantic City, N. J. |
| CITY OF GALLOPING TINTYPES | Hollywood, Calif. |
| CITY OF GARDENS | Montebello, Calif. |
| CITY OF GIANT INDUSTRY | Rochester, N. Y. |
| CITY OF GIGANTIC INDUSTRIES, UN-PARALLELED SCHOOLS | Pine Bluff, Ark. |
| CITY OF GOLDEN DREAMS | New York, N. Y. |
| CITY OF GOOD HEALTH, LIVING AND BUSINESS | Upland, Calif. |
| CITY OF GOOD HOMES | Wyandotte, Mich. |
| CITY OF GOOD LIVING | Anaheim, Calif. |
| CITY OF GOOD LIVING | St. Petersburg, Fla. |
| CITY OF GOOD LIVING | Slidell, La. |
| CITY OF GOOD NEIGHBORS | Buffalo, N. Y. |
| CITY OF GOOD WATER | Buckley, Wash. |
| CITY OF GOVERNORS | Bellefonte, Pa. |
| CITY OF GOVERNORS | Huntsville, Ala. |
| CITY OF GOVERNORS | Rochester, N. H. |
| CITY OF GRACIOUS LIVING | El Cerrito, Calif. |
| CITY OF GRACIOUS LIVING | Houston, Tex. |
| CITY OF GRACIOUS LIVING | Huntsville, Ala. |
| CITY OF GRACIOUS LIVING | Sanford, Fla. |
| CITY OF GRACIOUS LIVING | Yonkers, N. Y. |
| CITY OF GREAT INDUSTRY | Rochester, N. Y. |
| CITY OF GROWING INDUSTRIES | New Kensington, Pa. |
| CITY OF HEALING WATERS | Hot Springs, S. D. |
| CITY OF HEALTH | San Rafael, Calif. |
| CITY OF HEALTH AND RECREATION | Atlantic City, N. J. |
| CITY OF HEALTH, HISTORY, HOSPI-TALITY | Tombstone, Ariz. |

| | |
|---|---|
| CITY OF HEAT | Thermopolis, Wyo. |
| CITY OF HILLS | Lynchburg, Va. |
| CITY OF HILLS | Oneonta, N. Y. |
| CITY OF HILLS | Somerville, Mass. |
| CITY OF HISTORIC CHARM | De Pere, Wis. |
| CITY OF HISTORIC LORE | Wheeling, W. Va. |
| CITY OF HISTORICAL CHARM | Savannah, Ga. |
| CITY OF HISTORICAL HERITAGE | Fayetteville, N. C. |
| CITY OF HISTORY | Muskogee, Okla. |
| CITY OF HISTORY AND ROMANCE | Charleston, S. C. |
| CITY OF HISTORY AND ROMANCE | Monterey, Calif. |
| CITY OF HISTORY, CULTURE, EDU-CATION, INDUSTRY | Winston-Salem, N.C. |
| CITY OF HOME OWNERS | Altoona, Pa. |
| CITY OF HOMES | Albany, Calif. |
| CITY OF HOMES | Albany, Ga. |
| CITY OF HOMES | Atlanta, Ga. |
| CITY OF HOMES | Auburn, Me. |
| CITY OF HOMES | Brooklyn, N. Y. |
| CITY OF HOMES | Buffalo, N. Y. |
| CITY OF HOMES | Dallas, Tex. |
| CITY OF HOMES | Fort Myers, Fla. |
| CITY OF HOMES | Lakewood, Ohio |
| CITY OF HOMES | Louisville, Ky. |
| CITY OF HOMES | Milwaukee, Wis. |
| CITY OF HOMES | Montebello, Calif. |
| CITY OF HOMES | Newnan, Ga. |
| CITY OF HOMES | Niagara Falls, N. Y. |
| CITY OF HOMES | Norwalk, Conn. |
| CITY OF HOMES | Philadelphia, Pa. |
| CITY OF HOMES | Port Arthur, Tex. |
| CITY OF HOMES | Portland, Ore. |
| CITY OF HOMES | Richmond Heights, Mo. |
| CITY OF HOMES | Rochester, N. Y. |
| CITY OF HOMES | Royal Oak, Mich. |
| CITY OF HOMES | St. Petersburg, Fla. |
| CITY OF HOMES | Salem, Mass. |
| CITY OF HOMES | Seattle, Wash. |
| CITY OF HOMES | Somerville, Mass. |
| CITY OF HOMES | Springfield, Mass. |
| CITY OF HOMES | Vero Beach, Fla. |
| CITY OF HOMES | Winter Haven, Fla. |
| CITY OF HOMES | Winter Park, Fla. |
| CITY OF HOMES AND DIVERSIFIED INDUSTRIES | West Allis, Wis. |
| CITY OF HOMES AND GRACIOUS LIV-ING | Melrose, Mass. |

| | |
|---|---|
| CITY OF HOMES AND INDUSTRY | East Point, Ga. |
| CITY OF HOMES AND INDUSTRY | Pueblo, Colo. |
| CITY OF HOMES AND PARKS | Burlington, Vt. |
| CITY OF HOMES, CHURCHES AND FINE SCHOOLS | Moscow, Idaho |
| CITY OF HOMES, SCHOOLS AND CHURCHES | Yoakum, Tex. |
| CITY OF HOSPITALITY | Decatur, Ala. |
| CITY OF HOSPITALITY | Fullerton, Calif. |
| CITY OF HOSPITALITY | Memphis, Tenn. |
| CITY OF HOSPITALITY AND CHARM | Plant City, Fla. |
| CITY OF HOUSES WITHOUT STREETS | Washington, D. C. |
| CITY OF HUGUENOTS | New Rochelle, N. Y. |
| CITY OF HUNDRED LAKES | Winter Haven, Fla. |
| CITY OF ILLUSION | Virginia City, Nev. |
| CITY OF INDIVIDUALITY AND CHARM | Riverside, Calif. |
| CITY OF INDUSTRIAL OPPORTUNITY | Benicia, Calif. |
| CITY OF INDUSTRIAL OPPORTUNITY | Helena, Ark. |
| CITY OF INDUSTRIAL OPPORTUNITY | Petersburg, Va. |
| CITY OF INDUSTRIAL OPPORTUNITY | Warren, Pa. |
| CITY OF INDUSTRIAL PEACE | Garfield, N. J. |
| CITY OF INDUSTRIAL POTENTIAL-ITIES | Moundsville, W. Va. |
| CITY OF INDUSTRY | Dayton, Ohio |
| CITY OF INDUSTRY | Minneapolis, Minn. |
| CITY OF INDUSTRY | Montebello, Calif. |
| CITY OF INDUSTRY | Newark, N. J. |
| CITY OF INDUSTRY | Newburyport, Mass. |
| CITY OF INDUSTRY | Niagara Falls, N. Y. |
| CITY OF INDUSTRY | Wichita, Kan. |
| CITY OF INDUSTRY AND OPPORTUN-ITY | Lynchburg, Va. |
| CITY OF INDUSTRY IN THE LAND OF SAGE AND SUN | Rock Springs, Wyo. |
| CITY OF INDUSTRY, RECREATION, BUSINESS | Oshkosh, Wis. |
| CITY OF INVESTMENTS WHERE COMMERCE AND INDUSTRY THRIVE | Long Beach, Calif. |
| CITY OF LAKE WORTH WHERE THE FUN BEGINS | Lake Worth, Fla. |
| CITY OF ISLANDS | New York, N. Y. |
| CITY OF ISMS | Syracuse, N. Y. |
| CITY OF KIND HEARTS | Boston, Mass. |
| CITY OF LAKES | Fort Worth, Tex. |
| CITY OF LAKES | La Porte, Ind. |
| CITY OF LAKES | Lakeland, Fla. |
| CITY OF LAKES | Minneapolis, Minn. |
| CITY OF LAKES AND MILLS | Minneapolis, Minn. |

| | |
|---|---|
| CITY OF LEARNING | St. Louis, Mo. |
| CITY OF LIGHTS | Fort Morgan, Colo. |
| CITY OF LIQUID GOLD | Hastings, Neb. |
| CITY OF LIQUID SUNSHINE | Los Angeles, Calif. |
| CITY OF LITTLE WEDDING CHURCHES | Las Vegas, Nev. |
| CITY OF LIVING AND LEARNING | Claremont, Calif. |
| CITY OF LITTLE MEN | Boys Town, Neb. |
| CITY OF LOST FOOTSTEPS | Washington, D. C. |
| CITY OF LOVELY GARDENS | Hartsville, S. C. |
| CITY OF LUCK | Las Vegas, Nev. |
| CITY OF MAGIC | Lowell, Mass. |
| CITY OF MAGIC | Schenectady, N. Y. |
| CITY OF MAGIC ISLANDS AND WATER-<br>WAYS | Miami Beach, Fla. |
| CITY OF MAGNIFICENT CHURCHES,<br>BEAUTIFUL HOMES | Pine Bluff, Ark. |
| CITY OF MAGNIFICENT DISTANCES | Washington, D. C. |
| CITY OF MAGNIFICENT MOUNTAINS | Fort Collins, Colo. |
| CITY OF MAGNIFICENT STORES | Wheeling, W. Va. |
| CITY OF MAGNOLIAS | Houston, Tex. |
| CITY OF MAKE BELIEVE | Los Angeles, Calif. |
| CITY OF MANIFOLD ADVANTAGES | Agusta, Me. |
| CITY OF MANY ADVENTURES | San Francisco, Calif. |
| CITY OF MANY CULTURAL ADVAN-<br>TAGES | Marietta, Ohio |
| CITY OF MANY INDUSTRIES | Rochester, N. Y. |
| CITY OF MINERAL SPRINGS | San Bernardino,<br>Calif. |
| CITY OF MIRACLES | San Francisco, Calif. |
| CITY OF MISSIONS | San Antonio, Tex. |
| CITY OF MOLLY PITCHER | Carlisle, Pa. |
| CITY OF MONUMENTS | Richmond, Va. |
| CITY OF NOTIONS | Boston, Mass. |
| CITY OF OAKS | Bartow, Fla. |
| CITY OF OAKS | Raleigh, N. C. |
| CITY OF OAKS | Tuscaloosa, Ala. |
| CITY OF OAKS AND AZALEAS | Bartow, Fla. |
| CITY OF ONE HUNDRED HILLS | San Francisco, Calif. |
| CITY OF ONE HUNDRED LAKES | Winter Haven, Fla. |
| CITY OF ONE HUNDRED LAKES<br>AND STREAMS | Superior, Wis. |
| CITY OF ONE THOUSAND LAKES | Oklahoma City,<br>Okla. |
| CITY OF OPPORTUNITIES | Brunswick, Ga. |
| CITY OF OPPORTUNITIES | Miami, Fla. |
| CITY OF OPPORTUNITIES | Saginaw, Mich. |
| CITY OF OPPORTUNITIES | Salt Lake City, Utah |

277

| | |
|---|---|
| CITY OF OPPORTUNITY | Akron, Ohio |
| CITY OF OPPORTUNITY | Albany, Ga. |
| CITY OF OPPORTUNITY | Bristol, Conn. |
| CITY OF OPPORTUNITY | Cleveland, Miss. |
| CITY OF OPPORTUNITY | Conway, Ark. |
| CITY OF OPPORTUNITY | Dallas, Tex. |
| CITY OF OPPORTUNITY | Evansville, Ind. |
| CITY OF OPPORTUNITY | Manchester, N. H. |
| CITY OF OPPORTUNITY | Memphis, Tenn. |
| CITY OF OPPORTUNITY | Montgomery, Ala. |
| CITY OF OPPORTUNITY | Nashville, Tenn. |
| CITY OF OPPORTUNITY | Oshkosh, Wis. |
| CITY OF OPPORTUNITY, RECRE-ATION, RETIREMENT | Warsaw, Mo. |
| CITY OF ORCHIDS | Hilo, Hawaii |
| CITY OF ORCHESTRAS | New York, N. Y. |
| CITY OF ORDERLY GROWTH | Salem, Ore. |
| CITY OF OUTSTANDING EDUCA-TIONAL ADVANTAGES | Florence, Ala. |
| CITY OF PALMS | Fort Myers, Fla. |
| CITY OF PALMS | McAllen, Tex. |
| CITY OF PALMS | Pharr, Tex. |
| CITY OF PANORAMIC BOULEVARDS | Fort Collins, Colo. |
| CITY OF PAPER | Camas, Wash. |
| CITY OF PARKS | Madison, Wis. |
| CITY OF PARKS | Merrill, Wis. |
| CITY OF PAUL REVERE | Boston, Mass. |
| CITY OF PEACE | Salem, Mass. |
| CITY OF PEACE AND PLENTY | Pine Bluff, Ark. |
| CITY OF PEACHES | Brigham City, Utah |
| CITY OF PENN | Philadelphia, Pa. |
| CITY OF PEOPLE | Demopolis, Ala. |
| CITY OF PERSONALITY | Cincinnati, Ohio |
| CITY OF PINES AND FLOWERS | Dothan, Ala. |
| CITY OF PLEASANT LIVING | Pensacola, Fla. |
| CITY OF PLEASANT LIVING AND INDUSTRY | Watertown, N. Y. |
| CITY OF PLEASANT MEMORIES | Jacksonville, Fla. |
| CITY OF PLENTIFUL PLAINS | Fort Collins, Colo. |
| CITY OF PRESIDENTS | Quincy, Mass. |
| CITY OF PRIDE AND PROGRESS | San Pablo, Calif. |
| CITY OF PROGRESS | Dayton, Ohio |
| CITY OF PROGRESS | Dubuque, Iowa |
| CITY OF PROGRESS | Edgewater, Fla. |
| CITY OF PROGRESS | Jesup, Ga. |
| CITY OF PROGRESS | North Bend, Ore. |
| CITY OF PROGRESS | Reading, Pa. |
| CITY OF PROGRESS | Springfield, Ohio |

278

| | |
|---|---|
| CITY OF PROGRESS | Statesville, N. C. |
| CITY OF PROGRESS | Titusville, Fla. |
| CITY OF PROGRESS AND OPPORTUN-ITY | Phenix City, Ala. |
| CITY OF PROGRESS AND PROSPERITY | Oakland, Calif. |
| CITY OF PROGRESS AND SECURITY | Hawthorne, Calif. |
| CITY OF PROGRESS WITH PRIDE AND PURPOSE | Marshalltown, Iowa |
| CITY OF PROGRESSIVE OUTLOOK | Buffalo, N. Y. |
| CITY OF PROSPERITY | Worcester, Mass. |
| CITY OF PURE WATER | Zephyrville, Fla. |
| CITY OF QUALITY PRODUCTS | Rochester, N. Y. |
| CITY OF RECEPTIONS | Washington, D. C. |
| CITY OF RECREATION AND CULTURE | Omaha, Neb. |
| CITY OF RESEARCH | Stamford, Conn. |
| CITY OF RESOURCES | Santa Ana, Calif. |
| CITY OF RICH CULTURAL AND RESI-DENTIAL CHARM | Jackson, Miss. |
| CITY OF ROCKS | Nashville, Tenn. |
| CITY OF ROMANCE AND REBELLION | Richmond, Va. |
| CITY OF ROSES | Cape Giradeau, Mo. |
| CITY OF ROSES | Holly Springs, Miss. |
| CITY OF ROSES | Lovell, Wyo. |
| CITY OF ROSES | Little Rock, Ark. |
| CITY OF ROSES | New Castle, Ind. |
| CITY OF ROSES | Pana, Ill. |
| CITY OF ROSES | Paramount, Calif. |
| CITY OF ROSES | Pasadena, Calif. |
| CITY OF ROSES | Portland, Ore. |
| CITY OF ROSES | Thomasville, Ga. |
| CITY OF RUGS | Amsterdam, N. Y. |
| CITY OF SALT | Syracuse, N. Y. |
| CITY OF SCENIC MARVELS | Niagara Falls, N. Y. |
| CITY OF SCIENCE | Norwalk, Conn. |
| CITY OF SECESSION | Charleston, S. C. |
| CITY OF SECLUSION | Seldovia, Alaska |
| CITY OF SERENE LIVING | Laguna Beach, Calif. |
| CITY OF SEVEN HILLS | Brooksville, Fla. |
| CITY OF SEVEN HILLS | Richmond, Va. |
| CITY OF SEVEN HILLS | Rome, Ga. |
| CITY OF SEVEN HILLS | Seattle, Wash. |
| CITY OF SEVEN VALLEYS | Cassville, Mo. |
| CITY OF SEVEN WONDERS | Flagstaff, Ariz. |
| CITY OF SHADY WALKS AND PLEA-SANT LAWNS | Dayton, Wash. |
| CITY OF SHIPS AND SHIPBUILDING | Newport News, Va. |
| CITY OF SHOES | Brockton, Mass. |
| CITY OF SHOES | Lynn, Mass. |

| | |
|---|---|
| CITY OF SIX FLAGS | Mobile, Ala. |
| CITY OF SKYSCRAPERS | New York, N. Y. |
| CITY OF SMILES | Superior, Wis. |
| CITY OF SMOKESTACKS | Everett, Wash. |
| CITY OF SOLES | Lynn, Mass. |
| CITY OF SOUTHERN CHARM | Savannah, Ga. |
| CITY OF SOUTHERN FRIENDLINESS AND CHARM | Gonzales, La. |
| CITY OF SPAS | Ashland, Ore. |
| CITY OF SPINDLES | Lowell, Mass. |
| CITY OF SPRINGS | Neosho, Mo. |
| CITY OF STEEL | Pittsburgh, Pa. |
| CITY OF STRAITS | Detroit, Mich. |
| CITY OF STREETS WITHOUT HOUSES | Washington, D. C. |
| CITY OF SUCCESSFUL DIVERSIFIED INDUSTRY | Utica, N. Y. |
| CITY OF SUN AND FUN, SAND 'N SEA | Old Orchard Beach, Me. |
| CITY OF SUNSHINE | Colorado Springs. Colo. |
| CITY OF SUNSHINE | Los Angeles, Calif. |
| CITY OF SUNSHINE | Tucson, Ariz. |
| CITY OF SUNSHINE AND SILVER | Tombstone, Ariz. |
| CITY OF SUPERLATIVES | New York, N. Y. |
| CITY OF THE BELLES | Bellefonte, Pa. |
| CITY OF THE BIG SHOULDERS | Chicago, Ill. |
| CITY OF THE CARILLON | Lake Wales, Fla. |
| CITY OF THE FALLS | Louisville, Ky. |
| CITY OF THE FIRST AUTOMOBILE | Kokomo, Ind. |
| CITY OF THE FRENCH | St. Louis, Mo. |
| CITY OF THE FRIENDLY PEOPLE | Apalachicola, Fla. |
| CITY OF THE FUTURE | Cape Coral, Fla. |
| CITY OF THE FUTURE | Kansas City, Mo. |
| CITY OF THE FUTURE | New Haven, Conn. |
| CITY OF THE GAULS | Gallipolis, Ohio |
| CITY OF THE GOLDEN GATE | San Francisco, Calif. |
| CITY OF THE GREAT SMOKIES | Knoxville, Tenn. |
| CITY OF THE GREEN LIGHT | Eau Claire, Wis. |
| CITY OF THE HOUR | Dallas, Tex. |
| CITY OF THE LAKES | Chicago, Ill. |
| CITY OF THE LAKES | Laconia, N. H. |
| CITY OF THE LAKES AND PRAIRIES | Chicago, Ill. |
| CITY OF THE LONGEST SUNDAY | Pittsburgh, Pa. |
| CITY OF THE MOUNTAIN PEAKS | San Luis Obispo, Calif. |
| CITY OF THE NORTHLAND | Superior, Wis. |

| | |
|---|---|
| CITY OF THE PEOPLE | Demopolis, Ala. |
| CITY OF THE PLAINS | Abilene, Kan. |
| CITY OF THE PLAINS | Childress, Tex. |
| CITY OF THE PLAINS | Denver, Colo. |
| CITY OF THE PLAINS | Sacramento, Calif. |
| CITY OF THE PLAINS | Syracuse, N. Y. |
| CITY OF THE SAINTS | Salt Lake City, Utah |
| CITY OF THE SEVEN HILLS | Rome, Ga. |
| CITY OF THE SLAIN | Arlington, Va. |
| CITY OF THE STRAITS | Detroit, Mich. |
| CITY OF THE TWIN SPIRES | Ripon. Wis. |
| CITY OF THE UNBURIED DEAD | St. Petersburg, Fla. |
| CITY OF THE UNEXPECTED | Pittsburgh, Pa. |
| CITY OF THE VIOLET CROWN | Austin, Tex. |
| CITY OF THE WORLD | New York, N. Y. |
| CITY OF 13 HIGHWAYS | Hawkinsville, Ga. |
| CITY OF THREE CAPITALS | Little Rock, Ark. |
| CITY OF THRIVING INDUSTRIES | Wheeling, W. Va. |
| CITY OF TOBACCO | Quincy, Fla. |
| CITY OF TOWERS | New York, N. Y. |
| CITY OF TRADITION | Memphis, Tenn. |
| CITY OF TRANSFORMATIONS | Chelsea, Mass. |
| CITY OF TREES | Boise, Idaho |
| CITY OF TREES | Buffalo, N. Y. |
| CITY OF TREES | Forsyth, Mont. |
| CITY OF TREES | Los Altos, Calif. |
| CITY OF TREES | Marmarth, N. D. |
| CITY OF TREES | Sacramento, Calif. |
| CITY OF TREES WITHOUT HOUSES | Washington, D. C. |
| CITY OF TWENTIETH CENTURY AMERICA | Detroit, Mich. |
| CITY OF UNEXCELLED OPPORTUN-ITIES FOR BUSINESS AND INDUSTRY | Salem, Ore. |
| CITY OF UNINTERRUPTED ELECTRIC POWER | Holyoke, Mass. |
| CITY OF VARIED INDUSTRIES | Rochester, N. Y. |
| CITY OF VILLAGE CHARM | Manchester, Conn. |
| CITY OF WASHINGTON | Washington, D. C. |
| CITY OF WESTERN CHARM AND HOSPITALITY | Fort Worth, Tex. |
| CITY OF WINDS | Chicago, Ill. |
| CITY OF WITCHES | Salem, Mass. |
| CITY OF WONDERFUL LIVING WITH INDUSTRIAL PROSPERITY | Parkersburg, W. Va. |
| CITY OF WONDERFUL WATER | Stevens Point, Wis. |
| CITY OF YEAR-AROUND RECREATION | Augusta, Me. |
| CITY OF YOUNG MEN | Summerville, Ga. |
| CITY OF YOUR FUTURE | Fort Smith, Ark. |

CITY OF YOUTH, INDUSTRY, RECRE-
ATION                                       Lone Star, Tex.
CITY ON A MOUNTAIN                          Duluth, Minn.
CITY ON FLORIDA'S FAMOUS EAST
COAST AND THE INDIAN RIVER                  Edgewater, Fla.
CITY ON THE COOL GULF COAST                 Panama City, Fla.
CITY ON THE CROSSROADS OF THE
EXPRESSWAYS                                 Foxboro, Mass.
CITY ON THE DAN                             Danville, Va.
CITY ON THE GO                              Jacksonville, N. C.
CITY ON THE GOLDEN HILLS                    San Francisco, Calif.
CITY ON THE GROW                            Shreveport, La.
CITY ON THE GROW                            Waco, Tex.
CITY ON THE GULF                            Naples, Fla.
CITY ON THE GULF OF MEXICO                  St. Petersburg
                                            Beach, Fla.
CITY ON THE HIGHWAY OF PROGRESS             Colonial Heights, Va.
CITY ON THE HIGHWAY TO HEAVEN               Salida, Colo.
CITY ON THE HILL                            Paris, Me.
CITY ON THE LAKES                           Laconia, N. H.
CITY ON THE LAZY BLUE WATERS
OF THE GULF OF MEXICO                       Longboat Key, Fla.
CITY ON THE MOVE                            Denton, Tex.
CITY ON THE MOVE                            Macon, Ga.
CITY ON THE MOVE                            Oak Ridge, Tenn.
CITY ON THE MOVE                            Rockmart, Ga.
CITY ON THE TOP OF THE ROCKIES              Anaconda, Mont.
CITY PLANNED FOR PERFECT LIVING             Coral Gables, Fla.
CITY PLEDGED TO PROGRESS                    Peoria, Ill.
CITY PRACTICAL THAT VISION BUILT            Longview, Wash.
CITY PROGRAMMED FOR PROGRESS                Palm Bay, Fla.
CITY PROGRESSIVE                            Greensburg, Pa.
CITY READY FOR TOMORROW                     Jonesboro, Ark.
CITY RICH IN HISTORY                        Morristown, Tenn.
CITY RICH IN HISTORY WITH A
WEALTH OF CHARM                             Winchester, Va.
CITY RICH IN TRADITION AND OPPOR-
TUNITY                                      Springfield, Mass.
CITY RICH IN WESTERN TRADITION              Prescott, Ariz.
CITY RIGHT IN THE CENTER OF
THINGS                                      Pompano Beach, Fla.
CITY SET ON A HILL                          Angwin, Calif.
CITY SITUATED IN STRATEGIC NORTH-
WEST LOUISIANA                              Bossier City, La.
CITY SUBSTANTIAL                            Frankfort, Ind.
CITY THAT BELONGS TO THE WORLD              New York, N. Y.
CITY THAT BUILT ITS SEAPORT                 Houston, Tex.
CITY THAT CAME BACK                         Alton, Ill.

| | |
|---|---|
| CITY THAT CHARMS | Ontario, Calif. |
| CITY THAT CLIMATE BUILT | San Clemente, Calif. |
| CITY THAT COOPERATES | Cleveland, Ohio |
| CITY THAT DOES THINGS | Norfolk, Va. |
| CITY THAT HAS EVERYTHING FOR ENJOYABLE LIVING | Tavares, Fla. |
| CITY THAT HAS EVERYTHING FOR EVERYONE--ANYTIME | Las Vegas, Nev. |
| CITY THAT HAS EVERYTHING FOR INDUSTRY | Jersey City, N. J. |
| CITY THAT HAS SOMETHING FOR YOU | Stockton, Calif. |
| CITY THAT HAS THE RESOURCES TO FIT YOUR BUSINESS NEEDS | Indianapolis, Ind. |
| CITY THAT HOLDS THE KEY TO MID-AMERICA | Keokuk, Iowa |
| CITY THAT IS ATTRACTING NEW INDUSTRY | Keokuk, Iowa |
| CITY THAT IS BIG ENOUGH TO SERVE YOU, YET SMALL ENOUGH TO KNOW YOU | Dickinson, N. D. |
| CITY THAT IS BIG ENOUGH TO SERVE YOU AND SMALL ENOUGH TO KNOW YOU | Concordia, Kan. |
| CITY THAT IS FRIENDLY, PROGRESSIVE, ALIVE | Enderlin, N. D. |
| CITY THAT IS JUST FOR FUN | Palm Springs, Calif. |
| CITY THAT IS NEAR EVERYTHING | Atwater, Calif. |
| CITY THAT KNOWS WHERE IT IS GOING | El Cerrito, Calif. |
| CITY THAT IS ONLY TWO HOURS TO THE SIERRAS OR THE SEA | Modesto, Calif. |
| CITY THAT IS STILL A FRONTIER TOWN | Las Vegas, Nev. |
| CITY THAT LIGHTS AND HAULS THE WORLD | Schenectady, N. Y. |
| CITY THAT MEANS BUSINESS AND THE GOOD LIFE TOO | Jackson, Miss. |
| CITY THAT NEVER SLEEPS | New York, N. Y. |
| CITY THAT PROGRESS BUILT | Fayetteville, Ark. |
| CITY THAT PUTS BUSINESS ON THE GO | Harrisburg, Pa. |
| CITY THAT SAVED THE UNION | Virginia City, Nev. |
| CITY THAT SAYS WELCOME NEIGHBOR | Madison, S. D. |
| CITY THAT SMILES BACK | Corinth, Miss. |
| CITY THAT STARTED WITH A PLAN | Margate, Fla. |
| CITY THAT TREES BUILT | Berlin, N. H. |

| | |
|---|---|
| CITY THAT TURNED BACK TIME | Williamsburg, Va. |
| CITY THAT'S A STUDY IN CON-<br>TRASTS | Pompano Beach, Fla. |
| CITY THAT'S 'DUBLIN' DAILY | Dublin, Ga. |
| CITY THAT'S SCENIC, BUSY AND<br>FRIENDLY | Clifton Forge, Va. |
| CITY THE DEPRESSION PASSED UP | Bronson, Mich. |
| CITY THERE'S A LOT TO LIKE<br>ABOUT | Ocean City, Md. |
| CITY THRIVING FROM THE FERTILE<br>BANKS OF OLE MAN RIVER | Dyersburg, Tenn. |
| CITY TIME FORGOT | Galena, Ill. |
| CITY TO GROW WITH | Lone Star, Tex. |
| CITY TO WATCH | Minneapolis, Minn. |
| CITY WAY DOWN UPON THE SUWAN-<br>NEE RIVER | Cross City, Fla. |
| CITY WHERE A NEW SOUTH IS IN THE<br>MAKING | Jackson, Miss. |
| CITY WHERE A WEALTH OF PLEA-<br>SURE AWAITS YOU SPRING OR<br>SUMMER, FALL OR WINTER | Tampa, Fla. |
| CITY WHERE ADVANTAGES ABOUND<br>FOR BUSINESS | Salem, Ore. |
| CITY WHERE AGRICULTURE AND IN-<br>DUSTRY MEET | Fremont, Neb. |
| CITY WHERE AGRICULTURE AND IN-<br>DUSTRIES MEET | Tracy, Calif. |
| CITY WHERE AMBITION MEETS OP-<br>PORTUNITY | Livonia, Mich. |
| CITY WHERE AMERICA BEGAN IN THE<br>WEST | Monterey, Calif. |
| CITY WHERE BEER IS FAMOUS | Milwaukee, Wis. |
| CITY WHERE BUSINESS AND FRIEND-<br>SHIP THRIVE | Sanford, N. C. |
| CITY WHERE BUSINESS AND HAPPY<br>LIVING FLOURISH | Ogden, Utah |
| CITY WHERE BUSINESS AND INDUSTRY<br>THRIVE AND PEOPLE ENJOY A WIDE<br>VARIETY OF YEAR AROUND RECRE-<br>ATION | Athens, Tenn. |
| CITY WHERE CALIFORNIA AND MEX-<br>ICO MEET THE BLUE PACIFIC | San Diego, Calif. |
| CITY WHERE CALIFORNIA BEGAN | Sacramento, Calif. |
| CITY WHERE CALIFORNIA BEGAN | San Diego, Calif. |
| CITY WHERE CIVIC PRIDE IS CITY-<br>WIDE | Carrabelle, Fla. |
| CITY WHERE COAL AND IRON MEET | Toledo, Ohio |
| CITY WHERE COAL MEETS IRON | Ashland, Ky. |

| | |
|---|---|
| CITY WHERE COMMERCE, FARMING, INDUSTRY AND EDUCATION THRIVE TOGETHER | Blair, Neb. |
| CITY WHERE COTTON IS KING | Blytheville, Ark. |
| CITY WHERE DIXIE WELCOMES YOU | Corinth, Miss. |
| CITY WHERE FAMILIES ENJOY FLORIDA LIVING IN A BEAUTIFUL AND HISTORIC SETTING | Quincy, Fla. |
| CITY WHERE "FISH ARE JUMPIN' AND THE LIVIN' IS EASY" | Stockton, Mo. |
| CITY WHERE FOLKS ARE NOT TOO BUSY TO BE FRIENDLY | Bowling Green, Ky. |
| CITY WHERE GAMBLING REIGNS SUPREME | Las Vegas, Nev. |
| CITY WHERE GAME IN ITS WILD STATE ABOUNDS | Stockton, Mo. |
| CITY WHERE GOOD LIVING IS THE CUSTOM | Lynchburg, Va. |
| CITY WHERE GRACIOUS LIVING AND FINE CHURCHES OFFER A LIFE OF CONTENTMENT FOR BUSINESSMAN, WORKER, RETIRED AND THE SPORTSMAN | El Dorado Springs, Mo. |
| CITY WHERE GREAT EAST TEXAS MEETS THE SEA | Beaumont, Tex. |
| CITY WHERE GROWTH HAS BECOME A HABIT | Odessa, Tex. |
| CITY WHERE HISTORIC PRIDE AND CIVIC PROGRESS UNITE IN THE INDUSTRIAL AND CULTURAL HEART OF NORTHWEST FLORIDA | Quincy, Fla. |
| CITY WHERE HISTORY AND PROGRESS JOIN HANDS | Nacogdoches, Tex. |
| CITY WHERE HISTORY BLENDS WITH PROGRESS | Salem, Mass. |
| CITY WHERE HISTORIC YESTERDAY GREETS DYNAMIC TOMORROW | Bingham, Me. |
| CITY WHERE HISTORIC YESTERDAY GREETS DYNAMIC TOMORROW | Moscow, Me. |
| CITY WHERE HOSPITALITY IS A TRADITION | Santa Barbara, Calif. |
| CITY WHERE HOSPITALITY NEVER CEASES | Henderson, N. C. |
| CITY WHERE HOSPITALITY OF THE SOUTH BEGINS | Florence, Ky. |
| CITY WHERE INDUSTRIAL AND AGRICULTURAL ACTIVITIES ARE BLEND- | |

285

| | |
|---|---|
| ED WITH DAIRYING AND LIVESTOCK PRODUCTION | Columbus, Miss. |
| CITY WHERE INDUSTRY, AGRICULTURE, AND CULTURAL LIFE ALL BAL-ANCE | Tupelo, Miss. |
| CITY WHERE INDUSTRY AND EDUCA-TION MEET | Blacksburg, Va. |
| CITY WHERE INDUSTRY AND RECRE-ATION MEET | Palatka, Fla. |
| CITY WHERE INDUSTRY FINDS A FAVORABLE CLIMATE | Lakeland, Fla. |
| CITY WHERE INDUSTRY IS WANTED AND GROWING | Chula Vista, Calif. |
| CITY WHERE INDUSTRY PROFITS | Atmore, Ala. |
| CITY WHERE INDUSTRY PROSPERS, YOU WILL TOO | Nazareth, Pa. |
| CITY WHERE INDUSTRY THRIVES | Watertown, N. Y. |
| CITY WHERE IT'S JUNE IN JANUARY ALONG THE ROMANTIC APACHE TRAIL | Mesa, Ariz. |
| CITY WHERE LAND AND WATER MEET | Annapolis, Md. |
| CITY WHERE LIFE IS DIFFERENT | Biddeford, Me. |
| CITY WHERE LIFE IS DIFFERENT | Saco, Me. |
| CITY WHERE LIFE IS DIFFERENT | San Antonio, Tex. |
| CITY WHERE LIFE IS LIVED EVERY DAY OF THE YEAR | Englewood, Fla. |
| CITY WHERE LIFE IS WORTH LIVING | Dania, Fla. |
| CITY WHERE MAIN STREET MEETS THE RIVER AND JOINS MAIN STREET MID-AMERICA | Greenville, Miss. |
| CITY WHERE MAIN STREET MEETS THE WORLD | Beaumont, Tex. |
| CITY WHERE MEXICO MEETS UNCLE SAM | Brownsville, Tex. |
| CITY WHERE MODERN AMERICA BE-GAN | Lawrence, Mass. |
| CITY WHERE MOUNTAINS AND PLAINS MEET | Boulder, Colo. |
| CITY WHERE NATURE SMILES THE YEAR 'ROUND | Fortuna, Calif. |
| CITY WHERE NORTH AND SOUTH MEET EAST AND WEST | Salina, Kan. |
| CITY WHERE NORTH AND SOUTH MEET EAST AND WEST | Sedalia, Mo. |
| CITY WHERE OIL AND WATER MIX | Lovington, N. M. |
| CITY WHERE OIL AND WATER MIX | Powell, Wyo. |
| CITY WHERE OIL FLOWS, GAS BLOWS AND GLASS GLOWS | Okmulgee, Okla. |

| | |
|---|---|
| CITY WHERE PAST AND FUTURE MAKE A PROSPEROUS PRESENT | San Rafael, Calif. |
| CITY WHERE PEOPLE ARE HAPPY AND INDUSTRY FLOURISHES | East Point, Ga. |
| CITY WHERE PEOPLE LIKE TO LIVE | Homer, Alaska |
| CITY WHERE PEOPLE PLAY AND PROSPER | Manhattan, Kan. |
| CITY WHERE PLEASURE BEGINS | West Palm Beach, Fla. |
| CITY WHERE POTATOES ARE KING | Antigo, Wis. |
| CITY WHERE PROGRESS AND PLEASURES ARE PARTNERS | Douglas, Ariz. |
| CITY WHERE PROGRESS PROFITS GROWTH | Leavenworth, Kan. |
| CITY WHERE RAIL MEETS WATER | Kalama, Wash. |
| CITY WHERE RIVER, AIR, RAIL AND HIGHWAY MEET | Decatur, Ill. |
| CITY WHERE SCENIC GRANDEUR, HISTORY, LEGEND AND A BUSTLING MODERN ECONOMY ARE BLENDED INTO EVERYDAY LIFE | Sitka, Alaska |
| CITY WHERE SHE DANCED | Salome, Ariz. |
| CITY WHERE SOUTHERN HOSPITALITY BEGINS | Portsmouth, Ohio |
| CITY WHERE SPRING SPENDS THE SUMMER | Superior, Wis. |
| CITY WHERE SPRING SPENDS THE WINTER | Asheville, N. C. |
| CITY WHERE STRANGERS BECOME FRIENDS | Wareham, Mass. |
| CITY WHERE SUMMER WINTERS | Chandler, Ariz. |
| CITY WHERE SUMMER WINTERS | Phoenix, Ariz. |
| CITY WHERE SUMMERS ARE MILD AND WINTERS ARE WARM | National City, Calif. |
| CITY WHERE TEXAS MEETS THE SEA | Corpus Christi, Tex. |
| CITY WHERE THE ACCENT IS ON FAMILY | Independence, Kan. |
| CITY WHERE THE ACTION IS | Atlantic City, N. J. |
| CITY WHERE THE ACTION IS | Las Vegas, Nev. |
| CITY WHERE THE ADIRONDACKS MEET LAKE CHAMPLAIN | Westport, N. Y. |
| CITY WHERE THE AMERICAN TROPICS BEGIN | Fort Myers, Fla. |
| CITY WHERE THE BLUE RIDGE PARKWAY JOINS THE SKYLINE DRIVE | Waynesboro, Va. |
| CITY WHERE THE BREEZES BLOW | Jamestown, R. I. |
| CITY WHERE THE CHARM, CULTURE AND TRADITION OF THE OLD | |

| | |
|---|---|
| SOUTH BLEND IN A MODERN CITY | Natchez, Miss. |
| CITY WHERE THE DELTA BEGINS | Yazoo City, Miss. |
| CITY WHERE THE FAR EAST MEETS THE FAR WEST | San Francisco, Calif. |
| CITY WHERE THE FIGHT FOR TEXAS LIBERTY BEGINS | Gonzales, Tex. |
| CITY WHERE THE FUN BEGINS AND NEVER ENDS | Las Vegas, Nev. |
| CITY WHERE THE FUN OF LIVING COMES "NATURALLY" | La Belle, Fla. |
| CITY WHERE THE HERITAGE OF THE PAST LENDS WARMTH TO THE PRESENT | Guilford, Conn. |
| CITY WHERE THE HISTORY OF THE WEST BEGINS | Fort Leavenworth, Kan. |
| CITY WHERE THE HOSPITALITY OF THE OLD WEST REMAINS | Sidney, Neb. |
| CITY WHERE THE INDUSTRIAL EAST MEETS THE AGRICULTURAL WEST | Sioux City, Iowa |
| CITY WHERE THE LAND MEETS THE WATER | Wareham, Mass. |
| CITY WHERE THE MIGHTY SMITHY STANDS | Birmingham, Ala. |
| CITY WHERE THE MISSISSIPPI BECOMES MIGHTY | St. Cloud, Minn. |
| CITY WHERE THE MOUNTAIN MEETS THE SEA | Santa Monica, Calif. |
| CITY WHERE THE MOUNTAINS MEET THE SEA | Camden, Me. |
| CITY WHERE THE MOUNTAINS MEET THE SEA | Port Angeles, Wash. |
| CITY WHERE THE MOUNTAINS MEET THE SKY | Bluefield, W. Va. |
| CITY WHERE THE NORTH BEGINS | Harrison, Mich. |
| CITY WHERE THE NORTH BEGINS AND THE PURE WATERS FLOW | White Cloud, Mich. |
| CITY WHERE THE OLD AND THE NEW COMBINE | Quincy, Fla. |
| CITY WHERE THE OLD SOUTH AND THE NEW SOUTH MEET | Jackson, Miss. |
| CITY WHERE THE OLD SOUTH STILL LIVES | Natchez, Miss. |
| CITY WHERE THE PALMS MEET THE SEA | Miami Beach, Fla. |
| CITY WHERE THE PARTRIDGE FINDS A REFUGE | Bena, Minn. |
| CITY WHERE THE PINES MEET THE | |

|  |  |
|---|---|
| SEA | Virginia Beach, Va. |
| CITY WHERE THE PRAIRIE MEETS THE SEA | Duluth, Minn. |
| CITY WHERE THE RAILS AND THE TRAILS BEGIN | Lander, Wyo. |
| CITY WHERE THE SANTA FE TRAIL OF THE PRAIRIES MEETS THE MOUNTAINS OF THE HISTORICAL WEST | Trinidad, Colo. |
| CITY WHERE THE SEAWAY MEETS THE TURNPIKE | Toledo, Ohio |
| CITY WHERE THE SHENANDOAH NATIONAL PARK BEGINS | Front Royal, Va. |
| CITY WHERE THE SKYLINE DRIVE BEGINS | Front Royal, Va. |
| CITY WHERE THE SOUTH BEGINS AT THE GATEWAY TO THE BEAUTIFUL SHENANDOAH VALLEY | Winchester, Va. |
| CITY WHERE THE SOUTHEAST GETS ITS MONEY | Charlotte, N. C. |
| CITY WHERE THE SUMMER TRAILS BEGIN | Bay City, Mich. |
| CITY WHERE THE SUN BEAMS BRIGHTER WITH "OLE" FLORIDA'S HOSPITALITY | Plant City, Fla. |
| CITY WHERE THE SUN SPENDS THE WINTER | Pismo Beach, Calif. |
| CITY WHERE THE TRAIL ENDS AND THE SEA BEGINS | Homer, Alaska |
| CITY WHERE THE TRAIL MEETS RAIL | Burlingame, Kan. |
| CITY WHERE THE TROPICS BEGIN | Lake Worth, Fla. |
| CITY WHERE THE WELCOME'S WARM AS THE SUNSHINE | Miami Beach, Fla. |
| CITY WHERE THE WEST BEGINS | Fort Worth, Tex. |
| CITY WHERE THE WEST BEGINS | Independence, Mo. |
| CITY WHERE THE WEST BEGINS | Williston, N. D. |
| CITY WHERE THE WEST REMAINS | Sheridan, Wyo. |
| CITY WHERE THE WILDERNESS BEGINS | Ely, Minn. |
| CITY WHERE THE WORLD BATHES AND PLAYS | Hot Springs, Ark. |
| CITY WHERE THERE ARE NO STRANGERS. . .JUST NEW FRIENDS | York, Neb. |
| CITY WHERE THINGS ARE HAPPENING | Waterbury, Conn. |
| CITY WHERE THINGS ARE SHIPSHAPE AND BRISTOL FAST | Bristol, R. I. |

| | |
|---|---|
| CITY WHERE TRADITION LINGERS | Marblehead, Mass. |
| CITY WHERE VERMONT BEGINS | Brattleboro, Vt. |
| CITY WHERE VISITORS MEET HOS-<br>PITALITY | Lawrence, Mass. |
| CITY WHERE WATER MEANS PLEA-<br>SURE, PROGRESS AND PROSPERITY | Orange, Tex. |
| CITY WHERE WHEAT GROWS AND OIL<br>FLOWS | Pampa, Tex. |
| CITY WHERE WILSHIRE BOULEVARD<br>MEETS THE PACIFIC | Santa Monica, Calif. |
| CITY WHERE WINTER WEARS A TAN | Tucson, Ariz. |
| CITY WHERE WORK AND PLAY ARE<br>ONLY MINUTES AWAY | Palatka, Fla. |
| CITY WHERE YEAR-ROUND LIVING IS<br>A PLEASURE | Chula Vista, Calif. |
| CITY WHERE YOU CAN HAVE FUN<br>AND LIVE BETTER | Belleview, Fla. |
| CITY WHERE YOU CAN LIVE AND<br>ENJOY LIFE | Pass Christian, Miss. |
| CITY WHERE YOU CAN LIVE IN THE<br>CITY LIMITS AND BE ON THE LAKE | Stockton, Mo. |
| CITY WHERE YOU CAN WORK, LIVE,<br>PLAY, THE WESTERN WAY | Yuma, Ariz. |
| CITY WHERE YOUR DREAM VACA-<br>TION CAN BECOME A REALITY | Yankton, S. D. |
| CITY WHERE YOU HAVE THE SPLEN-<br>DOR OF FOUR SEASONS | Stockton, Mo. |
| CITY WHERE YOUR DREAMS OF FLOR-<br>IDA LIVING COME TRUE | Hallandale, Fla. |
| CITY WHERE YOUR SHIP COMES IN | Gulfport, Miss. |
| CITY WHERE YOUR VACATION DREAMS<br>ARE FULFILLED | Pompano Beach,<br>Fla. |
| CITY WHICH TOPS THE WORLD FOR<br>SUNSHINE AND SOCIABILITY | Chula Vista, Calif. |
| CITY WITH A BIG FUTURE | Chowchilla, Calif. |
| CITY WITH A BLENDING OF PAST AND<br>PRESENT ON THE BANKS OF THE<br>MERRIMAC | Newburyport, Mass. |
| CITY WITH A BRIGHT FUTURE | Slidell, La. |
| CITY WITH A BUILT-IN FUTURE | Sunnyvale, Calif. |
| CITY WITH A FUTURE | Bartlesville, Okla. |
| CITY WITH A FUTURE | Bloomington, Minn. |
| CITY WITH A FUTURE | Cape Coral, Fla. |
| CITY WITH A FUTURE | Dallas, Tex. |
| CITY WITH A FUTURE | Greensburg, Ind. |
| CITY WITH A FUTURE | Greenwood, Miss. |
| CITY WITH A FUTURE | Gulfport, Miss. |

| | |
|---|---|
| CITY WITH A FUTURE | Henderson, N. C. |
| CITY WITH A FUTURE | Jamestown, N. D. |
| CITY WITH A FUTURE | Port St. Joe, Fla. |
| CITY WITH A FUTURE | San Bruno, Calif. |
| CITY WITH A FUTURE | Trenton, Mo. |
| CITY WITH A FUTURE | Waukesha, Wis. |
| CITY WITH A FUTURE FOR ALL IN-DUSTRY | Victoria, Tex. |
| CITY WITH A FUTURE TO SHARE | Glendive, Mont. |
| CITY WITH A FUTURE UNLIMITED | Downey, Calif. |
| CITY WITH A GREAT CIVIC PRIDE AND A SOUND BUSINESS CLIMATE | Alexander City, Ala. |
| CITY WITH A GREAT POTENTIAL FOR GROWTH | Marshall, Mo. |
| CITY WITH A HEART | Grand Forks, N. D. |
| CITY WITH A HEART | Holly Hill, Fla. |
| CITY WITH A HEART | Valentine, Neb. |
| CITY WITH A HEART IN THE HEART OF DIXIE | Birmingham, Ala. |
| CITY WITH A HOLE IN THE MIDDLE | Lake Tahoe, Calif. |
| CITY WITH A MILLION AMBASSADORS | St. Petersburg, Fla. |
| CITY WITH A PAST | Petersburg, Va. |
| CITY WITH A PLANNED FUTURE | New Castle Ind. |
| CITY WITH A SPARKLE | Clearwater, Fla. |
| CITY WITH A VIEW | El Cerrito, Calif. |
| CITY WITH AN AREA OF AGRICUL-TURAL ACHIEVEMENT | Pahokee, Fla. |
| CITY WITH AN ARISTOCRATIC PAST | Greenwood, Miss. |
| CITY WITH AN EXCITING FUTURE | Greenwood, Miss. |
| CITY WITH EVERYTHING | New York, N. Y. |
| CITY WITH FORESIGHT | Grand Junction, Colo. |
| CITY WITH FUTURE UNLIMITED | Huron, S. D. |
| CITY WITH ITS SIGHTS ON ITS FU-TURE | New Castle, Pa. |
| CITY WITH NATURAL BEAUTY THE YEAR 'ROUND | Trinity, Tex. |
| CITY WITH OPPORTUNITY FOR ALL | Decatur, Ala. |
| CITY WITH PROMISE | Sparks, Nev. |
| CITY WITH ROOM TO STRETCH AND GROW IN | Atmore, Ala. |
| CITY WITH SMALL TOWN HOSPITAL-ITY | Trussville, Ala. |
| CITY WITH THE MILE LONG MALL | Avon Park, Fla. |
| CITY WITH THE NATION'S MOST PER-FECT YEAR 'ROUND CLIMATE | San Mateo, Calif. |
| CITY WITH THE PLANNED FUTURE | Harrisonburg, Va. |
| CITY WITH THE WORLD'S WHITEST BEACHES | Panama City, Fla. |

| | |
|---|---|
| CITY WITH TWO FACES | Chicago, Ill. |
| CITY WITH UNEXCELLED OPPORTUN-ITIES FOR GOOD LIVING | Orlando, Fla. |
| CITY WITH UNITY IN THE COMMUN-ITY | Concordia, Kan. |
| CITY WITHOUT A TOOTHACHE | Hereford, Tex. |
| CITY WITHOUT CITY LIMITS | Tupelo, Miss. |
| CITY WITHOUT CLOCKS | Las Vegas, Nev. |
| CITY WITHOUT LIMITS | Tupelo, Miss. |
| CITY WITHOUT PRECEDENT, WITHOUT COMPARISON | Atlanta, Ga. |
| CITY WONDER-FULL FOR BUSINESS | Lakeland, Fla. |
| CITY WORTH LOOKING INTO | Fort Worth, Tex. |
| CITY WORTH WHILE | St. Joseph, Mo. |
| CITY WORTHY OF A NOBLE NAME | Lincoln, Neb. |
| CITY YOU CAN BE PROUD TO LIVE AND WORK IN | East Point, Ga. |
| CIVICS CENTER OF THE MIDLAND EMPIRE | Billings, Mont. |
| CLAM TOWN | Norwalk, Conn. |
| CLAREMONT, THE BEAUTIFUL | Claremont, Calif. |
| CLASSIC CITY | Boston, Mass. |
| CLASSIC CITY OF THE SOUTH | Athens, Ga. |
| CLAY CENTER | Perth Amboy, N. J. |
| CLAY CITY | Brazil, Ind. |
| CLAY PIPE CENTER OF THE WORLD | Dennison, Ohio |
| CLAY PIPE CENTER OF THE WORLD | Uhrichsville, Ohio |
| CLEAN AND QUIET RESORT | Stone Harbor, N. J. |
| CLEAN COLORFUL TULIP CITY ON SCENIC LAKE MACATAWA | Holland, Mich. |
| CLEANEST BEACH IN THE WORLD | Old Orchard Beach, Me. |
| CLEANEST BIG CITY IN THE WORLD | New York, N. Y. |
| CLEANEST CITY IN LOUISIANA | Franklin, La. |
| CLEANEST CITY IN THE UNITED STATES | Morristown, Tenn. |
| CLEVELAND WITH PALM TREES | Los Angeles, Calif. |
| CLIPPER CITY | Manitowoc, Wis. |
| CLOCK CITY | Thomaston, Conn. |
| CLOCK CENTER OF THE WORLD | Bristol, Conn. |
| CLOSEST STATE TO HEAVEN | Salida, Colo. |
| CLOTHING CENTER OF THE SOUTH | Bremen, Ga. |
| CLOUD CITY | Leadville, Colo. |
| COAL BAY | Colby, Wash. |
| COAL CITY | Pittsburgh, Pa. |
| COAL CITY | Pottsville, Pa. |
| COASTAL TOWN OF CHARM AND BEAUTY | Yarmouth, Me. |

| | |
|---|---|
| COASTLINE OF HEALTH AND HAPPI-NESS | Atlantic City, N. J. |
| COCKADE CITY | Petersburg, Va. |
| COCKADE CITY | Richmond, Va. |
| COCKADE OF THE UNION | Petersburg, Va. |
| COCKPIT OF THE CIVIL WAR | Fredericksburg, Va. |
| COKE CITY | Uniontown, Pa. |
| COLISEUM CITY | New York, N. Y. |
| COLLAR CITY | Troy, N. Y. |
| COLLARD AND PICKLE CAPITAL | Cairo, Ga. |
| COLLECTION OF FREEWAYS IN SEARCH OF A CITY | Los Angeles, Calif. |
| COLLEGE CITY | Galesburg, Ill. |
| COLLEGE CITY | Lewisburg, Pa. |
| COLLEGE TOWN AMID THE ORANGE GROVES | Claremont, Calif. |
| COLONIAL CAPITAL OF THE EASTERN SHORE | Easton, Md. |
| COLONIAL CAPITAL OF VIRGINIA | Williamsburg, Va. |
| COLONIAL CITY | Kingston, N. Y. |
| COLONY CITY | Fitzgerald, Ga. |
| COLORADO'S SECOND CITY | Pueblo, Colo. |
| COLORFUL KEY CENTER FOR DE-FENSE ACTIVITIES | Jacksonville, Fla. |
| COLUMBIA CITY | Vancouver, Wash. |
| COMB CITY | Leominster, Mass. |
| COMING CITY OF THE GREAT NORTH-WEST | Pierre, S. D. |
| COMING VEGAS | Lake Tahoe, Calif. |
| COMMAND POST FOR THE NATION'S MANNED SPACE EXPLORATION | Houston, Tex. |
| COMMENCEMENT CITY | Tacoma, Wash. |
| COMMERCIAL CENTER IN THE PA-CIFIC NORTHWEST | Seattle, Wash. |
| COMMERCIAL CENTER OF IRRIGATED IDAHO | Gooding, Idaho |
| COMMERCIAL CENTER OF THE MID-LAND EMPIRE | Billings, Mont. |
| COMMERCIAL, CULTURAL AND IN-DUSTRIAL CENTER OF SOUTH AR-KANSAS | El Dorado, Ark. |
| COMMERCIAL EMPIRE OF THE UNITED STATES | Washington, D. C. |
| COMMERCIAL EMPORIUM | New York, N. Y. |
| COMMERCIAL METROPOLIS OF WEST TENNESSEE | Memphis, Tenn. |
| COMMUNICATION CENTER OF FLOR-IDA | Jacksonville, Fla. |

| | |
|---|---|
| COMMUNITY OF CRAFTSMEN | York, Pa. |
| COMMUNITY OF CULTURE AND TRA-<br>DITIONS | Lynchburg, Va. |
| COMMUNITY OF EIGHT THRILLING<br>ATTRACTIONS | Silver Springs, Fla. |
| COMMUNITY OF FRIENDLY PEOPLE | Decatur, Ark. |
| COMMUNITY OF HOSPITABLE PEOPLE | Jefferson, Iowa |
| COMMUNITY OF OPPORTUNITY | Malone, N. Y. |
| COMMUNITY OF PROGRESS | Goldsboro, N. C. |
| COMMUNITY OF SUBSTANCE | Norwalk, Conn. |
| COMMUNITY OF THE DEODARS | Altadena, Calif. |
| COMMUNITY OF TREES | Los Altos, Calif. |
| COMMUNITY ON THE MOVE | Rutland, Vt. |
| COMMUNITY ON THE MOVE FOR A<br>CENTURY AND A HALF WITH MORE<br>TO OFFER FOR THE FUTURE | Ogdensburg, N. Y. |
| COMMUNITY PLANNED FOR PLEA-<br>SANT LIVING | Indiantown, Fla. |
| COMMUNITY PROGRESSIVE | Greensburg, Pa. |
| COMMUNITY THAT BUILDS HEALTH<br>MINDS AND BODIES | Blacksburg, Va. |
| COMMUNITY THAT HAS EVERYTHING | Greenport, N. Y. |
| COMMUNITY WELL PLANNED, WELL<br>DEVELOPED, WELL EQUIPPED FOR<br>COMMERCE, INDUSTRY AND FAM-<br>ILY LIFE | East Point, Ga. |
| COMMUNITY WHERE BUSINESS AND<br>PLEASURE LIVE IN COMPLETE<br>HARMONY | Dunnellon, Fla. |
| COMMUNITY WHERE LIVING IS AT<br>ITS BEST | Ephrata, Pa. |
| COMMUNITY WHERE THE BIG BASS<br>BITE | Leesburg, Fla. |
| COMMUNITY WHERE THE FUTURE<br>MAY LEARN FROM THE PAST | Williamsburg, Va. |
| COMMUNITY WHERE YOU CAN LIVE,<br>WORK, RELAX | Haines City, Fla. |
| COMMUNITY WHERE YOU WORK AND<br>PLAY THE SAME DAY | Dunnellon, Fla. |
| COMMUNITY WITH A HEART IN THE<br>HEART OF FABULOUS FLORIDA | Leesburg, Fla. |
| COMMUNITY WITH ITS SITES SET ON<br>TOMORROW | Elgin, Ill. |
| COMMUNITY WORKING TOGETHER FOR<br>THE FUTURE | Tupelo, Miss. |
| COMMUTER'S HAVEN | Newton, Mass. |
| COMPLETE COMMUNITY | Manhattan, Kan. |
| COMPLETE SHOPPING CENTER | Meriden, Conn. |

294

| | |
|---|---|
| COMPLETE VACATION RESORT CITY | Key Colony Beach, Fla. |
| CONCENTRATOR CITY | Miami, Ariz. |
| CONEY ISLAND OF THE WEST | Saltair, Utah |
| CONFEDERATE CAPITAL | Richmond, Va. |
| CONFEDERATE STATE CAPITAL OF KENTUCKY | Bowling Green, Ky. |
| CONFEDERATE SUPPLY DEPOT | Atlanta, Ga. |
| CONSERVATIVE CINCINNATI | Cincinnati, Ohio |
| CONSTITUTION CITY | Port St. Joe, Fla. |
| CONSUMER COOPERATIVE CENTER OF THE UNITED STATES | Superior, Wis. |
| CONTENTED CITY | Cincinnati, Ohio |
| CONTINENTAL CROSSROADS | Minot, N. D. |
| CONVENIENT VACATIONLAND | Pompano Beach, Fla. |
| CONVENTION AND RECREATION CENTER OF THE NORTHWEST | Coeur D'Alene, Idaho |
| CONVENTION CAPITAL OF THE WEST | Las Vegas, Nev. |
| CONVENTION CENTER OF THE GREAT SMOKIES | Gatlinburg, Tenn. |
| CONVENTION CENTER OF THE UNITED STATES | Miami Beach, Fla. |
| CONVENTION CITY | Baltimore, Md. |
| CONVENTION CITY | Casper, Wyo. |
| CONVENTION CITY | Chicago, Ill. |
| CONVENTION CITY | Denver, Colo. |
| CONVENTION CITY | Jefferson City, Mo. |
| CONVENTION CITY | Juneau, Alaska |
| CONVENTION CITY | Louisville, Ky. |
| CONVENTION CITY | Portland, Ore. |
| CONVENTION CITY | St. Louis, Mo. |
| CONVENTION CITY | Salina, Kan. |
| CONVENTION CITY | Saratoga Springs, N. Y. |
| CONVENTION CITY | Sedalia, Mo. |
| CONVENTION CITY IN THE HEART OF THE SOUTH | Memphis, Tenn. |
| CONVENTION CITY OF IOWA | Marshalltown, Iowa |
| CONVENTION CITY OF THE EAST | Hartford, Conn. |
| CONVENTION CITY OF THE GREAT SMOKIES | Gatlinburg, Tenn. |
| CONVENTION HEADQUARTERS FOR THE DAKOTAS | Huron, S. D. |
| CONVENTION HUB OF THE DAKOTAS | Aberdeen, S.D. |
| COOL AND SUNNY PARADISE | Stowe, Vt. |
| COON CAPITOL OF THE WORLD | Rogersville, Mo. |
| COOLEST SUMMER CITY | Duluth, Minn. |

| | |
|---|---|
| COPPER CITY | Butte, Mont. |
| COPPER CITY | Rome, N. Y. |
| COPPER CITY | Valdez, Alaska |
| CORDAGE CITY | Auburn, N. Y. |
| CORN CITY | Toledo, Ohio |
| CORNCOB PIPE CAPITAL OF THE WORLD | Washington, Mo. |
| CORNHUSKER CAPITAL CITY | Lincoln, Neb. |
| CORNOPOLIS | Chicago, Ill. |
| CORNTOWN | Cornelius, Ore. |
| COSMOPOLITAN CITY | San Francisco, Calif. |
| COSMOPOLITAN CITY OF THE WEST | San Francisco, Calif. |
| COSMOPOLITAN COMMUNITY WITH THE WARMTH OF A SMALL TOWN | Cocoa Beach, Fla. |
| COSMOPOLITAN SAN FRANCISCO | San Francisco, Calif. |
| COSMOPOLITAN SEAPORT | Seattle, Wash. |
| COTTON CENTER | Memphis, Tenn. |
| COTTONSEED OIL CAPITAL OF THE WORLD | Lubbock, Tex. |
| COTTON TOWN OF THE U. S. A. | Paterson, N. J. |
| COTTONWOOD CITY | Leavenworth, Kan. |
| COUNTRY MUSIC CAPITAL OF THE NORTH | Flint, Mich. |
| COUNTRY MUSIC CAPITAL OF THE WORLD | Nashville, Tenn. |
| COUNTRY WHERE THE CLIMATE INVITES YOU OUT-OF-DOORS | Prineville, Ore. |
| COUNTRY'S GREATEST RAIL CENTER | Chicago, Ill. |
| COUNTRY'S LARGEST LUMBER SHIP- PING CENTER | Portland, Ore. |
| COUNTY SEAT OF COCONIMO COUNTY | Flagstaff, Ariz. |
| COUNTY SEAT OF CORTLAND COUNTY | Cortland, N. Y. |
| COUNTY SEAT OF LOVELY LAKE COUNTY | Tavares, Fla. |
| COURT CITY OF A NATION | Washington, D. C. |
| COURTEOUS CAPITAL CITY | Harrisburg, Pa. |
| COVERED BRIDGE CAPITAL OF THE WORLD | Rockville, Ind. |
| COW CAPITAL | Wichita, Kan. |
| COW CAPITAL OF FLORIDA | Kissimmee, Fla. |
| COW CAPITAL OF THE WEST | Miles City, Mont. |
| COW TOWN | Coffeyville, Kan. |
| COW TOWN | Fort Worth, Tex. |
| COW TOWN | Medora, N. D. |
| COW TOWN | Wayland, Mich. |

| | |
|---|---|
| COW TOWN OF THE SOUTH | Montgomery, Ala. |
| COWBOY BOOT CAPITAL | Olathe, Kan. |
| COWBOY CAPITAL | Dodge City, Kan. |
| COWBOY CAPITAL | Kenton, Okla. |
| COWBOY CAPITAL | Prescott, Ariz. |
| COWBOY CAPITAL OF NEBRASKA | Ogallala, Neb. |
| COWBOY CAPITAL OF OREGON | Prineville, Ore. |
| COWBOY CAPITAL OF THE WORLD | Dodge City, Kan. |
| CRAB TOWN | Hampton, Va. |
| CRABTOWN | Annapolis, Md. |
| CRABTOWN-ON-THE-BAY | Annapolis, Md. |
| CRADLE AND THE GRAVE OF THE CONFEDERACY | Abbeville, S. C. |
| CRADLE OF AMERICAN INDEPENDENCE | Providence, R. I. |
| CRADLE OF AMERICAN INDUSTRY | Paterson, N. J. |
| CRADLE OF ARKANSAS HISTORY | Washington, Ark. |
| CRADLE OF AMERICAN LIBERTY | Taunton, Mass. |
| CRADLE OF AVIATION | Dayton, Ohio |
| CRADLE OF CREATIVITY | Dayton, Ohio |
| CRADLE OF DENTAL EDUCATION | Bainbridge, Ohio |
| CRADLE OF GEORGIA | Savannah, Ga. |
| CRADLE OF INDUSTRY | Springfield, Vt. |
| CRADLE OF LIBERTY | Concord, Mass. |
| CRADLE OF LIBERTY | Lexington, Mass. |
| CRADLE OF LIBERTY | Philadelphia, Pa. |
| CRADLE OF LOUISIANA OIL | Jennings, La. |
| CRADLE OF NAVAL AVIATION | Pensacola, Fla. |
| CRADLE OF PACIFIC NORTHWEST HISTORY | Walla Walla, Wash. |
| CRADLE OF SECESSION | Charleston, S. C. |
| CRADLE OF SQUARE RIGGERS | Mystic, Conn. |
| CRADLE OF TEXAS | San Augustine, Tex. |
| CRADLE OF TEXAS LIBERTY | San Antonio, Tex. |
| CRADLE OF THE AMERICAN CIRCUS | Delavan, Wis. |
| CRADLE OF THE AMERICAN CIRCUS | Somers, N. Y. |
| CRADLE OF THE AMERICAN REVOLUTION | Boston, Mass. |
| CRADLE OF THE AMERICAN TEXTILE INDUSTRY | Pawtucket, R. I. |
| CRADLE OF THE AMERICAN UNION | Albany, N. Y. |
| CRADLE OF THE COLONY | Edenton, N. C. |
| CRADLE OF THE CONFEDERACY | Montgomery, Ala. |
| CRADLE OF THE MEXICAN WAR | Fort Jessup, La. |
| CRADLE OF THE REVOLUTION | Midway, Ga. |
| CRADLE OF THE REVOLUTION | Philadelphia, Pa. |
| CRADLE OF THE STEEL INDUSTRY | Johnstown, Pa. |
| CRADLE OF THE TROTTER | Goshen, N. Y. |

| | |
|---|---|
| CRAPE MYRTLE CITY | Henderson, Tex. |
| CRAPE MYRTLE CITY | Jackson, Miss. |
| CRAWFISH CAPITAL OF THE WORLD | Breaux Bridge, La. |
| CRAWFISH TOWN | New Orleans, La. |
| CREAM CITY | Milwaukee, Wis. |
| CREAM WHITE CITY OF THE UNSALT-ED SEAS | Milwaukee, Wis. |
| CRESCENT CITY | Appleton, Wis. |
| CRESCENT CITY | Hilo, Hawaii |
| CRESCENT CITY | New Orleans, La. |
| CRESCENT CITY OF THE NORTHWEST | Galena, Ill. |
| CRIME CAPITAL | Chicago, Ill. |
| CROSSPADS OF THE NATION | Washington, Pa. |
| CROSSROADS CITY | El Paso, Tex. |
| CROSSROADS FOR NORTH-SOUTH EAST-WEST TRAFFIC | Alma, Ark. |
| CROSSROADS OF ALASKA | Tok, Alaska |
| CROSSROADS OF AMERICA | El Paso, Tex. |
| CROSSROADS OF AMERICA | Indianapolis, Ind. |
| CROSSROADS OF AMERICA | Joplin, Mo. |
| CROSSROADS OF AMERICA | Seymour, Ind. |
| CROSSROADS OF AMERICAN HISTORY | Carlisle, Pa. |
| CROSSROADS OF CALIFORNIA | Manteca, Calif. |
| CROSSROADS OF CONNECTICUT | Waterbury, Conn. |
| CROSSROADS OF FLORIDA | Tavares, Fla. |
| CROSSROADS OF HISTORY | Carlisle, Pa. |
| CROSSROADS OF HISTORY | Petersburg, Va. |
| CROSSROADS OF INDUSTRIAL DE-VELOPMENT | Hudson, Mass. |
| CROSSROADS OF LOUISIANA | Alexandria, La. |
| CROSSROADS OF LOUISIANA | Pineville, La. |
| CROSSROADS OF MID-AMERICA | Carthage, Mo. |
| CROSSROADS OF MID AMERICA | Joplin, Mo. |
| CROSSROADS OF NEW ENGLAND | Springfield, Mass. |
| CROSSROADS OF NEW ENGLAND | Westboro, Mass. |
| CROSSROADS OF NEW YORK | Utica, N. Y. |
| CROSSROADS OF NEW YORK STATE | Syracuse, N. Y. |
| CROSSROADS OF NORTHERN NEW ENGLAND | Wells River, Vt. |
| CROSSROADS OF SOUTHERN INDIANA | Paoli, Ind. |
| CROSSROADS OF SOUTHERN INDIANA | Seymour, Ind. |
| CROSSROADS OF THE ADIRONDACKS | Tupper Lake, N. Y. |
| CROSSROADS OF THE CONTINENT | Carbondale, Ill. |
| CROSSROADS OF THE AMERICAS | El Paso, Tex. |
| CROSSROADS OF THE MID-SOUTH | Memphis, Tenn. |
| CROSSROADS OF THE MIDDLE WEST | Rockford, Ill. |
| CROSSROADS OF THE NATION | Cincinnati, Ohio |
| CROSSROADS OF THE NATION | Hastings, Neb. |

| | |
|---|---|
| CROSSROADS OF THE NATION | Omaha, Neb. |
| CROSSROADS OF THE NATION | Sioux Falls, S. D. |
| CROSSROADS OF THE PACIFIC | Honolulu, Hawaii |
| CROSSROADS OF THE NEW SOUTH | Spartanburg, S. C. |
| CROSSROADS OF THE OLD AND THE NEW SOUTH | Jackson, Miss. |
| CROSSROADS OF THE SOUTH | Jackson, Miss. |
| CROSSROADS OF THE SOUTH | La Grange, Ga. |
| CROSSROADS OF THE WEST | Salt Lake City, Utah |
| CROSSROADS OF THE WORLD | Anchorage, Alaska |
| CROSSROADS OF THE WORLD | New York, N. Y. |
| CROSSROADS OF THE WORLD | Washington, D. C. |
| CROSSROADS OF TOMORROW | Hazleton, Pa. |
| CROSSROADS OF TOMORROW | Statesville, N. C. |
| CROSSROADS OF WISCONSIN | Marshfield, Wis. |
| CROSSROADS OF YOUR NATIONAL MARKET | Dayton, Ohio |
| CROSSROADS TO THE GULF | Alvin, Tex. |
| CROSSROADS TO THE UNIVERSE | Melbourne, Fla. |
| CROSSROADS TO WONDERLAND | Salida, Colo. |
| CROWN CITY | Pasadena, Calif. |
| CROWN CITY OF THE VALLEY | Pasadena, Calif. |
| CROWN JEWEL OF THE FLORIDA KEYS | Islamorada, Fla. |
| CROWN OF THE VALLEY | Pasadena, Calif. |
| CRUISE CAPITAL OF THE SOUTH | Port Everglades, Fla. |
| CRUISE CAPITAL OF THE WORLD | Dania, Fla. |
| CUISINE CAPITAL OF THE WORLD | New York, N. Y. |
| CRUMPTOWN | Memphis, Tenn. |
| CRUTCH CAPITAL OF THE WORLD | Rumney, N. H. |
| CRYSTAL CENTER OF THE WORLD | Carlisle, Pa. |
| CRYSTAL CITY | Corning, N. Y. |
| CULTURAL AND ECONOMIC CENTER OF SOUTHEASTERN NEW ENGLAND | Providence, R. I. |
| CULTURAL CENTER | Madison, Wis. |
| CULTURAL CENTER OF THE ADIRONDACKS | Schroon Lake, N. Y. |
| CULTURAL CENTER OF THE NATION | New York, N. Y. |
| CULTURAL CENTER OF THE SOUTHWEST | Houston, Tex. |
| CULTURAL CENTER OF THE WEST | San Francisco, Calif. |
| CULTURAL HUB | Stamford, Conn. |
| CUYUNA CAPITAL | Crosby, Minn. |
| CZECH BETHLEHEM | Racine, Wis. |
| CZECH CAPITAL OF NEBRASKA | Wilber, Neb. |

| | |
|---|---|
| DAIRY, AGRICULTURAL AND INDUSTRIAL CENTER | Springfield, Mo. |
| DAIRY CENTER OF THE SOUTH | Starkville, Miss. |
| DAIRY CITY | Elkland, Pa. |
| DAM END OF SANTA CLARA COUNTY | Morgan Hill, Calif. |
| DANCINGEST TOWN IN THE UNITED STATES | Hendersonville, N.C. |
| DANISH CAPITAL OF THE UNITED STATES | Racine, Wis. |
| DATE CAPITAL OF THE UNITED STATES | Indio, Calif. |
| DEAN OF THE 27 SPRINGFIELDS IN THE U. S. A. | Springfield, Mass. |
| DEEP SOUTH OF TEXAS | Bay City, Tex. |
| DEEP WATER | Chelan, Wash. |
| DEEP WATER PORT | Jacksonville, Fla. |
| DELAWARE'S SUMMER CAPITAL | Rehoboth Beach, Del. |
| DELIGHTFUL RESIDENTIAL COMMUNITY IN THE HEART OF THE PALM BEACHES | Palm Springs, Fla. |
| DENVER OF OREGON | Baker, Ore. |
| DENVER OF SOUTH DAKOTA | Rapid City, S. D. |
| DEPOT SPRINGS | Cheney, Wash. |
| DERBY CITY | Norwalk, Conn. |
| DERRICK CITY | Oil City, Pa. |
| DESERET | Salt Lake City, Utah |
| DESERT BABYLON | Las Vegas, Nev. |
| DESERT COMMUNITY | Ridgecrest, Calif. |
| DESERT WONDERLAND | Indio, Calif. |
| DETROIT OF AIRPLANES | Los Angeles, Calif. |
| DETROIT OF THE WEST | Oakland, Calif. |
| DETROIT THE BEAUTIFUL | Detroit, Mich. |
| DEUTSCH-ATHENS | Milwaukee, Wis. |
| DIAMOND CITY | Wilkes-Barre, Pa. |
| DIMPLE OF THE BLUEGRASS | Lexington, Ky. |
| DIMPLE OF THE UNIVERSE | Nashville, Tenn. |
| DISTINGUISHED AND FRIENDLY COMMUNITY | Amherst, Mass. |
| DISTRIBUTION CENTER OF THE SOUTHEAST | Augusta, Ga. |
| DISTRIBUTION CENTER OF THE SOUTHEAST | Jacksonville, Fla. |
| DISTRIBUTION CENTER FOR THE GREAT NORTHWEST | Fargo, N. D. |
| DISTRIBUTION CENTER OF THE NORTHEAST | Springfield, Mass. |

| | |
|---|---|
| DISTRIBUTION POINT, U. S. A. | York, Pa. |
| DISTRICT INCOMPARABLE | Oroville, Calif. |
| DIVERSIFIED AGRICULTURAL AND INDUSTRIAL COMMUNITY | Pierce City, Mo. |
| DIVERSIFIED CITY | Waycross, Ga. |
| DIVERSIFIED COMMUNITY | Frankfort, Ky. |
| DIVERSIFIED INDUSTRY CITY | East Point, Ga. |
| DIVERSIFIED MANUFACTURING COMMUNITY | Framingham, Mass. |
| DIXIE GATEWAY | Covington, Ky. |
| DOGWOOD CITY | Atlanta, Ga. |
| DON'T OVERLOOK OVERBROOK | Overbrook, Kan. |
| DORMATORY OF NEW YORK | Brooklyn, N. Y. |
| DORP | Schenectady, N. Y. |
| DREAM CITY COME TRUE | Hollywood, Fla. |
| DREAM TOWN | Greenfield, Mass. |
| DRUID CITY | Tuscaloosa, Ala. |
| DUAL CITIES | Minneapolis, and St. Paul, Minn. |
| DUCK HUNTING CAPITAL OF THE WORLD | Stuttgart, Ark. |
| DUCKS' PUDDLE | Drakes Branch, Va. |
| DUDE RANCH CAPITAL OF THE WORLD | Wickenburg, Ariz. |
| DUKE CITY | Albuquerque, N. M. |
| DUNGENESS CRAB CAPITAL OF THE WORLD | Newport, Ore. |
| DUPONT TOWN | Wilmington, Del. |
| DUPONTONIA | Wilmington, Del. |
| DUTCH CITY | Holland, Mich. |
| DUTCHTOWN | Aurora, Ore. |
| DYNAMIC AREA OF GROWTH | Aliquippa, Pa. |
| DYNAMIC CITY | Detroit, Mich. |
| DYNAMIC CITY | Douglasville, Ga. |
| DYNAMIC CITY | El Cerrito, Calif. |
| DYNAMIC DAVENPORT | Davenport, Iowa |
| DYNAMIC DETROIT | Detroit, Mich. |
| DYNAMIC METROPOLIS OF THE ROCKY MOUNTAIN EMPIRE | Denver, Colo. |
| DYNAMO OF DIXIE | Chattanooga, Tenn. |

E

| | |
|---|---|
| EARLY WEST IN MODERN SPLENDOR | Las Vegas, Nev. |
| EARTHQUAKE CITY | Charleston, S. C. |
| EAST COAST MEGALOPOLIS | Hartford, Conn. |
| EASTERN APPROACH TO BERTHOUD PASS | Empire, Colo. |
| EASTERN CONNECTICUT CENTER | Willimantic, Conn. |

301

| | |
|---|---|
| EASTERN GATEWAY TO BUCKTAIL STATE PARK | Lock Haven, Pa. |
| EASTERN GATEWAY TO HILLSBOR-OUGH COUNTY | Plant City, Fla. |
| EASTERN GATEWAY TO JACKSON COUNTY | Sneads, Fla. |
| EASTERN GATEWAY TO LAUREL HIGHLANDS | Somerset, Pa. |
| EASTERN GATEWAY TO MT. RANIER NATIONAL PARK | Yakima, Wash. |
| EASTERN GATEWAY TO NEBRASKA-LAND | Blair, Neb. |
| EASTERN GATEWAY TO THE BLACK HILLS | Rapid City, S. D. |
| EASTERN GATEWAY TO THE MOUN-TAINOUS BLACK HILLS WHERE EAST MEETS WEST AND THE FRIENDLY HOSPITALITY | Rapid City, S. D. |
| EASTERN GATEWAY TO THE OZARKS | Poplar Bluff, Mo. |
| EASTERN SHORE OF MOBILE BAY | Fairhope, Ala. |
| EASTERLY GATEWAY TO THE LAKES AND WHITE MOUNTAINS REGION | Dover, N. H. |
| ECONOMY GATEWAY | New Bedford, Mass. |
| EDEN OF OHIO | Sabina, Ohio |
| EDEN OF THE CLOSEST STATE TO HEAVEN | Fort Collins, Colo. |
| EDINBURGH OF AMERICA | Albany, N. Y. |
| EDUCATIONAL CAPITAL | Jackson, Miss. |
| EDUCATIONAL CENTER | Ithaca, N. Y. |
| EDUCATIONAL CENTER | Mitchell, S. D. |
| EDUCATIONAL CENTER OF THE WEST | Emporia, Kan. |
| EDUCATIONAL, CULTURAL AND BUS-INESS CENTER | Holly Springs, Miss. |
| EDUCATION, CULTURE, BUSINESS DISTRIBUTION CENTER OF THE ST. LAWRENCE VALLEY | Potsdam, N. Y. |
| EDUCATIONAL-CULTURAL COMMUN-ITY | State College, Pa. |
| EGG BASKET OF THE WORLD | Petaluma, Calif. |
| EL-AY | Los Angeles, Calif. |
| ELAY | Los Angeles, Calif. |
| ELECTRIC CITY | Great Falls, Mont. |
| ELECTRIC CITY | Kaukauna, Wis. |
| ELECTRIC CITY | Schenectady, N. Y. |
| ELECTRIC CITY | Scranton, Pa. |
| ELECTRIC CITY OF THE FUTURE | Buffalo, N. Y. |
| ELECTRICAL CENTER OF AMERICA | Sheffield, Ala. |
| ELECTRICAL CITY | Schenectady, N. Y. |

| | |
|---|---|
| ELECTRONIC CENTER OF THE SOUTHWEST | Fort Huachuca, Ariz. |
| ELECTRONIC CITY OF THE SOUTH-WEST | Richardson, Tex. |
| ELECTRONICS AEROSPACE CENTER | Dallas, Tex. |
| ELECTRONICS CAPITAL OF THE MIDWEST | Ogallala, Neb. |
| ELECTRONICS CAPITOL OF THE WORLD | Syracuse, N. Y. |
| ELLENVILLE IS EVERYTHINGVILLE | Ellenville, N. Y. |
| ELLWOOD CITY ENCOURAGES ENTERPRISE | Ellwood City, Pa. |
| ELM CITY | New Haven, Conn. |
| ELM CITY | Waterville, Me. |
| EMBRYONIC CAPITAL | Washington, D. C. |
| EMERGING INDUSTRIAL CENTER | Birmingham, Ala. |
| EMERGING METROPOLIS | Rochester, N. Y. |
| EMPIRE CITY | New York, N. Y. |
| ENCAMPMENT CITY | Palacios, Tex. |
| ENERGY CAPITAL OF THE WEST | Farmington, N. M. |
| ENGINEERS' TOWN | Coulee City, Wash. |
| ENJOYMENT IN HISTORY RELIVED | Ogdensburg, N. Y. |
| ENTERTAINMENT CAPITAL OF THE WORLD | Las Vegas, Nev. |
| ENTERTAINMENT CAPITAL OF THE WORLD | New York, N. Y. |
| ENTIRE CITY OF FRIENDLY PEOPLE | Ogdensburg, N. Y. |
| ENTRANCE TO SAM HOUSTON NATIONAL FOREST | Cleveland, Tex. |
| ENTRANCE TO THE CHAIN-O-LAKES | Elk Rapids, Mich. |
| ESKIMO VILLAGE | Kotzebue, Alaska |
| ESSEN OF AMERICA | Bridgeport, Conn. |
| ESTABLISHED CITY | Muskogee, Okla. |
| EVERGREEN CITY | Sheboygan, Wis. |
| EVERGREEN PLAYGROUND | Seattle, Wash. |
| EVERGREEN PLAYGROUND | Tacoma, Wash. |
| EVERYTHING YOUR VACATION HEART DESIRES CAN BE FOUND IN RIVIERA BEACH | Riviera Beach, Fla. |
| EXCITING CITY | Los Angeles, Calif. |
| EXCITING CITY OF WELCOME | Honolulu, Hawaii |
| EXCITING INTERNATIONAL CITY | El Paso, Tex. |
| EXCITING WORLD CITY | Los Angeles, Calif. |
| EXECUTIVE CITY | Washington, D. C. |
| EXPOSITION CITY | San Francisco, Calif. |
| EYE OF THE COMMONWEALTH | Southbridge, Mass. |

303

F

| | |
|---|---|
| FABULOUS CITY | Los Angeles, Calif. |
| FABULOUS CITY IN THE SUN | Miami Beach, Fla. |
| FAIR CITY | Huron, S. D. |
| FAIR CITY | Largo, Fla. |
| FAIR CITY | Syracuse, N. Y. |
| FAIR LITTLE CITY | Tulsa, Okla. |
| FAIR PLAY CITY | Jersey Shore, Pa. |
| FAIR WHITE CITY | Milwaukee, Wis. |
| FAIRYLAND | Hollywood, Calif. |
| FAITHFUL CITY | Worcester, Mass. |
| FALLS | Fall City, Wash. |
| FALLS | Tumwater, Wash. |
| FALLS CITIES | Jeffersonville, Ind. |
| FALLS CITIES | Louisville, Ky. |
| FALLS CITIES | New Albany, Ind. |
| FALLS CITY | Louisville, Ky. |
| FAMED GOLD RUSH TOWN | Nome, Alaska |
| FAMILY CITY | Anaheim, Calif. |
| FAMILY CITY | St. Louis, Mo. |
| FAMILY COMMUNITY | Castro Valley, Calif. |
| FAMILY COMMUNITY FOR YOUR MAINE VACATION | Harrison, Me. |
| FAMILY OASIS OF SAFE OCEAN BEACHES | Pompano Beach, Fla. |
| FAMILY TOWN | Garden City, Kan. |
| FAMILY VACATION RESORT | China, Me. |
| FAMILY VACATION SPOT | Wildwood, N. J. |
| FAMILY VACATIONLAND | Schroon Lake, N. Y. |
| FAMOUS PLAYGROUND OF THE WONDROUS NORTHWEST | Coeur d'Alene, Idaho |
| FAMOUS WINTER RESORT FOR NORTHERN INVALIDS AND PLEASURE SEEKERS | Thomasville, Ga. |
| FAR AWAY ISLAND | Nantucket, Mass. |
| FAR AWAY LAND | Nantucket, Mass. |
| FARM MACHINERY CAPITAL OF AMERICA | Moline, Ill. |
| FARTHEST INLAND DEEP WATER PORT | Baton Rouge, La. |
| FASCINATING FOOTHILLS CITY | Fort Collins, Colo. |
| FASHION CAPITAL OF THE NATION | Houston, Tex. |
| FASHION CAPITAL OF THE WORLD | New York, N. Y. |
| FAST GROWING CITY | West Palm Beach, Fla. |

| | |
|---|---|
| FAST GROWING INDUSTRIAL COMMUNITY | Richmond, Calif. |
| FAST-GROWING NERVE CENTER FOR AMERICA'S GREAT NORTHLAND EMPIRE | Minneapolis, Minn. |
| FASTEST GROWING AREA IN VIRGINIA | Suffolk, Va. |
| FASTEST GROWING CHEMICAL CENTER IN THE GREAT MIDWEST | Joplin, Mo. |
| FASTEST GROWING CITY | Dallas, Tex. |
| FASTEST GROWING CITY IN EASTERN ARKANSAS | West Memphis, Ark. |
| FASTEST GROWING CITY IN LOS ANGELES COUNTY | Montebello, Calif. |
| FASTEST GROWING CITY IN MASSACHUSETTS | Quincy, Mass. |
| FASTEST GROWING CITY IN NEW ENGLAND | Chicopee, Mass. |
| FASTEST GROWING CITY IN THE COUNTY | Stamford, Conn. |
| FASTEST GROWING CITY IN TEXAS | Corpus Christi, Tex. |
| FASTEST GROWING CITY IN THE NORTHWEST | Bismarck, N.D. |
| FASTEST GROWING CITY IN THE STATE | Hastings, Neb. |
| FASTEST GROWING CITY IN THE UPPER MIDWEST | Rapid City, S.D. |
| FASTEST GROWING COMMUNITY IN MAINE | Norway, Me. |
| FASTEST GROWING COMMUNITY IN MAINE | Paris, Me. |
| FASTEST GROWING DEEP WATER SEAPORT IN MAINE | Searsport, Me. |
| FASTEST GROWING FRIENDLY RETIREMENT COMMUNITY | DeBary, Fla. |
| FASTEST GROWING INDUSTRIAL AREA IN THE SOUTHEAST | Hialeah, Fla. |
| FASTEST GROWING MOUNTAIN RESORT | Gatlinburg, Tenn. |
| FASTEST GROWING MUNICIPALITY IN THE STATE | Stamford, Conn. |
| FASTEST GROWING OF THE NATION'S MAJOR CITIES | Houston, Tex. |
| FASTEST GROWING TOWN IN HILLSBORO COUNTY | Merrimack, N.H. |
| FATHER KNICKERBOCKER | New York, N.Y. |
| FAVORED VACATION PACKAGE OF WESTERN AMERICA | Las Vegas, Nev. |

305

| | |
|---|---|
| FAVORITE FAMILY SEASIDE RE-SORT | Hampton Beach, N. H. |
| FAVORSBURG | Pataha, Wash. |
| FEDERAL CAPITAL | Washington, D. C. |
| FEDERAL CITY | Atlanta, Ga. |
| FEDERAL CITY | Paterson, N. J. |
| FEDERAL CITY | Washington, D. C. |
| FEDERAL SEAT | Washington, D. C. |
| FEDERAL SITE | Washington, D. C. |
| FEDERAL TOWN | Washington, D. C. |
| FEEDER CALF CAPITAL OF THE WORLD | Unionville, Mo. |
| FEEDER PIG CAPITOL OF THE WORLD | West Plains, Mo. |
| FERN CITY OF FLORIDA | Apopka, Fla. |
| FIGHTIN'EST TOWN ON THE RIVER | Lancaster, Ore. |
| FILBERT CENTER OF THE UNITED STATES | Hillsboro, Ore. |
| FILM CAPITAL | Hollywood, Calif. |
| FILM CAPITAL OF THE WORLD | Hollywood, Calif. |
| FILM CITY | Hollywood, Calif. |
| FILMDOM | Hollywood, Calif. |
| FILMLAND | Hollywood, Calif. |
| FINANCIAL CENTER | Midland, Tex. |
| FINANCIAL CENTER OF ALASKA | Anchorage, Alaska |
| FINANCE CENTER OF FLORIDA | Jacksonville, Fla. |
| FINANCIAL CENTER OF THE DEL-MAR-VA PENINSULA | Wilmington, Del. |
| FINANCIAL CENTER OF THE SOUTH-WEST | Dallas, Tex. |
| FINANCIAL CAPITAL OF THE WORLD | New York, N. Y. |
| FINANCIAL CENTER OF THE WEST | San Francisco, Calif. |
| FINANCIAL CENTER OF THE WORLD | San Francisco, Calif. |
| FINE PLACE TO LIVE | Boynton Beach, Fla. |
| FINE RESIDENTIAL CITY | Fargo, N. D. |
| FINE WRITING PAPER CENTER OF THE WORLD | Holyoke, Mass. |
| FINEST BEACH IN THE WORLD | Old Orchard Beach, Me. |
| FINEST HOME AND CULTURAL COM-MUNITY IN SOUTHERN CALIFORNIA | Whittier, Calif. |
| FINEST IN TENNIS ON THE JERSEY COAST | Stone Harbor, N. J. |
| FINEST NEW ENGLAND VILLAGE IN THE MIDDLE WEST | Evanston, Ill. |

| | |
|---|---|
| FIRE CLAY AND HORSE CAPITAL OF THE WORLD | Mexico, Mo. |
| FIRECLAY CAPITAL | Mexico, Mo. |
| FIRECLAY CAPITAL OF THE WORLD | Mexico, Mo. |
| FIRST AMERICAN CAPITAL WEST OF THE ROCKIES | Monterey, Calif. |
| FIRST AND LAST MAJOR U.S. PORT OF CALL ON THE SEAWAY ROUTE | Buffalo, N.Y. |
| FIRST CAPITAL CITY | Sitka, Alaska |
| FIRST CAPITAL OF ARIZONA | Prescott, Ariz. |
| FIRST CAPITAL OF MISSOURI | St. Charles, Mo. |
| FIRST CAPITAL OF NEW YORK | Kingston, N.Y. |
| FIRST CAPITAL OF THE REPUBLIC OF TEXAS | West Columbia, Tex. |
| FIRST CAPITAL OF THE STATE | Huntsville, Ala. |
| FIRST CAPITAL OF THE UNITED STATES | York, Pa. |
| FIRST CHOICE IN FAMILY RESORTS | Ocean City, N.J. |
| FIRST CITY | Ketchikan, Alaska |
| FIRST CITY | Memphis, Tenn. |
| FIRST CITY IN AMERICAN SPIRIT | Cleveland, Ohio |
| FIRST CITY IN FAMOUS PALM BEACH COUNTY | Jupiter, Fla. |
| FIRST CITY IN TEXAS | Houston, Tex. |
| FIRST CITY OF AMERICA'S FIRST VACATIONLAND | Providence, R.I. |
| FIRST CITY OF KANSAS | Leavenworth, Kan. |
| FIRST CITY OF THE FIRST STATE | Wilmington, Del. |
| FIRST CITY OF THE SOUTH | Savannah, Ga. |
| FIRST CITY OF THE WORLD | New York, N.Y. |
| FIRST COTTON PORT | Houston, Tex. |
| FIRST ELECTRICALLY LIGHTED CITY IN THE WORLD | Wabash, Ind. |
| FIRST ON THE FUN COAST OF FLORIDA | West Palm Beach, Fla. |
| FIRST PEACE TIME CAPITOL OF THE UNITED STATES | Annapolis, Md. |
| FIRST PORT ON THE COLUMBIA | Astoria, Ore. |
| FIRST SKI-CLUB CITY | Berlin, N.H. |
| FIRST STOP OF THE EASTWIND | Chatham, Mass. |
| FIRST TERRITORIAL CAPITAL | Lewiston, Idaho |
| FIRST TOWN OF AMERICA | Plymouth, Mass. |
| FIRST TVA CITY | Tupelo, Miss. |
| FISH CITY | Lake Andes, S.D. |
| FISHERMAN'S HARBOR | Coyle, Wash. |
| FISHERMAN'S PARADISE | Belmar, N.J. |
| FISHERMAN'S PARADISE | Bonita Springs, Fla. |

| | |
|---|---|
| FISHERMAN'S PARADISE | Carrabelle, Fla. |
| FISHERMAN'S PARADISE | Everglades, Fla. |
| FISHERMAN'S PARADISE | Marathon, Fla. |
| FISHERMAN'S PARADISE | St. Cloud, Fla. |
| FISHERMAN'S PARADISE | Salem, Ore. |
| FISHERMAN'S PARADISE OF THE NORTH ATLANTIC | New Shoreham, R. I. |
| FISHING AND HUNTING HEADQUARTERS FOR GIGANTIC LAKE GARRISON | Garrison, N. D. |
| FISHING CAPITAL OF THE OZARKS | Mountain Home, Ark. |
| FISHING SHANGRI-LA OF THE SOUTH | Marksville, La. |
| FIVE MILES OF HEALTH AND HAPPINESS | Wildwood, N. J. |
| FIVE MILES OF SMILES, SEA, SAND AND FUN | Salisbury Beach, Mass. |
| FIVE STAR CITY IN THE VALLEY OF THE SUN | Chandler, Ariz. |
| FLICKER CAPITAL | Hollywood, Calif. |
| FLICKER CITY | Hollywood, Calif. |
| FLICKER LANE | Hollywood, Calif. |
| FLOOD CITY | Johnstown, Pa. |
| FLOOD FREE CITY | Johnstown, Pa. |
| FLORAL CITY | Cincinnati, Ohio |
| FLORAL METROPLIS OF EAST TEXAS | Tyler, Tex. |
| FLORIDA PLUS CITY | Pensacola, Fla. |
| FLORIDA'S ALL-YEAR RESORT | West Palm Beach, Fla. |
| FLORIDA'S ATTRACTION SHOWPLACE | Lake Wales, Fla. |
| FLORIDA'S BIGGEST LITTLE TOWN | Davenport, Fla. |
| FLORIDA'S BOATING CAPITAL ON THE GULF | Dunedin, Fla. |
| FLORIDA'S CENTER FOR SCIENCE, EDUCATION, MEDICINE | Gainesville, Fla. |
| FLORIDA'S CITY BEAUTIFUL | Orlando, Fla. |
| FLORIDA'S CITY OF FIVE FLAGS | Pensacola, Fla. |
| FLORIDA'S COMPLETE FAMILY OUTDOOR RECREATION CENTER | Lake Hampton, Fla. |
| FLORIDA'S CONVENTION CITY | Tampa, Fla. |
| FLORIDA'S COUNTRY CLUB TOWN | Lehigh Acres, Fla. |
| FLORIDA'S DEEP WATER HARBER | Port Everglades, Fla. |
| FLORIDA'S DISSIMILAR RESORT | Delray Beach, Fla. |
| FLORIDA'S EIGHTH CITY | Lakeland, Fla. |
| FLORIDA'S ENTERTAINMENT CAPITAL | Sarasota, Fla. |
| FLORIDA'S FABULOUS FRONTIER COAST | Port St. Joe, Fla. |

| | |
|---|---|
| FLORIDA'S FASTEST GROWING CITY | Hialeah, Fla. |
| FLORIDA'S FINEST AGRICULTURAL, INDUSTRIAL AND RESORT COMMUNITY | Fort Pierce, Fla. |
| FLORIDA'S GATEWAY CITY | Jacksonville, Fla. |
| FLORIDA'S GOLFINGEST CITY | Hollywood, Fla. |
| FLORIDA'S GREAT GULF BEACH RESORT AREA | Sarasota, Fla. |
| FLORIDA'S GULF COAST METROPOLIS | Tampa, Fla. |
| FLORIDA'S HUB OF FUN | Jacksonville, Fla. |
| FLORIDA'S LAST FRONTIER | Belleview, Fla. |
| FLORIDA'S MAGIC CITY | Miami, Fla. |
| FLORIDA'S METROPOLITAN DISTRIBUTING CENTER | Tampa, Fla. |
| FLORIDA'S MOST FRIENDLY COMMUNITY | Largo, Fla. |
| FLORIDA'S NEW GATEWAY | Lake City, Fla. |
| FLORIDA'S NEWEST CONVENTION CITY | Clearwater, Fla. |
| FLORIDA'S NEWEST METROPOLITAN INDUSTRIAL AREA | Daytona Beach, Fla. |
| FLORIDA'S POTATO CAPITAL | Hastings, Fla. |
| FLORIDA'S SECOND LARGEST CITY | Tampa, Fla. |
| FLORIDA'S SHOWCASE COMMUNITY | Coral Gables, Fla. |
| FLORIDA'S TRANSPORTATION HUB | Orlando, Fla. |
| FLORIDA'S TREASURE CITY | Tampa, Fla. |
| FLORIDA'S TROPICAL PARADISE | Fort Lauderdale, Fla. |
| FLORIDA'S VACATION CAPITAL | Daytona Beach, Fla. |
| FLORIDA'S WATERFRONT WONDERLAND | Cape Coral, Fla. |
| FLORIDA'S WEST COAST BEACH RESORT | Longboat Key, Fla. |
| FLORIDA'S WEST COAST'S FINEST VACATION SPOT | Casey Key, Fla. |
| FLORIDA'S WINTER STRAWBERRY MARKET | Starke, Fla. |
| FLORIDA'S YEAR 'ROUND CITY | Tampa, Fla. |
| FLORIDA'S YEAR ROUND PLAYGROUND | Daytona Beach, Fla. |
| FLOUR CITY | Buffalo, N. Y. |
| FLOUR CITY | Minneapolis, Minn. |
| FLOUR CITY | Rochester, N. Y. |
| FLOUR MILLING CAPITAL OF THE WORLD | Buffalo, N. Y. |
| FLOUR MILLING CAPITAL OF THE WORLD | Minneapolis, Minn. |
| FLOWER BOX CITY | Neosho, Mo. |
| FLOWER CITY | Rochester, N. Y. |

| | |
|---|---|
| FLOWER CITY | Springfield, Ill. |
| FLOWER CITY | Springfield, Ohio |
| FLOWER, FRUIT, VEGETABLE CENTER | Hendersonville, N.C. |
| FLOWER TOWN IN THE PINES | Summerville, S.C. |
| FLOWERBOX CITY | Neosho, Mo. |
| FOAM CITY | Milwaukee, Wis. |
| FOCAL POINT OF INDUSTRIAL AMERICA | Aliquippa, Pa. |
| FOOD BASKET OF THE WORLD | Fargo, N.D. |
| FOOD EMPORIUM | Wishram, Wash. |
| FOOT OF THE ADIRONDACKS | Amsterdam, N.Y. |
| FOOTBALL CAPITAL OF THE SOUTH | Birmingham, Ala. |
| FOOTHILLS OF THE CATSKILLS | Walton, N.Y. |
| FORDTOWN | Detroit, Mich. |
| FOREMOST INDUSTRIAL CENTER OF IOWA | Sioux City, Iowa |
| FOREST CITY | Cleveland, Ohio |
| FOREST CITY | Middletown, Conn. |
| FOREST CITY | Portland, Me. |
| FOREST CITY | Rockford, Ill. |
| FOREST CITY | Savannah, Ga. |
| FOREST CITY | Wausau, Wis. |
| FOREST CITY OF THE SOUTH | Savannah, Ga. |
| FOREST PRODUCTS CAPITAL OF AMERICA | Tacoma, Wash. |
| FORESTRY CAPITAL OF FLORIDA | Lake City, Fla. |
| FORESTRY CAPITAL OF THE NATION | Crossett, Ark. |
| FORGE OF THE UNIVERSE | Pittsburg, Pa. |
| FORMER CAPITAL OF THE CHEROKEE INDIAN NATION | Tahlequah, Okla. |
| FORMER CAPITAL OF THE CHICKASAW NATION | Tupelo, Miss. |
| FORT LAUDERDALE OF THE EASTERN SHORE | Ocean City, Md. |
| FORT TOWN | Fort Worth, Tex. |
| FORTUNATE ISLAND | Monhegan, Me. |
| FOUNDLING CAPITAL | Washington, D.C. |
| FOUNTAIN CITY | De Soto, Mo. |
| FOUNTAIN CITY | Fond du Lac, Wis. |
| FOUNTAIN CITY | Pueblo, Colo. |
| FOUNTAIN OF YOUTH CITY | St. Augustine, Fla. |
| FOUR FLAGS CITY | Niles, Mich. |
| FOUR LAKE CITY | Madison, Wis. |
| FOUR LAKES CITY | Madison, Wis. |
| FOUR-LEAF CLOVER CITY | Decatur, Ala. |
| FOUR MOUNTAINS OF FUN | Killington, Vt. |
| FOUR-SEASON AREA | Springfield, Vt. |

| | |
|---|---|
| FOUR SEASON CITY | Superior, Wis. |
| FOUR-SEASON COMMUNITY | Newport, Vt. |
| FOUR SEASON RESORT AND CUL-<br>TURAL CENTER | Manchester, Vt. |
| FOUR-SEASON RESORT FOR HEALTH,<br>REST AND PLEASURE | Atlantic City, N. J. |
| FOUR SEASON'S PLAYGROUND | Marquette, Mich. |
| FRATERNAL CAPITAL OF THE<br>SOUTHWEST | Guthrie, Okla. |
| FREE STATE OF BEXAR | San Antonio, Tex. |
| FRENCH LOUISIANA | Lafayette, La. |
| FRIENDLIEST AREA IN NORTHERN<br>LOWER MICHIGAN | Cadillac, Mich. |
| FRIENDLIEST CITY | Rochester, N. Y. |
| FRIENDLIEST CITY IN THE STATE | Lebanon, Ind. |
| FRIENDLIEST CITY ON ANY INTER-<br>NATIONAL BORDER | Ogdensburg, N. Y. |
| FRIENDLIEST LITTLE "BIG TOWN"<br>IN KENTUCKY | Murray, Ky. |
| FRIENDLIEST LITTLE CITY | Avon Park, Fla. |
| FRIENDLIEST LITTLE CITY IN NE-<br>BRASKA | Burwell, Neb. |
| FRIENDLIEST SPOT ON THE KING'S<br>HIGHWAY | San Bruno, Calif. |
| FRIENDLIEST TOWN | Greenwich, Conn. |
| FRIENDLIEST TOWN IN AMERICA | Tryon, N. C. |
| FRIENDLIEST TOWN IN NEW ENGLAND | Skowhegan, Me. |
| FRIENDLIEST TOWN IN OKLAHOMA | Drumright, Okla. |
| FRIENDLIEST TOWN ON EARTH | Clarksville, Va. |
| FRIENDLIEST TOWN ON THE LAKE | Mabank, Tex. |
| FRIENDLY AND PROGRESSIVE CITY | Mason City, Iowa |
| FRIENDLY CITY | Albertville, Ala. |
| FRIENDLY CITY | Algona, Iowa |
| FRIENDLY CITY | Augusta, Ga. |
| FRIENDLY CITY | Austin, Tex. |
| FRIENDLY CITY | Bradenton, Fla. |
| FRIENDLY CITY | Carrollton, Ga. |
| FRIENDLY CITY | Chehalis, Wash. |
| FRIENDLY CITY | Columbus, Miss. |
| FRIENDLY CITY | Cordova, Alaska |
| FRIENDLY CITY | Douglas, Ga. |
| FRIENDLY CITY | Fort Worth, Tex. |
| FRIENDLY CITY | Fortuna, Calif |
| FRIENDLY CITY | Fredericksburg, Va. |
| FRIENDLY CITY | Hazlehurst, Ga. |
| FRIENDLY CITY | Huntsville, Ark. |
| FRIENDLY CITY | Jackson, Miss. |
| FRIENDLY CITY | Johnston, R. I. |

311

| | |
|---|---|
| FRIENDLY CITY | Johnstown, Pa. |
| FRIENDLY CITY | Kaukauna, Wis. |
| FRIENDLY CITY | Long Beach, Miss. |
| FRIENDLY CITY | Lynchburg, Va. |
| FRIENDLY CITY | Milwaukee, Wis. |
| FRIENDLY CITY | New York, N. Y. |
| FRIENDLY CITY | Owosso, Mich. |
| FRIENDLY CITY | Pampa, Tex. |
| FRIENDLY CITY | Porterville, Calif. |
| FRIENDLY CITY | Scranton, Pa. |
| FRIENDLY CITY | Spokane, Wash. |
| FRIENDLY CITY | Starke, Fla. |
| FRIENDLY CITY IN THE HEART OF GEORGIA | Macon, Ga. |
| FRIENDLY CITY IN THE HEART OF THE OLD WEST | Douglas, Ariz. |
| FRIENDLY CITY IN THE SKY | Denver, Colo. |
| FRIENDLY CITY OF ENDLESS CHARM | Jacksonville, Fla. |
| FRIENDLY CITY OF PROGRESS | Goldsboro, N. C. |
| FRIENDLY CITY OF THE HIGHLANDS | Frostproof, Fla. |
| FRIENDLY CITY OF THE SOUTHWEST | Fort Worth, Tex. |
| FRIENDLY CITY ON THE OREGON TRAIL | Baker, Ore. |
| FRIENDLY CITY WITH A FUTURE | Jeannette, Pa. |
| FRIENDLY COMMUNITY | Grove, Okla. |
| FRIENDLY COMMUNITY IN MARTIN COUNTY | Jensen Beach, Fla. |
| FRIENDLY COMMUNITY OF BEAUTY AND INDUSTRY | Upper Sandusky, Ohio |
| FRIENDLY COMMUNITY, THE HOME OF FRIENDLY PEOPLE | Ash Grove, Mo. |
| FRIENDLY DOOR TO WISCONSIN'S INDIANHEAD COUNTRY | Eau Claire, Wis. |
| FRIENDLY FABULOUS FLAGSTAFF | Flagstaff, Ariz. |
| FRIENDLY FOLK'S VILLAGE | Plainfield, Ind. |
| FRIENDLY FRONTIER CITY | Fairbanks, Alaska |
| FRIENDLY ISLAND | Marthas Vineyard, Mass. |
| FRIENDLY LITTLE CITY IN THE PROSPEROUS SHOSHONE VALLEY | Powell, Wyo. |
| FRIENDLY PLACE TO LIVE AND WORK | Barre, Vt. |
| FRIENDLY PROSPEROUS TOWN | Fryeburg, Me. |
| FRIENDLY RESORT CITY | Bradley Beach, N. J. |
| FRIENDLY TOWN | Clayton, N. M. |
| FRIENDLY TOWN | Johnston, R. I. |
| FRIENDLY TOWN OF FRIENDLY PEO- PLE | Raritan, N. J. |

| | |
|---|---|
| FRIENDLY VILLAGE | Harrison, Me. |
| FRIENDLY VILLAGE | Mattituck, N. Y. |
| FRIENDLY VILLAGE | Prentice, Wis. |
| FRISCO | San Francisco, Calif. |
| FROG AND TOE | New York, N. Y. |
| FROG LEVEL | Clinchport, Va. |
| FROG MARKET OF THE NATION | Rayne, La. |
| FRONT DOOR ENTRANCE TO AN ALASKA VACATION | Anchorage, Alaska |
| FRONT OFFICE OF AMERICAN BUSINESS | New York, N. Y. |
| FRONTIER OF INDUSTRIAL OPPORTUNITY | Laurel, Mont. |
| FROSTY CITY | Somerset, Pa. |
| FRUIT BOWL OF THE NATION | Yakima, Wash. |
| FRUIT CAKE CAPITAL | Claxton, Ga. |
| FUDGE CAPITAL OF THE WORLD | Mackinac Island, Mich. |
| FUN CAPITAL OF THE SOUTH | Daytona Beach, Fla. |
| FUN CAPITAL OF THE VACATION STATE | Billings, Mont. |
| FUN CAPITAL OF THE WORLD | Las Vegas, Nev. |
| FUN CAPITOL OF SOUTHERN OREGON | Medford, Ore. |
| FUN CITY | New York, N. Y. |
| FUN-CITY-ON-THE-HUDSON | New York, N. Y. |
| FUN COUNTRY, U. S. A. | Saratoga Springs, N. Y. |
| FUN FESTIVAL PLACE | Miami Beach, Fla. |
| FUN N' CONVENTION CITY | Anaheim, Calif. |
| FUN'N EXCITEMENT CENTER | Scottsdale, Ariz. |
| FUN PLACE | Denton, Tex. |
| FUN SHINES BRIGHTEST IN THE SUMMER TIME | Virginia Beach, Va. |
| FUN SPOT OF THE SOUTHWEST | Fort Worth, Tex. |
| FUN-TIER CAPITAL OF TEXAS | Austin, Tex. |
| FUN TOWN | Park Falls, Wis. |
| FURNITURE CAPITAL OF AMERICA | Grand Rapids, Mich. |
| FURNITURE CENTER OF THE WORLD | Grand Rapids, Mich. |
| FURNITURE CITY | Grand Rapids, Mich. |
| FURNITURE CITY | High Point, N. C. |
| FURNITURE CITY | Martinsville, Va. |
| FURNITURE CITY OF THE WORLD | High Point, N. C. |
| FURNITURE PRODUCTION CENTER OF THE U. S. | High Point, N. C. |
| FURNITURE, THREAD AND STEEL CITY | Toccoa, Ga. |
| FUTURE GREAT CITY | Pierre, S. D. |

313

| | |
|---|---|
| FUTURE GREAT CITY OF THE WORLD | St. Louis, Mo. |
| FUTURE INDUSTRIAL CAPITAL OF THE SOUTH SHORE | Braintree, Mass. |
| FUTURE MANUFACTURING CENTER OF THE WEST WHERE RAIL AND WATER TRANSPORTATION MEET | Petaluma, Calif. |
| FUTURE MINDED CITY | Chicopee, Mass. |

## G

| | |
|---|---|
| GABLE TOWN | Danville, Ind. |
| GAMBLER'S MECCA | Las Vegas, Nev. |
| GAMBLER'S PARADISE ON EARTH | Las Vegas, Nev. |
| GAMBLING QUEEN | Muskegon, Mich. |
| GAMECOCK CITY | Sumter, S. C. |
| GANGLAND | Chicago, Ill. |
| GAP | Pennington Gap, Va. |
| GARDEN CITY | Basin, Wyo. |
| GARDEN CITY | Beverly, Mass. |
| GARDEN CITY | Cedar Falls, Iowa |
| GARDEN CITY | Chicago, Ill. |
| GARDEN CITY | Missoula, Mont. |
| GARDEN CITY | Newton, Mass. |
| GARDEN CITY | San Jose, Calif. |
| GARDEN CITY | Savannah, Ga. |
| GARDEN CITY OF CLARK COUNTY | Boulder City, Nev. |
| GARDEN CITY OF SOUTHERN NEVADA | Boulder City, Nev. |
| GARDEN CITY OF THE SOUTH | Augusta, Ga. |
| GARDEN OF THE GLADES | Pahokee, Fla. |
| GARDEN OF MAINE | Houlton, Me. |
| GARDEN SPOT FOR GOLF | Virginia Beach, Va. |
| GARDEN SPOT OF LOUISIANA | Jennings, La. |
| GARDEN SPOT OF NORTHWEST FLORIDA | Monticello, Fla. |
| GARDEN SPOT OF PENNSYLVANIA | Mount Joy, Pa. |
| GARDEN SPOT OF SOUTHERN INDIANA | Washington, Ind. |
| GARDEN SPOT OF THE GARDEN STATE | Hammonton, N. J. |
| GARDEN SPOT OF THE PALM BEACHES | Palm Springs, Fla. |
| GARDEN SPOT OF THE PENINSULA | Palo Alto, Calif. |
| GARDEN SPOT OF THE SOUTH | Pensacola, Fla. |
| GARDEN SPOT OF THE WEST | Garden City, Kan. |
| GARDEN SPOT OF THE WORLD | Beverly Hills, Calif. |
| GARDEN SPOT OF THE WORLD FAMOUS SANTA CLARA VALLEY | Los Altos, Calif. |
| GARRISON CITY | Dover, N. H. |
| GAS CAPITAL OF THE WORLD | Hugoton, Kan. |
| GAS HOUSE OF THE NATION | Washington, D. C. |

| | |
|---|---|
| GATE CITY | Atlanta, Ga. |
| GATE CITY | Chattanooga, Tenn. |
| GATE CITY | Denison, Tex. |
| GATE CITY | Keokuk, Iowa |
| GATE CITY | Laredo, Tex. |
| GATE CITY | Nashua, N. H. |
| GATE CITY | Rapid City, S. D. |
| GATE CITY | Raton, N. M. |
| GATE CITY | San Bernardino, Calif. |
| GATE CITY | Winona, Minn. |
| GATE CITY OF FLORIDA | Jacksonville, Fla. |
| GATE CITY OF NEW HAMPSHIRE | Nashua, N. H. |
| GATE CITY OF THE WEST | Omaha, Neb. |
| GATE CITY TO THE GREAT NORTH-WEST | Pocatello, Idaho |
| GATE CITY TO THE SOUTH | Atlanta, Ga. |
| GATE TO THE OLD SOUTH | Rocky Mount, N. C. |
| GATE TO THE SPORTSMAN'S EDEN | Ely, Minn. |
| GATEWAY | Ashland, Ore. |
| GATEWAY ARCH CITY | St. Louis, Mo. |
| GATEWAY BETWEEN EAST AND WEST | Pittsburgh, Pa. |
| GATEWAY CENTER | Pittsburgh, Pa. |
| GATEWAY CITY | Fargo, N. D. |
| GATEWAY CITY | Huntington, W. Va. |
| GATEWAY CITY | Jacksonville, Fla. |
| GATEWAY CITY | La Crosse, Wis. |
| GATEWAY CITY | Laredo, Tex. |
| GATEWAY CITY | Louisville, Ky. |
| GATEWAY CITY | Minneapolis, Minn. |
| GATEWAY CITY | Seward, Alaska |
| GATEWAY CITY TO THE HILLS | Rapid City, S. D. |
| GATEWAY CITY TO CANADA | Buffalo, N. Y. |
| GATEWAY CITY TO THE BREAD BASKET OF THE WORLD | Fargo, N. D. |
| GATEWAY FROM SOUTH AND WEST TO OZARK PLAYGROUNDS | Pryor, Okla. |
| GATEWAY OF AMERICA'S SCENIC WONDERLAND | Dickinson, N. D. |
| GATEWAY OF KANSAS | Shawnee, Kan. |
| GATEWAY OF LAKE SUPERIOR | Sault Ste. Marie, Mich. |
| GATEWAY OF NEW ENGLAND | Norwalk, Conn. |
| GATEWAY OF SOUTHERN INDIANA | Seymour, Ind. |
| GATEWAY OF SOUTHERN NEW ENGLAND | Providence, R. I. |
| GATEWAY OF THE ADIRONDACKS | Utica, N. Y. |
| GATEWAY OF THE AMERICAS | Miami, Fla. |

| | |
|---|---|
| GATEWAY OF THE LAKE REGION | Leesburg, Ind. |
| GATEWAY OF THE NORTH | Massena, N.Y. |
| GATEWAY OF THE SOUTH | Atlanta, Ga. |
| GATEWAY OF THE SOUTH | Nashville, Tenn. |
| GATEWAY OF THE SOUTHEAST | Augusta, Ga. |
| GATEWAY OF THE WEST | St. Louis, Mo. |
| GATEWAY OF VAST FARM AND IN- | |
| DUSTRIAL MARKETS | Gary, Ind. |
| GATEWAY OF WEST TEXAS | Fort Worth, Tex. |
| GATEWAY PORT OF ALASKA | Ketchikan, Alaska |
| GATEWAY RESORT TOWN OF YOUR | |
| SMOKIES | Gatlinburg, Tenn. |
| GATEWAY TO A FABULOUS MARKET | East Brunswick, N.J. |
| GATEWAY TO ADVENTURE | Ketchikan, Alaska |
| GATEWAY TO ADVENTURE ON NORTH | |
| AMERICA'S SPECTACULAR MARINE | |
| HIGHWAY | Ketchikan, Alaska |
| GATEWAY TO ALASKA | Seattle, Wash. |
| GATEWAY TO ALL FLORIDA | Jacksonville, Fla. |
| GATEWAY TO ALL FLORIDA | Perry, Fla. |
| GATEWAY TO ALL NEW ENGLAND | Norwalk, Conn. |
| GATEWAY TO AMERICA'S LAST | |
| WILDERNESS | Sun Valley, Idaho |
| GATEWAY TO AMERICA'S WONDER- | |
| LAND | Billings, Mont. |
| GATEWAY TO ANCIENT CITIES | Mountainair, N.M. |
| GATEWAY TO ARIZONA'S SCENIC AND | |
| RECREATIONAL AREA | Globe, Ariz. |
| GATEWAY TO BLUE SHOALS LAKE | |
| AND DAM | Flippin, Ark. |
| GATEWAY TO BROWN COUNTY | Morgantown, Ind. |
| GATEWAY TO CALIFORNIA | San Diego, Calif. |
| GATEWAY TO CAMP PENDLETON | Oceanside, Calif. |
| GATEWAY TO CANADA'S ST. LAW- | |
| RENCE SEAWAY | Fort Kent, Me. |
| GATEWAY TO CANDLEWOOD LAKE | Danbury, Conn. |
| GATEWAY TO CAPE COD | New Bedford, Mass. |
| GATEWAY TO CHIRICAHUA NATIONAL | |
| MONUMENT | Bowie, Ariz. |
| GATEWAY TO COLORADO'S SCENIC | |
| REGION | Boulder, Colo. |
| GATEWAY TO COTEAU LAKE REGION | Webster, S.D. |
| GATEWAY TO DEATH VALLEY | Beatty, Nev. |
| GATEWAY TO EAST TEXAS' ENCHANT- | |
| ING VACATIONLAND | Jasper, Tex. |
| GATEWAY TO EASTERN MICHIGAN | Royal Oak, Mich. |
| GATEWAY TO EGYPT | Centralia, Ill. |
| GATEWAY TO FLORIDA | Pensacola, Fla. |

| | |
|---|---|
| GATEWAY TO FORT HUACHUCA | Bisbee, Ariz. |
| GATEWAY TO FT. HOOD | Kileen, Tex. |
| GATEWAY TO FOUR OZARK VACA-<br>TION AREAS | Springfield, Mo. |
| GATEWAY TO GARRISON DAM | Minot, N. D. |
| GATEWAY TO GIANT GREER'S FERRY<br>LAKE | Heber Springs, Ark. |
| GATEWAY TO GLACIER BAY NA-<br>TIONAL MONUMENT | Juneau, Alaska |
| GATEWAY TO HISTORYLAND | Fredericksburg, Va. |
| GATEWAY TO HOPILAND AND NAVAJO-<br>LAND | Winslow, Ariz. |
| GATEWAY TO HOOVER DAM | Kingman, Ariz. |
| GATEWAY TO INDIANA DUNES | Gary, Ind. |
| GATEWAY TO INTERNATIONAL FUN<br>FOR THE ENTIRE FAMILY | Ogdensburg, N. Y. |
| GATEWAY TO ISLE ROYALE NATIONAL<br>PARK | Grand Portage, Minn. |
| GATEWAY TO KENAI PENINSULA | Seward, Alaska |
| GATEWAY TO LAKE ERIE | Sandusky, Ohio |
| GATEWAY TO LAKE LANIER | Cumming, Ga. |
| GATEWAY TO LAKE MEAD AND<br>HOOVER DAM | Las Vegas, Nev. |
| GATEWAY TO LAKE NORFOLK | Mountain Home, Ark. |
| GATEWAY TO LAKE OF THE OZARKS | Eldon, Mo. |
| GATEWAY TO LAKE TAHOE AND<br>YOSEMITE VALLEY | Carson City, Nev. |
| GATEWAY TO LAKE "WHITNEY" | Cleburne, Tex. |
| GATEWAY TO MACKINAC ISLAND AND<br>UPPER PENINSULA OF MICHIGAN | Mackinaw City, Mich. |
| GATEWAY TO MAINE | Biddeford, Me. |
| GATEWAY TO MAINE | Kittery, Me. |
| GATEWAY TO MAINE | Saco, Me. |
| GATEWAY TO MAINE FROM THE<br>WHITE MOUNTAINS | Bethel, Me. |
| GATEWAY TO MEXICO | El Paso, Tex. |
| GATEWAY TO MEXICO | Laredo, Tex. |
| GATEWAY TO MEXICO | San Antonio, Tex. |
| GATEWAY TO MICHIGAN | New Buffalo, Mich. |
| GATEWAY TO MONUMENT VALLEY | Kayenta, Ariz. |
| GATEWAY TO MT. MAGAZINE | Paris, Ark. |
| GATEWAY TO MOUNT RANIER | Tacoma, Wash. |
| GATEWAY TO MUIR WOODS | Mill Valley, Calif. |
| GATEWAY TO NEBRASKA'S VACA-<br>TIONLAND | Omaha, Neb. |
| GATEWAY TO NEW ENGLAND | Danbury, Conn. |
| GATEWAY TO NEW ENGLAND | Greenwich, Conn. |
| GATEWAY TO NIAGARA FALLS | Williamsville, N. Y. |

| | |
|---|---|
| GATEWAY TO NOVA | Edgewater, Fla. |
| GATEWAY TO OCALA NATIONAL FOREST | Umatilla, Fla. |
| GATEWAY TO OKEFENOKEE SWAMP | Waycross, Ga. |
| GATEWAY TO OLD MEXICO | San Antonio, Tex. |
| GATEWAY TO OUTDOOR FISHING AND HUNTING ACTIVITIES | Monett, Mo. |
| GATEWAY TO PADRE ISLAND | Corpus Christi, Tex. |
| GATEWAY TO PICTURED ROCKS | Munising, Mich. |
| GATEWAY TO PICTURESQUE CANADA | Buffalo, N. Y. |
| GATEWAY TO PICTURESQUE PRECISION VALLEY | Springfield, Vt. |
| GATEWAY TO PITTSBURGH | Monroeville, Pa. |
| GATEWAY TO PLEASURE | Las Vegas, Nev. |
| GATEWAY TO RANGELEY AND SUGARLOAF | Farmington, Me. |
| GATEWAY TO REAL VACATION PLEASURE | Jackman, Me. |
| GATEWAY TO ROOSEVELT NATIONAL FOREST AND ROCKY MOUNTAIN NATIONAL PARK | Boulder, Colo. |
| GATEWAY TO "SAILFISH ALLEY" | Boynton Beach, Fla. |
| GATEWAY TO SALT AND FRESHWATER FISHING, HUNTING, SCENIC BEAUTY AND FUN | Ketchikan, Alaska |
| GATEWAY TO SAN LUIS REY MISSION | Oceanside, Calif. |
| GATEWAY TO SCENIC ADVENTURE | Ely, Nev. |
| GATEWAY TO SCENIC BOSTON MOUNTAINS | Fayetteville, Ark. |
| GATEWAY TO SCENIC SOUTHERN INDIANA | Greater Bloomington, Ind. |
| GATEWAY TO SLEEPING BEAR DUNES | Honor, Mich. |
| GATEWAY TO SMUGGLER'S NOTCH | Stowe, Vt. |
| GATEWAY TO SONOYTA, MEXICO AND THE GULF OF LOWER CALIFORNIA | Ajo, Ariz. |
| GATEWAY TO SOUTH DAKOTA'S VACATION WONDERLAND | Yankton, S. D. |
| GATEWAY TO SOUTHEAST ARKANSAS | Pine Bluff, Ark. |
| GATEWAY TO SPACE | St. Louis, Mo. |
| GATEWAY TO TEXAS | Jefferson, Tex. |
| GATEWAY TO TEXAS AND THE ASTRODOME | Orange, Tex. |
| GATEWAY TO THE (See also under "Gateway of" and "Gateway to") | |
| GATEWAY TO THE ADIRONDACKS | Glens Falls, N. Y. |

318

| | |
|---|---|
| GATEWAY TO THE ADIRONDACKS | Lake Luzerne, N. Y. |
| GATEWAY TO THE ADIRONDACKS | Utica, N. Y. |
| GATEWAY TO THE ADIRONDACKS AND THE 1000 ISLAND REGION | Carthage, N. Y. |
| GATEWAY TO THE ALLAGASH COUNTY | Fort Kent, Me. |
| GATEWAY TO THE AMERICAN WEST | St. Louis, Mo. |
| GATEWAY TO THE APALACHICOLA SYSTEM | Apalachicola, Fla. |
| GATEWAY TO THE ARCTIC | Fairbanks, Alaska |
| GATEWAY TO THE BADLANDS | Kadoka, S. D. |
| GATEWAY TO THE BADLANDS AND THE PINE RIDGE INDIAN RESERVATION | Kadoka, S. D. |
| GATEWAY TO THE BADLANDS NATIONAL PARK | Wall, S. D. |
| GATEWAY TO THE BASS CAPITAL OF THE WORLD | Crescent City, Fla. |
| GATEWAY TO THE BAUXITE FIELDS | Benton, Ark. |
| GATEWAY TO THE BEAR RIVER MIGRATORY BIRD REFUGE | Brigham, Utah |
| GATEWAY TO THE BERKSHIRES | Winsted, Conn. |
| GATEWAY TO THE BLACK HILLS | Pierre, S. D. |
| GATEWAY TO THE BLACK HILLS | Winner, S. D. |
| GATEWAY TO THE BEAUTIFUL OZARK PLAYGROUND | Fort Smith, Ark. |
| GATEWAY TO THE BLACK HILLS | Rapid City, S. D. |
| GATEWAY TO THE BOSTON MOUNTAINS | Fayetteville, Ark. |
| GATEWAY TO THE CANYONLANDS AND HIGHLAND OF SOUTHEASTERN UTAH | Price, Utah |
| GATEWAY TO THE CARIBBEAN | Tampa, Fla. |
| GATEWAY TO THE CAROLINA SEA ISLANDS | Beaufort, S. C. |
| GATEWAY TO THE CATSKILLS | Kingston, N. Y. |
| GATEWAY TO THE CENTERS OF THE AEROSPACE INDUSTRY | St. Louis, Mo. |
| GATEWAY TO THE DAKOTAS | Sioux Falls, S. D. |
| GATEWAY TO THE DELTA | Yazoo City, Miss. |
| GATEWAY TO THE DESERT AND IDYLLWILD MOUNTAIN RESORT | Banning, Calif. |
| GATEWAY TO THE EVERGLADES | Fort Lauderdale, Fla. |
| GATEWAY TO THE FAMED NORTHWOODS | St. Paul, Minn. |
| GATEWAY TO THE FAMOUS GOLD COAST | Hobe Sound, Fla. |

| | |
|---|---|
| GATEWAY TO THE FAMOUS SAND-<br>HILLS | Sanford, N. C. |
| GATEWAY TO THE FAR EAST | San Francisco, Calif. |
| GATEWAY TO THE FISH RIVER CHAIN<br>OF LAKES | Fort Kent, Me. |
| GATEWAY TO THE FRIENDLY CITY | Concord, N. C. |
| GATEWAY TO THE FUTURE IN SPACE | Picayune, Miss. |
| GATEWAY TO THE GALAXIES | Titusville, Fla. |
| GATEWAY TO THE GILA WILDERNESS | Silver City, N. M. |
| GATEWAY TO THE GRAND STRAND | Conway, S. C. |
| GATEWAY TO THE GREAT COAL<br>FIELDS OF SOUTHERN WEST VIR-<br>GINIA | Bluefield, W. Va. |
| GATEWAY TO THE GREAT MAD RIVER<br>VALLEY | Blue Lake, Calif. |
| GATEWAY TO THE GREAT NORTH-<br>WEST MARKET | Salem, Ore. |
| GATEWAY TO THE GREAT SMOKIES | Gatlinburg, Tenn. |
| GATEWAY TO THE GREAK SMOKY<br>MOUNTAINS NATIONAL PARK | Cherokee, N. C. |
| GATEWAY TO THE GREAT SMOKY<br>MOUNTAINS NATIONAL PARK | Knoxville, Tenn. |
| GATEWAY TO THE GREAT SMOKY<br>MOUNTAINS NATIONAL PARK | Waynesville, N. C. |
| GATEWAY TO THE GREAT TAHOE<br>NATIONAL FOREST | Nevada City, Calif. |
| GATEWAY TO THE GREATEST VA-<br>CATION LAND IN MID-AMERICA | Henderson, Ky. |
| GATEWAY TO THE GULF COAST | Pensacola, Fla. |
| GATEWAY TO THE GULF OF MEXICO | Surfside, Tex. |
| GATEWAY TO THE HAMPTONS | Riverhead, N. Y. |
| GATEWAY TO THE HEARTLAND OF<br>AMERICA | Buffalo, N. Y. |
| GATEWAY TO THE HISTORIC NORTH-<br>WEST | Glendive, Mont. |
| GATEWAY TO THE HOLIDAY HIGH-<br>LANDS | Haines City, Fla. |
| GATEWAY TO THE INDIANA LAKE<br>AREA | Warsaw, Ind. |
| GATEWAY TO THE INTERIOR | Valdez, Alaska |
| GATEWAY TO THE LAKE MEAD<br>RECREATIONAL AREA | Boulder City, Nev. |
| GATEWAY TO THE LAKE OF THE<br>OZARKS | Sedalia, Mo. |
| GATEWAY TO THE LAKE REGION | Webster, S. D. |
| GATEWAY TO THE LAKES | Cleveland, Tex. |
| GATEWAY TO THE LAKES | Drumright, Okla. |
| GATEWAY TO THE LAKES AND | |

| | |
|---|---|
| STREAMS OF THE THUNDER MOUNTAIN REGION | Crivitz, Wis. |
| GATEWAY TO THE LAND O'LAKES | Sedalia, Mo. |
| GATEWAY TO THE LITCHFIELD HILLS | Waterbury, Conn. |
| GATEWAY TO THE MAMMOTH CAVE | Cave City, Ky. |
| GATEWAY TO THE MIDWEST | Canton, Ohio |
| GATEWAY TO THE MISS UNIVERSE HIGHWAY | New Castle, Pa. |
| GATEWAY TO THE MISSILE TEST CENTER | Eau Gallie, Fla. |
| GATEWAY TO THE MOUNT MANSFIELD AREA | Waterbury, Vt. |
| GATEWAY TO THE NEBRASKA PAN-HANDLE | Ogallala, Neb. |
| GATEWAY TO THE NEWTON HILLS STATE PARK | Canton, S. D. |
| GATEWAY TO THE NORTH | Clare, Mich. |
| GATEWAY TO THE NORTH | Fort Anne, N. Y. |
| GATEWAY TO THE NORTH WOODS | Bangor, Me. |
| GATEWAY TO THE NORTHERN INDIANA LAKE REGION | Fort Wayne, Ind. |
| GATEWAY TO THE NORTHWEST | Bentonville, Ark. |
| GATEWAY TO THE NORTHWEST | St. Paul, Minn. |
| GATEWAY TO THE OHIO LAKE ERIE ISLANDS | Sandusky, Ohio |
| GATEWAY TO THE OLD WESTERN RESERVE | Youngstown, Ohio |
| GATEWAY TO THE OLD WESTERN RESERVE | Zanesville, Ohio |
| GATEWAY TO THE ORANGE EMPIRE | Baldwin Park, Calif. |
| GATEWAY TO THE ORIENT | San Francisco, Calif. |
| GATEWAY TO THE ORIENT | Seattle, Wash. |
| GATEWAY TO THE OZARKS | Dover, Ark. |
| GATEWAY TO THE OZARKS | Joplin, Mo. |
| GATEWAY TO THE PALMETTO STATE | Dillon, S. C. |
| GATEWAY TO THE PALMETTO STATE | Latta, S. C. |
| GATEWAY TO THE PENNSYLVANIA DUTCH COUNTRY | Downingtown, Pa. |
| GATEWAY TO THE PINES | Mineola, Tex. |
| GATEWAY TO THE POCONOS | Stroudsburg, Pa. |
| GATEWAY TO THE POUDRE | Fort Collins, Colo. |
| GATEWAY TO THE PROPOSED SLEEP-ING BEAR NATIONAL PARK | Frankfort, Mich. |
| GATEWAY TO THE RANGELEY LAKES | Farmington, Me. |
| GATEWAY TO THE ROCKIES | Denver, Colo. |
| GATEWAY TO THE ROCKIES | Limon, Colo. |
| GATEWAY TO THE ROUTT NATIONAL FOREST | Steamboat Springs, Colo. |

| | |
|---|---|
| GATEWAY TO THE RUBY MOUNTAINS | Wells, Nev. |
| GATEWAY TO THE ST. LAWRENCE POWER AND SEAWAY | Watertown, N.Y. |
| GATEWAY TO THE SAN FERNANDO VALLEY | North Hollywood, Calif. |
| GATEWAY TO THE SAN GABRIELS | Azuza, Calif. |
| GATEWAY TO THE SAN JOAQUIN VALLEY | Stockton, Calif. |
| GATEWAY TO THE SAND DUNE MOUNTAINS | Mears, Mich. |
| GATEWAY TO THE SMOKIES | Gatlinburg, Tenn. |
| GATEWAY TO THE SMOKIES | Johnson City, Tenn. |
| GATEWAY TO THE SMOKIES | Knoxville, Tenn. |
| GATEWAY TO THE SMOKIES | Newport, Tenn. |
| GATEWAY TO THE SMOKY MOUNTAINS | Erwin, Tenn. |
| GATEWAY TO THE SOUTH | Annapolis, Md. |
| GATEWAY TO THE SOUTH | Cincinnati, Ohio |
| GATEWAY TO THE SOUTH | Columbia, S.C. |
| GATEWAY TO THE SOUTH | Henderson, N.C. |
| GATEWAY TO THE SOUTH | Louisville, Ky. |
| GATEWAY TO THE SOUTH | Memphis, Tenn. |
| GATEWAY TO THE SOUTH | Richmond, Va. |
| GATEWAY TO THE SOUTH | Willow Springs, Mo. |
| GATEWAY TO THE SOUTHERN CATSKILLS | Harriman, N.Y. |
| GATEWAY TO THE SOUTHERN OZARKS | Springfield, Mo. |
| GATEWAY TO THE SOUTHWEST | Christiansburg, Va. |
| GATEWAY TO THE SOUTHWEST | West Memphis, Ark. |
| GATEWAY TO THE SPACE PROGRAM | Eau Gallie, Fla. |
| GATEWAY TO THE SPORTSMAN'S EDEN | Ely, Minn. |
| GATEWAY TO THE SPORTSMAN'S PARADISE | Nevada City, Calif. |
| GATEWAY TO THE STIKINE | Wrangell, Alaska |
| GATEWAY TO THE TEN THOUSAND ISLANDS | Naples, Fla. |
| GATEWAY TO THE THOUSAND IS-LANDS | Cape Vincent, N.Y. |
| GATEWAY TO THE THOUSAND IS-LANDS | Watertown, N.Y. |
| GATEWAY TO THE TOLLROADS | Westchester, Ill. |
| GATEWAY TO THE TROPICS | Belleview, Fla. |
| GATEWAY TO THE UNITED STATES | Philadelphia, Pa. |
| GATEWAY TO THE VALLEY OF PER-FECT APPLES | Wenatchee, Wash. |
| GATEWAY TO THE VOLCANOES | Hilo, Hawaii |

| | |
|---|---|
| GATEWAY TO THE WATER WONDER-<br>LAND | Grand Rapids, Mich. |
| GATEWAY TO THE WATER WONDER-<br>LAND | Morley, Mich. |
| GATEWAY TO THE WEST | Billings, Mont. |
| GATEWAY TO THE WEST | Dickinson, N. D. |
| GATEWAY TO THE WEST | Fort Worth, Tex. |
| GATEWAY TO THE WEST | Independence, Mo. |
| GATEWAY TO THE WEST | Omaha, Neb. |
| GATEWAY TO THE WEST | Pittsburgh, Pa. |
| GATEWAY TO THE WEST | St. Louis, Mo. |
| GATEWAY TO THE WEST | Schenectady, N. Y. |
| GATEWAY TO THE WEST | Sioux Falls, S. D. |
| GATEWAY TO THE WEST AND<br>SOUTHWEST | Kansas City, Mo. |
| GATEWAY TO THE WEST WHERE<br>THE OHIO AND THE BEAVER<br>RIVERS MEET | Rochester, Pa. |
| GATEWAY TO WESTERN WYOMING'S<br>WONDERLAND | Kemmerer, Wyo. |
| GATEWAY TO THE WHITEMAN AIR<br>FORCE BASE | Knob Noster, Mo. |
| GATEWAY TO THE WHITE MOUN-<br>TAINS | Franklin, N. H. |
| GATEWAY TO THE WINNESHIEK | Prairie du Chien,<br>Wis. |
| GATEWAY TO THE WORLD | Duluth, Minn. |
| GATEWAY TO THE WORLD | New Orleans, La. |
| GATEWAY TO THE YUKON | Skagway, Alaska |
| GATEWAY TO THREE LOCAL SLOGAN<br>STATES, VIRGINIA, TENNESSEE,<br>NORTH CAROLINA | Damascus, Va. |
| GATEWAY TO TROPICAL FLORIDA | New Port Richey,<br>Fla. |
| GATEWAY TO TROPICAL FLORIDA | Palmetto, Fla. |
| GATEWAY TO TROPICAL FLORIDA'S<br>FIRST RESORT | Jupiter, Fla. |
| GATEWAY TO TWELVE BEAUTIFUL<br>LAKES | Theresa, N. Y. |
| GATEWAY TO UPSTATE | Middletown, N. Y. |
| GATEWAY TO VACATIONLAND | Massena, N. Y. |
| GATEWAY TO VACATIONLAND | Portland, Me. |
| GATEWAY TO VACATIONLAND | Provo, Utah |
| GATEWAY TO VACATIONLAND | Rochester, N. H. |
| GATEWAY TO VACATIONLAND | Rochester, N. Y. |
| GATEWAY TO VAST FARM AND IN-<br>DUSTRIAL MARKETS | Gary, Ind. |
| GATEWAY TO WALLOWA NATIONAL | |

| | |
|---|---|
| FOREST | Enterprise, Ore. |
| GATEWAY TO "WANDERLAND" IN MOHAVE COUNTY, ARIZONA | Kingman, Ariz. |
| GATEWAY TO WEST BEND GROTTO | Algona, Iowa |
| GATEWAY TO WEST TEXAS | Fort Worth, Tex. |
| GATEWAY TO WORLD PORTS | Tampa, Fla. |
| GATEWAY TO YELLOWSTONE AND TETON NATIONAL PARKS | Rock Springs, Wyo. |
| GATEWAY TO YOSEMITE | Merced, Calif. |
| GATEWAY TO YOSEMITE SEQUOIA AND KING CANYON PARKS | Fresno, Calif. |
| GATEWAY TO YOUR GEORGIA VACATIONLAND | Brunswick, Ga. |
| GATEWAY TO ZANE GREY'S TONTO BASIN AND NAVAJOLAND | Winslow, Ariz. |
| GEM CAPITAL OF THE WORLD | Franklin, N. C. |
| GEM CITY | Dayton, Ohio |
| GEM CITY | Laramie, Wyo. |
| GEM CITY | Palatka, Fla. |
| GEM CITY | Pulaski, Va. |
| GEM CITY | Quincy, Ill. |
| GEM CITY | Redlands, Calif. |
| GEM CITY | St. Paul, Minn. |
| GEM CITY | Salida, Colo. |
| GEM CITY IN ARIZONA'S VALLEY OF THE SUN | Mesa, Ariz. |
| GEM CITY IN THE HEART OF THE GREAT MISSISSIPPI VALLEY | Quincy, Ill. |
| GEM CITY OF CEDAR EMPIRE | Coquille, Ore. |
| GEM CITY OF OHIO | Dayton, Ohio |
| GEM CITY OF SOUTHERN ALABAMA | Andalusia, Ala. |
| GEM CITY OF THE FOOTHILLS | Los Gatos, Calif. |
| GEM CITY OF THE FOOTHILLS | Monrovia, Calif. |
| GEM CITY OF THE LAKES | Erie, Pa. |
| GEM CITY OF THE MIDDLE WEST | Quincy, Ill. |
| GEM CITY OF THE ROCKIES | Ouray, Colo. |
| GEM CITY OF THE WABASH | Attica, Ind. |
| GEM CITY OF THE WEALTHY SAN JOAQUIN VALLEY | Madera, Calif. |
| GEM CITY OF THE WEST | Quincy, Ill. |
| GEM OF BEACHES | Long Beach, Calif. |
| GEM OF FLORIDA'S KEYS | Key Colony Beach, Fla. |
| GEM OF PENOBSCOT BAY | Camden, Me. |
| GEM OF THE CASCADES | Diamond Lake, Ore. |
| GEM OF THE FLORIDA EAST COAST | Vero Beach, Fla. |
| GEM OF THE GOLD COAST | Pompano Beach, Fla. |
| GEM OF THE HILLS | Clermont, Fla. |

| | |
|---|---|
| GEM OF THE JERSEY COAST | Avalon, N. J. |
| GEM OF THE NOOKSACK VALLEY | Ferndale, Wash. |
| GEM OF THE OCEAN | Salida, Colo. |
| GEM OF THE PLAINS | Abilene, Kan. |
| GEM OF THE PRAIRIES | Chicago, Ill. |
| GEM OF THE ROCKIES | Ouray, Colo. |
| GEM OF THE VALLEY | Redlands, Calif. |
| GEM ON THE OCEAN | Lantana, Fla. |
| GENEROUS PEOPLE | Puyallup, Wash. |
| GENTILE PEOPLE | Corinne, Utah |
| GEOGRAPHIC CENTER OF INDUSTRIAL SOUTHERN ILLINOIS | West Frankfort, Ill. |
| GEOGRAPHIC CENTER OF THE OIL INDUSTRY IN THE ROCKY MOUNTAINS | Casper, Wyo. |
| GEOGRAPHIC CULTURAL AND ECONOMIC CENTER | Little Rock, Ark. |
| GEOGRAPHIC HEART OF THE STATE | Wisconsin Rapids, Wis. |
| GEOGRAPHICAL CENTER OF MAGIC VALLEY | Jerome, Idaho |
| GEOGRAPHICAL CENTER OF MICHIGAN | St. Louis, Mich. |
| GEOGRAPHICAL CENTER OF THE METROPOLITAN BOSTON AREA | Cambridge, Mass. |
| GEOGRAPHICAL CENTER OF THE SOUTH | Huntsville, Ala. |
| GEOGRAPHICAL CROSSROADS OF LOUISIANA | Alexandria, La. |
| GEORGE WASHINGTON'S BOYHOOD HOME | Fredericksburg, Va. |
| GEORGIA VACATIONLAND | Brunswick, Ga. |
| GEORGIA VACATIONLAND | Sea Island, Ga. |
| GEORGIA VACATIONLAND | St. Simons Island, Ga. |
| GEORGIA'S COLONIAL CAPITAL | Savannah, Ga. |
| GEORGIA'S COLONIAL CAPITAL CITY | Savannah, Ga. |
| GEORGIA'S CRADLE OF THE REVOLUTION | Midway, Ga. |
| GEORGIA'S FABULOUS YEAR ROUND BEACH RESORT | Jekyll Island, Ga. |
| GEORGIA'S FIRST CITY | Savannah, Ga. |
| GEORGIA'S FIRST INLAND PORT | Bainbridge, Ga. |
| GEORGIA'S GOLDEN ISLES | Brunswick, Ga. |
| GEORGIA'S ISLAND OF FRIENDLINESS AND HOSPITALITY | Jekyll Island, Ga. |
| GEORGIA'S MOBILE HOME CENTER | Americus, Ga. |
| GEORGIA'S MOUNTAIN RESORT | Clayton, Ga. |

| | |
|---|---|
| GEORGIA'S OCEAN PORT | Brunswick, Ga. |
| GEORGIA'S PLAYGROUND FOR FAMILY FUN | Jekyll Island, Ga. |
| GEORGIA'S SECOND OLDEST CITY | Augusta, Ga. |
| GEORGIA'S "WELCOME WORLD" CITY | Waycross, Ga. |
| GEORGIA'S YEAR-ROUND FAMILY BEACH RESORT | Jekyll Island, Ga. |
| GEORGIA'S YEAR ROUND FAMILY RESORT | Jekyll Island, Ga. |
| GERMAN ATHENS | Milwaukee, Wis. |
| GIBRALTAR OF AMERICA | Vicksburg, Miss. |
| GIBRALTAR OF DEMOCRACY | Hoboken, N. J. |
| GIBRALTAR OF LOUISIANA | Vicksburg, Miss. |
| GIBRALTAR OF THE CONFEDERACY | Vicksburg, Miss. |
| GIBRALTAR OF THE SOUTH | Vicksburg, Miss. |
| GLADIOLI CAPITAL OF THE WORLD | Fort Myers, Fla. |
| GLAMOUR AND ACTION CAPITAL OF THE WORLD | Las Vegas, Nev. |
| GLAMOUR CITY | Hollywood, Calif. |
| GLASS CAPITAL OF THE WORLD | Toledo, Ohio |
| GLASS CENTER | Toledo, Ohio |
| GLASS CITY | Jeannette, Pa. |
| GLEN | Singers Glen, Va. |
| GLIDER CAPITAL OF AMERICA | Elmira, N. Y. |
| GLIDER CAPITAL OF THE WORLD | Elmira, N. Y. |
| GLIDING AND SOARING CENTER OF THE UNITED STATES | Frankfort, Mich. |
| GLORIOUS PAST...A BRILLIANT PRESENT...LOOKING FORWARD TO AN EXCITING FUTURE | Philadelphia, Pa. |
| GOAT CREEK | Mazama, Wash. |
| GOLD COAST CITY | Miami Beach, Fla. |
| GOLD COAST IN FLORIDA | Lake Worth, Fla. |
| GOLD COAST OF OREGON | Baker, Ore. |
| GOLDEN AGE HAVEN | Concord, Mass. |
| GOLDEN BUCKLE ON THE COTTON BELT | Clarksdale, Miss. |
| GOLDEN BUCKLE ON THE WHEAT BELT | Colby, Kan. |
| GOLDEN CITY | Sacramento, Calif. |
| GOLDEN CITY | San Francisco, Calif. |
| GOLDEN CITY OF THE GOLD COAST | Boca Raton, Fla. |
| GOLDEN COAST OF FLORIDA | Palm Beach, Fla. |
| GOLDEN GATE CITY | San Francisco, Calif. |
| GOLDEN GATEWAY TO THE GREAT GULF SOUTHWEST | Marshall, Tex. |

326

| | |
|---|---|
| GOLDEN HEART OF ALASKA | Fairbanks, Alaska |
| GOLDEN HEART METROPOLIS OF THE INTERIOR | Fairbanks, Alaska |
| GOLDEN HEART OF THE NORTH | Fairbanks, Alaska |
| GOLDEN ISLE IN A BY-GONE GOLDEN AGE | Jekyll Island, Ga. |
| GOLDEN ISLES OF GEORGIA | St. Simons Island, Ga. |
| GOLDEN ISLES OF GEORGIA | Sea Islands, Ga. |
| GOLDEN RULE CITY | Columbia, S. C. |
| GOLF CAPITAL OF AMERICA | Augusta, Ga. |
| GOLF CAPITAL OF PENNSYLVANIA | Hershey, Pa. |
| GOLF CAPITAL OF THE MIDWEST | Chicago, Ill. |
| GOLF CAPITAL OF THE U. S. | Augusta, Ga. |
| GOLF CAPITAL OF THE WORLD | Palm Springs, Calif. |
| GOLFING CAPITAL OF FLORIDA | Sebring, Fla. |
| GOLFTOWN, U. S. A. | Pinehurst, N. C. |
| GOLIATH OF ALL NORTH-EASTERN NORTH AMERICA | Mount Washington, N. H. |
| GOOD CAMPING GROUND | Mukilteo, Wash. |
| GOOD HOME TOWN | Roby, Tex. |
| GOOD LITTLE TOWN | Willits, Calif. |
| GOOD PLACE IN WHICH TO WORK AND LIVE | Coatesville, Pa. |
| GOOD PLACE TO AIM FOR | Cleveland, Tenn. |
| GOOD PLACE TO KNOW, GO, VISIT, STAY | Willcox, Ariz. |
| GOOD PLACE TO LIVE | Aberdeen, S. D. |
| GOOD PLACE TO LIVE | Chula Vista, Calif. |
| GOOD PLACE TO LIVE AND WORK | Blacksburg, Va. |
| GOOD PLACE TO LIVE--BETTER | Brandon, Fla. |
| GOOD PLACE TO LIVE, TO WORK AND TO REAR YOUR FAMILY | East Point, Ga. |
| GOOD PLACE TO LIVE, WORK AND DO BUSINESS | Keokuk, Iowa |
| GOOD PLACE TO LIVE, WORK AND ENJOY LIFE | Sedalia, Mo. |
| GOOD PLACE TO LIVE, WORK AND PLAY | Canton, Ill. |
| GOOD PLACE TO LIVE, WORK AND PLAY | Ellwood City, Pa. |
| GOOD PLACE TO LIVE, WORK AND PLAY | Fremont, Neb. |
| GOOD PLACE TO LIVE, WORK AND PLAY | Groveland, Fla. |
| GOOD PLACE TO LIVE, WORK AND PLAY | New Albany, Ind. |

| | |
|---|---|
| GOOD PLACE TO VISIT | Sebring, Fla. |
| GOOD PLACE TO VISIT, A GOOD PLACE TO LIVE | Dickinson, N. D. |
| GOOD PLACE TO WORK AND LIVE | Grand Island, Neb. |
| GOOD PLACE TO WORK...IN AND FROM | Falls Church, Va. |
| GOOD PLACE TO WORK, LIVE AND PLAY | Williston, N. D. |
| GOOD SIZE TOWN FOR KNOWING YOUR NEIGHBOR | Abilene, Kan. |
| GOOSE CAPITAL OF THE WORLD | Cairo, Ill. |
| GOOSETOWN | Wilbur, Wash. |
| GOTHAM | New York, N. Y. |
| GOVERNMENTAL, EDUCATIONAL, RECREATIONAL CENTER | Albany, N. Y. |
| GRANARY OF THE CONFEDERACY | Edinburg, Va. |
| GRAND CANYON OF THE EAST | Ausable Chasm, N.Y. |
| GRAND CENTRAL STATION OF THE UNDERGROUND RAILROAD | Fountain City, Ind. |
| GRAND EMPORIUM OF THE WEST | Washington, D. C. |
| GRAND METROPOLIS | Washington, D. C. |
| GRANITE CENTER | Hardwick, Vt. |
| GRANITE CENTER OF THE WORLD | Barre, Vt. |
| GRANITE CENTER OF THE WORLD | Elberton, Ga. |
| GRANITE CITY | Ashland, Ore. |
| GRANITE CITY | Elberton, Ga. |
| GRANITE CITY | Milbank, S. D. |
| GRANITE CITY | Quincy, Mass. |
| GRANITE CITY | St. Cloud, Minn. |
| GRANITE CITY | Spencer, S. D. |
| GRASS LANDS | Palouse, Wash. |
| GRASS ROOTS OF AMERICA | Orfordville, Wis. |
| GRASSY PLACE | Kennewick, Wash. |
| GRAVEYARD OF THE ATLANTIC | Hatteras, N. C. |
| GREAT AMERICAN SHRINE | Springfield, Ill. |
| GREAT CONVENTION-VACATION LO-CATION | Las Vegas, Nev. |
| GREAT DISMAL | Washington, D. C. |
| GREAT FOR BUSINESS, GREAT FOR LIVING AND GROWING GREATER | Milwaukee, Wis. |
| GREAT INTERMOUNTAIN TRANSPOR-TATION CENTER | Billings, Mont. |
| GREAT PLACE TO LIVE | Gonzalez, Tex. |
| GREAT PLACE TO VACATION, A WONDERFUL PLACE TO LIVE | Sea Island, Ga. |
| GREAT PLACE TO VISIT, A WONDER-FUL PLACE TO LIVE | Carrabelle, Fla. |
| GREAT RIVER CITY | St. Louis, Mo. |

328

| | |
|---|---|
| GREAT SALT LAKE CITY | Salt Lake City, Utah |
| GREAT SERBONIAN BOG | Washington, D. C. |
| GREAT SMOKIES' MOUNTAIN LAKE NEIGHBOR | Murphy, N. C. |
| GREAT SOUTH GATE | New Orleans, La. |
| GREAT SPORTS RESORT COMMUNITY | Seattle, Wash. |
| GREAT WHITE CITY | Washington, D. C. |
| GREATER MIAMI MEANS MORE | Miami, Fla. |
| GREATEST ALL-YEAR ROUND VACATION CITY | New York, N. Y. |
| GREATEST AUTOMOBILE CAPITAL | Detroit, Mich. |
| GREATEST CITY'S GREATEST BOROUGH | Brooklyn, N. Y. |
| GREATEST INDUSTRIAL CENTER IN THE WORLD | New York, N. Y. |
| GREATEST LUMBER MARKET IN THE WORLD | Bangor, Me. |
| GREATEST PRIMARY WINTER WHEAT MARKET | Kansas City, Mo. |
| GREATEST SHOW IN TOBACCOLAND | Wilson, N. C. |
| GREATEST STEEL CITY IN THE WORLD | Pittsburgh, Pa. |
| GREATEST TOWN FOR FISHING IN NEW ENGLAND | Marblehead, Mass. |
| GREATEST VACATION SPOT OF ALL | Miami, Fla. |
| GREEN BEAN CENTER | Stayton, Ore. |
| GREEN FELT JUNGLE | Las Vegas, Nev. |
| GREEN MOUNTAIN CITY | Montpelier, Vt. |
| GREEN SPOT IN ARIZONA'S FAMOUS VALLEY OF THE SUN | Chandler, Ariz. |
| GREENEST SPOT IN THE GOLDEN SPREAD OF TEXAS | Shamrock, Tex. |
| GREENWICH VILLAGE OF THE WEST | Sausalito, Calif. |
| GRETNA GREEN | Elkton, Md. |
| GRETNA GREEN | Ripley, N. Y. |
| GRETNA GREEN OF MARYLAND | Elkton, Md. |
| GREYHOUND CITY | Abilene, Kan. |
| GROWING CENTER OF ADMINISTRATIVE OFFICES | San Mateo, Calif. |
| GROWING CITY | Casper, Wyo. |
| GROWING CITY | Sioux Falls, S. D. |
| GROWING CITY OF INDUSTRY AND RECREATION | Fort Smith, Ark. |
| GROWING CITY OF OPPORTUNITY | Abilene, Kan. |
| GROWING CITY OF THE LOWER RIO GRANDE VALLEY OF TEXAS | Harlingen, Tex. |
| GROWING COMMUNITY CENTERED IN | |

| | |
|---|---|
| A GROWING MARKET | Bellingham, Mass. |
| GROWING GRAFTON LEADS NORTH DAKOTA | Grafton, N. D. |
| GROWING INDUSTRIAL CENTER OF NORTHWESTERN PENNSYLVANIA | Bradford, Pa. |
| GROWING INDUSTRIAL, FINANCIAL AND EDUCATIONAL CENTER | Louisville, Ky. |
| GROWING PROGRESSIVE COMMUNITY | Somerset, Pa. |
| GROWINGEST CITY IN LOUISIANA | Bossier City, La. |
| GROWINGEST CITY IN THE SOUTH | Orlando, Fla. |
| GROWTH MARKET IN LORAIN COUNTY | Elyria, Ohio |
| GUIDED MISSILE RESEARCH AND SPACE FLIGHT CENTER | Huntsville, Ala. |
| GULF CITY | Mobile, Ala. |
| GULF CITY | New Orleans, La. |
| GULF COAST CITY | Pensacola, Fla. |
| GUNSTOCK CAPITOL OF THE WORLD | Warsaw, Mo. |
| GYPSUM CITY | Fort Dodge, Iowa |

## H

| | |
|---|---|
| H-BOMB'S HOME TOWN | Ellenton, S. C. |
| HALF WAY AND A PLACE TO STAY | Kinsley, Kan. |
| HANDICRAFT CAPITAL OF THE UNITED STATES | Gatlinburg, Tenn. |
| HANGMAN CREEK | Latah, Wash. |
| HANGTOWN | Placerville, Calif. |
| HAPPY HOLLOW | Roda, Va. |
| HAPPY LIFE CITY | Salem, Ore. |
| HAPPY PEOPLE PLACE | St. Petersburg, Fla. |
| HARBOR CITY | Eau Gallie, Fla. |
| HARBOR CITY | Erie, Pa. |
| HARBOR OF THE AIR | Inglewood, Calif. |
| HARDWARE CITY | New Britain, Conn. |
| HARDWARE CITY OF THE WORLD | New Britain, Conn. |
| HARMONY | Hamilton, Va. |
| HARTFORD OF THE SOUTH | Jacksonville, Fla. |
| HARTFORD OF THE WEST | Lincoln, Neb. |
| HAT CITY | Danbury, Conn. |
| HAT CITY OF THE WORLD | Danbury, Conn. |
| HAT TOWN | Norwalk, Conn. |
| HAVEN FOR INDUSTRY, COMMERCE AND GOOD LIVING | Niles, Ohio |
| HAVEN TO RETIRE IN, AWAY FROM THE RUSH | Stockton, Mo. |
| HAY FEVER RELIEF HAVEN OF AMERICA | Duluth, Minn. |
| HEAD OF ELK | Elkton, Md. |

330

| | |
|---|---|
| HEADQUARTERS CITY | Grand Junction, Colo. |
| HEADQUARTERS CITY OF EAST SAN GABRIEL VALLEY | West Covina, Calif. |
| HEADQUARTERS CITY OF THE PERMIAN BASIN | Midland, Tex. |
| HEADQUARTERS OF LAKE LIVINGSTON | Trinity, Tex. |
| HEADQUARTERS OF THE BIG HORN NATIONAL FOREST | Sheridan, Wyo. |
| HEADQUARTERS OF THE INTERNATIONAL OIL TOOL TRADE | Houston, Tex. |
| HEADQUARTERS OF WORLD BANKING | New York, N. Y. |
| HEADWATERS OF STOCKTON LAKE | Greenfield, Mo. |
| HEADWATERS OF THE MISSISSIPPI | Bemidji, Minn. |
| HEALTH CENTER AND PRINCIPAL TRADE CENTER OF NORTH CENTRAL KANSAS | Abilene, Kan. |
| HEALTH CENTER OF THE WEST | Thermopolis, Wyo. |
| HEALTH CITY | Battle Creek, Mich. |
| HEALTH CITY | Mount Clemens, Mich. |
| HEALTH CITY, U. S. A. | Asbury Park, N. J. |
| HEALTH FOOD CITY | Battle Creek, Mich. |
| HEART AND HUB OF DELAWARE COUNTY | Walton, N. Y. |
| HEART CITY OF THE SANDHILLS | Valentine, Neb. |
| HEART OF A DISPERSED CITY OF TOWNS | West Frankfort, Ill. |
| HEART OF ALABAMA | Montevallo, Ala. |
| HEART OF A GREAT STATE | Columbus, Ohio |
| HEART OF A HUNTER'S PARADISE | Price, Utah |
| HEART OF AMERICA | Frankfort, Ky. |
| HEART OF AMERICA | Kansas City, Mo. |
| HEART OF AMERICA | Washington, D. C. |
| HEART OF AMERICA'S INDUSTRIAL WAR FRONT | Kearny, N. J. |
| HEART OF AMERICA'S NEW COMMERCIAL FRONTIER | New Orleans, La. |
| HEART OF AMERICA'S NUMBER ONE AGRICULTURAL AREA | Stockton, Calif. |
| HEART OF AMERICA'S WORKSHOP | Akron, Ohio |
| HEART OF AMISH TERRITORY SWISS CHEESE | Berlin, Ohio |
| HEART OF CALIFORNIA | Sacramento, Calif. |
| HEART OF CAPE COD | Dennis, Mass. |
| HEART OF CONNECTICUT | Meriden, Conn. |
| HEART OF DELAWARE | Milford, Del. |
| HEART OF DISTRIBUTION | Harrisburg, Pa. |

331

| | |
|---|---|
| HEART OF DIXIE | New Orleans, La. |
| HEART OF DOWN RIVER'S CHEM-ICAL EMPIRE | Wyandotte, Mich. |
| HEART OF EASTERN GEORGIA AND WESTERN SOUTH CAROLINA | Augusta, Ga. |
| HEART OF EASTERN NORTH CARO-LINA | Goldsboro, N.C. |
| HEART OF FLORIDA | Haines City, Fla. |
| HEART OF FLORIDA'S CITRUS IN-DUSTRY | Winter Haven, Fla. |
| HEART OF FLORIDA'S CROWN | Starke, Fla. |
| HEART OF FLORIDA'S FUN-LAND | Ocala, Fla. |
| HEART OF FLORIDA'S MIRACLE STRIP | Fort Walton, Fla. |
| HEART OF FLORIDA'S STRAWBERRY MARKET | Starke, Fla. |
| HEART OF FLORIDA'S THOROUGHBRED COUNTRY | Ocala, Fla. |
| HEART OF GEORGIA | Macon, Ga. |
| HEART OF GOOD LIVING | Castro Valley, Calif. |
| HEART OF HISTORIC AMERICA | West Chester, Pa. |
| HEART OF HISTORIC VIRGINIA | Charlottesville, Va. |
| HEART OF HISTORY AND ROMANCE IN KANSAS | Abilene, Kan. |
| HEART OF HUNTING LAND | Sylvester, Ga. |
| HEART OF INDUSTRIAL AMERICA | Delphos, Ohio |
| HEART OF INDUSTRY | Frederick, Md. |
| HEART OF KENTUCKY | Frankfort, Ky. |
| HEART OF KENTUCKY'S BLUE GRASS REGION | Lexington, Ky. |
| HEART OF MARVELOUS MARIN COUNTY | San Rafael, Calif. |
| HEART OF MARYLAND | Annapolis, Md. |
| HEART OF MONTANA'S MAGICLAND | Butte, Mont. |
| HEART OF NEW ENGLAND | Somerville, Mass. |
| HEART OF NEW ENGLAND | Southbridge, Mass. |
| HEART OF NEW YORK STATE | Syracuse, N.Y. |
| HEART OF NORTH CAROLINA | Sanford, N.C. |
| HEART OF NORTH CAROLINA'S HOLI-DAY HIGHLAND | Blowing Rock, N.C. |
| HEART OF NORTH DAKOTA | Grand Forks, N.D. |
| HEART OF NORTH MISSISSIPPI AND BEAUTIFUL GRENADA LAKE | Grenada, Miss. |
| HEART OF ORANGE COUNTY | Westminster, Calif. |
| HEART OF RHODE ISLAND | East Greenwich, R.I. |
| HEART OF TEXAS | Brady, Tex. |
| HEART OF THE ADIRONDACK VACA-TIONLAND | Schroon Lake, N.Y. |
| HEART OF THE ADIRONDACKS | Indian Lake, N.Y. |

| | |
|---|---|
| HEART OF THE AMERICAN RIVIERA | Foley, Ala. |
| HEART OF THE ANTELOPE VALLEY | Lancaster, Calif. |
| HEART OF THE BAY STATE | Worcester, Mass. |
| HEART OF THE BERKSHIRES | Pittsfield, Mass. |
| HEART OF THE BLACKSTONE VALLEY | Pawtucket, R. I. |
| HEART OF THE CITRUS INDUSTRY | Lakeland, Fla. |
| HEART OF THE COMMONWEALTH | Harrisburg, Pa. |
| HEART OF THE COMMONWEALTH | Worcester, Mass. |
| HEART OF THE CORN COUNTRY | Monona, Iowa |
| HEART OF THE EMERALD EMPIRE IN THE NORTH IDAHO SCENIC LAND | Coeur d'Alene, Idaho |
| HEART OF THE FABULOUS GULF COAST COUNTRY | Biloxi, Miss. |
| HEART OF THE FAMOUS BERKSHIRE HILLS | Pittsfield, Mass. |
| HEART OF THE FAMOUS NORTH SHORE | Beverly, Mass. |
| HEART OF THE FAMOUS ST. LAW-RENCE SEAWAY | Massena, N. Y. |
| HEART OF THE FINGER LAKES VA-CATIONLAND | Geneva, N. Y. |
| HEART OF THE FLORIDA KEYS | Marathon, Fla. |
| HEART OF THE FOX VALLEY AREA | Oshkosh, Wis. |
| HEART OF THE FRUIT BELT | Benton Harbor, Mich. |
| HEART OF THE GOLD COAST | Deerfield Beach, Fla. |
| HEART OF THE GOLD COAST | Hollywood, Fla. |
| HEART OF THE GOLD COAST | Pompano Beach, Fla. |
| HEART OF THE GREEN MOUNTAINS | Rutland, Vt. |
| HEART OF THE HARBOR | Wilmington, Del. |
| HEART OF THE INDIANA LAKE COUN-TRY | Albion, Ind. |
| HEART OF THE INLAND EMPIRE | Spokane, Wash. |
| HEART OF THE LAKE COUNTRY | Watkins Glen, N. Y. |
| HEART OF THE LEATHERSTOCKING LAND | Cooperstown, N. Y. |
| HEART OF THE MASSACHUSETTS VACATIONLAND | Worcester, Mass. |
| HEART OF THE MIDWEST | St. Louis, Mo. |
| HEART OF THE NATION | Wahoo, Neb. |
| HEART OF THE NATION'S HERITAGE | Alexandria, Va. |
| HEART OF THE NEW ENGLAND TOBACCO FARMLAND | Windsor, Conn. |
| HEART OF THE NEW SOUTH | Meridian, Miss. |

| | |
|---|---|
| HEART OF THE OLD DOMINION | Blackstone, Va. |
| HEART OF THE OLD SOUTHWEST | Tucson, Ariz. |
| HEART OF THE PACIFIC WONDER-LAND | Salem, Ore. |
| HEART OF THE PALM BEACHES | Lake Worth, Fla. |
| HEART OF THE PENNSYLVANIA DUTCH COUNTRY | Lancaster, Pa. |
| HEART OF THE PIEDMONT | Charlotte, N.C. |
| HEART OF THE PIONEER VALLEY | Northampton, Mass. |
| HEART OF THE POTOMAC HIGH-LANDS | Cumberland, Md. |
| HEART OF THE REGION | Naples, Me. |
| HEART OF THE ROCKIES | Salida, Colo. |
| HEART OF THE ROMANTIC SOUTH-WEST IN THE VALLEY OF THE SUN | Mesa, Ariz. |
| HEART OF THE SCENIC SOUTHWEST | Tucson, Ariz. |
| HEART OF THE SOUTH GEORGIA EM-PIRE | Fitzgerald, Ga. |
| HEART OF THE SOUTHEAST | Macon, Ga. |
| HEART OF THE SUN COUNTRY | Phoenix, Ariz. |
| HEART OF THE TEXAS FUNTIER | Waco, Tex. |
| HEART OF THE TURPENTINE IN-DUSTRY | Pearson, Ga. |
| HEART OF THE U.S.A. | Effingham, Ill. |
| HEART OF THE UNITED STATES OF AMERICA | Kansas City, Mo. |
| HEART OF THE VALLEY | Corvallis, Ore. |
| HEART OF THE VALLEY THAT WARMS A NATION | Wilkes-Barre, Pa. |
| HEART OF THE WESTSIDE OF FRESNO COUNTY | Coalinga, Calif. |
| HEART OF THE WHEAT LAND | Goodland, Kan. |
| HEART OF THE WHITE MOUNTAINS | Bethlehem, N.H. |
| HEART OF THE YELLOWSTONE VAL-LEY | Sidney, Mont. |
| HEART OF TOBACCO LAND | Blackshear, Ga. |
| HEART OF WESTCHESTER | White Plains, N.Y. |
| HEART OF WESTERN NEVADA'S AGRICULTURAL REGION | Fallon, Nev. |
| HEART OF YOUR TEXAS MARKET | Brenham, Tex. |
| HEARTLAND OF INDUSTRY AND ELEC-TRONICS | Waltham, Mass. |
| HEARTLAND OF THE BEAVER LAKE AREA | Rogers, Ark. |
| HEIDELBERG OF AMERICA | Dubuque, Iowa |
| HELICOPTER CAPITAL OF THE WORLD | Ozark, Ala. |

| | |
|---|---|
| HELL ON WHEELS | Cheyenne, Wyo. |
| HELLS FORTY ACRES | San Carlos, Ariz. |
| HEMISFAIR CITY | San Antonio, Tex. |
| HIDDEN JEWEL OF CENTRAL FLOR-IDA | Lake Mary, Fla. |
| HIGH AND PLEASANT SITUATION | Culpeper, Va. |
| HIGH GRADE OIL METROPOLIS OF THE WORLD | Bradford, Pa. |
| HIGH POINT FOR TRAVEL FUN | Dallas, Tex. |
| HIGH POINT OF LONG BEACH ISLAND | Harvey Cedars, N.J. |
| HIGHEST CITY IN FLORIDA | Quincy, Fla. |
| HIGHEST INCORPORATED TOWN IN EASTERN AMERICA | Highlands, N.C. |
| HIGHWAY HUB | Lake City, Fla. |
| HILL CITY | Lynchburg, Va. |
| HILL CITY | Portland, Me. |
| HILL CITY | Vicksburg, Miss. |
| HILL TOP CITY | Eveleth, Minn. |
| HILL TOWN | Hillsville, Va. |
| HILLS AGAINST THE SKY TOWN | New London, Conn. |
| HISTORIC AND COLORFUL CAPITAL OF THE EMPIRE STATE | Albany, N.Y. |
| HISTORIC AND SCENIC LINCOLN | Lincoln, R.I. |
| HISTORIC BETHLEHEM | Bethlehem, Pa. |
| HISTORIC BROWNVILLE, WHERE NEBRASKA BEGINS | Brownville, Neb. |
| HISTORIC CENTER OF EAST TEXAS | Nacogdoches, Tex. |
| HISTORIC CENTER OF NORTH CARO-LINA | New Bern, N.C. |
| HISTORIC CITY | Williamsburg, Va. |
| HISTORIC CITY OF AMERICA | Natchez, Miss. |
| HISTORIC CITY OF THE BLACK HILLS | Deadwood, S.D. |
| HISTORIC DOORWAY TO COLORADO'S FINEST SEE AND SKI COUNTRY | Georgetown, Colo. |
| HISTORIC FRANKFORT | Frankfort, Ky. |
| HISTORIC SEAPORT CITY | Charleston, S.C. |
| HISTORIC SHOWPLACE OF AMERICA | Newport, R.I. |
| HISTORIC HOME TOWN OF GENERAL GEORGE WASHINGTON | Alexandria, Va. |
| HISTORIC TOWN OF THE OLD SOUTH... NOW A PROGRESSIVE CITY | Canton, Miss. |
| HISTORICAL AND CULTURAL CENTER | St. Louis, Mo. |
| HISTORICAL CITY | Prairie du Chien, Wis. |
| HISTORICAL CITY OF HOMES | Evanston, Ill. |
| HOCKEY CAPITAL OF THE NATION | Eveleth, Minn. |
| HOG CAPITAL OF THE WORLD | Kewanee, Ill. |
| HOGOPOLIS | Chicago, Ill. |

335

| | |
|---|---|
| HOIST CAPITAL OF AMERICA | Forrest City, Ark. |
| HOLE IN THE GROUND | Albany, Ore. |
| HOLE IN THE GROUND | Kahlotus, Wash. |
| HOLIDAY CITY | St. Louis, Mo. |
| HOLIDAY HARBOR OF VERMONT | Newport, Vt. |
| HOLIDAY HIGHLANDS | Winter Haven, Fla. |
| HOLLAND'S CORNER | Holland, Va. |
| HOLLY CITY OF AMERICA | Millville, N. J. |
| HOLSTEIN CAPITAL OF AMERICA | Northfield, Minn. |
| HOLY CITY | Charleston, S. C. |
| HOLY CITY | Lincoln, Neb. |
| HOLY CITY | Sunnyside, Wash. |
| HOME CITY | Brookings, S. D. |
| HOME CITY | Charlotte, N. C. |
| HOME CITY | Lewiston, Me. |
| HOME FOR YOUR BUSINESS | Portsmouth, R. I. |
| HOME FOR YOUR FAMILY | Portsmouth, R. I. |
| HOME MARKET FOR THE GREAT NORTHWEST | Sioux City, Iowa |
| HOME OF A YANKEE COUNT | Woburn, Mass. |
| HOME OF ABRAHAM LINCOLN | Springfield, Ill. |
| HOME OF AIR MATERIEL COMMAND | Warner Robins, Ga. |
| HOME OF AMERICA'S GREATEST PETROCHEMICAL INDUSTRY COMPLEX | Houston, Tex. |
| HOME OF AMERICA'S GREATEST SPA | Saratoga Springs, N. Y. |
| HOME OF ANDERSONVILLE | Americus, Ga. |
| HOME OF APLETS, THE CONFECTION OF THE FAIRIES | Cashmere, Wash. |
| HOME OF APPLE BLOSSOM FESTIVAL | Wenatchee, Wash. |
| HOME OF ARKANSAS POLYTECHNIC COLLEGE | Russellville, Ark. |
| HOME OF ASTRONAUT VIRGIL (GUS) GRISSOM | Mitchell, Ind. |
| HOME OF ASTRONAUTS | Houston, Tex. |
| HOME OF BAKED BEANS | Boston, Mass. |
| HOME OF BARTLETT PEARS | Ukiah, Calif. |
| HOME OF BASEBALL | Cooperstown, N. Y. |
| HOME OF BEAUTIFUL CYPRESS GARDENS | Winter Haven, Fla. |
| HOME OF BEN HUR | Crawfordsville, Ind. |
| HOME OF BETTER LIVING | Metter, Ga. |
| HOME OF BUFFALO BILL | North Platte, Neb. |
| HOME OF BUICK | Flint, Mich. |
| HOME OF CASEY JONES | Jackson, Tenn. |
| HOME OF CHAMPIONS | Minden, La. |

336

| | |
|---|---|
| HOME OF CHAMPIONSHIP COWBOYS | Nowata, Okla. |
| HOME OF DELTA STATE COLLEGE | Cleveland, Miss. |
| HOME OF DENISON DAM | Denison, Tex. |
| HOME OF DIAMOND PRODUCTS | Tulsa, Okla. |
| HOME OF DIAMOND WALNUTS | Stockton, Calif. |
| HOME OF DISNEYLAND | Anaheim, Calif. |
| HOME OF EAST TEXAS' PEACH FESTIVAL | Pittsburg, Tex. |
| HOME OF EGLIN AIR FORCE BASE | Niceville, Fla. |
| HOME OF EISENHOWER'S BIRTHPLACE | Denison, Tex. |
| HOME OF EISENHOWER'S BIRTHPLACE AND DENISON DAM-LAKE TEXOMA | Denison, Tex. |
| HOME OF FAMOUS SAND HILL BEEF | Bassett, Neb. |
| HOME OF FISHINGEST BRIDGE | Pine Island, Fla. |
| HOME OF FLORENCE STATE COLLEGE | Florence, Ala. |
| HOME OF FORT RUCKER, THE ARMY AVIATION CENTER | Ozark, Ala. |
| HOME OF FORT STEWART | Hinesville, Ga. |
| HOME OF FOUR WHEEL DRIVE TRUCKS | Clintonville, Wis. |
| HOME OF FRANKLIN DELANO ROOSEVELT | Hyde Park, N. Y. |
| HOME OF FRIENDLY PEOPLE | Pierre, S. D. |
| HOME OF FRONTIER DAYS | Cheyenne, Wyo. |
| HOME OF GEORGE M. VERITY | Keokuk, Iowa |
| HOME OF GEORGIA BELLE PEACH | Commerce, Ga. |
| HOME OF GORDON COLLEGE | Barnesville, Ga. |
| HOME OF HAROLD WARP'S PIONEER VILLAGE | Minden, Neb. |
| HOME OF HEALTH, HISTORY AND HORSES | Saratoga Springs, N. Y. |
| HOME OF HELEN KELLER | Tuscumbia, Ala. |
| HOME OF HISTORICAL FORT SIDNEY | Sidney, Neb. |
| HOME OF HOSPITALITY | Jasper, Ala. |
| HOME OF IDAHO'S GREATEST MINES | Kellogg, Idaho |
| HOME OF ILLUMINATED CASCADES | Jackson, Mich. |
| HOME OF JAMES FENIMORE COOPER | Cooperstown, N. Y. |
| HOME OF JESSE JAMES | Saint Joseph, Mo. |
| HOME OF LADY BIRD JOHNSON | Marshall, Tex. |
| HOME OF LAKE McCONAUGY AND KINGSLEY DAM | Ogallala, Neb. |
| HOME OF LATEX RUBBER | Dover, Del. |
| HOME OF LITTLE STEEL | Warren, Ohio |
| HOME OF LOUISIANA STATE UNIVERSITY | Baton Rouge, La. |
| HOME OF L. B. J. | Stonewall, Tex. |

337

| | |
|---|---|
| HOME OF MINUTE TAPIOCA | Orange, Mass. |
| HOME OF MISS AMERICA 1954 | Ephrata, Pa. |
| HOME OF MISSISSIPPI'S ANNUAL DEEP SEA FISHING RODEO | Gulfport, Miss. |
| HOME OF MORE THAN 4,000 COMMERICAL TRAVELERS | Springfield, Mass. |
| HOME OF NATIONAL INDUSTRIES | Camden, N. J. |
| HOME OF NORTHWEST COMMUNITY COLLEGE | Powell, Wyo. |
| HOME OF 'OLD HICKORY' HAM AND BACON | Crane, Mo. |
| HOME OF OLD SEA CAPTAINS | Searsport, Me. |
| HOME OF 'OLE MISS' | Oxford, Miss. |
| HOME OF ONE OF THE NATION'S LARGEST SKILLED TECHNICAL WORK FORCES | Rochester, N. Y. |
| HOME OF OUR FIRST PRESIDENT | Mount Vernon, Va. |
| HOME OF PARRIS ISLAND | Beaufort, S. C. |
| HOME OF PAUL BUNYAN | Bemidji, Minn. |
| HOME OF PLANTERS PEANUTS | Suffolk, Va. |
| HOME OF PROSPEROUS AGRICULTURE BUSINESS AND INDUSTRY | McKinney, Tex. |
| HOME OF PURE WATER | Ocean City, Fla. |
| HOME OF QUAKER OATS | Cedar Rapids, Iowa |
| HOME OF RAINBOW SPRINGS | Dunnellon, Fla. |
| HOME OF SAKAKAWEA | Stanton, N. D. |
| HOME OF SANDWICH GLASS | Sandwich, Mass. |
| HOME OF SANTA CLAUS | North Pole, Alaska |
| HOME OF SOUTH CAROLINA'S LITTLE ARLINGTON | Florence, S. C. |
| HOME OF SOUTH DAKOTA STATE COLLEGE | Brookings, S. D. |
| HOME OF STANFORD UNIVERSITY | Palo Alto, Calif. |
| HOME OF STATE COLLEGE OF WASHINGTON | Pullman, Wash. |
| HOME OF STATE'S FIRST INDUSTRIAL TRAINING CENTER | Burlington, N. C. |
| HOME OF STETSON UNIVERSITY | De Land, Fla. |
| HOME OF STETSON UNIVERSITY AND FLORIDA MILITARY SCHOOL | De Land, Fla. |
| HOME OF TEN THOUSAND FRIENDLY PEOPLE | Flagstaff, Ariz. |
| HOME OF SUNSHINE AND FLOWERS | San Leandro, Calif. |
| HOME OF TEXAS DOGWOOD TRAILS | Palestine, Tex. |
| HOME OF TEXAS TECH | Lubbock, Tex. |
| HOME OF TEXTILES | West Point, Ga. |
| HOME OF THE ALBEMARLE PIPPIN | Charlottesville, Va. |
| HOME OF THE APPLE BLOSSOM | |

338

| | |
|---|---|
| FESTIVAL | Winchester, Va. |
| HOME OF THE ATLANTIC SEA BEES | North Kingstown, R. I. |
| HOME OF THE ATHLETICS | Kansas City, Mo. |
| HOME OF THE BIG BLACK BASS | Lake Village, Ark. |
| HOME OF THE BIG RED APPLE | Cornelia, Ga. |
| HOME OF THE BOLL WEEVIL MONU-MENT | Enterprise, Ala. |
| HOME OF THE BRAVES | Milwaukee, Wis. |
| HOME OF THE BREVARD MUSIC CEN-TER | Brevard, N. C. |
| HOME OF THE CHRISTMAS TREE INDUSTRY | Cook, Minn. |
| HOME OF THE COLORADO AGGIES | Fort Collins, Colo. |
| HOME OF THE COMSTOCK LODE | Virginia City, Nev. |
| HOME OF CONTENTED COWS | Carnation, Wash. |
| HOME OF THE DAN RIVER MILLS | Danville, Va. |
| HOME OF THE EAST TEXAS PEACH FESTIVAL | Hughes Springs, Tex. |
| HOME OF THE EVIL SPIRITS | Enumclaw, Wash. |
| HOME OF THE FABULOUS SUN DEVIL ATHLETIC TEAM AND ARIZONA STATE UNIVERSITY | Tempe, Ariz. |
| HOME OF THE FAMED BLACK HILLS ROUND-UP | Belle Fourche, S. D. |
| HOME OF THE FAMOUS "FIRST MON-DAY" TRADES DAY | Canton, Tex. |
| HOME OF THE FAMOUS "JACKSON-BORO LEGEND" | Sylvania, Ga. |
| HOME OF THE FAMOUS PLUTO MIN-ERAL SPRINGS | French Lick, Ind. |
| HOME OF THE FAMOUS SILVER KING TARPON | Punta Gorda, Fla. |
| HOME OF THE FIRST FULLY AUTO-MATIC NON-ATTENDED DIAL TELE-PHONE SWITCHBOARD IN THE UNITED STATES | Ketchum, Okla. |
| HOME OF THE FLAME TOKAY GRAPE | Lodi, Calif. |
| HOME OF THE FLORIDA DERBY | Hallandale, Fla. |
| HOME OF THE GAMEY BLACK BASS | Cape Vincent, N. Y. |
| HOME OF THE GIANT OAHE DAM | Pierre, S. D. |
| HOME OF THE GREEN SEA HORSE | Sealevel, N. C. |
| HOME OF THE HODAG | Rhinelander, Wis. |
| HOME OF THE HOMELESS BALLET | Boston, Mass. |
| HOME OF THE "HORN OF THE WEST" | Boone, N. C. |
| HOME OF THE INTERNATIONAL PETROLEUM EXPOSITION | Tulsa, Okla. |

339

| | |
|---|---|
| HOME OF THE JICARILLA APACHE TRIBE | Dulce, N. M. |
| HOME OF THE JUBILEE | Fairhope, Ala. |
| HOME OF THE KENTUCKY DERBY | Louisville, Ky. |
| HOME OF THE LARGEST COPPER PRODUCING SMELTER AND SMOKE-STACK IN THE WORLD | Anaconda, Mont. |
| HOME OF THE LOOP | Chicago, Ill. |
| HOME OF THE MAHANAY MEMORIAL CARILLON TOWER | Jefferson, Iowa |
| HOME OF THE MERCER MUSEUM | Doylestown, Pa. |
| HOME OF THE METERED MAID SYS-TEM | Stamford, Conn. |
| HOME OF THE MIGHTY M | Monticello, N. Y. |
| HOME OF THE MINING BARONS | Spokane, Wash. |
| HOME OF THE MISS UNIVERSE PAGEANT | Long Beach, Calif. |
| HOME OF THE MULE-TAIL DEER | Alturas, Calif. |
| HOME OF THE "MUSIC MAN" | Mason City, Iowa |
| HOME OF THE NATIONAL BASS ROUND-UP | Pocomoke City, Md. |
| HOME OF THE NATIONAL COTTON PICKING CONTEST | Blytheville, Ark. |
| HOME OF THE NATIONAL PEANUT FESTIVAL | Dothan, Ala. |
| HOME OF THE NATION'S BUILDING STONE | Bedford, Ind. |
| HOME OF THE NORBERTINES | De Pere, Wis. |
| HOME OF THE ORANGE | Riverside, Calif. |
| HOME OF THE ORIGINAL LONG HORNS | Valentine, Neb. |
| HOME OF THE ORIGINAL TROUT DER-BY | Livingston, Mont. |
| HOME OF THE PACIFIC FLEET | Bremerton, Wash. |
| HOME OF THE PACKERS | Green Bay, Wis. |
| HOME OF THE PIONEER FLORIDA MUSEUM | Dade City, Fla. |
| HOME OF THE PORTSMOUTH COM-PACT | Portsmouth, R. I. |
| HOME OF THE RAINBOW TROUT | Diamond Lake, Ore. |
| HOME OF THE RIPON ALMOND BLOS-SOM FESTIVAL | Ripon, Calif. |
| HOME OF THE ROBERT E. LEE | New Albany, Ind. |
| HOME OF THE SMITHFIELD HAM | Smithfield, Va. |
| HOME OF THE SNAKE RIVER STAMPEDE | Nampa, Idaho |
| HOME OF THE STATE FAIR | Sedalia, Mo. |
| HOME OF THE STRAWBERRY FES- | |

340

| | |
|---|---|
| TIVAL | Marysville, Wash. |
| HOME OF THE TANGERINE | Brooksville, Fla. |
| HOME OF THE TENNESSEE VALLEY INDUSTRIAL DISTRICT | Morristown, Tenn. |
| HOME OF THE TEXAS GRAPEFRUIT | Mission, Tex. |
| HOME OF THE UNIVERSITY OF ARIZONA | Tucson, Ariz. |
| HOME OF THE UNIVERSITY OF COLORADO | Boulder, Colo. |
| HOME OF THE UNIVERSITY OF FLORIDA | Gainesville, Fla. |
| HOME OF THE UNIVERSITY OF GEORGIA | Athens, Ga. |
| HOME OF THE UNIVERSITY OF NORTH DAKOTA | Grand Forks, N. D. |
| HOME OF THE UNIVERSITY OF SOUTH DAKOTA | Vermillion, S. D. |
| HOME OF THE UNIVERSITY OF WISCONSIN | Madison, Wis. |
| HOME OF THE WINTER WHITE HOUSE | Palm Beach, Fla. |
| HOME OF THE WORLD CHAMPION CLEARWATER BOMBERS | Clearwater, Fla. |
| HOME OF THE WORLD FAMOUS ANNUAL SHENANDOAH APPLE BLOSSOM FESTIVAL | Winchester, Va. |
| HOME OF THE WORLD-FAMOUS BLACK HILLS PASSION PLAY | Spearfish, S. D. |
| HOME OF THE WORLD FAMOUS GLASS BOTTOM BOATS | Silver Springs, Fla. |
| HOME OF THE WORLD FAMOUS CLAXTON FRUIT CAKE | Claxton, Ga. |
| HOME OF THE WORLD-FAMOUS MOUNT RUSHMORE NATIONAL MEMORIAL | Keystone, S. D. |
| HOME OF THE WORLD FAMOUS STOCKTON CHEESE | Stockton Springs, Me. |
| HOME OF THE WORLD'S FINEST CATFISH | Osceola, Mo. |
| HOME OF THE WORLD'S FINEST GRANITE | Snyder, Okla. |
| HOME OF THE WORLD'S LARGEST BASS | Dunnellon, Fla. |
| HOME OF THE WORLD'S LARGEST BEAR | Kodiak, Alaska |
| HOME OF THE WORLD'S LARGEST BLACK WALNUT PROCESSING PLANT | Stockton Springs, Me. |
| HOME OF THE WORLD'S LARGEST | |

341

| | |
|---|---|
| BREWERY | St. Louis, Mo. |
| HOME OF THE WORLD'S LARGEST BUFFALO | Jamestown, N. D. |
| HOME OF THE WORLD'S LARGEST MINERAL HOT SPRINGS | Thermopolis, Wyo. |
| HOME OF THE WORLD'S LARGEST SINGLE-UNIT TEXTILE MILL | Danville, Va. |
| HOME OF THE WORLD'S LARGEST WALNUT TREE | Gustine, Calif. |
| HOME OF THE WORLD'S ONLY CORN PALACE | Mitchell, S. D. |
| HOME OF THE WORLD'S ONLY LAND-LOCKED STRIPED ROCK BASS | Summerton, S. C. |
| HOME OF THE WRIGHT BROTHERS | Dayton, Ohio |
| HOME OF THE WYANDOT INDIANS | Upper Sandusky, Ohio |
| HOME OF THEODORE ROOSEVELT | Oyster Bay, N. Y. |
| HOME OF VULCAN | Birmingham, Ala. |
| HOME OF WARTHER MUSEUM | Dover, Ohio |
| HOME OF WEST VIRGINIA UNIVER-SITY | Morgantown, W. Va. |
| HOME OF WORLD FAMOUS CARTH-AGE MARBLE | Carthage, Mo. |
| HOME OF WORLD FAMOUS FRONT STREET AND BOOT HILL | Dodge City, Kan. |
| HOME OF WORLD FAMOUS SEA CAPTAINS | Searsport, Me. |
| HOME OF YACHTSMEN | Mystic, Conn. |
| "HOME ON THE RANGE" BIRTHPLACE | Smith Center, Kan. |
| HOME TOWN IN THE AMERICAN TROPICS | Fort Lauderdale, Fla. |
| HOME TOWN OF GEORGE WASHING-TON | Alexandria, Va. |
| HOME TOWN OF LYNDON B. JOHNSON | Johnson City, Tex. |
| HOME TOWN OF RICHARD NIXON | Whittier, Calif. |
| HOME TOWN OF SOUTHERN OREGON | Ashland, Ore. |
| HOMESEEKER'S PARADISE | Brookhaven, Miss. |
| HOMETOWN, U. S. A. | Glens Falls, N. Y. |
| HOMOCIDE HEADQUARTERS | Memphis, Tenn. |
| HOMESTEADER'S PARADISE | Palestine, Tex. |
| HONEY CAPITAL OF THE UNITED STATES | Uvalde, Tex. |
| HONEY CAPITAL OF THE WORLD | Uvalde, Tex. |
| HONEYMOON CITY | Niagara Falls, N. Y. |
| HONG KONG OF THE HUDSON | New York, N. Y. |
| HOOSIER ATHENS | Crawfordsville, Ind. |
| HOOSIER CAPITAL | Indianapolis, Ind. |

| | |
|---|---|
| HOOSIER CITY | Indianapolis, Ind. |
| HORN OF THE WEST | Boone, N. C. |
| HORNETS' NEST | Charlotte, N. C. |
| HORSE PLAINS | Hillyard, Wash. |
| HOSPITALITY CAPITAL OF THE NEW SOUTH | Brookhaven, Miss. |
| HOSPITALITY CENTER OF ALASKA | Petersburg, Alaska |
| HOSPITALITY CITY | Gulfport, Miss. |
| HOSPITALITY CITY OF THE ROCKIES | Salida, Colo. |
| HOST CITY | Norfolk, Neb. |
| HOST CITY OF THE NATION | Chicago, Ill. |
| HOST CITY OF THE SUNLAND EMPIRE | El Paso, Tex. |
| HOST CITY TO CONVENTIONS | Harrisburg, Pa. |
| HOST OF THE WORLD | New York, N. Y. |
| HOST RESORT TO THE NATION | Gatlinburg, Tenn. |
| HOST TO THE WEST'S SCENIC WONDER-WAYS | Provo, Utah |
| HOST WITH THE MOST | Atlantic City, N. J. |
| HOST WITHOUT PARALLEL | Springfield, Mass. |
| HOSTESS CITY OF THE SOUTH | Savannah, Ga. |
| HOTTEST TOWN | Quartzsite, Ariz. |
| HOUSE BUILT ON SAND | Los Angeles, Calif. |
| HUB | Boston, Mass. |
| HUB | Casper, Wyo. |
| HUB | Proctor, Minn. |
| HUB | San Anselmo, Calif. |
| HUB | Snohomish, Wash. |
| HUB CITY | Aberdeen, S. D. |
| HUB CITY | Albany, Ore. |
| HUB CITY | Alexandria, La. |
| HUB CITY | Anchorage, Alaska |
| HUB CITY | Brainerd, Minn. |
| HUB CITY | Camilla, Ga. |
| HUB CITY | Casper, Wyo. |
| HUB CITY | Centralia, Wash. |
| HUB CITY | Colton, Calif. |
| HUB CITY | Compton, Calif. |
| HUB CITY | Robertsdale, Ala. |
| HUB CITY IN THE HEART OF FLORIDA'S WEST COUNTRY | Crestview, Fla. |
| HUB CITY OF GOOD LIVING | Chattahoochee, Fla. |
| HUB CITY OF NORTHWEST FLORIDA | Crestview, Fla. |
| HUB CITY OF RECREATION | Chattahoochee, Fla. |
| HUB CITY OF SOUTH TEXAS | Yoakum, Tex. |
| HUB CITY OF SOUTHWESTERN WASHINGTON | Centralia, Wash. |
| HUB CITY OF THE DAKOTAS | Aberdeen, S. D. |

343

| | |
|---|---|
| HUB CITY OF THE SCENIC SOUTH-WEST | Las Vegas, Nev. |
| HUB CITY OF THE SOUTH PLAINS | Lubbock, Tex. |
| HUB CITY OF THE SOUTHEAST | Spartanburg, S. C. |
| HUB CITY OF THE WORLD | New York, N. Y. |
| HUB CITY OF TRANSPORTATION | Chattahoochee, Fla. |
| HUB CITY OF WESTERN COLORADO AND EASTERN UTAH | Grand Junction, Colo. |
| HUB OF A $500,000,000 TRADING AREA | Lima, Ohio |
| HUB OF A NEW WORLD | Cambridge, Mass. |
| HUB OF A VAST SCENIC AND SPORTS WONDERLAND | Las Vegas, Nev. |
| HUB OF AGRICULTURE | Lubbock, Tex. |
| HUB OF ALL SOUTH FLORIDA'S SUN-FUN VACATIONLAND | Miami, Fla. |
| HUB OF AMERICAN INLAND NAVIGATION | St. Louis, Mo. |
| HUB OF AMERICAN MERCHANDISING | Chicago, Ill. |
| HUB OF ARIZONA'S LUMBER INDUSTRY | Flagstaff, Ariz. |
| HUB OF AROOSTOOK COUNTY | Caribou, Me. |
| HUB OF BANKING AND INSURANCE INTERESTS | Fort Worth, Tex. |
| HUB OF BEAUTY | Lubbock, Tex. |
| HUB OF CENTRAL OREGON | Redmond, Ore. |
| HUB OF CIVIC PRIDE | Lubbock, Tex. |
| HUB OF COASTAL CAROLINA | New Bern, N. C. |
| HUB OF CONNECTICUT'S NAUGATUCK RIVER VALLEY | Naugatuck, Conn. |
| HUB OF EASTERN LONG ISLAND | Riverhead, N. Y. |
| HUB OF EDUCATION | Lubbock, Tex. |
| HUB OF FAST TRANSPORTATION | Chicopee, Mass. |
| HUB OF FLORIDA | Clermont, Fla. |
| HUB OF FLORIDA'S SCENIC WONDERLAND | Lakeland, Fla. |
| HUB OF FUN | Jacksonville, Fla. |
| HUB OF HISTORIC OHIO | Springfield, Ohio |
| HUB OF HISTORIC SHRINES | Portsmouth, Va. |
| HUB OF HISTORICAL OHIO | Springfield, Ohio |
| HUB OF HISTORY | Frederick, Md. |
| HUB OF HISTORY | Jacksonville, Fla. |
| HUB OF HOMES AND INDUSTRIES | Ambler, Pa. |
| HUB OF ILLINOIS | Bloomington, Ill. |
| HUB OF INDUSTRIAL AMERICA | Meadville, Pa. |
| HUB OF INDUSTRY AND OIL | Lubbock, Tex. |
| HUB OF LAKE SUPERIOR'S BEAUTIFUL SOUTH SHORE DRIVE | Port Wing, Wis. |

| | |
|---|---|
| HUB OF LIVESTOCK PROCESSING | Lubbock, Tex. |
| HUB OF MICHIGAN | St. Johns, Mich. |
| HUB OF MONTANA'S VAST VACA-TION LAND | Laurel, Mont. |
| HUB OF NASSAU | Hempstead, N. Y. |
| HUB OF NASSAU COUNTY | Hempstead, N. Y. |
| HUB OF NEW ENGLAND | Boston, Mass. |
| HUB OF NEW YORK'S BOATING CEN-TER | City Island, N. Y. |
| HUB OF NORTH AMERICA | Superior, Wis. |
| HUB OF NORTH CENTRAL FLORIDA'S SCENIC WONDERLAND | Lake City, Fla. |
| HUB OF NORTHEAST OREGON | La Grande, Ore. |
| HUB OF NORTHERN VIRGINIA | Culpeper, Va. |
| HUB OF NORTHWEST GEORGIA | Rome, Ga. |
| HUB OF PINELLAS COUNTY | Largo, Fla. |
| HUB OF PINELLAS COUNTY | Pinellas Park, Fla. |
| HUB OF PROGRESS | Jacksonville, Fla. |
| HUB OF RECREATIONAL NORTH DAKOTA | Minot, N. D. |
| HUB OF SCENIC AND HISTORIC WEST-ERN VIRGINIA | Waynesboro, Va. |
| HUB OF SOUTHWEST ALABAMA | Monroeville, Ala. |
| HUB OF SOUTHWEST VIRGINIA | Wytheville, Va. |
| HUB OF SOUTHWESTERN LOUISIANA | Lafayette, La. |
| HUB OF TEXAS | Waco, Tex. |
| HUB OF THE AMERICAS | New Orleans, La. |
| HUB OF THE BEAUTIFUL FLATHEAD VALLEY | Kalispell, Mont. |
| HUB OF THE CHATTAHOOCHEE VAL-LEY | Phenix City, Ala. |
| HUB OF THE COMMONWEALTH | Boston, Mass. |
| HUB OF THE DELTA | Cleveland, Miss. |
| HUB OF THE EMPIRE STATE | Syracuse, N. Y. |
| HUB OF THE EMPIRE STATE | Utica, N. Y. |
| HUB OF THE EMPIRE STATE'S CAP-ITAL DISTRICT | Albany, N. Y. |
| HUB OF THE FABULOUS GOLDEN GULF COAST | Pasadena, Tex. |
| HUB OF THE FABULOUS GULF COAST | Pasadena, Calif. |
| HUB OF THE FASTEST GROWING COUNTY IN THE STATE | Waukesha, Wis. |
| HUB OF THE FLORIDA PENINSULA | Sebring, Fla. |
| HUB OF THE GREAT APALACHICOLA VALLEY | Blountstown, Fla. |
| HUB OF THE GREAT NIAGARA FRUIT BELT | Lockport, N. Y. |
| HUB OF THE GREAT NORTH-CENTRAL | |

| | |
|---|---|
| INDUSTRIAL AND AGRICULTURAL AMERICA | Fort Wayne, Ind. |
| HUB OF THE GREAT LEHIGH VALLEY | Bethlehem, Pa. |
| HUB OF THE GREAT ORANGE, GRAPE-FRUIT AND WINTER STRAWBERRY PRODUCING SECTION IN THE UNITED STATES | Tampa, Fla. |
| HUB OF THE GREAT SOUTHWEST | Oklahoma City, Okla. |
| HUB OF THE GREATER LEHIGH VAL-LEY | Allentown, Pa. |
| HUB OF THE HARLEM VALLEY | Brewster, N. Y. |
| HUB OF THE HIGHWAYS | Mercer, Pa. |
| HUB OF THE "HOLIDAY HIGHLANDS" | Boone, N. C. |
| HUB OF THE INDUSTRIAL GULF COAST | Liberty, Tex. |
| HUB OF THE INTERNATIONAL SOUTH-WEST | El Paso, Tex. |
| HUB OF THE INTERSTATE AND U. S. HIGHWAYS | Harrisburg, Pa. |
| HUB OF THE KENAI PENINSULA | Soldatna, Alaska |
| HUB OF THE MAGIC VALLEY | Twin Falls, Idaho |
| HUB OF THE NATION | Kearney, Neb. |
| HUB OF THE NATION-WIDE TRANS-PORTATION SYSTEM | Indianapolis, Ind. |
| HUB OF THE NEW HIGH-SPEED IN-TERSTATE HIGHWAY SYSTEM | St. Louis, Mo. |
| HUB OF THE NORTH ALABAMA RE-SORT AREAS | Decatur, Ala. |
| HUB OF THE OZARKS | Harrison, Ark. |
| HUB OF THE PLAINS | Lubbock, Tex. |
| HUB OF THE POWERFUL TENNESSEE VALLEY | Huntsville, Ala. |
| HUB OF THE RICHEST FARMING DIS-TRICT OF THE UNITED STATES | Mount Joy, Pa. |
| HUB OF THE SCENIC HISTORIC TIDE-WATER REGION AT THE BASE OF CHESAPEAKE BAY | Portsmouth, Va. |
| HUB OF THE SCENIC OZARKS | Cassville, Mo. |
| HUB OF THE SCENIC WEST | Grand Junction, Colo. |
| HUB OF THE SOLAR SYSTEM | Boston, Mass. |
| HUB OF THE SOUTHEAST | Atlanta, Ga. |
| HUB OF THE SOUTHEAST | Gaffney, S. C. |
| HUB OF THE UNIVERSE | Boston, Mass. |
| HUB OF THE VALLEY OF PARKS | Corbin, Ky. |
| HUB OF THE WILLAMETTE VALLEY | Albany, Ore. |
| HUB OF THE WINTER GARDEN | Carrizo, Tex. |
| HUB OF THLINGIT TOTEM LAND | Wrangell, Alaska |

| | |
|---|---|
| HUB OF TRANSPORT | New York, N. Y. |
| HUB TOWN | Boston, Mass. |
| HUDSON OF THE WEST | Byron, Ill. |
| HUNTER'S RENDEZVOUS | Blackduck, Minn. |
| HYDRO-ELECTRIC CITY | Watertown, N. Y. |

I

| | |
|---|---|
| ICE MINE CITY | Coudersport, Pa. |
| IDAHO'S FARM MARKET | Caldwell, Idaho |
| IDAHO'S FINEST RESIDENTIAL COMMUNITY | Twin Falls, Idaho |
| IDAHO'S OLDEST INCORPORATED CITY | Lewiston, Idaho |
| IDAHO'S ONLY SEAPORT | Lewiston, Idaho |
| IDEAL AMERICAN CITY | St. Paul, Minn. |
| IDEAL CITY | Atlanta, Ga. |
| IDEAL CITY | Malden, Mass. |
| IDEAL CITY IN ALL SEASONS | New London, Conn. |
| IDEAL COMMUNITY | Corvallis, Ore. |
| IDEAL COMMUNITY IN WHICH TO LIVE, WORK, AND PLAY | West Caldwell, N. J. |
| IDEAL CONVENTION AND VACATION CITY | Madison, Wis. |
| IDEAL CONVENTION CITY | Atlanta, Ga. |
| IDEAL CONVENTION CITY | Jacksonville, Fla. |
| IDEAL FAMILY COMMUNITY | Palm Springs, Fla. |
| IDEAL HOME AND RECREATIONAL CENTER | Palo Alto, Calif. |
| IDEAL HOME CITY | Austin, Tex. |
| IDEAL HOME COMMUNITY | Douglas, Alaska |
| IDEAL HOME COMMUNITY | Evanston, Ill. |
| IDEAL INDUSTRIAL TOWN | Mount Joy, Pa. |
| IDEAL LIVING CITY IN THE HEART OF FLORIDA | High Springs, Fla. |
| IDEAL LOCATION FOR VACATION AND HOME | Belleview, Fla. |
| IDEAL PLACE IN WHICH TO LIVE, WORK AND PLAY | Bethel, Me. |
| IDEAL PLACE TO STAY OR PLAY | Carthage, Mo. |
| IDEAL PLACE TO WORK AND LIVE | Bloomsburg, Pa. |
| IDEAL PLACE TO WORK, LIVE, PLAY | Jacksonville, Fla. |
| IDEAL RESIDENTIAL CITY | Syracuse, N. Y. |
| IDEAL SPOT FOR RETIREMENT | Bonifay, Fla. |
| IDEAL TOWN | Haydenville, Ohio |
| IDEAL TOWN IN WHICH TO LIVE, WORK, SHOP AND PLAY | Riverhead, N. Y. |

347

| | |
|---|---|
| IDEAL VACATION RESORT | Long Beach, N. Y. |
| IDEAL VACATION RESORT AND YEAR 'ROUND RESIDENTIAL COMMUNITY | Long Beach, N. Y. |
| IDEAL VACATIONLAND | Brunswick, Ga. |
| IDEAL WORKING CITY | Lewiston, Me. |
| IDEAL YEAR ROUND COMMUNITY | Anaheim, Calif. |
| IDEAL YEAR ROUND RESORT | Daytona Beach, Fla. |
| IDEAL YEAR ROUND VACATION SPOT | Jacksonville, Fla. |
| ILLINOIS' CAPITAL CITY | Springfield, Ill. |
| ILLINOIS' SECOND CITY | Peoria, Ill. |
| ILLINOIS' SECOND INDUSTRIAL CITY | Rockford, Ill. |
| ILLINOIS' SECOND LARGEST CITY | Rockford, Ill. |
| IMMIGRANT CITY | Lawrence, Mass. |
| IMPERIAL POLK | Lakeland, Fla. |
| IMPORTANT CONVENTION AND CONFERENCE CITY | Springfield, Ill. |
| IMPORTANT LIVESTOCK CENTER | Fargo, N. D. |
| INDIAN CAPITAL | Gallup, N. M. |
| INDIAN CAPITAL OF THE WORLD | Gallup, N. M. |
| INDIAN VILLAGE | Upper Sandusky, Ohio |
| INDIANA'S FINEST HOME TOWN | La Porte, Ind. |
| INDIANA'S GATEWAY CITY | Jeffersonville, Ind. |
| INDIANA'S SUMMER PLAYGROUND | Michigan City, Ind. |
| INDIANAPOLIS OF THE EAST | Thompson, Conn. |
| INDUSTRIAL, AGRICULTURAL AND EDUCATIONAL CENTER OF THE SOUTH PLAINS OF TEXAS | Lubbock, Tex. |
| INDUSTRIAL AND CULTURAL CENTER OF NEW JERSEY | New Brunswick, N.J. |
| INDUSTRIAL AND DISTRIBUTING CENTER OF THE PACIFIC COAST EMPIRE | Stockton, Calif. |
| INDUSTRIAL AND DISTRIBUTION CENTER | Jacksonville, Fla. |
| INDUSTRIAL AND RECREATIONAL CENTER OF EAST ALABAMA | Alexander City, Ala. |
| INDUSTRIAL AND RECREATIONAL PARADISE | Pascagoula, Miss. |
| INDUSTRIAL AND RESORT CENTER | Panama City, Fla. |
| INDUSTRIAL AND TRADING CENTER OF EAST ALABAMA | Opelika, Ala. |
| INDUSTRIAL CAPITAL | Jackson, Miss. |
| INDUSTRIAL CAPITAL OF AMERICA | Bridgeport, Conn. |
| INDUSTRIAL CAPITAL OF CALIFORNIA | Pittsburg, Calif. |
| INDUSTRIAL CAPITAL OF CONNECTICUT | Bridgeport, Conn. |
| INDUSTRIAL CENTER | Lewiston, Me. |

348

| | |
|---|---|
| INDUSTRIAL CENTER | Ludlow, Mass. |
| INDUSTRIAL CENTER | Portsmouth, Va. |
| INDUSTRIAL CENTER | Saginaw, Mich. |
| INDUSTRIAL CENTER OF THE GREAT SOUTH | Birmingham, Ala. |
| INDUSTRIAL CENTER OF THE PAN-HANDLE | Borger, Tex. |
| INDUSTRIAL CENTER OF THE RED RIVER VALLEY | Paris, Tex. |
| INDUSTRIAL CENTER OF THE SOUTH | Pasadena, Tex. |
| INDUSTRIAL CENTER OF THE SOUTH-EAST | Birmingham, Ala. |
| INDUSTRIAL CENTER OF VERMONT | Springfield, Vt. |
| INDUSTRIAL CENTER OF WEST FLOR-IDA | Pensacola, Fla. |
| INDUSTRIAL CITY | Brockton, Mass. |
| INDUSTRIAL CITY | Colton, Calif. |
| INDUSTRIAL CITY | High Point, N.C. |
| INDUSTRIAL CITY | Holyoke, Mass. |
| INDUSTRIAL CITY | Milwaukee, Wis. |
| INDUSTRIAL CITY | Pittsfield, Mass. |
| INDUSTRIAL CITY | Sidney, Ohio |
| INDUSTRIAL CITY BEAUTIFUL | Birmingham, Ala. |
| INDUSTRIAL CITY OF DIXIE | Birmingham, Ala. |
| INDUSTRIAL CITY OF IOWA | Sioux City, Iowa |
| INDUSTRIAL CITY OF NORTH ALA-BAMA | Huntsville, Ala. |
| INDUSTRIAL CITY OF THE SOUTH | Birmingham, Ala. |
| INDUSTRIAL CITY OF THE WEST | Pittsburg, Calif. |
| INDUSTRIAL CITY OF THE WEST | Pittsburg, Pa. |
| INDUSTRIAL, COMMERCIAL AND CULTURAL CAPITAL | Denver, Colo. |
| INDUSTRIAL DYNAMO | Islip, N.Y. |
| INDUSTRIAL FRONTIER OF AMERICA | Oklahoma City, Okla. |
| INDUSTRIAL FRONTIER OF THE MAGIC LOWER RIO GRANDE VAL-LEY OF TEXAS | Pharr, Tex. |
| INDUSTRIAL, GEOGRAPHICAL HISTORIC AND TRANSPORTATION CENTER OF VIRGINIA | Lynchburg, Va. |
| INDUSTRIAL GIANT OF FAR SOUTH-WEST TEXAS | Beaumont, Tex. |
| INDUSTRIAL HALF-SISTER | Everett, Mass. |
| INDUSTRIAL HEART OF FLORIDA'S FUTURE | Quincy, Fla. |
| INDUSTRIAL HEART OF MAINE | Auburn, Me. |
| INDUSTRIAL HEART OF MAINE | Lewiston, Me. |
| INDUSTRIAL HEART OF THE NAUGA- | |

349

| | |
|---|---|
| TUCK VALLEY | Ansonia, Conn. |
| INDUSTRIAL HUB OF FLORIDA | Tampa, Fla. |
| INDUSTRIAL HUB OF THE WEST | Stockton, Calif. |
| INDUSTRIAL METROPOLIS | Reading, Pa. |
| INDUSTRIAL PARADISE | Brookhaven, Miss. |
| INDUSTRIAL ROCKET CENTER | Marshall, Tex. |
| INDUSTRIAL VACATION AND SEA-FOOD SHOPPING CENTER | Norfolk, Va. |
| INEVITABLE SPA CITY | Saratoga Springs, N. Y. |
| INLAND CITY BEAUTIFUL | Pomona, Calif. |
| INLAND METROPOLIS | Birmingham, Ala. |
| INLAND PARADISE OF FLORIDA | Haines City, Fla. |
| INNKEEPER'S CITY | Memphis, Tenn. |
| INSURANCE CAPITAL OF THE WORLD | Hartford, Conn. |
| INSURANCE CENTER OF THE SOUTH | Jacksonville, Fla. |
| INSURANCE CITY | Atlanta, Ga. |
| INSURANCE CITY | Hartford, Conn. |
| INTERESTING PAST, A PROSPEROUS PRESENT, AN UNLIMITED FUTURE | Richmond, Va. |
| INTERNATIONAL CITY | Calais, Me. |
| INTERNATIONAL CITY | El Paso, Tex. |
| INTERNATIONAL CITY | Long Beach, Calif. |
| INTERNATIONAL CITY | New Orleans, La. |
| INTERNATIONAL MELTING POT | Seattle, Wash. |
| INTERNATIONAL POLAR AIR CROSS-ROADS OF THE WORLD | Anchorage, Alaska |
| IOWA'S INDUSTRIAL, SCENIC AND CULTURED CITY | Dubuque, Iowa |
| IOWA'S OWN CITY | Des Moines, Iowa |
| IRIS CITY | Nashville, Tenn. |
| IRON CITY | Bessemer, Ala. |
| IRON CITY | Pittsburgh, Pa. |
| IRON CITY ON THE TENNESSEE RIVER | Sheffield, Ala. |
| IRON MOUNTAIN CITY | Lebanon, Pa. |
| IRON ORE CAPITAL OF THE WORLD | Hibbing, Minn. |
| IRON ORE CITY | Connellsville, Pa. |
| ISLAND CITY OF OLD WORLD CHARM | Key West, Fla. |
| ISLAND OF EASY LIVING | Peaks Island, Me. |
| ISLAND PARADISE | Key Biscayne, Fla. |
| ISLAND PARADISE MINUTES FROM MIAMI | Key Biscayne, Fla. |
| ISLAND YOU'LL LOVE | Anna Maria, Fla. |
| ISLAND WHERE THE SAND WHISPERS TO THE SEA | Jekyll Island, Ga. |
| ISLE OF PLEASANT LIVING | Alameda, Calif. |
| ITALY OF AMERICA | San Diego, Calif. |

IT'S PLEASANT TO LIVE IN       Bloomington, Ill.

## J

| | |
|---|---|
| JACARANDA CITY WITH THE MILE LONG MALL | Avon Park, Fla. |
| JACKSONOPOLIS | Jackson, Mich. |
| JAMBALAYA CAPITAL OF THE WORLD | Gonzales, La. |
| JAWBONE FLATS | Clarkston, Wash. |
| JAX | Jacksonville, Fla. |
| JEFF CITY | Jefferson City, Mo. |
| JEFFERSON'S COUNTRY | Charlottesville, Va. |
| JET TRANSPORT CAPITAL OF THE WORLD | Renton, Wash. |
| JEWEL CITY | Glendale, Calif. |
| JEWEL CITY OF CALIFORNIA | San Diego, Calif. |
| JEWEL CITY OF THE SUNSHINE STATE | Miami, Fla. |
| JEWEL CITY OF THE FLORIDA WEST COAST | Fort Myers, Fla. |
| JEWEL OF THE GEM STATE | Burley, Idaho |
| JEWEL ON THE GULF OF MEXICO | Corpus Christi, Tex. |
| JIMTOWN | Jamestown, N. D. |
| JONES BEACH OF NEW ENGLAND | Salisbury Beach, Mass. |
| JONQUIL CITY | Smyrna, Ga. |
| JUMPER'S FLATS | Waterville, Wash. |
| JUNCTION | Gretna, Va. |
| JUST A REAL NICE TOWN | Plant City, Fla. |

## K

| | |
|---|---|
| KANSAS CITY OF ALASKA | Fairbanks, Alaska |
| KANSAS' PREMIER CITY | Wichita, Kan. |
| KANSAS WATER SPORTS CAPITAL | Manhattan, Kan. |
| KAOLIN CENTER OF THE WORLD | Sandersville, Ga. |
| KEY CITY | Dubuque, Iowa |
| KEY CITY | Port Townsend, Wash. |
| KEY CITY | Vicksburg, Miss. |
| KEY CITY IN THE LOWER RIO GRANDE VALLEY | Harlingen, Tex. |
| KEY CITY OF CENTRAL NORTHWEST WISCONSIN | Eau Claire, Wis. |
| KEY CITY OF IOWA | Dubuque, Iowa |
| KEY CITY OF NAUGATUCK VALLEY | Waterbury, Conn. |
| KEY CITY OF PUGET SOUND | Port Townsend, Wash. |

| | |
|---|---|
| KEY CITY OF THE BLACK HILLS | Sturgis, S. D. |
| KEY CITY OF WEST TEXAS | Abilene, Tex. |
| KEY JUNCTION TO THE SOUTHEAST | Thomasville, Ga. |
| KEY NATIONAL DEFENSE CENTER | Jacksonville, Fla. |
| KEY OF THE GREAT VALLEY | New Orleans, La. |
| KEY SHOPPING AND MANUFACTUR- ING CENTER | Madison, Wis. |
| KEY SPOT IN THE FUTURE OF KAY- SINGER RESERVOIR | Osceola, Mo. |
| KING CRAB CAPITAL OF THE WORLD | Kodiak, Alaska |
| KING OF POWER | Niagara Falls, N. Y. |
| KINGDOM OF OPPORTUNITY | Blountstown, Fla. |
| KINGDOM OF THE SUN | Dunnellon, Fla. |
| KINGDOM OF THE SUN | San Diego, Calif. |
| KISSINGEN OF AMERICA | Glenwood Springs, Colo. |
| KODAK CITY | Rochester, N. Y. |
| KOPPER KETTLE | Van Buren, Ark. |
| KRINGLEVILLE | Racine, Wis. |

## L

| | |
|---|---|
| L. A. | Los Angeles, Calif. |
| LADINO CLOVER CENTER OF AMER- ICA | Oakdale, Calif. |
| LAKE CAPITAL OF THE HOOSIER STATE | Elkhart, Ind. |
| LAKE CITY | Chicago, Ill. |
| LAKE CITY | Fort Worth, Tex. |
| LAKE CITY | Madison, Wis. |
| LAKE CITY | Watertown, S. D. |
| LAKE ERIE'S VACATION CITY | Cleveland, Ohio |
| LAKE ONTARIO'S WESTERNMOST AMERICAN SEAPORT | Rochester, N. Y. |
| LAKE TROUT CAPITAL | Hovland, Minn. |
| LAKEWAY TO THE SMOKIES | Morristown, Tenn. |
| LAMB AND CATTLE CAPITAL OF THE WEST | Fort Collins, Colo. |
| LAND OF AMAZING VARIETY AND CONTRASTS | Burlington, Vt. |
| LAND OF BEAUTIFUL LAKES | Speculator, N. Y. |
| LAND OF BERRIES | Utsaladdy, Wash. |
| LAND OF BREAD | Kittitas, Wash. |
| LAND OF BUSINESS OPPORTUNITY | Fargo, N. D. |
| LAND OF CHEESE, TREES AND OCEAN BREEZE | Tillamook, Ore. |
| LAND OF CHIEF WABASIS | Belding, Mich. |
| LAND OF CONTRAST | Arcadia, Fla. |

| | |
|---|---|
| LAND OF CROSSES | Auriesville, N. Y. |
| LAND OF ENCHANTING WATERS | New Bern, N. C. |
| LAND OF FLOWERS | De Land, Fla. |
| LAND OF FLOWING SPRINGS | Youngstown, Ohio |
| LAND OF GOOD LIVING | Ruston, La. |
| LAND OF INCREDIBLE BEAUTY AND GREAT LIVABILITY | Medford, Ore. |
| LAND OF HAZEL NUTS | Tukwila, Wash. |
| LAND OF INDUSTRIAL OPPORTUN- ITIES | Long Beach, Calif. |
| LAND OF LAKES AND TROUT STREAMS | Murphy, N. C. |
| LAND OF LAKES SHOPPING CENTER | El Dorado Springs, Mo. |
| LAND OF LONGTAILS | Madison, S. D. |
| LAND OF OPPORTUNITY | Belleview, Fla. |
| LAND OF OPPORTUNITY | Morgan Hill, Calif. |
| LAND OF OUTDOOR FUN | Henderson, Ky. |
| LAND OF PERPETUAL HARVEST | Glendale, Ariz. |
| LAND OF PERPETUAL PROSPERITY | Oklahoma City, Okla. |
| LAND OF PLAY AND PLENTY | Virginia Beach, Va. |
| LAND OF PROMISE | Delano, Calif. |
| LAND OF PROMISE | Hollywood, Calif. |
| LAND OF ROMANCE AND RECRE- ATION | Sacramento, Calif. |
| LAND OF SHINING MOUNTAINS | Billings, Mont. |
| LAND OF SUNSHINE | De Land, Fla. |
| LAND OF SURPRISING CONTRASTS | New York, N. Y. |
| LAND OF THE AFTERNOON | Los Angeles, Calif. |
| LAND OF THE BIG INCH | Houston, Tex. |
| LAND OF THE ENDLESS MOUNTAINS | Emporium, Pa. |
| LAND OF THE OLD SOUTH | St. Simons Island, Ga. |
| LAND OF THE OLD SOUTH | Sea Island, Ga. |
| LAND OF THE PILGRIMS, SUN AND SAND | Plymouth, Mass. |
| LAND OF THE PINES | Alberta, Va. |
| LAND OF THE SKY | Asheville, N. C. |
| LAND OF THE SKY | Murphy, N. C. |
| LAND OF THE TREMBLING EARTH | Folkston, Ga. |
| LAND OF THE TREMBLING EARTH | Waycross, Ga. |
| LAND OF WASHINGTON | Fredericksburg, Va. |
| LAND WHERE HISTORY WAS MADE | Ticonderoga, N. Y. |
| LANDING | Fall City, Wash. |
| LARGEST CITY FOR ITS SIZE | Taunton, Mass. |
| LARGEST CITY IN NORTHERN ARI- ZONA | Winslow, Ariz. |

353

| | |
|---|---|
| LARGEST CITY IN THE LARGEST STATE | Anchorage, Alaska |
| LARGEST CITY IN THE MOST FAVORED CLIMATE AREA IN AMERICA | El Paso, Tex. |
| LARGEST CITY IN THE SOUTH | Houston, Tex. |
| LARGEST CITY IN THE SOUTHWEST | Houston, Tex. |
| LARGEST CITY OF CONTRA COSTA COUNTY | Richmond, Calif. |
| LARGEST COTTON MANUFACTURING CENTER IN THE STATE | La Grange, Ga. |
| LARGEST GHOST TOWN IN AMERICA | Jerome, Ariz. |
| LARGEST INDUSTRIAL CITY IN WESTERN MASSACHUSETTS | Holyoke, Mass. |
| LARGEST INDUSTRIAL CITY OF ITS SIZE IN OHIO | Barberton, Ohio |
| LARGEST INSURANCE CENTER IN THE WEST | Des Moines, Iowa |
| LARGEST METROPOLIS IN THE MISSISSIPPI VALLEY | St. Louis, Mo. |
| LARGEST PECAN SHIPPING CENTER IN AMERICA | Chandler, Okla. |
| LARGEST PORT IN THE LOWER EAST COAST | Port Everglades, Fla. |
| LARGEST RESORT CENTER IN INDIANA | Michigan City, Ind. |
| LARGEST SHOPPING CENTER IN THE POMME DE TERRE AREA | Bolivar, Mo. |
| LARGEST SMALL CITY IN INDIANA | Mitchell, Ind. |
| LARGEST WATERMELON SHIPPING CENTER IN CALIFORNIA | Kingsburg, Calif. |
| LAS DIABLOS | Los Angels, Calif. |
| LAS VEGAS ON THE POTOMAC | Colonial Beach, Va. |
| LAST CAPITAL OF THE CONFEDERACY | Danville, Va. |
| LAST OF THE OLD WEST AND THE BEST OF THE NEW | Jackson, Wyo. |
| LAST OF THE WESTERN FRONTIER | Sweetwater, Tex. |
| LAST OUTPOST OF CIVILIZATION | St. Charles, Mo. |
| LAST PLACE ON THE MAP | Ogden, Kan. |
| LAUNCH PAD TO PROGRESS | Merritt Island, Fla. |
| LAUREL CITY | Winsted, Conn. |
| LAWN CITY | Cedar Falls, Iowa |
| LEADING COMMERCIAL FINANCIAL AND DISTRIBUTION CENTER | Houston, Tex. |
| LEADING CONVENTION CITY IN THE COUNTRY | Chicago, Ill. |
| LEADING ENTERTAINMENT MECCA | Las Vegas, Nev. |

354

| | |
|---|---|
| LEADING FAMILY RESORT SUMMER AND WINTER | Pacific Grove, Calif. |
| LEADING INDUSTRIAL CITY IN ARKANSAS | Fort Smith, Ark. |
| LEADING INDUSTRIAL CITY OF THE SOUTHWEST | Houston, Tex. |
| LEADING ISLAND CITY OF THE SOUTH | San Bernardino, Calif. |
| LEADING RESORT CITY | Augusta, Ga. |
| LEADING SCALLOP PORT OF THE WORLD | New Bedford, Mass. |
| LEADING SPOT COTTON MARKET | Houston, Tex. |
| LEATHER CITY | Buford, Ga. |
| LEATHER CITY | Peabody, Mass. |
| LEMON CAPITAL | Corona, Calif. |
| LEMON CAPITAL OF THE WORLD | Chula Vista, Calif. |
| LEMON CENTER | Santa Paula, Calif. |
| LETTUCE CENTER OF THE NATION | Aguila, Ariz. |
| LEXINGTON OF TEXAS | Gonzalez, Tex. |
| LIGHTING CAPITAL OF THE WORLD | Cleveland, Ohio |
| LILAC CITY | Fort Collins, Colo. |
| LILAC CITY | Lincoln, Neb. |
| LILAC TOWN | Lombard, Ill. |
| LIMBERLOST COUNTRY | Geneva, Ind. |
| LIMESTONE CITY | Rogers City, Mich. |
| LINCOLN CITY | Boonville, Ind. |
| LITERARY EMPORIUM | Boston, Mass. |
| LITTLE CAPITAL | Denver, Colo. |
| LITTLE CITY IN THE ADIRONDACKS | Saranac Lake, N. Y. |
| LITTLE CITY IN THE WOODS | Kingfield, Me. |
| LITTLE CITY OF BIG OPPORTUNITY | Newberry, Fla. |
| LITTLE CITY OF CHARM | Mesa, Ariz. |
| LITTLE CITY WITH THE BIG INFERIORITY COMPLEX | San Pablo, Calif. |
| LITTLE DENMARK | Solvang, Calif. |
| LITTLE DETROIT | Connersville, Ind. |
| LITTLE EDEN | Hoboken, N. J. |
| LITTLE HEIDELBERG OF AMERICA | Dubuque, Iowa |
| LITTLE HOLLAND | Garibaldi, Ore. |
| LITTLE HOLLYWOOD | Kanab, Utah |
| LITTLE ITALY | Independence, La. |
| LITTLE LAS VEGAS | Gardena, Calif. |
| LITTLE LOUISVILLE OF THE SOUTHWEST | Seiling, Okla. |
| LITTLE LUNNON (LONDON) | Colorado Springs, Colo. |
| LITTLE NEW YORK | Welch, W. Va. |

| | |
|---|---|
| LITTLE NORWAY OF ALASKA | Petersburg, Alaska |
| LITTLE PORTAGE | Seattle, Wash. |
| LITTLE SEA BY THE SEA OF HAPPY REST AND REVERIE | Terminal Island, Calif. |
| LITTLE STUMPTOWN | Portland, Ore. |
| LITTLE SWITZERLAND | Ashfield, Mass. |
| LITTLE SWITZERLAND | New Glarus, Wis. |
| LITTLE SWITZERLAND | West Portal, N. J. |
| LITTLE SWITZERLAND OF AMERICA | Eureka Springs, Ark. |
| LITTLE VENICE | Skamokawa, Wash. |
| LITTLE WHITE HOUSE | Manchester, Ga. |
| LITTLE WHITE HOUSE CITY | Warm Springs, Ga. |
| LIVESTOCK, GRAIN AND INDUSTRIAL CAPITAL OF THE GREAT NORTH-WEST | Sioux City, Iowa |
| LIVING PAGE FROM TEXAS HISTORY | Jefferson, Tex. |
| LOBSTER CENTER OF THE WORLD | Bar Harbor, Me. |
| LOCK CITY | Stamford, Conn. |
| LONESOMEST TOWN IN THE WORLD | Jordan, Mont. |
| LONG ISLAND'S OCEAN PLAYGROUND | Hampton Bays, N. Y. |
| LONG ISLAND'S WORLD FAMOUS OCEAN PLAYGROUND | Hampton, N. Y. |
| LOOKOUT CITY | Ebensburg, Pa. |
| LOOM CITY | Rockville, Conn. |
| LOST ANGELS | Los Angeles, Calif. |
| LOST RESORT | Palm Springs, Calif. |
| LOUISIANA'S CLEANEST CITY | Jennings, La. |
| LOUISIANA'S FASTEST GROWING CITY | Baton Rouge, La. |
| LOVELIEST MODERN CITY IN MID-AMERICA | Lincoln, Neb. |
| LOVELIEST SITE IN THE WORLD FOR A TOWN | Emporia, Kan. |
| LOVELIEST VILLAGE OF THE PLAINS | Auburn, Ala. |
| LOVELY GATEWAY TO THE PASSES | Salida, Colo. |
| LOWELL OF THE SOUTH | Augusta, Ga. |
| LOWELL OF THE WEST | Petaluma, Calif. |
| LUDLOW IS A SNOW TOWN, LUDLOW IS A FUN TOWN, LUDLOW HAS EVERYTHING | Ludlow, Vt. |
| LUMBER CAPITAL | Tacoma, Wash. |
| LUMBER CAPITAL OF ALASKA | Wrangell, Alaska |
| LUMBER CAPITAL OF AMERICA | Tacoma, Wash. |
| LUMBER CAPITAL OF THE NATION | Roseburg, Ore. |
| LUMBER CAPITAL OF THE WORLD | Tacoma, Wash. |
| LUMBER CITY | Bangor, Me. |
| LUMBER CITY | Williamsport, Pa. |

| | |
|---|---|
| LUMBER CITY OF THE WORLD | Muskegon, Mich. |
| LUMBER EXPORT CAPITAL OF ALASKA | Wrangell, Alaska |
| LUMBER INDUSTRY'S CAPITAL | Portland, Ore. |
| LUMBER MANUFACTURING CENTER OF THE PACIFIC NORTHWEST | Portland, Ore. |
| LUMBER PORT OF THE WORLD | Coos Bay, Ore. |
| LUMBER QUEEN | Muskegon, Mich. |
| LUMBER QUEEN OF THE WORLD | Muskegon, Mich. |
| LUMBERING CENTER | Everett, Wash. |
| LUNCHBURG | Lynchburg, Va. |
| LUNCHSTONE | Blackstone, Va. |
| LUXURY RESORT TOWN | Las Vegas, Nev. |
| LYONS OF AMERICA | Paterson, N. J. |

M

| | |
|---|---|
| MACHINE CITY | Lynn, Mass. |
| MAGIC CITY | Anacortes, Wash. |
| MAGIC CITY | Anniston, Ala. |
| MAGIC CITY | Barberton, Ohio |
| MAGIC CITY | Billings, Mont. |
| MAGIC CITY | Birmingham, Ala. |
| MAGIC CITY | Florence, S. C. |
| MAGIC CITY | Gary, Ind. |
| MAGIC CITY | Leadville, Colo. |
| MAGIC CITY | Marceline, Mo. |
| MAGIC CITY | Miami, Fla. |
| MAGIC CITY | Miami Beach, Fla. |
| MAGIC CITY | Minot, N. D. |
| MAGIC CITY | Moberly, Mo. |
| MAGIC CITY | Muncie, Ind. |
| MAGIC CITY | Roanoke, Va. |
| MAGIC CITY | Schenectady, N. Y. |
| MAGIC CITY | Tulsa, Okla. |
| MAGIC CITY OF THE GREEN EMPIRE | Bogalusa, La. |
| MAGIC CITY OF THE PLAINS | Casper, Wyo. |
| MAGIC CITY OF THE PLAINS | Cheyenne, Wyo. |
| MAGIC CITY OF THE SOUTH | Birmingham, Ala. |
| MAGIC CITY OF THE SOUTH | Roanoke, Va. |
| MAGIC CITY OF THE WEST | Cheyenne, Wyo. |
| MAGIC CITY OF VIRGINIA | Roanoke, Va. |
| MAGIC LITTLE CITY | Whittier, Calif. |
| MAGIC MASCOT OF THE PLAINS | Wichita, Kan. |
| MAGNIFICENT CAPITAL | Washington, D. C. |
| MAGNIFICENT MOUNTAIN WONDERLAND | Long Lake, N. Y. |

| | |
|---|---|
| MAGNOLIA CITY | Houston, Tex. |
| MAGNOLIA STATE'S INDUSTRIAL CITY | Laurel, Miss. |
| MAGNOLIA'S LARGEST INDUSTRIAL CITY | Laurel, Miss. |
| MAIN STREET OF NORTHWEST ARKANSAS | Springdale, Ark. |
| "MAINE" IDEA IN RECREATION | Kennebunk, Me. |
| MAINE'S FASTEST GROWING INDUSTRIAL AND RECREATIONAL AREA | Norway, Me. |
| MAINE'S FASTEST GROWING INDUSTRIAL AND RECREATIONAL AREA | Paris, Me. |
| MAINE'S MOST FAMOUS COAST RESORT | Bar Harbor, Me. |
| MAINE'S MOST ENCHANTING ISLAND | Vinalhaven, Me. |
| MAINE'S OUTSTANDING WINTER SPORTS CENTER | Rumford, Me. |
| MAINLINE CITY | Fargo, N. D. |
| MAJOR CULTURAL CENTER OF THE WORLD | Boston, Mass. |
| MAJOR GLASS CENTER | Corning, N. Y. |
| MAJOR INSURANCE CITY | Hartford, Conn. |
| MAJOR MARKET OF YORK COUNTY | Biddeford, Me. |
| MAJOR MARKET OF YORK COUNTY | Saco, Me. |
| MAJOR WORLD TOOL AND DIE TRAINING CENTER | South Bend, Ind. |
| MANCHESTER OF AMERICA | Lowell, Mass. |
| MANCHESTER OF AMERICA | Manchester, N. H. |
| MANUFACTURING AND INDUSTRIAL METROPOLIS OF THE SOUTHEAST | Atlanta, Ga. |
| MANUFACTURING CITY | Oneonta, N. Y. |
| MANUFACTURING CITY OF THE PACIFIC | Stockton, Calif. |
| MANUFACTURING CITY OF THE ROCKY MOUNTAIN REGIONS | Pueblo, Colo. |
| MANUFACTURING RESEARCH AND DEVELOPMENT CENTER OF THE SOUTHWEST | Plano, Tex. |
| MAPLE CENTER OF THE WORLD | St. Johnsbury, Vt. |
| MAPLE CITY | Goshen, Ind. |
| MAPLE CITY | La Porte, Ind. |
| MAPLE CITY OF MICHIGAN | Adrian, Mich. |
| MAPLE SUGAR CENTER OF THE WORLD | St. Johnsbury, Vt. |
| MARBLE CAPITAL OF THE UNITED STATES | Proctor, Vt. |
| MARBLE CITY | Knoxville, Tenn. |
| MARBLE CITY | Rutland, Vt. |

| | |
|---|---|
| MARBLE CITY | Sylacauga, Ala. |
| MARDI GRAS METROPOLIS | New Orleans, La. |
| MARKET OF THREE BARBARIAN TRIBES | San Francisco, Calif. |
| MARKETING AND SHOPPING CENTER | Mitchell, S. D. |
| MARYLAND'S LARGEST CITY | Baltimore, Md. |
| MARYLAND'S PLAYGROUND | Ocean City, Md. |
| MEADOW CITY | Las Vegas, N. M. |
| MEADOW CITY | Northampton, Mass. |
| MECCA FOR CHAMPIONS IN MANY FIELDS | Palm Beach, Fla. |
| MECCA FOR HISTORY LOVERS | Gonzalez, Tex. |
| MECCA OF CRACKPOTS | Los Angeles, Calif. |
| MECCA OF TELEPHONE MEN | New York, N. Y. |
| MEDICAL CENTER | Fort Worth, Tex. |
| MEDICAL CENTER | Mitchell, S. D. |
| MEDICAL CENTER | Paducah, Ky. |
| MEDICAL CENTER OF THE MISSIS-SIPPI DELTA | Greenwood, Miss. |
| MEDICAL CENTER OF NORTH AMER-ICA | Bismarck, N. D. |
| MEDICAL CENTER OF WESTERN MONTANA | Missoula, Mont. |
| MELTING POT | New York, N. Y. |
| MEMPHIS OF THE AMERICAN NILE | St. Louis, Mo. |
| MERCANTILE CENTER | Fitchburg, Mass. |
| METROPOLIS | New York, N. Y. |
| METROPOLIS IN A FOREST OF TREES | Buffalo, N. Y. |
| METROPOLIS OF A CONTINENT | New York, N. Y. |
| METROPOLIS OF A FAST GROWING COMMERCIAL AND AGRICULTURAL AREA | Harrison, Ark. |
| METROPOLIS OF A NEW SOUTH | Atlanta, Ga. |
| METROPOLIS OF AMERICA | New York, N. Y. |
| METROPOLIS OF AN AGRICULTURAL EMPIRE | Amarillo, Tex. |
| METROPOLIS OF CENTRAL AND NORTHWEST KANSAS | Salina, Kan. |
| METROPOLIS OF "DUTCHLAND" | Lancaster, Pa. |
| METROPOLIS OF EASTERN NEVADA | Elko, Nev. |
| METROPOLIS OF EAST TENNESSEE | Knoxville, Tenn. |
| METROPOLIS OF INDUSTRY | Cedar Rapids, Iowa |
| METROPOLIS OF ISMS | Los Angeles, Calif. |
| METROPOLIS OF NEW ENGLAND | Boston, Mass. |
| METROPOLIS OF NEW MEXICO | Albuquerque, N. M. |
| METROPOLIS OF NORTH DAKOTA | Fargo, N. D. |

| | |
|---|---|
| METROPOLIS OF NORTH TEXAS | Dallas, Tex. |
| METROPOLIS OF NORTHERN NEW YORK | Watertown, N. Y. |
| METROPOLIS OF SOUTHEASTERN FLORIDA | Miami, Fla. |
| METROPOLIS OF SOUTHERN NEVADA | Las Vegas, Nev. |
| METROPOLIS OF THE COUNTRY | Washington, D. C. |
| METROPOLIS OF THE DESERT | Phoenix, Ariz. |
| METROPOLIS OF THE INLAND EMPIRE | Spokane, Wash. |
| METROPOLIS OF THE MAGIC VALLEY | Brownsville, Tex. |
| METROPOLIS OF THE MISSISSIPPI DELTA | Greenville, Miss. |
| METROPOLIS OF THE MISSOURI VALLEY | Kansas City, Mo. |
| METROPOLIS OF THE NEW SOUTH | Louisville, Ky. |
| METROPOLIS OF THE NORTHEAST | Bangor, Me. |
| METROPOLIS OF THE NORTHWEST | Pierre, S. D. |
| METROPOLIS OF THE PACIFIC COAST | Los Angeles, Calif. |
| METROPOLIS OF THE PACIFIC NORTHWEST | Seattle, Wash. |
| METROPOLIS OF THE PANHANDLE | Amarillo, Tex. |
| METROPOLIS OF THE PENOBSCOT BAY REGION | Rockland, Me. |
| METROPOLIS OF THE PINE RIDGE RESERVATION COUNTRY | Martin, S. D. |
| METROPOLIS OF THE SOUTH | New Orleans, La. |
| METROPOLIS OF THE SOUTHERN WEST VIRGINIA COAL FIELDS | Bluefield, W. Va. |
| METROPOLIS OF THE SOUTHWEST | Dallas, Tex. |
| METROPOLIS OF THE STATE OF OREGON | Portland, Ore. |
| METROPOLIS OF THE UNSALTED SEAS | Duluth, Minn. |
| METROPOLIS OF THE WEST | Chicago, Ill. |
| METROPOLIS OF THE WEST | Houston, Tex. |
| METROPOLIS OF THE WEST | Los Angeles, Calif. |
| METROPOLIS OF VASHON ISLAND | Vashon, Wash. |
| METROPOLIS OF WEST FLORIDA | Pensacola, Fla. |
| METROPOLIS OF WESTERN MASSACHUSETTS | Springfield, Mass. |
| METROPOLITAN CENTER OF MCKEAN COUNTY | Bradford, Pa. |
| METROPOLITAN CENTER OF TROPICAL FLORIDA'S FIRST RESORT AREA | W. Palm Beach, Fla. |

| | |
|---|---|
| METROPOLITAN CITY | New York, N. Y. |
| METROPOLITAN CITY | Washington, D. C. |
| METROPOLITAN COMMUNITY OF OP-<br>PORTUNITY | Beloit, Wis. |
| MIAMI BEACH OF THE NORTH | Montauk, N. Y. |
| MICHIGAN'S DYNAMIC CITY | Dearborn, Mich. |
| MICHIGAN'S FASTEST GROWING CITY | Dearborn, Mich. |
| MICHIGAN'S FASTEST GROWING COM-<br>MUNITY | Dearborn, Mich. |
| MICHIGAN'S MOST FAMOUS SUMMER<br>RESORT | Benton Harbor, Mich. |
| MICHIGAN'S MOST RENOWNED PHAN-<br>TOM CITY | White Rock, Mich. |
| MID-AMERICA'S FAST GROWING<br>EXCITING NEW PLAYGROUND | Garrison, N. D. |
| MID-AMERICA'S FINEST VACATION-<br>LAND | Angola, Ind. |
| MID-AMERICA'S INDUSTRIAL CENTER | Anderson, Ind. |
| MID-SOUTH RESORT | Southern Pines, N. C. |
| MID-WAY CITY | Melbourne, Fla. |
| MIDDLE OF MARKETING AMERICA | Columbus, Ohio |
| MIDDLE TOWN OF NEW ENGLAND | Pittsfield, Mass. |
| MIDDLETOWN, U. S. A. | Muncie, Ind. |
| MIDDLEWEST CENTER FOR DIVER-<br>SIFIED MANUFACTURE | Milwaukee, Wis. |
| MIDGET CITY | Colby, Wis. |
| MIDLAND EMPIRE CITY | Billings, Mont. |
| MIDLAND METROPOLIS | Chicago, Ill. |
| MIDWEST GOLF CAPITAL | Chicago, Ill. |
| MIDWEST METROPOLIS | Chicago, Ill. |
| MIDWEST'S WINTER SPORTS MECCA | Three Lakes, Wis. |
| MIGHTY CAPITAL | Washington, D. C. |
| MIGHTY MANHATTAN | New York, N. Y. |
| MIGHTY METROPOLIS | Chicago, Ill. |
| MILE HIGH CITY | Denver, Colo. |
| MILE HIGH CITY | Lead, S. D. |
| MILE HIGH CITY | Prescott, Ariz. |
| MILE HIGH CITY OF HEALTH | Prescott, Ariz. |
| MILE SQUARE CITY | Hoboken, N. J. |
| MILK CENTER OF THE WORLD | Harvard, Ill. |
| MILK CITY | Carnation, Wash. |
| MILLION DOLLAR CAMP | Tok, Alaska |
| MILL TOWN | Pittsfield, Mass. |
| MILLTOWN | Minneapolis, Minn. |
| MILWAUKEE THE BEAUTIFUL | Milwaukee, Wis. |
| MILWAUKEE OF THE EAST | Newark, N. J. |

| | |
|---|---|
| MINERAL CITY | Spruce Pine, N.C. |
| MINERAL CITY OF THE SOUTH | Birmingham, Ala. |
| MINERAL POCKET OF NEW ENGLAND | Cumberland, R.I. |
| MINERAL SPRINGS CITY | Bedford, Pa. |
| MINERAL SPRINGS CITY | Bedford, Va. |
| MINING TOWN WITH A HEART | Denver, Colo. |
| MINNEAPOLIS OF THE WEST | Spokane, Wash. |
| MINNESOTA'S OUTDOOR PLAYGROUND | Winona, Minn. |
| MIRACLE CITY | Houston, Tex. |
| MIRACLE CITY OF THE GOLD COAST | Deerfield Beach, Fla. |
| MIRACLE CITY OF THE MIDWEST | Chicago, Ill. |
| MISSILE CAPITAL OF THE WEST | Santa Maria, Calif. |
| MISSILE CITY | Titusville, Fla. |
| MISSILE LAND, U.S.A. | Cocoa Beach, Fla. |
| MISSING CITY OF MARIN | San Rafael, Calif. |
| MISSION CITY | Riverside, Calif. |
| MISSION CITY | San Antonio, Tex. |
| MISSISSIPPI'S BEST EXAMPLE OF THE NEW SOUTH | Tupelo, Miss. |
| MISSISSIPPI'S FINEST EXAMPLE OF THE NEW SOUTH | Tupelo, Miss. |
| MISSISSIPPI'S GREAT RESORT AND HISTORIC CENTER | Biloxi, Miss. |
| MISSISSIPPI'S INDUSTRIAL CITY | Laurel, Miss. |
| MISSISSIPPI'S INDUSTRIAL SEAPORT | Pascagoula, Miss. |
| MISSISSIPPI'S LARGEST RIVER PORT | Greenville, Miss. |
| MISSISSIPPI'S THRIVING INDUSTRIAL CENTER | Yazoo City, Miss. |
| MISSOURI'S MOST INDUSTRIALLY DI-VERSIFIED SMALL CITY | Washington, Mo. |
| MOBTOWN | Baltimore, Md. |
| MODEL CITY | Anniston, Ala. |
| MODEL CITY | Commerce, Calif. |
| MODEL CITY | Quincy, Ill. |
| MODEL CITY OF ALABAMA | Anniston, Ala. |
| MODEL FAMILY RESORT, SUMMER AND WINTER | Pacific Grove, Calif. |
| MODEL MINING COMMUNITY | Carbonado, Wash. |
| MODEL MUNICIPALITY | Monroe, Wash. |
| MODEL VILLAGE | Coleraine, Minn. |
| MODERN AMERICAN ATHENS | Lowell, Mass. |
| MODERN ATHENS | Boston, Mass. |
| MODERN ATHENS | Cleveland, Ohio |
| MODERN CITY | Commerce, Calif. |
| MODERN CITY | Lynchburg, Va. |
| MODERN CITY | Marshfield, Wis. |
| MODERN CITY | Portsmouth, Va. |

| | |
|---|---|
| MODERN CITY OF GREAT HISTORICAL INTEREST | Philadelphia, Pa. |
| MODERN CITY ON THE MOVE | Orlando, Fla. |
| MODERN CITY WITH A COLONIAL SETTING | Annapolis, Md. |
| MODERN CITY WITH A PROUD HERITAGE | Providence, R. I. |
| MODERN GOMORRAH | New York, N. Y. |
| MODERN LITTLE CITY | Belmar, N. J. |
| MODERN PHOENIX | Cloquet, Minn. |
| MODERN ROME | Richmond, Va. |
| MODERN TOWN FOR MODERN LIVING | Vidalia, Ga. |
| MODERN TOWN RICH IN HISTORY | Wiscasset, Me. |
| MONEY HOLE | Conconully, Wash. |
| MONEY TOWN | New York, N. Y. |
| MONTANA'S FRIENDLY COMMUNITY | Cut Bank, Mont. |
| MONTANA'S LARGEST AND FRIENDLIEST CITY | Great Falls, Mont. |
| MONTANA'S ONLY BILLION DOLLAR MARKET | Billings, Mont. |
| MONTE CARLO OF THE WEST | Las Vegas, Nev. |
| MONUMENT CITY | Richmond, Va. |
| MONUMENTAL CITY | Baltimore, Md. |
| MORMON CITY | Salt Lake City, Utah |
| MORMON'S MECCA | Salt Lake City, Utah |
| MOST AIR-MINDED CITY IN THE WORLD | Anchorage, Alaska |
| MOST ACCESSIBLE CITY | Torrington, Conn. |
| MOST ACCESSIBLE CITY ON THE NORTH AMERICAN CONTINENT | Buffalo, N. Y. |
| MOST BEAUTIFUL CITY | Detroit, Mich. |
| MOST BEAUTIFUL CITY IN AMERICA | Washington, D. C. |
| MOST BEAUTIFUL COLLEGE TOWN IN AMERICA | Princeton, N. J. |
| MOST BEAUTIFUL LITTLE CITY IN AMERICA | Madison, Wis. |
| MOST BEAUTIFUL OF ALL WESTERN CITIES | Quincy, Ill. |
| MOST BEAUTIFUL VILLAGE IN NEW YORK STATE | Fredonia, N. Y. |
| MOST BRIDGED CITY IN THE WORLD | Pittsburgh, Pa. |
| MOST COLORFUL EXCITING CITY IN THE WORLD | New York, N. Y. |
| MOST COMPLETE YEAR-'ROUND RESORT TOWN IN THE WHITE MOUNTAINS | North Conway, N. H. |
| MOST EASTERN WESTERN METROPOLIS | Tulsa, Okla. |

| | |
|---|---|
| MOST HISTORIC CITY IN THE EAST | Salem, Mass. |
| MOST HISTORIC CITY IN THE NORTH-WEST TERRITORY | Marietta, Ohio |
| MOST HISTORIC SPOT IN NORTH DA-KOTA | Stanton, N. D. |
| MOST NORTHERN SOUTHERN CITY | Tulsa, Okla. |
| MOST OPPORTUNE LOCALITY OF THE MIDDLE WEST | Warsaw, Okla. |
| MOST POPULAR SUMMER RESORT IN NEW ENGLAND | Rockport, Mass. |
| MOST PROMISING INDUSTRIAL COM-MUNITY OF THE FUTURE | Colonial Heights, Va. |
| MOST SCENIC CITY ON THE CONTI-NENT | Seattle, Wash. |
| MOST TYPICAL WESTERN CITY IN WYOMING | Evanston, Wyo. |
| MOST VERSATILE PORT ON THE WEST COAST | Long Beach, Calif. |
| MOTEL CITY | Perry, Ga. |
| MOTHER CITY | Yankton, S. D. |
| MOTHER CITY OF AMERICA | Boston, Mass. |
| MOTHER CITY OF AN EMPIRE | San Antonio, Tex. |
| MOTHER CITY OF GEORGIA | Savannah, Ga. |
| MOTHER CITY OF THE DAKOTAS | Yankton, S. D. |
| MOTHER OF COUNTIES | Fayette, Mo. |
| MOTHER OF THE WEST | Marshall, Mo. |
| MOTHER OF TOWNS | Farmington, Conn. |
| MOTHER OF TOWNS | Mexico, N. Y. |
| MOTION PICTURE CENTER OF THE WORLD | Los Angeles, Calif. |
| MOTOR CAPITAL OF THE WORLD | Detroit, Mich. |
| MOTOR CITY | Detroit, Mich. |
| MOUND CITY | St. Louis, Mo. |
| MOUNT VERNON OF TEXAS | Huntsville, Tex. |
| MOUNT ZION | Montesano, Wash. |
| MOUNTAIN CITY | Altoona, Pa. |
| MOUNTAIN CITY | Chattanooga, Tenn. |
| MOUNTAIN GATEWAY | Cleveland, Ga. |
| MOUNTAIN LAKE VACATIONLAND | Murphy, N. C. |
| MOVIE CITY | Los Angeles, Calif. |
| MOVIE-MAKING CITY | New York, N. Y. |
| MOVIE VILLAGE | Hollywood, Calif. |
| MOVIELAND | Hollywood, Calif. |
| MUD HEN CITY | Toledo, Ohio |
| MUD HOLE CITY | Washington, D. C. |
| MUNICIPAL POEM OF BEAUTY, SUN-SHINE, HEALTH, PROSPERITY AND | |

| | |
|---|---|
| HAPPINESS | Whittier, Calif. |
| MURDER CAPITAL OF AMERICA | Memphis, Tenn. |
| MURDER CAPITAL OF THE WORLD | Birmingham, Ala. |
| MURDER CAPITAL OF THE WORLD | Dallas, Tex. |
| MURDER CAPITAL OF THE WORLD | Houston, Tex. |
| MURDER CITY | Los Angeles, Calif. |
| MUSHROOM CAPITAL | Mesick, Mich. |
| MUSHROOM CITY | San Francisco, Calif. |
| MUSHROOMOPOLIS | Kansas City, Mo. |
| MUSIC CENTER OF THE SOUTH | Brevard, N. C. |
| MUSIC CITY, U. S. A. | Nashville, Tenn. |
| MUSICAL INSTRUMENT CAPITAL OF THE WORLD | Elkhart, Ind. |
| MUSKIE CAPITAL OF NEW YORK | Bemus Point, N. Y. |
| MUSKY CAPITOL | Hayward, Wis. |

N

| | |
|---|---|
| NAIL CITY | Wheeling, W. Va. |
| NAPLES OF AMERICA | Munising, Mich. |
| NATIONAL ANTHEM CITY | Baltimore, Md. |
| NATIONAL CAPITAL | Washington, D. C. |
| NATIONAL, INDUSTRIAL, SCIENTIFIC, EDUCATIONAL AND CULTURAL CENTER | Buffalo, N. Y. |
| NATION'S BEST RECREATIONAL AREA-FOUR SEASON FUN | Biddeford, Me. |
| NATION'S BIRTHPLACE | Plymouth, Mass. |
| NATION'S CAPITAL | Washington, D. C. |
| NATION'S CLEANEST CITY | Memphis, Tenn. |
| NATION'S FINEST WINTER SPORTS CENTER | Lake Placid, N. Y. |
| NATION'S FIRST CITY | New York, N. Y. |
| NATION'S GREAT ALL-YEAR RESORT | Asbury Park, N. J. |
| NATION'S GREAT ALL-YEAR RESORT CITY-BY-THE-SEA | Asbury Park, N. J. |
| NATION'S GREAT NEW CONVENTION CITY | Las Vegas, Nev. |
| NATION'S GREAT RESORT CITY-BY-THE-SEA | Asbury Park, N. J. |
| NATION'S GREATEST CITY | New York, N. Y. |
| NATION'S GREATEST HISTORIC SHRINE | Gettysburg, Pa. |
| NATION'S HEADQUARTERS | Washington, D. C. |
| NATION'S HEALTH RESORT | Hot Springs, Ark. |
| NATION'S HOTTEST TOWN | Quartzsite, Ariz. |
| NATION'S INSURANCE CAPITAL | Hartford, Conn. |

| | |
|---|---|
| NATION'S LARGEST BASQUE COLONY | Boise, Idaho |
| NATION'S LARGEST COMMUNICATIONS CENTER | New York, N.Y. |
| NATION'S LARGEST PORT | New York, N.Y. |
| NATION'S LARGEST WINTER WHEAT MARKET | Kansas City, Mo. |
| NATION'S MOST BEAUTIFUL CITY | Seattle, Wash. |
| NATION'S MOST EXCITING NEW CONVENTION CENTER | Houston, Tex. |
| NATION'S MOST HISTORIC AREA | Beaufort, S.C. |
| NATION'S MOST HOSPITABLE CITY | Baltimore, Md. |
| NATION'S NO. 1 CONVENTION CITY | Chicago, Ill. |
| NATION'S NO. 3 POTATO CENTER, SOON THE FIRST | Grafton, S.D. |
| NATION'S OLDEST CITY | St. Augustine, Fla. |
| NATION'S OLDEST SEASHORE RESORT | Cape May, N.J. |
| NATION'S OTHER CAPITAL | Key West, Fla. |
| NATION'S PEONY CENTER | Van Wert, Ohio |
| NATION'S RESIDENTIAL RESEARCH CENTER | Monroeville, Pa. |
| NATION'S SAFEST BEACH | White Lake, N.C. |
| NATION'S SEAFOOD CENTER | Biloxi, Miss. |
| NATION'S SECOND LARGEST MACHINE-TOOL CENTER | Rockford, Ill. |
| NATION'S SMOG CAPITAL | Los Angeles, Calif. |
| NATION'S SOUTHERNMOST CITY | Key West, Fla. |
| NATION'S STATE | Washington, D.C. |
| NATION'S SUGAR BOWL | Pahokee, Fla. |
| NATION'S SUMMER CAPITAL | Rehoboth Beach, Del. |
| NATION'S THOROUGHFARE | Louisville, Ky. |
| NATION'S WESTERN CAPITAL | San Francisco, Calif. |
| NATION'S WOOD CAPITAL | Jasper, Ind. |
| NATIVE CITY OF BENJAMIN FRANKLIN | Philadelphia, Pa. |
| NATURAL CITY | Huron, S.D. |
| NATURAL GAS CAPITAL OF THE U.S. | Hugoton, Kan. |
| NATURAL GAS CITY | Bradford, Pa. |
| NATURAL GAS PIPELINE CAPITAL OF THE NATION | Houston, Tex. |
| NATURAL GATEWAY TO SOUTHERN CALIFORNIA'S ENDLESS CHARM | Long Beach, Calif. |
| NATURAL LOCATION FOR AGRICULTURAL INDUSTRY | Fargo, N.D. |
| NATURAL PORT CITY | Apalachicola, Fla. |
| NATURAL TRADING CENTER | Merrill, Wis. |
| NATURE'S AIR CONDITIONED CITY | Bluefield, W.Va. |

| | |
|---|---|
| NATURE'S AIRCONDITIONED CITY | Bluefield, Va. |
| NATURE'S GIFT TO TEXAS | Houston, Tex. |
| NATURE'S GIFT TO THE GOLD COAST | Pass Christian, Miss. |
| NATURE'S MIGHTY MASTERPIECE | Niagara Falls, N. Y. |
| NATURE'S PLAY GROUND | Libby, Mont. |
| NATURE'S UNDERWATER FAIRYLAND | Silver Springs, Fla. |
| NATURE'S WONDERLAND | Salida, Colo. |
| NAVAL CENTER | Newport, R. I. |
| NAVAL CENTER OF THE SOUTH | Jacksonville, Fla. |
| NAVAL STORES CAPITAL OF THE WORLD | Valdosta, Ga. |
| NAVY TOWN | Vallejo, Calif. |
| NAVY'S FIRST CITY OF THE SEA | Portsmouth, Va. |
| NEAR TO EVERYTHING EVERYWHERE | Lebanon, Mo. |
| NEARBY WONDER OF THE WORLD | Niagara Falls, N. Y. |
| NEAREST FLORIDA RESORT TO MOST OF THE NATION | Pensacola, Fla. |
| NEAREST METROPOLITAN CENTER TO ALL FIVE GATEWAYS OF RANIER NATIONAL PARK | Tacoma, Wash. |
| NEBRASKA'S FRIENDLY CITY | Plainview, Neb. |
| NEBRASKA'S GAME PARADISE | Norfolk, Neb. |
| NEBRASKA'S SPORT CENTER | Ogallala, Neb. |
| NEBRASKA'S THIRD CITY | Grand Island, Neb. |
| NEBRASKALAND'S BIG GAME CAPITAL | Chadron, Neb. |
| NEIGHBORLY FRIENDLY COMMUNITY | Fontana, Calif. |
| NEIGHBORLY SATISFYING COMMUN- ITY FOR LIVING | Plant City, Fla. |
| NEPTUNE TOWNSHIP'S OCEAN FRONT | Ocean Grove, N. J. |
| NERVE CENTER OF ALASKA | Anchorage, Alaska |
| NEVADA'S LARGEST CITY | Las Vegas, Nev. |
| NEVER-CLOSED CASINO CITY | Las Vegas, Nev. |
| NEW CAPITAL | Washington, D. C. |
| NEW CAR CAPITAL OF ARIZONA | Glendale, Ariz. |
| NEW CITY IN THE OLD SOUTH | Shreveport, La. |
| NEW CITY OF WASHINGTON | Washington, D. C. |
| NEW ENGLAND GARDEN SPOT | Norwalk, Conn. |
| NEW ENGLAND'S PLAYGROUND ON THE ATLANTIC | Salisbury Beach, Mass. |
| NEW ENGLAND'S TREASURE HOUSE | Salem, Mass. |
| NEW HEIGHT IN AMERICAN SKIING | Jackson, Wyo. |
| NEW HELVETIA | Sacramento, Calif. |
| NEW INDUSTRIAL FRONTIER OF THE SOUTHWEST | Odessa, Tex. |
| NEW JERUSALEM | Salt Lake City, Utah |

| | |
|---|---|
| NEW KIND OF CITY | Atlanta, Ga. |
| NEW MARKET | Tumwater, Wash. |
| NEW NATIONAL CITY | Atlanta, Ga. |
| NEW PLAYGROUND OF AMERICA | Pompano Beach, Fla. |
| NEW PUEBLO | Tucson, Ariz. |
| NEW RESORT AREA OF FLORIDA | Fort Myers, Fla. |
| NEW SETTLEMENT | Washington, D. C. |
| NEW WORLD PORT | Portsmouth, N. H. |
| NEW YORK OF NEBRASKA | Omaha, Neb. |
| NEW YORK OF THE SOUTH | Atlanta, Ga. |
| NEW YORK STATE'S COMPLETE ALL-SEASON RESORT | Lake Placid, N. Y. |
| NEW YORK STATE'S FIRST CAPITAL | Kingston, N. Y. |
| NEW YORK'S FIRST CAPITAL | Kingston, N. Y. |
| NEW YORK'S LAKE ERIE VACATION-LAND IN BEAUTIFUL CHAUTAUQUA COUNTY | Dunkirk, N. Y. |
| NEWARKS | Los Angeles, Calif. |
| NEWPORT OF CHICAGO SOCIETY | Lake Geneva, Wis. |
| NEWPORT OF THE EASTERN SHORE | Easton, Md. |
| NEWPORT OF THE PACIFIC | Santa Barbara, Calif. |
| NEWPORT OF THE SOUTH | Beaufort, S. C. |
| NEWPORT OF THE WEST | Colorado Springs, Colo. |
| NEWS CAPITAL OF THE WORLD | Washington, D. C. |
| NEXT STATION TO HEAVEN | New Canaan, Conn. |
| NIAGARA OF PENNSYLVANIA | Bushkill, Pa. |
| NIAGARA OF THE SOUTH | Muscle Shoals, Ala. |
| NIAGARA OF THE WEST | Great Falls, Mont. |
| NICE PLACE TO LIVE | Chowchilla, Calif. |
| NINE HILLS | Richmond, Va. |
| NINETEEN SUBURBS IN SEARCH OF A METROPOLIS | Los Angeles, Calif. |
| NORTH CAROLINA'S PLEASURE IS-LAND | Ocracoke, N. C. |
| NORTH CENTRAL FLORIDA'S SHOP-PING CENTER | Gainesville, Fla. |
| NORTH CENTRAL FLORIDA'S SHOP-PING HEADQUARTERS | Gainesville, Fla. |
| NORTH DAKOTA'S FAVORITE CON-VENTION CITY | Minot, N. D. |
| NORTH DAKOTA'S QUEEN CITY | Dickinson, N. D. |
| NORTH FLORIDA'S GRETNA GREEN | Macclenny, Fla. |
| NORTH GATEWAY TO THE KAYSINGER DAM AND RESERVOIR AREA | Windsor, Mo. |
| NORTH NEBRASKA'S LARGEST CITY | Norfolk, Neb. |

| | |
|---|---|
| NORTH SHORE HAVEN | Beaver Bay, Minn. |
| NORTH STAR CITY | St. Paul, Minn. |
| NORTHEASTERN GATEWAY TO THE GRAND LAKE RESORT AREA | Seneca, Mo. |
| NORTHEASTERN NORTH CAROLINA INDUSTRIAL CENTER | Roanoke Rapids, N. C. |
| NORTHEASTERNMOST CITY IN THE U. S. | Caribou, Me. |
| NORTHERN ENTRANCE TO THE SKY-LINE DRIVE, SHENANDOAH NATIONAL PARK | Front Royal, Va. |
| NORTHERN GATEWAY TO ALABAMA | Decatur, Ill. |
| NORTHERN GATEWAY TO BROWARD COUNTY | Deerfield Beach, Fla. |
| NORTHERN GATEWAY TO THE BAD-LANDS NATIONAL MONUMENT | Wall, S. D. |
| NORTHERN GATEWAY TO THE BEAU-TIFUL SHENANDOAH VALLEY | Winchester, Va. |
| NORTHERN GATEWAY TO THE BLACK HILLS | Belle Fourche, S. D. |
| NORTHERN GATEWAY TO THE NAT-URAL PARADISE BAXTER PARK | Patten, Me. |
| NORTHERN GATEWAY TO THE SHENANDOAH VALLEY | Winchester, Va. |
| NORTHERN MICHIGAN'S SHOPPING CENTER | Petoskey, Mich. |
| NORTHERN NEW MEXICO'S MOST UNIQUE VACATIONLAND | Taos, N. M. |
| NORTHERN PIKE CAPITAL OF THE WORLD | Mobridge, S. D. |
| NORTHERNMOST OASIS IN AMERICA | Twenty-Nine Palms, Calif. |
| NORTHWEST ARKANSAS' LARGEST CITY | Fayetteville, Ark. |
| NORTHWEST GATEWAY | Seattle, Wash. |
| NORTHWEST MONTANA'S BUSINESS AND SHOPPING CENTER | Kalispell, Mont. |
| NUMBER ONE HOST OF THE JERSEY COAST | Atlantic City, N. J. |

O

| | |
|---|---|
| OAK CITY | Raleigh, N. C. |
| OASIS IN MOUNTAIN COUNTRY | Powell, Wyo. |
| OASIS IN THE DESERT | Palm Springs, Calif. |
| OASIS OF NEVADA | Fallon, Nev. |

369

| | |
|---|---|
| OCEAN CITY | Fernandina Beach, Fla. |
| OCOSTA BY THE SEA | Ocosta, Wash. |
| OFFICIAL COWBOY CAPITAL OF NEBRASKA | Ogallala, Neb. |
| OGUNQUIT IS THE SEA | Ogunquit, Me. |
| OHIO'S BEAUTIFUL CAPITAL | Columbus, Ohio |
| OHIO'S CITY OF FRIENDS | Salem, Ohio |
| OHIO'S FIRST CAPITAL | Chillicothe, Ohio |
| OHIO'S FIRST CITY | Marietta, Ohio |
| OHIO'S MOST PROGRESSIVE CITY | Fairborn, Ohio |
| OHIO'S OLDEST AND MOST BEAUTIFUL CITY | Marietta, Ohio |
| OIL AND GAS CENTER OF THE GREAT ANADARKO BASIN | Perryton, Tex. |
| OIL CAPITAL | Jackson, Miss. |
| OIL CAPITAL | Mount Pleasant, Mich. |
| OIL CAPITAL | Tulsa, Okla. |
| OIL CAPITAL IN THE HEART OF THE WHEAT BELT | Great Bend, Kan. |
| OIL CAPITAL OF ALABAMA | Citronelle, Ala. |
| OIL CAPITAL OF ALASKA | Kenai, Alaska |
| OIL CAPITAL OF ARKANSAS | El Dorado, Ark. |
| OIL CAPITAL OF MISSISSIPPI | Yazoo City, Miss. |
| OIL CAPITAL OF MONTANA | Cut Bank, Mont. |
| OIL CAPITAL OF SOUTHWEST NE-BRASKA | Mc Cook, Neb. |
| OIL CAPITAL OF THE ROCKIES | Casper, Wyo. |
| OIL CAPITAL OF THE WORLD | Tulsa, Okla. |
| OIL CENTER | Midland, Tex. |
| OIL CENTER FOR MISSISSIPPI | Jackson, Miss. |
| OIL CENTER OF ILLINOIS | Centralia, Ill. |
| OIL CENTER OF THE WORLD | Houston, Tex. |
| OIL CITY | Bayonne, N. J. |
| OIL CITY | Casper, Wyo. |
| OIL CITY | Glenrock, Wyo. |
| OIL CITY | Montpelier, Ind. |
| OIL CITY OF THE SOUTHWEST | Odessa, Tex. |
| OIL, GAS, STEEL, CHEMICAL, CLAY, LUMBER CENTER | Marshall, Tex. |
| OIL WELL CEMENTING CAPITAL OF THE WORLD | Duncan, Tex. |
| OLD CHI | Chicago, Ill. |
| OLD CITY WITH A NEW FUTURE | Apalachicola, Fla. |
| OLD DORP | Schenectady, N. Y. |
| OLD FRENCH TOWN | New Orleans, La. |
| OLD GARRISON | San Antonio, Tex. |

| | |
|---|---|
| OLD GOLD HILL | San Francisco, Calif. |
| OLD MAID CITY, LOOKING UNDER HER BED EVERY NIGHT FOR AN OCEAN | Duluth, Minn. |
| OLD MART | Clarksville, Va. |
| OLD PUEBLO | Los Angeles, Calif. |
| OLD PUEBLO | Tucson, Ariz. |
| OLD SLAVE MARKET | Louisville, Ga. |
| OLD TOWN BY THE SEA | Portsmouth, N. H. |
| OLD WEST'S NEWEST CITY | New Town, N. D. |
| OLDEST AND QUAINTEST CITY IN THE UNITED STATES | Santa Fe, N. M. |
| OLDEST CHARTERED CITY IN THE UNITED STATES | Albany, N. Y. |
| OLDEST CITY IN THE UNITED STATES | St. Augustine, Fla. |
| OLDEST CITY IN THE UNITED STATES OPERATING UNDER ITS ORIGINAL CHARTER | Albany, N. Y. |
| OLDEST CITY WEST OF THE MISSISSIPPI | Ste Genevieve, Mo. |
| OLDEST CONTINUOUS ENGLISH-SPEAKING SETTLEMENT IN AMERICA | Hampton, Va. |
| OLDEST FRENCH CITY IN THE U. S. | Biloxi, Miss. |
| OLDEST INLAND CITY IN THE UNITED STATES | Lancaster, Pa. |
| OLDEST PORT IN THE WEST GULF | Galveston, Tex. |
| OLDEST SETTLEMENT IN MINNESOTA | Grand Portage, Minn. |
| OLDEST SPORT FISHING CENTER IN VIRGINIA | Wachapreague, Va. |
| OLDEST SUMMER RESORT IN AMERICA | Wolfeboro, N. H. |
| OLDEST TOWN IN NEVADA | Genoa, Nev. |
| OLDEST TOWN IN WEST VIRGINIA | Shepherdstown, W.Va. |
| OLDEST WHITE SETTLEMENT IN THE STATE | Salina, Okla. |
| OLEANDER CITY | Galveston, Tex. |
| OLEANDER CITY BY THE SEA | Galveston, Tex. |
| OLEMAN HOUSE | Port Madison, Wash. |
| OLYMPIC VILLAGE | Lake Placid, N. Y. |
| ONCE CONFEDERATE CAPITAL OF AMERICA | Cassville, Mo. |
| ONE HUNDRED SQUARE MILES OF PICTURESQUE PLEASURE | Marthas Vineyard, Mass. |

371

| | |
|---|---|
| ONE OF AMERICA'S FASTEST GROWING CITIES | Las Vegas, Nev. |
| ONE OF AMERICA'S FASTEST GROWING CITIES | Twin Falls, Idaho |
| ONE OF AMERICA'S FIFTY BEST VACATION SPOTS | Bemidji, Minn. |
| ONE OF AMERICA'S FOREMOST ALL-YEAR RESORTS | Asbury Park, N. J. |
| ONE OF AMERICA'S GREAT CITIES | Toledo, Ohio |
| ONE OF AMERICA'S GREATEST PLAYGROUNDS | St. Petersburg, Fla. |
| ONE OF AMERICA'S MOST IMPORTANT INLAND PORT CENTERS | Buffalo, N. Y. |
| ONE OF AMERICA'S MOST INTERESTING CITIES | Chattanooga, Tenn. |
| ONE OF AMERICA'S MOST INTERESTING CITIES | Montgomery, Ala. |
| ONE OF AMERICA'S MOST UNIQUE CITIES | Butte, Mont. |
| ONE OF AMERICA'S OLDEST PLAYGROUNDS | Lake Placid, N. Y. |
| ONE OF AMERICA'S OUTSTANDING CITIES | Newark, N. J. |
| ONE OF CALIFORNIA'S CHOICEST COMMUNITIES | Burlingame, Calif. |
| ONE OF FLORIDA'S FINEST SMALLER COMMUNITIES | Lake Alfred, Fla. |
| ONE OF GEORGIA'S GOLDEN ISLES | Jekyll Island, Ga. |
| ONE OF MISSISSIPPI'S FASTEST GROWING CITIES | Greenville, Miss. |
| ONE OF NEW ENGLAND'S MOST FAMOUS COAST RESORTS | Wells, Me. |
| ONE OF PENNSYLVANIA'S FASTEST GROWING COMMUNITIES | Ambler, Pa. |
| ONE OF THE BUSIEST FRESHWATER PORTS IN THE WORLD | Toledo, Ohio |
| ONE OF THE COUNTRY'S LEADING BURLEY MARKETS | Greenville, Tenn. |
| ONE OF THE FASTEST DEVELOPING AREAS IN THE NATION | Clarksville, Tenn. |
| ONE OF THE FASTEST GROWING AREAS IN THE NATION | Lorain, Ohio |
| ONE OF THE FASTEST GROWING CITIES IN THE NATION | Jackson, Miss. |
| ONE OF THE FASTEST GROWING RESORT CENTERS | Naples, Fla. |
| ONE OF THE FIRST AMERICAN CITIES OF THE INDUSTRIAL AGE | New Haven, Conn. |

| | |
|---|---|
| ONE OF THE GREAT NATURAL WONDERS OF THE WORLD | Silver Springs, Fla. |
| ONE OF THE LEADING HEALTH AND TOURIST RESORTS OF THE EAST | Asheville, N. C. |
| ONE OF THE LEADING TOBACCO MARKETS FOR BRIGHT LEAF TOBACCO | Henderson, N. C. |
| ONE OF THE MOST ACCESSIBLE CITIES IN THE EASTERN STATES | Springfield, Mass. |
| ONE OF THE MOST COLORFUL CITIES IN AMERICA | Butte, Mont. |
| ONE OF THE MOST FASIONABLE WINTER RESORTS OF THE SOUTH | Aiken, S. C. |
| ONE OF THE MOST FAVORABLE WINTER RESORTS OF THE SOUTH | Aiken, S. C. |
| ONE OF THE NATION'S LARGEST SPRING LAMB PRODUCING CENTERS | Lexington, Ky. |
| ONE OF THE SOUTH'S FASTEST GROWING CITIES | Jackson, Miss. |
| ONE OF THE SOUTH'S FOREMOST EDUCATIONAL CENTERS | Lexington, Ky. |
| ONE OF THE WORLD'S GREAT AIRPLANE MANUFACTURING CENTERS | Wichita, Kan. |
| ONE OF THE WORLD'S LARGEST LONG-STAPLE COTTON MARKETS | Greenwood, Miss. |
| ONE OF THE WORLD'S LARGEST MANUFACTURERS OF CIGARETTES | Richmond, Va. |
| ONE OF THE WORLD'S LARGEST ROSE GROWING CENTERS | Pana, Ill. |
| ONE OF THE WORLD'S LEADING CONVENTION CENTERS | Albuquerque, N. M. |
| ONE OF WISCONSIN'S FASTEST GROWING CITIES | Beloit, Wis. |
| ONLY CEDARTOWN IN THE U. S. A. | Cedartown, Ga. |
| ONLY ELECTRIC-LIGHTED CEMETERY IN THE UNITED STATES | Butte, Mont. |
| ONLY GRAND FORKS IN THE NATION | Grand Forks, N. D. |
| ONLY HENNIKER ON EARTH | Henniker, N. H. |
| ONLY TOWN IN THE UNITED STATES WITH AN APOSTROPHE IN ITS NAME | Coeur d'Alene, Idaho |
| ONLY TWIN CITIES IN SOUTH CAROLINA | Batesburg, S. C. |
| ONLY TWIN CITIES IN SOUTH CAROLINA | Leesville, S. C. |
| OPPORTUNITY CITY | Indianapolis, Ind. |

| | |
|---|---|
| OPPORTUNITY FOR HISTORY | Gonzalez, Tex. |
| OPTIMIST CITY | Sheridan, Wyo. |
| ORANGE CAPITAL OF THE WORLD | Eustis, Fla. |
| ORCHARD CITY | Burlington, Iowa |
| ORCHID CAPITAL OF HAWAII | Hilo, Hawaii |
| ORE AND GRAIN PORT | Duluth, Minn. |
| OREGON'S BEAUTIFUL CAPITAL CITY | Salem, Ore. |
| OREGON'S OWN HOMEBASE FOR FUN, CULTURE AND SCENIC SPLENDOR | Forest Grove, Ore. |
| ORGAN TOWN | Brattleboro, Vt. |
| ORIGINAL SITE OF CALIFORNICATION | Los Angeles, Calif. |
| ORIGINAL WINTER RESORT OF THE SOUTH | Thomasville, Ga. |
| OUR LADY OF THE ANGELS | Port Angeles, Wash. |
| OUTDOORMAN'S PARADISE | Bristol, Tenn. |
| OUTSTANDING AMERICAN CITY | Cambridge, Mass. |
| OVER A MILE HIGH, A MILE LONG, A MILE WIDE AND A MILE DEEP | Lead, S. D. |
| OVERGROWN COUNTRY TOWN | Cleveland, Ohio |
| OVERGROWN COW TOWN | Kansas City, Mo. |
| OVERGROWN SMALL TOWN | Detroit, Mich. |
| OVERGROWN VILLAGE | Buffalo, N. Y. |
| OYSTER CENTER OF THE STATE | Houma, La. |
| OZARK WONDERLAND | Harrison, Ark. |
| OZARK'S WESTERN GATEWAY | Vinita, Okla. |

P

| | |
|---|---|
| PACEMAKER OF THE PIEDMONT | Gastonia, N. C. |
| PACESETTER OF PROGRESS | Philadelphia, Pa. |
| PACIFIC NORTHWEST'S MOST PRO-GRESSIVE COMMUNITY | Boise, Idaho |
| PACKERS' TOWN | Green Bay, Wis. |
| PAINCOURT | St. Louis, Mo. |
| PAINTERS' PARADISE | Copperhill, Tenn. |
| PALACE OF KING COTTON | Waco, Tex. |
| PALM CITY | Phoenix, Ariz. |
| PALMETTO CITY | Charleston, S. C. |
| PANAMA PORT | Pensacola, Fla. |
| PANCAKE CENTER | Liberal, Kan. |
| PANCAKE CENTER OF THE WORLD | Liberal, Kan. |
| PANHANDLER'S HEAVEN | Boston, Mass. |
| PANTHER CITY | Fort Worth, Tex. |
| PAPER CITY | Holyoke, Mass. |
| PAPER CITY | Johnsonburg, Pa. |
| PAPER CITY | Neenah, Wis. |
| PAPER CITY OF THE WORLD | Neenah, Wis. |
| PARADISE IN A NUT SHELL | Walnut Creek, Calif. |

374

| | |
|---|---|
| PARADISE IN THE PINES | Crockett, Tex. |
| PARADISE OF FISHING, HUNTING AND SWIMMING | Blountstown, Fla. |
| PARADISE OF NEW ENGLAND | Salem, Mass. |
| PARADISE OF THE SOUTH | Miami, Fla. |
| PARADISE SULLIED | Los Angeles, Calif. |
| PARENT OF THE WEST | St. Louis, Mo. |
| PARIS OF AMERICA | Cincinnati, Ohio |
| PARIS OF AMERICA | New Orleans, La. |
| PARIS OF AMERICA | San Francisco, Calif. |
| PARIS OF THE PACIFIC | Sitka, Alaska |
| PARISH OF UNITY | South Berwick, Me. |
| PARK CITY | Bridgeport, Conn. |
| PARK CITY | New Rochelle, N. Y. |
| PARK PLACE | Monroe, Wash. |
| PARKING LOT CITY | St. Louis, Mo. |
| PARLOR CITY | Binghamton, N. Y. |
| PARLOR CITY | Cedar Rapids, Iowa |
| PARROT'S PARADISE | Ormond Beach, Fla. |
| PATHWAY TO PROGRESS | Buffalo, N. Y. |
| PAUL BUNYAN'S CAPITAL | Brainerd, Minn. |
| PEACEFUL VALLEY IN THE HEART OF THE GREEN MOUNTAINS | Waitsfield, Vt. |
| PEACH BOWL OF THE UNITED STATES | Marysville, Calif. |
| PEACH BOWL OF THE UNITED STATES | Yuba City, Calif. |
| PEACH CAPITAL OF ARKANSAS | Nashville, Ark. |
| PEACH CAPITAL OF TEXAS | Stonewall, Tex. |
| PEACH CAPITAL OF THE WORLD | Modesto, Calif. |
| PEACH CENTER | Fort Valley, Ga. |
| PEACH CENTER OF TEXAS | Johnson City, Tex. |
| PEANUT CAPITAL OF THE WORLD | Blakely, Ga. |
| PEANUT CAPITAL OF THE WORLD | Enterprise, Ala. |
| PEANUT CITY | Suffolk, Va. |
| PEAR CITY | Medford, Ore. |
| PEARL CITY | Muscatine, Iowa |
| PEARL OF THE SOUTH | Anniston, Ala. |
| PECAN CAPITAL OF THE WORLD | Chandler, Okla. |
| PEERLESS PRINCESS OF THE PLAINS | Wichita, Kan. |
| PENN STATE CITY | State College, Pa. |
| PENN'S TOWN | Reading, Pa. |
| PENNSYLVANIA ATHENS | Wellsboro, Pa. |
| PENNSYLVANIA'S ABOVE-AVERAGE MARKET OF INDUSTRY AND AGRICULTURE | Lancaster, Pa. |
| PENNSYLVANIA'S CAPITAL CITY | Harrisburg, Pa. |

| | |
|---|---|
| PENNSYLVANIA'S HIGHEST CITY | Hazleton, Pa. |
| PENNSYLVANIA'S NEW VACATION-LAND | Huntingdon, Pa. |
| PEONY CAPITOL OF THE WORLD | Sarcoxie, Mo. |
| PEONY CENTER OF THE WORLD | Faribault, Minn. |
| PEOPLES' CITY | Demopolis, Ala. |
| PERCHVILLE, U. S. A. | Tawas City, Mich. |
| PERFECT PLACE FOR GROWING UP | Brookhaven, Miss. |
| PERFECT PLAYGROUND FOR THE YOUNG IN HEART | Pompana Beach, Fla. |
| PERFECT SPOT TO WORK, TO PLAY, TO ENJOY LIFE | Dothan, Ala. |
| PERFECT VACATION SPOT | Rockaway Beach, Mo. |
| PERMANENT HOME OF THE PINE | Cass Lake, Minn. |
| PERRY DAVIS' PAIN KILLER CITY | Providence, R. I. |
| PETROLEUM WORLD CENTER | Houston, Tex. |
| PETUNIA CAPITAL | New Hampton, Iowa |
| PETUNIA CAPITAL OF THE WORLD | Webster, S. D. |
| PHEASANT CAPITAL OF KANSAS | Norton, Kan. |
| PHEASANT CAPITAL OF THE WORLD | Huron, S. D. |
| PHEASANT CAPITAL OF THE WORLD | Sioux Falls, S. D. |
| PHEASANT COUNTRY | Denver, Iowa |
| PHEASANT PARADISE OF AMERICA | Howard, S. D. |
| PHENOMINAL EXAMPLE OF AMERICAN GROWTH | Aliquippa, Pa. |
| PHILLY | Philadelphia, Pa. |
| PHOENIX CITY | Chicago, Ill. |
| PHOENIX OF THE PACIFIC | San Francisco, Calif. |
| PHOTOGENIC SUN CAPITAL OF THE EAST | Miami Beach, Fla. |
| PHOTOGRAPHER'S PARADISE | Valdez, Alaska |
| PHOTOGRAPHIC AND OPTICAL CENTER OF THE WORLD | Rochester, N. Y. |
| PHOTOGRAPHY CAPITAL | Rochester, N. Y. |
| PICNIC CITY | Mobile, Ala. |
| PICTURESQUE HEART OF CENTRAL FLORIDA | Haines City, Fla. |
| PICTURESQUE OLD WORLD VILLAGE | St. Donatus, Iowa |
| PIG'S EYE | St. Paul, Minn. |
| PIGOPOLIS | Chicago, Ill. |
| PIGOPOLIS | Cincinnati, Ohio |
| PILGRIM LAND | Plymouth, Mass. |
| PIMIENTO CENTER OF THE WORLD | Griffin, Ga. |
| PINE TREE COUNTRY | Swainsboro, Ga. |
| PINHOOK | Independence, Va. |
| PIONEER MORMON CITY | Provo, Utah |

| | |
|---|---|
| PIONEER RESORT TOWN | Winslow, Ark. |
| PIONEERING CENTER OF AVIATION | Dayton, Ohio |
| PIPELINE CAPITAL OF THE WORLD | Drumright, Okla. |
| PIPELINE CAPITOL OF AMERICA | Shreveport, La. |
| PIPELINE CENTER OF THE NATION | Lima, Ohio |
| PITTSBURGH OF NEW JERSEY | Dover, N. J. |
| PITTSBURGH OF THE BIG WEST | Terre Haute, Ind. |
| PITTSBURGH OF THE SOUTH | Birmingham, Ala. |
| PITTSBURGH OF THE WEST | Joliet, Ill. |
| PIVOT CITY OF THE CENTRAL SOUTH | Shreveport, La. |
| PIVOT CITY OF THE GREAT LAKES | Toledo, Ohio |
| PIVOT CITY OF THE SOUTH | Shreveport, La. |
| PIVOT OF THE PIEDMONT | Greensboro, N. C. |
| PLACE BY THE WINDING RIVER | Haverhill, Mass. |
| PLACE IN THE SUN TO VISIT, TO PLAY, TO WORK, TO LIVE | Edgewater, Fla. |
| PLACE FOR VACATIONS YEAR 'ROUND AND FOR YEAR 'ROUND LIVING | Fryeburg, Me. |
| PLACE OF GOOD ABODE | Memphis, Tenn. |
| PLACE OF MANY WATERS | Walla Walla, Wash. |
| PLACE TO ENJOY YOURSELF | Missoula, Mont. |
| PLACE TO LIVE | Norwalk, Conn. |
| PLACE TO LIVE | Washington, Mo. |
| PLACE TO LIVE, A PLACE TO WORK | Anderson, S. C. |
| PLACE TO LIVE, RELAX AND PLAY-- NIGHT AND DAY | Wareham, Mass. |
| PLACE TO LIVE, RELAX AND PLAY... ON MILES OF WATER | Ruskin, Fla. |
| PLACE TO LIVE, WORK OR PLAY | Denmark, Me. |
| PLACE TO GO IN FLORIDA | Fort Lauderdale, Fla. |
| PLACE WHERE CALIFORNIA BEGAN | San Diego, Calif. |
| PLACE WHERE EVERY DAY'S A HOLIDAY | Las Vegas, Nev. |
| PLACE WHERE FUN NEVER STOPS | Los Angeles, Calif. |
| PLACE WHERE LAKE MEETS FOREST | Grand Marais, Minn. |
| PLACE WHERE THE SUNSHINE AND SEA MEET | Blue Lake, Calif. |
| PLAINS EMPIRE CITY | Aberdeen, Wash. |
| PLANK ISLAND | Amarillo, Tex. |
| PLANNED GROWING CITY | Garden Grove, Calif. |
| PLAY AROUND THE CLOCK TIME | Las Vegas, Nev. |
| PLAYGROUND FOR VACATIONERS | Gonzalez, Tex. |
| PLAYGROUND OF PAUL BUNYON | Blaney Park, Mich. |
| PLAYGROUND OF PRESIDENTS | Superior, Wis. |
| PLAYGROUND OF SOUTHERN CALIFORNIA | San Bernardino, Calif. |

| | |
|---|---|
| PLAYGROUND OF THE ADIRONDACKS | Schroon Lake, N. Y. |
| PLAYGROUND OF THE AMERICAS | Miami, Fla. |
| PLAYGROUND OF THE AMERICAS | Miami Beach, Fla. |
| PLAYGROUND OF THE DESERT | Las Vegas, Nev. |
| PLAYGROUND OF THE DUNES | Gary, Ind. |
| PLAYGROUND OF THE NORTHWEST | Seaside, Ore. |
| PLAYGROUND OF THE "NOW" SET | Las Vegas, Nev. |
| PLAYGROUND OF THE WORLD | Atlantic City, N. J. |
| PLAYGROUND OF THE WORLD | Las Vegas, Nev. |
| PLAYGROUND OF VACATIONLAND | Old Orchard Beach, Me. |
| | |
| PLAYTOWN, U. S. A. | Decatur, Ill. |
| PLAYTOWN, U. S. A. | Las Vegas, Nev. |
| PLEASANT ALL YEAR VACATION CENTER | Pensacola, Fla. |
| PLEASANT PLACE TO LIVE AND WORK | Altoona, Pa. |
| PLEASANT PLACE TO VISIT | Mitchell, S. D. |
| PLOUGH-SHARE CITY | York, Pa. |
| PLOW CITY | Moline, Ill. |
| PLUMB LINE PORT TO PANAMA | Charleston, S. C. |
| PLYMOUTH OF THE PACIFIC COAST | San Diego, Calif. |
| PLYMOUTH OF THE WEST | San Diego, Calif. |
| PLYMOUTH OF THE WESTERN RE-SERVE | Conneaut, Ohio |
| PLYWOOD CAPITAL OF THE WORLD | New Albany, Ind. |
| POINSETTIA CITY | Ventura, Calif. |
| POINT OF OPPORTUNITY | West Point, Miss. |
| POKER CITY | Gardena, Calif. |
| POKER-PLAYING CAPITAL OF THE WEST | Gardena, Calif. |
| POLISH CITY | Hamtramck, Mich. |
| POLISH CITY IN TEXAS | Panna Maria, Tex. |
| POLITICAL FRONT | Washington, D. C. |
| POLK COUNTY'S LARGEST CITY | Lakeland, Fla. |
| POLO CAPITAL OF THE SOUTH | Aiken, S. C. |
| PONY EXPRESS CITY | Gothenburg, Neb. |
| POOR MAN'S PARADISE | San Francisco, Calif. |
| | |
| POPULAR CONVENTION CITY | Asheville, N. C. |
| POPULAR CONVENTION CITY | Duluth, Minn. |
| POPULAR SUMMER RESORT | Brevard, N. C. |
| POPULAR VACATION LAND | Jacksonville, Fla. |
| POPULATION CENTER | Worcester, Mass. |
| POPULATION CENTER OF TEXAS | Temple, Tex. |
| POPULATION CENTER, U. S. A. | Centralia, Ill. |
| PORK CITY | Chicago, Ill. |

| PORKOPOLIS | Chicago, Ill. |
| PORKOPOLIS | Cincinnati, Ohio |
| PORKOPOLIS OF IOWA | Burlington, Iowa |
| PORT AND PLAYGROUND OF THE SOUTHWEST | Galveston, Tex. |
| PORT CITY | Beaumont, Tex. |
| PORT CITY | Mobile, Ala. |
| PORT CITY | Portsmouth, N. H. |
| PORT CITY OF THE CORN BELT | Muscatine, Iowa |
| PORT CITY OF THE DELTA | Greenville, Miss. |
| PORT O' MISSING MEN | San Francisco, Calif. |
| PORT OF DISTINCTION | Green Bay, Wis. |
| PORT OF ENTRY | Port Townsend, Wash. |
| PORT OF ENTRY TO THE MISSOURI GREAT LAKES | Yankton, S. D. |
| PORT OF FRIENDLINESS | Avalon, Calif. |
| PORT OF GOLD | San Francisco, Calif. |
| PORT OF HOSPITALITY ON THE GREAT FATHER OF WATERS | Davenport, Iowa |
| PORT OF LAST CALL | Mystic, Conn. |
| PORT OF MANY PORTS | New York, N. Y. |
| PORT OF PERSONAL SERVICE | Wilmington, Del. |
| PORT OF SEA CAPTAINS | Coupeville, Wash. |
| PORT OF THE PILGRIMS | Provincetown, Mass. |
| PORT OF THE SOUTHWEST | Galveston, Tex. |
| PORTAGE | Granite Falls, Wash. |
| PORTAGE CITY | Hollidaysburg, Pa. |
| PORTAL TO ROMANCE | Sitka, Alaska |
| PORTAL TO THE QUINT STATES | Salida, Colo. |
| POSTMARK OF DISTINCTIVE TRADE-MARKS | Hamilton, Ohio |
| POST CITY | Lawton, Okla. |
| POTATO CAPITAL OF THE WEST | Monte Vista, Colo. |
| POTATO CAPITOL | Shafter, Calif. |
| POTTERY CENTER | East Liverpool, Ohio |
| POTTERY CITY | Zanesville, Ohio |
| POULTRY CAPITAL OF THE WORLD | Gainesville, Ga. |
| POWER CITY | American Falls, Idaho |
| POWER CITY | Fulton, N. Y. |
| POWER CITY | Keokuk, Iowa |
| POWER CITY | Niagara Falls, N. Y. |
| POWER CITY | Rochester, N. Y. |
| POWER CITY | Stanton, N. D. |

| | |
|---|---|
| POWER CITY OF SCENIC WONDERS | Niagara Falls, N. Y. |
| POWERHOUSE OF THE NIAGARA FRONTIER | Niagara Falls, N. Y. |
| PRAIRIE | Chicago, Ill. |
| PRAIRIE CITY | Bloomington, Ill. |
| PRALINE CAPITAL OF THE WORLD | Bay St. Louis, Miss. |
| PRECISION CITY | Waltham, Mass. |
| PREEMINENT VACATION CENTER | Asheville, N. C. |
| PRETTIEST LITTLE TOWN THIS SIDE OF HEAVEN | Winter Haven, Fla. |
| PRETTIEST RESORT IN THE WORLD | Daytona Beach, Fla. |
| PRETTIEST SMALL TOWN BETWEEN NEW YORK AND MAINE | Manning, S. C. |
| PRETTIEST SMALL TOWN BETWEEN NEW YORK AND MIAMI | Manning, S. C. |
| PRETTIEST TOWN IN DIXIE | Cheraw, S. C. |
| PRETZEL CITY | Lancaster, Pa. |
| PRETZEL CITY | Reading, Pa. |
| PRIDE OF THE MISSISSIPPI VALLEY | St. Louis, Mo. |
| PRIDE OF THE PACIFIC | Long Beach, Calif. |
| PRIME BEEF CENTER OF THE WORLD | De Witt, Iowa |
| PRIME BEEF CENTER OF THE WORLD | Monmouth, Ill. |
| PRIME RESIDENTIAL COMMUNITY IN THE BAY AREA | El Cerrito, Calif. |
| PRINCESS CITY OF PUGET SOUND | Edmonds, Wash. |
| PRISON CITY | Jackson, Mich. |
| PRIVATE FLYING CAPITAL OF THE WORLD | Lock Haven, Pa. |
| PROBLEM CAPITOL OF THE WORLD | Washington, D. C. |
| PROFIT CENTER OF THE SOUTHWEST | Phoenix, Ariz. |
| PROGRESS CITY OF THE ROCKIES | Casper, Wyo. |
| PROGRESS THROUGH VISION | Hershey, Pa. |
| PROGRESSIVE AMERICAN CITY | Springfield, Ill. |
| PROGRESSIVE CITY | Athens, Tenn. |
| PROGRESSIVE CITY | Augusta, Ga. |
| PROGRESSIVE CITY | Brunswick, Ga. |
| PROGRESSIVE CITY | Eau Gallie, Fla. |
| PROGRESSIVE CITY | Grand Isle, Neb. |
| PROGRESSIVE CITY | Keokuk, Iowa |
| PROGRESSIVE CITY | Memphis, Tenn. |
| PROGRESSIVE CITY | Peoria, Ill. |
| PROGRESSIVE CITY | Sioux Falls, S. D. |
| PROGRESSIVE CITY PLANNING TODAY FOR THE EVENTS OF TOMORROW | Brunswick, Ga. |
| PROGRESSIVE CITY WITH A BRIGHT FUTURE | Norwalk, Conn. |

| | |
|---|---|
| PROGRESSIVE CITY WITH THE RICH HERITAGE AND CHARM OF THE OLD RIVER DAYS | Davenport, Iowa |
| PROGRESSIVE COMMUNITY | Belleview, Fla. |
| PROGRESSIVE COMMUNITY | Clewiston, Fla. |
| PROGRESSIVE COMMUNITY | Moultrie, Ga. |
| PROGRESSIVE COMMUNITY WITH A BRIGHT FUTURE | Belleview, Fla. |
| PROGRESSIVE GATEWAY CITY TO THE DAKOTAS | Sioux Falls, S. D. |
| PROGRESSIVE METROPOLIS | Lynchburg, Va. |
| PROGRESSIVE, PROSPEROUS AND PEACEFUL COMMUNITY | Lewiston, Me. |
| PROGRESSIVELY GROWING WELL-SEASONED CITY | Springfield, Ohio |
| PROUD CITY | Bridgeport, Conn. |
| PROUD CITY WITH A BRIGHT FUTURE | Maiden, Mass. |
| PROUD PORT OF THE PACIFIC | Long Beach, Calif. |
| PROUDEST SMALL TOWN IN AMER-ICA | Cadiz, Ohio |
| PROVEN PROGRESSIVE CITY | Salina, Kan. |
| PUMPKIN CAPITAL OF THE WORLD | Eureka, Ill. |
| PURPLE MARTIN CAPITAL OF THE WORLD | Griggsville, Ill. |
| PURE BRED JERSEY CAPITAL OF AMERICA | Carthage, Mo. |
| PURITAN CITY | Boston, Mass. |
| PURITAN ZION | Boston, Mass. |
| PUSH ROOT | Lander, Wyo. |

Q

| | |
|---|---|
| QUAD CITIES | East Moline, Moline, Rock Island, Ill., and Davenport, Iowa |
| QUAIL HAVEN | Cedar Vale, Kan. |
| QUAKER CITY | Newberg, Ore. |
| QUAKER CITY | Philadelphia, Pa. |
| QUAKER CITY | Salem, Ohio |
| QUAKER CITY | Whittier, Calif. |
| QUAKER CITY OF THE WEST | Richmond, Ind. |
| QUAKER TOWN | Wilmington, Del. |
| QUAKERTOWN | Philadelphia, Pa. |
| QUALITY CITY | Niagara Falls, N. Y. |
| QUALITY CITY | Rochester, N. Y. |
| QUEEN CITY | Allentown, Pa. |
| QUEEN CITY | Alma, Ga. |
| QUEEN CITY | Bangor, Me. |

| | |
|---|---|
| QUEEN CITY | Burlington, Vt. |
| QUEEN CITY | Charlotte, N. C. |
| QUEEN CITY | Cincinnati, Ohio |
| QUEEN CITY | Cumberland, Md. |
| QUEEN CITY | Davenport, Iowa |
| QUEEN CITY | Dickinson, N. D. |
| QUEEN CITY | Galveston, Tex. |
| QUEEN CITY | Manchester, N. H. |
| QUEEN CITY | Marinette, Wis. |
| QUEEN CITY | San Francisco, Calif. |
| QUEEN CITY | Seattle, Wash. |
| QUEEN CITY | Sioux Falls, S. D. |
| QUEEN CITY | Spearfish, S. D. |
| QUEEN CITY | Williamsport, Pa. |
| QUEEN CITY IN THE GARDEN STATE | Plainfield, N. J. |
| QUEEN CITY OF ALABAMA | Gadsden, Ala. |
| QUEEN CITY OF FLORIDA'S SUGAR BOWL | Clewiston, Fla. |
| QUEEN CITY OF LAKE SUPERIOR | Marquette, Mich. |
| QUEEN CITY OF NEW HAMPSHIRE | Manchester, N. H. |
| QUEEN CITY OF NEW JERSEY | Plainfield, N. J. |
| QUEEN CITY OF SOUTHEAST KANSAS | Independence, Kan. |
| QUEEN CITY OF THE ARK-LA-TEX AREA | Shreveport, La. |
| QUEEN CITY OF THE BLACK BELT | Selma, Ala. |
| QUEEN CITY OF THE BORDER | Caldwell, Kan. |
| QUEEN CITY OF THE CHEROKEE STRIP | Enid, Okla. |
| QUEEN CITY OF THE COOSA | Gadsden, Ala. |
| QUEEN CITY OF THE COW TOWNS | Dodge City, Kan. |
| QUEEN CITY OF THE EAST | Bangor, Me. |
| QUEEN CITY OF THE GAS BELT | Marion, Ind. |
| QUEEN CITY OF THE GOLDEN VALLEY | Clinton, Mo. |
| QUEEN CITY OF THE GREAT LAKES | Buffalo, N. Y. |
| QUEEN CITY OF THE HILLS | Spearfish, S. D. |
| QUEEN CITY OF THE HUDSON | Yonkers, N. Y. |
| QUEEN CITY OF THE IRON RANGE | Virginia, Minn. |
| QUEEN CITY OF THE LAKES | Buffalo, N. Y. |
| QUEEN CITY OF THE LEHIGH VALLEY | Allentown, Pa. |
| QUEEN CITY OF THE MERRIMAC VALLEY | Manchester, N. H. |
| QUEEN CITY OF THE MIDLAND EMPIRE | Billings, Mont. |
| QUEEN CITY OF THE MISSISSIPPI | St. Louis, Mo. |
| QUEEN CITY OF THE MOUNTAINS | Knoxville, Tenn. |
| QUEEN CITY OF THE NORTHLAND | Marquette, Mich. |

| | |
|---|---|
| QUEEN CITY OF THE NORTHWEST | Dubuque, Iowa |
| QUEEN CITY OF THE OHIO | Cincinnati, Ohio |
| QUEEN CITY OF THE OHIO RIVER | Cincinnati, Ohio |
| QUEEN CITY OF THE OTTER TAIL EMPIRE | Fergus Falls, Minn. |
| QUEEN CITY OF THE OUACHITA | Camden, Ark. |
| QUEEN CITY OF THE OZARKS | Springfield, Mo. |
| QUEEN CITY OF THE PACIFIC | San Francisco, Calif. |
| QUEEN CITY OF THE PACIFIC | Seattle, Wash. |
| QUEEN CITY OF THE PACIFIC COAST | San Francisco, Calif. |
| QUEEN CITY OF THE PANHANDLE | Amarillo, Tex. |
| QUEEN CITY OF THE PLAINS | Denver, Colo. |
| QUEEN CITY OF THE PLAINS | Fort Worth, Tex. |
| QUEEN CITY OF THE PRAIRIES | Dickinson, N. D. |
| QUEEN CITY OF THE PRAIRIES | Fort Worth, Tex. |
| QUEEN CITY OF THE PRAIRIES | Sedalia, Mo. |
| QUEEN CITY OF THE RANGE | Virginia, Minn. |
| QUEEN CITY OF THE RIO GRANDE | Del Rio, Tex. |
| QUEEN CITY OF THE SEA | Charleston, S. C. |
| QUEEN CITY OF THE SHENANDOAH VALLEY | Staunton, Va. |
| QUEEN CITY OF THE SOUND | New Rochelle, N. Y. |
| QUEEN CITY OF THE SOUND | Seattle, Wash. |
| QUEEN CITY OF THE SOUTH | Charleston, S. C. |
| QUEEN CITY OF THE SOUTH | Richmond, Va. |
| QUEEN CITY OF THE TECHE | New Iberia, La. |
| QUEEN CITY OF THE TRAILS | Independence, Mo. |
| QUEEN CITY OF THE WEST | Cincinnati, Ohio |
| QUEEN CITY OF THE WEST | Denver, Colo. |
| QUEEN CITY OF THE WEST | San Francisco, Calif. |
| QUEEN CITY OF VERMONT | Burlington, Vt. |
| QUEEN OF AMERICA'S LAKES | Lake George, N. Y. |
| QUEEN OF AMERICAN LAKES | Lake George, N. Y. |
| QUEEN OF BEAUTY | Niagara Falls, N. Y. |
| QUEEN OF COW TOWNS | Dodge City, Kan. |
| QUEEN OF LAKE ERIE | Cleveland, Ohio |
| QUEEN OF RESORTS | Atlantic City, N. J. |
| QUEEN OF SUMMER RESORTS | Newport, R. I. |
| QUEEN OF THE AMERICAN LAKES | Lake George, N. Y. |
| QUEEN OF THE AMERICAN NILE | Memphis, Tenn. |
| QUEEN OF THE BEACHES | Long Beach, Calif. |
| QUEEN OF THE BRAZOS | Waco, Tex. |
| QUEEN OF THE COMSTOCK LODE | Virginia City, Nev. |
| QUEEN OF THE COW COUNTRIES | Los Angeles, Calif. |
| QUEEN OF THE COW TOWNS | Dodge City, Kan. |

| | |
|---|---|
| QUEEN OF THE GOLDEN EMPIRE | Sacramento, Calif. |
| QUEEN OF THE HILLS | Piedmont, Calif. |
| QUEEN OF THE LAKES | Buffalo, N. Y. |
| QUEEN OF THE LAKES | Chicago, Ill. |
| QUEEN OF THE MISSIONS | Santa Barbara, Calif. |
| QUEEN OF THE MOUNTAINS | Helena, Mont. |
| QUEEN OF THE NECHES | Beaumont, Tex. |
| QUEEN OF THE OHIO | Cincinnati, Ohio |
| QUEEN OF THE PACIFIC | San Francisco, Calif. |
| QUEEN OF THE RESORTS | Newport, R. I. |
| QUEEN OF THE SILVER CAMPS | Tonopah, Nev. |
| QUEEN OF THE SOUTH | New Orleans, La. |
| QUEEN OF THE SPAS | Saratoga Springs, N. Y. |
| QUEEN OF THE VALLEY | Glendale, Calif. |
| QUEEN OF THE WEST | Cincinnati, Ohio |
| QUEEN OF WORLD RESORTS | Newport, R. I. |
| QUEEN ON THE JAMES | Richmond, Va. |
| QUEEN SHOE CITY OF THE WORLD | Haverhill, Mass. |
| QUEEN VILLAGE OF THE ADIRON-DACKS | Warrensburg, N. Y. |

# R

| | |
|---|---|
| RADIANT GARDEN SPOT OF CALI-FORNIA | Redlands, Calif. |
| RAGTOWN | Altoona, Ga. |
| RAIL AND HARBOR CITY | Elizabeth, N. J. |
| RAIL CENTER | Buffalo, N. Y. |
| RAIL CENTER OF NEW ENGLAND | Worcester, Mass. |
| RAILROAD CENTER | Pierre, S. D. |
| RAILROAD CENTER SINCE 1850 | Crestline, Ohio |
| RAILROAD CITY | Altoona, Pa. |
| RAILROAD CITY | Atlanta, Ga. |
| RAILROAD CITY | Indianapolis, Ind. |
| RAILROAD CITY | St. Albans, Vt. |
| RAILROAD TOWN | Pierre, S. D. |
| RAILROAD METROPOLIS OF THE WEST | Milwaukee, Wis. |
| RAISIN CAPITAL OF THE WORLD | Selma, Calif. |
| RAISIN CENTER OF THE WORLD | Fresno, Calif. |
| RAISINLAND, U. S. A. | Dinuba, Calif. |
| RANCHING CENTER | Elko, Nev. |
| RAPID CITY | Cedar Rapids, Iowa |
| RAZOR CLAM CAPITAL OF THE WORLD | Cordova, Alaska |

| | |
|---|---|
| REAL HOOSIER CITY | New Albany, Ind. |
| REAL PARADISE FOR FAMILY LIVING | Crestview, Fla. |
| REAL WESTERN CITY | Pierre, S. D. |
| REBEL CAPITAL | Philadelphia, Pa. |
| RECREATION AND INDUSTRIAL CENTER OF EAST TEXAS | Marshall, Tex. |
| RECREATION CENTER | Anaheim, Calif. |
| RECREATION CENTER | Midland, Tex. |
| RECREATION CENTER OF THE WEST | Thermopolis, Wyo. |
| RECREATION CROSSROADS OF VERMONT | Waterbury, Vt. |
| RECREATION HUB OF THE HISTORICAL COLORFUL WEST | Sidney, Neb. |
| RECREATION PARADISE ON BEAUTIFUL LEWIS AND CLARK LAKE | Yankton, S. D. |
| RECREATIONAL CENTER | Madison, Wis. |
| RECREATIONAL CENTER | Mitchell, S. D. |
| RECREATIONAL CENTER FOR GENERATIONS | Bridgeport, Conn. |
| RECREATIONAL, EDUCATIONAL AND CULTURAL CENTER OF NORTHEASTERN OHIO | Youngstown, Ohio |
| RECREATIONAL INDUSTRIAL CITY | Duluth, Minn. |
| RECREATIONAL MECCA OF THE FABULOUS SOUTHEASTERN COAST OF FLORIDA | Lake Worth, Fla. |
| RECREATIONAL SLUM | Lake Tahoe, Calif. |
| RED LIGHT QUEEN | Muskegon, Mich. |
| RED ROSE CITY | Lancaster, Pa. |
| REFRIGERATION CAPITAL OF THE WORLD | Evansville, Ind. |
| REFUGE FROM RESORTS | Naples, Fla. |
| REGION OF GREAT NATURAL WONDERS | Belleview, Fla. |
| RENAISSANCE CITY OF AMERICA | Pittsburgh, Pa. |
| RESEARCH CENTER OF THE MIDWEST | Ann Arbor, Mich. |
| RESEARCH CITY | Stamford, Conn. |
| RESIDENTIAL HAVEN | Islip, N. Y. |
| RESIDENTIAL RESEARCH CENTER OF THE NATION | Monroeville, Pa. |
| RESORT AND CONVENTION PLAYGROUND OF THE ALLEGHENIES | Bedford, Pa. |
| RESORT AREA | Daytona Beach, Fla. |
| RESORT AREA OF CAPE KENNEDY | Cocoa Beach, Fla. |
| RESORT AREA OF THE ADIRONDACKS | Lake George, N. Y. |
| RESORT CITY OF BLUE RIDGE | Hendersonville, N. C. |
| RESORT OF ENJOYMENT | Asbury Park, N. J. |

385

| | |
|---|---|
| RESORT TOWN, U. S. A. | Estes Park, Colo. |
| RESORT TOWN WHERE THE FISHERMAN IS KING | Marathon, Fla. |
| RESORT WHERE FUN NEVER SETS | Surfside, Fla. |
| RESTING PLACE OF UNKNOWN AMERICAN SOLDIER | Arlington, Va. |
| RESTORED COLONIAL CITY | Williamsburg, Va. |
| RETAIL CENTER OF SOUTHWEST NEBRASKA AND NORTHEAST KANSAS | McCook, Neb. |
| RETAIL SHOPPING CENTER OF THE PENINSULA | San Mateo, Calif. |
| RETAIL, WHOLESALE, INDUSTRIAL, MEDICAL INSTITUTION CENTER OF KENTUCKY | Lexington, Ky. |
| RETIRE, RELAX, RELIVE | Ormand-by-the-Sea, Fla. |
| RETIREMENT CENTER | Harlingen, Tex. |
| RETIREMENT CENTER OF THE NATION | Tucson, Ariz. |
| RHODE ISLAND'S MOST HISTORIC TOWN | Newport, R. I. |
| RICE CAPITAL OF LOUISIANA | Crowley, La. |
| RICE CAPITAL OF LOUISIANA | Lake Charles, La. |
| RICE CAPITAL OF THE WORLD | Crowley, La. |
| RICE CENTER OF AMERICA | Crowley, La. |
| RICE CENTER OF THE U. S. A. | Hazen, Ark. |
| RICE CITY OF AMERICA | Crowley, La. |
| RICH AGRICULTURAL AND INDUSTRIAL HEARTLAND OF MID-AMERICA | Rockford, Ill. |
| RICHEST HILL ON EARTH | Butte, Mont. |
| RICHEST SQUARE MILE ON EARTH | Central City, Colo. |
| RICHEST TOWN IN THE WORLD | Brookline, Mass. |
| RICHEST VILLAGE ON EARTH | Hibbing, Minn. |
| RIFLE CITY | Springfield, Mass. |
| RIGHT CLIMATE FOR BUSINESS AND FAMILY LIVING | Bonifay, Fla. |
| RIVIERA OF AMERICA | Miami Beach, Fla. |
| ROBBERS' ROOST | Ellensburg, Wash. |
| ROBBERS' ROOST | Fruitland, Wash. |
| ROCK CAPITAL OF THE NATION | Dubois, Wyo. |
| ROCK CITY | Nashville, Tenn. |
| ROCK CITY | Wabash, Ind. |
| ROCK FISH CAPITAL OF THE WORLD | Weldon, N. C. |
| ROCKET CAPITAL OF THE NATION | Huntsville, Ala. |
| ROCKET CITY | Alamogordo, N. M. |
| ROCKET CITY | Huntsville, Ala. |

| | |
|---|---|
| ROCKET CITY, U. S. A. | Huntsville, Ala. |
| ROCKFISH CAPITAL | Weldon, N. C. |
| RODEO CITY | Ellensburg, Wash. |
| RODEO OF THE OZARKS TOWN | Springdale, Ark. |
| ROGER WILLIAMS CITY | Providence, R. I. |
| ROLLICKING, HILARIOUS TENT AND SHACK CITY | Lawton, Okla. |
| ROMAN GODDESS OF FRUIT TREES | Pomona, Wash. |
| ROOF GARDEN OF AMERICA | Salida, Colo. |
| ROOF GARDEN OF FLORIDA | Lake Placid, Fla. |
| ROOF GARDEN OF PENNSYLVANIA | Somerset, Pa. |
| ROOF GARDEN OF TEXAS | Alpine, Tex. |
| ROOF GARDEN RESORT OF TEXAS | Alpine, Tex. |
| ROSE CAPITAL | Tyler, Tex. |
| ROSE CAPITAL OF AMERICA | Newark, N. Y. |
| ROSE CAPITAL OF TEXAS | Tyler, Tex. |
| ROSE CAPITAL OF THE WORLD | Columbus, Ohio |
| ROSE CAPITAL OF THE WORLD | Tyler, Tex. |
| ROSE CENTER OF THE UNITED STATES | Richmond, Ind. |
| ROSE CITY | Jackson, Mich. |
| ROSE CITY | Madison, N. J. |
| ROSE CITY | Manheim, Pa. |
| ROSE CITY | Pleasantville, Iowa |
| ROSE CITY | Portland, Ore. |
| ROSE CITY | Thomasville, Ga. |
| ROSE OF NEW ENGLAND | Norwich, Conn. |
| ROSE TOWN | Lowell, Wyo. |
| ROUND-UP CITY | Pendleton, Ore. |
| ROYAL CITY | Santa Fe, N. M. |
| RUBBER CAPITAL OF THE UNITED STATES | Akron, Ohio |
| RUBBER CAPITAL OF THE WORLD | Akron, Ohio |
| RUBBER CITY | Akron, Ohio |
| RUSSIAN-AMERICAN CAPITAL | Sitka, Alaska |

S

| | |
|---|---|
| SACTO | Sacramento, Calif. |
| SADDLE HORSE CAPITAL OF THE WORLD | Mexico, Mo. |
| SAFE PLACE FOR CHILDREN | Jamestown, R. I. |
| SAFEST SPOT IN THE WORLD | Fort Collins, Colo. |
| SAILFISH CAPITAL OF THE WORLD | Stuart, Fla. |
| ST. ANTHONY'S TOWN | San Antonio, Tex. |
| ST. MORITZ OF THE ROCKIES | Anaconda, Mont. |
| ST. PETERSBURG OF TOM SAWYER | Hannibal, Mo. |
| SAINTLY CITY | St. Paul, Minn. |

387

| | |
|---|---|
| SAINTS REST | Oak Park, Ill. |
| SALAD BOWL OF AMERICA | Ruskin, Fla. |
| SALAD BOWL OF THE NATION | Ruskin, Fla. |
| SALMON CAPITAL OF ALASKA | Ketchikan, Alaska |
| SALMON CAPITAL OF THE WORLD | Ketchikan, Alaska |
| SALMON CITY | Astoria, Ore. |
| SALOON QUEEN | Muskegon, Mich. |
| SALT CITY | Hutchinson, Kan. |
| SALT CITY | Manistee, Mich. |
| SALT CITY | Syracuse, N. Y. |
| SALT WATER PEOPLE | Quilcene, Wash. |
| SALT WATER TROUT CAPITAL OF THE WORLD | Cocoa, Fla. |
| SAN BERDOO | San Bernardino, Calif. |
| SAND HILLS OF THE EASTERN BAR-BARIANS | San Francisco, Calif. |
| SANTA'S LOOKOUT | Middletown, Mass. |
| SANTA'S VILLAGE | Dundee, Ill. |
| SANTA'S VILLAGE | Jefferson, N. H. |
| SANTA'S VILLAGE | Lancaster, N. H. |
| SANTA'S WORKSHOP | North Pole, N. Y. |
| SARATOGA OF THE WEST | Waukesha, Wis. |
| SARDINE CAPITAL OF THE U. S. | Eastport, Me. |
| SATANIC CITY | Devils Lake, N. D. |
| SATURDAY TOWN | Decatur, Ala. |
| SAWDUST CITY | Lock Haven, Pa. |
| SAWDUST CITY | Minneapolis, Minn. |
| SAWDUST CITY | Muskegon, Mich. |
| SAWDUST CITY | Oshkosh, Wis. |
| SAWDUST CITY OF AMERICA | Williamsport, Pa. |
| SCENIC AND RECREATION CENTER OF ALASKA | Juneau, Alaska |
| SCENIC CALIFORNIA'S SCENIC PLAYGROUND | Santa Cruz, Calif. |
| SCENIC CAPITAL OF CENTRAL PENNSYLVANIA | Williamsport, Pa. |
| SCENIC CENTER OF THE SOUTH | Chattanooga, Tenn. |
| SCENIC CITY | Berlin, Pa. |
| SCENIC CITY OF FIVE FLAGS AT THE TOP OF THE GULF OF MEXICO | Pensacola, Fla. |
| SCENIC CITY OF NIGHTLESS SUMMER DAYS | Juneau, Alaska |
| SCENIC CITY OF SOUTHERN MINNESOTA | Redwood Falls, Minn. |

| | |
|---|---|
| SCENIC GATEWAY | Laurel, Mont. |
| SCENIC GATEWAY TO AMERICA | Niagara Falls, N.Y. |
| SCENIC HEALTH RESORT OF CALIFORNIA | Elsinore, Calif. |
| SCENIC HUB OF THE GOLDEN STATE | Fresno, Calif. |
| SCENIC LAND OF THE STANDING STONE | Huntingdon, Pa. |
| SCENIC SPORTLAND | Las Vegas, Nev. |
| SCHOLARSHIP CITY | Fall River, Mass. |
| SCIENCE CITY | New York, N.Y. |
| SCIENTIFIC CENTER | Rolla, Mo. |
| SCRAPPLE CITY | Allentown, Pa. |
| SCREENLAND | Hollywood, Calif. |
| SEA AND SAND VACATIONLAND | Sea Isle City, N.J. |
| SEA GATE TO THE SOUTHWEST | Lake Charles, La. |
| SEA TURTLE CAPITAL OF THE WORLD | Jensen Beach, Fla. |
| SEAFOOD CAPITAL OF THE WORLD | Crisfield, Md. |
| SEAPORT FOR THE LANDLOCKED STATE OF IDAHO | Lewiston, Idaho |
| SEAPORT OF IOWA | Los Angeles, Calif. |
| SEAPORT OF THE WEST | Galveston, Tex. |
| SEAPORT VILLAGE | Mystic, Conn. |
| SEAT OF EMPIRE | New York, N.Y. |
| SEAWAY VACATIONLAND | Massena, N.Y. |
| SECOND LARGEST AIRCRAFT PRODUCTION CENTER IN THE COUNTRY | Fort Worth, Tex. |
| SECOND LARGEST GRAIN SHIPPING CENTER OF THE NORTHWEST | Craigmont, Idaho |
| SECOND LARGEST RAILROAD CENTER IN THE UNITED STATES | Buffalo, N.Y. |
| SECOND MURDER CITY | Los Angeles, Calif. |
| SECOND OLDEST SETTLEMENT IN OKLAHOMA | Vinita, Okla. |
| SECOND ROME | Washington, D.C. |
| SEDATE CAPITAL OF THE BIBLE BELT | Oklahoma City, Okla. |
| SENTINEL CITY IN THE PINES | Prescott, Ariz. |
| SERVICE CENTER FOR INDUSTRIAL AGRICULTURE | Scotts Bluff, Neb. |
| SHADE TOBACCO CAPITAL | Quincy, Fla. |
| SHADE-GROWN TOBACCO CAPITAL | Quincy, Fla. |
| SHAKE-RAG | Mineral Point, Wis. |
| SHANGRI-LA OF ALASKA | Homer, Alaska |
| SHANGRI-LA OF THE WESTERN HEMISPHERE | Miami Beach, Fla. |
| SHIP-BUILDING CITY | Chester, Pa. |

389

| | |
|---|---|
| SHIPBUILDING CITY | Quincy, Mass. |
| SHIP HARBOR | Anacortes, Wash. |
| SHIPPING CENTER OF THE SOUTH-WEST | Dodge City, Kan. |
| SHIPPING CITY | Bath, Me. |
| SHIRE CITY OF ANDROSCOGGIN COUNTY | Auburn, Me. |
| SHIRE CITY OF WALDO COUNTY | Belfast, Me. |
| SHIRE TOWN AND HUB OF THE COUNTY | Farmington, Me. |
| SHOE AND SLIPPER CITY | Norwalk, Conn. |
| SHOE CAPITAL OF THE WORLD | Lynn, Mass. |
| SHOE CITY | Auburn, Me. |
| SHOE CITY | Hanover, Pa. |
| SHOE CITY | Johnson City, N. Y. |
| SHOE CITY | Lynn, Mass. |
| SHOE TOWN | Haverhill, Mass. |
| SHOPPING CENTER OF CHESTER COUNTY | West Chester, Pa. |
| SHOPPING CENTER OF NORTHERN MAINE | Houlton, Me. |
| SHOPPING CENTER OF THE APPA-LACHIANS | Bristol, Tenn. and Bristol, Va. |
| SHOPPING CENTER OF THE RARITAN BAY AREA | Perth Amboy, N. J. |
| SHOPPING CENTER OF WESTERN VIRGINIA | Roanoke, Va. |
| SHORE VILLAGE | Guilford, Conn. |
| SHOVEL CITY OF THE WORLD | Marion, Ohio |
| SHOW COUNTRY OF NEW ENGLAND | Pittsfield, Mass. |
| SHOW PLACE OF SOUTHERN CALI-FORNIA | Redlands, Calif. |
| SHOWBOAT CITY | St. Louis, Mo. |
| SHOWPLACE OF SOUTHEAST ALASKA | Sitka, Alaska |
| SHOWPLACE OF THE LAKES | Mackinac Island, Mich. |
| SHRIMP CAPITAL OF ALASKA | Petersburg, Alaska |
| SHRINE OF OLD HOMES | Guilford, Conn. |
| SHRINE OF THE SOUTH | Lexington, Va. |
| SHUFFLEBOARD CAPITAL | Lake Worth, Fla. |
| SIERRA "CONEY ISLAND" | Lake Tahoe, Calif. |
| SIGHT-SEEING CITY OF THE MIDDLE WEST | Leavenworth, Kan. |
| SIGHTSEEING CENTER OF FLORIDA | Tampa, Fla. |
| SIGHTSEEING HUB OF THE WEST COAST OF CENTRAL FLORIDA | Brandon, Fla. |
| SILK CITY | Paterson, N. J. |
| SILVER BOOM TOWN | Austin, Nev. |

| | |
|---|---|
| SILVER CITY | Meriden, Conn. |
| SILVER DOLLAR CITY | Billings, Mont. |
| SILVER QUEEN OF THE ROCKIES | Georgetown, Colo. |
| SILVER TOWN | Tonopah, Nev. |
| SIN CITY | Atolia, Calif. |
| SIN CITY | Las Vegas, Nev. |
| SIN CITY | Port Chester, N. Y. |
| SINEMA LAND | Hollywood, Calif. |
| SISTER CITY OF THE SUN | Miami Beach, Fla. |
| SITE OF THE OAHE DAM | Pierre, S. D. |
| SKI CAPITAL OF COLORADO | Georgetown, Colo. |
| SKI CAPITAL OF THE EAST | Stowe, Vt. |
| SKI CAPITOL OF MICHIGAN | Gaylord, Mich. |
| SKI CAPITAL U. S. A. | Aspen, Colo. |
| SKI CROSSROADS OF THE WORLD | St. Johnsbury, Vt. |
| SKI TOWN, U. S. A. | Steamboat Springs, Colo. |
| | |
| SKIER'S HEAVEN | Snow, Vt. |
| SKINNER'S MUDHOLE | Eugene, Ore. |
| SKY CITY | Acoma, N. M. |
| SKYLINE OF ROMANCE | Atlantic City, N. J. |
| SLASH TOWN | Ashland, Va. |
| SLAUGHTER HOUSE | Auburn, Wash. |
| SLED DOG CENTER OF THE U. S. | Wonalancet, N. H. |
| SLEEPY TOWN | Philadelphia, Pa. |
| SMALL TOWN WITH A BIG WELCOME | Saratoga, Wyo. |
| SMALL TOWN WITH THE BUSTLING ACTIVITY OF A GROWING CITY | Maitland, Fla. |
| SMALLEST CAPITAL IN AMERICA | Carson City, Nev. |
| SMALLEST CAPITAL IN THE WORLD | Carson City, Nev. |
| SMELTER CITY | Anaconda, Mont. |
| SMILE OF THE GREAT SPIRIT | Winnipesaukee, N. H. |
| SMOG CITY | Los Angeles, Calif. |
| SMOKE ON THE WATER | Skamokawa, Wash. |
| SMOKELESS COAL CAPITAL OF THE WORLD | Beckley, W. Va. |
| SMOKY CITY | Pittsburgh, Pa. |
| SMOOTH WATER | Sequim, Wash. |
| SNAPSHOT CITY | Rochester, N. Y. |
| SNOW PARADISE | Stowe, Vt. |
| SNOWSHOE TOWN OF AMERICA | Norway, Me. |
| SO NEAR TO SO MUCH | Cleveland, Miss. |
| SOBER-MINDED | Dedham, Mass. |
| SODOM-BY-THE-SEA | Coney Island, N. Y. |
| SODOM OF THE SOUTH | Memphis, Tenn. |
| SOIL PIPE CENTER OF THE WORLD | Anniston, Ala. |
| SOO | Saulte Ste. Marie, Mich. |

| | |
|---|---|
| SOLID CITY | St. Louis, Mo. |
| SOUR DOUGH FLATS | Waterville, Wash. |
| SOURCE OF THE AU SABLE | Grayling, Mich. |
| SOUTH ARKANSAS' BUSY PORT CITY | Camden, Ark. |
| SOUTH CAROLINA'S CAPITAL CITY | Columbia, S. C. |
| SOUTH DAKOTA'S CITY OF OPPOR-TUNITY | Mitchell, S. D. |
| SOUTH DAKOTA'S NEWEST CONVEN-TION CITY | Watertown, S. D. |
| SOUTH DAKOTA'S OPPORTUNITY CITY | Mitchell, S. D. |
| SOUTH FLORIDA HUB | Hialeah, Fla. |
| SOUTH FLORIDA'S OLDEST PIONEER VILLAGE | Bradenton, Fla. |
| SOUTH GEORGIA'S MARKET PLACE | Moultrie, Ga. |
| SOUTH SEA ISLES OF AMERICA | Miami, Fla. |
| SOUTHEASTERN ENTRANCE TO THE REDWOOD EMPIRE | Napa, Calif. |
| SOUTHEASTERN GATEWAY TO VER-MONT | Brattleboro, Vt. |
| SOUTHERN CALIFORNIA'S BIG "OH" | San Luis Obispo, Calif. |
| SOUTHERN CALIFORNIA'S DESERT PLAYGROUND | Indio, Calif. |
| SOUTHERN CALIFORNIA'S MOST MODERN RESORT | Portofino, Calif. |
| SOUTHERN CROSSROADS CITY | Atlanta, Ga. |
| SOUTHERN GATEWAY | Moose Lake, Minn. |
| SOUTHERN GATEWAY OF NEW ENG-LAND | Providence, R. I. |
| SOUTHERN GATEWAY TO THE BLACK HILLS | Chadron, Neb. |
| SOUTHERN GATEWAY TO THE BLACK HILLS | Hot Springs, S. D. |
| SOUTHERN GATEWAY TO THE LEWIS AND CLARK LAKE | Norfolk, Neb. |
| SOUTHERN GATEWAY TO THE SMOKIES | Murphy, N. C. |
| SOUTHERN HOLIDAY HIGHLAND | Blowing Rock, N. C. |
| SOUTHERN KENTUCKY'S LARGEST SHOPPING CENTER | Bowling Green, Ky. |
| SOUTHERNMOST CITY IN THE CON-TINENTAL UNITED STATES | Key West, Fla. |
| SOUTHLAND AT ITS BEST | Tallahassee, Fla. |
| SOUTH'S FASTEST GROWING CITY | East Point, Ga. |
| SOUTH'S GREATEST CITY | New Orleans, La. |
| SOUTH'S LARGEST PRODUCER OF COTTON CLOTH | Spartanburg, S. C. |

| | |
|---|---|
| SOUTH'S MOST BEAUTIFUL AND IN-<br>TERESTING CITY | Macon, Ga. |
| SOUTH'S MOST STRATEGIC AND<br>DISTRIBUTION CENTER | Decatur, Ala. |
| SOUTH'S MOST STRATEGIC INDUS-<br>TRIAL AND DISTRIBUTIONAL CEN-<br>TER | Decatur, Ala. |
| SOUTH'S NO. 1 CRUISE SHIP PORT | Port Everglades,<br>Fla. |
| SOUTH'S OLDEST INDUSTRIAL CITY | Columbus, Ga. |
| SOUTHWEST ARKANSAS' MOST CON-<br>VENIENTLY LOCATED CITY | Hope, Ark. |
| SOUTHWEST SUN COUNTRY | Tucson, Ariz. |
| SOUTHWEST'S FOREMOST EDUCA-<br>TIONAL CENTER | Houston, Tex. |
| SOUTHWEST'S GREATEST HEALTH<br>RESORT | Marlin, Tex. |
| SOUTHWEST'S LEADING FINANCIAL<br>MANUFACTURING AND DISTRIBU-<br>TION CENTER | Dallas, Tex. |
| SOUTHWEST'S SIGHTSEEING CENTER | Phoenix, Ariz. |
| SOUTHWESTERN FACTORY CITY | Fort Smith, Ark. |
| SOUTHWESTERN GATEWAY TO THE<br>HISTORIC FOUR SEASON VACA-<br>TIONLAND | Bennington, Vt. |
| SOYBEAN CAPITAL OF THE WORLD | Decatur, Ill. |
| SOYBEAN CENTER | Decatur, Ill. |
| SPA CITY | Saratoga Springs,<br>N. Y. |
| SPACE AGE CITY | Danbury, Conn. |
| SPACE AGE CITY | Muscle Shoals, Ala. |
| SPACE AGE COMMUNITY | Blacksburg, Va. |
| SPACE CAPITAL OF THE NATION | Huntsville, Ala. |
| SPACE CAPITAL OF THE WORLD | Huntsville, Ala. |
| SPACE CENTER | Houston, Tex. |
| SPACE CITY, U. S. A. | Houston, Tex. |
| SPACE HEADQUARTERS, U. S. A. | Houston, Tex. |
| SPACE HUB | Cape Canaveral,<br>Fla. |
| SPACE PORT USA | Galveston, Tex. |
| SPACEPORT, U. S. A. | Cape Kennedy, Fla. |
| SPANISH PEANUT CENTER OF THE<br>WORLD | Dawson, Ga. |
| SPANISH TOWN | Half Moon Bay,<br>Calif. |
| SPANISH TOWN | Tampa, Fla. |
| SPANISH VILLAGE | San Clemente, Calif. |
| SPARKLING CITY BY THE SEA | Corpus Christi, Tex. |

| | |
|---|---|
| SPARKLING SAND, GOLDEN SUNSHINE ON THE ATLANTIC SHORE | Pompano Beach, Fla. |
| SPAWNING GROUND OF REALTORS | Los Angeles, Calif. |
| SPEARHEAD OF THE NEW SOUTH | Charlotte, N. C. |
| SPECTACULAR CONVENTION CENTER | Las Vegas, Nev. |
| SPLENDOR OF THE WEST | Las Vegas, Nev. |
| SPINACH CAPITAL OF THE WORLD | Crystal City, Tex. |
| SPINDLE CITY | Fall River, Mass. |
| SPINDLE CITY | Lewiston, Me. |
| SPINDLE CITY | Lowell, Mass. |
| SPINSTER CITY | Portland, Ore. |
| SPOKANE OF OREGON | Eugene, Ore. |
| SPONGE CITY | Tarpon Springs, Fla. |
| SPOONBILL CAPITAL OF THE WORLD | Warsaw, Mo. |
| SPORT CENTER OF THE SOUTH | Aiken, S. C. |
| SPORT PARACHUTING CENTER OF U. S. A. | Orange, Mass. |
| SPORTFISHING CAPITAL OF THE WORLD | Islamorada, Fla. |
| SPORTLAND OF THE GULF | Mobile, Ala. |
| SPORTS CENTER OF THE SOUTHWEST | Dallas, Tex. |
| SPORTSMAN'S PARADISE | Apalachicola, Fla. |
| SPORTSMAN'S PARADISE | Chincoteague, Va. |
| SPORTSMAN'S PARADISE | Clinton, Mo. |
| SPORTSMAN'S PARADISE | Greenwood, Miss. |
| SPORTSMAN'S PARADISE | Laurel, Mont. |
| SPORTSMAN'S PARADISE | Punta Gorda, Fla. |
| SPORTSMAN'S PARADISE | Salida, Colo. |
| SPORTSMAN'S TOWN | Bishop, Calif. |
| SPORTSMAN'S TOWN | Umatilla, Fla. |
| SPOT FOR A HOME AND A LIFE OF JOY | Grove, Okla. |
| SPRING CITY | Waukesna, Wis. |
| SPRINGBOARD INTO THE FOUR-SEASON AREA | Springfield, Vt. |
| SPRINGS OF HEALTH AND PITS OF WEALTH | Buhl, Minn. |
| SPRINGTIME CITY | Clearwater, Fla. |
| SQUAW HARBOR | Anacortes, Wash. |
| SQUAWKIEWOOD | Hollywood, Calif. |
| SQUIRE CITY | Springdale, Wash. |
| STAGE COACH TOWN | Fort Worth, Tex. |
| STAR CITY | Lafayette, Ind. |
| STAR CITY OF THE SOUTH | Roanoke, Va. |
| STAR CITY WITH A GREAT FUTURE | Bethlehem, Pa. |
| STAR OF THE BIG SKY COUNTRY | Billings, Mont. |

| | |
|---|---|
| STAR OF THE NORTH | Malone, N. Y. |
| STAR OF THE SOUTHLAND | Long Beach, Calif. |
| STARDOM | Hollywood, Calif. |
| STARLAND | Hollywood, Calif. |
| STATE CITY | Harrisburg, Pa. |
| STATES LARGEST OCEANSIDE RESORT TOWN | Carolina Beach, N.C. |
| STEAK CAPITAL OF THE WORLD | Omaha, Neb. |
| STEAK CENTER OF THE NATION | Kansas City, Mo. |
| STEAMTOWN, U. S. A. | North Walpole, N. H. |
| STEEL CAPITAL OF THE WORLD | Pittsburgh, Pa. |
| STEEL CITY | Bethlehem, Pa. |
| STEEL CITY | Gary, Ind. |
| STEEL CITY | Pittsburgh, Pa. |
| STEEL CITY | Portsmouth, Ohio |
| STEEL CITY OF THE WEST | Pueblo, Colo. |
| STEEL-MAKING CITY | Gary, Ind. |
| STILL WATER | Sequim, Wash. |
| STONE CITY | Bedford, Ind. |
| STORYTOWN, U. S. A. | Lake George, N. Y. |
| STOVE CITY | Taunton, Mass. |
| STRATEGIC GEOGRAPHICAL LOCATION FOR INDUSTRY | Hurst, Tex. |
| STRAWBERRY CAPITAL OF ALASKA | Haines, Alaska |
| STRAWBERRY CAPITAL OF AMERICA | Hammond, La. |
| STRAWBERRY CAPITAL OF THE WORLD | Watsonville, Calif. |
| STRAWBERRY CAPITAL OF TEXAS | Poteet, Tex. |
| STRAWBERRY CITY | Starke, Fla. |
| STRING TOWN | Bremerton, Wash. |
| STRING TOWN | Manette, Wash. |
| STRONG WATER | Shelton, Wash. |
| STUDIOLAND | Hollywood, Calif. |
| STUDY IN CONTRASTS | Pompano Beach, Fla. |
| SUB-TREASURY OF THE PACIFIC NORTHWEST | Portland, Ore. |
| SUBURB OF WASHINGTON | Chevy Chase, Md. |
| SUGAR BOWL OF AMERICA | Pahokee, Fla. |
| SUGAR BOWL OF THE SOUTHEAST | Savannah, Ga. |
| SUICIDE CAPITAL OF THE UNITED STATES | San Francisco, Calif. |
| SUMMER AND HEALTH RESORT | Hendersonville, N. C. |
| SUMMER AND WINTER PARADISE | Somerset, Pa. |
| SUMMER AND WINTER YEAR 'ROUND RESORT | St. Augustine, Fla. |

| | |
|---|---|
| SUMMER CAPITAL | Portland, Ore. |
| SUMMER CAPITAL OF AMERICA | Superior, Wis. |
| SUMMER CAPITAL OF SOCIETY | Newport, R. I. |
| SUMMER CITY | Duluth, Minn. |
| SUMMER FUN CAPITAL OF THE SOUTH | Daytona Beach, Fla. |
| SUMMER RESORT | Newport, R. I. |
| SUMMER VACATIONLAND AND WINTER WONDERLAND | Lake Placid, N. Y. |
| SUMMER WONDERLAND | Mackinac Island, Mich. |
| SUMMIT CITY | Akron, Ohio |
| SUMMIT CITY | Fort Wayne, Ind. |
| SUMMIT CITY | Kane, Pa. |
| SUMMIT TOWN | Glassboro, N. J. |
| SUN AND FUN CAPITAL OF THE WORLD | Miami Beach, Fla. |
| SUN AND FUN! SAND N' SEA | Old Orchard Beach, Me. |
| SUN CITY | Corpus Christi, Tex. |
| SUN CITY OF THE BIG SKY COUNTRY | Billings, Mont. |
| SUN, FUN AND ACTION TOWN | Las Vegas, Nev. |
| SUN SMILES HAPPILY ON INDUSTRY IN RIVIERA BEACH WHERE THERE IS EVERYTHING TO MAKE YOU HAPPY | Riviera Beach, Fla. |
| SUNNY COMMUNITY OF LEISURELY LIVING AND HAPPY HOLIDAYS | Surfside, Fla. |
| SUNRISE OF OPPORTUNITY | Brooksville, Fla. |
| SUNSHINE CAPITAL OF THE SOUTHWEST | Tucson, Ariz. |
| SUNSHINE CAPITAL OF THE UNITED STATES | Yuma, Ariz. |
| SUNSHINE CAPITAL OF THE WORLD | Miami, Fla. |
| SUNSHINE CITY | Fort Lauderdale, Fla. |
| SUNSHINE CITY | St. Petersburg, Fla. |
| SUNSHINE CITY | Sarasota, Fla. |
| SUNSHINE CITY | Tucson, Ariz. |
| SUNSHINE TOWN | Newport, N. H. |
| SUPER CITY | New York, N. Y. |
| SURFING CAPITAL OF THE SOUTH | Cocoa Beach, Fla. |
| SWEATSHIRT CAPITAL OF THE WORLD | Martinsville, Va. |
| SWEET WINE CAPITAL OF THE WORLD | Fresno, Calif. |
| SWEETHEART OF SOUTH TEXAS | Alice, Tex. |
| SWEETHEART TOWN | Loveland, Colo. |

396

| | |
|---|---|
| SWELL PLACE TO LIVE | Tempe, Ariz. |
| SWIMMING POOL CITY | Palm Springs, Calif. |
| SWISS CHEESE CAPITAL OF THE UNITED STATES | Monroe, Wis. |
| SWISS CHEESE CENTER OF OHIO | Sugarcreek, Ohio |
| SWITCHBACK CITY | Mauch Chunk, Pa. |
| SWITZERLAND OF ALASKA | Valdez, Alaska |
| SWITZERLAND OF AMERICA | Afton, Wyo. |
| SWITZERLAND OF AMERICA | Baker, Ore. |
| SWITZERLAND OF AMERICA | Durango, Colo. |
| SWITZERLAND OF AMERICA | Ouray, Colo. |
| SWITZERLAND OF AMERICA | Terre Haute, Ind. |
| SWITZERLAND OF IOWA | Decorah, Iowa |
| SWITZERLAND OF MAINE | Jackman, Me. |
| SWITZERLAND OF THE CATSKILLS | Hancock, N. Y. |
| SYCAMORE CITY | Terre Haute, Ind. |

## T

| | |
|---|---|
| TABLE-LAND | Mesa, Wash. |
| TABLE WINE CENTER OF THE WORLD | Napa, Calif. |
| TABLE WINE CENTER OF THE WORLD | St. Helena, Calif. |
| TAILHOLD | Rogue River, Ore. |
| TAILHOLT | Carrollton, Ind. |
| TALL TOWER TOWN | Raymond, Me. |
| TALLEST TOWN IN OREGON | Lakeview, Ore. |
| TANNERY CITY | Blossburg, Pa. |
| TANNING CITY | Woburn, Mass. |
| TARGET OF OPPORTUNITY | Waco, Tex. |
| TARRARA CITY | Boykins, Va. |
| TATER TOWN | Gleason, Tenn. |
| TATERVILLE | Gleason, Tenn. |
| TAXPAYER'S HAVEN | Hialeah, Fla. |
| TELEGRAPHIC HUB | Syracuse, N. Y. |
| TENNESSEE'S BEAUTY SPOT | Nashville, Tenn. |
| TENNIS CAPITAL OF THE WORLD | Salisbury, Md. |
| TENT CITY | Wildwood, N. J. |
| TENT TOWN | Douglas, Wyo. |
| TERRACE CITY | Yonkers, N. Y. |
| TEXAS' FIRST STOP | Denison, Tex. |
| TEXAS' LARGEST ISOLATED MARKET | Lubbock, Tex. |
| TEXAS' ONLY ATLAS MISSILE SITES | Abilene, Tex. |
| TEXAS'S SPARKLING CITY BY THE SEA | Corpus Christi, Tex. |
| TEXTILE CENTER OF THE WORLD | Greenville, S. C. |
| TEXTILE CITY | Reading, Pa. |

397

| | |
|---|---|
| THERE'S MORE IN MILWAUKEE | Milwaukee, Wis. |
| THERE'S SOMETHING FOR EVERYONE IN HOLLYWOOD | Hollywood, Calif. |
| THERMOPYLAE OF MIDDLE TENNES- SEE | Tullahoma, Tenn. |
| THIRD LARGEST TOBACCO MARKET IN VIRGINIA | South Hill, Va. |
| THIS PLEASANT LAND AMONG THE MOUNTAINS | Manchester, Vt. |
| THOROUGHBRED CAPITAL OF FLOR- IDA | Ocala, Fla. |
| THOROUGHBRED, STANDARDBRED AND SADDLE HORSE CENTER OF AMERICA | Lexington, Ky. |
| THREAD CITY | Willimantic, Conn. |
| THREE FORKS | Pullman, Wash. |
| THREE SPITS | Bangor, Wash. |
| THRESHOLD OF THEODORE ROOSE- VELT NATIONAL MEMORIAL PARK | Dickinson, N. D. |
| THRIFTY NEW ENGLAND COMMUNITY STEEPED IN COLONIAL TRADITION AND DEMOCRACY | Norwalk, Conn. |
| THRIVING CAPITAL CITY | Montgomery, Ala. |
| TIDE-WATER CITY | Troy, N. Y. |
| TIMBER CAPITAL OF THE NATION | Roseburg, Ore. |
| TIMELESS WONDERLAND | San Francisco, Calif. |
| TIN HORN VILLAGE | Newton, Mass. |
| TIP OF CAPE COD | Provincetown, Mass. |
| TIRE CAPITAL OF THE WORLD | Akron, Ohio |
| TIRE CITY OF THE UNITED STATES | Akron, Ohio |
| TIRE CORD CAPITAL OF THE U. S. | Thomaston, Ga. |
| TITLETOWN, U. S. A. | Green Bay, Wis. |
| TOBACCO AND FARMING CENTER | Clayton, N. C. |
| TOBACCO CAPITAL OF SOUTH CARO- LINA | Mullins. S. C. |
| TOBACCO CAPITAL OF THE WORLD | Richmond, Va. |
| TOBACCO CENTER | Lyons, Ga. |
| TOBACCO CENTER | Viroqua, Wis. |
| TODAY'S CITY WITH TOMORROW'S VISION | Ottumwa, Iowa |
| TOMATO CAPITAL OF SOUTH CEN- TRAL TEXAS | Yoakum, Tex. |
| TOMATO CAPITAL OF THE WORLD | Dania, Fla. |
| TOMATO CAPITAL OF THE OZARKS | Green Forest, Ark. |
| TOMATO CENTER OF THE WORLD | Dania, Fla. |
| TOMATO PLANT CAPITAL | Tifton, Ga. |
| TOP OF THE WORLD | Point Barrow, |

| | Alaska |
|---|---|
| TOPS IN SUN'N FUN | St. Petersburg, Fla. |
| TOTEM CITY | Ketchikan, Alaska |
| TOUR ENTRANCE TO THE KENNEDY SPACE CENTER | Titusville, Fla. |
| TOURIST AND CONVENTION CENTER | Jacksonville, Fla. |
| TOURIST CITY | Statesboro, Ga. |
| TOURIST MECCA AND ANTIQUES CENTER OF THE SOUTH | Dania, Fla. |
| TOURIST MECCA OF EAST TEXAS | Jacksonville, Tex. |
| TOURIST MECCA OF THE SOUTH | Allendale, S. C. |
| TOURIST'S PARADISE | Index, Wash. |
| TOUROPOLIS OF AMERICA | Flagstaff, Ariz. |
| TOWER TREE CITY | Greensburg, Ind. |
| TOWN BLESSED BY AN IDEAL YEAR 'ROUND CLIMATE | Las Vegas, Nev. |
| TOWN FOR THOSE IN LOVE WITH LIFE | Marietta, Ohio |
| TOWN IN THE GATEWAY TO THE BEAUTIFUL RED SECTION OF FLORIDA | Davenport, Fla. |
| TOWN JUST RITE FOR YOUR PLANT SITE | Houlton, Me. |
| TOWN OF HAPPY HOMES | Greenwood, Ind. |
| TOWN OF HOMES | Westport, Conn. |
| TOWN OF HOSPITALITY AND PROGRESS | Victoria, Va. |
| TOWN OF MANY OPPORTUNITIES | Uvalde, Tex. |
| TOWN OF MILLIONAIRES | Brookline, Mass. |
| TOWN OF SANDY BEACHES | Sebago Lake, Me. |
| TOWN OF SCHOOLS--AND A COLLEGE | Wellesley, Mass. |
| TOWN OF TUMBLING WATERS | Shelburne Falls, Mass. |
| TOWN OF "UP AND DOWN" | Eureka Springs, Ark. |
| TOWN ON THE RIDGE IN THE HEART OF ORANGELAND | Davenport, Fla. |
| TOWN RICH IN HISTORY | Manassas, Va. |
| TOWN THAT CHANGED AMERICA'S VIEWPOINT ON RETIREMENT LIVING | Sun City, Ariz. |
| TOWN THAT GAVE THE WORLD A GREAT IDEA | Nebraska City, Neb. |
| TOWN THAT HAS BECOME A UNIVERSITY | Winter Park, Fla. |
| TOWN THAT IS GOING PLACES | Meredith, N. H. |
| TOWN THAT "JACK" BUILT | Joplin, Mo. |
| TOWN THAT MOVED OVERNIGHT | Hibbing, Minn. |

| | |
|---|---|
| TOWN THAT OUTLIVES AND OUT-GROWS THE OIL BOOM | Titusville, Pa. |
| TOWN THAT ROSES BUILT | Pasadena, Calif. |
| TOWN THE ATOM BUILT | Richland, Wash. |
| TOWN TO GROW WITH | East Windsor Hill, Conn. |
| TOWN TOO TOUGH TO DIE | Tombstone, Ariz. |
| TOWN TWO MILES LONG AND TWO YARDS WIDE | St. Francisville, La. |
| TOWN WHERE INDUSTRY'S CONTRIBUTION TO THE COMMUNITY IS APPRECIATED | Foley, Ala. |
| TOWN WHERE NATURAL BEAUTY AND INDUSTRY MEET TO CREATE | Mount Joy, Pa. |
| TOWN WHERE OIL DERRICKS LOOM IN ALMOST ANY YARD | Oklahoma City, Okla. |
| TOWN WHERE RAIL MEETS WATER | Kalama, Wash. |
| TOWN WHERE THE ACTION IS | Custer City, S. D. |
| TOWN WHERE THE OFFICE LEDGER HAS REPLACED THE HORSE PISTOL | Oklahoma City, Okla. |
| TOWN WHERE SUMMER IS AIR-CONDITIONED | Chatham, Mass. |
| TOWN WHERE THE TROUT LEAP IN MAIN STREET | Saratoga, Wyo. |
| TOWN WHERE YOUR SUMMER FUN BEGINS | Riverhead, N. Y. |
| TOWN WHICH HELD THE KEY | Orondo, Wash. |
| TOWN WITH A GUNSMOKE FLAVOR | Custer City, S. D. |
| TOWN WITH A FUTURE | Stratford, Conn. |
| TOWN WITH A HEART | Salida, Colo. |
| TOWN WITH A SPLIT PERSONALITY | Islip, N. Y. |
| TOWN WITH GROW POWER | South Windsor, Conn. |
| TOWN WITH THE MOST TO OFFER INDUSTRY | Columbus, Miss. |
| TOY TOWN | Winchendon, Mass. |
| TRACK AND FIELD TOWN, U. S. A. | Jemez Pueblo, N. M. |
| TRADE CAPITAL OF FLORIDA'S WEST COAST | Tampa, Fla. |
| TRADE CENTER FOR SOUTHEAST ARKANSAS | Pine Bluff, Ark. |
| TRADE CENTER OF MID-EAST NEBRASKA | Fremont, Neb. |
| TRADE CENTER OF SOUTHWEST GEORGIA | Albany, Ga. |
| TRADE CENTER OF THE RICH BLUE GRASS, TOBACCO AND LIVESTOCK REGION | Lexington, Ky. |

| | |
|---|---|
| TRADING CENTER | New Bedford, Mass. |
| TRADING CENTER | Raleigh, N. C. |
| TRADING CENTER | Wheeling, W. Va. |
| TRADING CENTER OF EAST ALA- BAMA | Opelika, Ala. |
| TRADING CENTER OF THE INLAND EMPIRE | Spokane, Wash. |
| TRAIL'S END | International Falls, Minn. |
| TRANQUIL LIVING IN A NATURAL PARADISE | La Belle, Fla. |
| TRANSPORT CENTER OF THE NA- TION | Buffalo, N. Y. |
| TRANSPORTATION CENTER | Midland, Tex. |
| TRANSPORTATION CENTER OF NORTH AMERICA | Superior, Wis. |
| TRANSPORTATION CITY | Cumberland, Md. |
| TRANSPORTATION CITY | Easton, Pa. |
| TRANSPORTATION HUB OF THE WEST | Ogden, Utah |
| TRANSPORTATION KING OF THE MID- EAST | Harrisburg, Pa. |
| TREASURE CITY | Tampa, Fla. |
| TREASURE ISLAND OF THE SOUTH- WEST | Galveston, Tex. |
| TREE CITY | Boise, Idaho |
| TREE CITY | Greensburg, Ind. |
| TREMONT | Boston, Mass. |
| TRI-CITIES | Bristol, Johnstown City and Kings- port, Tenn. |
| TRI-CITIES | Draper, Leaksville and Spray, N. C. |
| TRI-CITIES | Florence, Sheffield and Tuscumbia, Ala. |
| TRI-CITIES | Kennewick, Pasco and Richland, Wash. |
| TRI-CITIES | Moline and Rock Island, Ill., and Davenport, Iowa |
| TRI-COUNTY CITY THAT IS FRIEND- LY, PROGRESSIVE, ALIVE | Enderlin, N. D. |
| TRI-COUNTY TRADING CENTER | Aurora, Mo. |
| TRI-STATE CAPITAL | Memphis, Tenn. |
| TRIMOUNTAIN CITY | Boston, Mass. |
| TROPIC METROPOLIS | Miami, Fla. |

| | |
|---|---|
| TROPICAL FLORIDA'S FIRST RESORT | West Palm Beach, Fla. |
| TROPICAL ISLAND WONDERLAND IN THE GULF OF MEXICO | Fort Myers Beach, Fla. |
| TROPICAL WONDERLAND | Fort Lauderdale, Fla. |
| TRUE CENTER OF THE RICH RED RIVER VALLEY | Grafton, N. D. |
| TRULY COLONIAL TOWN | Clinton, Conn. |
| TRULY IZAAK WALTON'S HEADQUAR-TERS | Pompano Beach, Fla. |
| TRULY YEAR 'ROUND VACATION LAND | Wells, N. Y. |
| TUBE CITY | McKeesport, Pa. |
| TUFTED TEXTILE CENTER OF THE WORLD | Dalton, Ga. |
| TULIP CENTER OF AMERICA | Holland, Mich. |
| TULIP CITY | Bellingham, Wash. |
| TULIP CITY | Holland, Mich. |
| TUNG OIL CENTER OF AMERICA | Picayune, Miss. |
| TUNG TREE CAPITAL OF THE WORLD | Picayune, Miss. |
| TUNNEL CITY | Greensburg, Pa. |
| TURKEY CAPITAL | Aitkin, Minn. |
| TURKEY CAPITAL OF ARKANSAS | Berryville, Ark. |
| TURKEY CAPITAL OF MINNESOTA | Worthington, Minn. |
| TURKEY CAPITAL OF THE EAST | Harrisonburg, Va. |
| TURKEY CAPITAL OF THE NATION | Harrisonburg, Va. |
| TURKEY CAPITAL OF THE OZARKS | Berryville, Ark. |
| TURKEY CAPITAL OF THE WORLD | Worthington, Minn. |
| TURPENTINE CAPITAL OF THE WORLD | Baxley, Ga. |
| TUSSELBURGH | Alton, Ill. |
| TWENTY-FOUR HOUR GAMBLING CITY | Las Vegas, Nev. |
| TWENTY-THOUSAND ACRE PLAY-GROUND | Del Monte Park, Calif. |
| TWIN CITIES | Aberdeen, Wash. , and Hoquiam, Wash. |
| TWIN CITIES | Alcoa, Tenn. and Maryville, Tenn. |
| TWIN CITIES | Auburn, Me. , and Lewiston, Me. |
| TWIN CITIES | Bangor, Me. , and Brewer, Me. |

| | |
|---|---|
| TWIN CITIES | Benton Harbor, Mich., and St. Joseph, Mich. |
| TWIN CITIES | Biddeford, Me., and Saco, Me. |
| TWIN CITIES | Bluefield, Va., and Bluefield, W. Va. |
| TWIN CITIES | Bluefield, W. Va., and Bluefield, Va. |
| TWIN CITIES | Brewer, Me., and Bangor, Me. |
| TWIN CITIES | Bristol, Tenn., and Bristol, Va. |
| TWIN CITIES | Bristol, Va., and Bristol, Tenn. |
| TWIN CITIES | Central Falls, R. I., and Pawtucket, R. I. |
| TWIN CITIES | Champaign, Ill., and Urbana, Ill. |
| TWIN CITIES | Gardnerville, Nev., and Minden, Nev. |
| TWIN CITIES | Helena, Ark., and West Helena, Ark. |
| TWIN CITIES | Hoquiam, Wash., and Aberdeen, Wash. |
| TWIN CITIES | Lafayette, Ind., and West Lafayette, Ind. |
| TWIN CITIES | Lewiston, Me., and Auburn, Me. |
| TWIN CITIES | Maryville, Tenn., and Alcoa, Tenn. |
| TWIN CITIES | Menasha, Wis., and Neenah, Wis. |
| TWIN CITIES | Miami, Fla., and Miami Beach, Fla. |
| TWIN CITIES | Miami Beach, Fla., and Miami, Fla. |
| TWIN CITIES | Minden, Nev., and Gardnerville, Nev. |
| TWIN CITIES | Minneapolis, Minn., and St. Paul, Minn. |
| TWIN CITIES | Monroe, La., and West Monroe, La. |
| TWIN CITIES | Neenah, Wis., and Menasha, Wis. |

| | |
|---|---|
| TWIN CITIES | Pawtucket, R. I. , and Central Falls, R. I. |
| TWIN CITIES | Saco, Me. , and Biddeford, Me. |
| TWIN CITIES | St. Joseph, Mich. , and Benton Harbor, Mich. |
| TWIN CITIES | St. Paul, Minn. , and Minneapolis, Minn. |
| TWIN CITIES | Texarkana, Ark. , and Texarkana, Tex. |
| TWIN CITIES | Texarkana, Tex. , and Texarkana, Ark. |
| TWIN CITIES | Urbana, Ill. , and Champaign, Ill. |
| TWIN CITIES | West Helena, Ark. , and Helena, Ark. |
| TWIN CITIES | West Lafayette, Ind. , and Lafayette, Ind. |
| TWIN CITIES | West Monroe, La. , and Monroe, La. |
| TWIN CITIES | Winston-Salem, N.C. |
| TWIN CITIES BY THE TRUCKEE | Reno, Nev. , and Sparks, Nev. |
| TWIN CITIES BY THE TRUCKEE | Sparks, Nev. , and Reno, Nev. |
| TWIN CITIES OF THE NORTHERN BLACK HILLS OF SOUTH DAKOTA | Deadwood, S. D. |
| TWIN CITIES OF THE NORTHERN BLACK HILLS OF SOUTH DAKOTA | Lead, S. D. |
| TWIN CITIES OF THE OUACHITA | Monroe, La. , and West Monroe, La. |
| TWIN CITIES ON THE BAY | Niceville, Fla. , and Valparaiso, Fla. |
| TWIN CITIES ON THE BAY | Valparaiso, Fla. , and Niceville, Fla. |
| TWIN CITIES ON THE RED RIVER IN THE HEART OF LOUISIANA | Alexandria, La. , and Pineville, La. |
| TWIN CITY | Bloomington, Ill. , and Normal, Ill. |
| TWIN CITY | Minneapolis and St. Paul, Minn. |

| | |
|---|---|
| TWIN CITY | Normal, Ill., and Bloomington, Ill. |
| TWIN CITY | Norwalk, Conn., and South Norwalk, Conn. |
| TWIN CITY | St. Paul and Minneapolis, Minn. |
| TWIN CITY | South Norwalk, Conn., and Norwalk, Conn. |
| TWIN CITY | Sun City, Ariz., and Youngstown, Ariz. |
| TWIN CITY | Winston-Salem, N.C. |
| TWIN CITY | Youngstown, Ariz., and Sun City, Ariz. |
| TWIN LAKES CAPITAL OF THE OZARKS | Forsyth, Mo. |
| TWIN PORTS | Duluth, Minn., and Superior, Wis. |
| TWIN PORTS | Superior, Wis., and Duluth, Minn. |
| TWIN TOWNS | Damariscotta, Me., and Newcastle, Me. |
| TWIN TOWNS | Newcastle, Me., and Damariscotta, Me. |
| TWIN VILLAGES | Damariscotta and Newcastle, Me. |
| TWIN VILLAGES | Newcastle and Damariscotta, Me. |
| TWINS | Minneapolis and St. Paul, Minn. |
| TWINS | St. Paul and Minneapolis, Minn. |
| TYPEWRITER CAPITAL OF THE WORLD | Cortland, N.Y. |
| TYPICAL AMERICAN CITY | Middletown, Ind. |
| TYPICAL AMERICAN CITY | Muncie, Ind. |
| TYPICAL AMERICAN CITY | Owatonna, Minn. |
| TYPICAL NEW ENGLAND CITY | Norton, Mass. |
| TYPICAL OZARK HOME TOWN | Gentry, Ark. |
| TYPICAL RESORT CITY | Pensacola, Fla. |

# U

| | |
|---|---|
| ULTIMATE CITY | Litchfield, Conn. |
| ULTIMATE CITY | Los Angeles, Calif. |
| ULTRA MODERN CITY | Palo Alto, Calif. |
| UNDERWATER MOTION PICTURE CAPITAL OF THE WORLD | Silver Springs, Fla. |
| UNITED NATIONS' CONFERENCE CENTER | San Francisco, Calif. |
| UNIVERSITY CITY | Cambridge, Mass. |
| UNIVERSITY CITY | Gainesville, Fla. |
| UNIVERSITY CITY | Vermillion, S. D. |
| UNIVERSITY OF LIGHT | Cleveland, Ohio |
| UNIVERSITY OF TELEPHONY | New York, N. Y. |
| UNSAINTED ANTHONY | San Antonio, Tex. |
| UNSPOILED BEAUTY SPOT OF NORTHERN MAINE | Patten, Me. |
| UP AND COMING TOWN | Sanford, Me. |
| UPPER SANDUSKY WEST | Los Angeles, Calif. |
| UP-TO-DATE OLDEST TOWN IN LOUISIANA | Natchitoches, La. |
| URANIUM CAPITAL OF THE WORLD | Grand Junction, Colo. |
| URANIUM CAPITAL OF THE WORLD | Grants, N. M. |
| URANIUM CAPITAL OF THE WORLD | Moab, Utah |
| URANIUM CENTER OF SOUTH DAKOTA | Edgemont, S. D. |
| UTAH ZION | Salt Lake City, Utah |
| UTOPIA OF THE NORTH ATLANTIC | New London, Conn. |

# V

| | |
|---|---|
| VACATION AND HEALTH RESORT | Waynesville, N. C. |
| VACATION CAPITAL OF THE APPALACHIAN HIGHLANDS | Elkins, W. Va. |
| VACATION CAPITAL OF THE NATION | Atlantic City, N. J. |
| VACATION CENTER | Portsmouth, R. I. |
| VACATION CENTER | Watkins Glen, N. Y. |
| VACATION CENTER OF A FABULOUS LAND OF CONTRASTS | Grand Junction, Colo. |
| VACATION CITY | Cleveland, Ohio |
| VACATION CITY | New York, N. Y. |
| VACATION CITY | St. Louis, Mo. |
| VACATION CITY ON CASCO BAY | Portland, Me. |
| VACATION CITY SUPREME | Atlantic City, N. J. |
| VACATION FOR A LIFETIME | Lakeland, Fla. |

| | |
|---|---|
| VACATION FUN SPOT OF WESTERN MAINE | Bridgton, Me. |
| VACATION LAND | Chula Vista, Calif. |
| VACATION LAND | Wadena, Minn. |
| VACATION LAND IN THE CENTER OF THE BERKSHIRES | Pittsfield, Mass. |
| VACATION OR YEAR ROUND HOME CITY | Scituate, Mass. |
| VACATION WONDERLAND | Morristown, Tenn. |
| VACATION WONDERLAND | Park Falls, Wis. |
| VACATIONER'S DREAMLAND | Bonita Springs, Fla. |
| VACATIONER'S PARADISE | Shelter Islands, N. Y. |
| VACATIONIST'S PARADISE | Virginia Beach, Va. |
| VACATIONER'S PARADISE | Walker, Minn. |
| VACATIONLAND FOR THE WHOLE FAMILY | Fort Pierce, Fla. |
| VACATIONLAND OF A THOUSAND PLEASURES | Miami Beach, Fla. |
| VACATIONLAND OF NORTHERN WISCONSIN | Park Falls, Wis. |
| VACATIONLAND OF UNLIMITED ENJOYMENT | Speculator, N. Y. |
| VACATIONLAND, U. S. A. | Eastham, Mass. |
| VACATIONLAND, U. S. A. | Miami Beach, Fla. |
| VACATIONLAND, U. S. A. | Norfolk, Va. |
| VACATIONLAND UNLIMITED | Medford, Ore. |
| VACATIONLAND WITHOUT EQUAL | Treasure Island, Fla. |
| VALE OF BEAUTY | Valdosta, Ga. |
| VALENTINE HAS EVERYTHING | Valentine, Neb. |
| VALLEY IN THE SUN | Phoenix, Ariz. |
| VALLEY OF THE GARDENS | Santa Maria, Calif. |
| VALLEY OF VAPORS | Hot Springs, Ark. |
| VALLEY'S COLLEGE TOWN | Tempe, Ariz. |
| VAPOR CITY | Hot Springs, Ark. |
| VARIETY OF RECREATIONAL OPPORTUNITIES | Stockton, Calif. |
| VATICAN CITY | St. Louis, Mo. |
| VEGETABLE BOWL | Zellwood, Fla. |
| VEHICLE CITY | Flint, Mich. |
| VENICE OF AMERICA | Annapolis, Md. |
| VENICE OF AMERICA | Fort Lauderdale, Fla. |
| VENICE OF AMERICA | Houma, La. |
| VENICE OF AMERICA | Stone Harbor, N. J. |
| VENICE OF AMERICA | Syracuse, N. Y. |
| VENICE OF AMERICA | Wickford, R. I. |
| VENICE OF PUGET SOUND | La Conner, Wash. |
| VENICE OF THE NORTHWEST | Willapa, Wash. |
| VENICE OF THE PACIFIC | Union, Wash. |

| | |
|---|---|
| VENICE OF THE PRAIRIE | San Antonio, Tex. |
| VENICE OF THE SOUTH | Tarpon Springs, Fla. |
| VERMONT'S MOST HISTORIC TOWN | Bennington, Vt. |
| VERMONT'S RECREATION CROSS-ROADS | Waterbury, Vt. |
| VERSATILE CITY | Rome, Ga. |
| VERY CENTER OF THE SUNSHINE STATE | Lake Weir, Fla. |
| VERY HEART OF FLORIDA | Orlando, Fla. |
| VILLAGE BEAUTIFUL | Williamstown, Mass. |
| VILLAGE NOT FOR TOURISTS, NOT FOR EXCITEMENT BUT FOR MODEST TRANQUIL HEALTHFUL LIVING | Lake Mary, Fla. |
| VILLAGE IDEAL FOR RETIREMENT FOR RAISING A FAMILY AND FOR PLACID EVERYDAY LIVING | Lake Mary, Fla. |
| VILLAGE OF BREATH-TAKING BEAUTY AND ENCHANTMENT | North Pole, N.Y. |
| VILLAGE OF CITY CHARM | Manchester, Conn. |
| VILLAGE OF DESTINY | Gilbert, Minn. |
| VILLAGE OF ENCHANTMENT | North Pole, N.Y. |
| VILLAGE OF FRIENDLY FOLK | Plainfield, Ind. |
| VILLAGE OF GREAT MUSEUMS | Cooperstown, N.Y. |
| VILLAGE OF MUSEUMS | Cooperstown, N.Y. |
| VILLAGE OF THE PLAINS | Auburn, Ala. |
| VILLAGE RIGHT IN THE MIDDLE OF THINGS ON BEAUTIFUL CHAUTAUQUA LAKE | Bemus Point, N.Y. |
| VILLAGE WHERE NATURE SMILES | Cooperstown, N.Y. |
| VILLAGE WHERE THE PINES MEET THE SEA | Cambria Village, Calif. |
| VILLAGE WITH A PAST, THE CITY WITH A FUTURE | Kenai, Alaska |
| VIRGIN CAPITAL | Washington, D.C. |
| VIRGINIA'S ATLANTIC CITY | Virginia Beach, Va. |
| VIRGINIA'S BIGGEST LITTLE CITY | Harrisonburg, Va. |
| VIRGINIA COLONY'S ELEGANT OLD CAPITAL | Williamsburg, Va. |
| VIRGINIA'S INLAND PORT | Hopewell, Va. |
| VIRGINIA'S LARGEST MARKET FOR BRIGHT LEAF TOBACCO | Danville, Va. |
| VIRGINIA'S VACATION PARADISE ON BEAUTIFUL BUGGS ISLAND LAKE | Clarksville, Va. |
| VISUALLY EXCITING CITY | Seattle, Wash. |
| VIVID CAPITAL OF THE OLD SOUTH | Jackson, Miss. |

| | |
|---|---|
| WALKING HORSE CAPITAL OF THE WORLD | Shelbyville, Tenn. |
| WALL STREET OF THE SOUTH | Nashville, Tenn. |
| WALNUT CITY | McMinnville, Ore. |
| WASHINGTON, B. C. --BEFORE CORN | Washington, D. C. |
| WASHINGTON-BY-THE-SEA | Rehoboth Beach, Del. |
| WATER CITY | Madison, S. D. |
| WATER POLO CAPITAL OF FLORIDA | Boca Raton, Fla. |
| WATER WONDERLAND | Orange, Tex. |
| WATERCRESS CAPITAL OF THE WORLD | Huntsville, Ala. |
| WATERFALLS | Tumwater, Wash. |
| WATERFRONT WONDERLAND | Cape Coral, Fla. |
| WATERING-POT OF AMERICA | Utica, N. Y. |
| WATERLOO OF THE REVOLUTION | Yorktown, Va. |
| WATERMELON CAPITAL | Chiefland, Fla. |
| WATERMELON CAPITAL | Immokalee, Fla. |
| WATERMELON CAPITAL OF FLOR-IDA | Immokalee, Fla. |
| WATERMELON CAPITAL OF FLOR-IDA | Leesburg, Fla. |
| WATERMELON CAPITAL OF THE U. S. | Hope, Ark. |
| WATERMELON CAPITAL OF THE WORLD | Weatherford, Tex. |
| WATERMELON CENTER | Mineola, Tex. |
| WATERMELON CENTER FESTIVAL | Chiefland, Fla. |
| WATERSTOWN | Pataha, Wash. |
| WEEDLESS CITY | Kane, Pa. |
| WELCOME STATION CITY | Sylvania, Ga. |
| WELCOME TO THE CITY OF LAKES | Lakeland, Fla. |
| WELL BALANCED CITY WITH OPPOR-TUNITIES FOR ALL | Norwalk, Conn. |
| WELL-BALANCED COMMUNITY | Greenfield, Mass. |
| WELL-BALANCED COMMUNITY | Lockport, N. Y. |
| WELL-BALANCED METROPOLIS | Atlanta, Ga. |
| WEST GATE TO THE LAND-O-LAKES | Butler, Mo. |
| WEST POINT OF THE SOUTH | Fort Benning, Ga. |
| WEST TEXAS INDUSTRIAL CITY | Sweetwater, Tex. |
| WESTERN CAPITAL | Denver, Colo. |
| WESTERN CITY OF SHIPS | Oakland, Calif. |
| WESTERN GATE | San Francisco, Calif. |
| WESTERN GATE TO MEXICO | Tucson, Ariz. |
| WESTERN GATEWAY CITY | Mariposa, Calif. |
| WESTERN GATEWAY TO THE NA-TION'S CAPITAL | Bethesda, Md. |

| | |
|---|---|
| WESTERN GATEWAY TO THE SKYLINE DRIVE | New Market, Va. |
| WESTERN MECCA FOR ENJOYMENT UNLIMITED | Boise, Idaho |
| WESTERN METROPOLIS | Chicago, Ill. |
| WESTERN OREGON'S LEADING INDUSTRIAL AND MARKETING CENTER | Eugene, Ore. |
| WESTERN SHANGRI-LA | Upland, Calif. |
| WESTERN WATER GATE | Everglades, Fla. |
| WESTERN WATER GATEWAY | Everglades, Fla. |
| WESTERNMOST PORT ON AMERICA'S FOURTH SEACOAST | Duluth, Minn. |
| WESTERNMOST SUBURB OF DES MOINES | Los Angeles, Calif. |
| WEST'S FASTEST-GROWING TRANSPORTATION AND INDUSTRIAL CENTER | Ogden, Utah |
| WEST'S MOST WESTERN COMMUNITY | Scottsdale, Ariz. |
| WEST'S MOST WESTERN TOWN | Scottsdale, Ariz. |
| WHALING CAPITAL OF THE WORLD | New Bedford, Mass. |
| WHALING CITY | New Bedford, Mass. |
| WHALING CITY | New London, Conn. |
| WHAT WE MAKE MAKES US | Gastonia, N. C. |
| WHEAT CAPITAL OF THE WORLD | Wellington, Kan. |
| WHEAT HEART OF THE NATION | Perryton, Tex. |
| WHEN YOU SEE SAN ANTONIO, YOU SEE TEXAS | San Antonio, Tex. |
| WHIP CITY | Westfield, Mass. |
| WHISKEY TOWN | Peoria, Ill. |
| WHITE CITY | Chicago, Ill. |
| WHITE COLLAR CITY | Denver, Colo. |
| WHITE LEGHORN CITY OF THE WEST | Petaluma, Calif. |
| WHITE MARLIN CAPITAL OF THE WORLD | Ocean City, Md. |
| WHITE ROSE CITY | York, Pa. |
| WHITE STALLION | Touchet, Wash. |
| WICKEDEST CITY IN AMERICA | Phenix City, Ala. |
| WICKEDEST LITTLE CITY IN AMERICA | Dodge City, Kan. |
| WIDEST STREET IN THE WORLD | Greenwood, S. C. |
| WILDERNESS CAPITAL OF LINCOLN'S LAND | Vandalia, Ill. |
| WILDERNESS CITY | Washington, D. C. |
| WILLIAMSBURG OF TEXAS | Jefferson, Tex. |
| WILLIAMSBURG OF THE MID WEST | Washington, Mo. |
| WILLIAMSBURG OF THE NORTH | Bennington, Vt. |
| WILLIAMSBURG OF THE SEA | Mystic, Conn. |

410

| | |
|---|---|
| WINDY CITY | Chicago, Ill. |
| WINE AND OLIVE COLONY | Demopolis, Ala. |
| WINTER AND SUMMER PLAYGROUND | Steamboat Springs, Colo. |
| WINTER AND SUMMER VACATION CENTER OF FLORIDA | Eustis, Fla. |
| WINTER CAPITAL OF AMERICA | New Orleans, La. |
| WINTER GOLF CAPITAL OF AMERICA | Atlanta, Ga. |
| WINTER GOLF CAPITAL OF AMERICA | Pinehurst, N.C. |
| WINTER GOLF CAPITAL OF THE WORLD | Augusta, Ga. |
| WINTER GOLF CAPITAL OF THE WORLD | Palm Springs, Calif. |
| WINTER GOLF MECCA | Palm Desert, Calif. |
| WINTER HOME OF THE NATIONAL LEAGUE PHILADELPHIA "PHILLIES" | Clearwater, Fla. |
| WINTER PLAYGROUND | Great Barrington, Mass. |
| WINTER PLAYGROUND OF AMERICA | San Antonio, Tex. |
| WINTER SPORTS CAPITAL OF THE NATION | St. Paul, Minn. |
| WINTER SPORTS CITY | Kane, Pa. |
| WINTER STRAWBERRY CAPITAL OF THE WORLD | Plant City, Fla. |
| WISCONSIN'S BEAUTIFUL CAPITOL CITY | Milwaukee, Wis. |
| WISCONSIN'S SECOND CITY | Racine, Wis. |
| WITCH CITY | Salem, Mass. |
| WITCHCRAFT CITY | Salem, Mass. |
| WIZARD'S CLIP | Middleway, W. Va. |
| WONDER CITY | Decatur, Ala. |
| WONDER CITY | Hopewell, Va. |
| WONDER CITY | New York, N. Y. |
| WONDER CITY IN THE MIDDLE OF THE LAND OF LAKES | El Dorado Springs, Mo. |
| WONDER CITY OF AMERICA | Buffalo, N. Y. |
| WONDER CITY OF THE WORLD | Miami, Fla. |
| WONDER CONVENTION CITY | Scranton, Pa. |
| WONDERFUL PLACE OF RECREATIONAL ENJOYMENT | Tucumcari, N. M. |
| WONDERFUL PLACE TO LIVE | Augusta, Ga. |
| WONDERFUL PLACE TO LIVE | Mitchell, S. D. |
| WONDERFUL PLACE TO LIVE | Sebring, Fla. |
| WONDERFUL PLACE TO LIVE | Tyler, Tex. |
| WONDERFUL PLACE TO LIVE, TO WORK, TO PLAY | Augusta, Ga. |

411

| | |
|---|---|
| WONDERFUL PLACE TO LIVE, TO WORK AND PLAY | Portland, Me. |
| WONDERFUL PLACE TO LIVE AND WORK | Garland, Tex. |
| WONDERFUL PLACE TO LIVE, WORK, PLAY | New Britain, Conn. |
| WONDERFUL PLACE TO REAR YOUR FAMILY BENEATH WIDE-OPEN MISSOURI SKIES | Stockton, Mo. |
| WONDERFUL PLACE TO VISIT AND A BETTER PLACE TO LIVE | Waynesboro, Va. |
| WONDERFUL WEATHER LAND | Tucson, Ariz. |
| WONDERLAND OF AMERICA | Boulder, Colo. |
| WONDERLAND OF LAKES | Bridgton, Me. |
| WONDERLAND OF THE TEN THOUSAND ISLANDS | Everglades, Fla. |
| WOODS | Boise, Idaho |
| WOODS | Middletown, R. I. |
| WOOL CITY | Eaton Rapids, Mich. |
| WOOLWORTH TOWN | Watertown, N. Y. |
| WORK CLOTHING CENTER OF THE WORLD | Winder, Ga. |
| WORKING CITY | Lewiston, Me. |
| WORLD CAPITAL OF FASHION | New York, N. Y. |
| WORLD CAPITAL OF THE ORANGE-GROWING INDUSTRY | Eustis, Fla. |
| WORLD CENTER OF OCEANOLOGY | Long Beach, Calif. |
| WORLD FAMOUS MANUFACTURING CENTER | Dayton, Ohio |
| WORLD FAMOUS RESORT AND CONVENTION CENTER | Las Vegas, Nev. |
| WORLD GLIDING CENTER | Bishop, Calif. |
| WORLD OF VARIETY | Los Angeles, Calif. |
| WORLD PORT | Seattle, Wash. |
| WORLD RENOWNED STRIP | Las Vegas, Nev. |
| WORLD'S BEST BEACH | Cocoa Beach, Fla. |
| WORLD'S BEST LITTLE TOWN | Bedford, Pa. |
| WORLD'S BEST TOBACCO MARKET | Danville, Va. |
| WORLD'S CAPITAL CITY | New York, N. Y. |
| WORLD'S CELERY CENTER | Sanford, Fla. |
| WORLD'S CENTRAL LIVESTOCK MARKET | Sioux City, Iowa |
| WORLD'S CITRUS CENTER | Lakeland, Fla. |
| WORLD'S EGG BASKET | Petaluma, Calif. |
| WORLD'S FAIR CITY | Chicago, Ill. |
| WORLD'S FAIR CITY | New York, N. Y. |
| WORLD'S FINANCIAL CAPITAL | New York, N. Y. |

| | |
|---|---|
| WORLD'S FINEST AND SAFEST BATHING BEACH | Wildwood, N. J. |
| WORLD'S FINEST BEACH | Jacksonville Beach, Fla. |
| WORLD'S FINEST NATURAL WHITE SAND BEACHES | Longboat Key, Fla. |
| WORLD'S FIRST RODEO | Pecos, Tex. |
| WORLD'S GREATEST HALIBUT PORT | Seattle, Wash. |
| WORLD'S GREATEST HARBOR | Hampton Roads, Va. |
| WORLD'S GREATEST HARBOR | Newport News, Va. |
| WORLD'S GREATEST MULE MARKET | Galesburg, Ill. |
| WORLD'S GREATEST RESORT | Miami Beach, Fla. |
| WORLD'S GREATEST STOREHOUSE OF RAW MATERIAL | Fort Worth, Tex. |
| WORLD'S GREATEST WORKSHOP | Philadelphia, Pa. |
| WORLD'S HEART TRANSPLANT CAPITAL | Houston, Tex. |
| WORLD'S LARGEST ANTHRACITE COAL MINING CITY | Scranton, Pa. |
| WORLD'S LARGEST ART POTTERY CITY | Macomb, Ill. |
| WORLD'S LARGEST BLACK WALNUT FACTORY | Gravette, Ark. |
| WORLD'S LARGEST CARDINAL GARDENS | Griggsville, Ill. |
| WORLD'S LARGEST COAL-SHIPPING PORT | Toledo, Ohio |
| WORLD'S LARGEST FRESH WATER PORT | Philadelphia, Pa. |
| WORLD'S LARGEST FAMILY RESORT | Daytona Beach, Fla. |
| WORLD'S LARGEST GAMBLING CENTER | Las Vegas, Nev. |
| WORLD'S LARGEST HARDWOOD LUMBER MARKET | Memphis, Tenn. |
| WORLD'S LARGEST IMPORT EXPORT AIR CARGO TERMINAL | Miami, Fla. |
| WORLD'S LARGEST LILAC CENTER | Rochester, N. Y. |
| WORLD'S LARGEST LIVESTOCK AND MEAT PACKING CENTER | Omaha, Neb. |
| WORLD'S LARGEST LOOSE-LEAF TOBACCO MARKET | Lexington, Ky. |
| WORLD'S LARGEST LUMBER SHIPPING PORT | Coos Bay, Ore. |
| WORLD'S LARGEST MINERAL HOT SPRINGS | Thermopolis, Wyo. |
| WORLD'S LARGEST MOBILE HOME MANUFACTURING CENTER | Elkhart, Ind. |
| WORLD'S LARGEST PEANUT CENTER | Suffolk, Va. |

| | |
|---|---|
| WORLD'S LARGEST RAILROAD CENTER | Chicago, Ill. |
| WORLD'S LARGEST SAFEST BATHING BEACH | New Smyrna, Fla. |
| WORLD'S LARGEST SEED AND NURSERY CENTER | Shenandoah, Iowa |
| WORLD'S LARGEST SHALLOW OIL FIELD | Nowata, Okla. |
| WORLD'S LARGEST SPANISH PEANUT MARKET | Dawson, Ga. |
| WORLD'S LARGEST SPOT COTTON MARKET | Memphis, Tenn. |
| WORLD'S LARGEST SPECIALTY JEWELRY MANUFACTURING CENTER | Plainville, Mass. |
| WORLD'S LIVELIEST GHOST TOWN | Virginia City, Nev. |
| WORLD'S LUCKIEST FISHING VILLAGE | Destin, Fla. |
| WORLD'S METROPOLIS | New York, N. Y. |
| WORLD'S MOST BEAUTIFUL CITY | Washington, D. C. |
| WORLD'S MOST EXCITING ALL YEAR ROUND VACATION CENTER | New York, N. Y. |
| WORLD'S MOST FAMOUS BEACH | Daytona Beach, Fla. |
| WORLD'S MOST FAMOUS PLAYGROUND | Santa Cruz, Calif. |
| WORLD'S OYSTER CAPITAL | Norwalk, Conn. |
| WORLD'S PETROLEUM CAPITAL | Houston, Tex. |
| WORLD'S PLAYGROUND | Atlantic City, N. J. |
| WORLD'S PREMIER WINTER RESORT | Palm Beach, Fla. |
| WORLD'S RAILROAD CAPITAL | Chicago, Ill. |
| WORLD'S RAILROAD MECCA | Chicago, Ill. |
| WORLD'S SADDLE HORSE CAPITAL | Mexico, Mo. |
| WORLD'S SAFEST BATHING BEACH | Edgewater, Fla. |
| WORLD'S SALMON CAPITAL | Ketchikan, Alaska |
| WORLD'S SPINACH CAPITAL | Crystal City, Tex. |
| WORLD'S SUBMARINE CAPITAL | Groton, Conn. |
| WORLD'S TURKEY CAPITAL | Harrisonburg, Va. |
| WORLD'S WINTER GOLF CAPITAL | Palm Springs, Calif. |
| WORLD'S WORKSHOP | Pittsburgh, Pa. |
| WORSTED MILL CAPITAL OF THE WORLD | Lawrence, Mass. |
| WURST CITY OF THE WORLD | Sheboygan, Wis. |
| WYOMING'S BIG LITTLE TOWN | Glendo, Wyo. |
| WYOMING'S MOST PROGRESSIVE CITY | Casper, Wyo. |
| WYOMING'S YEAR 'ROUND HEALTH AND SCENIC CENTER | Thermopolis, Wyo. |

Y

| | |
|---|---|
| "Y" BRIDGE CITY | Zanesville, Ohio |

414

| | |
|---|---|
| YACHTING CAPITAL OF NEW ENG-LAND | Boothbay Harbor, Me. |
| YACHTING CAPITAL OF THE WORLD | Marblehead, Mass. |
| YACHTING CAPITAL OF THE WORLD | Newport, R. I. |
| YACHTING CENTER OF THE WORLD | Marblehead, Mass. |
| YANKEE ATHENS | New Haven, Conn. |
| YANKEE CITY | Newburyport, Mass. |
| YEAR AROUND LIVING AT ITS BEST | Lake Weir, Fla. |
| YEAR AROUND PLAYGROUND | Rutland, Vt. |
| YEAR ROUND CENTER FOR MAJOR SPECTATOR EVENTS | Las Vegas, Nev. |
| YEAR-ROUND CONVENTION AND MEETING CENTER | Jekyll Island, Ga. |
| YEAR 'ROUND CONVENTION AND RESORT METROPOLIS OF THE PACIFIC | Long Beach, Calif. |
| YEAR-ROUND CONVENTION CITY | Los Angeles, Calif. |
| YEAR ROUND GOLF CAPITAL OF THE WORLD | Monterey, Calif. |
| YEAR-ROUND HEALTH AND RECRE-ATIONAL RESORT | Kane, Pa. |
| YEAR ROUND PLAYGROUND | Duluth, Minn. |
| YEAR ROUND PLAYGROUND OF THE AMERICAS | Miami Beach, Fla. |
| YEAR ROUND PLAYGROUND OF THE PACIFIC | Long Beach, Calif. |
| YEAR 'ROUND RESORT AND CONVEN-TION CENTER | Biloxi, Miss. |
| YEAR ROUND SPORTSMAN'S PARA-DISE | Okeechobee, Fla. |
| YEAR-ROUND SPORTSMAN'S PARA-DISE | Philipsburg, Mont. |
| YEAR ROUND VACATION PLAYLAND | Atlantic City, N. J. |
| YEAR ROUND VACATION TOWN IN THE WHITE MOUNTAINS | North Conway, N. H. |
| YEAR ROUND VACATIONLAND | Burlington, Vt. |
| YEAR 'ROUND VACATIONLAND | Old Forge, N. Y. |
| YOSEMITE OF ARIZONA | Portal, Ariz. |
| YOSEMITE OF TEXAS | Junction, Tex. |
| YOSEMITE OF THE EAST | Ausable Chasm, N.Y. |
| YOUNG CAPITAL | Washington, D. C. |
| YOUNG MAN'S CAPITAL OF THE WORLD | Tulsa, Okla. |
| YOUNGEST BIG CITY IN THE UNITED STATES | Phoenix, Ariz. |
| YOUNGEST OF THE WORLD'S GREAT CITIES | Birmingham, Ala. |

| | |
|---|---|
| YOUR COOL MOUNTAIN VACATION-<br>LAND | Hendersonville, N.C. |
| YOUR ONE-STOP SPORTS PARADISE | Valentine, Neb. |
| YOUR VACATION CENTER | Watkins Glen, N.Y. |
| YOUR TROPICAL "HOME TOWN" | Englewood, Fla. |
| YOUTHFUL COMMUNITY | Pittsfield, Mass. |

## Z

| | |
|---|---|
| ZENITH CITY | Duluth, Minn. |
| ZENITH CITY OF THE UNSALTED<br>SEAS | Duluth, Minn. |
| ZION | Salt Lake City, Mo. |

## All-American Cities

| | |
|---|---|
| Albuquerque, N. M. | 1957 |
| Alexandria, Va. | 1963 |
| Allentown, Pa. | 1962 |
| Alton, Ill. | 1959 |
| Altus, Okla. | 1956 |
| Anacortes, Wash. | 1961 |
| Anchorage, Alaska | 1956,  1965 |
| Ann Arbor, Mich. | 1966 |
| Asheville, N. C. | 1951 |
| Atlanta, Ga. | 1951 |
| Auburn, Me. | 1967 |
| Aztec, N. M. | 1963 |
| | |
| Baltimore, Md. | 1952 |
| Bartlesville, Okla. | 1962 |
| Bayonne, N. J. | 1949 |
| Bellevue, Wash. | 1955 |
| Bemidji, Minn. | 1952 |
| Bloomington, Ill. | 1955 |
| Bloomington, Ind. | 1958 |
| Bloomington, Minn. | 1960 |
| Bluefield, W. Va. | 1964 |
| Boston, Mass. | 1949,  1951,  1962 |
| Brattleboro, Vt. | 1956 |
| Brookfield, Ill. | 1952 |
| | |
| Cambridge, Ohio | 1955 |
| Canton, Ohio | 1953 |
| Cape Girardeau, Mo. | 1967 |
| Chattanooga, Tenn. | 1962 |
| Chicago, Ill. | 1954 |
| Cincinnati, Ohio | 1949, 1950 |
| Clarksburg, W. Va. | 1957 |
| Clearfield, Pa. | 1966 |
| Cleveland, Ohio | 1949 |
| Cohoes, N. Y. | 1966 |
| Columbia, S. C. | 1951, 1964 |
| Columbus, Ohio | 1958 |
| Compton, Calif. | 1952 |
| | |
| Dayton, Ohio | 1951 |

| | | |
|---|---|---|
| Daytona Beach, Fla. | 1953 | |
| Decatur, Ark. | 1954 | |
| Decatur, Ill. | 1960 | |
| Des Moines, Iowa | 1949 | |
| De Soto, Mo. | 1953, | 1959 |
| Detroit, Mich. | 1966 | |
| | | |
| East Providence, R. I. | 1960 | |
| East St. Louis, Mo. | 1959 | |
| Elgin, Ill. | 1956 | |
| | | |
| Falls Church, Va. | 1961 | |
| Fargo, N. D. | 1959 | |
| Flat River, Mo. | 1965 | |
| Flint, Mich. | 1953 | |
| Florence, S. C. | 1965 | |
| Fort Worth, Tex. | 1964 | |
| Fresno, Calif. | 1967 | |
| | | |
| Galesburg, Ill. | 1957 | |
| Galveston, Tex. | 1961 | |
| Gastonia, N. C. | 1963 | |
| Grafton, W. Va. | 1962 | |
| Grand Island, Neb. | 1955, | 1967 |
| Grand Junction, Colo. | 1962 | |
| Grand Rapids, Mich. | 1949, | 1960 |
| Granite City, Ill. | 1958 | |
| Green Bay, Wis. | 1964 | |
| Greensboro, N. C. | 1966 | |
| | | |
| Hartford, Conn. | 1950, | 1961 |
| Hayden, Ariz. | 1958 | |
| Hazleton, Pa. | 1964 | |
| Hickory, N. C. | 1967 | |
| High Point, N. C. | 1962 | |
| Highland Park, Ill. | 1958 | |
| Hopkinsville, Ky. | 1964 | |
| Huntington, W. Va. | 1958 | |
| | | |
| Independence, Mo. | 1961 | |
| | | |
| Joliet, Ill. | 1955 | |
| | | |
| Kalamazoo, Mich. | 1951 | |
| Kansas City, Mo. | 1950, | 1951 |
| Keene, N. H. | 1964 | |
| Ketchikan, Alaska | 1957 | |
| Knoxville, Tenn. | 1962 | |

| La Crosse, Wis. | 1965 | |
| Lamar, Colo. | 1959 | |
| Las Vegas, Nev. | 1960 | |
| Laurinburg, N. C. | 1956, | 1967 |
| Leadville, Colo. | 1958 | |
| Leavenworth, Wash. | 1967 | |
| Louisville, Ky | 1963 | |
| Lynwood, Calif. | 1961 | |
| | | |
| Malden, Mass. | 1966 | |
| Manhattan, Kan. | 1952 | |
| Mexico, Mo. | 1954 | |
| Miami, Fla. | 1952, | 1957 |
| Michigan City, Ind. | 1965 | |
| Middletown, Ohio | 1957 | |
| Milton, Ore. | 1961 | |
| Minneapolis, Minn. | 1952, | 1963 |
| Modesto, Calif. | 1954 | |
| Montclair, N. J. | 1950 | |
| Mount Vernon, Ill. | 1951 | |
| Mount Vernon, Ohio | 1965 | |
| | | |
| Neosho, Mo. | 1957 | |
| Newark, N. J. | 1954 | |
| Newburgh, N. Y. | 1952 | |
| New Haven, Conn. | 1958 | |
| New Orleans, La. | 1950 | |
| Niles, Ill. | 1964 | |
| Norfolk, Va. | 1959 | |
| | | |
| Oakland, Calif. | 1956 | |
| Ogallala, Neb. | 1965 | |
| Oil City, Pa. | 1963 | |
| Omaha, Neb. | 1957 | |
| Owensboro, Ky. | 1952 | |
| | | |
| Park Forest, Ill. | 1953 | | |
| Pawtucket, R. I. | 1951 | | |
| Peoria, Ill. | 1953, | 1966 | |
| Petersburg, Va. | 1953 | | |
| Phenix City, Ala. | 1955 | | |
| Philadelphia, Pa. | 1949, | 1951, | 1957 |
| Phoenix, Ariz. | 1950, | 1958 | |
| Pikeville, Ky. | 1965 | | |
| Pinellas Co. , Fla. | 1966 | | |
| Pittsburgh, Pa. | 1949 | | |
| Port Angeles, Wash. | 1953 | | |
| Port Huron, Mich. | 1955 | | |

| | |
|---|---|
| Portland, Me. | 1950 |
| Poughkeepsie, N. Y. | 1949 |
| Presque Isle, Me. | 1966 |
| Pueblo, Colo. | 1954 |
| | |
| Quincy, Ill. | 1962 |
| | |
| Radford, Va. | 1960 |
| Reading, Pa. | 1955 |
| Richfield, Minn. | 1954 |
| Richland, Wash. | 1960 |
| Richmond, Calif. | 1953 |
| Richmond, Va. | 1950, 1966 |
| Riverside, Calif. | 1955 |
| Roanoke, Va. | 1952 |
| Rock Island, Ill. | 1954 |
| Rockville, Md. | 1954, 1961 |
| Roseville, Calif. | 1963 |
| Royal Oak, Mich. | 1967 |
| | |
| St. Louis, Mo. | 1956 |
| St. Paul, Minn. | 1955 |
| Salem, Ore. | 1960 |
| Salisbury, N. C. | 1961 |
| San Antonio, Tex. | 1949, 1951 |
| San Diego, Calif. | 1962 |
| San Jose, Calif. | 1960 |
| Santa Fe Springs, Calif. | 1959 |
| Savannah, Ga. | 1955 |
| Scranton, Pa. | 1953 |
| Seattle, Wash. | 1959, 1966 |
| Seward, Alaska | 1963, 1965 |
| Sheridan, Wyo. | 1958 |
| Shreveport, La. | 1953 |
| Sidney, Ohio | 1963 |
| Sioux City, Iowa | 1961 |
| South Bend, Ind. | 1967 |
| South Portland, Me. | 1964 |
| Springfield, Mo. | 1956 |
| | |
| Tacoma, Wash. | 1956 |
| Toledo, Ohio | 1950 |
| Torrance, Calif. | 1956 |
| Tupelo, Miss. | 1967 |
| | |
| Valdez, Alaska | 1965 |
| Vallejo, Calif. | 1959 |
| Vancouver, Wash. | 1957 |

| | |
|---|---|
| Warren, Ohio | 1954 |
| Westport, Conn. | 1958 |
| Wheaton, Ill. | 1967 |
| White Bear Lake, Minn. | 1964 |
| Wichita, Kan. | 1961 |
| Wilmington, N. C. | 1965 |
| Winston-Salem, N. C. | 1959, 1964 |
| Woodbridge, N. J. | 1963 |
| Woodstock, Ill. | 1963 |
| Woonsocket, R. I. | 1952 |
| Worcester, Mass. | 1949, 1961, 1965 |
| | |
| Yankton, S. D. | 1957 |
| Youngstown, Ohio | 1950 |
| | |
| Zanesville, Ohio | 1956 |

# Geographical Index
## States

### ALABAMA

The Cornucopia of the South, The Cotton State (cotton plantations), The Heart of Dixie, The Heart of the Deep South, The Land of Flowers, The Land of Opportunity, The Lizard State (lizards), The Pioneer Space Capital of the World, The Star of the South, The State of Productive Farms, The Vacationland, The Yellowhammer State (the uniforms of the Confederate soldiers had a home-dyed yellow tinge)

### ALASKA

America's Last Frontier, America's Last Great Frontier, America's Last Outpost, America's Last Primeval Wilderness, America's Newest Gayest Frontier, America's Northern Frontier, American Land of the Midnight Sun, The Arctic Land of the Eskimo, The Arctic Treasureland, The Beautiful Northland of Opportunity, The Big Land, The Big State, The Eskimoland, The Far North Frontier, The Great Bear's Cub, The Great Land, Johnson's Polar Bear Garden, The Land of Adventure, The Land of Now (title of book by D.A. Noonan), The Land of Opportunity, The Land of Promise, The Land of Tomorrow, The Land of Yesterday, Today and Tomorrow, The Land of the Midnight Sun, The Land where the Summer Sun Never Sets, The Last American Frontier (the 49th state, admitted Jan. 3, 1959), The Last Frontier, The Midnight Sunland, The Nation's New Playground, The New Frontier, The Northern Wonderland, The Northernmost State, Seward's Folly (William Henry Seward, U.S. Secretary of State, advocated and negotiated purchase from Russia for $7,200,000), Seward's Ice Box (U.S. Secretary of State arranged for Alaska's purchase from Russia), The State of Contrasts, Uncle Sam's Icebox, The Vacationland of Opportunity, The Wonderland Unsurpassed

### ARIZONA

Amazing Arizona, where You Can Always Expect to Enjoy the Unexpected, The Apache State (Indian tribes), The Aztec State

(Aztec names), The Baby State (48th state, admitted February 14, 1912), The Canyon State, The Copper State (copper production), Friendly Arizona, The Grand Canyon State, The Healthful State, The Italy of America (scenic), The Land of Sunshine and Scenic Grandeur, The Land where the Sun Spends the Winter, One of America's Most Popular Playgrounds, The Sand Hill State (desert), The State where You Can Always Expect to Enjoy the Unexpected, The Sunset Land, The Sunset State, The Vacation State of the Nation, The Valentine State (admitted on Valentine Day, February 14, 1912), The Wonderland, The Youngest State (the 48th state, admitted Feb. 14, 1912)

## ARKANSAS

The Bear State (bears), The Bowie State (bowie knives used), The Guinea Pig State (proving ground for experiments of Department of Agriculture), The Home of the Peach, Strawberry and Vine, The Hot Water State (numerous hot springs), The Land of Opportunity, The Land of Majestic Beauty, The Nation's Cool Green Paradise, The Toothpick State (bowie knives in handles), The Wonder State

## CALIFORNIA

America's Number One Market, The Cornucopia of the World, The El Dorado State, The Eureka State, The Gateway to the Pacific, The Golden State (gold discovered in 1848; golden poppies each spring), The Grape State (grape production), The Land of Discoveries, The Land of Gold, The Land of Living Color, The Land of Opportunity, The Land of Promise, The Land of Sunshine and Flowers, The Sunshine Empire, The Wine Land of America

## COLORADO

America's Vacation Paradise, The Buffalo Plains State, The Centennial State (admitted August 1, 1876, the hundredth anniversary of the Declaration of Independence), The Colorful Colorado, The Gateway to the Rocky Mountain West, The Glorious Vacation Playground, The Highest State (highest mean elevation, 54 of its peaks over 14,000 feet in height), The Highest State in the Union (average altitude 6,800 feet), The Land of Contrasts, The Lead State (lead production), The Rocky Mountain Empire, The Silver State (silver production), The Ski Country, U.S.A., The State of Magnificent Scenery, The Switzerland of America (numerous high mountains),

The Top of the Nation (mountain peaks), The Top Vacation
State of the Nation, The Vacation Country, The Winter Paradise of America

## CONNECTICUT

The Arsenal of the Nation, The Blue Law State (New Haven
blue laws), The Brownstone State (quarries), The Constitu-
tion State (1639, first written constitution, the Fundamental
Orders, official nickname, enacted by Public Act 121, Jan.
session 1959), The Doorway to Nostalgic New England, The
Freestone State (freestone quarries), The Holiday State, The
Insurance State, The Land of Steady Habits, The Nutmeg
State (wooden nutmegs), The State Alive with Variety and
Fun to See, The Wooden Nutmeg State

## DELAWARE

The Blue Hen State (a fighting hen popular in the Revolutionary War for its bravery), The Blue Hen's Chickens State
(see above), The Diamond State (because it is small in size
yet important), The Economic Sunshine State, The First State
(Delaware on December 7, 1787 was the first state to ratify
the Constitution), New Sweden (name of fort built in 1638
by Peter Minuit whose expedition was sent out by Queen
Christiana), The Peach State (used in the 1840's), Uncle
Sam's Pocket Handkerchief

## FLORIDA

The Airconditioned State, The Alligator State (alligators),
America's Dream Vacation State, The Everglades State (ever-
glades), Fabulous Florida, The Gateway to the World, The
Gulf State (on Gulf of Mexico), The Land of Flowers, The
Land of Fun, Sun and Sand, The Land of Sunshine, The Ma-
rina Capital of the U. S. A., The National Country, The New
American Frontier, The Orange Land, The Orange State
(orange and citrus production), The Peninsula State (geograph-
ical), The Scenic Wonderland, The Southernmost State, The
Sports Capital of the World, The State of Festivals, Theatre,
Museums and Music, The Sunshine State, The U. S. Gateway
to Latin America, Winter Salad Bowl

## GEORGIA

The Airlift Center of the World, The Buzzard State, The
Cracker State, The Different Vacation State, The Empire

State of the South, The Goober State, The Land of Blossoms and Relaxed Living, The Land of Peanuts, Pecans and Peaches, The Pace Setter of the South, The Peach State, The South's Empire State, The State of Adventure, The State of Incredible Variety, The Yankee Land of the South, Year 'Round Vacation Wonderland

## HAWAII

The All-American Playground, The Aloha State (official nickname enacted by Joint Resolution No. 1, April 23, 1959, 30th Territorial Legislature), The Convention Center of the Pacific, The Fiftieth State of Enchantment, The Gateway to the Orient, The Gateway to the Pacific, The Gem of the Pacific, The Island Paradise, The Island State, The Jewel of the Pacific, The Land of Leisure, The Orchid Isle, The Paradise of the Pacific, The Pineapple State (second and most important product), The Playground of the Pacific, The Scenic Isle, The State at the Crossroads of the Pacific, The Tropical Paradise, The Window on the East, The Youngest State (the 50th state, admitted Aug. 21, 1959), Your Dreamland of Pleasure

## IDAHO

The Gem State, The Gem of the Mountain States, The Gem of the Mountains, The Land of Pleasure, The Place to Go, The State of Shining Mountains, The Vacation Land, The Vacation Land of Your Fondest Dreams, The Vacation Wonderland

## ILLINOIS

The Corn Belt State, The Corn State, The Crossroads of America, Egypt, The Garden of the West, The Great Lakes State, The Heart of the Nation, The Hub of the Nation, The Jubilee State for '68, The Land of Lincoln, The Land of the Illini, The Livestock Feeding State, The Prairie State, The Sucker State, The Vacation Target for Millions of Americans, The Vacationland

## INDIANA

The Center of the Commercial Universe, The Crossroads of America (official nickname enacted March 2, 1937, House Joint Resolution No. 6, chapter 312), The Hoosier State (claimed to originate from early pioneer greeting "Who'shyer"), The State of Surprises

# IOWA

The Beautiful Land, The Beautiful Land Between Two Great
Rivers, The Brightest Star in the American Constellation,
The Food Market of the World, The Greatest Food Producing
Area in the World, The Haven for the Traveler, The Hawk-
eye State (Indian Chief Hawkeye), The Land of the Rolling
Prairie, The Land Rich in History, Heritage and Hospitality,
The Last Frontier of Industrial Development, The Leading
Farm Crop, The Peerless State, The State where the West
Begins and Progress Never Ceases, The Vacation Haven in
Mid-Nation

# KANSAS

Bleeding Kansas (the seven hectic years, 1854-1861, while
slavery was at stake), The Breadbasket of the Nation, The
Central State (geographical location), The "Clean Air" Country, The Cyclone State, The First in Clean Air, The Friendly State, The Garden of the West, The Garden State, The
Grasshopper State, The Great State, The Jayhawk State (ir-
regular troops and pillaging bands in Civil War--one of several explanations, a bird), Midway U. S. A. (center of travel
and transportation, commerce and industry), The Salt of the
Earth (enough salt reserves to provide the U. S. for 375,000
years at the present rate of use), The Squatter State (squat-
ters who arrived about 1854), The Sunflower State, The
Wheat State, The Wheat State of America, The Wheatheart
of the Nation (first in wheat production and flour milling)

# KENTUCKY

The Blue Grass Region, The Bluegrass State (blueish tinged
grass), The Corncracker State (corn-cracker birds), The
Dark and Bloody Ground State (battleground of Indian tribes),
The Hemp State, One Hundred Vacation Lands Into One, The
Pioneer Commonwealth, The State where Big Things Are
Happening, The Tobacco State, The Vacation Center of Amer-
ica, The Vacation Paradise

# LOUISIANA

The Bayou State, The Bayou Wonderland, The Child of the
Mississippi River, The Creole State (creoles of French and
Spanish descent), The Holland of America (numerous canals),

427

The Lovely Louisiana, The Nation's Growth Frontier, The Nation's Industrial Frontier, Nature's Cornucopia, The Pelican State (the brown pelican native to the shore), The Picturesque Historic Land of Early America, The Right to Profit State, The Sportsman's Paradise, The State That Has to be Seen to be Believed, The Sugar State, The Variety Vacationland

## MAINE

America's Top Vacation Land, The Angler's Paradise, The Border State, The Complete Vacationland, The Convention State, The Down East State, The Four-Season State, The Great Place to Live, Laze, Locate, The Great Recreation Center, The Health Resort of America, The Land of Remembered Vacations, Lobsterland, The Lumber State, The Nation's Vacationland, The Old Dirigo State (state motto "Dirigo"), The Pine Tree State (pine tree depicted on the coat-of-arms), The Place to Live, Work and Play, The Playground of the Nation, The Polar Star State, The Scenic Wonderland, The State where Every Season Is Vacation Time, State where History and Hospitality Began, The Summer Playground of the Nation, The Switzerland of America (scenic), The Vacationland, The World of Good That Awaits You

## MARYLAND

The Cockade State (a type of hat worn by patricians), The Delightful Land, The Delightsome Land, The Free State, The Monumental State (because of its monuments, principally in Baltimore), The Old Line State (the dividing line between the crown land grants of William Penn and Lord Baltimore), The Oyster State (oyster fisheries), The Queen State (named for Queen Henrietta Maria), The Star-Spangled Banner State

## MASSACHUSETTS

The Baked Bean State, The Bay State (Massachusetts Bay), The Bean Eating State, The Bean State, The Birthplace of American Democracy, The Birthplace of American Freedom, The Custodian of America's Heritage, The Custodian of America's Historical Heritage, The Four-Season Vacationland, The Historic Vacationland, The Most Varied State of the Fifty, The Old Bay State, The Old Colony State, The Puritan State, The Space Center of the World, The Vacationland of Fun and Plenty, The Wellspring of Art and Culture, The World of Fun and Relaxation, The Year 'Round Vacationland

428

# MICHIGAN

The Auto State, The Automobile State, The Big Fish State,
The Four Season Vacation Fun Land, The Great Lake State,
The Jewel of Many Facets, The Lady of the Lake (Lake
Michigan), The Lake State (touches Lakes Michigan, Superior,
Erie, Huron and St. Clair), One of the Great Resort States
of the Middle West, The Peninsula State, The Playtime Country, The Tourist Empire of the Inland Seas, The Water Wonderland, The Water-Winter Wonderland, The Winter Wonderland, The Wolverine State, The Wonderland of 11,000 Lakes

# MINNESOTA

The Bread and Butter State (flour and dairy industry), The
Gopher State (gophers), The Lake State (14,215 lakes over
10 acres in size), The Land of 10,000 Lakes (see above),
The Nation's Vacation Land, The New England of the West,
The North Star State (the state seal has the motto L'Etoile
du Nord, the star of the north), The Playground of 10,000
Lakes, The Rich and Varied Land, The United Nations in
Miniature, The Wheat State

# MISSISSIPPI

A Great Agricultural State, America's State of Opportunity,
The Bayou State (bayous, rivulets), The Border-eagle State
(eagle depicted on the coat-of-arms), The Cotton Kingdom,
The Crossroads of the South, The Eagle State (see above),
The Fastest Growing Cattle State, The Fun-Filled Vacation
Land, The Gateway to the Southland, The Groundhog State,
The Heart of the Deep South, The Hospitality State, The Mag-
nolia State (magnolia trees), The Mud-cat State (name for
catfish), The Mud-waddler State, The State of Opportunity,
The State of the Future, The State Rich in Beauty and Abundant Resources, The State where Cotton Is Still King, The Tad-
pole State (young French settlers; "frogs" being nickname
applied to their elders), Variety Vacationland for All the
Family

# MISSOURI

The Bullion State (Thomas Hart Benton, known as Old Bullion),
The Cave State (26 caves open), The Family Vacationland, The
Fire Clay Capital, The Heart of America, The Heartland of
Hospitality, The Iron Mountain State (Iron Mountain), The
Lead State (lead production), Little Dixie, Memorable Mis-

souri, The Mother of the West, The National Gateway to the Frontierlands, The Ozark State (Ozark Mountain), The Pennsylvania of the West, The Puke State, The Show Me State, The Vacation Capital of the Midwest, The World's Saddle Horse Capital

## MONTANA

The Big Ski Country, The Big Sky Country, The Big Sky Vacationland, The Bonanza State, The Four Season Vacationland, The Land of Enchantment, The Land of Scenic Splendor, The Land of the Shining Mountains, The Lead State (lead production), The Singed Cat State, The Stub Toe State, The Treasure State, The Vacation State, The Wonderland

## NEBRASKA

The Antelope State (antelopes), The Beef State (cattle production), The Big Country, The Birthplace of Rodeo, The Black Water State (dark soil which makes water appear dark), The Bug-eating State (bull bats which eat bugs), The Corn Husking State, The Cornhusker State, The Land of the Oregon Trail and the Pony Express, The Land where the West Begins, The Leisureland State, The Nation's Mixed-bag Capital (77, 227 square miles of diversified hunting), Nebraskaland, The Sportsman's Paradise, The State on the March, The State where the West Begins, The Tall Corn State, The Treeplanter State, The Western Playground

## NEVADA

The Battle Born State (Nevada was made a territory in 1861 and admitted as a state in 1864 during the Civil War), The Entertainment Capital of the World, The Mining State, The Nation's Fastest Growing State, One Sound State (slogan because of good financial condition in 1929-1933 depression), The Sage State (prevalence of wild sage), The Sage-hen State (a common-type of fowl), The Sagebrush State (wild sage), The Silver State (silver mines), The State where Man and Nature Gamble, The Vacation State, Your Vacation State

## NEW HAMPSHIRE

The Granite State (granite is the bedrock underlying most of the surface), The Land of Peace and Beauty, The Land of Scenic Splendor, The Mother of Rivers, The Old Man of the Mountain State (rock formation), The Scenic State, The State in the Heart of New England, The State of Surprise, The

Switzerland of America (scenic), The White Mountain State (White Mountains), The Yankee Playland

## NEW JERSEY

The Adaptable State, The Camden and Amboy State (Camden and Amboy Railroad), The Center of World Transportation, The Clam State (seafood production), The Cockpit of History, The Cockpit of the Revolution (used in 1776), The Crossroads of the East, The Crossroads State, The Energy-packed State, The Foreigner State (see New Spain State), The Garden State, The Garden State for Pleasure and Business, The Geographic Center of the World's Richest Market, History's Main Road, The Hub of Commerce, The Industrial Park State (more industrial parks per square mile than any other state), The Jersey Blue State (blue uniforms worn by Revolutionary Army troops, or blue laws), The Land of Amazing Advantages, The Land of Amazing Industrial Advantages, The Mosquito State, Nature's Showcase, The New Spain State (in 1812 Joseph Bonaparte, king of Spain, fled to Bordentown, N. J., where he bought 1, 400 acres), The Pathway of the Revolution (nearly 100 battles were fought on New Jersey soil), The Riviera of America, The Sharpbacks State, The Small State, Big in Agriculture, Big in Industry, The State of Camden and Amboy (see above), The State of Spain (see above), The State where You Come for a Visit and Come Back for a Lifetime, U. S. Gateway to the World, The Vacationland the Year 'Round

## NEW MEXICO

The Cactus Land (profusion of cactus), The Colorful State, The Land of the Cactus (cactus plants), The Land of Enchantment, The Land of Hearts' Desire, The Land of Opportunity, The Land of Sunshine, The Land of the Delight-Makers (from the book "The Delight Makers" by Adolf Bandelier), The Playground of the Southwest, The Space Age Research Center for the Free World, The Spanish State, The State of Diversity, The State of Spain State, The Sunshine State, The Unspoiled Empire, Vacation and Industrial Nucleus of the Southwest, The Vermin State

## NEW YORK

America's Cultural Capital, The Center of American Culture, The Empire State, The Excelsior State (motto), The Gateway to Expo 67 (International Fair at Montreal, Canada), The Host State for the World's Fair, The Knickerbocker State (short loose trousers worn by the early Dutch settlers), The Nation's Showcase, The Seat of Empire, The State That Has Everything, The Vacation Empire, The Vacation Variety, The World of Scenic Beauty, The Year-Round Vacationland

## NORTH CAROLINA

The Dixie Dynamo, The Game Fish Junction, The Goodliest Land Under the Cape of Heaven, The Ireland of America, The Land of Beginnings (site of the first settlement in America, Roanoke Island), The Land of the Sky (many mountain peaks), Nature's Mineral Specimen Case (over 300 different minerals found), The Old North State (north of South Carolina), The Rip Van Winkle State (used in the 1830's when it was undeveloped and backward), The Second Nazareth, The Tarheel State (a derisive name applied by Mississippi soldiers to North Carolinians who failed to hold their position, and did not put tar on their heels), The Turpentine State (product obtained from the pine trees), The Variety Vacationland, The Year-Round Mid-South, The Year 'Round Vacation State

## NORTH DAKOTA

America's Newest Family Vacationland, The Crossroads of All America, The Flickertail State (the flickertail squirrel), The Friendly State, The Great Central State (center of the wheat belt), The Land of the Dakotas (Dakota Indians), The Land of Fresh Horizons, The Land of the Long North Furrow, The Land of the North Furrow, The Land of Theodore Roosevelt and General Custer, The Peace Garden State, The Sioux State (Indian tribe) The State where the Sunshine Speaks the Winter, Visit North Dakota for Family Water Fun

## OHIO

The Buckeye State (buckeye or horse-chestnut, buckeye resemblance to the seed, both in color, shape and appearance to the eye of the buck), The Gateway State (to the Northwest Territory), The Gateway to the Northwest Territory, The Land of History, The Land of Opportunity, The Modern Mother of Presidents (birthplace of Grant, Hayes, Garfield, B. Harrison, McKinley, Taft and Harding), The Mother of Presidents, The Oldest State West of the Thirteen Original Colonies, The State on the Move, The State where History and the Present Make Your Visit Delightful, The Tomato State (first in tomato production under glass, 500 acres of greenhouses), The Yankee State (because of its free institutions), The "You-Name-It-We-Make-It" State

432

## OKLAHOMA

America's Newest Vacationland, America's Vacation Treasureland, America's Year Round Adventureland, The Boomers' Paradise (the "boomers" who opened Oklahoma, April 22, 1889), The Empire State Dedicated to Progress, The Heart of the Cow Country, The Land of the Red Men, The Sooner State ("sooners" were those who entered Oklahoma sooner than the designated legal time), The State of Industry, The State Pioneering in Progress, The State With New Ideas, The State where the Wind Comes Sweepin' Down the Plains, The Vacation Adventureland

## OREGON

America's Finest Vacationland, America's Northwest Playland, The Beaver State, The Cool, Green Vacationland, The Hard-case State (rough life of the early settlers), The Land of Exciting Contrasts, The Land of Opportunity, The Land where Dreams Come True, Nature's Wonderland, The Pacific Wonderland, The Scenic State, The State of Excitement, The Sunset State, The Threshold of Paradise, The Web-foot State (excessive rain in winter) The Welcome State

## PENNSYLVANIA

The Birth State of the Nation (Declaration of American Independence signed, July 4, 1776), The Birthplace of a Nation, The Coal State (coal mines), The Keystone State (central geographical position among the thirteen original colonies), The Nation's Family Playground, The Nation's Ideal Family Playground, The Quaker State (founded in 1680 by William Penn), The State of Excitement, The State of 1001 Vacation Pleasures, The Steel State (industry), The Tourist State, The Workshop of the World

## RHODE ISLAND

America's First Vacationland, The American Venice, The Land of Roger Williams (founded Providence 1636), Little Rhody, The Nation's First Tourist Host, Our Social Capital, The Plantation State (the State of Rhode Island and Providence Plantations), The Southern Gateway of New England

## SOUTH CAROLINA

The Iodine State, The Keystone of the South Atlantic Seaboard (wedge shape), The Land of Recreation and Progress, The

Palmetto State (tree), The Rice State (rice production), The Sand-lapper State (humorous, designation of poor people who lapped up sand for subsistence), The State That Forgot (title of book by W. Ball), The State where Resources and Markets Meet, The Swamp State (rice fields), The Wonderful Iodine State

## SOUTH DAKOTA

The Artesian State (artesian wells), The Blizzard State (gales, storms), The Coyote State (coyotes), The Friendly Land of Infinite Variety, The Frontier of Pleasure, The Land of Infinite Variety, The Land of Plenty, The Land of Wonder, The Pheasant Capital of the World, The State With Many Landscapes, The Sunshine State, The Swiagecat State

## TENNESSEE

America At Its Best, America's Central Vacation Land, America's Most Interesting State, The Big Bend State (Indian name for the Tennessee River), The Hog and Hominy State (leader in corn and pork products in the 1830's), The Interstate State, The Lion's Den State, The Mother of Southwestern Statesmen (Jackson, Polk, Andrew Johnson), The Nation's Most Interesting State, The River With the Big Bend (the Tennessee River), The Scenic Wonderland, The State where Every Season is Vacation Time, The Three States in One, The Volunteer State (on May 26, 1847 during the Mexican War, Governor Aaron Vail Brown called for 2, 800 volunteers and 30, 000 responded)

## TEXAS

America's Fun-tier, The Banner State (descriptive word, leading, excelling, etc. ), The Beef State (cattle production), The Blizzard State (dust storms and wind storms), The Jumbo State (referring to size, name of large elephant exhibited by P. T. Barnum), The Land of Opportunity, The Land of Promise (title of book by Joseph Lynn Clark), The Lone Star State (single star in its coat-of-arms and flag), The New World of Adventure, The Republic, The State of the Confederacy

## UTAH

The Beehive State (emblem on the coat-of-arms of Utah), The Center of Scenic America, The Colorful Vacation Land, The Deseret State (the name by which Utah was known in 1849-

1850), The Friendly State, The Good Highway State, The
Honey State (the product found in beehives), The Hub of the
West, The Land of Blossoming Valleys, The Land of Color,
The Land of Color and Contrasts, The Land of Contrasts,
The Land of Endless Scenic Discovery, The Land of Honey
Bees, The Land of Mormons (the Book of Mormon, or Golden
Bible written by the prophet Mormon), The Land of the
Saints (the Mormons whose official church name is the Church
of Jesus Christ of the Latter-Day Saints), The Magic Land
of Colorful Past and Interesting Future, The Mormon State,
Nature's Wonderland, The Salt Lake State (the Great Salt
Lake, area 1,500 square miles), The World of Scenic Beauty,
The Year 'Round Paradise

## VERMONT

The Beauty State of New England, The Beckoning Country,
Every American's Second State, Everybody's Second State,
Everything for Outdoor Living, The Four-Season State, The
Four Seasons' Recreation State, The Green Mountain State
(name of the mountain range), The Ski State of the East
The State Where Profit and Pleasure are Part of the Eco-
nomic Mix

## VIRGINA

America's Historyland, The Ancient Dominion, The Battlefield of the Civil War, The Beckoning Land, The Birthplace
of Eight Presidents (Washington, Jefferson, Madison, Monroe, W.H. Harrison, Tyler, Taylor and Wilson), The Birthplace of the Nation, The Cavalier State (cavaliers settled in
Virginia sided with the king against the Parliament), The
Commonwealth (term applied to Virginia in its first constitution, adopted June 29, 1776), The Land of Romance, The
Mother of Presidents, The Mother of States (the first state
to be settled, the 1609 charter embraced West Virginia, Kentucky, Ohio, Illinois, Indiana, Wisconsin and parts of Minnesota), The Mother of States and Statesmen, The Mother of
Statesmen (Washington, Jefferson, Madison, Monroe, Marshall,
Mason, Patrick Henry, Richard Henry Lee, Payton Randolph,
Jr.), The Old Dominion State (Charles II called the colony
"the old dominion" because of its loyalty to the Crown)

## WASHINGTON

The Boating Capital of the World, The Chinook State (Chinook
division of Indians) (for its salmon industry), The Clam Grab-
bers, The Evergreen State (forests of fir and pine) (green

firs), The Exciting State of Contrasts, The Gateway to Alaska and the Orient, The State of Contrasts, The State of Exciting Contrasts, The Surprising State

## WEST VIRGINIA

The Appalachian State, The Free State, The Fuel State, The Land for Relaxation, The Land of Growth and Grandeur, The Land of Resourcefulness and Relaxation, The Little Mountain State (Allegheny Mountains), The Mountain State, The Panhandle State (descriptive of shape), The Place to See; The Place to Be; for Industry, for Vacations, The State of Dynamic Industry, The Switzerland of America (scenic), The Vacationland of the East

## WISCONSIN

America's Dairyland, The Badger State (so-called because the early settlers lived underground), The Cheese Capital of the Nation, The Copper State (copper mines), The Four Season Vacationland, The Land That Was Made for Vacations, The Nation's Finest Vacationland, The Playground of the Middle West, The Vacation Land For All, Wonderful Wisconsin

## WYOMING

The Cowboy State, The Equality State (equal suffrage extended to women in 1869), The Equality Suffrage State, The Gateway to the Scenic Wonders of the Great West, The Land of Cattle and Sheep, The Land of the Purple Sage, The Mountain Wonderland, The Sagebrush State (wild sage growing in the deserts), The Sanctuary of Peace, The Vacation Wonderland, The Wonderland of America, Wonderful Wyoming

A

| | |
|---|---|
| ADAPTABLE STATE | New Jersey |
| AIRCONDITIONED STATE | Florida |
| AIRLIFT CENTER OF THE WORLD | Georgia |
| ALL-AMERICAN PLAYGROUND | Hawaii |
| ALLIGATOR STATE | Florida |
| ALOHA STATE | Hawaii |
| AMAZING ARIZONA WHERE YOU CAN ALWAYS EXPECT TO ENJOY THE UN- EXPECTED | Arizona |
| AMERICA AT ITS BEST | Tennessee |
| AMERICA'S CENTRAL VACATION LAND | Tennessee |
| AMERICA'S CULTURAL CAPITAL | New York |
| AMERICA'S DAIRYLAND | Wisconsin |
| AMERICA'S DREAM VACATION STATE | Florida |
| AMERICA'S FINEST VACATIONLAND | Oregon |
| AMERICA'S FIRST VACATIONLAND | Rhode Island |
| AMERICA'S FUN-TIER | Texas |
| AMERICA'S HISTORYLAND | Virginia |
| AMERICA'S LAST FRONTIER | Alaska |
| AMERICA'S LAST GREAT FRONTIER | Alaska |
| AMERICA'S LAST OUTPOST | Alaska |
| AMERICA'S LAST PRIMEVAL WILDER- NESS | Alaska |
| AMERICA'S MOST INTERESTING STATE | Tennessee |
| AMERICA'S NEWEST FAMILY VACATION- LAND | North Dakota |
| AMERICA'S NEWEST GAYEST FRONTIER | Alaska |
| AMERICA'S NEWEST VACATIONLAND | Oklahoma |
| AMERICA'S NORTHERN FRONTIER | Alaska |
| AMERICA'S NUMBER ONE MARKET | California |
| AMERICA'S NORTHWEST PLAYLAND | Oregon |
| AMERICA'S STATE OF OPPORTUNITY | Mississippi |
| AMERICA'S TOP VACATION LAND | Maine |
| AMERICA'S VACATION PARADISE | Colorado |
| AMERICA'S VACATION TREASURELAND | Oklahoma |
| AMERICA'S YEAR ROUND ADVENTURE- LAND | Oklahoma |

| | |
|---|---|
| AMERICAN LAND OF THE MIDNIGHT SUN | Alaska |
| AMERICAN VENICE | Rhode Island |
| ANCIENT DOMINION | Virginia |
| ANGLER'S PARADISE | Maine |
| ANTELOPE STATE | Nebraska |
| APACHE STATE | Arizona |
| APPALACHIAN STATE | West Virginia |
| ARCTIC LAND OF THE ESKIMO | Alaska |
| ARCTIC TREASURELAND | Alaska |
| ARSENAL OF THE NATION | Connecticut |
| ARTESIAN STATE | South Dakota |
| AUTO STATE | Michigan |
| AUTOMOBILE STATE | Michigan |
| AZTEC STATE | Arizona |

B

| | |
|---|---|
| BABY STATE | Arizona |
| BADGER STATE | Wisconsin |
| BAKED BEAN STATE | Massachusetts |
| BANNER STATE | Texas |
| BATTLE-BORN STATE | Nevada |
| BATTLEFIELD OF THE CIVIL WAR | Virginia |
| BAY STATE | Massachusetts |
| BAYOU STATE | Louisiana |
| BAYOU STATE | Mississippi |
| BAYOU WONDERLAND | Louisiana |
| BEAN EATING STATE | Massachusetts |
| BEAN STATE | Massachusetts |
| BEAR STATE | Arkansas |
| BEAUTIFUL LAND | Iowa |
| BEAUTIFUL LAND BETWEEN TWO GREAT RIVERS | Iowa |
| BEAUTIFUL NORTHLAND OF OPPORTUNITY | Alaska |
| BEAUTY STATE OF NEW ENGLAND | Vermont |
| BEAVER STATE | Oregon |
| BECKONING COUNTRY | Vermont |
| BECKONING LAND | Virginia |
| BEEF STATE | Nebraska |
| BEEF STATE | Texas |
| BEEHIVE STATE | Utah |
| BIG BEND COUNTRY | Texas |
| BIG BEND STATE | Tennessee |
| BIG COUNTRY | Nebraska |
| BIG FISH STATE | Michigan |

438

| | |
|---|---|
| BIG LAND | Alaska |
| BIG SKI COUNTRY | Montana |
| BIG SKY COUNTRY | Montana |
| BIG SKY VACATIONLAND | Montana |
| BIG STATE | Alaska |
| BIRTH STATE OF THE NATION | Pennsylvania |
| BIRTHPLACE OF A NATION | Pennsylvania |
| BIRTHPLACE OF AMERICAN DEMOC- | |
| RACY | Massachusetts |
| BIRTHPLACE OF AMERICAN FREEDOM | Massachusetts |
| BIRTHPLACE OF EIGHT PRESIDENTS | Virginia |
| BIRTHPLACE OF RODEO | Nebraska |
| BIRTHPLACE OF THE NATION | Virginia |
| BLACK WATER STATE | Nebraska |
| BLEEDING KANSAS | Kansas |
| BLIZZARD STATE | South Dakota |
| BLIZZARD STATE | Texas |
| BLUE GRASS REGION | Kentucky |
| BLUEGRASS STATE | Kentucky |
| BLUE HEN STATE | Delaware |
| BLUE HEN'S CHICKENS STATE | Delaware |
| BLUE LAW STATE | Connecticut |
| BOATING CAPITAL OF THE WORLD | Washington |
| BONANZA STATE | Montana |
| BOOMERS' PARADISE | Oklahoma |
| BORDER-EAGLE STATE | Mississippi |
| BORDER STATE | Maine |
| BOWIE STATE | Arkansas |
| BREAD AND BUTTER STATE | Minnesota |
| BREADBASKET OF THE NATION | Kansas |
| BRIGHTEST STAR IN THE AMERICAN | |
| CONSTELLATION | Iowa |
| BROWNSTONE STATE | Connecticut |
| BUCKEYE STATE | Ohio |
| BUFFALO PLAINS STATE | Colorado |
| BUG-EATING STATE | Nebraska |
| BULLION STATE | Missouri |
| BUZZARD STATE | Georgia |

C

| | |
|---|---|
| CACTUS LAND | New Mexico |
| CAMDEN AND AMBOY STATE | New Jersey |
| CANYON STATE | Arizona |
| CAVALIER STATE | Virginia |
| CAVE STATE | Missouri |
| CENTENNIAL STATE | Colorado |
| CENTER OF AMERICAN CULTURE | New York |
| CENTER OF SCENIC AMERICA | Utah |

| | |
|---|---|
| CENTER OF THE COMMERCIAL UNIVERSE | Indiana |
| CENTER OF WORLD TRANSPORTATION | New Jersey |
| CENTRAL STATE | Kansas |
| CHEESE CAPITAL OF THE NATION | Wisconsin |
| CHILD OF THE MISSISSIPPI RIVER | Louisiana |
| CHINOOK STATE | Washington |
| CLAM GRABBERS | Washington |
| CLAM STATE | New Jersey |
| "CLEAN AIR" COUNTRY | Kansas |
| COAL STATE | Pennsylvania |
| COCKADE STATE | Maryland |
| COCKPIT OF HISTORY | New Jersey |
| COCKPIT OF REVOLUTION | New Jersey |
| COLORFUL COLORADO | Colorado |
| COLORFUL STATE | New Mexico |
| COLORFUL VACATION LAND | Utah |
| COMMONWEALTH | Virginia |
| COMPLETE VACATIONLAND | Maine |
| CONSITUTION STATE | Connecticut |
| CONVENTION CENTER OF THE PACIFIC | Hawaii |
| CONVENTION STATE | Maine |
| COOL GREEN VACATIONLAND | Oregon |
| COPPER STATE | Arizona |
| COPPER STATE | Wisconsin |
| COMPLETE VACATIONLAND | Maine |
| CORN BELT STATE | Illinois |
| CORN STATE | Illinois |
| CORN-CRACKER STATE | Kentucky |
| CORNHUSKER STATE | Nebraska |
| CORN HUSKING STATE | Nebraska |
| CORNUCOPIA OF THE SOUTH | Alabama |
| CORNUCOPIA OF THE WORLD | California |
| COTTON KINGDOM | Mississippi |
| COTTON STATE | Alabama |
| COWBOY COUNTRY | Nebraska |
| COWBOY STATE | Wyoming |
| COYOTE STATE | South Dakota |
| CRACKER STATE | Georgia |
| CREOLE STATE | Louisiana |
| CROSSROADS OF ALL AMERICA | North Dakota |
| CROSSROADS OF AMERICA | Illinois |
| CROSSROADS OF AMERICA | Indiana |
| CROSSROADS OF THE EAST | New Jersey |
| CROSSROADS OF THE SOUTH | Mississippi |
| CROSSROADS OF THE WORLD | Alaska |

440

"CROSSROADS" STATE                              New Jersey
CUSTODIAN OF AMERICA'S HERITAGE                  Massachusetts
CUSTODIAN OF AMERICA'S HISTORICAL
   HERITAGE                                      Massachusetts
CYCLONE STATE                                    Kansas

D

DARK AND BLOODY GROUND STATE                     Kentucky
DELIGHTFUL LAND                                  Maryland
DELIGHTSOME LAND                                 Maryland
DESERET STATE                                    Utah
DIAMOND STATE                                    Delaware
DIFFERENT VACATION STATE                         Georgia
DIXIE DYNAMO                                      North Carolina
DOORWAY TO NOSTALGIC NEW ENG-
   LAND                                          Connecticut
DOWN EAST STATE                                  Maine

E

EAGLE STATE                                      Mississippi
ECONOMIC SUNSHINE STATE                          Delaware
EGYPT                                            Illinois
EL DORADO STATE                                  California
EMPIRE DEDICATED TO PROGRESS                     Oklahoma
EMPIRE STATE                                     New York
EMPIRE STATE OF THE SOUTH                        Georgia
ENERGY-PACKED STATE                              New Jersey
ENTERTAINMENT CAPITAL OF THE
   WORLD                                         Nevada
EQUALITY STATE                                   Wyoming
EQUALITY SUFFRAGE STAGE                          Wyoming
ESKIMOLAND                                       Alaska
EUREKA STATE                                     California
EVERGLADES STATE                                 Florida
EVERGREEN STATE                                  Washington
EVERY AMERICAN'S SECOND STATE                    Vermont
EVERYBODY'S SECOND STATE                         Vermont
EVERYTHING FOR OUTDOOR LIVING                    Vermont
EXCELSIOR STATE                                  New York
EXCITING STATE OF CONTRASTS                      Washington

F

FABULOUS FLORIDA                                 Florida
FAMILY VACATION LAND                             Missouri
FAR NORTH FRONTIER                               Alaska

441

| | |
|---|---|
| FASTEST GROWING CATTLE STATE | Mississippi |
| FIFTIETH STATE OF ENCHANTMENT | Hawaii |
| FIRE CLAY CAPITAL | Missouri |
| FIRST IN CLEAN AIR | Kansas |
| FIRST STATE | Delaware |
| FLICKERTAIL STATE | North Dakota |
| FOOD MARKET OF THE WORLD | Iowa |
| FOREIGNER STATE | New Jersey |
| FOUR SEASONS' RECREATION STATE | Vermont |
| FOUR-SEASON STATE | Maine |
| FOUR SEASON STATE | Vermont |
| FOUR SEASON VACATION FUN LAND | Michigan |
| FOUR-SEASON VACATIONLAND | Massachusetts |
| FOUR SEASON VACATIONLAND | Montana |
| FOUR SEASON VACATIONLAND | Wisconsin |
| FREE STATE | Maryland |
| FREE STATE | West Virginia |
| FREESTONE STATE | Connecticut |
| FRIENDLY ARIZONA | Arizona |
| FRIENDLY LAND OF INFINITE VARIETY | South Dakota |
| FRIENDLY STATE | Kansas |
| FRIENDLY STATE | North Dakota |
| FRIENDLY STATE | Utah |
| FRONTIER OF PLEASURE | South Dakota |
| FRONTIER OF PLEASURE ON THE OLD WEST TRAIL | South Dakota |
| FUEL STATE | West Virginia |
| FUN-FILLED VACATION LAND | Mississippi |

G

| | |
|---|---|
| GAME FISH JUNCTION | North Carolina |
| GARDEN OF THE WEST | Illinois |
| GARDEN OF THE WEST | Kansas |
| GARDEN STATE | Kansas |
| GARDEN STATE | New Jersey |
| GARDEN SPOT FOR PLEASURE AND BUSINESS | New Jersey |
| GATEWAY STATE | Ohio |
| GATEWAY TO ALASKA AND THE ORIENT | Washington |
| GATEWAY TO EXPO 67 | New York |
| GATEWAY TO THE NORTHWEST TERRITORY | Ohio |
| GATEWAY TO THE ORIENT | Hawaii |
| GATEWAY TO THE PACIFIC | California |
| GATEWAY TO THE PACIFIC | Hawaii |
| GATEWAY TO THE ROCKY MOUNTAIN | |

| | |
|---|---|
| WEST | Colorado |
| GATEWAY TO THE SCENIC WONDERS | |
| OF THE GREAT WEST | Wyoming |
| GATEWAY TO THE SOUTHLAND | Mississippi |
| GATEWAY TO THE WORLD | Florida |
| GATEWAY TO WHERE THE WEST BEGAN | South Dakota |
| GEM OF THE MOUNTAIN STATES | Idaho |
| GEM OF THE MOUNTAINS | Idaho |
| GEM OF THE PACIFIC | Hawaii |
| GEM STATE | Idaho |
| GEOGRAPHIC CENTER OF THE WORLD'S | |
| RICHEST MARKET | New Jersey |
| GLORIOUS VACATION PLAYGROUND | Colorado |
| GOLDEN STATE | California |
| GOOBER STATE | Georgia |
| GOOD HIGHWAY STATE | Utah |
| GOODLIEST LAND UNDER THE CAPE OF | |
| HEAVEN | North Carolina |
| GOPHER STATE | Minnesota |
| GRAND CANYON STATE | Arizona |
| GRANITE STATE | New Hampshire |
| GRAPE STATE | California |
| GRASSHOPPER STATE | Kansas |
| GREAT AGRICULTURAL STATE | Mississippi |
| GREAT BEAR'S CUB | Alaska |
| GREAT CENTRAL STATE | North Dakota |
| GREAT LAKE STATE | Michigan |
| GREAT LAKES STATE | Illinois |
| GREAT LAND | Alaska |
| GREAT PLACE TO LIVE, LAZE, LO- | |
| CATE | Maine |
| GREAT RECREATION STATE | Maine |
| GREAT STATE | Kansas |
| GREATEST FOOD PRODUCING AREA | |
| IN THE WORLD | Iowa |
| GREEN MOUNTAIN STATE | Vermont |
| GROUNDHOG STATE | Mississippi |
| GUINEA PIG STATE | Arkansas |
| GULF STATE | Florida |

H

| | |
|---|---|
| HARD-CASE STATE | Oregon |
| HAVEN FOR THE TRAVELER | Iowa |
| HAWKEYE STATE | Iowa |
| HEALTH RESORT OF AMERICA | Maine |
| HEALTHFUL STATE | Arizona |
| HEART OF AMERICA | Missouri |

| | |
|---|---|
| HEART OF DIXIE | Alabama |
| HEART OF THE COW COUNTRY | Oklahoma |
| HEART OF THE DEEP SOUTH | Alabama |
| HEART OF THE DEEP SOUTH | Mississippi |
| HEART OF THE NATION | Illinois |
| HEARTLAND OF HOSPITALITY | Missouri |
| HEMP STATE | Kentucky |
| HIGHEST STATE | Colorado |
| HIGHEST STATE IN THE UNION | Colorado |
| HISTORIC VACATIONLAND | Massachusetts |
| HISTORY'S MAIN ROAD | New Jersey |
| HOG AND HOMINY STATE | Tennessee |
| HOLIDAY STATE | Connecticut |
| HOLLAND OF AMERICA | Louisiana |
| HOME OF THE PEACH, STRAWBERRY AND VINE | Arkansas |
| HONEY STATE | Utah |
| HOOSIER STATE | Indiana |
| HOSPITALITY STATE | Mississippi |
| HOST STATE FOR THE WORLD'S FAIR | New York |
| HOT-WATER STATE | Arkansas |
| HUB OF COMMERCE | New Jersey |
| HUB OF THE NATION | Illinois |
| HUB OF THE WEST | Utah |

I

| | |
|---|---|
| IDAHO IS WHAT THE REST OF THE WORLD WOULD LIKE TO BE | Idaho |
| INDUSTRIAL PARK STATE | New Jersey |
| INSURANCE STATE | Connecticut |
| INTERSTATE STATE | Tennessee |
| IODINE STATE | South Carolina |
| IRELAND OF AMERICA | North Carolina |
| IRON MOUNTAIN STATE | Missouri |
| ISLAND PARADISE | Hawaii |
| ISLAND STATE | Hawaii |
| ITALY OF AMERICA | Arizona |

J

| | |
|---|---|
| JAYHAWKER STATE | Kansas |
| JERSEY BLUE STATE | New Jersey |
| JEWEL OF MANY FACETS | Michigan |
| JEWEL OF THE PACIFIC | Hawaii |
| JOHNSON'S POLAR BEAR GARDEN | Alaska |
| JUBILEE STATE FOR '68 | Illinois |
| JUMBO STATE | Texas |

# K

| | |
|---|---|
| KEYSTONE STATE | Pennsylvania |
| KEYSTONE OF THE SOUTH ATLANTIC SEABOARD | South Carolina |
| KNICKERBOCKER STATE | New York |

# L

| | |
|---|---|
| LADY OF THE LAKE | Michigan |
| LAKE STATE | Michigan |
| LAKE STATE | Minnesota |
| LAND FOR RELAXATION | West Virginia |
| LAND MADE FOR VACATIONS | Wisconsin |
| LAND OF ADVENTURE | Alaska |
| LAND OF AMAZING ADVANTAGES | New Jersey |
| LAND OF AMAZING INDUSTRIAL ADVANTAGES | New Jersey |
| LAND OF BEGINNINGS | North Carolina |
| LAND OF BLOSSOMING VALLEYS | Utah |
| LAND OF BLOSSOMS AND RELAXED LIVING | Georgia |
| LAND OF CATTLE AND SHEEP | Wyoming |
| LAND OF COLOR | Utah |
| LAND OF COLOR AND CONTRASTS | Utah |
| LAND OF CONTRASTS | Colorado |
| LAND OF CONTRASTS | Utah |
| LAND OF DISCOVERIES | California |
| LAND OF ENCHANTMENT | Montana |
| LAND OF ENCHANTMENT | New Mexico |
| LAND OF ENDLESS SCENIC DISCOVERY | Utah |
| LAND OF EXCITING CONTRASTS | Oregon |
| LAND OF FLOWERS | Alabama |
| LAND OF FLOWERS | Florida |
| LAND OF FRESH HORIZONS | North Dakota |
| LAND OF FUN, SUN AND SAND | Florida |
| LAND OF GOLD | California |
| LAND OF GROWTH AND GRANDEUR | West Virginia |
| LAND OF HEARTS' DESIRE | New Mexico |
| LAND OF HISTORY | Ohio |
| LAND OF HONEY BEES | Utah |
| LAND OF INFINITE VARIETY | South Dakota |
| LAND OF LAKES AND PRAIRIES | Minnesota |
| LAND OF LEISURE | Hawaii |
| LAND OF LINCOLN | Illinois |
| LAND OF LIVING COLOR | California |
| LAND OF MAJESTIC BEAUTY | Arkansas |
| LAND OF NOW | Alaska |

445

| | |
|---|---|
| LAND OF OPPORTUNITY | Alabama |
| LAND OF OPPORTUNITY | Alaska |
| LAND OF OPPORTUNITY | Arkansas |
| LAND OF OPPORTUNITY | New Mexico |
| LAND OF OPPORTUNITY | Ohio |
| LAND OF OPPORTUNITY | Oregon |
| LAND OF OPPORTUNITY | Texas |
| LAND OF PEACE AND BEAUTY | New Hampshire |
| LAND OF PEANUTS, PECANS AND PEACHES | Georgia |
| LAND OF PLEASURE | Idaho |
| LAND OF PLENTY | South Dakota |
| LAND OF PROMISE | Alaska |
| LAND OF PROMISE | California |
| LAND OF PROMISE | Texas |
| LAND OF RECREATION AND PROGRESS | South Carolina |
| LAND OF REMEMBERED VACATIONS | Maine |
| LAND OF RESOURCEFULNESS AND RE-LAXATION | West Virginia |
| LAND OF ROGER WILLIAMS | Rhode Island |
| LAND OF ROMANCE | Virginia |
| LAND OF SCENIC SPLENDOR | Montana |
| LAND OF SCENIC SPLENDOR | New Hampshire |
| LAND OF STEADY HABITS | Connecticut |
| LAND OF SUNSHINE | Florida |
| LAND OF SUNSHINE | New Mexico |
| LAND OF SUNSHINE AND FLOWERS | California |
| LAND OF SUNSHINE AND SCENIC GRANDEUR | Arizona |
| LAND OF TEN THOUSAND (10, 000) LAKES | Minnesota |
| LAND OF THE CACTUS | New Mexico |
| LAND OF THE DAKOTAS | North Dakota |
| LAND OF THE DELIGHT-MAKERS | New Mexico |
| LAND OF THE ILLINI | Illinois |
| LAND OF THE LONG NORTH FURROW | North Dakota |
| LAND OF THE MIDNIGHT SUN | Alaska |
| LAND OF THE MORMONS | Utah |
| LAND OF THE NORTH FURROW | North Dakota |
| LAND OF THE OLD WEST | South Dakota |
| LAND OF THE OREGON TRAIL AND THE PONY EXPRESS | Nebraska |
| LAND OF THE PURPLE SAGE | Wyoming |
| LAND OF THE RED MEN | Oklahoma |
| LAND OF THE ROLLING PRAIRIE | Iowa |
| LAND OF THE SAINTS | Utah |
| LAND OF THE SHINING MOUNTAINS | Montana |
| LAND OF THE SKY | North Carolina |

| | |
|---|---|
| LAND OF THEODORE ROOSEVELT AND GENERAL CUSTER | North Dakota |
| LAND OF TOMORROW | Alaska |
| LAND OF WONDER | South Dakota |
| LAND OF YESTERDAY, TODAY AND TOMORROW | Alaska |
| LAND RICH IN HISTORY, HERITAGE AND HOSPITALITY | Iowa |
| LAND THAT WAS MADE FOR VACATIONS | Wisconsin |
| LAND WHERE DREAMS COME TRUE | Oregon |
| LAND WHERE THE SUMMER SUN NEVER SETS | Alaska |
| LAND WHERE THE SUN SPENDS THE WINTER | Arizona |
| LAND WHERE THE WEST BEGINS | Nebraska |
| LAST AMERICAN FRONTIER | Alaska |
| LAST FRONTIER | Alaska |
| LAST FRONTIER OF INDUSTRIAL DEVELOPMENT | Iowa |
| LEAD STATE | Colorado |
| LEAD STATE | Missouri |
| LEAD STATE | Montana |
| LEADING FARM CROP STATE | Iowa |
| LEISURELAND STATE | Nebraska |
| LION'S DEN STATE | Tennessee |
| LITTLE DIXIE | Missouri |
| LITTLE MOUNTAIN STATE | West Virginia |
| LITTLE RHODY | Rhode Island |
| LIVESTOCK FEEDING STATE | Illinois |
| LIZARD STATE | Alabama |
| LOBSTERLAND | Maine |
| LONE STAR STATE | Texas |
| LOVELY LOUISIANA | Louisiana |
| LUMBER STATE | Maine |

## M

| | |
|---|---|
| MAGIC LAND OF COLORFUL PAST AND INTERESTING FUTURE | Utah |
| MAGNOLIA STATE | Mississippi |
| MARINA CAPITAL OF THE U. S. A. | Florida |
| MEMORABLE MISSOURI | Missouri |
| MIDNIGHT SUNLAND | Alaska |
| MIDWAY, U. S. A. | Kansas |
| MINING STATE | Nevada |
| MODERN MOTHER OF PRESIDENTS | Ohio |
| MONUMENTAL STATE | Maryland |

| | |
|---|---|
| MORMON STATE | Utah |
| MOSQUITO STATE | New Jersey |
| MOST VARIED STATE OF THE FIFTY | Massachusetts |
| MOTHER OF PRESIDENTS | Ohio |
| MOTHER OF PRESIDENTS | Virginia |
| MOTHER OF RIVERS | New Hampshire |
| MOTHER OF SOUTH-WESTERN STATES-MEN | Tennessee |
| MOTHER OF STATES | Virginia |
| MOTHER OF STATES AND STATESMEN | Virginia |
| MOTHER OF STATESMEN | Virginia |
| MOTHER OF THE WEST | Missouri |
| MOUNTAIN STATE | West Virginia |
| MOUNTAIN WONDERLAND | Wyoming |
| MUD-CAT STATE | Mississippi |
| MUD-WADDLER STATE | Mississippi |

## N

| | |
|---|---|
| NATIONAL COUNTRY | Florida |
| NATIONAL GATEWAY TO THE FRONTIERLANDS | Missouri |
| NATION'S COOL GREEN PARADISE | Arkansas |
| NATION'S FAMILY PLAYGROUND | Pennsylvania |
| NATION'S FASTEST GROWING STATE | Nevada |
| NATION'S FINEST VACATIONLAND | Wisconsin |
| NATION'S FIRST TOURIST HOST | Rhode Island |
| NATION'S GROWTH FRONTIER | Louisiana |
| NATION'S IDEAL FAMILY PLAYGROUND | Pennsylvania |
| NATION'S INDUSTRIAL FRONTIER | Louisiana |
| NATION'S MIXED-BAG CAPITAL | Nebraska |
| NATION'S MOST INTERESTING STATE | Tennessee |
| NATION'S NEW PLAYGROUND | Alaska |
| NATION'S NUMBER ONE INDUSTRIAL STATE | Connecticut |
| NATION'S SHOWCASE | New York |
| NATION'S VACATIONLAND | Maine |
| NATION'S VACATION LAND | Minnesota |
| NATION'S WONDERLAND | Oregon |
| NATURE'S CORNUCOPIA | Louisiana |
| NATURE'S MINERAL SPECIMEN CASE | North Carolina |
| NATURE'S SHOWCASE | New Jersey |
| NATURE'S WONDERLAND | Utah |
| NEBRASKALAND | Nebraska |
| NERVE CENTER FOR WORLD TRADE | New Jersey |
| NEW AMERICAN FRONTIER | Florida |
| NEW ENGLAND OF THE WEST | Minnesota |
| NEW FRONTIER | Alaska |

| | |
|---|---|
| NEW SPAIN STATE | New Jersey |
| NEW SWEDEN | Delaware |
| NEW WORLD OF ADVENTURE | Texas |
| NORTH STAR STATE · | Minnesota |
| NORTHERN WONDERLAND | Alaska |
| NORTHERNMOST STATE | Alaska |
| NUTMEG STATE | Connecticut |

O

| | |
|---|---|
| OLD BAY STATE | Massachusetts |
| OLD COLONY STATE | Massachusetts |
| OLD DIRIGO STATE | Maine |
| OLD DOMINION STATE | Virginia |
| OLD LINE STATE | Maryland |
| OLD MAN OF THE MOUNTAIN STATE | New Hampshire |
| OLD NORTH STATE | North Carolina |
| OLDEST STATE WEST OF THE THIR-<br>TEEN ORIGINAL COLONIES | Ohio |
| ONE HUNDRED VACATION LANDS<br>INTO ONE | Kentucky |
| ONE OF AMERICA'S MOST POPULAR<br>PLAYGROUNDS | Arizona |
| ONE OF THE GREAT RESORT STATES<br>OF THE MIDDLE WEST | Michigan |
| ONE SOUND STATE | Nevada |
| ORANGE LAND | Florida |
| ORANGE STATE | Florida |
| ORCHID ISLE | Hawaii |
| OUR SOCIAL CAPITAL | Rhode Island |
| OYSTER STATE | Maryland |
| OZARK STATE | Missouri |

P

| | |
|---|---|
| PACE SETTER OF THE SOUTH | Georgia |
| PACIFIC WONDERLAND | Oregon |
| PALMETTO STATE | South Carolina |
| PANHANDLE STATE | West Virginia |
| PARADISE OF THE PACIFIC | Hawaii |
| PATHWAY OF THE REVOLUTION | New Jersey |
| PEACE GARDEN STATE | North Dakota |
| PEACH STATE | Delaware |
| PEACH STATE | Georgia |
| PEERLESS STATE | Iowa |
| PELICAN STATE | Louisiana |
| PENINSULA STATE | Florida |
| PENINSULA STATE | Michigan |

| | |
|---|---|
| PENNSYLVANIA OF THE WEST | Missouri |
| PHEASANT CAPITAL OF THE WORLD | South Dakota |
| PICTURESQUE HISTORIC LAND OF EARLY AMERICA | Louisiana |
| PINE TREE STATE | Maine |
| PINEAPPLE STATE | Hawaii |
| PIONEER COMMONWEALTH | Kentucky |
| PIONEER SPACE CAPITAL OF THE WORLD | Alabama |
| PLACE FOR ALL SEASONS | New York |
| PLACE TO GO | Idaho |
| PLACE TO LIVE WORK, AND PLAY | Maine |
| PLACE TO SEE; THE PLACE TO BE; FOR INDUSTRY, FOR VACATIONS | West Virginia |
| PLANTATION STATE | Rhode Island |
| PLAYGROUND OF TEN THOUSAND LAKES | Minnesota |
| PLAYGROUND OF THE MIDDLE WEST | Wisconsin |
| PLAYGROUND OF THE NATION | Maine |
| PLAYGROUND OF THE PACIFIC | Hawaii |
| PLAYGROUND OF THE SOUTHWEST | New Mexico |
| PLAYTIME COUNTRY | Michigan |
| POLAR STAR STATE | Maine |
| PRAIRIE STATE | Illinois |
| PUKE STATE | Missouri |
| PURITAN STATE | Massachusetts |

Q

| | |
|---|---|
| QUAKER STATE | Pennsylvania |
| QUEEN STATE | Maryland |

R

| | |
|---|---|
| REPUBLIC | Texas |
| RICE STATE | South Carolina |
| RICH AND VARIED LAND | Minnesota |
| RIGHT TO PROFIT STATE | Louisiana |
| RIP VAN WINKLE STATE | North Carolina |
| RIVER WITH THE BIG BEND | Tennessee |
| RIVIERA OF AMERICA | New Jersey |
| ROCKY MOUNTAIN EMPIRE | Colorado |

S

| | |
|---|---|
| SAGE STATE | Nevada |
| SAGEBRUSH STATE | Nevada |
| SAGEBRUSH STATE | Wyoming |

| | |
|---|---|
| SAGE-HEN STATE | Nevada |
| SALT LAKE STATE | Utah |
| SALT OF THE EARTH | Kansas |
| SANCTUARY OF PEACE | Wyoming |
| SAND HILL STATE | Arizona |
| SAND-LAPPER STATE | South Carolina |
| SCENIC ISLE | Hawaii |
| SCENIC STATE | Oregon |
| SCENIC STATE | New Hampshire |
| SCENIC WONDERLAND | Florida |
| SCENIC WONDERLAND | Maine |
| SCENIC WONDERLAND | Tennessee |
| SEAT OF EMPIRE | New York |
| SECOND NAZARETH | North Carolina |
| SEWARD'S FOLLY | Alaska |
| SEWARD'S ICE BOX | Alaska |
| SHARPBACKS STATE | New Jersey |
| SHOW ME STATE | Missouri |
| SILVER STATE | Colorado |
| SILVER STATE | Nevada |
| SINGED CAT STATE | Montana |
| SIOUX STATE | North Dakota |
| SKI COUNTRY, U. S. A. | Colorado |
| SKI STATE OF THE EAST | Vermont |
| SKIINGEST STATE IN THE EAST | New York |
| SMALL STATE, BIG IN AGRICULTURE, BIG IN INDUSTRY | New Jersey |
| SOONER STATE | Oklahoma |
| SOUTHERN GATEWAY OF NEW ENG-LAND | Rhode Island |
| SOUTHERNMOST STATE | Florida |
| SOUTH'S EMPIRE STATE | Georgia |
| SPACE AGE RESEARCH CENTER FOR THE FREE WORLD | New Mexico |
| SPACE CENTER OF THE WORLD | Massachusetts |
| SPANISH STATE | New Mexico |
| SPORTS CAPITAL OF THE WORLD | Florida |
| SPORTSMAN'S PARADISE | Louisiana |
| SPORTSMAN'S PARADISE | Maine |
| SPORTSMAN'S PARADISE | Nebraska |
| SQUATTER STATE | Kansas |
| STAR OF THE SOUTH | Alabama |
| STAR-SPANGLED BANNER STATE | Maryland |
| STATE ALIVE WITH VARIETY AND FUN TO SEE | Connecticut |
| STATE AT THE CROSSROADS OF THE PACIFIC | Hawaii |
| STATE IN THE HEART OF NEW ENG- | |

LAND, A LAND OF PEACE AND
BEAUTY                                   New Hampshire
STATE OF ADVENTURE                       Georgia
STATE OF CAMDEN AND AMBOY                New Jersey
STATE OF CONTRASTS                       Alaska
STATE OF CONTRASTS                       Washington
STATE OF DIVERSITY                       New Mexico
STATE OF DYNAMIC INDUSTRY                West Virginia
STATE OF EXCITEMENT                      Oregon
STATE OF EXCITEMENT                      Pennsylvania
STATE OF EXCITING CONTRASTS             Washington
STATE OF FESTIVALS, THEATRE,
MUSEUMS AND MUSIC                        Florida
STATE OF INCREDITABLE VARIETY            Georgia
STATE OF INDUSTRY                        Oklahoma
STATE OF MAGNIFICENT SCENERY             Colorado
STATE OF ONE THOUSAND AND ONE
VACATION PLEASURES                       Pennsylvania
STATE OF OPPORTUNITY                     Mississippi
STATE OF PRODUCTIVE FARMS                Alabama
STATE OF SHINING MOUNTAINS               Idaho
STATE OF SPAIN                           New Jersey
STATE OF SPAIN STATE                     New Mexico
STATE OF SURPRISE                        New Hampshire
STATE OF SURPRISES                       Indiana
STATE OF THE CONFEDERACY                 Texas
STATE OF THE FUTURE                      Mississippi
STATE ON THE MARCH                       Nebraska
STATE ON THE MOVE                        Ohio
STATE PIONEERING IN PROGRESS             Oklahoma
STATE RICH IN BEAUTY AND ABUNDANT
RESOURCES                                Mississippi
STATE THAT FORGOT                        South Carolina
STATE THAT'S GEARED FOR PROFIT           South Dakota
STATE THAT HAS EVERYTHING                New York
STATE THAT HAS TO BE SEEN TO BE
BELIEVED                                 Louisiana
STATE WHERE BIG THINGS ARE HAP-
PENING                                   Kentucky
STATE WHERE COTTON IS STILL KING         Mississippi
STATE WHERE EVERY SEASON IS VA-
CATION TIME                              Maine
STATE WHERE EVERY SEASON IS VA-
CATION TIME                              Tennessee
STATE WHERE HISTORY AND HOSPI-
TALITY BEGAN                             Massachusetts
STATE WHERE HISTORY AND THE
PRESENT MAKE YOUR VISIT DE-

| | |
|---|---|
| LIGHTFUL | Ohio |
| STATE WHERE MAN AND NATURE GAMBLE | Nevada |
| STATE WHERE PROFIT AND PLEASURE ARE PART OF THE ECONOMIC MIX | Vermont |
| STATE WHERE RESOURCES AND MARKETS MEET | South Carolina |
| STATE WHERE THE FUN BEGINS ON THE OLD WEST TRAIL | South Dakota |
| STATE WHERE THE SUNSHINE SPENDS THE WINTER | North Dakota |
| STATE WHERE THE WEST BEGINS | Nebraska |
| STATE WHERE THE WEST BEGINS AND PROGRESS NEVER CEASES | Iowa |
| STATE WHERE THE WIND COMES SWEEPIN' DOWN THE PLAINS | Oklahoma |
| STATE WHERE YOU CAN ALWAYS EXPECT TO ENJOY THE UNEXPECTED | Arizona |
| STATE WHERE YOU COME FOR A VISIT AND COME BACK FOR A LIFETIME | New Jersey |
| STATE WITH MANY LANDSCAPES | South Dakota |
| STATE WITH NEW IDEAS | Oklahoma |
| STEEL STATE | Pennsylvania |
| STUB TOE STATE | Montana |
| SUCKER STATE | Illinois |
| SUGAR STATE | Louisiana |
| SUMMER PLAYGROUND OF THE NATION | Maine |
| SUNFLOWER STATE | Kansas |
| SUNSET LAND | Arizona |
| SUNSET STATE | Arizona |
| SUNSET STATE | Oregon |
| SUNSHINE EMPIRE | California |
| SUNSHINE PENINSULA | Florida |
| SUNSHINE STATE | Florida |
| SUNSHINE STATE | New Mexico |
| SUNSHINE STATE | South Dakota |
| SURPRISING STATE | Washington |
| SWAMP STATE | South Carolina |
| SWIAGECAT STATE | South Dakota |
| SWITZERLAND OF AMERICA | Colorado |
| SWITZERLAND OF AMERICA | Maine |
| SWITZERLAND OF AMERICA | New Hampshire |
| SWITZERLAND OF AMERICA | West Virginia |

T

| | |
|---|---|
| TADPOLE STATE | Mississippi |
| TALL CORN STATE | Nebraska |

| | |
|---|---|
| TARHEEL STATE | North Carolina |
| THREE STATES IN ONE | Tennessee |
| THRESHOLD OF PARADISE | Oregon |
| TOBACCO STATE | Kentucky |
| TOMATO STATE | Ohio |
| TOOTHPICK STATE | Arkansas |
| TOP OF THE NATION | Colorado |
| TOP VACATION STATE OF THE NATION | Colorado |
| TOURIST EMPIRE OF THE INLAND SEAS | Michigan |
| TOURIST STATE | Pennsylvania |
| TREASURE STATE | Montana |
| TREEPLANTER STATE | Nebraska |
| TROPICAL PARADISE | Hawaii |
| TURPENTINE STATE | North Carolina |

## U

| | |
|---|---|
| UNCLE SAM'S ICEBOX | Alaska |
| UNCLE SAM'S POCKET HANDKER-CHIEF | Delaware |
| UNITED NATIONS IN MINIATURE | Minnesota |
| U. S. GATEWAY TO LATIN AMERICA | Florida |
| U. S. GATEWAY TO THE WORLD | New Jersey |
| UNSPOILED EMPIRE | New Mexico |

## V

| | |
|---|---|
| VACATION ADVENTURELAND | Oklahoma |
| VACATION AND INDUSTRIAL NUCLEUS OF THE SOUTH WEST | New Mexico |
| VACATION CAPITAL OF THE MID-WEST | Missouri |
| VACATION CENTER OF AMERICA | Kentucky |
| VACATION COUNTRY | Colorado |
| VACATION EMPIRE | New York |
| VACATION HAVEN IN MID-NATION | Iowa |
| VACATION LAND | Idaho |
| VACATION LAND FOR ALL | Wisconsin |
| VACATION LAND OF FUN AND PLENTY | Massachusetts |
| VACATION LAND OF YOUR FONDEST DREAMS | Idaho |
| VACATION PARADISE | Kentucky |
| VACATION STATE | Montana |
| VACATION STATE | Nevada |
| VACATION WONDERLAND | Wyoming |
| VACATIONLAND | Alabama |
| VACATIONLAND | New York |

| | |
|---|---|
| VACATIONLAND OF OPPORTUNITY | Alaska |
| VACATIONLAND OF THE EAST | West Virginia |
| VACATION STATE OF THE NATION | Arizona |
| VACATION TARGET FOR MILLIONS OF AMERICANS | Illinois |
| VACATION VARIETY | New York |
| VACATION WONDERLAND | Idaho |
| VACATIONLAND | Illinois |
| VACATIONLAND | Maine |
| VACATIONLAND THE YEAR 'ROUND | New Jersey |
| VALENTINE STATE | Arizona |
| VARIETY VACATIONLAND | Louisiana |
| VARIETY VACATIONLAND | North Carolina |
| VARIETY VACATIONLAND FOR ALL THE FAMILY | Mississippi |
| VERMIN STATE | New Mexico |
| VISIT NORTH DAKOTA FOR FAMILY WATER FUN | North Dakota |
| VOLUNTEER STATE | Tennessee |

## W

| | |
|---|---|
| WATER WONDERLAND | Michigan |
| WATER-WINTER WONDERLAND | Michigan |
| WEB-FOOT STATE | Oregon |
| WELCOME STATE | Oregon |
| WELLSPRING OF ART AND CULTURE | Massachusetts |
| WESTERN PLAYGROUND | Nebraska |
| WHEAT STATE | Kansas |
| WHEAT STATE | Minnesota |
| WHEAT STATE OF AMERICA | Kansas |
| WHEATHEART OF THE NATION | Kansas |
| WHITE MOUNTAIN STATE | New Hampshire |
| WINDOW ON THE EAST | Hawaii |
| WINE LAND OF AMERICA | California |
| WINTER PARADISE OF AMERICA | Colorado |
| WINTER SALAD BOWL | Florida |
| WINTER WONDERLAND | Michigan |
| WOLVERINE STATE | Michigan |
| WONDER STATE | Arkansas |
| WONDERFUL IODINE STATE | South Carolina |
| WONDERFUL WISCONSIN | Wisconsin |
| WONDERFUL WYOMING | Wyoming |
| WONDERLAND | Arizona |
| WONDERLAND | Montana |
| WONDERLAND OF AMERICA | Wyoming |
| WONDERLAND OF 11,000 LAKES | Michigan |
| WONDERLAND UNSURPASSED | Alaska |

| | |
|---|---|
| WOODEN NUTMEG STATE | Connecticut |
| WORKSHOP OF THE WORLD | Pennsylvania |
| WORLD OF FUN AND RELAXATION | Massachusetts |
| WORLD OF GOOD THAT AWAITS YOU | Maine |
| WORLD OF SCENIC BEAUTY | New York |
| WORLD OF SCENIC BEAUTY | Utah |
| WORLD'S SADDLE HORSE CAPITAL | Missouri |

## Y

| | |
|---|---|
| YANKEE LAND OF THE SOUTH | Georgia |
| YANKEE PLAYLAND | New Hampshire |
| YANKEE STATE | Ohio |
| YEAR ROUND MID-SOUTH | North Carolina |
| YEAR 'ROUND PARADISE | Utah |
| YEAR 'ROUND VACATION STATE | North Carolina |
| YEAR 'ROUND VACATION WONDERLAND | Georgia |
| YEAR 'ROUND VACATIONLAND | Massachusetts |
| YEAR-ROUND VACATIONLAND | New York |
| YELLOWHAMMER STATE | Alabama |
| "YOU-NAME-IT-WE-MAKE-IT" STATE | Ohio |
| YOUNGEST STATE | Arizona |
| YOUNGEST STATE | Hawaii |
| YOUR DREAMLAND OF PLEASURE | Hawaii |
| YOUR FOUR-SEASON VACATIONLAND | Massachusetts |
| YOUR VACATION STATE | Nevada |

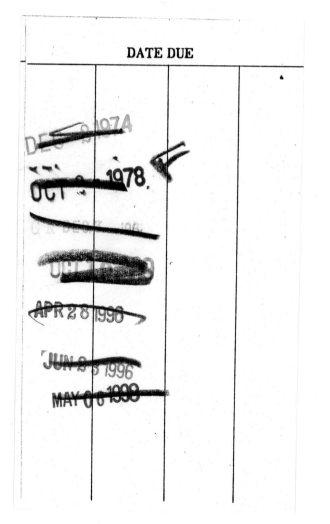